Microsoft Word for Windows 95:
The Complete Reference

About the Authors...

Mary Campbell, co-author of **Quicken 4 for Windows Made Easy** and author of many **Answers: Certified Tech Support** books, has written and co-authored dozens of acclaimed books on a large variety of computer topics. As a widely read author and corporate trainer, she has taught thousands of users about many popular software programs.

Gabrielle A. Lawrence, a software support manager at Relational Systems, has developed manuals and help facilities, trained users, and worked with programmers to make software easier to use. She has over ten years of experience helping people and software get along.

Microsoft Word for Windows 95: The Complete Reference

Mary Campbell
Gabrielle Lawrence

Osborne **McGraw-Hill**

Berkeley New York St. Louis San Francisco
Auckland Bogotá Hamburg London Madrid
Mexico City Milan Montreal New Delhi Panama City
Paris São Paulo Singapore Sydney
Tokyo Toronto

Osborne **McGraw-Hill**
2600 Tenth Street
Berkeley, California 94710
U.S.A.

For information on translations or book distributors outside the U.S.A., or to arrange bulk purchase discounts for sales promotions, premiums, or fundraisers, please contact Osborne **McGraw-Hill** at the above address.

Microsoft Word for Windows 95: The Complete Reference

1234567890 DOC 998765

ISBN 0-07-882150-9

Publisher
  Lawrence Levitsky

Acquisitions Editor
  Joanne Cuthbertson

Project Editor
  Wendy Rinaldi

Copy Editors
  Kathryn Hashimoto
  Jan Jue

Indexer
  Richard Shrout

Proofreader
  Pat Mannion

Computer Designer
  Peter F. Hancik

Illustrator
  Marla J. Shelasky

Quality Control Specialist
  Joe Scuderi

Cover Design
  Compass Marketing

Contents at a Glance

Part I   Word Basics

	1	The Word Window	. . . .	3
	2	Creating and Editing a Document	. . . .	23
	3	Formatting Documents	. . . .	45

Part II   Alphabetical Reference

	4	Word Features	. . . .	61

Part III   Special Features

	5	Exchanging Data with Other Applications	. . . .	557
	6	Desktop Publishing in Word	. . . .	575

7   Adding Sophistication to Merge and Macro Features   603
8   Using Word in a Workgroup Environment   639
9   Using the Internet Assistant with Word   657

Part IV Appendixes

A   Installing Word for Windows 95   677
B   Switching from WordPerfect to Word for Windows   .   681
C   Word for Windows Buttons   685
D   Templates   713

Contents

Acknowledgments xiii
Introduction xv

Part I
Word Basics

1 The Word Window 3
  Starting and Ending a Word for Windows
    Session 4
    Starting a Word for Windows Session 4
    Ending a Word for Windows Session 5
  The Word Application Window 5
    Document Windows 6
    Elements of the Word Window 7
  Using the Mouse 11
    Mouse Actions 11
    Mouse Pointer Shapes 12
  Using the Keyboard 12

The Function Keys 13
Working in Dialog Boxes 13
Command Buttons 14
Text Boxes 14
List Boxes 15
Option Buttons and Check Boxes 16
Tabbed Sections 17
Arranging Your Workspace 17
Sizing Windows 17
Moving Windows 18
Closing Windows 19
Accessing Help 19
Showing a Help Window 19
Moving Among Help Topics 20
Index and Find 21
The Answer Wizard 22
Dialog Box and Screen Help 22

2 Creating and Editing a Document 23
Creating a Document 24
Creating Additional New Documents 24
Switching Among Documents 25
Entering Text 25
Typing in the Document Window 25
Ending a Paragraph 27
Using the Tab Key 27
Editing a Document 28
Navigating Within a Document 28
Making Corrections 30
Selecting Text 31
Moving and Copying Text by Dragging and
Dropping 32
Deleting Selected Text 33
Inserting Text 34
Copying Text 35
Undoing Edits 35
Saving and Opening Your Documents 36
Saving for the First Time 36
Subsequent Saves 38
Closing the Document 38
Opening an Existing Document 38
Checking the Spelling and Grammar of Your
Document 39

The AutoCorrect Feature 40
Using the Grammar Checker 40
Printing the Document 41
Changing the View 41

‖‖‖‖ 3 Formatting Documents 45
Character Formatting 46
Font Settings 47
Size Settings 49
Character Style Settings 49
Position Settings 50
Paragraph Formatting 51
Alignment Settings 52
Indentation Settings 53
Spacing Settings 54
Page Formatting 55
Margin Settings 56
Page Size Settings 57
Orientation Setting 57

Part II

Alphabetical Reference

‖‖‖‖ 4 Word Features 61

Part III

Special Features

‖‖‖‖ 5 Exchanging Data with Other
Applications 557
Why Use Embedding and Linking? 560
Understanding Windows OLE 563
Working with Linked and Embedded Objects in
Word 563
What Happens to Data When You Link or
Embed It 564
Updating Data from Linked and Embedded
Objects 565
Changing the Data Shown in a Link 567
Switching Between Linked and Embedded
Objects 567
Fields Used for Linked and Embedded Data . . . 568

Word Documents as Linked and Embedded
   Data 569
Working with Documents of Other Document
   Types 570
  Linked and Inserted Documents 571
  Converting Documents 571
  Document Type Registrations 573

6 Desktop Publishing in Word 575
How You Can Use Desktop Publishing 576
Basic Steps in Desktop Publishing 576
  Learning About Design 577
Specialized Terms and Ideas 578
Creating Sample Documents 582
  Business Cards 582
  Letterheads 585
  Brochures 588
  Flyers or Announcements 590
  Greeting Cards 591
  Reports 593
  Forms 596
  Newsletters 598

7 Adding Sophistication to Merge and
Macro Features 603
Macros 604
  Using the Macro Recorder 604
  Using the Macro Toolbar to Edit and Test a
    Macro 604
  Using the WordBasic Programming Language
    to Create Macros 607
  The Building Blocks of Your Macro 608
  Some Macro Examples 613
  The Word Dialog Editor 618
  Where Macros Are Stored 622
  Automatic Macros 623
  What to Do When Your Macros Don't Work . . . 623
Mail Merge 624
  Putting Together a Long-Term Merge
    Strategy 625
  Merge Documents Other Than Form Letters . . . 625
  Utilizing the Full Potential of Word Fields 630
  Solving Merge Problems 636

||||| 8 Using Word in a Workgroup
Environment 639
Workgroup Options 640
Some Workgroup Scenarios 641
Network Options 643
Routing Documents to Network Users 644
Using Word's Protection Features 645
Word's Support of Local and Remote
Workgroup Activities 645
Revision Marks 646
Master Documents and Subdocuments 647
Annotating Documents 650
Templates 651
Routing Documents with Microsoft Mail 654
Binder 654

||||| 9 Using the Internet Assistant with Word . . 657
World Wide Web 658
HTML Codes 659
Page Structure and Character Formatting 660
Hypertext Links 661
Graphics 662
Using the Internet Assistant to Create Web
Pages 662
Starting the Internet Assistant 663
Creating a New Web Document 663
Converting a Word Document for Use on the
Web 664
Word Styles and Commands for Adding
HTML Codes to a Web Document 665
Viewing the HTML Codes in a Web
Document 669
Adding Graphics to Web Documents 670
Using the Internet Assistant to Create Forms . . . 671

Part IV

Appendixes

||||| A Installing Word for Windows 95 677
Hardware Requirements 678
Hard Disk Space Requirements 678
Installing Word 678

Updating Word 679

▮▮▮▮▮ B Switching from WordPerfect to Word
for Windows 681
WordPerfect Help in Word 684

▮▮▮▮▮ C Word for Windows Buttons 685

▮▮▮▮▮ D Templates 713
Creating a Document from a Template 714
A Look at Each of the Templates 715
Agenda Wizard 715
Award Wizard 715
Brochure Template 716
Calendar Wizard 717
Directory Template 717
Fax Wizard 718
Fax Cover Sheet Templates 719
Invoice Template 719
Letter Wizard 719
Letter Templates 720
Manual Template 720
Memo Wizard 720
Memo Templates 721
Newsletter Wizard 721
Newsletter Template 722
Normal Template 722
Pleading Wizard 723
Press Release Templates 723
Purchase Order Template 723
Report Templates 724
Resume Wizard 724
Resume Templates 725
Table Wizard 725
Thesis Template 726
Weekly Time Sheet Template 727
Altering a Template 727
Creating Your Own Templates 728

▮▮▮▮▮ Index 729

Acknowledgments

The efforts of many individuals played an important part in completing this book. Without the team of experts who lent their assistance to this book, it would not have been possible. I would like to offer my special thanks to the following individuals:

David Campbell, who did a fantastic job of reviewing the manuscript. David's suggestions helped to insure that the book met the needs of users at all levels.

Joanne Cuthbertson, Acquisitions Editor, for her help on all phases of the project from lining up beta software to reading over chapters to insure that they were clear.

Wendy Rinaldi, Project Editor, for an incredible job of keeping all the pieces of this project together and moving it through the system despite almost impossible time schedules. Special thanks to Kathryn Hashimoto and Jan Jue, who both did a wonderful job of copy editing and Pat Mannion who did a great job proofreading. Also thanks to all the people in production that were responsible for the design and layout of the pages of this book.

The graphics you see in the book came from several sources. Jim Anderton at A. J. Graphics provided the samples of Yesterday's Art. Jim markets an interesting collection of clip art and provided some of the clip art for this book. His graphics are the ones that look like sketches. Jim Haney at New Vision Technologies Inc. provided us with Presentation Task Force that has 3,500 pieces of CGM clipart to add to Word documents. Another source of graphics was CorelDRAW!. CorelDRAW! is known for its graphics editing features that go beyond the capabilities of Word's drawing features. Julia Galla and Micheal Bellefeuille at CorelDRAW! were particularly helpful.

Introduction

This book is for all Word for Windows users. If you have used an earlier version of Word for Windows you will find that this book will help you make a quick transition to the new release of Microsoft Word for Windows 95. Chapter 4, the Command Reference, includes full coverage of all of the new features of Windows 95, as well as all the existing features, options, and procedures of Microsoft Word for Windows 3.1. When you are ready to look at more advanced applications, you'll find ideas in Chapters 5 through 8 that discuss the benefits of desktop publishing, file transfer, macros, mail merge, and workgroup options.

If you are new to Word for Windows you will find the help you need in the first three chapters to get you up and running quickly. You will then be ready to access any of the commands and features in Chapter 4.

How This Book Is Organized

The information in this book is organized into eight chapters. The first three provide the basics to getting started with Word. You will learn how to create, save, and print a Word document with the instructions provided. You will even learn some of the formatting basics needed to tailor the appearance of your document to meet your exact needs.

Chapter 4 is the largest section of the book. It is a comprehensive Comand Reference. It is organized alphabetically making it easy to look up any specific topic or feature. Cross-referenced entries are amply provided throughout Chapter 4 to make it easy to find related topics.

There are consistent sections that can be used within each topic although many of them are optional. The sections you will find throughout the Command Reference are:

- Step-by-step procedures
- Options to change the many standard featues of Word for Windows
- Hints that describe interesting points about the special features of Word for Windows
- Related Topics to direct you to more information on similar Word for Windows features

The last four chapters provide more detail on individualized topics. They cover desktop publishing, sharing data with other applications, macros and mail merge, and workgroups and networking. These chapters have more of an application perspective and provide specific examples in each area. The appendices cover installation and provide reference information on templates, icons, and Word commands for WordPerfect users.

Conventions Used

This book uses several conventions to help you understand when the text refers to a key, menu command, or other word feature. If you prefer to use the keyboard to make menu selections, you will also find underlined mnemonics that can be used when choosing a menu selection.

All function keys and keyboard selections are shown in small capital letters. For example, you will see F1 and ENTER when you need to press a specific key. If you need to press two keys at the same time, they will be joined with a plus symbol (+) as in SHIFT+ENTER. If two keys must be pressed sequentially, a comma (,) is used to separate them as in HOME, LEFT ARROW.

Any data preceded by the word "enter" or "type" is shown in boldface. This will clarify exactly how much data you are expected to type.

About the Rules Boxes

Over the years I have taught thousands of people how to use word processing programs. I have listened to the requests of many students in writing this book by incorporating some of the information they indicated they wanted close at hand such as state code abbreviations and rules for capitalization. Although I couldn't answer all of the requests and still cover the needed Word features, I did try to include the things that were requested most frequently. All of the additional information has been placed in rules boxes scattered throughout the text:

Rule Box	**Page**
Rules for Entering Numbers	26
Rules for Comma Placement	42
Guidelines for Using Character Styles	51
Common Abbreviations	62
Rules for Creating Correctly Spelled Plurals	80
Rules for Using the Correct Date Format	131
State Code Abbreviations	171
Problem Homonyms to Watch For	225
Rules for Correcting Wordiness and Redundancy	227
Footnote Forms	237
Rules for Adjectives and Adverbs	267
Rules for Using Pronouns Correctly	269
Rules for Hyphenation	299
Forms of Address	355
Rules for Abbreviating Degrees and Professional Associations	356
Rules for Quotes	463
Aligning Entries in Tables	515
Problem Verbs	526
Linking and Embedding Data	558
Rules for Using Specialized Characters	581
Things to Watch Out for When Writing Macros	611
Adding Emotional Impact to Your E-mail Messages	644

These rules boxes present information relating to grammar and punctuation to conform with commonly accepted business standards. Sometimes this information might conform to *The Chicago Manual of Style, 14th Edition* (The University of Chicago Press, 1993), *Webster's Secretarial Handbook* (Merriam-Webster), *The Gregg Reference Manual, 7th Edition* (Glencoe, 1992), and *Webster's Guide to Business Correspondence Handbook* (Merriam-Webster, 1988.) Where all of the sources agree, common business practice would dictate the use of the common suggestion. In other cases, there is a discrepancy in the advice presented by the various sources. Since *The Chicago Manual of Style* is oriented toward the publishing industry and *Webster's* references are oriented toward business correspondence, it is no surprise that they might differ. The information presented might conform to some of the rules from each, or a common business practice may suggest yet another solution.

What's New in Word for Windows 95

Microsoft Word for Windows 95 has many new features as well as some retooled features. These new features make the leading Windows word processing program even better. Some of the most important new features are:

Feature	Function
Address Book	Stores names and addresses so you can use them when creating envelopes, labels, and form letters
Answer Wizard	Locates help topics that answer your questions
AutoFormat	Automatically makes formatting adjustments as you type your document to create headings, bullets, and special characters
Document Properties	Besides the more enhanced document properties provided by Word, you can also create your own custom properties
Language Switching	As you change the language in Windows 95, Word changes the language setting for a document
Scrap	Stores a piece of Word document outside of Word so you can place it in another Word document or within another application's data
Spell-It	Automatically marks the misspelled words in a document
Tip Wizard	Displays suggestions for how to better use Word features to perform the tasks you are currently performing
WordMail	Word can provide a consistent interface for your E-mail service

PART ONE

Word Basics

Chapter One

The Word Window

Before you create your first document in Word for Windows, you need to master a few basics for both the Word and Windows programs. You need to learn about Windows applications; windows, menus, and dialog boxes; mouse and keyboard techniques; and how to use online help. If you have used other Windows applications, you will be familiar with some of these tasks and techniques and can skim through this chapter quickly to look for items that may not be familiar. If you are new to Windows and Windows applications, you will want to take your time and read through the basics slowly—preferably with Word for Windows on the screen in front of you—to familiarize yourself with the tools to use Word productively. Learning these basics will make you more comfortable as you begin learning how to create a Word letter or report.

In this chapter, you will learn how to start and end a Word for Windows session. You will find out what the various screen elements do for you, and you will explore fundamental techniques for using the mouse and keyboard. You will also learn about common screen elements, such as the status bar, the toolbars, the ruler, and dialog boxes. To complete your introduction to the basic building blocks, you will learn about Word's online Help feature. After reading this chapter, you will be ready to complete your first document by following the directions in Chapter 2.

TIP: The features described in this book apply to Word for Windows 7, although many instructions will work correctly if you are using Word for Windows 6.

Throughout the first three chapters, you will see the icon that appears to the left of this paragraph. The text accompanying this icon will always refer you to Word features that are more advanced than the basics offered in the chapter.

Starting and Ending a Word for Windows Session

To use Word for Windows, you must have two programs loaded into the memory of your system: Windows 95 and Word for Windows. Windows must be started first and is automatically loaded when you turn on your computer.

Starting a Word for Windows Session

Once Windows is up and running, starting a Word session is easy. To start Word, click the Start button, click Programs, and select the Microsoft Word or Microsoft Office folder and then the Microsoft Word program. You can also start Word for Windows in the following other ways:

- Open the folder that contains the Word for Windows program item (it may be initially called WINWORD). You can do this in the Windows Explorer program or through the My Computer folder.

- Double-click the Word for Windows shortcut icon if you have added a shortcut for Word for Windows to your desktop.

- Open any Word document—either through Documents on the Start button or from any open folder.

NOTE: Unless a different version of Word is specifically noted, you can assume that Word always refers to the current release, Word for Windows 7.

When Word has finished loading, you may see a Tip of the Day (explained later in this chapter, in the "Accessing Help" section); you can remove this tip by pressing ENTER or clicking OK.

NOTE: To make sure that you do not have memory problems when you run Word, you will want about 8MB of memory. If you have more memory, you can have more applications open at once. Although 4MB is the stated minimum, you may not be happy with Word's performance with this amount of memory.

Ending a Word for Windows Session

To end a Word for Windows session, choose E̲xit from the F̲ile menu. You can also click Word's Close button (the one with an X), press ALT+F4, double-click the program icon in the upper-left corner, or click the program icon once, then click Close. Ending the session closes all open document windows (you'll learn about these shortly) and the Word application window. If you have not saved the current document or any other document you have open, Word prompts you about saving it, to prevent your losing unsaved work as you exit Word. At this point, you can save the document using the Save As dialog box.

TIP: Menu selections have underlined letters that indicate which key you can press to select an item. For example, to select F̲ile, you can press F once the menu is activated. To activate Word's menu with the keyboard, press the ALT key.

The Word Application Window

When you start Word, your first screen looks like Figure 1-1; this is the Word application window. This window is normally *maximized*, which means it fills your entire screen—you do not see the windows of other open Windows applications or your Windows desktop.

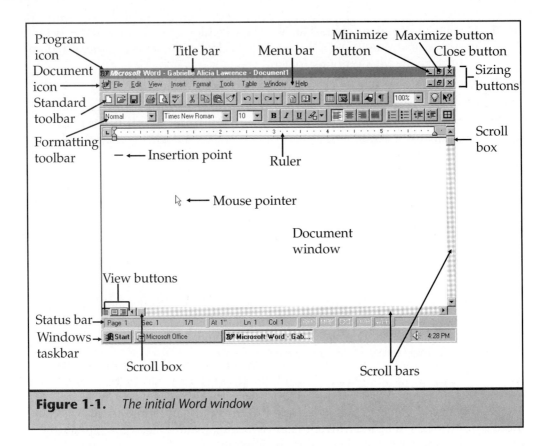

Figure 1-1. *The initial Word window*

The Word window contains a document window (described below), which is also maximized. When a document window is maximized, that document takes up the entire space of the Word window. If you want to see more than one document at a time, you can make the current document window smaller. Most of the time, however, you will work with both the Word window and the document window maximized, because you can see more of a document this way.

Document Windows

A *document window* contains all of your text for a memo, report, or chapter. Word for Windows lets you have many documents open at one time, each one in its own document window. You can quickly switch and transfer data among multiple open documents or compare one document to another. The document window at the top of the stack that you are working on is called the *active window*. It is the one that contains the insertion point, and its title bar has a different color or intensity than the other title bars.

Elements of the Word Window

The Word window has many different elements. At first it might seem a bit cluttered, but each element is an important tool, ready when you need it. The elements of the screen are organized to make them easy to use—just as you might organize the objects on your desk. Figure 1-1 shows the Word window with the following items labeled: title bar, menu bar, Standard and Formatting toolbars, ruler, scroll bars, status bar, insertion point, and mouse pointer.

In the sections that follow, you will take a closer look at how each of these tools can make your Word for Windows sessions productive and efficient.

Title Bar

The *title bar* appears at the top of the window, and it describes the window's contents. With a document window maximized in the Word window, as in Figure 1-1, Word's title bar shows the contents of the application window "Microsoft Word," the licensed Word user's name, and the name of the maximized document, "Document1." If the document window was not maximized, the document window would have a separate title bar containing the name of the document.

Besides describing the window's contents, the title bar contains the application window's program icon on the left end and three sizing buttons on the right end. You can click the program icon to display a menu of options or to close the window.

Later in this chapter, you will learn how the sizing buttons let you change the size of a window (maximizing, minimizing, and restoring). A title bar will show two of the possible three buttons in addition to the Close button.

Menu Bar

The *menu bar* offers a horizontal list of menus; these menus are the primary method of accessing Word commands. Most Word features are available through the menus. You can access the menus with either the keyboard or the mouse. Figure 1-2 shows what the File menu looks like when it is opened or "pulled down" from the menu bar.

To pull down a menu with the mouse, click the menu name in the menu bar. Then click the desired menu command or option to select it from the pull-down menu.

Using the keyboard, you press ALT to first activate the menu bar. To pull down one of the menus, press the letter that is underlined in the menu title, such as F for File. Once the pull-down menu is open, press the underlined letter of the menu command or option you wish to use. You can also press the arrow keys to move horizontally among menus in the menu bar or vertically among the commands in a pulled-down menu. As you move from menu to menu or command to command, the status bar will display a description of the highlighted item. To select the highlighted menu or command, press ENTER.

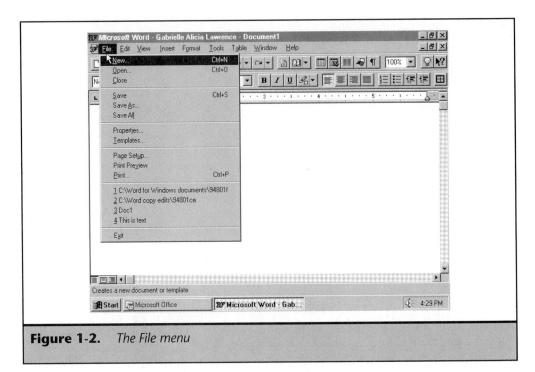

Figure 1-2.   *The File menu*

 **NOTE:** *In this book, Word commands are expressed as the series of selections from the menus; for example, File | Save means selecting File from the menu bar and then choosing Save.*

Standard Toolbar

Word has several toolbars. The *Standard toolbar* displays buttons representing the most popular Word features. By clicking one of these buttons with the mouse, you can quickly access the feature.

In Figure 1-1, the toolbar appears near the top of the window, under the menu bar. Word lets you move it to another location. You can also remove the toolbar altogether if you are not using it or if you wish to display more of the document in the window. Word's View | Toolbars command sets which toolbars display.

 TIP: *The status bar displays a description of a particular button on the toolbar when you move the mouse pointer to a toolbar button. When you move the mouse pointer to a button for more than a second or two, the name of the button and possibly a shortcut are displayed next to the button in addition to the status bar entry.*

The features invoked when you click toolbar buttons are introduced in Chapter 4. Word has eight toolbars that you can display by right-clicking the Standard toolbar and then selecting from the shortcut menu. Several of Word's features, such as View | Outline and View | Header and Footer, also display specialized toolbars. Also, you can create your own custom toolbars. The "Toolbars" section in Chapter 4 explains how to switch to other toolbars, how to reposition or remove the toolbars, and how to change the items available on a toolbar.

Formatting Toolbar

The *Formatting toolbar,* located beneath the Standard toolbar, provides many of the features needed to format text in a document. You can use the Formatting toolbar to make characters and paragraphs look different. You can apply styles to your text, change the typeface or size of selected text, change the alignment of paragraphs, or apply boldface, italic, or underlining to text. The Formatting toolbar is designed to be used with a mouse, but you can also use keyboard shortcuts to access some of the features represented by the buttons.

Ruler

The *ruler* tells you how your document is laid out on the page, showing you the margins of a paragraph, any paragraph indentation settings, and tab stops to which you can quickly move by pressing the TAB key. The ruler appears horizontally beneath the Formatting toolbar when the document is maximized. When the document window is not maximized, the ruler appears at the top of the document window. You can also set a document to display a vertical ruler to display heights.

To learn about how to change ruler settings with the mouse, look under "Ruler" in Chapter 4. To learn about the tab stops that a ruler displays, see "Tabs" in Chapter 4.

Scroll Bars

Scroll bars, which appear at the bottom and right of the window shown in Figure 1-1, let you move through large documents quickly. With a mouse, you can click the arrow buttons on these scroll bars to change the part of the document currently displayed in the window. The small box that appears within the scroll bars is the *scroll box;* it indicates the relative position of the section you are viewing within the document. Chapter 2 explains how to use the scroll bars to change the section of the document that appears in the window.

The three buttons to the left of the horizontal scroll bar are the View buttons; they allow you to change the way you view the document.

 The vertical scroll bar contains, in addition to the arrow buttons and scroll box, a splitter box that you can use to divide a document window into two parts, or panes, as described in Chapter 4. "Viewing Documents" in Chapter 4 also tells you how to use the View buttons to change the view of a document.

Status Bar

The *status bar* at the bottom of the window displays information about what is going on in Word. This bar is divided into sections for different kinds of information. The far left end of the status bar tells you what page you are on, which section of the document you are in, and how many pages are in the document. The next section tells you the distance between the top of the page and the current position of your insertion point, the number of that line, and how many characters are between the left margin and the current position of your insertion point. Next, the status bar contains the indicators that show when various features are turned on, such as overtype, revision mode, or spelling.

The information in the status bar depends on your current activity. For instance, when you highlight a menu command or point with the mouse to screen elements such as the toolbar buttons, the status bar tells you what task that command or button will perform. This special information temporarily overlays the standard status bar display. When you use certain keyboard shortcuts for commands, such as F2 or SHIFT+F2, the status bar displays a message asking for more information about that command and lets you enter your response. The status bar can also tell you the status of a command as Word is performing it—for example, how much of the document has been saved.

Insertion Point

The *insertion point* is a marker on the screen that indicates where you are in a document. You may be more familiar with the term "cursor," but throughout this book we will use insertion point. The characters you type appear at the insertion point. In addition to this marker, information on the left side of the status bar tells you where the insertion point is in the document (as described in the previous section). Before entering text, editing text, or doing anything else with your documents, you will want to know exactly where the insertion point is.

Windows Taskbar

The bottom of your screen may show the Windows taskbar. This taskbar includes the Start button to launch other applications and icons for the different tasks that you have open. These tasks include folders you have open and other applications you have running. You can select the task to work on by clicking the icon.

Using the Mouse

Using the mouse is the simplest way to get around in Word. The mouse controls a mouse pointer that moves across the screen as you move the mouse around your desktop. A mouse lets you point to and select objects on the screen to perform actions, rather than using the keyboard. This is often called *pointing and clicking*. For example, by pointing and clicking on the scroll bar arrows, you can move through a document quickly. A few actions, such as a SHIFT+click, require the use of the mouse and keyboard at the same time.

Other pointing devices, such as a trackball or stylus, can be used in a similar way.

Mouse Actions

To use the mouse in Windows, you have to master a few basic techniques: drag, click, right-click, and double-click.

All of these techniques require you to press the mouse button and release it. For dragging, clicking, and double-clicking, you use the left button on the mouse. Only for right-clicking do you use the right mouse button. You will never need the center button of a three-button mouse with Word for Windows.

For clicking, right-clicking, and double-clicking, you *press and quickly release* the mouse button; for dragging (or moving) an object with the mouse, however, you have to *press and hold* the mouse button. Place the mouse pointer on the object you wish to drag. Then press the left mouse button and hold it down. *Without releasing the button*, drag the mouse pointer to where you want the object to appear, and then release the mouse button. Chapter 2 teaches you how to use dragging to select text in a document.

You can click with the mouse to to select something. Point to the object you want to select, then press the left mouse button once and quickly release it.

Right-clicking opens *shortcut menus*. You point to an object or location on the screen, and press the right mouse button once.

Double-clicking usually selects an object or carries out an action. To double-click an object, point to that object and press the left mouse button twice in quick succession. You may have already used a double-click on the Microsoft Word for Windows icon to start the Word application.

> **TIP:** *You can change the clicking speed required for recognition of a double-click, as well as which mouse button is designated as the primary mouse button (left or right). These changes are made through the Control Panel (available through Settings in the Start button). If you find that your double-clicks are frequently interpreted by Word as a single click, you can change the double-click speed setting to a lower number to allow more time between clicks. Left-handed people often swap the left/right button setting to make the mouse easier to use with their left hand.*

In Chapter 2, you learn about selecting and rearranging text. In Chapter 3, you learn about how to change the appearance of selected text. These options use the mouse actions you have just learned.

Mouse Pointer Shapes

The mouse pointer marks the location of the mouse on the screen and shows you which object will be affected by your next mouse action. The mouse pointer changes its shape frequently as you use it. These shapes indicate that certain options are available and tell you about what is occurring at the moment. When you know the shapes of the mouse pointer, you can use Word and other Windows applications more efficiently. Table 1-1 shows you some of the mouse pointer shapes and their meanings.

Using the Keyboard

Your mouse lets you do some things on the screen more easily, but you will also use the keyboard frequently in Word. As you are typing, you may find it easier to enter a command using a keyboard technique rather than the mouse. Anything that you can do with the mouse can also be done with the keyboard. Word also has many valuable command shortcuts that are accomplished from the keyboard. In addition to using the

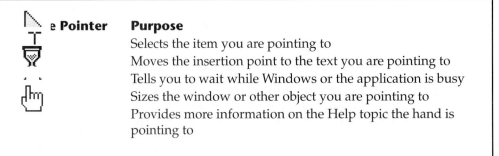

e Pointer	Purpose
	Selects the item you are pointing to
	Moves the insertion point to the text you are pointing to
	Tells you to wait while Windows or the application is busy
	Sizes the window or other object you are pointing to
	Provides more information on the Help topic the hand is pointing to

Table 1-1. *Mouse Pointers and Their Roles*

keyboard to enter text and commands, you use it to move the insertion point in a document to where you want to add or remove text.

There are several available layouts for keyboards. One of the most common is the IBM Enhanced keyboard, shown in Figure 1-3. If you are using another keyboard, you will find the same keys, just in different positions.

In Chapter 2, you learn about using the keyboard and mouse to move through a document you are creating. Keyboard or mouse--the choice is yours, since the results are the same. Use whichever technique you find more convenient.

The Function Keys

The function keys are the keys labeled F1 through F12; on most keyboards these keys are usually positioned along the top. By pressing the function keys, you can quickly perform tasks in Word. Function keys combined with the CTRL, ALT, or SHIFT keys provide *keyboard shortcuts* for the most popular features.

Word has assigned tasks to the function keys. An important function key that you will use from the beginning is F1. This key accesses the online Help that you will learn more about later in this chapter. The other function keys will be explained when their features are introduced.

Working in Dialog Boxes

Dialog boxes are small windows that appear on your screen when Word needs information from you in order to carry out a command. They contain some objects you

Figure 1-3. *The IBM enhanced keyboard*

have not yet encountered in this introduction to the Word window: command buttons, text boxes, list boxes, option buttons, and check boxes. These objects are identified in Figure 1-4.

The contents of a dialog box will depend on what command or feature you have selected. However, all dialog boxes behave the same—whether you are describing how you want text to appear, the document you want to see on the screen, or the graphic image you want to add, you will do similar things in every dialog box. To make dialog boxes easier to use, Word may even change the display in a dialog box as you make selections, removing components that are no longer appropriate. The prompts that appear in a dialog box will clearly identify the information that is required.

To make a selection within a dialog box, you first move to an element of the dialog box by clicking it. If you want to use your keyboard, all elements in the dialog box have an underlined letter. You can move to an element in the dialog box by pressing ALT and the underlined letter, or by pressing TAB until the element is highlighted.

Command Buttons

Command buttons appear in every dialog box. When you select one of these buttons, an action is carried out. If the text on the button displays an ellipsis, selecting the button opens another dialog box. To select a command button, you can click it, or you can press ALT and the underlined letter on the button (or press TAB until the button is highlighted) and then press ENTER.

Two command buttons appear in nearly every dialog box: the OK button and the Cancel button (see Figure 1-4):

- ■ Clicking the OK button starts the action for which you opened the dialog box, using the information you provide in the dialog box. The OK button has no underlined letter, but you can select it from the keyboard by pressing ENTER when the button has an extra outline around it, as it does in Figure 1-4.

- ■ Clicking the Cancel button closes the dialog box without carrying out any action. You can also select Cancel from the keyboard by pressing ESC.

Text Boxes

Another important element of dialog boxes is the *text box*, into which you can type information. For example, in Figure 1-4, you can set the font for text by typing a size into the Size text box.

Text boxes can occur independently, or they can be attached to a list box (explained just below). If a text box is independent, you can type the required information into it. If the text box is attached to a list box, you have a choice: you can either type information directly into the text box, or you can choose an option from the list box, and Word will put that option into the text box.

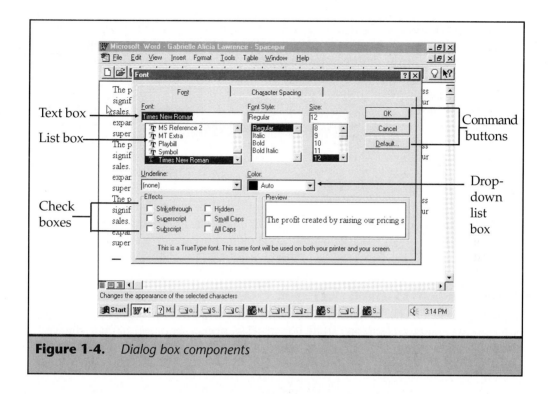

Figure 1-4. *Dialog box components*

Sometimes a text box calls for a number to be entered. When a text box has a set of up- and down-arrow buttons on the right side, you can increase or decrease the number in the text box by clicking the appropriate arrow button, as well as by simply typing a new number. This special type of text box is sometimes referred to as a *spin box*. It is used for setting page margins, for example.

List Boxes

In dialog boxes, you frequently need to make selections from lists. Lists can be in either list boxes or drop-down list boxes (you can see examples of both in Figure 1-4). A *list box*, such as the Font list box in Figure 1-4, displays a number of choices. When the list is longer than the box, a scroll bar appears at the side of the box, and you can use it to move through the list to find the selection you need. You select an item on the list by clicking it or highlighting it with the arrow keys and pressing ENTER.

The list boxes in Figure 1-4 have attached text boxes. Only some list boxes have text boxes attached. The adjoining text boxes show the item that is currently selected in the list. You can also type an entry in the text box, rather than selecting it from the list. A list box not shown with a text box looks just like the list boxes that you see below the Font, Font Style, and Size text boxes.

The Underline box in Figure 1-4 is a *drop-down list box*. The selection that appears in the box is the current selection for that list. To view the entire list, as shown here, you must click the arrow button or move to Underline and press DOWN ARROW:

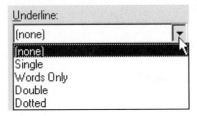

Most drop-down lists require that you select one of the items listed rather than type it in. Select the item with the usual mouse or keyboard method; or, if you press a letter key, Word will select the next item in the list that starts with that letter.

Option Buttons and Check Boxes

Option buttons and check boxes are two more ways to specify settings in Word. *Option buttons* (also called *radio buttons*) allow you to select from a set of mutually exclusive options. Option buttons appear in sets, like these:

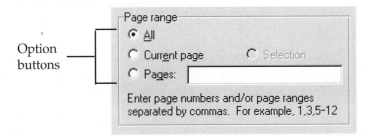

You can select one and only one option button from a set. For example, the Print dialog box has option buttons to select the amount you want to print. You can select only one of the following option buttons: All, Current Page, or Pav:\y\a1
es. When you select one, the others in the set are deselected (turned off). The selected option button has the dark circle in the middle; the unselected ones are clear.

Check boxes turn features on or off. The All Caps check box in Figure 1-4 is currently turned on. You can tell this because the check box is filled with an X. If All Caps were turned off, the check box would be empty, and this character formatting option would not be added.

Tabbed Sections

Word for Windows has divided some of its dialog boxes into *tabbed sections*; in Figure 1-4 you can see the tabs for Font and Character Spacing at the top of the dialog box. To see the desired set of dialog box options, click the desired tab or press CTRL+TAB or CTRL+SHIFT+TAB until the tab you want is on top of the "stack."

TIP: You can use either a mouse or the keyboard to make dialog box selections. It is the final selection in a dialog box when you select OK or another button, so you will have some time to make a correction if you select the wrong option before you process your entries.

Arranging Your Workspace

To use Word and your computer effectively, you need to see what you want to work with. To accomplish this, you need to be able to position your Word window and the document windows that you have open. You can size, move, and close your windows. While the focus in this section is on windows in Word, many of these window control features work for any window in Windows.

Sizing Windows

You can change the size of document windows within the Word application window, and you can also size the Word application window itself. Sizing lets you display several applications or documents on the screen at the same time. You can allocate how much of the screen Word uses versus other applications. And when Word is the active application, you can decide how much space each document uses within the Word window. The directions for sizing both types of window are the same, except a document window cannot appear outside the Word window.

Windows applications have three techniques for sizing windows: you can maximize, minimize, and restore. When you maximize a window, it takes up all the available space, and you can see the maximum amount of text and data. In Figure 1-1, both the application window and document window are maximized.

To maximize a window, you can either click the Maximize button (the middle sizing button on the right end of the bar) or click on the program or document icon and select Maximize.

TIP: You can display the menu for a program icon by pressing ALT+SPACEBAR. You can display the menu for a document icon by pressing ALT+- (hyphen).

When you minimize a window, it is reduced to an icon. You may want to minimize the Word window when you want to make room on your screen to work with another application window. To minimize a window, click the Minimize button, or click the program or document icon and then select Mi̱nimize.

The third sizing technique is Restore. When you click the Restore button or select the Ṟestore command, the window is changed to an intermediate size; it's not maximized, but it's not an icon, either. A window at this intermediate size has window borders that are lines surrounding the entire window. In this state, you can change the size of the window to any size you want. The Restore button replaces the Maximize button when the window is not maximized.

Using the mouse to size a window is easy once you have practiced a few times. Point the mouse at the window's border. When the mouse is correctly positioned, the mouse pointer turns into a double-headed arrow (see Table 1-1). Then drag the border to where you want that side of the window to be. The double-headed arrow points in the two directions in which you can move the border. For example, when you point to the lower-right window corner, the mouse pointer changes to a double-diagonal arrow, telling you that you can move that corner in or out diagonally, to shrink or enlarge the window size.

TIP: *You cannot size a maximized window.*

Sizing a window with the keyboard is almost as easy. Select S̱ize from the program or document icon's menu. A four-headed arrow will appear. Press an arrow key to move to one of the window borders, and the pointer will move to that border and become a double-headed arrow. Then use the arrow keys to move the border; when the window is correctly sized, press ENTER.

TIP: *Word has several function key combinations that you can use to size a window. CTRL+F10 maximizes a document window, and ALT+F10 maximizes an application window. CTRL+F5 restores a document window's size, and ALT+F5 restores an application window's size. CTRL+F8 lets you size a document window using the arrow keys.*

Moving Windows

After you have sized the windows on your screen, you may want to arrange them in some fashion by moving them. You use the same methods for moving document and application windows, using either the mouse or the keyboard. (Maximized windows cannot be moved, since they occupy all the available space.)

Moving a window with the mouse is a one-step operation. Simply point the mouse at the title bar and drag it to a new location. This moves the window to that location.

To move a window using the keyboard, select M̱ove from the icon's menu. Then use the arrow keys to move the title bar to a new location. Press ENTER when the window is correctly located, and the window will be redrawn in the new location.

TIP: *When moving a document window, you can press* CTRL+F7 *instead of selecting Move from the window icon's menu.*

Closing Windows

In Word, you need to close both document and application windows. When you are done with a document, close it to free up the memory that document used and to make sure any changes that you have made are saved. When you are done with Word, you will want to close Word, Exit the program, and free up the memory Word uses. All windows have a Close box in the upper-right corner—it is the one with the X. When you close a window, Word checks if the document needs to be saved. If the document does need to be saved, you see the prompt for saving the document or leaving it without saving changes. Besides closing windows with the Close box, you can also select the File | Close command, press CTRL+F4, press CTRL+W, double-click the program's or document's icon, or click the document's icon in the upper-left corner and select Close.

TIP: *Dialog boxes also have a Close button so you can close the dialog box without carrying out any action, similar to the Cancel button or* ESC.

Accessing Help

Word's online Help feature is the perfect way to answer a quick question about any of the program's features. Word for Windows Help is a separate application and appears in its own window. When you open Word for Windows Help, it replaces any other Help window you have open at the time. Word has multiple types of help to answer your questions.

You already have seen several examples of help that Word provides to guide you through its features. When you start Word, you may see the Tip of the Day, which offers pointers about Word features you may want to use. Also, Word displays toolbar button names when you point to them for a couple of seconds. And in the status bar, you can see help about where you are in a document, the command you are pointing to, or the dialog box you are working with.

Showing a Help Window

Help is always easy to access: Just press F1. When you press F1, Word guesses about what topic you want to know about; this is called *context-sensitive* help, because it is based on what you are doing when you press F1. For example, if you press F1 in the middle of selecting a command from a menu, the Help window displays information about the command you have highlighted before pressing F1.

The Help application window opens with Word's best guess. Word also has a Help Topics window, which appears when Word cannot tell what specific task you want information about. Figure 1-5 shows the Word Help Topics window.

You can also access Help by opening the Help menu and selecting one of the options there. If you select Microsoft Word Help Topics, the Help window opens with Word's Help Topics shown in Figure 1-5. You can also select Answer Wizard to go directly to the Answer Wizard which is available through the Help Topics window. If you have previously used the WordPerfect program, look into WordPerfect Help. The help supplied by this command will assist you in translating your WordPerfect skills into fluency with Word for Windows. About Microsoft Word shows your copyright information, product ID number, and provides buttons to open the System Info program and to open Help to show how to get technical support.

Moving Among Help Topics

Next to each of the main topics in the Help Topics window are book icons. If you click on any one, the book icon changes to an open book, and you can see other books

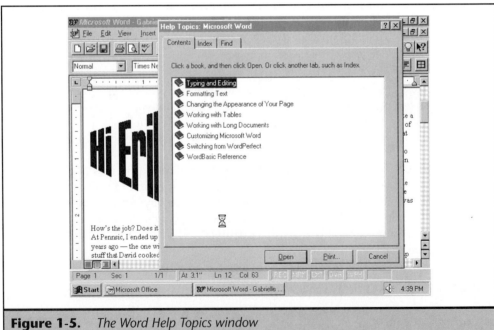

Figure 1-5.   *The Word Help Topics window*

(documents) that are part of it. Figure 1-6 shows the Help Topics window after clicking the Typing and Editing topic and then clicking the Typing and Selecting topic from the second-level list. The icons containing question marks are help topics that you can display by double-clicking them.

When you are finished with a Help window, put it away with the Close button or click one of the other buttons to switch to a different topic. You can always return to the Help Topics window by selecting the Help Topics button.

READY
for
MORE
　　　　　"Help" in Chapter 4 describes more of what is available through Word's Help feature.

Index and Find

The Index and Find tabbed sections can also help you find the topic that answers your questions. Select the Index tab in the Help Topics window to switch to the Index window. In the text box at the top part of the window, type the word or phrase you are curious about. The list box just below will shift to display the subjects that match what

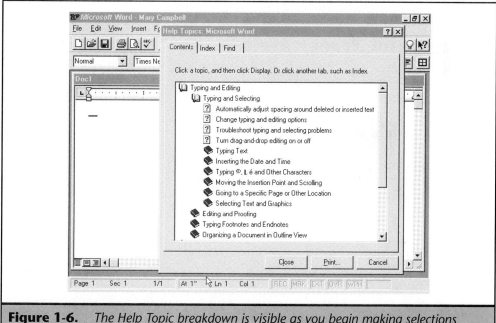

Figure 1-6. *The Help Topic breakdown is visible as you begin making selections*

you type. You can add or remove text to refind your match. You can also double-click the topic that appeals to you to switch to that help information.

The Find feature creates an index based on the text in Word's help file. Instead of looking for topics, you are looking at the words in the help topic. You might want to do this when you are looking for some information about a topic and you want to find help topics on other Word features that reference that topic. To use the Find feature, click the Find tab in the Help Topics window. Type the word or phrase that you want to locate, and the list box in the middle narrows down to words that match what you have typed. You can narrow down which help topics are listed in the list box at the bottom by selecting just the words in the middle list box that interest you. Double-click a topic from the bottom list box or highlight it and select Display. The Help window will then change to show the topic you selected.

The Answer Wizard

The Answer Wizard is an online assistant that you can ask questions. You can try out the Answer Wizard by moving to the Answer Wizard tab from the Help Topics window or by selecting Answer Wizard from the Help menu. Once at this tab, type what you want to learn how to do in the drop-down list box. Examples include: "Add space after a paragraph" or "Print my hidden topics." After typing the question that you want answered, select Search. The list box in the middle of the window now lists various help topics that might be related to your question. Double-click any topic or highlight it and select Display to see that topic.

Dialog Box and Screen Help

Word has two other features that help you learn about Word. When you click the Help button (the one with an arrow and question mark) on the Standard toolbar, you can point at other objects on the window to learn about them. For example, click on the Help button, then click on a topic that you want to learn about.

A second quick help feature is available in a dialog box. Dialog boxes with a question mark (?) button in their title bar can display information about any part of the dialog box. For example, when you select File | Open to open a file, you can click the ? button and then the Look In drop-down list box to learn how to change where Word looks for documents.

Chapter Two

Creating and Editing a Document

When you write a letter, you start with a clean sheet of paper. When you create a document with Word, you start with a new document, which is just like a clean sheet of paper. With it, you can get started creating your letter, report, or other text. In this chapter, you will learn how to create a document, edit it, save it, print it, and check its spelling—in other words, all the basics of document creation. When you finish, you will be ready to try other Word features.

The documents you will work with in this chapter use some of the formatting described in Chapters 3 and 4. As you learn more about Word, you will be able to incorporate more of these formatting features in your own documents.

Creating a Document

When you start a new Word session, Word always provides a new document, called Document1. This document is in a document window that is maximized, so it occupies as much of the Word window as possible. Document1 appears in the Word title bar; but later, when you save your document, the Document1 name will be replaced by the name you select for the document.

Once you have a blank document displayed, you are ready to start typing the text you want it to contain.

Creating Additional New Documents

Whenever you want to create a new letter, memo, or report, you will need a new document. But you need not close one document to open another; you can create a new document at any time while you are working with Word. When you are ready to create a new document, click the New button on the toolbar, shown in the margin.

This button creates a new document, with the initial name of Document# (the # represents the next unused document number). These document numbers help you identify the documents even before you have saved them with a unique name.

CAUTION: If you do not save your new document before exiting Word, you will lose the entire document. Word does prompt you to save changes before you exit it.

The other way you can create a new document is to select the File | New command. This opens the New dialog box, which has tabs for all the different types of document templates. Using a template provides some additional structure to the document (a *template* is a pattern that affects formatting and may even provide some of the document text). You can select from faxes, reports, letters, and resumes for some of the documents already set up for you. You will learn all about Word templates in Chapter 4. When you select OK in the New dialog box with the Normal template selected, Word creates a new document just as if you used the New button on the toolbar.

READY
for
MORE

Create and use templates when you want to give a set of documents a consistent appearance. Chapter 4 has more information about creating templates and using them. You can also use a Word wizard, which will help you create several types of documents. There are wizards for legal pleadings and other types of documents that function as templates with a little extra assistance. Word also includes the option to provide summary information in a new document; in Chapter 4, you will learn that this feature is now set with the Tools Options Save tab, which sets the prompt for summary information and other properties when saving a new document.

Switching Among Documents

When you have more than one document open, you need to be able to switch to the document you want. Two quick methods for doing this are the Window menu and CTRL+F6.

The bottom portion of the Window menu lists the documents currently open on your screen. Each of the documents has a number next to it; you can either type this number or click on the document name to switch to one of these open documents. While you can open as many documents as you want, Word has a limit of nine document names that can display in the Window menu. If you have more than nine open, you will see an option for More Windows to see additional documents.

Pressing CTRL+F6 switches from one document window to the next, following the same order in which documents are listed at the bottom of the Window menu.

READY
for
MORE

If you want to be able to see several documents at once, look at "Windows" in Chapter 4. "Viewing Documents" in Chapter 4 explains other options to change how you display documents. When displaying several document windows at once, you can also switch to the document you want by clicking it.

Entering Text

After opening a new document, you will want to enter text or other elements in that document. Entering text in an electronic Word document is the same as typing a document on a typewriter or writing with a pen on paper—with certain differences. You can correct anything on the screen without having to retype the entire document. Also, you must use a different technique for marking the end of lines and paragraphs.

Typing in the Document Window

Most of the techniques for typing with a computer are just like typing with a typewriter. For example, each time you press a key on the keyboard, the character on the key—a letter, number, or punctuation symbol—appears on the screen. If you press SHIFT, the capital letter (or the top character on the key) appears. Although Word doesn't impose many restrictions on what you enter in a document window, you will want to follow the usual rules for grammar and punctuation. Be sure to read the box on the following page containing "Rules for Entering Numbers."

Rules for Entering Numbers

Numbers are sometimes written as digits and sometimes spelled out in words. The following guidelines provide examples of when each method of recording numbers is most popular:

- Express monetary amounts as digits.

- Enter both words and numbers in legal documents, as in "one hundred fifty (150)."

- Use digits to represent measurements, ages, percentages, and decimals.

- Use words for numbers that start a sentence.

- In formal documents, spell out numbers that require one or two words.

- Use hyphens to separate compound words, such as "fifty-four."

- Use words for indefinite numbers, as in "Millions of people are affected."

- Numbers requiring three or more words should be expressed as digits, as in "253" or "21 million."

- In less formal documents, numbers below ten are always written as words ("three, four, five") unless they are combined in a sentence with numbers above ten, in which case they are all expressed with digits ("1, 25, and 53").

- Add an *s* to make digits plural, and either *s* or *es* for plurals of words that represent numbers.

Some other techniques work differently when you're typing on a computer. For example, on a typewriter, you have to press the RETURN key at the end of each line to mark its end. Word, however, will automatically wrap the line of text down to the next line when you run out of space at the right margin. You only press the ENTER key (the RETURN key's counterpart) when you want to signal the end of a paragraph. Because Word wraps text to fit the width of the lines, you can change margins after typing text, and the text will automatically size itself to the new margins. You also can let Word handle the page breaks; the program will automatically add a page break when the text fills a page.

When you lock the SHIFT key down on a typewriter, the letter keys you type produce all uppercase characters, and other keys produce their top characters. With the computer, when you press the CAPS LOCK key, the letter keys will produce capital letters; however, you still must press SHIFT to access the upper characters for the other keys. Also, pressing SHIFT does not release CAPS LOCK in the same way that it releases SHIFT LOCK on the typewriter.

Ending a Paragraph

To end a paragraph or short line in Word, press ENTER. When you press ENTER, you move to the next line, and an invisible paragraph symbol (¶) is entered in your document. Figure 2-1 contains several lines of text where ENTER was pressed to end the line.

CAUTION: Do not press ENTER to mark the end of a line within a paragraph. If you do so, you will have great difficulty formatting your document later, and you will lose one of the great advantages of using a word processor—automatic word wrap.

READY
for
MORE

If you want to see the paragraph symbols (¶), which indicate where you have pressed ENTER to move to the next line, or other "invisible" characters such as TAB, look at "Nonprinting Characters" in Chapter 4.

Using the Tab Key

Pressing the TAB key in Word moves you to the next tab stop, just as it does on a typewriter. *Tab stops* are positions on the page that you can easily move to by pressing TAB. In new documents, default tab stops are set every half-inch. When you press TAB,

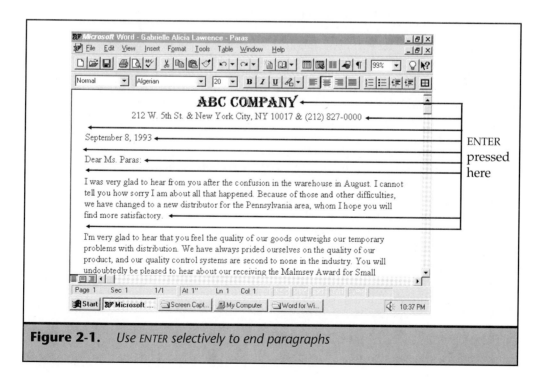

Figure 2-1. *Use ENTER selectively to end paragraphs*

the insertion point moves to the next tab stop and aligns the characters you type next with that tab position.

On a typewriter, you use a tab to indent the beginning of paragraphs. You can still do this in Word, but it's easier to use paragraph formatting, which lets you start a paragraph without pressing TAB. You find out how to do this in Chapter 3.

When you want to align text in Word, use TAB and not the SPACEBAR. Since Word can use attractive proportional fonts (these control the width of the characters), each character does not occupy the same amount of space. So if you use the SPACEBAR to align text, you will have jagged alignment, since each character does not use the same amount of space as an empty space. When you use TAB, the space used is an absolute measurement, and so the text always aligns on the same location on the page.

Word's initial tab stops are set every half-inch, but you can change them. "Tabs" in Chapter 4 tells you how to do this and explains right, center, and decimal tabs, which change the alignment of the text you enter at a tab stop. Rather than using TAB to create a table within a document, check out "Tables" in Chapter 4, which describes an easier method.

Editing a Document

No one creates a perfect document with the first draft. You will often need to edit your documents, either to refine your organization, correct mistakes, or reuse a document in a somewhat different context. Word gives you many efficient tools that make editing a simple task. Among other things, you can delete entire sections of text, copy them, or move them to different locations in your document.

Navigating Within a Document

The first step in learning how to edit your document is knowing how to move around in it as well as quickly through it.

Moving with the Mouse

Moving within a document using the mouse is easy: You point and click at a location in the document, and the insertion point moves there.

If the text you want to see is not currently displayed, use the document window's scroll bars to get there. Click the scroll bar arrow buttons to move one line up or down. Click to either side of the scroll box to move one window of text in that direction. Drag the scroll box to a new position in the scroll bar to move to that position in the document (this method involves some guesswork). Once you've displayed a new part of the document, click to move the insertion point to the exact desired location. Horizontal scrolling works the same way if the document is too wide to display on the screen all at once.

CAUTION: *The scroll bar changes the part of the document that is displayed, but it does not move the insertion point. Before you enter any text after scrolling, remember to click to move the insertion point to the place where you want it to be.*

Moving with the Keyboard

The keyboard offers a variety of methods for moving in a document. When you move with the keyboard, you move the insertion point itself, rather than just changing the display of the document. Here is a list of the movement keys:

Key	Moves You To
HOME	The beginning of the line
END	The end of the line
PGDN	One window down in the document
PGUP	One window up in the document
CTRL+HOME	The beginning of the document
CTRL+END	The end of the document
CTRL+LEFT ARROW	The beginning of the current or previous word
CTRL+RIGHT ARROW	The beginning of the next word
CTRL+UP ARROW	The beginning of the current paragraph or the previous one
CTRL+DOWN ARROW	The beginning of the following paragraph

These keystrokes may be very confusing at first, but rest assured, they will quickly become familiar and easy to use. Most Windows applications use the same keystrokes for similar movements.

TIP: *For a shortcut in moving through very long documents, see "Outlines" in Chapter 4.*

Moving to a Specific Page

In a long document, you will need to be able to quickly move from one page to another. Word lets you move to a specific page in a document using the Go To command. You can also move to other types of markers using this command, as you'll learn in Chapter 4.

To use Go To, select Edit | Go To or press F5; this opens the Go To dialog box. The Page option will already be selected. In the Enter Page Number text box, type the number of the page you want to move to, and select Go To. The insertion point will move to the beginning of the text on that page.

You can even type the plus (+) or minus (-) key in the Enter Page Number text box, followed by a number, to move a specific number of pages forward or backward in the document. For example, typing **+2** and selecting Next moves you two pages forward from the current location.

> **TIP:** *You can move to any of the last three locations where you made editing changes. Press* SHIFT+F5 *to cycle through the last three editing locations. These locations might even be in different documents.*

Making Corrections

As you type, you may find that you have misspelled words, used the wrong words, or simply mistyped something. Making corrections with Word is simple: you simply delete the characters on the screen and enter new ones.

Use the mouse or arrow keys to move the insertion point to the mistake that you want to correct. Position the insertion point just before or just after the characters to be deleted. Press DEL to delete the characters to the right of the insertion point, and press BACKSPACE to delete the characters to the left of the insertion point. If you want to delete one whole word, Word provides a shortcut. Press CTRL+BACKSPACE to delete the word before the insertion point and CTRL+DEL to delete the word after the insertion point.

After deleting the incorrect characters, you'll want to enter the correct ones. Just type them, starting with the insertion point at the correct location. Word inserts the characters you type at the insertion point.

You can also replace characters using overtype mode. (You can tell whether you are in overtype mode when you see OVR in the status bar, in either a black or bright display. OVR is dimmed, or grayed out, in the status bar when you are not in overtype mode.) In overtype mode, Word does not make space for the new characters you type. Instead, new characters replace the old characters. If you are inserting the same number of characters that you are deleting, using overtype mode is faster than deleting the old text and inserting the new. To switch to overtype mode, press the INS key or double-click the dimmed OVR in the status bar. To switch back to the default insert mode, press INS or double-click the OVR indicator again.

> **TIP:** *At certain times, you cannot use overtype mode. This includes when you have the Use Ins for Paste option turned on and when revision marks are turned on.*

NOTE: *If you delete a word at the end of a sentence or immediately before a closing parenthesis, colon, semicolon, question mark, or exclamation mark, Word also deletes the space before the word. Thus, the punctuation mark moves to the end of the word before the one you just deleted. This is called Smart Cut and Paste. This feature also applies when you copy text before a punctuation mark—Word adds a space to separate the inserted text from the surrounding words.*

Selecting Text

You have learned how to manipulate a single character of text, but you can also work with many characters at the same time—by selecting the text before taking an action. Selected text appears highlighted on your screen. Once text is selected, you can delete it, format it, copy it, or move it.

Selecting with the Mouse

Selecting text with the mouse lets you quickly choose the text you want to work with. First, move the mouse pointer to the beginning of the text you want to select and drag to the end of the text you want to select. The text between the point where you started to drag and where you release the mouse button becomes highlighted, marking it as the selected text. Another way to do this is to click at the beginning of the text you want to select, moving the insertion point there. Then hold down the SHIFT key while you click the end of the text to select. All of the text in between the two clicks will be highlighted. You can also do this by clicking the beginning location, clicking the EXT indicator in the status bar, and clicking the end of the text to select.

If you change your mind about what you are selecting, just click at another location in the document, or release the SHIFT key and press any arrow key.

Another way to use the mouse for selecting text is by using it with the selection bar. The *selection bar*—the blank area at the left of the text area—lets you select large areas of text quickly. When the mouse pointer is in the selection bar, it looks like an arrow pointing to the right.

When you click the mouse in the selection bar, the line of text immediately to the right of the pointer is selected. Click and drag the mouse up or down in the selection bar, and all of the lines to the right of where you drag in the selection bar will be selected. Another method is to click the selection bar multiple times: clicking once selects the current line, twice selects the current paragraph, and three times selects the entire document.

Here are additional options: Double-click a word to select it. Triple-click in the same spot, and you select the entire paragraph. To select an entire sentence, hold down CTRL when you click anywhere in the sentence.

Selecting with the Keyboard

To select text using the keyboard, you use the SHIFT key in combination with the movement keys. For example, pressing END moves the insertion point to the end of a line of text, but when you press SHIFT+END, you select all of the text from the insertion point's original location to the end of the line. You can use any of the movement keys or movement key combinations with SHIFT to select text.

If you change your mind about what you are selecting with the keyboard, you can use the arrow keys to leave out part of your original selection by holding down the SHIFT key. If you press an arrow key after releasing the SHIFT key, you'll have to make a new selection of the text you want to include.

To select an entire document, press CTRL and the 5 key in the middle of the numeric keypad.

Another way to select text with the keyboard is using the Extend key (F8). Press F8, and the EXT indicator appears in the status bar. (To turn Extend off, press ESC.) Then you can press the arrow keys to indicate the area of text you want to select.

Press F8 repeatedly, and you select a progressively larger section of text: first the word your insertion point is on, then that sentence, then that paragraph, then the section, and then the entire document. To reverse directions, selecting progressively smaller sections of text, press SHIFT+F8 repeatedly.

You can also type a character after pressing F8, and Word will select all the text between the insertion point and the next occurrence of that character in the document. For example, if you press F8 and then type a period, you'll select from your current location to the end of that sentence.

TIP: *When you already have text selected and you type more text, Word's default action is to replace the selected text with the text you are typing. However, Word has an editing option that you can set if you do not want text you type to replace any text you have selected.*

Moving and Copying Text by Dragging and Dropping

Word provides a neat mouse shortcut for moving and copying text you have already selected. Drag the mouse from the selected text to where you want it moved. When you start dragging, the status bar will show the question, "Move to where?" The mouse pointer will be accompanied by a dashed bar with a box just below it, indicating where the selected text will be inserted. As you point to a new location, you have a bar showing where the text will be placed, as shown in the following illustration:

- Assign waste reduction goals for divisions
- Review latest EPA reports on clean-up at Massingham
- Compare waste production statistics of various divisions

When you release the mouse, the selected text is moved to the location of the dashed bar.

Copying selected text by dragging and dropping works the same way, except you hold down the CTRL key while you drag the selected text to a new location. The pointer will be accompanied by a plus sign (+) to the right, indicating that you are copying rather than moving. The status bar shows the message "Copy to where?" This drag-and-drop method of rearranging your document is quick and easy.

Deleting Selected Text

You can also select text that you do not want in its current location and delete it. You can delete text so that it is completely erased, or you can cut the text. When you cut text, it is removed from its current location in the document, but it can be pasted, or reinserted, into a document.

If you no longer want the text and wish to erase it completely, select it and press either the DEL or BACKSPACE key.

If you want to paste the text you are cutting into another location, you have two options: the Windows Clipboard and Word's Spike feature.

Cutting Text to the Clipboard or the Spike

Word and most other Windows applications use the Clipboard—a temporary storage location for cut data. You can put data into the Clipboard and take data from it. The Clipboard stores data from one source at a time, so when you put something into the Clipboard, you are discarding whatever was there before. The Clipboard is emptied when you leave Windows.

Word's Spike is another special location in memory. The Spike, too, holds data temporarily, but it only works within Word. The Spike lets you move data from one location to another among Word documents only.

The Spike has a few other differences from the Clipboard. When you add something to the Spike, it is appended to the end of the current Spike contents. Paragraph breaks are added between all the separate items added to the Spike. You can use the Spike to pick up text from different parts of a Word document and then dump all of it into another location. The Spike is emptied when you leave Word or when you put the Spike's contents into a document with CTRL+SHIFT+F3, as described shortly in the "Inserting Text" section.

When you select and cut text, it is sent either to the Clipboard or to the Spike, as follows:

■ To cut to the Clipboard, select the Cut command, either by clicking on the Cut tool on the toolbar or by selecting Edit I Cut. The selected text is deleted from your Word document and placed in the Windows Clipboard. From the Windows Clipboard, you can paste the selected text to another Windows application or into a Word document.

CAUTION: *When you cut or copy text to the Clipboard, the previous contents of the Clipboard are erased. You cannot cut two different selections of text to the Clipboard and then insert them both elsewhere.*

■ To cut to the Spike, press CTRL+F3. The selected text disappears from its current location in the document and is added to the Spike's current contents. From there, it can be inserted into any open Word document.

Inserting Text

When you cut text, either to the Windows Clipboard or to Word's Spike, you can paste (insert) that text into a Word document. This is a helpful technique when you are reorganizing a document. When you paste text, it is placed at the insertion point's location—even in overtype mode. So, whether you are pasting from the Clipboard or the Spike, you should always begin by moving the insertion point to where you want the text placed.

When the text you want to paste is in the Clipboard, you can either click the Paste button in the toolbar or select Edit I Paste. Word reads the contents of the Clipboard into your Word document at the insertion point's position. The text remains on the Clipboard, so if you want to paste it in another location in your document or into another document, simply reposition the insertion point and use the Paste command again. The text will stay in the Clipboard until you cut or copy a different piece of text.

When the text you want to paste is in the Spike, position the insertion point where you want the text placed and press CTRL+SHIFT+F3. All the contents of the Spike will be inserted into your document. If you have cut several selections of text onto the Spike, all of those selections will appear, in the same order in which you added them to the Spike. When you paste text from the Spike in this way, the Spike is emptied.

When you want to paste the same text from the Spike to several locations, you need to use another method of pasting text from the Spike. Rather than CTRL+SHIFT+F3, type **spike** where you want the text pasted, press the SPACEBAR, and press F3. Word replaces the word "spike" with the contents of the Spike. To insert the Spike's contents in another location, type **spike** again and press F3, or press CTRL+SHIFT+F3.

The Spike is a special implementation of the AutoText feature, discussed in Chapter 4.

Copying Text

You can copy text to the Clipboard without deleting it from its original location in your document. For example, if an address is used twice in a letter, you can copy the first occurrence of the address into another location without having to type it again and without its being deleted from the first location. You cannot copy text to the Spike.

The only difference between copying and cutting is how the text gets to the Clipboard. Whether the text was copied or cut to the Clipboard, you paste the text into your document in the same way.

To copy text to the Clipboard, select the text as you do for cutting. Then click the Copy button on the toolbar or select Edit I Copy. At this point, you will not see a change in your document—the selected text remains where it is and stays selected. However, a copy of that text is now in the Clipboard. Move your insertion point to where you want the copy to be inserted, and use the Paste command as described above in "Inserting Text."

 NOTE: You can also paste the data you copy into the Clipboard into a document in another application. The steps to insert the data into another application depend on the other application. See Chapter 4 for details on copying to the Clipboard.

 Word can create a scrap,–a piece of information that exists outside your document and on your desktop. You can use scraps to copy information between your document and other documents, including documents in other locations. See "Scrap" in Chapter 4 to learn more about this feature.

Undoing Edits

If you make an edit by mistake or you change your mind, Word can undo the effect of the last several edits you have made. You can restore text you have deleted, remove text you have pasted, and reverse the effect of other commands. The Undo feature also helps you recover from a mistyped command, such as pressing Y instead of N when prompted to confirm a command.

To undo your last action, either click the Undo button on the toolbar or select Edit I Undo. Note that the Undo menu command will change to indicate the command you last executed. For instance, the Undo menu command might read "Undo Paste," "Undo Delete Word," or "Undo Typing." You can also press CTRL+Z or ALT+BACKSPACE to undo an action, although with this method you do not see a description of what you are undoing.

If you need to reverse the effect of more than one action, click the arrow next to the Undo button in the toolbar. You'll see a drop-down list box that lists many of the edits you have made, in the reverse order in which you made them. When you click one of these actions, all of the changes—from the last one made to the one you clicked— are undone.

The Undo command does have limitations:

- Undo only remembers a limited number of changes, based on the amount of RAM (Random Access Memory) available.

- You can undo changes you make to your document on the screen, but you cannot undo changes that affect files saved to disk or printed, since these changes go beyond Word itself. For example, if you save a document over one you already have on disk, Undo cannot restore the disk file you have just overwritten.

- For Undo to remove the effect of a change you have made, you must use Undo before the change is forgotten. The oldest changes are forgotten when there is no more memory to add new changes.

Besides using Undo to reverse the effect of an action, you can also use Redo to reapply an action that you undid. See "Undoing and Redoing Actions" in Chapter 4 for more information about this feature. You may also want to look at "Repeating Actions" in Chapter 4 to see how you can have Word apply the same edits in several places.

Saving and Opening Your Documents

If you do not save your document to a disk file, the work you have put into it disappears when you close the document window or exit Word. Saving to a disk file lets you keep your document so that you can use it again later. The documents you no longer want to work with can be saved and closed, to get them out of your way. Then, to work with them again, you have to open them. The commands that save, close, and open documents have several shortcuts, summarized in Table 2-1.

CAUTION: Save often. A power surge or other incident can make your computer stop or crash, and you will lose any unsaved work. See "Save Options" in Chapter 4 to learn how to create timed backups of your documents as you are working.

Saving for the First Time

When you save a document for the first time, you need to give it a name. To save a document, select File | Save or Save As, or use one of the shortcuts in Table 2-1. Word opens the Save As dialog box, where you provide a name for the document. This dialog box also lets you designate where the document is saved (folder and drive) and whether it is saved in another application's format.

Command	Toolbar Icon	Function Key Combination	Ctrl Key Combination
File	Save	▯	SHIFT+F12	CTRL+S
File	Save As		F12	
File	Close		CTRL+F4	CTRL+W
File	Open	🗁	CTRL+F12	CTRL+O
File	New	🖫		CTRL+N

Table 2-1.   *Shortcuts for Saving, Closing, and Opening Documents*

Type the name for the document in the File Name drop-down list box. You can enter as many as 255 characters and use any characters except for /, \, :, *, ?, ", <, >, or |. This includes spaces. Choose a name that describes the contents of the document. For example, a letter to Jean Muraski might be named Letter to Jean Muraski. The list box above File Name lists all the files in the current folder. Files also have a document type that can set which documents are listed in the dialog box.

TIP: *Word, like other Windows 95 applications, assigns a DOS filename that includes a DOC file extension. You only need to care about this name when you share a document with another computer that is not running Windows 95.*

Once you select OK in the Save As dialog box, Word saves the document in a disk file, using the name you have provided. The document's name also appears in the title bar, as well as in the Window menu.

READY *for* **MORE**   *If you want to save a document and store it in another directory or on another drive, look at "Saving Documents" in Chapter 4 for how to change the location of where a document is saved. This section of Chapter 4 also has information about saving a document in different document types so you can use them with other applications.*

Subsequent Saves

You do not have to provide the document name every time you save a document. For subsequent saves after the first one, Word uses the settings from the first time you saved the document. You do not see the Save As dialog box, though you do see the message on the status bar telling you that Word is saving your document. You will see the message without the dialog box on subsequent saves whether you use the menu or the Save button on the toolbar.

If you want to save a document again with a different name, location, or type, you cannot use the File | Save command to do this. Instead, use the File | Save As command or one of its shortcuts. Saving with the Save As command does not delete the original document from the disk; it simply creates another copy of the document using a different name. You will see the same Save As dialog box that you saw when you first saved the document.

Closing the Document

When you have finished working with a document, you will want to put it away or close it. This is just like removing a letter from your desk. If you do not put Word documents away, they may get in the way of the documents you do want to work with; moreover, when you leave long documents open, they slow down Word's performance.

To close a document window, move to that document (making it active) and select the File | Close command or use one of its shortcuts. If the active document has not changed since the last time you saved it, Word immediately closes the document window. If you have changed the document since the last time you saved it, Word asks if you want to save your changes. If you select Yes, Word saves the changes just as if you used the File | Save command. If you select No, your changes are discarded. If the document has never before been saved, selecting Yes causes Word to display the Save As dialog box. You can then make the settings necessary to save the document, or you can choose Cancel to return to the active document without saving or closing.

Opening an Existing Document

Once you save a document to a disk and close it, you can open it and work with it again. When you open a file, you are reading it into your computer's memory.

 REMEMBER: Be sure to save the document again after opening it and editing it, or you will lose the changes that you make.

To open a file, select the File | Open command or use one of its shortcuts. You will see the Open dialog box, in which you can select the document you want to open. This dialog box has many of the same options as those for saving a document. In the File

Name text box, you can type the name of the document you want to open, or you can select it from the Name list box. When you have designated the correct document, select OK to open the document in a new document window.

TIP: *When you want to open a document that you have recently used, you have a shortcut. You can select one of the recently used documents from the bottom of the File menu. You can also select Documents from the Windows' Start menu and select the document from that menu.*

Checking the Spelling and Grammar of Your Document

Word's spell check feature locates misspelled words in your document and suggests the correct spelling. Word automatically marks potentially misspelled words. The spell checker also locates words with unusual capitalization and repeated words. Certainly, you can search the document for these mistakes yourself, but using the spell checker ensures that you do not accidentally overlook any.

READY *for* **MORE**

In Chapter 4, you learn about how you can check spelling through a dialog box as well as setting options that change how Word checks the spelling in your documents.

To check any misspelling, right-click one of the words that has the wavy red lines to display a menu, as shown here:

TIP: *If you don't see the wavy lines but you have the small dictionary icon at the end of the status bar with an X on it, your document has at least one word that is potentially misspelled. You can move to that location in the document by double-clicking that icon.*

At this point, the option you select tells Word what you want to do about the misspelled word:

- For most misspellings, Word supplies suggestions for the possible correct spelling of the word. If you want to use one of the suggestions, select it from the list.

- If you want to leave the word as is, select Ignore All. Word removes the wavy line in this instance and every other instance where this marked word appears.

- You may want to add the word to Word's dictionary by selecting the Add button; by doing this, every time the word subsequently appears during a spell check, Word will know how to spell it. You may want to add proper names, acronyms, and technical terms.

When a document does not contain any misspelled words, the dictionary in the status bar contains a check mark rather than an X.

The AutoCorrect Feature

The Spelling dialog box has a wonderful feature called *AutoCorrect*. This feature automatically corrects your "favorite" spelling mistakes (that is, the ones you tend to make most frequently). When you check the spelling of a document and a word is consistently misspelled, select AutoCorrect. Now, every time you type the misspelled word, Word automatically alters it to the correct spelling. Word already has a few automatic spelling corrections set up for you. To see AutoCorrect in action, type **teh** and a space, and watch Word convert it to "the" followed by a space.

Word lets you customize how the spell checker works. For example, you can create custom dictionary files and you can also purchase dictionary files for other languages or professions, such as a legal dictionary. To learn more about these features, look up "Spelling" in Chapter 4. Also, "AutoCorrect" in Chapter 4 describes the options available to change how AutoCorrect works, including new Word for Windows 7 features that correct borders, headings, and list formatting.

Using the Grammar Checker

Word does not check for misused words; for example, if "their" is used instead of "they're," Word won't identify it as incorrect as long as it's spelled correctly. The Tools | Grammar command can help you review your document for this type of error. However, even if you use Word's grammar checker, you should always proof your document yourself to catch mistakes that the computer cannot identify.

If you are responsible for putting together an important report, for instance, and you haven't had much writing practice lately, you may want to review a good source of grammar guidelines to give your writing a professional appearance. The box in this chapter, "Rules for Comma Placement," can help clarify at least one aspect of your writing.

NOTE: *If you select Tools | Grammar and you get the message that this part of Word is not installed, then you need to run the Setup program again to install this Word feature.*

Printing the Document

After you have created, edited, and saved a document, you will probably at some point want to print it. Printing a document in Word is as simple as selecting a command. When you are ready to print, press CTRL+P or select File | Print. You will see the Print dialog box, where you can make the appropriate settings. (You'll learn more about these settings in Chapter 4 under the section, "Printing.") Select OK and Word then prints your document. You can also click the Print button, shown here in the margin, to print if you want to use the default settings.

When you print a document in Windows, you send that document to the print folder. This folder contains all of the documents that you are printing. This process of grouping print jobs in the folder is called *spooling*. The Windows print spooler sends images for the final printed page to the printer using the printer's own language. Once the document is sent to the print folder, you can continue working with Word.

The Print dialog box has many options for changing how much of your document you print, how many copies, and so forth. "Printing" and "Print Options" in Chapter 4 contain more information about changing how Word prints the document. Many of the changes you make to a document are formatting changes to make the printed version look better. Chapter 3 describes some basic formatting, and Chapter 4 covers specific information about all of the formatting available for your Word documents.

Changing the View

You can change how your document is displayed while you edit it. The two most common editing views are normal view and page layout view. *Normal view* is what you have seen so far as you have worked through Chapter 1 and Chapter 2. *Page layout view* shows you how the document will look when you print it. Some Word screen elements, such as pictures, tables, and hidden characters, display differently in normal versus page layout view. Figure 2-2 shows the same document in both normal view and page layout view.

Rules for Comma Placement

Commas separate elements of sentences to make the meaning clearer. They are also used to separate phrases that are nonessential and that provide an aside from the main theme of the sentence. Correctly used, commas help add clarity to your sentences; when commas are missing or misused, the reader may have a less-than-perfect understanding of your material. Always use commas in these situations:

- To separate two parts of a compound sentence, as in "The weather was dismal, but we went despite it."

- After introductory phrases, such as "Loved by all," "Founded in 1901," and "Gripped by fear."

- To separate the city name from the state or country, as in "Cleveland, Ohio" and "Frankfurt, Germany."

- To separate each of three or more entries, as in "Peter, Paul, and Mary" and "red, green, or yellow."

- To isolate the name when an individual is addressed directly, as in "No, Jane, I cannot give you a raise this year."

- Between consecutive modifiers: "a beautiful, gentle child."

- To separate an individual's name from an employer's name, as in "Robert Eton, of General Motors."

- To separate nonessential clauses from the rest of a sentence. If the sentence makes sense without the clause, use commas. For example, "Marsha Taft, you must admit, is a dedicated, hard-working employee."

- To isolate "too" and other such words and expressions that help effect a transition: "He, too, was stricken ill while abroad."

- When omitting the comma would cause confusion, as in "To a great cook like Betty, Crocker's new book would be useless."

To switch to normal view, select View | Normal or click the Normal View button at the left end of the horizontal scroll bar. To switch to page layout view, select View | Page Layout or click the Page Layout View button, which is the second button from the left end on the horizontal scroll bar.

You can also preview what the printed output from a document will look like by selecting the Print Preview button in the toolbar or by selecting the File | Print Preview command. Word displays the document as Word will print it, as shown in Figure 2-3.

You can click the Print button on the toolbar to print the document as it currently appears. To exit the preview of the printed document, press ESC or click the Close button on the toolbar.

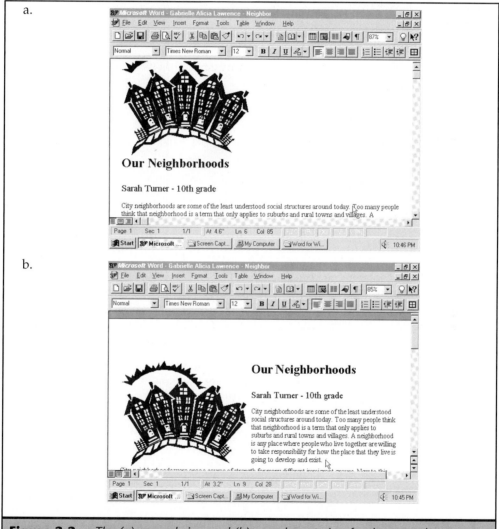

Figure 2-2. *The (a) normal view and (b) page layout view for the same document*

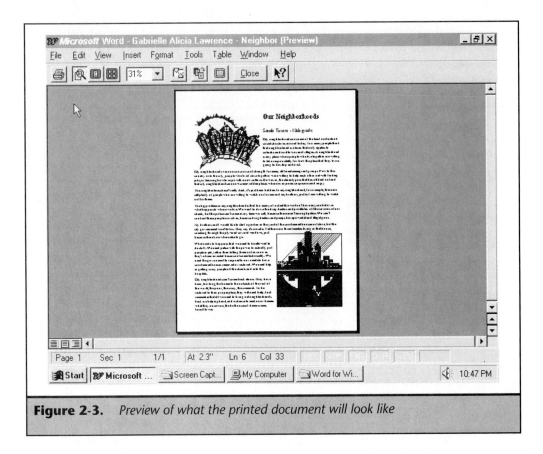

Figure 2-3.   *Preview of what the printed document will look like*

READY
for
MORE

Word also has an outline view and a master document view. Outline view is described further in Chapter 4. Master document view is described under "Master Documents" in Chapter 4. You can also view a document at various magnification levels when you want to see the document larger or smaller than it appears when printed. "Viewing Documents" in Chapter 4 discusses the View \ Zoom command, which lets you change the magnification level and other settings for previewing a document.

Chapter Three

Formatting Documents

Word's formatting options allow you to control the appearance of your documents. Up to now, you have learned about Word features that focus on entering text and making sure it's error-free, well organized, spelled correctly, and grammatical. The only formatting actions discussed so far have been pressing ENTER to end a short line or a paragraph and pressing TAB to indent the first line of a new paragraph. With just these fundamentals, you can create a memo or a report, since Word has default format options for essential elements such as margins and tab stops. These default formats provide an acceptable page layout for basic documents, and you have been using these defaults in your work so far. Now it's time to explore a few more elaborate formatting options, which will add visual impact to your documents.

Word for Windows offers a full range of formatting features. *Character formatting* allows you to change the appearance of one or more characters. You can display characters in a particular style, size, or font. *Paragraph formatting* lets you define the type of margins, indents, tabs, borders, and alignment you want to implement for a single paragraph or a set of paragraphs. With the *page layout options*, you can change the appearance of an entire page or the whole document, including its margins, paper size, and orientation.

In this chapter, you will learn the principles of all three types of formatting. In many instances there are several ways to apply the formatting, although only the simplest approach will be presented in this chapter. Chapter 4 offers additional formatting options. You'll want to read all the Ready for More paragraphs in this chapter, which call your attention to some of the more advanced formatting options that you can explore after mastering the basics.

Rest assured, however, that with just the basics presented in this chapter, you can effect some dramatic changes in your documents. Figure 3-1 previews one page, before and after formatting. Although the preview's small text size does not clearly show that the text on both pages is the same, you can still see how the formatting added to the page on the right has considerably improved the appearance of the page.

Character Formatting

When you format characters, you are changing the appearance of individual letters or symbols. You can change the formatting of one character, a group of characters, or every character in your document. Character formatting options let you change the size of characters, the font or typeface used for characters, or the style of characters by adding enhancements such as boldface or underlining. Character formatting gives you the greatest ability to control the appearance of your document and its impact on readers. You will quickly find these character formatting features indispensable. Notice how the character formatting of the document in Figure 3-2 prevents the document from looking boring.

You apply all character formatting in the same ways. One way is to set the format of characters and then type them. Your formatting affects only the text you type next, even if the insertion point is in the middle of an existing paragraph. Or, to change the character formatting of existing text, you must select the text before setting the format.

Word for Windows offers you several ways to change formatting options, so you can choose the method that works best for you. As mentioned earlier, only the easiest methods are covered in this chapter: The Formatting toolbar is used for most settings, because the toolbar is the easiest way to accomplish most formatting tasks. You will use the Font dialog box only for settings that cannot be changed using the Formatting toolbar. If you are interested in using other methods of character formatting, refer to the "Fonts" section in Chapter 4.

Font Settings

The most noticeable feature of a character is its font. *Fonts* are sets of alphabetic, numeric, or symbolic characters in various typefaces. For example, if your handwriting were converted to fonts, cursive and printing would be two separate fonts. The fonts you select for your document go a long way toward setting its tone, whether it is traditional, modernistic, or simply fun.

Fonts are either serif, sans serif, or decorative. Serif fonts have little lines or curves, called serifs, at the top and bottom of letters.

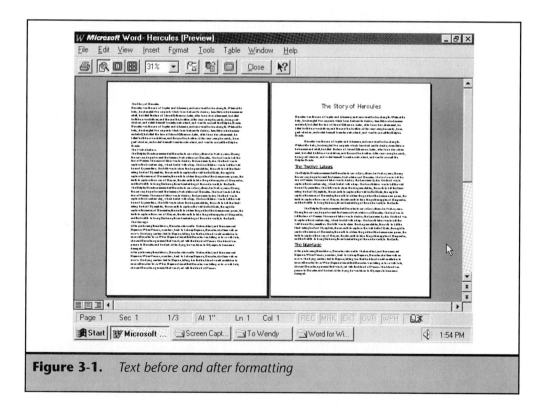

Figure 3-1.   *Text before and after formatting*

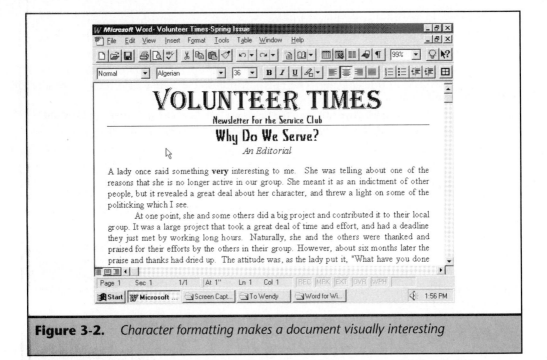

Figure 3-2. *Character formatting makes a document visually interesting*

- Serif fonts are usually used for the major body of text in a document, because they are "anchored" to the line by the serifs, making them easier to read. Also, since serif fonts are typically used in printed material, readers have more experience reading them.

- Sans serif fonts have no anchoring lines. Conventionally, sans serif fonts are used for headlines and short sections of text. They can be harder to read at length, but they have a clean line that stands out against serif text.

- Decorative fonts are highly embellished or distorted and provide a graphical element in your document. Never use decorative fonts for more than a few words, because they are hard to read.

In Figure 3-2, the text "Volunteer Times" is in a decorative font. It is very pretty, but you would not want to use this font for the entire document. The next two lines use the Kino MT font, which is a sans serif font. The rest of the text uses Times New Roman, a serif font.

To change the font of your text, first move the insertion point to where you plan to enter new text, or select the existing text you want to format. On the Formatting toolbar, click the arrow button for the drop-down list box that is second from the left. Choose the font you want to use from that list by clicking it.

CAUTION: *Avoid using more than three fonts in a document. Using too many fonts creates a document that is visually confusing for readers.*

Size Settings

Another way to change the appearance of text is to change its size. Many fonts come in a variety of sizes. Some fonts only have a few standard sizes, but others are scalable, which means they can be scaled to a number of different sizes. A font's size is specified as the font's height, measured in points. (A point is 1/72 of an inch.) Height rather than width is used as the measure, because some fonts have characters that vary in width.

The height specification is the height of the font's capital letters. A typical height for a text font you might use in a letter or report is 10 points. In *proportional fonts*, the letters have different widths even though the height of the capital letters is set the same. When you use a proportional font, an *I* takes up less space than a *W*. Some fonts have the same width for each letter and are called *monospaced fonts*. The width of the characters in a monospaced font is the same, always providing the same number of characters per inch. Look at a sample font to see if the characters are all the same size or proportionally sized.

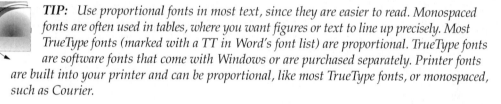

TIP: *Use proportional fonts in most text, since they are easier to read. Monospaced fonts are often used in tables, where you want figures or text to line up precisely. Most TrueType fonts (marked with a TT in Word's font list) are proportional. TrueType fonts are software fonts that come with Windows or are purchased separately. Printer fonts are built into your printer and can be proportional, like most TrueType fonts, or monospaced, such as Courier.*

To change font size, begin by positioning the insertion point or selecting some text. On the Formatting toolbar, click the arrow button for the drop-down list box that is third from the left. The sizes available for the chosen font appear in this list. Click on a size in the list. If the font is scalable, you can type a font size in this box to have Word scale the font to that size instead of selecting a size.

READY
for
MORE *Look up "Fonts" in Chapter 4 for more information on changing the font size and to get a better understanding of various font characteristics.*

Character Style Settings

A third way to emphasize text is to apply character styles. There are many character styles, but in all cases a style is applied to the particular size and font that is already established for the text. Word offers the familiar boldfacing, italic, and underlining styles, as well as several other character styles. Bold, Italic, and Underline buttons can be found on the Formatting toolbar. Other character styles can only be applied using the Font dialog box, available through the Format | Font command.

The less common character styles that Word for Windows provides include Strikethrough, Small Caps, All Caps, and a variety of Underline styles. Strikethrough places a horizontal line through the text; Small Caps displays lowercase letters as uppercase letters of a smaller font size; and All Caps displays all the text as uppercase letters. The default type of Underline is a single underline beneath all characters and spaces. You can also choose to underline only the words (not spaces) with a single line, to use a double underline, or to use a dotted underline.

 NOTE: Use character styles sparingly to emphasize important text. It is important to apply your style options in a consistent fashion. The box called "Guidelines for Using Character Styles" offers some commonly accepted conventions for applying character styles. Using the style options as suggested will greatly enhance their ability to increase the reader's attention to particular details.

To apply boldface, italic, or underlines to your text, begin by positioning the insertion point or selecting text. Next, click the appropriate button in the formatting toolbar. The Bold button is marked with a boldfaced **B**, the Italic button has an italicized *I*, and the Underline button has an underlined U. These buttons are toggles, which means that if the bold, italic, or underline style has already been applied to selected text, then clicking the appropriate button will turn the character style off.

To add other character styles to text, begin by positioning the insertion point or selecting text. Then select Format | Font. Select the check box for the style you want to use. If you are choosing an alternate underline style, you'll need to select it from the Underline drop-down list box. When you finish choosing the styles you want, select OK to apply them.

READY *You can look up each of the style options in Chapter 4 to get more information. Try some*
for   *of these topics: "Bold," "Underline," "All Caps," "Small Capitals," and "Text Color."*
MORE

Position Settings

You can change the vertical positioning of text, moving it above or below the normal line of text. *Superscript* text is raised just above the normal line of text; *subscript* text appears just beneath the normal line of text. Super- and subscript text is usually also reduced in size. Word calculates the precise size and position change individually for each font. A typical use for super- or subscript text is in formulas and in chemical symbols, such as H_2O.

To change text to sub- or superscript, position the insertion point where you want to enter the text or select existing characters. Select Format | Font, select the Subscript or Superscript check box; then select OK.

Guidelines for Using Character Styles

Changing a character style to boldface, underline, or italic can add visual interest and emphasis to document text. Avoiding overuse and inconsistent application of these features is an important element in the professional appearance of your document. Here are some ideas for applying these styles in your documents:

Italic

- Words and expressions from other languages.
- A word defined in a sentence, as in "The word *bare* is sometimes misspelled *bear*."
- Letters used as words, as in "Dot your *i's* and cross your *t's*."
- A term discussed in a sentence, as in "The term *gothic* has different meanings to different people."
- Titles of books, magazines, journals, movies, and plays.

Boldface

- To add emphasis to report headings and letterheads.
- To add emphasis to text in informal documents, such as newsletters.
- To distinguish user input when creating documentation for computer applications.

<u>Underline</u>

- To separate subtotals and totals in a column of numbers.
- In place of italics, if italics are not available.

See "Super/Subscript" in Chapter 4 for information on specifying the size or position of super- or subscript text.

Paragraph Formatting

When you format a paragraph, you are designating how the paragraph will appear on the page. You can set the alignment of the lines in the paragraph, the spacing between the lines in the paragraph, the spacing between paragraphs, the indentation for the entire paragraph, and the indentation of just the first line.

As with character formatting, there are several ways to change paragraph formatting settings. This chapter emphasizes techniques using the Formatting toolbar and the ruler to apply paragraph formatting. Spacing between lines and between paragraphs, however, must be set using the Paragraph dialog box, displayed with the Format | Paragraph command. These changes are on the Indents and Spacing tab, as shown here:

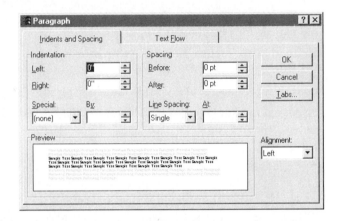

When you set a paragraph format, the format applies to the paragraph containing the insertion point, or for all paragraphs in which there is some selected text. If you create another paragraph after an existing paragraph by pressing ENTER, the new paragraph has the same format as the preceding one.

Other paragraph formatting features, not covered in this chapter, determine how page breaks affect the paragraph, the tab settings, and whether line numbers appear. Look in Chapter 4 under "Alignment," "Pagination," and "Spacing" for further information on these and other paragraph formatting features.

Alignment Settings

The *alignment* of a paragraph determines how the ends of the paragraph's lines line up with the margins of the page. You can left-align a paragraph to start the text at the left margin, leaving a "ragged edge" on the right side of the page. You can right-align the paragraph so that the left side is ragged. When you center-align the paragraph, you get an equal amount of space between each margin and the beginning and end of the lines. You can also justify the paragraph, so that the space between words is adjusted to fill the line completely, creating smooth left and right edges to the paragraph that

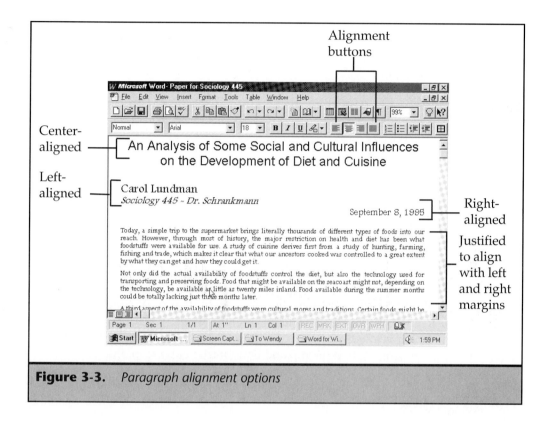

Figure 3-3. *Paragraph alignment options*

are even with the left and right margin settings. Figure 3-3 shows paragraphs with each of these four alignments.

To change the alignment of a paragraph, click on one of the four alignment buttons on the Formatting toolbar. These are the buttons marked in Figure 3-3. The lines on the buttons indicate the alignment each represents.

Indentation Settings

Indentation allows you to temporarily alter the location of text in relation to the current margin settings. With Word for Windows, you can set the indentation of a paragraph from either the left or right margin, and you can specify a separate indentation for the first line of a paragraph.

To set the indentation for an entire paragraph or set of paragraphs, first position the insertion point or select the paragraphs to be indented. Since the ruler is the easiest way to change indentation, select View | Ruler if you do not already see the ruler. Notice how the ruler has small triangles on the left and right sides of your paragraphs, as you can see in the following illustration:

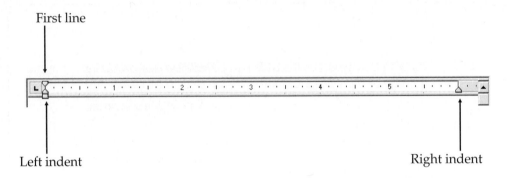

First line

Left indent   Right indent

To change the left side of a paragraph's indentation, drag the triangle for the left indent. To set the right indent for the paragraph, drag the single triangle at the right edge of the ruler to the desired location. To change the left indent for just the first line of a paragraph, drag the top of the double triangle that indicates the left indent. To set the left indent for everything *but* the first line, drag the bottom triangle of the two. To move the top *and* bottom of the double triangle together, even if they are separated in the ruler, move the bar below the bottom triangle as if you were changing the left indent for the entire paragraph. If the top and bottom triangles are in different locations when you do this, the bottom arrow will move to where you drag it, and the top arrow will move to a new position that is the same distance from the bottom arrow as before.

TIP: *Word's AutoFormat feature may change paragraph formatting, such as when you press TAB as the first entry for a paragraph. See "AutoFormat" in Chapter 4 to learn about other formatting changes that Word can make for you.*

Spacing Settings

Spacing indicates how close together lines are placed in the document. You can set two types of spacing for your document: the space between the lines within a paragraph, and the spacing between paragraphs. When you increase line spacing, you increase the amount of white space between the text lines within a paragraph. When you increase the space between paragraphs, you add extra white space between paragraphs.

Changing Spacing Within a Paragraph

When you want to change the line spacing within a paragraph, first position the insertion point or select the paragraph. Then select Format | Paragraph, which opens the Paragraph dialog box. Choose a setting in the Line Spacing drop-down list box.

There are two types of options for setting line spacing. You can either work with Word's calculations for the correct line spacing, or you can specify a line spacing to use. The line spacing default options are as follows:

■ For Single, Word calculates the height of each line based on the height of the capital letters in the largest font used on the line.

■ If you select 1.5 Lines or Double, Word simply multiplies the height it calculates for Single by 1.5 or 2.

■ You can also select Multiple and enter a value in the At text box, to have Word multiply the calculated height for the line by the value you enter. This lets you do double, triple, or quadruple spacing.

You can also specify line height more precisely:

■ Choose the At Least option, and enter a value in the At text box indicating the minimum line height you want Word to use. Word is able to increase the line spacing if needed to accommodate a large font.

■ If you choose Exactly and enter a value in the At text box, Word must use that value as the line height, even if this means printing one line on top of another.

Changing Spacing Between Paragraphs

You can add extra space before or after your paragraph. This is commonly done in block-style business letters, in which there is no other way to indicate separate paragraphs. To set space before or after a paragraph, select the paragraphs to be affected or position the insertion point. Select Format I Paragraph and enter a measurement in either the Before or the After text box in the Spacing area of the dialog box. The Before value designates how close the paragraph will be to the preceding paragraph. The After value designates how close the next paragraph will be to the formatted paragraph.

Page Formatting

When you specify page layout options, you control how the text is arranged on the page. You can set the size of the margins, that is, the distance between the edge of the text and the edges of the paper. You can designate what size of paper the text is formatted for, and whether the long or short edge of the paper is at the top (orientation).

Page formatting is done through the Page Setup dialog box, displayed by the File I Page Setup command. Unless you want to change the page formatting options for your entire document, you will want to first position the insertion point on the first page for which you want to change the settings, or select some text from each page for which you want to change the settings.

Margin Settings

The margins of your document are the areas of space between the edge of the paper and the edge of the text. There are four margins on every page: top, bottom, left, and right. You can set each one individually.

If you are planning to print on both sides of the paper, you will want to use mirror margins, in which the margins of facing pages mirror each other. When you use mirror margins, you set inside and outside margins rather than left and right ones. You can also define a *gutter*, which is the amount of the page you expect to lose if the pages of your document will be bound.

To change the margins, begin as usual by positioning the insertion point, or selecting the pages to be affected. Then select File | Page Setup and the Margins tab. Choose your settings as described just below, and select OK to apply the new margins.

Enter the desired margin measurements in the Top, Bottom, Left, and Right text boxes. The effect of your settings is shown in an example page in the Preview box. You can see these settings on the Margins tab shown here:

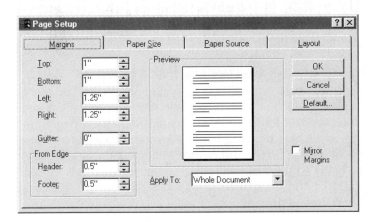

To create mirror margins, select the Mirror Margins check box. Notice that the Left and Right text boxes change to Inside and Outside and that there are now two example pages in Preview. The Inside margin measurement is used for the right margin of even-numbered pages and the left margin of odd-numbered pages. The Outside setting is used for the left margin of even-numbered pages and the right margin of odd-numbered pages.

If you plan to bind your pages along the left side, you will need to allow extra margin space there, since some of the page will be hidden by the binding. To allow extra space for binding, enter a value in the Gutter text box. This value is added to the inside or left margin. Defining the gutter and margin space separately allows you greater flexibility in reformatting the document if you change to a different binding technique or change the format of the pages.

Page Size Settings

You can control both the size and orientation of the page that Word uses when formatting the document. You probably work with standard letter-size pages, $8\frac{1}{2}$ by 11 inches, most of the time. All the predefined Word templates used for creating new documents use this size. When you print an envelope or on paper of a different size, it's important to specify that size, because Word uses page size in conjunction with other settings (such as margins) to determine where to place text.

To change the paper size for a page in your document, first position the insertion point or select the pages that will use the new size. Then select File | Page Setup and click the Paper Size tab.

Choose a paper size from the Paper Size drop-down list box. Word offers several standard paper sizes. If you are using paper of a different, nonstandard size, enter the paper's measurements in the Width and Height text boxes. Remember that the width of the paper is the measurement of the top of the page, and the height measurement is the side of the page.

As usual, select OK to use the new settings.

Orientation Setting

The orientation of the page determines whether the short edge of the paper is at the top or on the side. *Portrait orientation* uses the width measurement for the top of the page, and the height measurement for the side. With $8\frac{1}{2}$ x 11 paper, the top of the page is $8\frac{1}{2}$ inches, and 11 inches is the length of the document. When you change to *landscape orientation*, these measurements are reversed. Working in landscape mode is like writing on a standard sheet of paper that is turned sideways. Portrait orientation is used for most documents; landscape mode is often used with large tables, where the 11-inch width of the page is required in order to show many columns and to use a font size that is readable.

Changing the orientation of a page is easy; begin by positioning the insertion point or selecting some text on the pages to be affected. Select File | Page Setup and click the Paper Size tab. Choose Portrait or Landscape (notice that the values in the Width and Height text boxes exchange places). Then select OK.

PART TWO

Alphabetical
Reference

Chapter Four

Word Features

This chapter is a comprehensive A through Z reference to all the features found in Word for Windows. Each entry in the chapter includes a description of the feature along with other information, such as the procedure for using it, an explanation of the options available, helpful hints, as well as possible applications. Entries are classified alphabetically by the name of the Word feature, but cross-references are used generously throughout. This makes it easy for you to look up a feature if you know the Word command or even just a generic word processing term that refers to it.

Abbreviations

You can speed up your typing by substituting abbreviations in place of certain frequently used long words, names, and titles. For example, you can use the abbreviation ANSI in place of American National Standards Institute. If the use of abbreviations is not appropriate in your document, you can type the abbreviation and have Word automatically substitute the full name represented by the abbreviation with the AutoCorrect feature or only make the substitution when you want with the AutoText feature. In the case of the ANSI abbreviation just mentioned, for instance, after the document is typed you can use the AutoText or AutoCorrect feature to replace all occurrences of ANSI with the full name, American National Standard Institute.

Some abbreviations are widely used in technical documents, business memos, interoffice correspondence, and catalogs, and they will not need to be replaced. The box in this chapter, "Common Abbreviations," lists some abbreviations you can use with confidence that they will be recognized.

For more information on how to replace abbreviations with the names they represent, see "Find and Replace," "AutoText," and "AutoCorrect."

Common Abbreviations

In the lists of abbreviations that follow, you will want to take special note of capitalization and whether or not a period is used. The forms shown for each abbreviation are the ones in common use today, but for some words, there are several acceptable variations. The use of periods, again, conforms to standard usage, but many references drop nearly all periods in abbreviations, while some use periods in all abbreviations. You may want to see if the organization or group you are working with uses a single style manual so you can match your abbreviations to that style.

Word	Abbreviation	Word	Abbreviation
abbreviation	abbr.	additional	addl.
account	acct.	also known as	a.k.a.
Accounts Payable	AP	amount	amt.
Accounts Receivable	AR	anonymous	anon.
		associate	assoc.

Word	Abbreviation
Association	Assn.
assistant	asst.
attachment	att.
balance	bal.
building	bldg.
care of	c/o
central standard time	cst or CST
Chief Executive Officer	CEO
Chief Financial Officer	CFO
collect on delivery	c.o.d.
Company	Co.
continued	cont.
credit	cr.
debit	dr.
department	dept.
discount	dis.
eastern standard time	est or EST
enclosure	enc.
feet/foot	ft.
for example	e.g.
free on board	f.o.b.
gallon	gal.
inclusive	inc.
Incorporated	Inc.

Word	Abbreviation
miles per gallon	mpg or MPG
miles per hour	mph or MPH
mountain standard time	mst or MST
not available/not applicable	NA
ounce	oz.
pacific standard time	pst or PST
package	pkg.
pound or pounds	lb.
purchase order	PO
quart	qt.
quarterly	qtr.
return on investment	ROI
seconds	sec.
self-addressed stamped envelope	SASE
standard	std.
temperature or temporary	temp.
Universal Product Code	UPC
volume	vol.
with	w/
without	w/o
year	yr.

Accelerator Keys

Accelerator keys is another term for shortcut keys. See "Shortcut Keys."

Accepting Revisions

See "Revision and Annotation Merging" and "Comparing Versions."

Access

Microsoft Access is a database program that can provide data for Microsoft Word. This data can become the variable data to include in a mail merge document or provide a block of data that will appear in a document. See "Mail Merge" for information on how to create merge documents. See "Databases" for information on how you can put database data, such as what is available through Access, into Word.

Active Document

The *active document* is the one that currently contains the insertion point. When you type text or select commands, you affect the active document. You activate a document by clicking it or by selecting the window containing it from the Window menu.

Add-Ins

Add-ins in Word provide additional features beyond what is available in Word. To become available, they need to be loaded.

Procedure

1. Select File | Templates then select the Add button.

2. Select the file for the add-in and select OK.

3. Select OK again to put away the Templates and Add-ins dialog box.

At this point, your add-in is ready to use according to the instructions provided with the add-in.

CAUTION: *These steps are the generic steps for loading an add-in. Some add-ins include their own installation and starting procedure. You will want to follow the instructions that come with the add-in.*

TIP: *If you want the add-in loaded every time you start Word, put it in the Word Startup folder.*

Add/Edit Routing Slip

See "Electronic Mail."

A

Adding Borders to Graphics or Text

See "Borders and Shading."

Adding Numbers

See "Math Calculations."

Address Book

Word can use address books to store addresses, phone numbers, and other information about people you need to contact. You can use your address book to supply the address entered into a Word document. Besides the address book available from the Exchange Personal Address Book, Word can also use address books created with Schedule+. Using the procedure described below, you can use an address book to insert an address into any Word document.

Procedures

1. Move the insertion point to where you want the address placed.

2. Click the Address button on the Standard toolbar. The Address button looks like this:

3. Select the profiles to use for electronic mail from the Profile Name drop-down list box. If you want to use the same address book each time, select the Options button, then select Set as Default Profile. Select OK.

4. Modify the entries in the Post office and Mailbox text boxes if they are missing or incorrect.

5. Type the password in the Password text box. If you want the password automatically supplied, select the Remember Password check box. Select OK.

6. Select the person whose address you want to insert from the list box and choose OK.

Once you have performed these steps, you can add an address by just clicking the Address button and selecting one from the list. You can also select someone from the currently selected address book by clicking the down arrow at the end of the Address button and clicking the person whose address you want added to the document.

TIP: *An address book can also supply the addresses for envelopes, labels, and mail merges. See "Envelopes," "Labels," and "Mail Merge" to learn how to use these features, as well as how to use your address book as the source of address information.*

Addresses for Routing Documents

See "Electronic Mail."

Advance

In WordPerfect, you use the Advance feature to position text or graphics precisely on a page. In Word, you do this by inserting a frame around the text or graphic and then positioning the frame. For information on positioning frames, see "Frames." You can also use the ADVANCE field for the same effect as frames. See "Fields" for more information on how to use the ADVANCE field.

ADVANCE Field

The ADVANCE field positions text precisely. For more information, see "Fields."

Aligning a Frame

When you align a frame, you set its position on a page. See "Frames" to learn how to align or position frames.

Aligning Pages

See "Margins," "Page Setup," "Page Size and Orientation," and "Paper Source."

Aligning Text

See "Alignment," "Tabs," "Sections," and "Frames" for information on aligning text.

Alignment

Word offers you four ways to align paragraphs between the left and right margins. You can left-align, right-align, center, or justify paragraphs in Word. Alignment of text between the left and right margins is a paragraph formatting option.

Procedures

Alignment is a paragraph format option, applied using either the Formatting toolbar, the Paragraph dialog box, or shortcut keys. When you change the alignment, the new alignment affects the paragraph where the insertion point is, or all paragraphs containing selected text. If you press ENTER within a paragraph to create a new paragraph, then the new paragraph has the same alignment as the previous one.

Begin by selecting text or positioning the insertion point to indicate the paragraphs you want to realign. Then choose one of the following procedures.

TIP: *To revert to the default paragraph alignment, press CTRL+Q. This removes all direct paragraph formatting from the affected paragraphs, not just the alignment.*

With the Formatting Toolbar

Click on one of the following alignment buttons in the Formatting toolbar. The first button left-aligns, the second centers, the third right-aligns, and the fourth justifies.

With the Paragraph Dialog Box

You can also set the alignment by selecting Paragraph from the Format menu.

1. Select Format | Paragraph, or right-click in the selected area and select Paragraph from the shortcut menu.

2. Select the Indents and Spacing tab, if necessary.

3. Choose a setting from the Alignment drop-down list box, and select OK.

With the Shortcut Keys

Press one of the four shortcut key combinations shown in the following table:

Shortcut	Result
CTRL+L	Left-aligns paragraphs
CTRL+E	Centers paragraphs
CTRL+R	Right-aligns paragraphs
CTRL+J	Justifies paragraphs

Hints

Here are some hints about how alignment works and how it affects paragraphs that are indented.

What Alignments Look Like

When you change the alignment of a paragraph, you are changing how the words are arranged on the line between the left and right margins or indents. Figure 4-1 shows centered, right-aligned, and justified paragraphs used to create a flyer (this screen is in Page Layout view).

- In left-aligned paragraphs, each line starts at the left margin or indent and looks ragged along the right side, because each line has a slightly different length.

- Centered paragraphs have ragged edges on both the right and left sides. The center of each line is the midpoint between the left and right margins or indents.

- In right-aligned paragraphs, each line ends at the right margin or indent, so the left edge appears ragged.

- In justified paragraphs, Word adjusts the space between words to make each line start at the left margin or indent and end exactly at the right margin or indent. The last line of the paragraph is left-aligned.

Indented Paragraphs

When you apply an indent to a paragraph, you are effectively adding an additional margin to that paragraph. The alignment for the paragraph uses the additional margin for aligning the paragraph; therefore, the text is aligned using the indent rather than the margin set with the margin feature. For example, if you create a first-line indent of one-half inch and then justify the paragraph, the first line begins half an inch to the right of the left margin instead of at the left margin.

Applications

Left-alignment is the most common alignment for text documents, because it is the easiest to read.

Justified text works well in printed material, such as books, brochures, and newspapers. Justification should be used sparingly in documents that contain technical or long words, unless you are also planning to use hyphenation. Otherwise, you will have the occasional line that contains only one or two long words and a lot of white space.

Centering works best for titles, page numbers, and other headings. Remember that you can center paragraphs that contain only a single line. Do not center substantial sections of body text, because centered text is difficult to read for more than a few lines.

Right-alignment adds a modern flair to text, but it should be used sparingly because it is more difficult to read than left-aligned or justified text. Frequently,

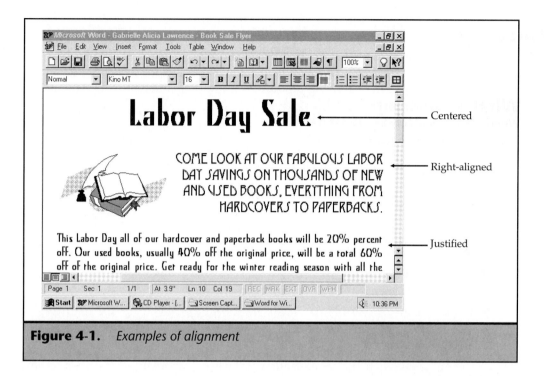

Figure 4-1. *Examples of alignment*

right-alignment is used in *sidebars,* which are thin columns of text that appear to one side of a wider column of main body text, providing explanations, quotations, or further insights to the main discussion.

Related Topics

Indents
Margins
Page Setup
Sections
Styles

All Caps

All Caps is a character formatting option that displays all characters as uppercase. All Caps can provide emphasis in titles and headings, and it can be used in scripts and speeches to make them easier to read.

Procedures

All Caps can be applied to new or existing text. To apply it to new text, first add the format and then type the text. To apply it to existing text, select the text and then add the style. Choose one of the following procedures for adding and removing All Caps.

With the Font Dialog Box

To apply or turn off All Caps:

1. Select Format | Font, or right-click the mouse in the selected text and select Font to open the Font dialog box.

2. Select the Font tab, if necessary.

3. Select the All Caps check box to turn the option on if you are applying this format or to turn it off if you are removing this format. Select OK.

With the Keyboard

Press CTRL+SHIFT+A to turn the All Caps format on and off.

Hints

You can put all text in capital letters as you type by pressing the CAPS LOCK key before typing. You can also change the capitalization of the text with features described under the topic "Capitalization."

Removing Formatting

You can remove this formatting by clearing the All Caps check box in the Fonts dialog box. Another way to remove All Caps is to select the text and press CTRL+SPACEBAR. This removes all character formatting from the selected text, not just All Caps.

Related Topics

Capitalization
Fonts

Alphabetizing

See "Sorting."

ALT Key

When you are using the keyboard, you use the ALT key in combination with other keys to select from menus and dialog boxes and to carry out commands and macros. Press

ALT when the insertion point is in a document to activate the menu bar, and then press the key for one of the underlined letters in the menu titles to open that menu. To select a command or option in a dialog box, press ALT and the key for the underlined letter in that command or option.

For information on how to use the ALT key with function keys, see "Function Keys."

Related Topics

Function Keys
Shortcut Keys

Anchoring

You can lock the position of a frame by anchoring it to a paragraph, character, or page. See "Frames" for more information.

Annotations

Annotations are initialed comments that can be added to a document and are typically used to let readers other than the author make comments to a document that has been protected. (In a protected document, the text is protected from changes except those made by the document's original author.) Annotations are indicated in the document text by an *annotation mark*, which consists of the initials of the user who entered it and a sequential number. The text of the annotation does not appear in the document but in a special Annotation pane.

Procedures

The following procedures will tell you how to prepare your document for annotations, how to create them, and how to edit and work with them.

Protecting and Unprotecting a Document

When you protect a document, no one can make changes to the text. People reviewing the protected document can make comments and suggest changes by using annotations. This protection can be turned off easily, however, unless you also select a password when you protect the document. The password must then be provided in order to unprotect the document.

To protect a document:

1. In the document to protect, select Tools | Protect Document to open the Protect Document dialog box.

2. Select Annotations. The other option buttons protect the document in different ways as described under "Locking and Protecting Documents."

3. To prevent another user from turning off your document protection, enter a password in the Password text box. The password can be up to 15 characters long. When you type the password, Word displays asterisks instead of the actual characters, so type the password carefully. When you're done, select OK.

TIP: *Case matters to passwords in Word so remember whether you use upper or lowercase letters.*

4. A Confirm Password dialog box appears. Type the password a second time and select OK. Entering the password a second time lets you make sure that a typing mistake didn't occur when first entering the password.

TIP: *Don't forget to record the password somewhere, so you won't forget it.*

To unprotect a document:

1. Select Tools | Unprotect Document.

2. If you assigned a password when you protected the document, you will have to provide the password before the document is unprotected, then select OK.

Inserting Annotations

When an annotation is inserted, Word adds an annotation mark to the document and formats it as hidden text. The annotation mark consists of the user's initials and a sequential number. The annotation text itself appears only in the Annotations pane.

To insert annotations:

1. Move the insertion point to where you want to add an annotation.

TIP: *If your annotation is about a specific sentence or phrase, highlight the sentence or phrase first. If you select text before creating an annotation, then that text will be selected and highlighted when the annotation is viewed. This can help the person reading your annotation recognize which text is being referred to.*

2. Select Insert | Annotation. Word inserts an annotation mark at the insertion point and opens the Annotations pane.

3. Type the annotation text, as shown in Figure 4-2.

4. Close the Annotations pane by clicking Close or pressing ALT+SHIFT+C.

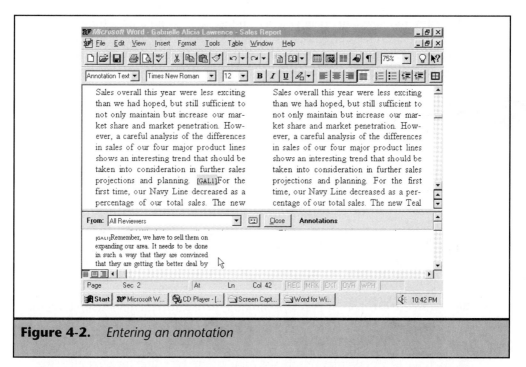

Figure 4-2. *Entering an annotation*

If you want to return to the document window without closing the Annotations pane, click on the document text or press F6. To switch back to the Annotations pane, select Insert | Annotation again, click on the open Annotations pane, or press F6.

Displaying Annotation Marks

Annotation marks are formatted as hidden text. To display them in the document, you have to display hidden text. You can do this temporarily by selecting the Show/Hide ¶ button (in the Standard toolbar), which shows the ¶ character, or by changing the View settings using the Tools | Options command.

Viewing Annotations

To view annotations, open the Annotations pane either by selecting View | Annotations or by double-clicking on an annotation mark in the document. You can also open the Annotations pane by holding down the CTRL key as you drag the split box down. The split box is the extra black bar at the top of the vertical scroll bar. You can also resize how much of the screen the Annotations pane occupies by dragging the split box up and down. Annotations in the document are hidden text so if you are not currently showing hidden text, you will only see existing annotation marks as well as other hidden text in the document while the Annotations pane is open.

With the Annotations pane open, you can choose to view all annotations or only those of a single reviewer. To view selected annotations, choose that reviewer's name in the From drop-down list box in the Annotations pane toolbar. You can open this list box by clicking it or by pressing ALT+SHIFT+R.

Going to an Annotation

Use the Edit | Go To command to move to a specific annotation quickly. To move to a specific annotation:

1. Select Edit | Go To, or press F5.

2. Select Annotations from the Go To What list box.

3. Use the Enter Reviewer's Name list box to specify the annotation you want, as follows:

   ■ To move to the next or previous annotation, leave the default entry, Any Reviewer, in the Enter Reviewer's Name drop-down list box and select Next or Previous.

   ■ To move to the next or previous annotation of a specific reviewer, select the reviewer from the Enter Reviewer's Name drop-down list box before selecting Next or Previous.

   ■ To move to a particular numbered annotation, type that number after the reviewer's name in the Enter Reviewer's Name text box and select Go To.

Editing Annotations

To edit an existing annotation, click the Annotations pane or press F6. (If the pane is not already open, you'll need to select View | Annotations first.) Then edit the annotation. You can either close the Annotations pane or leave it open, as instructed earlier in "Inserting Annotations." When a document is protected for annotations, changes that anyone makes to another person's annotations are marked with revision marks so you can track the changes that each person makes.

Deleting Annotations

To delete an existing annotation:

1. Display the annotation marks by selecting View | Annotations or by clicking the Show/Hide ¶ button in the Standard toolbar. Move to the mark for the annotation you want to delete.

2. Highlight the annotation mark in the document window and press DEL or BACKSPACE. The annotation mark and the annotation are deleted.

Pasting Annotations into Text

You can paste the text of an annotation from the Annotations pane into the document by cutting or copying the annotation in the pane to the Clipboard, moving to the document window, and pasting. (Remember that the document will have to be unprotected in order for you to paste in annotations.)

Printing Annotations

You can print annotations with the document or by themselves.

1. Select File | Print.
2. Select the Print What drop-down list box.

   ■ To print the document with its annotations, select Document from the drop-down list box.

   ■ To print annotations only, select Annotations and skip to step 4.

3. Select Options, then select the Annotations check box to print annotations with the document text.
4. Select OK to print.

When you print both the document and annotations, the annotations start on a new page after the text. The annotation text appears after the page number of the annotation mark, the user's initials, and an annotation number.

Creating or Reviewing Voice Annotations

If you have the appropriate equipment installed on your computer, you can create and review voice annotations. To record voice annotations, you need both a sound board and a microphone installed, but you only need the sound board to review voice annotations.

Creating voice annotations is not much different than creating text annotations. If you want to create a combined text and voice annotation, start by entering a text annotation as usual, then put the insertion point next to the annotation mark in the document and insert the voice annotation using the following steps:

1. Position the insertion point for inserting the voice annotation.
2. Select Insert | Annotation, and click the Insert Sound Object button in the Annotations pane toolbar.
3. Record your voice annotation, following the instructions for recording that come with your sound board and microphone.

4. If, when you finish recording, Word displays a message asking if you want to update the sound object, select <u>Y</u>es.

5. Select <u>C</u>lose or return to the document window.

Listening to sound annotations is also very similar to viewing your text annotations.

1. Select <u>V</u>iew | <u>A</u>nnotations.

2. In the Annotations pane, double-click the sound symbol for the voice annotation you want to hear.

3. When you're finished, select <u>C</u>lose or return to the document window.

Hints

Use annotations to get feedback from a number of people on a draft of a document. Word's annotations are easier to read and review than handwritten notes on printouts of the document.

You can also use annotations to get responses on proposals. Send the protected document file to everyone who may need to comment on the proposal, and request their comments. When the files come back to you, you can print the reviewers' comments and begin making any necessary adjustments to your proposal. Of course, you first need to check that your reviewers use Word for Windows and know how to add annotations.

Related Topics

Electronic Mail
Footnotes and Endnotes
Locking and Protecting Documents
Revision and Annotation Merging
Viewing Documents

ANSI Codes

The ANSI codes are a set of 256 characters standardized by the American National Standards Institute. Most fonts use this set of characters, so even if you change fonts in your document, the characters stay the same. For example, if you type the letter *J* in Times Roman font and then switch to Arial, the *J* does not become a Z, because both fonts use the same code for *J*.

Some fonts, usually called *symbol fonts*, do not correspond to the ANSI set of characters. For example, if you type a *J* in the Times Roman font and then change to the Wingdings font, your *J* becomes a smiley face.

See "Special Characters" for instructions on inserting symbol font characters, which do not change when you switch fonts.

Answer Wizard

The Answer Wizard is part of Word's help. It provides you information based on the text that you enter. You ask what you want to find and the Answer Wizard provides an answer. The Answer Wizard is one of the tabs available through Word's Help.

Procedures

1. Select Answer Wizard from the Help menu in Word. You can also select the Help Topics button from any open Word help window and move to the Answer Wizard tab.

2. Type a description of what you want to find. Examples include **Print my document sideways** or **Create a form letter**.

3. Select Search to find the topics that might answer your question. The list box in the middle of the dialog box now shows topics arranged by steps, by explanatory text, and by programming topics.

4. Move to any one of the topics and select Display to switch the Help window to that topic. You can return to the same list of topics by selecting the Help Topics button. When you select this button, you return to the same tab you were at the last time with the same topics listed.

Related Topic

Help

Antonyms

An antonym is a word that is the opposite of another word. Use the Thesaurus to find antonyms for words in your documents. See "Thesaurus" to learn more about this feature.

Append

See "Spike" for information on how to cut or copy multiple items and paste (append) them as a unit. See "Inserting Documents" for information on how to add one document to another.

Arithmetic

See "Math Calculations" for information on Word features to perform computations within your document.

Arranging Records

See "Sorting."

Arrow Keys

The arrow keys are used to navigate in documents (that is, to move the insertion point). For more information on using these keys, see "Moving the Insertion Point."

ASCII Text Files

ASCII text files contain characters only, with no formatting and no other extraneous special characters. You can save or retrieve ASCII text files in Word for Windows. Many programs can work with ASCII text files, so when you need to work with data in a program that cannot use the Windows Clipboard, such as a DOS-based program, save the file in an ASCII-format text file.

ASK Field

The ASK field prompts for information during a mail merge. See "Mail Merge" and "Fields."

Attaching Templates to Documents

See "Templates."

Attributes

If you are familiar with WordPerfect 5.1 or earlier, you may be accustomed to assigning colors to represent different types of character formatting and calling these color assignments *attributes*. Some people refer to character formatting as character attributes. In all views of Word for Windows, character formatting such as boldfacing, italic, and font size are displayed just as they will print, so you do not need to assign attributes.

For more information on Word for Windows views, see "Views." For more information on characters styles, see "Character Formats" in this chapter or review the "Character Formatting" section in Chapter 3.

Audio

You can record using a microphone and use sound clips in your Word document if your system has a sound board. See "Annotations" and "Sound" for more information.

AUTHOR Field

The AUTHOR field is used to insert the name of the author into the documents. See "DOCPROPERTY" and "INFO" under "Fields" for more information.

Authorities

Tables of authorities are used in a legal brief to list citations of court decisions and other legal documents and their location within the brief. The citations are sorted by type of source, so that citations referring to different levels of the court system appear separately. For example, the tables of authorities might include individual tables for citations from the Supreme Court, federal courts, and state courts; federal and state laws and regulations; and legal commentary. Creating a table of authorities is described in "Table of Authorities."

AutoCaption

See "Captions."

AutoCorrect

AutoCorrect automatically replaces text that you enter with other text that you have set up. It corrects many standard typographical mistakes. For instance, AutoCorrect will automatically do the following as you type:

- Make sure names of days and first words in sentences are capitalized
- Correct words that have the first two letters capitalized
- Correct text when you have unintentionally pressed the CAPS LOCK key
- Replace abbreviations with the words they represent
- Correct standard typographical errors

Rules for Creating Correctly Spelled Plurals

Although plurals are normally formed by adding *s* or *es* to the singular form of the noun, there are a number of exceptions. Some of the more common exceptions are the following:

- When a noun ends in a *y* preceded by a consonant, change the *y* to *i* and add *es*. For example, "trophy" becomes "trophies." If a vowel precedes the *y*, you can simply add an *s*. For example, "She received more than toys for Christmas."

- If the singular form of the noun ends in a silent *s*, the plural does not require the addition of a second *s*, although the *s* is typically pronounced in the plural form. For example, "General Smith's Special Forces Corps will receive their new orders on the same day as all the other corps on the base."

- Letters are made plural with either *s* or *'s* depending on whether they are uppercase or lowercase. For example, "Cross all your *t*'s," and "The degrees will be conferred for the Ph.D's on Thursday."

- Some singular nouns that end with an *o* preceded by a consonant take *es* to form the plural, and others simply take an *s*. For example, "Why did you direct the movers to put the pianos in the same room with the crates of potatoes?"

- Words ending in *ch* or *sh* form their plural with *es*. For example, "There are four churches in our community," and "I broke two dishes last night."

- Nouns that end in *s*, *x*, or *z* typically form plurals with *es*. For example, "We sent twelve faxes to him last week."

- Abbreviations normally are made plural by adding an *s* to the singular form. For example, "Col. 1 contains the answer, but the answer can be found in cols. 1 and 2." or "The YWCAs in Akron chose to centralize child care at the West Exchange Street YWCA."

- Proper names or nouns use an *s* or an *es* to create the plural. Never change the original spelling of the name or nouns when you make the plural. For example, "There are two Marys and three Felixes living in Winnebagos."

- Hyphenated words change from singular to plural by making the most important word plural. For example, "All the mothers-in-law were presented corsages," and "Follow-ups are scheduled on Wednesdays." Compound words that are spelled open (with a space rather than a hyphen) follow the same rule.

- Words of foreign derivation frequently use the foreign form for their plural. For example, "I measured the radii of the circles."

See the box, "Rules for Creating Correctly Spelled Plurals," for guidance on some mistakes you might make, so that you can create AutoCorrect entries for them.

Procedures

Before you can use AutoCorrect, you need to turn it on. If you want AutoCorrect to fill out abbreviations and correct standard errors, you first need to tell AutoCorrect what you want substituted.

Turning AutoCorrect On and Off

1. Select Tools | AutoCorrect.
2. Select the check boxes to indicate which features of AutoCorrect you want to use. If you want to turn AutoCorrect off, clear all of these check boxes. Then select OK.

Creating an AutoCorrect Entry

1. If you want to replace errors or abbreviations with long sections of text or with text that contains formatting, begin by creating the replacement text and selecting it.
2. Select Tools | AutoCorrect.
3. Select the Replace Text as You Type check box if it is not already selected.
4. In the Replace text box, enter the typographical error or abbreviation to be replaced.
5. In the With text box, enter the correct or expanded version of text. If you selected text before opening the AutoCorrect dialog box, that text now appears in the With text box. Also, the Plain Text and Formatted Text option buttons are activated. Select the appropriate option button:

   ■ Plain Text saves the text without formatting, so that it takes on the formatting that surrounds it when it is entered.

   ■ Formatted Text saves the text with its current formatting, so that it is always inserted with that formatting.

6. Select Add and then select OK.

Deleting or Editing an AutoCorrect Entry

1. If you want to replace the text supplied by an AutoCorrect entry with formatted text or a long text section, begin by creating and selecting the replacement text.
2. Select Tools | AutoCorrect.

3. In the list box under Replace Text as You Type, highlight the entry to be replaced.

4. To edit the entry, enter a new replacement text in the With text box, and then select Replace. To delete the entry, select Delete. Then select OK.

Options

The following options are available with AutoCorrect.

Correct TWo INitial CApitals

Select this check box to have Word for Windows automatically correct words beginning with two capitals so only the initial letter is capitalized. However, Word is smart enough to realize the words like CDs and LPs intentionally have the first two letters capitalized. You can prevent other words with unusual capitalization using AutoCorrect's exception list.

Capitalize First Letter of Sentences

Select this check box to have Word automatically capitalize the first word in a sentence. Word will capitalize any word that follows a period, question mark, or exclamation point when any letter comes before the punctuation and a space follows the punctuation.

Capitalize Names of Days

Select this check box to have Word for Windows automatically capitalize the days of the week when they are spelled out. If the day of the week is abbreviated, as in "Mon," the word will not be capitalized.

Correct Accidental Usage of cAPS LOCK Key

Select this check box to let Word automatically adjust after you have made entries with the CAPS LOCK button accidentally selected. With this checkbox selected, if you type a word with the first letter lower-case and the rest in uppercase while the CAPS LOCK key is on, Word switches the case of the letter and turns off the CAPS LOCK key.

Replace Text as You Type

Select this check box to have Word for Windows automatically replace text with other text, using the AutoCorrect entries that you have provided. Even if this check box is turned off, Word still replaces quotation marks and corrects capitalization.

 TIP: *Word has already built many of the entries in the AutoCorrect list based on its study of the most frequently misspelled words. Besides misspellings, AutoCorrect can also replace text with symbols such as replacing (tm) with the ™ symbol.*

E̲xceptions

AutoCorrect lets you create exceptions to AutoCorrect's rules by developing an exception list of words that intentionally have unusual capitalization and words that frequently do not indicate an end of a sentence. Select this button to open another dialog box where you can add to Word's exception list. The F̲irst Letter tab stores exceptions of words that do not indicate an end of a sentence such as abbreviations like abbr. and Jr. The I̲Nitial CAps tab stores exceptions to words that intentionally have two letters in uppercase. For either tab, you can type an entry then select A̲dd or highlight an existing entry and select D̲elete. The Au̲tomatically Add Words to List check box selects whether Word adds entries to either tab based on when you undo a change you have made. For example, suppose you typed **John Smith, Jr. is here** and Word made the I in "is" uppercase. After you make the I in "Is" lowercase, Word adds Jr. to the F̲irst Letter tab.

Hint

Even though you have created an AutoCorrect entry to replace certain text, there may be times when you want to enter that text without having Word correct it. In this case, you need to turn AutoCorrect off, enter the text, and then turn AutoCorrect back on. For example, if you need to enter "teh," perhaps as a demonstration or as a non-English word, you would turn AutoCorrect off, type **teh**, and then turn AutoCorrect back on; that way, AutoCorrect would not try to correct "teh" to "the."

Related Topics

Auto Format
AutoText
Find and Replace
Spelling

AutoFormat

The AutoFormat feature analyzes your document, then makes changes and applies styles based on its interpretations. AutoFormat can quickly convert a plain document into an attractively formatted document with little effort on your part. Word has expanded AutoFormat to make some changes as you type. For instance, AutoFormat will automatically do the following as you type:

- Apply headings and borders
- Add numbering or bullets to the paragraph formatting

- Replace straight quote marks (primes) with "curly quotes"
- Make the text after ordinal numbers such as 1st superscript
- Change fractions such as 1 / 2 to ½
- Replace symbols such as - - with —

Procedures

You can AutoFormat your document automatically, with or without reviewing it.

Automatically Format Your Document As You Type

As you type your document, if you have AutoFormat turned on and you type one of AutoFormat's entries that it will replace, then AutoFormat will make that change. If the TipWizard toolbar button is displayed, that toolbar will describe the change it has made along with buttons to turn that feature on or off as well as a button to undo the change. The settings controlling the changes that AutoFormat can make are described under "Options" below.

Formatting Your Document Automatically

To have Word AutoFormat your document and then give you the opportunity to review the changes:

1. Create the document.

2. Select Format | AutoFormat and then select OK. Word applies preliminary formatting to the document.

3. To review the changes made to your document, select Review Changes. The revision marks, which indicate where the document was changed, appear in the document, and the Review AutoFormat Changes dialog box appears. In this dialog box, you can choose to move to the next or last revision, or to reject any one change. When you are done, select Cancel.

4. If you want to use another set of styles in the document, select Style Gallery to get the Style Gallery dialog box. Choose a template from the Template list box, and examine the Preview of box to see how your document will look formatted with this other template. Select OK when you are ready, and the currently highlighted template will be used for the document.

5. To accept the changes made, select Accept. You can also choose to reject all of the changes made, by selecting Reject All.

TIP: *If you wish to AutoFormat your document without reviewing the changes, press CTRL+K or select the AutoFormat button as shown in the margin in the Standard toolbar.*

Options

Before letting Word AutoFormat your document, you can define AutoFormat options. Select Tools | Options and select the AutoFormat tab. You can also select the Options button in the AutoFormat dialog box, which opens the same Options dialog box automatically showing the AutoFormat tab. By default, all of the AutoFormat options are turned on. The options can be set separately for when you tell Word to AutoFormat a document and for when Word automatically formats the document as you type.

Headings

Select this check box when you want lines with less than a full line (20 percent shorter than the line length) made into a heading. When you press ENTER to end a short line that is 20 percent shorter than the line length and that line starts with a capital letter, Word assigns the Heading 1 style to that line. When AutoFormat applies headings as you type, paragraphs that end with ENTER pressed twice are assigned Heading 1 and Heading 2 styles depending on whether the title text is indented.

Borders

Select this check box when you want paragraphs that include three or more equal signs (=), hyphens (-), or underscores (_) to automatically replace these characters with a horizontal border at the bottom of the previous paragraph.

Automatic Bulleted Lists

Select this check box when you want lines that start with a *, o, >, -, or a symbol character to automatically have the bullet added to the paragraph's formatting—just as if you clicked on the Bullets button on the Formatting toolbar. Subsequent paragraphs continue to have the same formatting until you press ENTER twice or you press ENTER to start a new paragraph and then BACKSPACE.

Automatic Numbered Lists

Select this check box when you want lines that start with a number and a period to automatically have numbering added to the paragraph's formatting—just as if you clicked on the Numbering button on the Formatting toolbar. Subsequent paragraphs continue to have the same formatting until you press ENTER twice or you press ENTER to start a new paragraph and then BACKSPACE.

Straight Quotes to 'Smart Quotes'

Select this check box to have Word for Windows automatically replace straight quotation marks (primes or foot marks) with "smart quotes" (curly quotation marks).

Ordinals (1st) with Superscript

Select this check box to have Word automatically superscript the text after a number as in the 'rd' in 23rd to make it 23rd.

<u>F</u>ractions (1/2) with fraction character ($^1\!/_2$)

Select this check box to have Word automatically replace common fractions of $\frac{1}{2}$, $\frac{1}{4}$, $\frac{3}{4}$ and with their symbols.

Symbol Characters with Symbols

Select this check box to have Word automatically replace some characters with other ones such as replacing two hyphens with the em dash (—).

<u>S</u>tyles

Select the <u>S</u>tyles check box when you don't want AutoFormat to apply new styles to paragraphs that are already formatted with styles. This check box is only available when the <u>A</u>utoFormat option button is selected.

Related Topic

Styles

Automatic Backup

See "Saving Documents."

Automatic Font Substitution

There are two occasions when Word for Windows may automatically substitute one font for another. One is when you do not have both a screen and printer font for the font you choose. The other is when you retrieve a document that uses a font you do not have.

Fonts have various commands to tell your printer how to print them and to tell your computer monitor how to display them. If you have installed sets of fonts for your printer but have no equivalent screen fonts to tell your computer how to display them, then Word will use the closest available screen font to display the font on your monitor. *Closest* does not mean exact, however, so the appearance may well differ. Also, if you have installed screen fonts on your computer but do not have the equivalent printer font to tell your printer how to create them, then your printer will use the closest available printer font. If your printed document does not match what is appearing on your screen, switch to a font for which you *do* have both the screen and printer versions, such as TrueType Fonts.

If you retrieve a document that uses fonts not available on your system, Word will automatically substitute the font it thinks is closest, either in display or printing. You can either accept the substitutions or change the font using the usual font formatting methods.

You have another choice for dealing with this situation: You can select Tools | Options, select the Compatibility tab, and then select Font Substitution. Using the Font Substitution dialog box, change the font assigned to substitute for the font in the document. The advantage to doing this is that if you save the document with your changes and then retrieve it on another computer that does have the missing fonts installed, the document will not need reformatting—the file will use the fonts that were missing on your system. See "Compatibility Options" for more information on this font substitution feature.

Automatic Saving

See "Saving Documents."

AUTONUM Field

Use the AUTONUM field to insert paragraph numbers automatically. See "Fields" for more information.

AUTONUMLGL Field

Use the AUTONUMLGL field to insert legal format paragraph numbers automatically. See "Fields" for more information.

AUTONUMOUT Field

Use the AUTONUMOUT field to insert Outline format paragraph numbers automatically. See "Fields" for more information on this and other fields, and see "Outlines" for information on how outlines work.

AutoText

The AutoText feature lets you enter text into your document faster. You create an AutoText entry that defines what you will type in the document and the text that you want to replace it. Unlike AutoCorrect, with AutoText you choose when to have Word add the new text. This feature was called the Glossary feature in earlier versions.

Procedures

First create an AutoText entry. Then you can type text in the document and use AutoText to replace that text.

Creating an AutoText Entry

1. Enter the text you want to use as an AutoText entry in the document and select it. This is the actual text that you want inserted into the document.

2. Select Edit | AutoText.

3. Edit the text in the Name text box. This is what you will type into the document and that AutoText will replace. Make sure that this name is meaningful, so that you can easily remember it while you are typing your document.

4. By default, AutoText entries are available to all documents. If you want to restrict this AutoText entry so that it is only available to documents created with a certain template, choose that template from the Make AutoText Entry Available To drop-down list box.

5. You can choose to save the replacement text with the current formatting or without it, by selecting Formatted Text or Plain Text. If you select Plain Text, when the text is inserted, it will adopt the formatting of the text it replaces.

6. Select Add.

Using AutoText Entries

After your AutoText entries are created, you can use them in your document.

1. Type the name of the AutoText entry.

2. With the insertion point within or next to the AutoText name, press F3, or select Edit | AutoText and Insert. Word replaces the AutoText name with the text you have assigned to that name.

For example, in Figure 4-3 the company letterhead, which combines the company logo, slogan, and address, was inserted by typing an AutoText entry called **logo** and pressing F3. Now the user is ready to create the letter by simply typing it. Consider using AutoText to create your own letterhead when its text and graphic will also be used in flyers, memos, or other documents in different locations (see "Hints" in this section). Normally, a letterhead that will only be used for letters would be saved as a template.

Editing or Deleting AutoText Entries

If you want to replace or delete the AutoText entry's replacement text:

1. Enter and format the new text.

2. Select Edit | AutoText.

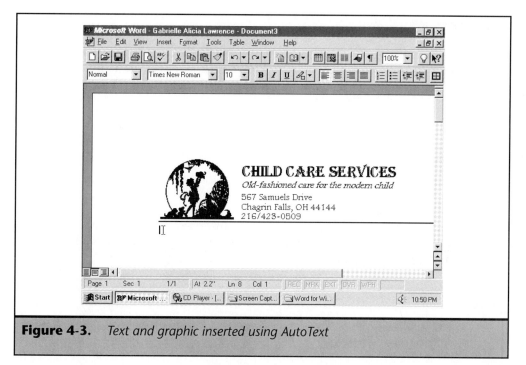

Figure 4-3. *Text and graphic inserted using AutoText*

3. In the <u>N</u>ame list box, highlight the name of the AutoText entry you are editing or deleting.

4. Select <u>A</u>dd to edit the entry or <u>D</u>elete to delete it. If you select <u>A</u>dd, Word displays a dialog box asking if you want to replace the current AutoText entry. Select <u>Y</u>es to do so.

5. Select OK.

Hints

AutoText can be used to insert either text and graphics. For example, you might save a company logo as an AutoText entry and use "logo" as the name.

If you use AutoText to insert a field, make sure to update the field by pressing F9 immediately after inserting the field. Otherwise, the field will display whatever it contained when you created the AutoText entry.

Related Topics

AutoCorrect
Find and Replace

AUTOTEXT Field

The AUTOTEXT field inserts an AutoText entry into the document. See "AutoText" for an explanation of how AutoText works and "Fields" for an explanation of this and other fields.

Backnotes

Backnotes is another name for endnotes. See "Footnotes and Endnotes."

Backspace Key

Use the BACKSPACE key to delete text: position the insertion point after the text to delete, and press BACKSPACE. Unlike the DEL key, which also deletes text, BACKSPACE removes text *behind* the insertion point.

Backup

See "Saving Documents."

BARCODE Field

Use the BARCODE field to insert a bar code for a zip code into your document. See "Fields" for information.

Bending Text

See "WordArt."

Binder

Microsoft Office includes a binder that allows you to organize your documents according to function rather than application. You can add Word documents to any binder. When a document is part of a binder, when you print, move or send it, every document that is part of the binder is included. From the binder, you can also edit each document in the binder in its original application.

Block

See "Selecting Text."

Block Protecting

In WordPerfect, block protection is a feature that keeps lines or paragraphs together on a page. See "Keeping Paragraphs Together on the Page" or "Keeping Lines on the Same Page" under "Pagination" for the equivalent features in Word for Windows.

Bold

Bold, or boldface, is a character style that produces heavy, dark characters. Bold is often used to provide emphasis in titles, headings, and important text.

Procedures

The Bold style can be applied either as you are typing or after you have typed the text. To apply the Bold format while typing, you add the format, type the text to be affected, and then remove the format. To apply it to existing text, select the text to be formatted and then add the format.

Adding and Removing Bold with the Font Dialog Box

1. Select Format | Font to open the Font dialog box. You can also right-click the mouse at the insertion point to open the shortcut menu, and then select Font.

2. Select Bold in the Font Style list box. If you are removing Bold, choose another style in the list box. Then select OK.

Adding and Removing Bold with the Toolbar

To either add or remove Bold, click on the Bold button (shown in the margin) in the Formatting toolbar.

Adding and Removing Bold with the Keyboard

To either add or remove Bold, press CTRL+B.

Hints

Another procedure for removing Bold from text is to select the text and press CTRL+SPACEBAR. This removes all character formatting from the selected text.

Many dot matrix printers print boldface text by overprinting it or by printing the text a second time, offsetting it slightly to make the lines of the letter thicker. If the bold style is not printing to your satisfaction, consult your printer's manual for options to change the way bold is created.

Related Topics

Character Formats
Fonts

BOOKMARK Field

Use the BOOKMARK field to insert text marked with a bookmark in another location of the document. See "Fields" for more information about this field. See "Bookmarks," just below, for more about working with bookmarks.

Bookmarks

Use Word's bookmarks feature to mark a position or some text in a document. You can reference these bookmarks in field names, or you can use them to quickly find a specific location in a document.

Procedures

The following procedures will tell you how to insert, move, delete, go to, or indicate bookmarks.

Inserting and Moving Bookmarks with the Dialog Box

1. Put the insertion point where you want to insert the bookmark. To mark text rather than a position in the document, select the text.

2. Select Edit | Bookmark to open the Bookmark dialog box. You can also open this dialog box by pressing CTRL+SHIFT+F5.

3. Type the name of the bookmark in the Bookmark Name text box. If you are moving the bookmark from a previous reference, select the bookmark name from the Bookmark Name list box. Bookmark names can be up to 40 characters long. You can only use letters, numbers, and underscore (_) characters in the name.

4. Select Add.

Removing Bookmarks

1. Select Edit | Bookmark to open the Bookmark dialog box.

2. Highlight the name of the bookmark you want to delete in the Bookmark Name list box, and select Delete.

3. Select Close to put away the Bookmark dialog box.

Going to Bookmarks with the Menus

1. Select Edit | Go To or press F5 to open the Go To dialog box.

2. Select Bookmark from the Go To What list box.

3. Type the bookmark name in the Enter Bookmark Name drop-down list box or select it from the list, and select OK.

NOTE: *You can also simply highlight the bookmark name in the Bookmark dialog box and select Go To.*

Showing or Hiding Bookmark Indicators

1. Select Tools | Options and the View tab.

2. Select or clear the Bookmarks check box.

3. Select OK.

You will see a large I for most bookmarks. Bookmarks that represent a selection instead of a single point in the document show brackets ([ ]) at their beginning and ending points. The bookmark indicators are shown here:

```
┌────────────── Bookmark ends for a selection ──────────────┐
│                                                           │
[Here are the features that you get when you upgrade to the new version:]
 •  [Phone and address book to automatically track the people you need to contact every day.
 •  [Daily planner built by the reminders that you enter.
Bookmark representing a single point
```

Hints

Bookmarks may seem a minor feature by themselves. However, bookmarks can be used by other Word for Windows functions to greatly enhance your productivity and flexibility. For example, you can use bookmarks with fields to create cross-references or to calculate values in your document. You can use them to copy text or graphics from one part of your document to another. You can also use bookmarks to move quickly to a specific part of the document using the Go To feature or to mark text for copying into another document.

Related Topics

Cross-References
Fields
Mail Merge

Borders and Shading

You can add borders around paragraphs or graphics. Frames often have borders.

Procedures

Borders can be applied to a single paragraph, a set of paragraphs, cells in a table, a graphic, or a frame. These options are described further in "Options," following this section. You can apply borders using menu commands or Word's Borders toolbar.

Applying Borders with the Borders Toolbar

You can apply borders and shading using the Borders toolbar, shown here:

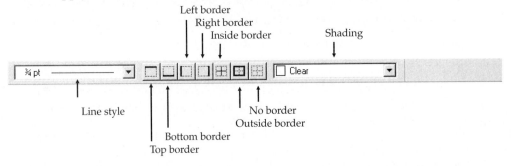

1. Display the Borders toolbar by clicking the Borders button, the last button in the Formatting toolbar, or by using the <u>V</u>iew | <u>T</u>oolbars command.

2. From the Line Style list box, choose a type of line for the border.

3. Choose one of the border buttons to designate the border part. The border part will use the last selected line style.

4. Choose a shading from the Shading list box.

5. Put away the Borders toolbar by selecting the Borders button again.

Applying Borders with the Menus

1. Select the item that you want to have the border.

2. Select Format | Borders and Shading to open the Paragraph Borders and Shading dialog box. The options in this dialog box depend on the type of item that you selected in step 1.

TIP: *You can right-click a frame and select Borders and Shading to quickly open the dialog box.*

3. Choose a line type under Line in the dialog box. If you choose None, you will remove lines.

4. Choose a color for the line from the Color drop-down list box. If color is not supported by your monitor or printer, when you print the border the line may appear in a shading or pattern used to represent the color, or the color setting may be ignored.

5. Set the borders to apply with the border sample. The borders indicated with markers are what will appear in the document, using the line style that you selected in the previous step. You can select the border parts using the mouse or the keyboard:

   ■ With the mouse, click the border parts that you want.

   ■ With the keyboard, press ALT+R to move to the border sample. Then press the arrow keys to cycle through the possible selections and press the SPACEBAR to toggle adding or removing the border from the current side.

TIP: *One shortcut for defining where you want borders to appear is to select one of the preset border options. The options available depend on the item you selected before opening the dialog box.*

6. If you started by selecting a paragraph or paragraphs, you can specify how close the text will be to the border by entering a value in the From Text text box.

7. Select OK.

Removing Borders

To remove a border, follow the steps given above for applying borders, and select "None" for the line type of each border that you want to remove.

Applying and Removing Shading

You can apply shading to paragraphs and tables but not to graphics. Shading changes the color or pattern of the background.

1. Select the paragraphs or cells you want to shade.

2. Select Format | Borders and Shading and select the Shading tab or button.

3. Select Custom to specify options for shading the selected object. Or select None to remove shading.

4. Choose an option from the Shading list box. Choices include a percentage shading and a line pattern.

5. Select a color from the Foreground drop-down list box, which is the color that appears above the Background color.

6. Select a color from the Background drop-down list box, which is the color that appears behind the Foreground color.

7. Select OK to return to the document.

If you selected colors and you have a noncolor printer, Word tries to simulate the colors using shading. If it cannot, or if your printer cannot print graphics, no shading is applied.

Options

Different border and shading options are provided, depending on what type of object you are applying them to.

Applying Borders to Paragraphs and Frames

When you add borders to paragraphs, the border settings become part of the paragraph formatting. In addition to the standard options for where borders can appear, you can specify how close the border comes to the paragraph text and add lines between paragraphs.

Paragraph borders use the same indent settings as the paragraph to which they are applied. Paragraphs that have different indents have separate borders. To allow paragraphs with separate indents to be inside the same border, convert the paragraphs to a table, and apply the format to the table.

In Figure 4-4, all five paragraphs were selected at once, and the preset option Shadow was applied (the shadow effect is more apparent when the text is printed than when it is onscreen). However, because of the different indents, you see three different shadow boxes on the page. Notice that the second paragraph in the third shadow box has a different left margin indent. Since the first-line indent is the same as the left margin indent of the surrounding paragraphs, this paragraph uses the same border.

You can also see in Figure 4-4 that a border can come very close to your text. You can increase the distance between the text and border by changing the value in the

From Text text box in the Borders dialog box. This value measures the distance in points, which are 1/72 of an inch, so you can fine-tune the distance between the text and border.

You can also add lines between paragraphs, whether you selected one paragraph or many. To add lines between paragraphs, select the line between the paragraphs in the border sample. When you add a line between paragraphs to a single paragraph, the line will appear when you create a new paragraph.

NOTE: *You cannot create both a frame border and a paragraph border for text within a frame. Only one border is allowed.*

Shading applies to entire paragraphs. If you want to change the background color for text that is less than an entire paragraph, Word's highlighting feature, as described under "Highlighting."

Applying Borders to Pictures

You can apply borders to pictures or graphics that you add to your Word document. Notice that there are no options for creating lines between pictures or for setting the distance between border and picture. You can, however, create white space between a graphic and its border, but not by changing the border settings. Instead, you apply *negative cropping* to the graphic, as described under "Graphics."

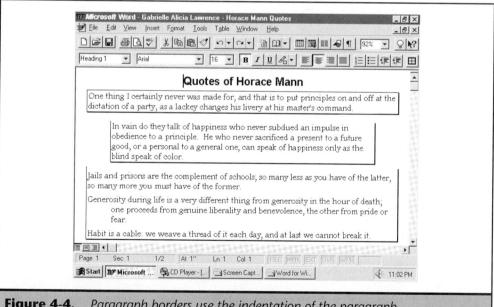

Figure 4-4. *Paragraph borders use the indentation of the paragraph*

You can also add a frame around a graphic, but that frame cannot have a border separate from the graphic border. The border applied to the graphic becomes the only border for both the graphic and frame. To create special effects, however, you can add graphics to tables. In the table, you can apply a graphic border and a table border.

Applying Borders to Tables

What you see in the border sample depends on whether you select a single cell, a single row, a single column, or cells from multiple columns and rows. If you select cells from multiple columns and rows, the Shadow preset option becomes Grid.

You can combine graphics and text with tables and use borders to create interesting effects, as you can see in Figure 4-5. In this figure, the first row of the table has double-line borders at the top and bottom. The figures are inside single, thin-line boxes. The text paragraphs are bordered by a double-line on the left.

Related Topics

Frames
Graphics
Pictures

Boxes

See "Borders and Shading" and "Frames."

Breaks

You can insert page breaks (see "Pagination"), column breaks (see "Columns"), and section breaks (see "Sections") in your document.

Bulleted List

To quickly create bulleted lists, use Word's Format I Bullets and Numbering command, as described in "Lists."

Bullets

Bullets are graphic symbols that are typically used to mark items in lists where numbering is not appropriate. You can insert bullets using the Insert I Symbol command, or you can convert a number of paragraphs into a bulleted list using

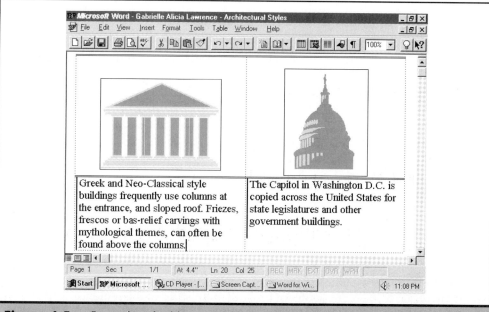

Figure 4-5.   *Examples of table paragraph and graphic borders*

Word's Format | Bullets and Numbering command. AutoFormat will automatically apply this format when you start a new paragraph with certain characters (*, o, >, -, or a symbol character) as described under "AutoFormat". For instructions on converting paragraphs into bulleted lists, see "Lists."

Calculations

See "Math Calculations."

Callouts

A *callout* is text with a line that points to some element in a picture or chart. You can create callouts using the Callout button on the Drawing toolbar. For information on using the Drawing toolbar and creating callouts, see "Drawing on a Document."

Cancel

See "Close Button."

Capitalization

You can change the capitalization of text in your document in the following ways:

- Press SHIFT and a letter key to type the capital of that letter.

- Press CAPS LOCK. All letters you type will be capitals. To turn off CAPS LOCK, press the key again.

- Apply the All Caps character format to text (see "All Caps").

- Select the text to be affected and press SHIFT+F3 repeatedly. As you press this key combination, the selected text changes from all lowercase letters to initial caps (the first letter of each word is uppercase and the rest is lowercase), and then to all caps. However, if you select a whole sentence or paragraph before using SHIFT+F3 to cycle through capitalization options, you do not get initial caps on all words in the sentence or paragraph. Word recognizes sentences and only capitalizes the first letter of the sentence.

- You can select the text, select Format | Change Case, choose a capitalization option, and select OK. This command has options for changing text into lowercase, uppercase, sentence (only the first letter of the sentence is capitalized), title case (first letter in each word is capitalized), and toggle case (uppercase becomes lowercase and vice versa).

 TIP: *Word's AutoCorrect feature can correct many capitalization mistakes including accidentally capitalizing the first and second letter of a word instead of just the first, and pressing the CAPS LOCK key to make uppercase letters lowercase and lowercase letters uppercase. See "AutoCorrect" for how you can make this feature work for you.*

Captions

You can add captions that number similar objects and include a short description or title for figures, tables, or other objects in a Word document. The figures and tables in this book show examples of captions.

Procedures

You can create individual captions, or you can have Word automatically create captions for objects of a specific type.

Creating Individual Captions

1. Select the object you want a caption for: a picture, frame, table, or other object inserted into your document.

CAUTION: *You can insert captions without selecting an object, in which case the caption is simply part of the normal text. However, the caption then serves no purpose.*

2. Select Insert | Caption.

3. Choose a label from the Label drop-down list box. If none of the labels there are appropriate, you can select New Label, type a new label, such as **Chart** or **Photograph**, and select OK.

4. From the Position drop-down list box, choose a location for the caption. You can put a caption above or below the object it labels.

5. If you do not want to use the default numbering system for objects, select Numbering.

   ■ Select a new numbering system from the Format drop-down list box.

   ■ To include chapter or section numbers in the caption (for instance, Table 2-4 would be the fourth table in the second chapter or section), select Include Chapter Numbers. Then choose the heading level to indicate chapter beginnings and the separator to use between chapter and object numbers.

   ■ Select OK when you are done. If you have not yet divided your document into chapters, Word reminds you to.

6. The Caption text box displays the current text of the caption, using the label and numbering format you selected. If you want to add a title or description to the caption, type it in the Caption text box.

7. Select OK to insert the caption for the currently selected object.

A caption for a graph in your document might look like the one above the pie chart in Figure 4-6.

Creating Captions with AutoCaption

1. Before inserting any of the objects you want to caption automatically, select Insert | Caption.

2. Select AutoCaption.

3. In the Add Captions While Inserting list box, select the check boxes for the items you want numbered and labeled automatically.

   For example, to add captions to all pictures added to your document, you could select Paintbrush Picture and Microsoft Word Picture together, because all pictures would be numbered together.

4. Under Options, you can choose where the caption is to appear, the text of the label, and a numbering format. You can also create a new label for the type of object you are working with. These options all work the same as described above for "Creating Individual Captions."

5. Select OK.

Hints

Word numbers each object with the same label sequentially; all the objects labeled with "Table" are in one list, all objects labeled with "Figure" are in another, and so forth.

To add text to a caption created with AutoCaption, just move to the caption in the document window and type the additional text you want to use.

If you delete an object that has a caption, you do not delete the caption. You will have to delete the caption separately. You delete a caption by highlighting the text and fields that make the caption and pressing DEL or BACKSPACE. Word renumbers the captions after you delete one.

Captions are created using SEQ (sequence) fields; see "Fields" in this chapter for details.

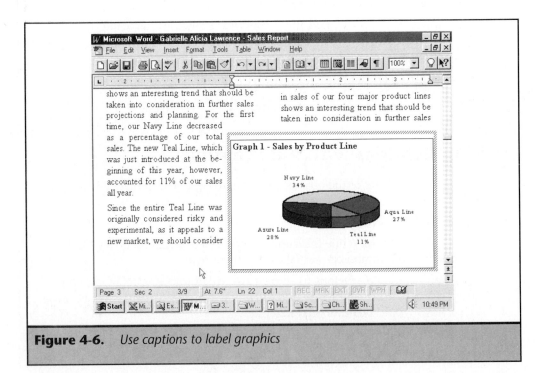

Figure 4-6.   *Use captions to label graphics*

Related Topics

Fields
Graphics
Objects
Tables

Cartridges

Most printers have installed printer fonts, which are stored in the printer's memory rather than the computer's. You can expand the variety of printer fonts on most laser printers by installing printer cartridges containing the necessary information for the added fonts. These fonts must also be installed in your system, so that Word and other Windows applications can access them. For a complete explanation on installing font cartridges, consult the documentation that comes with your cartridge.

Center Page

You can center the text between the top and bottom margins by changing the vertical alignment of the section. See "Sections" for more information.

Center Text

See "Alignment" and "Tabs."

Centimeters

Word's default unit of measurement is inches. However, you can change the default setting to centimeters. You can also enter specific measurements in centimeters at any time by including the centimeter abbreviation, cm, after the measurement.

See "General Options" for details on changing the default measurement unit.

Changing Case

See "All Caps" and "Capitalization."

Changing the Folder

You can easily change the folder where Word opens and stores document files. These steps are described under "Document Location Options."

Changing the Font

See "Fonts."

Chapter Numbers

You can include chapter numbers in the page numbers, captions, and indexes or tables of contents of your documents. Before doing so, you need to set up chapters in your document.

Procedures

Chapters in Word for Windows are sections of text that begin with a paragraph, usually a chapter title or number, that has a specific heading-level style applied to it. You can use any heading level to indicate the beginning of chapters, as long as that heading level is not used for any text other than the text marking the beginning of chapters. To make outlining your document easier, use the Heading 1 or Heading 2 styles, so that any headings within a chapter are of a lower-level heading. Thus, each chapter starts with a Heading 1 style and other heading levels below that are the headings within that chapter. These chapters can even be supplied as subdocuments so each chapter can be its own document.

When you create page numbers, caption numbers, and indexes or tables of contents, you can choose to include the chapter numbers. The steps needed to include the chapter numbers are described within these specific features, since the exact steps are different for each feature. When you include chapter numbers, choose the level of the heading indicating the beginning of each chapter as part of those features.

Related Topics

Captions
Index
Master Documents
Page Numbers

Character Formats

Character formats change the appearance of the characters in your document. You can change formats such as:

- Font or font size (see "Fonts")
- Attributes, such as boldface or underlining (see "Bold," "Italics," "Strikethrough," "Hidden Text," "Small Capitals," "All Caps," and "Underline")

- Text color (see "Text Color")
- Placement of the text above or below the baseline (see "Super/Subscript")
- Spacing between the characters (see "Spacing Characters")

Characters Per Inch

Characters per inch, or cpi, is a way of measuring the size of monospaced fonts, in which each character takes up the same space on a line. Word does not use cpi but rather measures fonts by determining the height of the font in points, which are 1/72 of an inch. See "Fonts."

Charts

Graphs are occasionally referred to as charts. For instructions on creating and editing a graph, see "Graphs."

Check Spelling

See "Spelling."

Clearing Tabs

See "Tabs."

Click

See "Mouse Pointer."

Clip Art

Clip art refers to graphic images saved in a file and available for use in computer programs. Word for Windows comes with several pieces of clip art, as does Windows itself. You can also purchase, from various companies, sets of clip art with specific themes, such as business, transportation, and holidays. See "Graphics" for information on importing and using clip art files in your Word for Windows documents.

Clipboard

The Windows Clipboard enables you to copy and move text, graphics, and other data within a Word for Windows document, between Word for Windows documents, or between Word for Windows and other applications, as shown in Figure 4-7. With the documents in Figure 4-7, Document 1 and Document 2 can be the same document, two documents in the same application, or documents in separate applications.

Most Windows applications can access the Clipboard. You can use the Clipboard to copy data from other applications to Word documents, or from Word documents to most other applications. Because of this, you can easily import graphics, text, and other information into a Word document, or export that information into another application's document. The one restriction on this operation is the type of data the other application can support. For example, when you copy part of Word into Microsoft Excel, some of the word processing features may not carry over if they are features that Microsoft Excel does not support.

How It Works

The Clipboard is a Windows feature that can be used in Word and in other Windows applications. You can also use the Clipboard to move text and other objects between Windows applications and some DOS applications that can run in a window.

When you cut or copy to the Clipboard, the items you select are read to the Clipboard in the format they are currently in. When you paste them into your document, they are simply read back into a document, just as if they were being entered originally.

The Clipboard can paste items in any format the original application supports, as well as in their original format. You can also use the Clipboard to create linked or embedded objects.

Procedures

The following steps explain how to copy and move text using the Clipboard and how to insert material from the Clipboard using different formats.

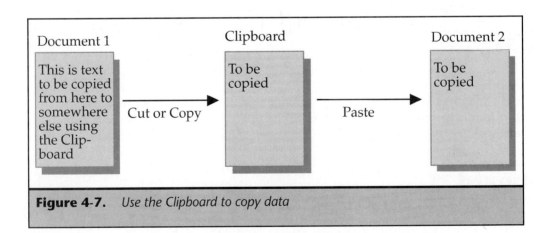

Figure 4-7.   *Use the Clipboard to copy data*

Moving (Cutting) with the Clipboard

1. Select the text or graphics you want to move.

2. Select Edit | Cut, or press CTRL+X, or click the Cut button in the Standard toolbar.

3. Place the insertion point where you want the text or graphics to appear.

4. Select Edit | Paste, or press CTRL+V, or click the Paste button in the Standard toolbar.

Copying with the Clipboard

1. Select the text or graphics you want to copy.

2. Select Edit | Copy, or press CTRL+C, or click the Copy button in the Standard toolbar.

3. Place the insertion point where you want the text or graphics copied.

4. Select Edit | Paste, or press CTRL+V, or click the Paste button in the Standard toolbar.

Pasting Something in a Different Format

By default, Word pastes text or graphics into your document using the original format—that is, the format of the source of the pasted object. For some types of objects, you can choose a different format when you paste into a Word document, using the Edit | Paste Special command. This feature is most useful when you want to use a specific format for inserting a graphic or when you want to link and embed the object.

1. Cut or copy the objects (text, graphics, or other data) to the Clipboard, from Word or another Windows application.

2. Place the insertion point where you want the data to appear in the Word document.

3. Select Edit | Paste Special, to open the Paste Special dialog box shown here:

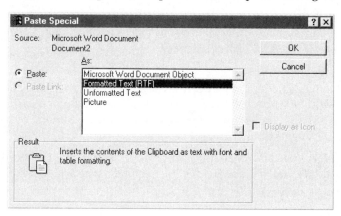

4. Choose a format from the <u>A</u>s list box; this is the format that will be used when the object is pasted in.

5. Select the <u>P</u>aste option button. (The Paste <u>L</u>ink button is used to create a link to the original application, which is the source of the pasted object. Links are explained under "Object Linking and Embedding.")

Related Topics

Drag and Drop
Object Linking and Embedding
Scrap
Spike

Close Button

Almost all dialog boxes and windows contain a Close button. Selecting this button closes the dialog box without applying any selections you have made in that dialog box. In a window, it closes the document, so you may see a prompt for saving your document. In a dialog box, you can select this button by pressing ESC.

Closing Documents

When you are finished using a document, you can close the document window containing it. This removes the document from your computer's memory. To edit the document again, you have to reopen it.

Procedures

1. To close a file, select <u>F</u>ile | <u>C</u>lose or click on its Close button.

 TIP: *You can also close a document window by double-clicking on the document window's document icon in the upper-left corner.*

2. If the document has never before been saved, or if you have made changes to the document since it was last saved, Word displays a dialog box asking you if you want to save the document. Select <u>Y</u>es to save the document, or <u>N</u>o to close the window without saving.

3. When you select <u>Y</u>es and the document has never before been saved, Word opens the Save As dialog box, where you specify a name and location for the

document. If the document has been previously saved, Word saves the document with the same filename.

Hint

If you choose <u>N</u>o when Word prompts you to save your changes, all your edits are lost and cannot be recovered. Even if you have enabled the Automatic Save feature, those changes, too, are lost. The Automatic Save feature saves to a temporary file, which can only be recovered when you are restarting Word after an unexpected system crash or reboot procedure that clears everything in memory. The temporary backup copy is discarded once you request a save operation, even if you choose not to save the file.

Related Topics

Exiting Word
Opening Documents
Saving Documents

Collapsing Text

You can expand or collapse an outline to display various levels of outline entries or body text within the outline. For information on this, see "Outlines."

Color

See "Text Color" for changing the color of text and "Highlighting" for changing the color behind the text.

Columns

In Word, you can create two types of columns: table columns and newspaper-style columns. In tables, text is arranged in columns and rows. Newspaper-style columns "snake" from the bottom of one column to the top of the next, as in magazine and newspaper columns. See "Tables" in this chapter to learn about table columns. Newspaper-style columns are discussed here.

Figure 4-8 shows one example of how columns can be used in a newsletter. Notice that the columns are unequal in width, allowing the main story to run in the large column on the left, with a less-significant story in the narrower column on the right. You can set the width of each column and the space that separates them. Columns are often used in newsletters to increase visual interest, and you can also fit more text on a page with the careful use of columns.

TIP: *If you have not used columns before, read the "Hints" section on columns before reading the procedures.*

Procedures

Columns only appear as side-by-side columns in Page Layout view. In Normal view, your columns appear using the correct width, but not all on one page. Instead, they appear after each other, separated by a column break line. Your text is formatted as columns, but it doesn't appear that way on the screen in this mode.

Creating Columns with the Standard Toolbar

When you use the Standard toolbar, the columns created are spaced one-half inch apart and are applied to the document section containing the insertion point or the selected text.

TIP: *See "Sections" for an explanation of what Word document sections are and how they affect formatting.*

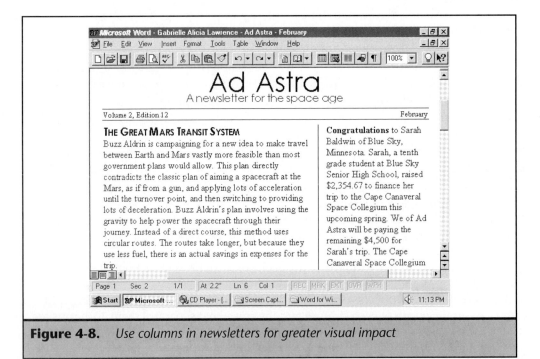

Figure 4-8.   *Use columns in newsletters for greater visual impact*

1. Put your insertion point in the section you want to format into columns, or select the text that you want to appear in columns.

2. Click the Columns button in the standard toolbar; Word displays this columns grid:

3. In the columns grid, click and drag to the right to select the number of columns you want. Word allows you as many columns as it can fit on your selected page size without letting the columns or the spaces between them become smaller than one-half inch.

Creating or Editing Columns with the Menus

1. Put your insertion point where you want columns to begin or in the column you want to edit.

2. Select Format I Columns.

3. Enter the number of columns you want, up to 45, in the Number of Columns text box. Initially, each column is the same width, and the space between columns is one-half inch. Word may actually create fewer columns if there isn't enough room on your selected page size.

4. To change the column widths or spacing between them, enter the measurements in the first Width or Spacing text boxes. When you are using varying widths for columns and spaces between them, start by clearing the Equal Column Width check box, then enter the measurements in the Width or Spacing text boxes for each column.

TIP: *The Spacing text box for each column refers to the space that appears after that column.*

5. To add a solid line in the space between columns, select the Line Between check box.

6. To have Word insert a column break at the insertion point in order to start a new column, select Start New Column. The text after the insertion point appears at the top of the next column.

7. In the Apply To drop-down list box, select what part of the document you want the column settings applied to, and select OK.

Adjusting Column Widths with the Ruler

You can use Word's ruler to change the widths of your column. However, if you want to have unequal columns, you must turn off the Equal Column Width check box in the Columns dialog box before you can separately set the column's widths. Otherwise, when you adjust the width of one column, all other columns are also adjusted. To adjust column widths with the ruler, you must use the mouse.

If you turned off the Equal Column Width check box, you can change a column width by dragging the dark gray area in the column marker shown below, and moving the entire column marker. Change the width of the space between columns by dragging the thin gray boxes at each side of the column marker as shown here:

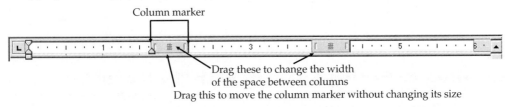

Column marker

Drag these to change the width
of the space between columns
Drag this to move the column marker without changing its size

When the Equal Column Width check box is selected, you can drag either column marker to the position you want it to hold. What you are doing is changing the column width by increasing or decreasing the space between the columns. Word rearranges the column markers for the other columns so that the columns and the space between them are all equal, and the columns fill the page from margin to margin.

Balancing Columns

When you reach the end of a section or a document that is formatted with columns, you may find that the length of the columns is too uneven. You can make Word balance the columns so that they are as close as possible to the same length, given the number of lines and line height. Figure 4-9 shows the visual effect of unbalanced and balanced columns.

1. Position your insertion point at the end of the text in columns.

2. Select Insert | Break.

3. In the Break dialog box, select the Continuous option button, and then select OK.

NOTE: *If you want to start a new page after the columns, do not select Next Page in the Break dialog box. Instead, select Continuous as instructed in step 3 above, and add a hard page break after the continuous section break.*

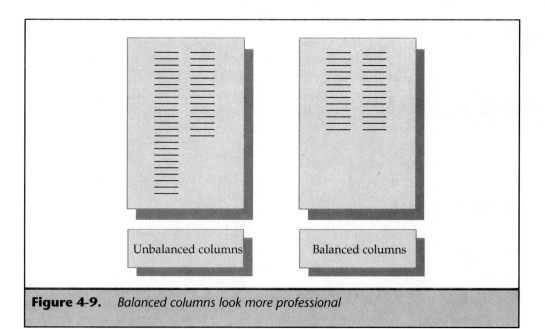

Figure 4-9.   *Balanced columns look more professional*

Hints

You can insert a column break, causing the text after the break to move to the top of the next column. Insert column breaks by pressing CTRL+SHIFT+ENTER or by selecting Insert | Break, choosing the Column Break option button, and selecting OK.

You can select columns of text using either the keyboard or the mouse.

- To select a column of text with the mouse, start at one corner of the column you want to select. Drag the mouse from there to the opposite corner.

- To select a column of text using the keyboard, position the insertion point in one corner of the column you want to select. Press CTRL+SHIFT+F8 and notice that the COL indicator is on where the EXT indicator normally appears. Use the arrow keys to move to the opposite corner. You can also use HOME to move to the beginning of a line in the column and END to move to the end of a line. When you are in Normal view, you can use PGUP and PGDN to move your selection a screen up or down; this doesn't work in Page Layout view.

Related Topics

Margins
Tables

C

Comments

See "Annotations" and "Hidden Text."

COMMENTS Field

The COMMENTS field inserts the contents of the Comments text box from the Properties dialog box into a document. See "Fields" and "Document Properties" for more information.

COMPARE Field

Use the COMPARE field to compare two values and determine if they are the same or different. See "Fields" for more information.

Comparing Versions

You can compare two versions of a document by adding revision marks to the document. Revision marks indicate where the two documents are different, by marking deleted, added, replaced, and moved text. You can have Word mark revisions as you are making them or add the revision marks using a saved file as the original version of the document.

Figure 4-10 shows revision marks in a document, added while the document was edited. Notice the deleted text indicated by strikethrough text, new text marked with underlining, and the revision bars on the outside edge to let you locate changes faster.

Procedures

The following procedures tell you how to add, customize, and review revision marks in your document.

Adding Revision Marks While Editing

1. Open the document you are going to revise.
2. Select Tools | Revisions to open the Revisions dialog box.

TIP: *You can quickly open the Revisions dialog box by double-clicking the MRK indicator in the status bar.*

3. Select the Mark Revisions While Editing check box. If you turn this option off, Word will stop marking revisions.

4. Select OK.

5. Edit your document, and you will see the revision marks appearing as you work.

Adding Revision Marks after Editing

1. Open the revised document.

2. Select Tools | Revisions and then Compare Versions, to open the Compare Versions dialog box. The options of this dialog box are the same as the Open dialog box.

3. Select the name of the file that is the original version of the document, and then OK. Word reads the two files and adds revision marks to the open document, marking how the open document is different from the original one.

TIP: *You can compare two documents with different document names by following the above steps.*

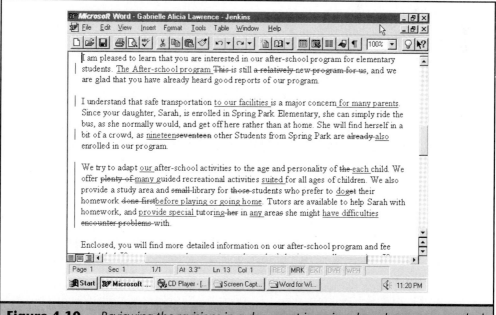

Figure 4-10. *Reviewing the revisions in a document is easier when changes are marked*

Designating Revision Marks Settings

1. Select Tools | Revisions and then Options. Word opens the Options dialog box with the Revisions tab selected. You can also open this dialog box with the Tools | Options command.

2. To tell Word how to mark new text, use the Mark drop-down list box under Inserted Text. You can choose bold, italic, underlined, double-underlined, or no marks at all. You can also choose a color for the marks from the Color drop-down list box. The default is to let Word pick a different color for each author who works on the document.

3. To tell Word how to mark deleted text, use the Mark drop-down list box under Deleted Text. You can choose hidden or strikethrough formats. You can also choose a color from the Color drop-down list box.

4. Specify where you want revision bars located (to indicate revised paragraphs), by choosing from the Mark drop-down list box. You can also choose a color from the Color drop-down list box.

5. Select OK twice.

Reviewing and Accepting/Rejecting Revisions

You can accept or reject individual revisions and deletions or all revisions in a document.

1. In a document with revision marks, select Tools | Revisions.

2. Select Review. Word opens a dialog box that you can use to search for revision marks.

3. Review the revisions by selecting Find or Find to move forward or backward through the document to the revision marks.

4. Select Accept to keep or Reject to discard each revision. You may want to select the Find Next After Accept/Reject check box to automatically move to the next revision mark as you accept or reject the current revision. If you change your mind, you can select Undo Last to reverse the last acceptance or rejection you made.

5. When finished, select Cancel.

Accepting or Undoing All Revisions

1. Select a section of text to accept/undo the revisions in the document. If you don't select a specific section of text, you will accept or reject all revisions in the document.

2. Select <u>T</u>ools | Re<u>v</u>isions.

3. Select <u>A</u>ccept All to keep all the revisions made to the selected text/document or Reject All to discard all the revisions made to the selected text/document.

 TIP: *You can use <u>E</u>dit | <u>U</u>ndo if you find you've accidentally selected the wrong option.*

4. Select OK.

Hints

Compare copies of legal documents, to ensure that you are aware of all changes to a document before you sign off on it. It would be very easy for a reviser to accidentally remove a vital phrase without quite realizing it. You can also emphasize text without using revision marks by adding a background color for a selection of text as described under "Highlighting."

Whether you compare versions of a document or have Word mark revisions while you edit, Word does not mark revisions to formatting, only revisions to the text.

As you are making changes to the document when revision marks are turned on, you may find it easier to see the end result by hiding revision marks. Hide revision marks by selecting <u>T</u>ools | Re<u>v</u>isions and clearing the Show Revisions on <u>S</u>creen check box.

You can also select whether the revisions appear when you print the document. To only print the revised version of the text, select <u>T</u>ools | Re<u>v</u>isions and clear the Show Revisions on <u>P</u>rinted Document check box.

This feature also works for locating coworkers' edits and checking if they have made their changes to the wrong version of the file.

Related Topic

Revision and Annotation Merging

Compatibility Options

Word for Windows lets you convert documents created by other programs so you can use them in Word. However, since many features work somewhat differently in various programs, the compatibility among formats is not complete. Word lets you change Compatibility options, which determine how Word handles certain features so it can work more like the program that created the document originally. You can also substitute a font if the original font is not available on your system.

Procedures

The Compatibility options do not change the document in question. Instead, they change how Word works with that document. If you save the document in its original format from Word, and open it again in the original program used to create it, the Compatibility options will not have changed anything in the file.

1. Select Tools | Options and select the Compatibility tab.

2. If there are fonts used in the document that are not available for Windows on your system, select Font Substitution. You're now in the Font Substitution dialog box.

3. In the Missing Document Font list box, highlight the font you don't have.

4. In the Substituted Font drop-down list box, select the font you want to use in place of the missing font.

> *NOTE: Select Default in the Substituted Font list box to tell Word to determine which font is closest to the missing one and use it. Remember, this does not change the font assigned to the text, merely the font used to display the text. If you want to change the font actually used to format the text in question, select Convert Permanently instead.*

5. Select OK.

6. Back in the Compatibility options, in the Recommended Options For drop-down list box, choose the program used to create the file originally. Word displays a selection of check boxes for options that can be adapted in the Options list box. The program that you choose determines which of these check boxes are selected or cleared. These are the recommended options for making Word work more like the selected program, but you are free to turn individual options on or off to suit yourself, your working style, or to simulate a program not included in the Recommended Options For list box.

7. When you are happy with the settings, select OK.

> *NOTE: There are a limited number of settings you can change through Compatibility Options. These settings are designed to let you match the way some other popular word processing programs create documents, but they won't turn Word into those programs.*

Related Topic

Opening Documents

Compose

Composing characters is a WordPerfect term referring to the process of entering characters that cannot be typed at the keyboard. See "Special Characters" for information on the equivalent process in Word for Windows.

Concordances

Concordances are files containing lists of words to be included as entries in indexes. See "Index" for more information.

Conditional End of Page

Conditional end of page is a WordPerfect feature for keeping paragraphs or lines together on a single page. See "Pagination" for information on the equivalent process in Word for Windows.

Continuation Notice

Footnotes and endnotes that appear on more than one page use continuation notices to tell readers that there is more text. See "Footnotes and Endnotes" for more information on how to create a continuation notice for your endnotes and footnotes.

Control Panel

The Control Panel is a Windows application used to control many settings and features for Windows and applications that run under Windows. You use the Control Panel to install fonts, install new printers, customize the colors used on the screen, and for many other tasks. You will want to review your Windows documentation for instructions on using the Control Panel.

Controlling Pagination

See "Pagination."

Convert

See "Document Management" and "Opening Documents" for how Word converts documents created by other programs and applications.

Convert Text to a Table

See "Tables."

Converting Documents or Files

See "Opening Documents."

Copy

See "Drag and Drop," "Clipboard," "Scrap," and "Spike."

Copying Formats

You can copy paragraph and character formatting from one section of text to another. Word for Windows offers the Format Painter button on the Standard toolbar to make copying formatting even easier.

Procedures

You can copy character or paragraph formatting using the Format Painter button or other options.

Copying Formatting with the Format Painter Button

1. Select the formatting you want to copy.

   - ■ Select text only, and the formatting of the first character will be copied.

   - ■ Select text and a paragraph mark, and the formatting of the first character as well as the paragraph formatting will be copied.

   - ■ Select only a paragraph mark, and the paragraph formatting only will be copied.

2. Click the Format Painter button on the Standard toolbar (shown in the margin). To copy the formatting to multiple locations, double-click the button.

3. Select the text to which you want to apply the copied formatting. To copy the formatting to another location, select another passage of text to format. If you double-clicked the Format Painter button, click the button again to stop applying the selected format.

Copying Paragraph Formats

Paragraph formats are saved with the paragraph character at the end of the paragraph. Copying this paragraph character also copies the paragraph formatting.

1. Select the paragraph mark at the end of the paragraph whose format you want to copy.
2. Select Edit | Copy, or press CTRL+C, or click the Copy button in the toolbar.
3. Put the insertion point at the end of the paragraph to which you want to apply the copied format.
4. Select Edit | Paste, or press CTRL+V, or click the Paste button.

Copying Formats Using the Keyboard

Besides copying formats using the Format Painter tool as described above, you can also use these shortcut keys:

- To copy the formatting, select the formatted text and press CTRL+SHIFT+C.
- To paste the formatting, select the text to format and press CTRL+SHIFT+V.

To use these shortcut keys, if you want to copy the paragraph formatting, you must select the end of the paragraph when you copy the formatting and the end of the paragraph when you paste it.

Hints

Copying formats can be useful in limited circumstances; however, you will want to explore Word for Windows's styles to apply formats. When you apply styles, you can quickly change the formatting of all text formatted with that style, rather than copying formats each time you want to change the formatting in your document.

Related Topic

Styles

Count

Word counts the number of words in your document each time you save it and records that value as part of the document's properties. See "Document Properties" and "Word Count" for instructions on finding out how many words are in your document.

Create a New Folder

You can create a new folder for storing Word documents by using Windows or while changing the default folder for Word documents.

Procedures

You can create the new folder for organizing your documents using Word or Windows.

Creating a New Folder from Word

1. Select Tools | Options and click the File Locations tab.
2. In the File Types list box, highlight Documents.
3. Select Modify and then the Create New Folder button.
4. Enter the name for the new folder in the Name text box and select OK.
5. Select the new folder from the list of folders.
6. Select OK again and then Close to return to the document.

 CAUTION: *This new folder is now the default location for saving and opening your Word documents.*

Creating a New Folder with Windows

1. Open a window that shows the contents of the folder where you want the new folder added. You can get to any folder on your computer using the My Computer icon or the Windows Explorer program.
2. Select File | New | Folder to create a new folder icon.
3. Enter the folder name below the folder's icon. Folder names, like filenames, can be up to 255 characters.
4. Select OK.

Hint

You may want to create a new folder in your WINWORD directory to store all document files, or you may want to create several folders to divide your documents by purpose or type. If you create a folder to store your working Word files, you may want to change the default Word folder so that accessing the documents will be easier. You can also add shortcuts to your most frequently used documents in your Favorites Folder as described under "Favorites Folder."

Related Topics

Changing the Folder
Document Location Options
Favorites Folder

CREATEDATE Field

Use the CREATEDATE field to insert into a document the date and time it was first saved. See "Fields" for more information.

Criteria

Word uses criteria in several instances. You provide criteria to select the files that you want to find or open, as described in "Document Management." Databases use criteria to select records from the database to include in a Word feature such as mail merge. Criteria for databases are described under "Databases." You also provide criteria when you are searching a document for text, as described under "Find and Replace."

Cropping a Graphic

Cropping a graphic means to cut it down, as you would trim a photograph. Cropping is usually done to isolate a specific part of the graphic or to remove unwanted white space at the edges. See "Graphics" for more information.

Cross-References

Cross-references appear in one location of the document showing text from another location or telling you where in the document you can find related information. For example, your document might include text similar to this: "...as you can see in *Table 1, New Program Items*, on page 4..." The table number, its caption, and its page number are supplied with cross-references. Cross-references created with Word means that Word takes responsibility for updating the references. Word has many options for creating cross-references. The cross-references can be to heading styles, bookmarks, footnotes and endnotes, and any item labeled with a caption.

Procedures

1. Place the insertion point in the document where you want to insert the cross-reference.

2. Type any lead-in or explanatory text you want to appear, such as "For further information, see".

3. Select Insert | Cross-reference.

4. In the Reference Type list box, choose the type of object or text you are referring to.

5. In the Insert Reference To list box, choose the type of reference you want to enter in the text.

6. In the For Which list box, select the specific object or text you are referring to.

7. Select Insert.

8. Select Close to put away the Cross-reference dialog box.

Hints

When you add a cross-reference, you are adding a field that displays the selected cross-reference. This means that if you see {REF} or {PAGEREF} field codes, the document is showing field codes instead of the results of the fields. You can switch between hiding and showing field codes by pressing ALT+F9. To delete a cross-reference, delete the field creating the cross-reference.

Related Topics

Bookmarks
Captions
Fields

Cursor Movement

The insertion point is sometimes called a *cursor*. You can use the keyboard to move the insertion point in your document, or you can use the mouse. For a full explanation of the keyboard options for moving the insertion point, see "Moving the Insertion Point."

Custom Dictionary

See "Spelling."

Customized Page Numbers

See "Page Numbers." You may also want to look at the explanation of the PAGE field under "Fields."

Customizing Menus

See "Menu Options."

Customizing the Keyboard

See "Keyboard Options."

Customizing the Toolbar

See "Toolbar Options."

Customizing Word for Windows

You can customize Word for Windows in many ways. The related topics in the following list explain how to customize the various features.

See This:	About Customizing This:
AutoFormat	How AutoFormat works with your document
Comparing Versions	How revisions are marked
Compatibility Options	How Word converts files
Edit Options	How you edit documents
File Location Options	Where Word expects to find documents
General Options	General features
Grammar Options	How Word checks the grammar in your documents
Keyboard Options	The shortcut keys
Menu Options	Word's menus
Print Options	How Word prints documents
Save Options	How Word saves documents
Spelling Options	How Word checks spelling in your document
Toolbar Options	The toolbars
User Info Options	The information Word maintains about you
View Options	The screen display for Word

Cutting

See "Drag and Drop," "Clipboard," and "Spike."

Dashes

You add em dashes (—) and en dashes (–) when you want a dash longer than the hyphen. Use the steps for entering these characters described under "Special Characters."

Data Form

See "Database Toolbar" for how you can work with databases and tables by using a form to add, remove, and change data.

DATABASE Field

The DATABASE field inserts the result of a database query into the document. For more information on this, see "Databases."

Database Toolbar

The Database toolbar provides many of the tools you will want to use when working with a database in a document. Databases in a Word document often appear as a table, so you can also use this toolbar as you work with tables. Most of the time, you use a database to supply the variable information that another document uses in a mail merge. Displaying the Database toolbar is done following the same steps as displaying any other toolbar. You can easily add the toolbar by selecting the View I Toolbars command, the Database check box, and OK. Once the Database toolbar appears, select from the following buttons to work with the data you have in the database.

Button	Button Name	Function
	Data Form	Displays a data form to enter new records into a database
	Manage Fields	Lets you add, remove, and rename the fields in a database
	Add New Record	Adds a new row to the end of a database for you to enter another record
	Delete Record	Removes the selected row from the database

Button	Button Name	Function
	Sort Ascending	Sorts the records in ascending order by the field containing the insertion point
	Sort Descending	Sorts the records in descending order by the field containing the insertion point
	Insert Database	Inserts an external database into the current document as if you selected the Insert	Database command
	Update Fields	Updates fields in the text that you have selected
	Find Record	Searches a field in the database for an entry you provide
	Mail Merge Main Document	Switches to the main document that uses the database as its source for data

Hints

The Data Form button opens a form like the one in Figure 4-11. From this form you can add, change, and remove data in the database or table. Making changes here makes changes to the underlying table or database, just as if you made the changes directly. Besides using the Database toolbar for modifying tables or databases, you can use many of the same features that you use on other Word tables.

Related Topics

Databases
Mail Merge
Tables
Toolbars

Databases

You use databases for Word's mail merge features. Word will accept the data for mail merge from Word documents, documents that Word can open with File | Open as well as Excel and 1-2-3 spreadsheets and Access databases. You can also open database files using OLE (object linking and embedding) features to display other databases in a Word document.

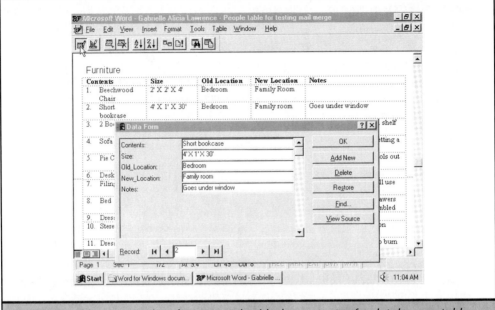

Figure 4-11. *Using a data form to work with the contents of a database or table*

You can insert data from a database into your Word document. When you use the database feature, the database can be any file that Word can read, which contains information you want to insert into your document—anything from a Microsoft Access database to a WordPerfect document. The word "database" is used to describe how the document is being used, rather than the format the document is in.

Procedure

1. Position your insertion point where you want the information from the database to appear. This information will be formatted in a table.

2. Select Insert | Database.

3. Select Get Data.

4. Select the document you want to use as the database, and select OK to open it. The options available are the same that you can use for opening any document.

   Depending on the type of document you are attempting to open, you may now be prompted to select a range of data from a spreadsheet or the specific table or query from the database. If so, select the appropriate unit of data to insert.

TIP: *If you do not know about working with spreadsheets and databases, you will want to look at the documentation or a book on these applications. The time investment will prevent a lot of frustration and ensure a successful application.*

5. Select Query Options to set rules for which data you want to use. You can choose to filter records, sort records, or select fields, depending on the tab you select in the Query Options dialog box. After setting options in this dialog box, as described below, select OK.

■ Select Filter Records to create a series of comparative rules to control which records are used. For each rule, select the field to compare in the Field box, how the comparison is to be done in the Comparison box, and enter the text or data to compare the field to in the Compare To box. You can combine rules with And or Or. And requires that both rules be met, while Or requires that either rule be met.

■ Select Sort Records to sort the records into an order before they are inserted into the current document. You can define three keys. For each key, select which field is being sorted, and whether the sort is ascending or descending. The lower keys are used when the higher level key results in a tie.

■ Choose Select Fields to set which fields to insert. You can use Select or Select All to transfer fields from the Fields in the Data Source list box to the Selected Fields list box. Use Remove or Remove All to remove fields from the Selected Fields list box.

6. Select Table AutoFormat to format the table that will appear in the current document. This feature works exactly like the Table AutoFormat feature described under "Tables."

7. Select Insert Data. Word displays a final dialog box with some final settings you can make for the data. Select OK when you are finished to actually insert the data.

■ Select All or From to set whether all or a limited number of records is inserted. If you select From, enter the first and last record number in the From and To text boxes.

■ Select the Insert Data as Field check box to insert all of the data and the table as a DATABASE field.

Hints

You will want to insert the data as a field if you need to be able to update the data. For example, you may insert the data from a spreadsheet into a report created in a Word document. If this report needs to be re-created regularly, such as in a monthly sales report, you will find it easier if you use a field.

When you insert the data as a field, any formatting you apply to the table in the document is lost when you update that field. When you do want to insert data as a field, make sure that you use the Table AutoFormat feature to format the table, ensuring that you do not lose the formatting, or add * mergeformat to the DATABASE field.

Related Topics

Inserting Documents
Mail Merge
Object Linking and Embedding
Opening Documents
Saving Documents
Tables

Date and Time

You can insert a date or time in your document. The date or time can be entered as text or as a field. When you add the date or time as a field, the field displays the current date or time and is updated each time you print the document. Depending on the viewing options you have set for fields, the dates and times appear as the codes Word uses to represent these dates and times or as the dates and times that the fields represent.

Procedures

You can insert the Date or Time field using the menus, shortcut keys, or, in a header or footer, using a toolbar button.

Using the Menus

1. Select Insert | Date and Time, opening the Date and Time dialog box.

2. Select a format for displaying the date and/or time from the Available Formats list box. By selecting one of the listed formats, you are selecting whether you are adding the date, the time, or both. The different purposes for different date and time formats are described in the box "Rules for Using the Correct Date Format."

3. Select the Update Automatically (Insert as Field) check box to add a DATE or TIME field to the document that will be updated each time you use the document. Clear this check box when you want the text of the date or time that does not change.

4. Select OK.

You can also enter a date and time with the Insert | Field command. However, selecting the appearance of the date and/or time is easier with the Insert | Date and Time command.

Using Shortcut Keys

■ Press ALT+SHIFT+D to insert a date.

■ Press ALT+SHIFT+T to insert a time.

These key combinations insert either the text or the field for the date and time, depending on whether the Update Automatically (Insert as Field) check box was selected the last time you used the Insert | Date and Time command.

The date or time you add has the same date or time format as the last date or time you added to a document. When you have not added a date or time, the date and time have the format set by the Regional Settings properties that you change through the Control Panel.

Rules for Using the Correct Date Format

Word supports many different date formats. Each of them is useful in different situations. If you want your documents to look professional, it is important to know when to pick a specific format. The following rules will help you decide the correct format whether you are inserting a date with Word or typing a date in a sentence.

■ Never use abbreviations when placing a date in the date line of a letter. For example, use March 23, 1996 and not Mar 23, 1996.

■ If you use only two of the three date components, no comma is needed. For example, May 1996 or May 5.

■ Decade references are always plural and written in numbers as in 1970s or the '70s.

■ Dates used in a sentence are typically written in a month, day, year sequence. For example, "The open house is scheduled for October 5, 1995." An altered day, month, year style is used in military correspondence and in foreign countries. For example, "General Smith has scheduled a meeting on 2 July 1996 for all base personnel." Note the absence of a comma in military-style dates.

■ Interoffice correspondence, business forms, and other informal notes are the only places where all numeric date entries are appropriate. For example, "Let's try to reschedule for 8/8/96."

- When the day precedes the month, the ordinal form is normally used. For example, "The movers are scheduled to come on the 12th of August." If you rewrite the sentence with the day following the month, the ordinal form is not appropriate. For example, "The movers are scheduled to come on August 12."

- In formal documents, always write the day and year in words. "The *twenty-first* of April *nineteen hundred ninety-six* is a memorable date." The year number can also be expressed as one thousand nine hundred ninety-six.

In a Header or Footer

When you are entering a header or footer, Word shows a Header and Footer toolbar. You select the Date or the Time button from this toolbar to enter a DATE or TIME field in your header. This toolbar and the date and time added to a header are shown here:

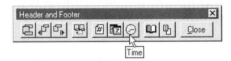

Hints

In a header or footer, use a DATE and TIME field instead of text when printing drafts of documents. The date and time on the document ensure that you are reviewing the most up-to-date draft, instead of an older one that might still be sitting on your desk.

When you move the insertion point to any part of the DATE or TIME field, the entire date and time is highlighted. Any changes you make to the shaded area are replaced when you print the document. You can also update a DATE or TIME field by moving to it and pressing F9. When you insert the text of the current date or time, you can edit the text just as if you typed the characters for the date and time yourself.

Related Topics

Databases
Fields
Headers and Footers

Date and Time Formats

See "Date and Time."

DATE Field

The DATE field inserts the current date. For more information on this, see "Date and Time."

DCA/RFT

See "Rich Text Format (RTF)."

DDE

See "Object Linking and Embedding."

Decimal Alignment

See "Tabs."

Default Folder

Word's default document folder is the folder that Word displays as the working folder when you first open or save a document during a work session. Word assumes that this is the folder containing your documents. When you first install Word, the default folder is the folder containing the Word program. To set the default folder, see "Document Location Options."

Default Options

See "Options." Many of Word's customizations are described with the features they alter.

Default Settings

See "Options." Many of Word's customizations are described with the features they alter.

Default Toolbar

Word's default toolbar, the Standard toolbar, is the toolbar saved in the Normal template. This toolbar is available to all documents. You can modify the toolbar and save the modified toolbar so that it is available for all documents or only those using a single template. For more information on modifying the default toolbar, see "Toolbar Options." See "Standard Toolbar" for a description of the buttons available through this toolbar.

Delete Documents

See "Document Management."

Delete Folder

You can delete a folder from within Word and move it and its contents to your Recycling Bin. Deleting a folder is done the same way you delete a document. Deleting documents is described under "Document Management."

Delete Formatting

See "Removing Formatting."

Deleting Text

You can delete text from your document permanently or delete text from your document to place it at another location. To learn how to delete text and then replace it in another location, another document, or another application, see "Clipboard" and "Spike."

Procedures

You can delete one character, one word, or selected text by following these instructions.

To Delete One Character

- Position the insertion point after the character and press BACKSPACE.
- Position the insertion point before the character and press DEL.

To Delete One Word

- Position the insertion point after the word and press CTRL+BACKSPACE.
- Position the insertion point before the word and press CTRL+DEL.

To Delete Selected Text

- Select the text you want to delete.
- Press DEL or BACKSPACE.

Hint

You can restore text you accidentally delete by selecting Edit | Undo. Word tracks the changes you make so you can undo one or more of the changes you have made.

Related Topics

Clipboard
Drag and Drop
Spike
Undoing and Redoing Actions

D

Dialog Boxes

Dialog boxes are special windows. You provide specifics for carrying out commands by selecting options in dialog boxes. Certain elements are common to all dialog boxes.

Options

You must select a dialog box element to make a change to its setting. You select, or move to, a dialog box element by clicking it with the mouse, or by pressing TAB and SHIFT+TAB so the dialog box element you want is highlighted or has an extra outline. Also, one letter in each part of a selectable element's label is underlined, just as one letter in all menu commands is underlined. You select or move to a dialog box element by pressing ALT and the underlined letter.

Text Boxes

You enter text in text boxes. For example, in the Go To dialog box, enter a page number where you want to go to in the Enter Page Number text box, shown here:

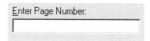

When the entire entry in the text box is highlighted, your entry will entirely replace the existing entry. Some text boxes are connected to list boxes. When you select an item in the list box, it appears in the text box. Other text boxes are followed by double arrows. By clicking on these arrows, or by pressing UP ARROW or DOWN ARROW in these text boxes, you change the number that appears in the dialog box.

List Boxes

There are two basic types of list boxes: list boxes and drop-down list boxes. List boxes are a set size and display several options, such as the Go to What list box, shown here:

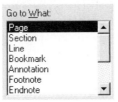

Drop-down list boxes initially look like text boxes followed by a down arrow button. Opening the drop-down list box displays the list box beneath the original box. After you a make a selection, the drop-down box closes again, and only the current setting is displayed.

Drop-down list boxes also come in two types. When the arrow is actually attached to the box, as in the Search drop-down list box shown below, you can only select an option from the list. Typing any character moves to the next item in the list that starts with the same character. If the arrow is slightly detached from the box, as in the Find What drop-down list box shown below, you can either select an option from the drop-down list, or you can type an entry.

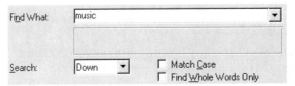

Check Boxes

Check boxes turn a feature on or off. When a check box is selected, the box has a check mark in it, and the feature is active. When it is cleared, the box is empty, and the feature is inactive. For example, the dialog box shown above has the Match Case and Find Whole Words Only check boxes. They are selected or cleared independently of one another.

Option Buttons

Option buttons appear in sets. Option buttons are sometimes called radio buttons. Each option button in a set indicates a possible setting for the feature. For example, the

Tabs dialog box has two sets of option buttons, which are shown below. Selecting an option button in a set clears the other option buttons.

Command Buttons

You select command buttons to carry out an action. Most dialog boxes have at least two buttons: OK and Cancel. Selecting OK closes the dialog box and carries out the command using the settings you have chosen in the dialog box. Selecting Cancel closes the dialog box without carrying out any command.

Command buttons always have some text on them that indicates what they do. Ellipses (three periods) after the text means that selecting the button opens another dialog box in which you can make further settings.

Tabs

Word has divided options in some dialog boxes into tabs that organize the dialog box options. You can switch between tabs to change which set of dialog box options you are working with. You switch between tabs by clicking them or pressing CTRL+TAB until the tab you want is in front. When a letter in the tab name is underlined, you can select the tab by pressing ALT and the underlined letter. With the Tools I Options command, you can also type the first letter of the tab. Tabs look like this:

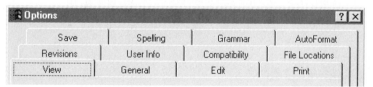

TIP: *If you want more information about a particular part of a dialog box, click on the ? button in the upper-right corner of the dialog box, then click on the part of the dialog box that you want to learn about.*

Dictionaries

See "Spelling."

Directories

Windows 95 calls directories *folders*. Word works with directories as folders, so all of Word's features for working with these documents are described under topics such as "Create a New Folder," "Delete Folder," "Folders," and "Document Location Options."

Display

To change the display of what you see on the screen, look at "View Options" as well as "Toolbars" for changing the appearance of the toolbars. To change how parts of your document appear, look under the document feature you want to customize. This includes character formats, paragraph formats, and page setup.

Display Print Queue

When you print in Word, Word sends the document to print to the print folder. This folder contains all of the documents from all applications that you are printing. You can view the print queue by opening the print folder. From here, you can change the print order of the items in the queue and delete them. For more instructions on using the Windows Print folder, see your Windows documentation.

DOCPROPERTY Field

The DOCPROPERTY field displays some information about a document's properties. See "Document Properties" for the types of information stored as document properties and see "Fields" for information about adding fields such as this one to your document.

Document Compare

See "Comparing Versions."

Document Location Options

Word uses several types of documents. In addition to the program's own documents, you have documents for your data, clip art for graphics, and templates to provide models for the appearance of your documents. To use these documents, Word needs to know where to find them. These locations are designated by File Location options available through the Tools | Options command. The settings for the document locations are saved as part of your user settings in Windows.

Procedure

1. Select Tools | Options and then the File Locations tab.

2. Select the type of documents and the folder you want to change in the File Types list box. The types of documents and their purpose include the following:

Document Type	Purpose
Documents	Where you keep most of your documents
Clipart Pictures	Where you want Word to look for graphics images when you use commands such as Insert	Picture
User Templates	Templates that are your own (versus shared with other users)
Workgroup Templates	Templates that you share with other users
User Options	Where Word records your customizing options
AutoSave Files	Where Word puts the automatically saved documents that are emergency backups in case your system fails
Dictionaries	Dictionary documents used for checking the spelling of documents
Startup	Templates and add-in programs that Word automatically loads

3. Select Modify. Then either type the path to select the folder where you want to store the selected type of document, or use the Look in list box and buttons to select a new location. You can also create the folder you want by selecting the Create New Folder button, typing a name for the folder, and selecting OK.

4. Select OK.

5. Repeat steps 2 through 4 for each location you want to change.

TIP: *The locations you specify can be altered. For example, when you select a particular folder when you save or open a document, you change the path of that document. Word will continue using the newly selected folder during the Word session.*

Hint

Use one folder for all of your currently-in-use Word for Windows documents, so that they are easy to retrieve and save. If all of them are in the same directory, you won't need to change directories to save or retrieve documents. However, over time this folder may become quite crowded. To prevent this, set up a regular schedule for transferring documents that you are not using to another folder or to archival floppy disks.

Document Management

With Word's document management tools, you can find documents using any information stored in the document, and open, delete, print, or copy multiple documents. These features are in addition to the ones that are available through Windows folder windows and the Windows Explorer.

Procedures

The following procedures tell you how to locate and work with documents.

Finding Documents

1. Select File | Open, to open the Open dialog box as shown in Figure 4-12.

   The list box in the middle of the dialog box shows what Word is looking at. You will see icons and names for folders and documents. Depending on which of several viewing options is selected, you may just see a list of names, names and some properties, or names and a preview of what the document looks like. Figure 4-12 shows a preview of the selected document.

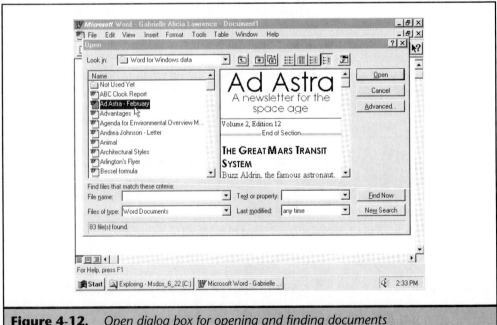

Figure 4-12.   *Open dialog box for opening and finding documents*

2. If the documents you want are not showing in the main list box, select them. You can change the drive where Word looks with the Look in drop-down list box. You can change folders using the Up One Level button shown below or by double-clicking any folder name that you want to move to. You can also choose which documents appear in the dialog box by using the Search options described in the "Options" section following.

 TIP: *You can also work with the contents of your Favorites folder by clicking the Look In Favorites button. See "Favorites Folder" for how you can select from and add to the contents of this folder.*

3. Carry out the desired action with the selected document(s). You can print, open, copy, or delete the document(s). For more information on these operations, see the "Options" section next.

4. When you are finished working with the documents, select Cancel to leave the dialog box without opening a document or select one of the documents and Open to start working with that document.

Options

The following sections describe the command options available through the Open dialog box. Many of these options are available through the shortcut menu that you see when you right-click any document in the main list box. Others are available through the Commands and Settings button shown here:

Changing What Appears in the List Box

The Open dialog box includes the following four buttons:

These four buttons are: List, Details, Properties, and Preview. By clicking these buttons, you set how documents and folders are listed in the main list box. Click List to display a list of documents and folders. Click Details to display the name, size, type, and last modified date for all of the documents listed in the window. Click Properties to display the document properties for the highlighted document. Click Preview to display the contents of the highlighted document.

Open

Select the Open button to open the documents selected in the main list box. You can also right-click one of the selected documents and choose Open. If you want to open any documents and ensure you don't save them with the same name, right-click them and select Open Read Only. You can also select Open Read Only from the menu that displays when you click the Commands and Settings button. Word will not let you save documents opened this way using the same name.

Delete

You can delete selected documents by right-clicking one of them and selecting Delete. Word prompts you to confirm that you want to move the documents to the recycle bin; select Yes to delete the documents, or No to halt the deletion.

Print

Right-click a document and select Print to print the documents selected in the main list box. You can also click the Commands and Settings button, then select Print to print the selected documents. Word displays the Print dialog box, which is identical to the dialog box for the File | Print command. Choose the settings in this dialog box and then select OK. The print options you choose will apply to all documents that you print from this dialog box. Word opens these documents and prints their contents.

Copy

Right-click a document and select Copy to copy the documents selected in the main list box. Then move to the folder where you want the document copied, right-click the folder, and select Paste. The copied documents have the same name as the original documents, but you can later rename them.

Rename

To change the name for any document listed, click the document's name so that the name appears highlighted with a box around it. At this point, you can type a new name to replace the existing one or edit the existing one. When you are finished, press ENTER or click another document.

Properties

To see the properties for any document, right-click the document and select Properties. You can also see the document's properties by clicking the Commands and Settings button, then selecting Properties. Word opens the Properties dialog box just as if you had opened the document and selected File | Properties. In this dialog box, you can see the information that identifies the document. See "Document Properties" for a complete explanation of the document properties. Even if multiple documents are selected, you will only change the properties of the one document selected when you chose Properties.

Sorting

You can change the order in which the documents are listed by clicking the Commands and Settings button, then selecting Sorting. In the Sort By dialog box, you can select File Name, Size, Files of Type, or Last Modified from the Sort Files By drop-down list box to determine how the documents are sorted in the Open dialog box. Select OK, and Word reorders the listed documents. You can change whether Word groups documents according to their folder when you are looking at more than one folder's documents. If the Open dialog box is listing documents from multiple folders, you can click on the Commands and Settings button, then select Group Files By Folder to turn this feature on or off. When this feature is on, the documents in each folder are listed and sorted as a group. When this feature is off, the documents from all folders in the main list box are sorted in the order you selected and are not first sorted by folder, which means that the documents you see may be stored in very different locations.

Search

The rest of the Open dialog box contains features for searching for documents. Several of the search options do not appear until you select the Advanced button. After you have specified the search you want Word to perform, select Find Now. The following sections describe the search options you can use to select which documents are shown.

FILE NAME AND TYPE   To search for a specific document name, type the name in the File Name drop-down list box. To search for a specific document type, select the type of document from the Files of Type drop-down list box.

You can include the ? and * wildcard characters in the document name. For example, entering EFR? in the File Name list box will find files such as EFR3, EFR4, and EFRT. However, Word would not find the file EFR010. To find this document, you would enter EFR*. Word will then find EFR3 and EFR010.

LAST MODIFIED DATE   You can find documents based on when you last modified them simply by making a selection from the Last Modified drop-down list box. For example, selecting Yesterday from the drop-down list box and clicking Find Now lists the documents that were last modified and saved yesterday.

FINDING TEXT OR PROPERTIES   You can find documents that contain specific text or have a specific value for one of the document's properties. All you have to do to find text is to type the text in the Text or Property drop-down list box. You can even use the * and ? wildcard characters, where * represents zero or more characters and ? represents a single character. When you click Find Now, the main list box shows the documents that contain that specific text—either in the main body of the document or in the document's properties. You can also look for an entry that you previously typed by selecting the past entry from the drop-down list portion of the Text or Property drop-down list box.

When you want to find an entry for a specific property or you want to find more than one item of text, you can do that with the advanced options. When you click Advanced, you can add criteria to the search for documents. Select the property you want searched from the Property drop-down list box in the Define More Criteria section of the dialog box. Selecting Any Text searches the document's text and properties, while selecting Contents searches the document's text without searching the document's properties. From the Condition drop-down list box next to it, you can choose values such as Equals or Is Less Than to choose the type of condition that you want to place on the property. In the Value text box, you can enter the value that you want as part of the criteria.

With the criteria selected, click the Add to List button to add the criteria at the top of the Find Files dialog box. You can further fine-tune the criteria you have added by clicking the Match All Word Forms or Match Case check box. The Match Case check box tells Word to be specific about uppercase or lowercase letters when it looks for documents that match the selected criteria. Match All Word Forms allows Word to match words when the ending letters are different, so for example, searching for "Jump" finds "Jumps" and "Jumping" as well. You can continue adding more criteria to the list by selecting the entries for the Property, Condition, and Value drop-down list boxes then selecting Add to List.

As you add more criteria, you choose whether you are joining the criteria with And or Or operators. Most of the time, you use And for finding documents that contain, for example, "Selling" And "Contract." However, you can join them with Or for finding documents containing "Selling" Or "Contract." While And is the default, you can switch between the two by selecting the And or Or option button before adding the criteria. If you add one that you do not want, just select it from the list box at the top of the dialog box and click the Delete button.

SAVING A SEARCH   Once you have set up a search that you plan to use repeatedly, you can save the search. Saved searches retain their criteria so you can easily repeat them. For instance, say you keep all your Word documents in three folders, and frequently use a search that only looks for *.DOC documents from those three folders.

To save a search, select the Advanced button in the Open dialog box, then the Save Search button. From the Save Search dialog box, type a description for the search, then select OK. When you are ready to use the same search, click the Commands and Settings button in the Open dialog box and select Saved Searches. The pop-up menu lists the searches you have saved. Click on the saved search you want, and the criteria and location where Word looks for documents changes to the settings saved in that search.

You can also open, delete, and rename searches by clicking on the Open Search button available in the same Advanced Find dialog box as the Save Search button. From the Open Search dialog box, you can highlight the search you want and click

Delete to remove the search. Click Rename, type a new name, and click OK to change the name assigned to the selected search. If you click Open, you use the selected search just as if you had used it by selecting it from the Open dialog box.

> **TIP:** *You can quickly remove the existing search criteria when you are about to supply new criteria. Select New Search from the Open or Advanced Find dialog box.*

Hints

With document operations such as copying, deleting, and printing, you can work with multiple documents. To select multiple documents, move to the first one and hold down the SHIFT key while either moving to or clicking the last document you want to select. Or hold down CTRL to select a noncontiguous group of documents. All of the documents you select will be included in the next document operation, if possible.

If you want to list all of your Word documents, specify the initial folder of the disk as the location to search, select Word Documents in the Files of Type drop-down list box, and then search all folders by selecting Search Subfolders from the menu that the Commands and Settings button displays. Once you have the Word documents listed, you can back them up by copying them to floppy disks.

Use the Preview or Properties view of a document to make sure you are opening, deleting, or printing the right document.

> **TIP:** *If you accidentally delete the wrong document, you can recover it if it is in your recycle bin.*

Related Topics

Document Properties
Favorites Folder

Document Margins

See "Margins."

Document Properties

Windows and its applications use properties to provide information about a document the way an adjective provides information on a noun. You can change what some of these properties are as well as look at the ones that Word sets. The properties available for your documents include information about when the document was created and last saved as well as statistics about the document's contents.

Procedure

1. Select File | Properties to open the Properties dialog box. The Properties window has five tabs, as described in greater detail below. You can switch through the tabs to see the different properties available.
2. Add or edit the document's properties in the Summary or Custom tab and review the properties that appear on the other tabs.
3. Select OK to return to the document.

Options

The options for document properties set the document information Word retains with the document. The tabs and their contents are described in the following sections.

General

The General tab contains document information similar to what you see when you look at a document's properties in a folder. This includes its name, type, size, location, and the date it was created, last saved, and last opened. You cannot change these entries.

Summary

The Summary tab is where you can alter properties specific to Word documents, such as Title, Subject, Author, Manager, Company, Category, Keywords, and Comments. The Title initially comes from the first paragraph in the document and the Author initially comes from the User Info tab available through the Tools | Options command. The information included in these text boxes should reflect characteristics of the document, making it easier to find if you should forget its name. After Template is the template that this document uses as its basis. You can also select whether Word saves a preview of the document to have something to look at in the Open dialog box by selecting or clearing the Save Preview Picture check box.

Statistics

The Statistics tab describes the statistics of the document, such as when you created, last saved, opened, or printed it. It also includes who last saved it, how many times it has been saved, how long you have edited, as well as the number of pages, paragraphs, lines, words, characters, and bytes.

Contents

The Contents tab contains the first paragraph in the document.

Custom

The Custom tab lets you create your own document properties. Type a property name in Name, the type of data it contains in Type, and the value for the property in Value. For example, a document that must be reviewed by several departments may have properties created that record when each department has finished reviewing it. You can even link a property to some or all of the document's content by assigning a bookmark to the text to include as the property; then when you add the property, select the Link to Content check box and select the bookmark from the Source drop-down list box (which replaces the Value text box once you select the Link to Content check box). Once you add the linked property, you will see a link next to the property in the list. If you don't want a custom property to appear in other applications, add an underline (_) as the first character for the property name.

Hints

You can use a document's properties in different ways. You can print it separately from a document; you can insert it into a document through fields; and you can search for specific information to select the documents you want to work with. To make sure a document includes the information that appears on the Summary tab and other property tabs, you can tell Word when you save a document to prompt you for this information.

Printing Document Properties

You can print a document's properties with the document or alone. To print a document's properties, select Summary Info from the Print What drop-down list box in the Print dialog box. To print the document properties along with the document it describes, select the Summary Info check box in the Print tab of the Options dialog box.

Inserting Document Property Values into the Document

You can insert the values for document properties into your document using fields. These field codes insert the current information from the Properties dialog box into your document. For further information on this feature, see "Fields."

Prompting for Document Properties

By default, you have to select File | Properties to open the Properties dialog box. You can also set Word to prompt you to add this information the first time you save a document.

To do this, open the Options dialog box by selecting Tools | Options, select the Save tab, then select the Prompt for Document Properties check box. The first time you save each document, Word opens the Properties dialog box so that you can fill in entries for the Summary and Custom tabs. If you do not want to supply this information for a particular document, you can select OK to close the dialog box and save the document.

Finding Documents

You can use document property information with the File | Open command to find a document whose name you have forgotten. See "Document Management" for a full explanation of how to use this command.

Related Topics

Fields
Document Management

Document Sharing

Word lets you share documents and data in several ways. When you are working with other users, you can password-protect your documents so they cannot be unintentionally revised, as described in "Saving Documents." If you want to share your documents with others to receive their comments, look at the suggestions under "Faxes" and "Annotations." To share data in one document with other documents, follow instructions in "Object Linking and Embedding." "Opening Documents" has various information about opening shared files, such as those on a network.

Document Summary

See "Document Properties."

Document Templates

See "Templates."

Document Window

A document window is a window that appears within the Word window and contains a document. Like other windows, it has a title bar, a document icon, sizing buttons, and a Close button. You can have as many document windows open as you have the memory for.

Procedures

You can move, size, arrange, and switch between your Word document windows.

Moving Between Open Windows

- Click on a portion of the open window when the windows are not maximized.
- Select Window, and then the window.
- Press CTRL+F6 or SHIFT+CTRL+F6 until the window you want is on top.

Opening a Second Window

You can open a second window for the same document. This lets you use separate windows for looking at different sections of the same document.

1. Make the current window active by moving to it.

2. Select Window | New Window.

   You can also split one window into two parts called *panes*. The steps for this are described in "Viewing Documents."

Arranging Windows

To have Word size and arrange your open document windows so that you see all of each window, as shown in Figure 4-13, select Window | Arrange All.

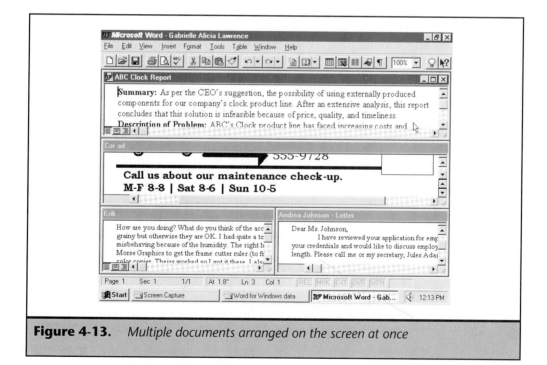

Figure 4-13. *Multiple documents arranged on the screen at once*

Sizing the Active Document Window

Windows has a few quick sizing options you can select using the sizing buttons in the document window's title bar. Clicking the Maximize button, double-clicking the document window's title bar, selecting Maximize in the document icon's menu, or pressing CTRL+F10 expands the window to fill the Word application window. You display the document icon's menu by clicking the icon or pressing ALT+-. You can also reduce document windows to an icon by clicking the Minimize button or selecting Minimize in the document icon's control menu.

To make a window any size you want, drag the window border to a new location. Notice how the mouse changes to a double arrow so you can drag the window's border to a new location. If you do not see a window border, click the Restore button first. You can also size a window by selecting Size from the document icon's menu or by pressing CTRL+F8. Then press an arrow key to move to the window border in the arrow's direction. The subsequent arrow keys you press will move that border. When you press ENTER, the window is sized to the selected size.

You cannot size minimized or maximized windows. You may need to select Restore from the document icon's menu or press CTRL+F5 before you size it. You can also restore a window size by clicking its Restore button in the title bar or by double-clicking the title bar. You also cannot make document windows larger than they appear when you maximize them.

Moving Document Windows

Drag the document window's title bar to where you want the window placed.

You can also move a window by selecting Move from the document icon's menu or by pressing CTRL+F7. Then press the arrow keys until the window outline is where you want the window placed. When you press ENTER, the window is moved to the outlined position.

You cannot move maximized windows. You can move a window so part of it does not appear within the Word window, but you cannot move the window outside of the area used by the Word application window.

Appearance

When the document window is not maximized, the ruler, if displayed, appears in the document window rather than the application window. The document window does not include menu bars or toolbars. Each window has its own scroll bars. Only the active window shows the Normal View, Page Layout View, and Outline View buttons.

When a document window is maximized, the document title appears in the application window's title bar. The document icon appears at the left end of the menu bar. The document window's sizing buttons appear at the right end of the menu bar.

Hints

You want document windows to be large enough so you are comfortable working with the text. Often, unless you are working with multiple documents at once, you will want to leave the document windows maximized to see as much as possible of the current document. You may want to show two documents simultaneously when dragging and dropping text between documents. If you want to see more of your document at once, try some of Word's Zooming options. You can also try changing the desktop area through the Control Panel to use a higher number of pixels. This makes the text smaller so you can see more.

Related Topic

Windows

DOS Text

Most applications can save their documents in a DOS text or ASCII format. DOS text or ASCII files contain no coding or formatting. Word can open DOS text files. Saving data as a DOS text file and opening it is often the least confusing method of transferring information from a nonWindows application into Word. Also, you can write programs for BASIC or Pascal in Word and then save the file in the DOS text format for future use. To save a document in a text format, look at "Saving Documents."

Dot Leaders

See "Tabs."

Double-Click

See "Mouse Techniques."

Double-Sided Printing

If your printer handles double-sided printing, you can print double-sided by selecting that Paper Size option. If double-sided pages are not an option on your printer, insert the pages in the printer twice. To print a double-sided document when your printer does not support double-sided printing, print all the odd pages, flip the paper, then print the even pages. To do this, select File | Print and select Odd Pages from the Print drop-down list box. Then select OK.

Once the odd pages are printed, put the pages back into the printer so printing occurs on the opposite side of the paper. For a dot-matrix printer, this means turning the paper around and rethreading it through the printer. In a laser printer, you will need to flip over the paper. Then print the even pages. Select File | Print and select Even Pages from the Print drop-down list box. Then select OK. If you plan to bind the double-sided pages, see "Margins" about adding a binding offset.

A neat trick for printing on two sides of the page using certain laser printers is after you print the odd pages, remove the pages without rearranging them, leaving page one at the bottom of the stack. If the last page of the document is an odd-numbered page, remove this page from the stack as you put the pages back into the laser printer's feeding tray with the printing face down. Also remember to keep track of which way the top of the page should face. When you print the even pages on a laser printer and page one is at the bottom of the stack, select the Reverse Print Order check box for Print options. This little trick means you do not have to rearrange pages so page one is at the top, then page three, and so on.

Double Spacing

See "Spacing."

Double Underline

See "Underline."

Drag

See "Mouse Techniques."

Drag and Drop

Word for Windows offers the ultimate in convenience for moving and copying text, a feature called Drag and Drop, which uses the mouse. You can drag and drop text between documents as long as both documents are simultaneously visible.

Procedures

Instructions on how to use the Drag and Drop feature are described below.

Copying Text with Drag and Drop

1. Select the text to copy by dragging the mouse across it.

2. Hold down the CTRL key.

3. Point the mouse at the selected text and press the mouse button.

4. Drag the text to a new location, then release the mouse button.

Moving Text with Drag and Drop

1. Select the text to move by dragging the mouse across it.

2. Point the mouse at the selected text and press the mouse button.

3. Drag the text to a new location in your document, and then release the mouse button.

Related Topics

Clipboard
Mouse Techniques
Scrap
Spike

Drawing Boxes and Lines in a Paragraph

See "Borders and Shading."

Drawing on a Document

Word lets you draw on a document. The drawing can be simple objects such as rectangles, lines, and circles, or it can be very complex. You can also insert other documents containing graphics into Word.

Procedures

The Drawing features you will use to create your drawings are described below.

Drawing in a Document

1. Click the Drawing button in the Standard toolbar.

D

You can also display this toolbar just like you display other toolbars, by selecting the <u>V</u>iew | <u>T</u>oolbars command, the Drawing check box, and OK.

Word displays a Drawing toolbar like the one shown in Figure 4-14. Using this toolbar, you can draw on top of the document. The tools available on this toolbar are described under "Drawing Toolbar."

2. Draw the desired object on the document.

For example, the text callouts to the two faces in Figure 4-14 were added using the Drawing toolbar. Most of the tools for drawing are similar to features present in most drawing packages. Drawn objects do not appear in Normal view, so when you display the Drawing toolbar, Word will switch you to Page Layout view. If you have the Drawing toolbar displayed and then switch to Normal view, when you select a button on the Drawing toolbar, Word will prompt you to select whether you want to switch to Page Layout view before continuing.

Hints

Holding down SHIFT while you draw a line only draws lines in 30-degree and 45-degree increments. Holding down SHIFT while you draw an ellipse or a rectangle makes the ellipse or rectangle a circle or square. If you press CTRL+SHIFT while you

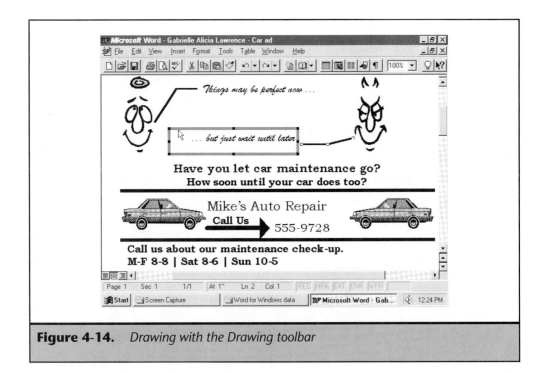

Figure 4-14.   *Drawing with the Drawing toolbar*

Button	Name	Function
	Line	Draws a straight line using the starting and ending points you provide
	Rectangle	Draws a rectangle using the two corners you provide
	Ellipse	Draws an ellipse or circle using the two points you provide
	Arc	Draws an arc using the starting and ending points you provide
	Freeform	Draws a freeform shape over the area you drag the mouse
	Text Box	Adds a text box to contain text or other effects for text that you want separated from the main part of a document
	Callout	Inserts a box of text that points to an object in the document
	Format Callout	Sets the appearance of the callout including how many lines can connect the callout to what it points to, the gap between the line and the text box, the angle, the length, the drop, whether the callout has a border, whether Word handles attaching the line between what you are pointing to and the callout, and whether the callout has an accent bar
	Fill Color	Sets the color of filled object drawn with Rectangle, Ellipse, Arc, Freeform, Text Box, and Callout buttons
	Line Color	Sets the color of lines drawn with Line and the border for filled objects drawn with Rectangle, Ellipse, Arc, Freeform, Text Box, and Callout buttons
	Line Style	Sets the style of the lines drawn with Line and the border for filled objects drawn with Rectangle, Ellipse, Arc, Freeform, Text Box, and Callout buttons

Table 4-1. *Word Drawing Toolbar*

Button	Name	Function
	Select Drawing Objects	Selects objects you click to be altered by the other buttons
	Bring to Front	Puts selected drawn objects in front of all others
	Send to Back	Puts selected drawn objects behind all others
	Bring in Front of Text	Puts selected drawn objects in front of document text
	Send Behind Text	Puts selected drawn objects behind document text
	Group	Puts selected drawn objects into a group so further customization, sizing, and placement affects all objects in the group equally
	Ungroup	Ungroups a group of objects in a group so you can change the objects individually
	Flip Horizontal	Flips the selected objects so what was on the left side is on the right and vice versa
	Flip Vertical	Flips the selected objects so what was on the top is on the bottom and vice versa
	Rotate Right	Rotates the selected objects ninety degrees to the right
	Reshape	Lets you adjust the points that define the selected freeform objects
	Snap to Grid	Causes subsequently placed drawn objects to start at the nearest grid point

Table 4-1. *Word Drawing Toolbar* (continued)

Button	Name	Function
	Align Drawing Objects	Aligns selected drawn objects relative to one another or the page
	Create Picture	Creates a picture frame that contains drawn objects, text, and imported graphics
	Insert Frame	Adds a frame around the selected drawn objects or adds an empty frame

Table 4-1.   *Word Drawing Toolbar* (continued)

draw an ellipse, you will draw a circle around the point you select before you drag the circle away from the center. SHIFT and CTRL+SHIFT work the same way for making squares out of rectangles.

Double-clicking a Drawing toolbar button keeps that tool selected until you click another button or type text. Use this feature to draw multiple lines, rectangles, ellipses, arcs, or freeform shapes.

When the Select Drawing Objects button is selected, drag the mouse over a rectangle to select the drawn objects included in the rectangle. You can also select multiple objects using the Select Drawing Objects button by holding down SHIFT while you click each object you want to add or remove from the current selection.

Related Topics

Drawing Toolbar
Layering Text and Graphics

Drawing Toolbar

The Drawing toolbar provides many of the tools you will want to use to draw in a document. These tools provide drawing capabilities. Display this toolbar by clicking the Drawing button in the Standard toolbar. Once the Drawing toolbar appears, you draw on a document by selecting the buttons and where you want to draw. Some of the buttons require that you select the drawn objects to change before you use the buttons on the Drawing toolbar. The Drawing toolbar has the buttons with the associated functions shown in Table 4-1.

You can also change the appearance of a drawn object by right-clicking it and selecting Format Drawing Object, by double-clicking it, or by selecting it and using the Format | Drawing Object command.

Related Topics

Drawing on a Document
Frames
Toolbars

Drop-Down Lists

Drop-down lists in a form make form completion easier by providing a list of predefined choices. Look at "Forms" for how to include drop-down lists in the forms you create.

Dropped Capitals

Word can create dropped capitals like the ones that you see at the beginning of books, magazines, and newspapers.

Procedure

1. Move to the paragraph where you want the dropped capital.

2. Select Format | Drop Cap.

3. Select Dropped as the style when you want the initial capital to occupy the beginning of the next several lines or In Margin when you want the initial capital to cause the paragraph to be indented by the space the capital requires.

4. Select the font for the initial capital from the Font drop-down list box when you want it to be a different font than the rest of the text.

5. Select the number of lines of document text the initial capital occupies in the Lines to Drop text box. This sets the size of the initial capital, but you can change it later by selecting the initial capital and changing its font size.

6. Select how much distance you want between the document text and the initial capital in the Distance from Text text box.

7. Select OK.

If you select more than one character before you select Format | Drop Cap, all the selected characters will be accented as shown in Figure 4-15. The effect for the word "Once" was created by selecting the text and then using Format | Drop Cap to make it drop in the margin (where the graphic image is added). The "F" later in the text is added by making it a dropped capital that uses three lines.

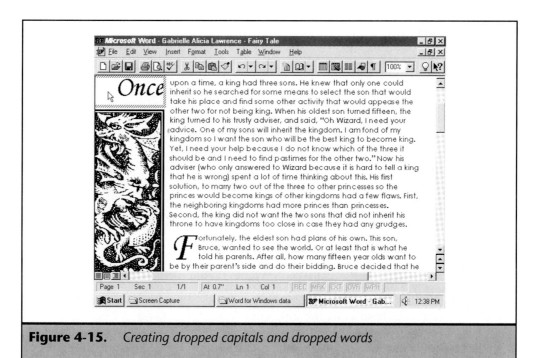

Figure 4-15. *Creating dropped capitals and dropped words*

Hints

If you need to alter the placement of the dropped capital on the page, do it by changing the paragraph formatting. You can also drag the margins on the rulers to shift a dropped capital's position. You can also change the alignment of a dropped capital without affecting the alignment of the paragraph that the dropped capital introduces. You change the font and size of the dropped capital using Font and Font Size in the Formatting toolbar.

If you no longer want a dropped capital used, select the dropped capital, select the Format | Drop Cap command, and select the None option under Position.

Edit Options

Word has several customization settings that change how you edit documents. These options are on the Edit tab in the dialog box that the Tools | Options command displays.

Procedure

1. Select Tools | Options.

2. Click the Edit tab.

3. Change the options described below. Select OK.

Options

The Edit options let you set how Word works when you are editing your documents.

Typing Replaces Selection

If this check box is selected, and you type while text is selected, your typed entry replaces the selected text. When this check box is cleared, the selected text becomes unselected so anything you type does not replace that text. Set this according to your preference for whether you want any selected text replaced when you start typing. By trying it both ways, you will find a preference.

Drag-and-Drop Text Editing

If this check box is selected, you can copy and move text by dragging it and dropping it with the mouse as described under "Drag and Drop." When this check box is cleared, you cannot use this method of rearranging your text.

Automatic Word Selection

If this check box is selected, Word selects the entire word when you select part of a word. When this check box is cleared, only the selected part of the word is included. For example, with this check box selected, if the insertion point is before the *m* in "automation" and you select *m* through the beginning of the next word, then Word selects "automation." If this check box is cleared, then Word selects "mation." This feature is smarter than blindly selecting whole words. You can wiggle the mouse to select just the first character in a word and Word will interpret your action to know that you want to select some characters from that word without selecting the whole word.

Use the INS Key for Paste

When this check box is selected and you press INS, Word pastes the Clipboard's contents at the insertion point. When this check box is cleared and you press INS, you switch between insert and overtype mode.

Overtype Mode

When this check box is selected, overtype mode is in effect so the characters you type replace the characters at the insertion point's location. When this check box is cleared, you are in insert mode. You can switch to overtype mode by pressing INS (assuming the Use the INS Key for Paste check box is cleared). You can continue switching between insert and overtype mode by double-clicking the OVR indicator on the status bar. You can't use overtype mode when revision marks are turned on so this check box will be grayed.

Use Smart Cut and Paste

When this check box is selected, Word will intelligently remove spaces before punctuation marks when you delete words before punctuation marks. When this check box is cleared, Word only deletes the text you select.

Use Tab and Backspace Keys to Set Left Indent

When this check box is selected, pressing TAB adds an indent to each new paragraph. Pressing BACKSPACE adds an indent to the left. Clearing this check box means that TAB and BACKSPACE always have the same meaning and effect.

Allow Accented Uppercase

When this check box is selected, Word assumes that accented characters at the beginning of words are acceptable. When this check box is cleared, features such as changing case and spelling assume that the first character in a word should have any accent mark removed.

Picture Editor

Selects the editor used to edit pictures. The options you have depend on the Word components and other applications you have installed on your computer.

Edit | AutoText

See "AutoText."

Edit | Bookmark

See "Bookmarks."

Edit | Clear

See "Clipboard" and "Spike."

Edit | Copy

See "Clipboard," "Scrap," and "Spike" as well as "Object Linking and Embedding" for when to use this command and others to share data between applications.

Edit | Cut

See "Clipboard," "Scrap," and "Spike" as well as "Object Linking and Embedding" for when to use this command and others to share data between applications.

Edit | Find

See "Find and Replace."

Edit | Go To

See "Bookmarks" and "Moving the Insertion Point."

Edit | Links

See "Object Linking and Embedding."

Edit | Object

See "Object Linking and Embedding."

Edit | Paste

See "Clipboard" and "Spike" as well as "Object Linking and Embedding" for when to use this command and others to share data between applications.

Edit | Paste Special

See "Clipboard," "Scrap," and "Spike" as well as "Object Linking and Embedding" for when to use this command and others to share data between applications.

Edit | Redo

See "Undoing and Redoing Actions."

Edit | Repeat

See "Repeating Actions."

Edit | Replace

See "Find and Replace."

Edit | Select All

See "Selecting Text."

Edit | Undo

See "Undoing and Redoing Actions."

Editing Documents

Editing is the process of creating and formatting a document. If you are unfamiliar with the steps involved in the process, see Chapters 1, 2, and 3 for a quick explanation of the basic features of editing. When you have read those chapters, you will be ready to return to this chapter, and research specific areas of interest.

Related Topic

Shortcut Keys

EDITTIME Field

The EDITTIME field inserts the amount of time a document is edited. For more information on this, look at the DOCPROPERTY and INFO fields under "Fields."

Electronic Mail

Word can work with Microsoft Exchange and other mailing systems to route Word documents to other users. Word and Microsoft Exchange can work together so you can send a document to one or many other Word users. Each of the document recipients can make revision marks on the document and send them back to you or to the next person in a chain of recipients. Since Word and Microsoft Exchange do much of the work, all you have to do is tell Word the document to send, to whom you want it sent, and whether you want each recipient to be sent the document at once or whether you want one recipient to look at it and pass it on to the next one.

If you want to send a Word document without using Microsoft Exchange, you can probably mail the document electronically anyway. If your electronic mail system is MAPI- or VIM-compliant, you have the commands in the File menu to send your documents electronically. Most electronic mail systems let you attach a file to a message.

E

You attach your Word document to a message and have the message and the attached file sent to the desired recipient. However, this is done through the electronic mail system and is not as convenient as the steps described in the previous paragraph.

Word's electronic mailing works with your address book. This address book is maintained by Microsoft Schedule+. You can add addresses from this address book directly into your document or as the recipient of electronic mail.

Procedures

The following procedures describe how to route a document to multiple users, and how to use Word to send electronic mail.

Routing a Document

1. Open the document to send.

2. Select File | Add Routing Slip.

3. Select the Address button.

4. Select the names of the people you want to receive the Word document and the Add button for each name.

5. Select OK.

6. Type any entries in the Subject and Message Text boxes that you want included in the document.

7. Select One After Another when you want the same document sent serially from one named recipient to the next, or select All At Once when you want to send the Word document to all recipients simultaneously.

8. Select from other options, including the following:

   ■ *Remove*   Removes the highlighted name from the list of recipients.

   ■ *Move*   Moves the highlighted name in the list of recipients up or down in the list.

   ■ *Return When Done*   Tells Word that after a recipient reviews the document, the recipient's copy of Word for Windows will send the copy of the document back to you.

   ■ *Track Status*   Tells Word to send a message back to you when the document is sent to the next person in the list.

   ■ *Protect For*   Protects users from making changes to the document that are not marked as changes. When Annotations is selected, document recipients can only make annotations to the document. When Revisions is selected, document recipients can make changes but they all use revision marks that cannot be turned off. When Forms is selected, document recipients can only make changes in the form fields.

■ *Clear*   Removes the settings made in other parts of the dialog box.

9. Select Route to send the document to the selected recipients, or select Add Slip if you want to continue editing the document before you select File | Send to send the document to the selected recipients.

Before the document is sent to the selected recipients, you can edit the routing slip by selecting File | Edit Routing Slip.

Sending Electronic Mail

1. Select File | Send.

   If the Mail as Attachment check box in the General tab of Tools | Options is selected, then the current document is picked up as an attachment to the note and you can see the Word icon for the document you are adding. If the Mail as Attachment check box is cleared, the contents of the document are added as the note's contents.

2. Type the recipients in the To and Cc text boxes.

   You can also add names for the To and Cc text boxes by selecting their buttons. For each recipient to add, highlight the name, then select To to add it to the To text box or Cc to add it to the Cc text box. Then select OK to return to the Microsoft Exchange dialog box. You can compare the recipients in the To and Cc text boxes to the names you have in your address book for your mail system by selecting the Tools | Check Names command. The names in the To and Cc text boxes that Word finds are underlined. You will see a message if one or more of the recipients are not in your address book.

3. Type the subject for the note in the Subject text box.

4. Change the message shown at the bottom. You can also select the Insert | File command and select a file to include as an attachment. Use this option when you want to attach a file other than the current one.

5. Select the File | Send command.

TIP: *You can use Word as your primary interface for your e-mail system. Look at Chapter 9 for more information on this and other features.*

TIP: *You can also send e-mail outside of Word by sending a document to Microsoft Exchange and completing the information you are prompted for.*

E

Make a Document Available to Other Microsoft Exchange Members

■ Select the File | Post to Exchange Folder command. Then, respond to the same window that you see when you use the File | Send command

Related Topic

Annotations
Microsoft Exchange

Embedded Objects

Embedded objects are objects such as text, graphs, or pictures that are created by another application and embedded in Word. The object, and all its relevant information, is saved in your Word document. You start the application used to create the object from within Word, edit the object, and then close the other application to continue working with Word. For more information, see "Object Linking and Embedding."

Embedding

Embedding allows you to add objects such as text, graphs, or pictures created by another application in your Word document. Embedded objects are saved in your Word document although you use the other application to modify the embedded objects. For more information, see "Object Linking and Embedding." Word includes several supplementary applications that can be used to create embedded objects. These applications include WordArt, the Equation Editor, and Microsoft Graph.

Related Topics

Equations
Graphics
Object Linking and Embedding
WordArt

Encapsulated PostScript (EPS) Files

Encapsulated PostScript (EPS) files is one of the file formats Word accepts for graphic images. You add these files as pictures to your Word documents. Look under "Graphics" for more information about bringing image files, such as those in an EPS format, into a Word document.

The way EPS files display in your Word documents depends on whether the file also includes a TIFF or WMF format picture of the EPS contents. If the EPS file does not contain a TIFF or WMF format image as part of its file, then the EPS file appears in your Word document as a boundary box, indicating that the file is an EPS file. When you print a document with an EPS file, if you have a PostScript printer, the PostScript image is printed. If you do not have a PostScript printer, Word prints the TIFF or WMF format image if the EPS file has one. If you do not have a PostScript printer and the EPS file does not include a TIFF or WMF format image, the printed document has an empty box indicating where the image is placed in the document.

E

Enclosures

When you are creating mail merge documents such as form letters to which you want to add enclosures, use the Insert | File command with the Link to File check box selected to include the selected documents in the final version of the form letters. This command adds the INCLUDETEXT field to the document. See "Inserting Documents" for how to use the Insert | File command and "Fields" for how to use the INCLUDETEXT field.

Endnotes

Endnotes let you attribute the source of your information in a document. Unlike footnotes, which are placed at the bottom of the page, endnotes are placed at the end of your document. Word arranges and places the endnotes for you. The features for endnotes are the same as footnotes and are described under "Footnotes and Endnotes."

Entering Special Characters

You can enter special characters besides the ones on your keyboard. The steps for doing this are described under "Special Characters."

Envelopes

Word makes it easy for you to create envelopes that can be printed just like your other print documents. Word can pick up addresses from your document to make entering the data easier. The envelope can either be printed at once or added to your document.

Procedure

1. Select the address in your document. If you do not select the address before the next step, Word searches the document for text that looks like an address. Word uses any set of several short lines as the address for the envelope. If you are uncertain that Word will pick up the appropriate address, select the text containing the address.

2. Select Tools | Envelopes and Labels. Word opens the Envelopes and Labels dialog box. You may need to select the Envelopes tab to see the options you want for addressing envelopes.

3. Check the address in the Delivery Address text box. The text box currently contains the address you selected or the address Word picked up from the document. You can enter new text, edit it, or delete it. You can also select an address from an available address book. Click the Address button above Delivery Address and connect to your address book. Then, choose someone from the list box or type their name in the text box provided and select OK.

4. Enter your return address in the Return Address text box if necessary. Word saves the return address as the default return address and automatically uses it the next time. You can also select an address from an available address book. Click the Address button above Return Address and perform the same steps as you do for the delivery address. If you do not want a return address included, select the Omit check box.

5. Change the options described in the next section. These options do not appear until you select the Options button.

6. Select Print or Add to Document. When you select Print, Word immediately prints the envelope you have defined. When you select Add to Document, Word adds the envelope as a separate section at the beginning of your current document. This section has the page number 0 (zero), so it does not disturb the page numbering for the remainder of your document.

   If you have changed the return address, when you complete the dialog box Word prompts for whether you want to save that return address as the default mailing address. Select Yes to save the address with the user information. Select No and the address is not used as the return address the next time. The default return address is one of Word's User Info options.

You can see how Word converts the information in the dialog box into an envelope by looking at Figure 4-16. Word has placed the contents of the addressee and return address in their correct locations.

TIP: *Word remembers the envelope addresses it created. You can return to an envelope address that you have already used by clicking the down arrow after the Address button and selecting the one you want from the list.*

Options

The following options are available in the Envelope Options dialog box that you see when you select Options in the Envelopes and Labels dialog box. The Envelope Options dialog box divides the options between the Envelope Options and Printing Options tabs.

Envelope Size

This drop-down list box selects the size of the envelope. The list includes a variety of sizes of envelopes including United States and European standard sizes.

E

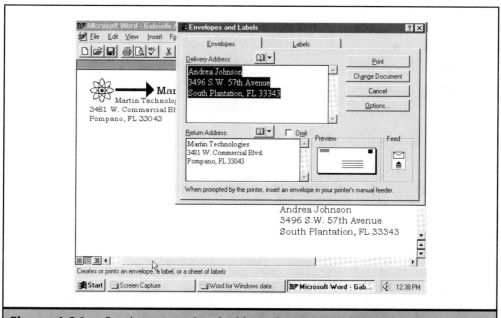

Figure 4-16. *Envelope created and addressed using Word for Windows*

Delivery Point Bar Code

When this check box is selected, Word adds the POSTNET bar code for the addressee zip code. The POSTNET bar code helps the post office promptly deliver the letter and can save you money with mass mailing. If you happen to still be using a daisy-wheel printer, you cannot print a POSTNET bar code.

FIM-A Courtesy Reply Mail

When this check box is selected, Word adds the facing identification mark (FIM) that identifies the front of the envelope to make presorting quicker for the post office when you are including a delivery point bar code. Daisy-wheel printers cannot print a POSTNET bar code.

Delivery Address

These options set the style and position of the address entered in the Delivery Address text box. Selecting Font and the font style and size sets the delivery address font and style. You can also select the Default button from the dialog box Font displays so that all envelopes created with the same template as the current document will use the same font style and size. From Left and From Top set the distance from the upper-left corner of the envelope where Word starts the delivery address. The default of Auto lets Word place it according to the envelope's size.

Return Address

These options set the style and position of the address entered in the Return Address text box. You have the same options as Delivery Address.

Feed Method

These options tell Word how envelopes are inserted into the printer. The six boxes select the alignment in the printer's feeder. The Face Up and Face Down radio buttons select whether you are putting envelopes face up or face down in the printer. Clockwise Rotation selects whether you are putting the envelopes in a reverse direction. Initially the options selected match what Word assumes works best for your printer so you only need to change the options if you want to feed the envelopes into the printer differently.

Feed From

This drop-down list box lets you select how the envelopes are inserted into the printer. You have any of the options listed to choose from, although the options Word lists depend on the printer you are using.

Hints

Even if you use envelopes with the return address preprinted, you can use the return address field to include your initials or name. This lets the recipient of your letter or mailed document know exactly who at your company mailed the letter.

State Code Abbreviations

State abbreviations are commonly used on most correspondence. You can use this handy list to look up the code for any state, the District of Columbia, or United States territories:

State	Abbreviation	State	Abbreviation
Alabama	AL	Montana	MT
Alaska	AK	Nebraska	NE
Arizona	AZ	Nevada	NV
Arkansas	AR	New Hampshire	NH
California	CA	New Jersey	NJ
Colorado	CO	New Mexico	NM
Connecticut	CT	New York	NY
Delaware	DE	North Carolina	NC
District of Columbia	DC	North Dakota	ND
Florida	FL	Ohio	OH
Georgia	GA	Oklahoma	OK
Guam	GU	Oregon	OR
Hawaii	HI	Pennsylvania	PA
Idaho	ID	Puerto Rico	PR
Illinois	IL	Rhode Island	RI
Indiana	IN	South Carolina	SC
Iowa	IA	South Dakota	SD
Kansas	KS	Tennessee	TN
Kentucky	KY	Texas	TX
Louisiana	LA	Utah	UT
Maine	ME	Vermont	VT
Maryland	MD	Virginia	VA
Massachusetts	MA	Virgin Islands	VI
Michigan	MI	Washington	WA
Minnesota	MN	West Virginia	WV
Mississippi	MS	Wisconsin	WI
Missouri	MO	Wyoming	WY

E

Be sure to use the correct two-letter abbreviation for the state. As a reminder, these are listed in the "State Code Abbreviations" box.

If you want to add further formatting to an envelope, add the envelope to the document. Once the letter is in the document, you can use other Word features such as adding graphics to the document.

You can also change the appearance and position of addresses on an envelope by changing styles. For example, documents using the Normal template use styles named Envelope Return and Envelope Address for the positioning and appearance of envelopes.

Changing the definition of the styles changes the appearance of envelopes. If you modify these styles in a template, you will change the appearance of all envelopes created for documents using that template.

Related Topics

Mail Merge
Printing
Styles

Environment Defaults

If you have used WordPerfect, you are accustomed to changing how WordPerfect behaves by changing the environment defaults. In Word, you change these settings somewhat differently. In the table below, the first column lists the WordPerfect environment defaults and the second column lists the topics in this chapter you should refer to for the comparable information in Word.

WordPerfect Environment Default	Word Topic
Allow Undo	Undoing and Redoing Actions (Undo is always available)
Back-Up Options	Save Options
Beep Options	General Options
Cursor Speed	Control Panel
Document Management/Summary	Save Options and Document Properties
Fast Save	Save Options
Format Document for Default Printer on Open	No parallel, since Word does this automatically
Hyphenation	Hyphenation
Language	Foreign Language Support
Units of Measure	General Options
WordPerfect 5.1 Keyboard	Control Panel and Appendix B
Auto Code Placement	No parallel, since Word handles where formatting starts and stops
WordPerfect 5.1 Cursor Movements	General Options
Delimited Text Options	Mail Merge

EPS

EPS (Encapsulated PostScript) is one of the many file formats Word accepts for graphic images. You add EPS files as pictures to your Word documents. Look under "Graphics" for more information about bringing graphics files, such as those in EPS format, into a

Word document. See "Encapsulated PostScript Files" for information on how these files display and print in your Word documents.

EQ Field

The EQ field creates an equation similar to ones created with the Equation Editor. For more information on this, see "Fields."

Equation Editor

See "Equations."

Equations

E

Use Word's supplementary application, the Equation Editor, when you need to enter an equation or formula into a document. The Equation Editor creates equations using mathematical and typesetting conventions. Since the equation is treated as a separate unit, any editing you do in your document has no effect on it. The Equation Editor is designed to make entering and placing mathematical characters easy.

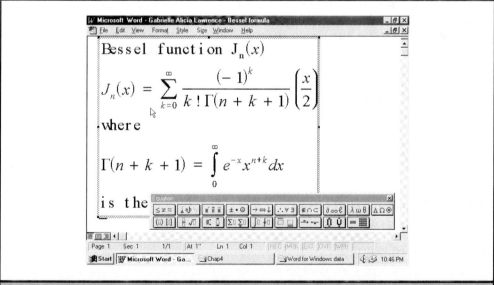

Figure 4-17. *Equations created with the Equation Editor*

TIP: *The Equation Editor must be installed before you can create equations with it. You may need to run Setup again to install this program. If you only want to create a simple equation, create it with the EQ field.*

Procedures

The following instructions describe how to use the Equation Editor to create an equation.

Starting the Equation Editor

1. Select Insert | Object.
2. Select Microsoft Equation 2.0 from the list and OK. If you do not see Microsoft Equation 2.0 in the list, it is not installed. Run Word's or Microsoft Office's Setup program to add this application to your computer.
3. Enter the equation. Figure 4-17 shows the Equation Editor with an equation completed.
4. Click outside of the area that the equation uses to leave Microsoft Equation.

Editing the Equation

To edit the equation, double-click the equation, select Edit | Equation Object | Edit, or right-click the equation and select Edit Equation. While you work on the equation, Microsoft Equation's menu and toolbars appear in place of Word's. You continue to work with the Equation Editor until you click outside of the area the equation uses.

You can also edit the equation in its own window by opening the Equation Editor as a separate application. To edit the equation in its own application window, right-click the equation and select Open Equation, or select the equation and the Edit | Equation Object | Open command. To leave the Equation Editor in its own window, you can use the File | Exit command.

TIP: *If you double-click an EQ field and the Equation Editor is installed, Word converts the EQ field into an Equation Editor embedded object and opens that object for editing.*

Entering an Equation

When you enter an equation in the Equation Editor, you are filling in slots. *Slots* are areas in the Equation Editor that you fill with characters and symbols. You can add more slots by adding templates, as described below. Equation Editor templates, such as fractions and matrices, are combinations of symbols and empty slots. The insertion point covers the slot you are currently working with. Press TAB to move to the next slot or SHIFT+TAB to go back to the previous slot. HOME and END move the insertion point to the beginning and end of a slot. Empty slots have an outlined box. An equation with empty slots looks like this:

The procedure for entering an equation depends on what you want to enter. You can enter letters, numbers, and symbols. You can also insert templates. Click or use the arrow keys to move to the part of the equation you want to edit. Symbols, templates, and embellishments are added using the *palettes*, which are the 19 buttons shown in the toolbar (see Figure 4-17). The palettes and the different items they add to an equation are shown in Table 4-2. To enter characters or symbols, or to set a position, follow one of these steps:

■ To enter numbers and letters, type the numbers and letters. To include spaces in the text, select <u>S</u>tyle | <u>T</u>ext and then type the text.

■ To enter a symbol, click a palette containing the symbol you want. Drag the mouse to the symbol. Releasing the mouse adds the selected symbol. Clicking another palette or part of the window unselects the chosen palette. When a palette is selected it looks like this:

■ To enter some symbols, select a style in the <u>S</u>tyle menu and type the character that creates the character you want. For example, select <u>S</u>tyle | <u>G</u>reek and let the Equation Editor convert the letters you type into their Greek characters. You can do this with symbols which are also inserted with the palettes.

■ To select a template, click the palette containing the template. Then click the button on the palette for the template. Clicking another palette or part of the window unselects the chosen palette. When you add templates, you see outlined boxes for the slots to fill with other characters.

■ To select an embellishment such as primes, click the palette containing the embellishment. Then click the button on the palette for the embellishment. Clicking another palette or part of the window unselects the chosen palette. The embellishment applies to the last character or symbol entered.

For example, to add "$J_n(x)$" as seen at the top of Figure 4-17, start by typing J. For the subscripted *n*, click the third palette in the second row, which has templates for

Palette	Adds
	Relational symbols such "not equals" or "approximately"
	Spaces and ellipses
	Embellishments such as primes and arrows
	Draws mathematical operators such as $\times$ and division signs
	Arrows
	Logical symbols
	Set theory symbols
	Miscellaneous symbols such as infinity and the degree symbol
	A lowercase Greek letter
	An uppercase Greek letter
	Template to put entries inside parentheses, braces, and brackets
	Template for fractions and radicals

Table 4-2.   *Equation Editor Palettes*

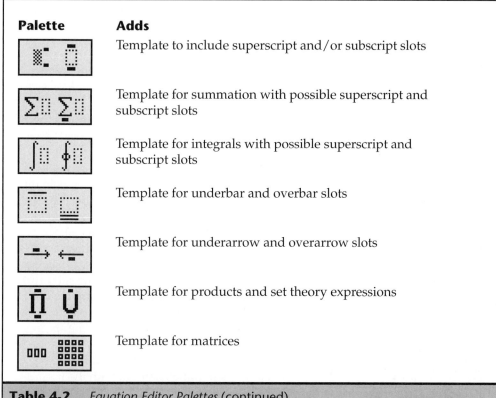

Palette	Adds
	Template to include superscript and/or subscript slots
	Template for summation with possible superscript and subscript slots
	Template for integrals with possible superscript and subscript slots
	Template for underbar and overbar slots
	Template for underarrow and overarrow slots
	Template for products and set theory expressions
	Template for matrices

Table 4-2. *Equation Editor Palettes* (continued)

subscript and superscript positions. Click the second button in this palette, and the Equation Editor adds an outline that is below the *J*. Type **n** and press RIGHT ARROW to move out of the slot. Next, click the first button in the first palette in the second row to add the parentheses. The size of parentheses inserted with a template is adjusted better than if you type them. Next, type **x** as the contents of the parentheses and press RIGHT ARROW. The rest of the formula is added the same way—using palettes to add templates for positioning options and symbols.

Formatting with the Equation Editor

The Equation Editor has several commands for changing the appearance of equations. By default, the Equation Editor uses settings that match the most commonly used typesetting and mathematical conventions. You can change several of these settings to get desired results. You can change font typefaces, font size, spacing, and alignment.

The style of the characters is defined in several ways. Some of the symbols require specific fonts, because only those fonts provide the desired characters. You can change the font of other text items. The easiest way to change the font is to select Style | Define. Choose a typeface for each style, and choose whether it uses boldface or italics. Then select the style from the Style pull-down menu and type the entries that use that style. If the style you want does not appear, select Style | Other, then select a typeface and whether characters using that typeface are also boldfaced or italicized.

The easiest way to set the font's size is to select Size and a font description. Select Size | Define to set the exact size. You can override the font size by selecting Size | Other and then typing the point size you want and OK.

You can either set the typeface and size before you enter the affected characters or you can select the characters and then the commands. You select characters in the Equation Editor just like you select text in Word: drag the mouse across the characters you want to select, or use SHIFT and the arrow keys.

Change the spacing to stretch or squeeze an equation to fit a particular space. Set the spacing by selecting Format | Spacing. From the Spacing dialog box, you can set t he distance between lines of equations, the horizontal and vertical distance between elements in a matrix, how high superscript characters are raised, how low subscript characters are dropped, the distance between a limit and the symbol using the limit, and whether the settings you enter become the new defaults. The spacing defaults are relative so they match the size of the characters. You can see a sample of the spacing you are setting with the diagram on the right side of the dialog box.

When several equations are in one Equation Editor object, you need to set an alignment between them. The most used alignment options are set with the Format menu. Using the options at the top of the Format pull-down menu, you can left-align, center, right-align, or align according to the equals sign or decimal point. The alignment you select applies to all of the equations in the Equation Editor object.

Shortcut Keys for the Equation Editor

The Equation Editor has many shortcut keys you can use to make selections. Table 4-3 shows the shortcut keys for menu commands. Table 4-4 shows the shortcut keys for entering popular symbols. Table 4-5 shows the shortcut keys for popular templates. Table 4-6 shows the shortcut keys for popular embellishments.

Besides the key combinations listed in the tables, the Equation Editor has a few other key combinations. If you want to insert a tab character in a slot, press CTRL+TAB. You can also press CTRL+G when you want only the next character to use the Symbol style, and press CTRL+B when you want only the next character to use the matrix-vector style.

Menu Command	Keyboard Shortcut
File I Update	F3
File I Exit and Return to Document	ALT+F4
Edit I Copy	CTRL+C
Edit I Clear	DEL
Edit I Cut	CTRL+X
Edit I Paste	CTRL+V
Edit I Select All	CTRL+A
Edit I Undo	CTRL+Z
View I 100%	CTRL+1
View I 200%	CTRL+2
View I 400%	CTRL+4
View I Redraw	CTRL+D
View I Show All	CTRL+Y
Format I Align Left	CTRL+SHIFT+L
Format I Align Center	CTRL+SHIFT+C
Format I Align Right	CTRL+SHIFT+R
Style I Math	CTRL+SHIFT+=
Style I Text	CTRL+SHIFT+E
Style I Function	CTRL+SHIFT+F
Style I Variable	CTRL+SHIFT+I
Style I Greek	CTRL+SHIFT+G
Style I Matrix-Vector	CTRL+SHIFT+B

Table 4-3. *Shortcut Keys for Equation Editor Commands*

TIP: *The Equation Editor also has shortcut keys to enter any symbol or template when you know its palette number and the number of the button within the palette. To insert a symbol, press* CTRL+SHIFT+S, *type a number between 1 and 9 for the palette number, followed by a number between 1 and 32 for the button number within the palette, and press* ENTER. *To insert a template, press* CTRL+SHIFT+T, *type a number between 1 and 9 for the palette number, followed by a number between 1 and 32 for the button number within the palette, and press* ENTER.

Symbol	Keyboard Shortcut
∞	CTRL+S I
→	CTRL+S A
∂	CTRL+S D
≤	CTRL+S <
≥	CTRL+S >
×	CTRL+S T
∈	CTRL+S E
∉	CTRL+S SHIFT+E
⊂	CTRL+S C
⊄	CTRL+S SHIFT+C

Table 4-4.   *Shortcut Keys for Symbols in the Equation Editor*

Hints

Sketch out the equation you want to enter before you start the Equation Editor. The sketch helps you figure out which symbols and position options you want in the Equation Editor and it gives you an idea of how the final result should look.

You do not need SPACEBAR to add spaces between parts of an equation. Most of the time, the Equation Editor adds spaces appropriately. When you do want to add spaces with SPACEBAR, select Style | Text first. While you can type symbols such as brackets and parentheses, use the palettes instead. The Equation Editor sizes and spaces characters added with the palettes to match typographical and mathematical conventions, preventing later spacing problems. You can nudge some things by pressing CTRL and an arrow key, as when you grab part of an equation, but use this only when the equation is completed and you are fine-tuning its appearance.

Working with an equation may be easier if you zoom it. You can enlarge an equation by selecting View | 200% or View | 400%. Select View | 100% to see the equation at its actual size. If the equation has clutter remaining as you edit the equation, select View | Redraw. To make the overall equation(s) larger or smaller, drag one of the four corners of the Equation Editor object while you are in Word.

You can enter more than one equation in an Equation Editor object. Press ENTER at the end of the equation to start the next line. Use multiple equations to group the equations together.

When you have more complex equations than you can create with the Equation Editor, consider getting MathType. MathType is an enhanced version of the Equation Editor. It provides features such as macros, customizable palettes, formatting that changes

Symbol	Template	Shortcut Keys
	Parentheses	CTRL+9 or CTRL+0 or CTRL+T (or)
	Brackets	CTRL+[or CTRL+] or CTRL+T [or]
	Braces	CTRL+{ or CTRL+} or CTRL+T { or }
	Fraction	CTRL+F or CTRL+T F
	Slash fraction	CTRL+/ or CTRL+T /
$X^{\Box}$	Superscript (high)	CTRL+H or CTRL+T H
$X_{\Box}$	Subscript (low)	CTRL+L or CTRL+T L
$X_{\Box}^{\Box}$	Joint sub/superscript	CTRL+J or CTRL+T J
	Integral	CTRL+I or CTRL+T I
	Absolute value	CTRL+T |
$\sqrt{\Box}$	Root	CTRL+R or CTRL+T R
$\sqrt[\Box]{\Box}$	nth root	CTRL+T N

Table 4-5. *Shortcut Keys for Templates in the Equation Editor*

E

$\sum$	Summation	CTRL+T S
$\prod$	Product	CTRL+T P
▯ ▯ ▯ ▯ ▯ ▯ ▯ ▯ ▯	Matrix template (3 × 3)	CTRL+T M
▯	Underscript (limit)	CTRL+T U
	Fraction	CTRL+T F

Table 4-5. *Shortcut Keys for Templates in the Equation Editor* (continued)

by pressing TAB, a TEX interface, and saving equations in EPS and WMF files. MathType is provided by Design Science. You can contact the company at (800) 827-0685.

To print your Equation Editor equations correctly, your printer must be able to print scalable fonts, such as the TrueType ones that the Equation Editor uses. If you change printers after you install the Equation Editor, you may need to reinstall the Equation Editor. Reinstalling Equation Editor is often the best solution if you have problems with equations printing or displaying incorrectly.

If you want to enter equations in other Windows applications, use the Clipboard in the Equation Editor to copy the equation to the Clipboard. Then switch to the other

Embellishments	Keyboard Shortcut
Overbar	CTRL+SHIFT+-
Tilde	CTRL+~ (CTRL+" on some keyboards)
Arrow (vector)	CTRL+ALT+-
Single prime	CTRL+ALT '
Double prime	CTRL+" (CTRL+~ on some keyboards)
Single dot	CTRL+ALT+.

Table 4-6. *Shortcut Keys for Embellishments in the Equation Editor*

application and paste the equation into that application's document. Applications that let you insert objects into their documents may include the Equation Editor in the list of acceptable objects to add. You can add the equations through these applications. However, you cannot run the Equation Editor independently.

Related Topic

Object Linking and Embedding

Erasing

You erase text as described under "Deleting Text." You can also erase documents as described under "Document Management."

E

Errors

If you run into a problem while working with Word, Word will display a message. These messages let you select OK to leave the message and continue working with Word. You can also display the Help window to show information about the message that Word has just displayed and possible causes for the error. You can also look at Word's Help Index, which includes Word's messages.

Excel

Excel is a spreadsheet application designed for the Windows environment. Word can open Excel spreadsheets, converting them into Word format as they are opened. For more information on opening these documents, see "Opening Documents" and "Inserting Spreadsheets." You can also embed Excel spreadsheets into Word documents and link Excel spreadsheets into Word documents. Word lets you start Excel from within Word by clicking the Microsoft Excel button in the Microsoft toolbar. You can also create a Microsoft Excel object that you want as part of your Word document by clicking the Insert Microsoft Excel Worksheet button in the Standard toolbar. Once you start Microsoft Excel, you are using Excel, not Word. You leave Excel and return to your Word document by clicking part of the document where the Excel data does not appear. If Excel appears in its own window, you can leave Excel by selecting File | Exit and Return to *document name*. A Word document with an Excel embedded document might look like Figure 4-18.

TIP: *You need to have Microsoft Excel for Windows installed on your computer to take advantage of sharing data between Word and Excel.*

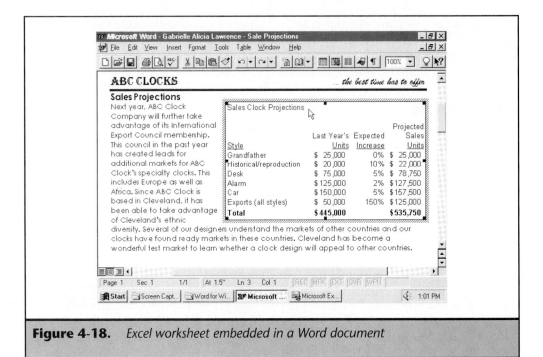

Figure 4-18.   *Excel worksheet embedded in a Word document*

Exchange

See "Microsoft Exchange."

Exchanging Data

See "Object Linking and Embedding."

Exclude Dictionary

See "Spelling."

Executing Macros

See "Macros."

Exiting Word

You must exit Word whenever you want to quit using Word completely. This removes Word from active memory and releases the memory for other applications.

Procedures

Exiting Word and closing Word's application window mean the same thing. If you close the application window, Word is exited. Exit Word following any of these procedures:

- Select File | Exit.
- Click the Close button in the application's title bar.
- Double-click the application's program icon.
- Press ALT+F4.

After doing any of these, the Word application window closes. To use Word again, you need to restart the application. When you exit Word, open documents that have not changed since they were saved close automatically. Word prompts you about saving documents that have changed since they were last saved or that were never saved. Select Yes for each document that you want to save and No for the documents you do not want to save. If the document has never been saved before, Word opens the Save As dialog box for you to specify a document name.

Expanding and Collapsing Outlines

See "Outlines" for details on creating and using outlines.

Exporting Word Documents

Exporting a Word document moves it into another format that other applications can use. Word can save documents in other formats by selecting a different type in the Save as Type drop-down list box. This drop-down list box and the other options for saving a document are described under "Saving Documents."

EXPRESSION = Field

The EXPRESSION = field returns the result of an expression or formula. For more information on this, see "Fields."

Extend Mode/Key

See "Selecting Text" for information on using extend mode when selecting text.

E

Fast Save

See "Save Options" and "Saving Documents."

Favorites Folder

To make it easier to work with the documents that you use most frequently, Word has a Favorites folder. This folder stores shortcuts to opening documents, not the actual documents. As you open documents from the Favorites folder, Word uses the shortcut to guide it to opening the original file in its other location. To open a document that you have added to the Favorites folder, click the Look In Favorites button, the first of the two buttons shown in the margin and then select the file from the list. This button and the Add to Favorites button (also shown in the margin) are at the top of the Open dialog box which you see when you select a document to open. The Look In Favorites button is also located in the Save As dialog box which you see when you go to save a document.

You can add items to the Favorites folder. Select the document, then click the Add to Favorites button. You can even add a folder to the Favorites location. For example, on a network, you can add a folder to the Favorites folder that represents data stored on another computer if you have the networking features enabled that allow you to see the folders on another computer. That way, you can quickly open files in that remote location by selecting the folder out of the Favorites folder and then selecting the document you wish to open.

Faxes

You can use Word to make faxing documents easier in several ways. Word has templates that guide you through creating fax cover letters. Select one of the Fax templates from the Letters & Faxes tab when you create a new document. These templates have ready-made fax forms into which you can insert the data applicable to the fax you are sending. There is also a Fax Wizard you can use to guide you through creating a fax cover letter. With either the Fax template or Fax Wizard, you just enter your information.

You can use Word with a fax board to fax Word documents directly from your computer to another fax. To do this, select your fax printer from the Name drop-down list box in the Print dialog box. To make this option available, you must install your fax board into your computer and in Windows. The directions that come with the fax board will guide you through these steps.

You can set Word to do a mail merge for records with fax numbers, as described in the following section.

Procedures for Mail Merges to Records with Fax Numbers

The procedure for setting up a mail merge to use only records with fax numbers has the same steps as selecting records using other criteria.

1. After setting up the main and data documents, select Tools | Mail Merge.

2. Select Query Options.

3. In the Field column, select the field with the fax number, and choose Is Not Blank in the Comparison column. Select OK.

4. Select Close or Merge.

Related Topics

Mail Merge
Printing

Fields

Fields are special codes. When Word prints a document, it substitutes something for each code in your document. For example, you can enter a date code in your document, and whenever you print the document, Word will substitute the current date in the code's location.

A field code consists of the following:

The opening field character, which is a { (curly brace)
The field code
Instructions, if required
General switches, if desired
The closing field character, which is a } (curly brace)

All Word fields are listed under "Options" in this section. Each field's description includes the field code, a description of what it inserts into your document, and an explanation of the possible instructions for that field. General switches, which most fields can use, are explained under "Other Options" in this section.

For information on specific fields used in mail merges, see "Mail Merge." If you want more information about a particular field than what is described here, press F1 for help to find the help information on the field.

Procedures

This section gives the procedures for the various ways to: enter fields in a document; display the results of field codes; update, edit, and format the results of field codes; move among field codes; print field codes; lock a field; and unlink a field from the updating process.

Entering a Field with the Menus

In addition to entering a field with the Insert | Field command described here, some fields can be inserted in other ways. For example, the DATE and TIME fields can be inserted using shortcut keys, or using the Insert | Date and Time command from the Insert menu. The fields that are not normally added with the Insert | Field command described below are instead added by using other Word features, such as using the Tools | Mail Merge command, Insert | File, or Edit | Paste Special commands.

1. Move the insertion point to the location in the document where you want the field added.

2. Select Insert | Field, to open the Field dialog box shown here:

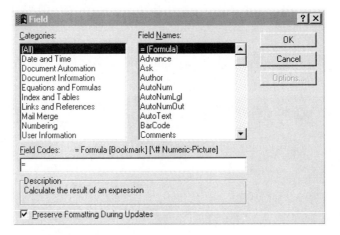

The Field Names list box displays the fields belonging to the category selected in the Categories list.

3. Change which fields are listed in the Field Names list box by selecting a different category under Categories. Then select a field from the Field Names list box.

Notice that the field code for the selected field appears in the Field Codes text box. Above this text box, Word displays other instructions the field code can use. Below the Field Codes box is a description of the code's purpose.

4. If needed, specify the options or instructions to add to the field code. Select the Options button and then choose from the options that are displayed for the field. Select OK to return to the Field dialog box. The Options button is dimmed when the selected field does not use additional options or instructions.

NOTE: *Besides using the method described above, you can also type the options, switches, and instructions in the Field Codes text box after the field name.*

5. Specify whether you want Word to replace the field's formatting when it updates the field. If you want Word to keep the field's formatting when it is updated, select the Preserve Formatting During Updates check box; turn off the check box when you want the formatting to be replaced.

6. Select OK.

Word now inserts the field into the document. Depending on your settings, Word displays either the field code or the field's result. See the upcoming procedure for "Switching Between Codes and Results" to learn how to change what Word displays. If you see the field codes, you can see how Word added the{ and } for you.

Entering a Field with Shortcut Keys

You can type the field name and any codes for a field you want to add into the document rather than using the Insert | Field command. Use this method of adding the field when you know the field code and any switches you want to add.

1. Move the insertion point to the location in the document where you want the field added.

2. Press CTRL+F9 to insert the opening and closing field code symbols, { and }. (You cannot type these characters on the keyboard, because Word will not recognize them as field codes.)

3. Type the field name and any options, switches, and instructions between the field code symbols.

4. Press F9 to update the field.

When you press F9, Word interprets the entry within the { } (curly braces) and updates the field you have entered. Depending on your settings, Word displays either the field code or the field's result. If Word does not understand what you typed in step 3 and Word is displaying field results, you may see a message such as "Error!" or "Error: Bookmark not defined."

> *TIP: You can change text you already have in a document into a field code. After typing the field name and its options or instructions, select the field name and options or instructions, and press CTRL+F9.*

Nesting Fields

You can use a field as part of the instructions for another field; this is called *nesting* fields. You can nest up to 20 fields in this fashion.

To insert a field within another field, position the insertion point directly after the field code of the existing field. Then insert the nested field using one of the methods described above.

Switching Between Codes and Results

You can switch between displaying the field codes and displaying the results of those field codes, using either the menus or shortcut keys.

- Press ALT+F9 to toggle between field codes and results. The toggle changes all fields in a document.

- Select Tools | Options, then the View tab, the Field Codes check box, and OK.

- Right-click the field and select Toggle Field Codes from the shortcut menu. This only affects the current field.

- Press SHIFT+F9 to toggle between a field's code and its results. The toggle changes only the current field.

> *NOTE: When you move the insertion point to any part of the field's code or result, the entire field is grayed out. This is due to the way shading fields are set, as described below.*

Shading Fields

1. Choose Tools | Options and select the View tab.

2. Select an option for how you want fields shaded by choosing one of the choices in the Field Shading drop-down list box: Always to all the time shade fields; When Selected to shade fields only when the insertion point is at the field; and Never to never shade a field.

3. Select OK.

Updating Fields

Updating a field makes the field's value the most current value. To update the results of a field code, you can do either:

- Press F9 with the insertion point inside the field.
- Right-click the field and select Update Field from the shortcut menu.

Word will also update the field's contents when you print the field. This assumes that Word is set to update fields when printing. To turn on this setting, select File | Print and then Options, the Update Fields check box, and OK.

Editing Fields

You can edit field codes just as you would edit other text in the document. You cannot edit the field results, however, because Word updates them and replaces them with the new field results.

1. Toggle your display so you see the field codes (see "Switching Between Codes and Results," just above).

2. Move the insertion point inside the field code, and modify the field code or instructions as needed.

3. When you're done, update the field, and then toggle back to displaying field results to check that the results are what you want.

Formatting Field Results

You can apply formatting directly to field results by selecting all or part of the field results and applying the format as you would to normal text. However, when you update the field, you may lose the formatting. You can designate whether a field will keep its formatting. To do this when you add the field with Insert | Field, turn on the Preserve Formatting During Updates check box, and the field results will retain the formatting as they change. If this check box is cleared, the field contents may have new formatting after the field is updated.

If you type the field code to add it, use the * mergeformat switch to tell Word to retain the formatting after the field is updated. The * mergeformat switch is added at the end of the field instructions, as in

{TIME * mergeformat}

Word adds this switch automatically with Insert | Field when the Preserve Formatting During Updates check box is selected. For more information about general switches, see "Switches" under "Other Options."

Moving Among Fields Only

You can quickly move from field to field in your document without having to search through the text to find the codes. When using this feature, you will not be able to move to fields that Word automatically formats as hidden text (the index entry, TOC entry, Referenced Document (RD) field types).

F

■ Press F11 to move to the next field.

■ Press SHIFT+F11 to move the previous field.

Printing Field Codes

In some situations, you may want to print your document showing the field codes rather than the field results. For instance, you might do this as documentation for a mail merge document, or to print a quick draft version of the document. Here are the steps:

1. Select File | Print, to open the Print dialog box.

2. Select Options, to open the Options dialog box displaying the print options.

3. Select the Field Codes check box.

4. Select OK twice to close the Options dialog box and then print the document.

REMEMBER: *Don't forget to turn off the Field Codes check box after you've finished printing field codes, so that Word will return to printing your document with the field results.*

Locking or Unlocking a Field

You can lock a field to temporarily prevent Word from updating it. This allows you to preserve the previous result of the field. If you manually try to update the field, Word beeps. For example, if you have a {USERNAME} field in a document and you want to continue to show your name even when someone else is working on the document, you would lock the {USERNAME} field.

1. Move the insertion point to inside the field.

2. Press CTRL+F11 to lock the field so that its results cannot be updated. Press SHIFT+CTRL+F11 to unlock a field so that its results can be updated again.

Unlinking a Field

To permanently prevent Word from updating a field's results, you can *unlink* the field. Most fields are linked to information; for example, the TIME field is linked to your system's internal clock. Unlinking the field means that it can no longer access that source of information and thus cannot be updated at all. When you unlink a field, you are permanently converting the field into its field's results. You will no longer see the field code for an unlinked field, even when you show field codes instead of field results.

CAUTION: *You cannot relink a field after unlinking it.*

To unlink a field, move the insertion point inside the field and press CTRL+SHIFT+F9.

Options

This section contains a list of the available fields. For each field, there is an example of the field code, an explanation of its purpose and its instructions, and any specific switches used with the field. For an explanation of the general switches that all fields can use, see "Other Options" at the end of this section. Fields relating to mail merge are also mentioned here, but they are more thoroughly explained in "Mail Merge."

- The field code itself appears in all capitals, with options or instructions in lowercase.

- If instructions or arguments are optional rather than required, they appear inside square brackets ([ ]).

- Any value that will be replaced by variable information appears in italic. For example, "*NewValue*" would be replaced by something else when you actually enter the field. If the variable is optional, the instruction will read ["*NewValue*"], for example.

- Spaces shown in field codes are not optional. You must include spaces between the field code and the options and between different options.

TIP: *Many of the fields use commas and backslashes (\) for specific purposes. When you need to include a comma or backslash for a different purpose, include an extra backslash. For example, a document name used within a field code might look like C:\\Word for Windows\\My Text.doc.*

The = Field

You can use the {=} field to evaluate an expression. After the =, you enter the formula you want calculated. You can use operators, functions, and bookmark names for the data you want the field to evaluate. An example might be

{=.07 *Subtotal}

where Subtotal is the bookmark that contains a number you want multiplied by 7 percent.

You can use the following operators and functions in your = fields.

NOTE: *In the following table, "on left" means before the operator or function; "on right" means after the operator or function.*

Operator	Effect
+	Adds value on left to value on right
–	Subtracts value on right from value on left
*	Multiplies value on left times value on right
/	Divides value on right by value on left
^	Raises value on left to the power of the value on right
%	Treats value on left as a percentage
=	Equals TRUE when value on left equals value on right
<=	Equals TRUE when value on left is less than or equals value on right
<	Equals TRUE when value on left is less than value on right
>=	Equals TRUE when value on left is greater than or equals value on right
>	Equals TRUE when value on left is greater than value on right
<>	Equals TRUE when value on left does not equal value on right

Function	Purpose
ABS(x)	Returns the absolute value of x
AND(x,y)	Equals TRUE when both x and y are true; equals FALSE in other cases
AVERAGE( )	Returns the average of the values in parentheses
COUNT( )	Counts the number of values in parentheses
DEFINED( )	Equals TRUE when bookmark in parentheses is a defined bookmark
FALSE	Equals a FALSE value to use as comparison with TRUE
IF(x,y,z)	Equals y when x is true, and z when x is false
INT(x)	Returns the integer of the sum of x
MAX( )	Returns the largest value among values in parentheses
MIN( )	Returns the lowest value among values in parentheses
MOD(x,y)	Returns the remainder when value of x is divided by value of y
NOT(x)	Equals TRUE when x equals FALSE; equals FALSE when x equals TRUE
OR(x,y)	Equals TRUE when either x or y are true; equals FALSE when both are false
PRODUCT( )	Multiplies the blocks of values in parentheses and totals the products

ROUND(*x,y*)	Rounds the value of x to the number of digits set by y
SIGN(x)	Returns 1 if value of x is positive, or –1 if x is negative, or 0 if x equals 0
SUM( )	Totals the values in parentheses
TRUE	Equals a TRUE value to use as comparison with FALSE

ADVANCE

The {ADVANCE} field shifts the text on the remainder of the line a number of points in any direction you select. After ADVANCE you enter the direction you want the text shifted: \l for left, \r for right, \u for up, \d for down, \x for left from the left margin of the column or frame, and \y for down from the top margin of the column or frame. After this switch is the number of points you want the entry shifted in that direction. For example, the field code

T{ADVANCE \d2 }E{ADVANCE \u2 }X

produces TEX. Notice that the second ADVANCE field code is after the *E* so the X is on the same level as the T.

ASK

The {ASK} field prompts the user to enter information during a mail merge. That text is then assigned a bookmark. You can use this field to take the text typed by the user and insert it into the merged document. See "Mail Merge" for more information.

AUTHOR

See "DOCPROPERTY" and "INFO" in this section for how to add the document's author.

AUTONUM

The {AUTONUM} field automatically numbers the paragraph on a particular level of an outline. This field is normally at the beginning of each paragraph you want numbered. This field cannot be nested inside an IF field, or locked or unlinked. The field's result is the paragraph's number. When Word counts the paragraphs to calculate the result, Word counts all paragraphs that are at the same outline level, starting fresh each time a paragraph with a higher outline level is encountered. For example, an {AUTONUM} field in the eleventh paragraph would result in 11.

AUTONUMLGL

The {AUTONUMLGL} field automatically numbers paragraphs in the legal format, which displays all outline levels for the paragraph. This field cannot be nested inside an IF field, or locked or unlinked. The field's result is the paragraph's number, including all outline levels. For example, an {AUTONUMLGL} field might show a result of 2.3.1; the paragraph referred to here is in the first third-level paragraph under the third second-level paragraph, under the second first-level paragraph. Legal documents use this numbering system to number paragraphs and outlines.

AUTONUMOUT

The {AUTONUMOUT} field automatically numbers paragraphs in the outline format. This field cannot be nested inside an IF field, or locked or unlinked. The field's result is the number or letter for the heading's position within an outline. When you use this field on a paragraph that does not have an outline level, it has the same result as the {AUTONUM} field. For instance, *II.* is the second first level paragraph in a document, and B. is the second second-level paragraph under a first-level heading. You can also easily add outline numbering using bullets and numbering as described under "Lists."

AUTOTEXT

The {AUTOTEXT} field returns the contents of an AutoText entry. Using this field instead of replacing the AutoText entry will update the document if the AutoText entry changes. After AUTOTEXT you enter the name of the AutoText entry to insert, as in {AUTOTEXT Call_Me}. The document will contain the expanded version of the AutoText entry, Call_Me.

BARCODE

The {BARCODE} field returns the POSTNET delivery-point bar code, using the information entered after BARCODE or the contents of the given bookmark. For example, {BARCODE 44406} displays its result as the POSTNET delivery-point bar code for zip code 44406. POSTNET delivery-point bar codes help the post office deliver mail promptly. When you are doing mass mailings, using the POSTNET delivery-point bar code may provide a discount for postage.

This field can use the following switches:

Switch	Result
\b	Tells Word that the information after BARCODE is a bookmark name.
\f	Tells Word to add a facing identification code. Follow \f with **"a"** when you want a courtesy reply mark. Follow \f with **"c"** when you want a business reply mark.
\u	Tells Word that the address is in the United States.

Bookmarks

The bookmark field, {*bookmark*}, returns the contents of the named bookmark. For example, if you have a bookmark named Sales that contains $569,349, inserting {Sales} as a field code will produce $569,349 as the field's results. You cannot use Insert I Field to add this field, so use CTRL+F9 instead and type the bookmark name before you press F9 to update the field.

If the bookmark includes a paragraph mark, then the paragraph that uses this field takes the same paragraph formatting. If the bookmark name matches the name of another Word field, put REF and a space before the bookmark name so Word knows to use the bookmark's contents rather than the other field. Word automatically adds REF to this type of field when you insert certain types of cross-references with the Insert I Cross-reference command (See "Cross-References").

Word has three switches you can use with this field:

- Use \f when you want the bookmark to include footnotes and endnotes from the text in the bookmark and you want Word to increment their number when they appear as part of the field.

- Use \n when you want paragraph numbering from the text in the bookmark to also appear where the text appears again as the {*bookmark*} field's results.

- Use \! when you want to limit the updating of fields within the text selected by the {*bookmark*} field. This switch is described under {INCLUDETEXT}.

COMMENTS
See "DOCPROPERTY" and "INFO" in this section to add the document's Comments property to your document.

COMPARE
The {COMPARE} field returns a 1 when the comparison of the two expressions using the operator you provide is TRUE, or a 0 when it isn't. The {COMPARE} field uses this format:

{COMPARE *expression1 operator expression2*}

Both expressions can be bookmarks, text in quotes, numbers, or results from other fields. The operator can be =, <=, <, >=, >, or <> as described for the = field. You can use the ? to represent any single character in either expression, and the * to represent zero or more characters in either expression.

For example, {COMPARE State="Ohio"} returns 1 when the bookmark State contains the text Ohio.

CREATEDATE
See CreateTime under "DOCPROPERTY" and "INFO" in this section.

DATABASE

The {DATABASE} field inserts a database query's results in a document. You can use this field to insert an SQL database query into a Word document. You may also add this field when you use the Insert | Database command.

This field uses several switches:

- Use the \c switch followed by the directions to the other application for the query you want included in Word.

- You can tell Word the location of the database using the \d switch; include two backslashes in the path information where you would otherwise use one, so Word will recognize the pathname.

- To include the SQL instructions that select the database records to insert as the field's result, include \s and the SQL instruction as part of the field information. *SQL instructions* are the Standard Query Language statements that select data from a database.

- To apply a Table AutoFormat format to the field's results, use the \l switch followed by the AutoFormat format name to apply to the field's results.

- The \b switch selects the part of the AutoFormat table format to apply to the {DATABASE} field's results. After \b is a number: 0 to use no table formatting; 1 to include the borders; 2 to include the shading; 4 to include the font; 8 to include the color; 16 to include the best fit settings; 32 to include the heading row; 64 to include the last row; 128 to include the first column; and 256 to include the last column. To combine features, add their numbers such as 33 to include any border and set the heading row.

- To specify the range of records from the database included in the query, use \f followed by the first record and \t followed by the last record.

- To insert the data at the beginning of the merge, use the \o switch.

DATE

The {DATE} field displays the date when the field was last updated. Use this field to insert the current date in a document. The resulting date is usually displayed in the default date format for Windows, but you can use the date-time picture switch (described in "Other Options" in this section) to format the date in another fashion. You can also include the \l switch when you want the {DATE} field to use the same date and time format as the last {DATE} field.

The {DATE} field can be added in more than one way, as described in "Date and Time" earlier in this chapter.

DOCPROPERTY

The {DOCPROPERTY} field inserts data from the Properties dialog box into your document. Use this field in place of {INFO} when you want to display, rather than change, a document's information. This field takes the format

{DOCPROPERTY "*Name*"}

Name is the document property value that you want inserted. Possible values include:

Author	CreateTime	Manager	Template
Bytes	Keywords	NameofApplication	Title
Category	LastPrinted	Pages	TotalEditingTime
Characters	LastSaved	Paragraph	Words
Comments	LastSavedTime	RevisionNumber	
Company	Lines	Subject	

Notice how these possible entries are the same ones that you see in the Properties dialog box except that the spaces have been removed. You can also return custom properties, but since these property names are defined by you, not Word, you must enter the property name yourself, as in {DOCPROPERTY "RecordNumber") to return the value of the custom RecordNumber property.

EDITTIME

See "INFO" and TotalEditingTime for "DOCPROPERTY" in this section.

EMBED

The {EMBED} field embeds an object in your Word document. Word adds this field for you when you embed an object. See "Object Linking and Embedding" for more information.

EQ

The {EQ} field creates an equation, similar to ones you can create with the Equation Editor. The {EQ} is useful if you did not install the Equation Editor or you want to add a formula inline with other text. When a formula is fairly complex, however, the Equation Editor is easier to use. You can double-click the {EQ} field to start the Equation Editor with the equation that this field creates.

This field uses many switches to tell Word the equation you want to create.

F

THE \A SWITCH   This switch draws a two-dimensional array using the entries in the parentheses that follow. The numbers for the array are separated by commas and fill up the array's size one row at a time. If the array has more than one column, include \co and the number of columns between \a and the opening parentheses for the number of columns in the array. You can also use \al after \a when you want the array elements left-aligned; \ar when you want the array elements right-aligned; or \ac when you want the array elements centered. When you want to set the vertical or horizontal spacing between the array element, use \a and then the \vs or \hs switches and a number of points. As an example of the \a switch, the field code {EQ \a \co3 (5, 6, 7, 1, 2, 3)} creates the following:

5 6 7
1 2 3

THE \B SWITCH   This switch draws parentheses or other characters around the element in parentheses. Without any switches modifying \b, \b draws parentheses. You can set the left side of the matching characters with \lc\ and a character, and the right side with \rc\ and a character. Another option is to set the character with \bc\ and a character. If the character after \c\ is an opening (, {, [, or <, Word draws the matching closing symbol around the element. If it is another character, Word uses the same character for both sides. For example, {EQ \b \bc\[(\a \co2 (1, 2, 3, 4))} returns

$$\begin{bmatrix} 12 \\ 34 \end{bmatrix}$$

THE \D SWITCH   This switch adjusts the position of the next entry (often it is something else created by the {EQ} field). At the end of the \d switch is an empty set of parentheses. You can include the following switches between the \d and the opening parentheses: \fo and a number of points to move forward the next element; \ba and a number of points to move backward the next element; and \li( ) to draw a line from the affected element to the next character.

THE \F SWITCH   Use \f followed by two entries in parentheses separated by commas to place the first entry as a fraction's numerator and the second entry as the fraction's denominator. For example, {EQ \f (7,8)} creates the fraction ⅞.

THE \I SWITCH   Use \i to create an integral sign ∫. After the \i are parentheses containing the lower limit, the upper limit, and the expression after the integral symbol, separated by commas. Before the opening parentheses, you can include \su to change the integral sign to a summation sign; \pr to change the integral sign to a pi character; \in to place the upper and lower limits to the right of the sign so the expression is more in line with the text; \fc \ and a character to place the character as a fixed-size character in place of the integral sign; or \vc \ and a character to place the character as a variable-size character in place of the integral sign.

THE \L SWITCH   The \l switch treats the series of elements entered in parentheses after the \l as a single element. Use this switch to create a series of entries that other switches will treat as a single unit.

THE \O SWITCH   With the \o switch you can combine characters by putting one on top of another (overstriking). Following \o are the characters that will be put on top of one another, in parentheses and separated by commas. Between the \o and the opening parentheses you can include \al to left-align the boxes that hold each overstruck character; \ac to center the boxes that hold each overstruck character; or \ar to right-align the boxes that hold each overstruck character.

THE \R SWITCH   The \r switch followed by one element in the parentheses puts the element in parentheses under a radical sign. You can also have two elements in parentheses, separated by commas, to tell the \r switch to put the first element above the radical sign and the second element under the radical sign.

THE \S SWITCH   The \s switch positions a single element as a superscript or subscript character. If you put multiple elements in the parentheses following the switch, the first element is superscript, and the next elements are placed in order below the first one and left-aligned. If you only use one element for this switch, you can also include the following switches to modify how the s\switch operates: \ai and a number of points to add above the line within the paragraph; \di and a number of points to add below the line within the paragraph; \up and a number of points to move the element up; and \do and a number of points to move the element down. For example, Sales{ EQ\s\do3 (last year) } displays as Sales_last year_.

THE \X SWITCH   You can add a box around an element by putting it in parentheses preceded by \x. If you want to specify the sides of the box you are drawing, insert one of the following between the \x and the element in parentheses: \to to draw the line that is the top of the box; \bo to draw the line that is the bottom of the box; \le to draw the line that is the left side of the box; or \ri to draw the line that is the right side of the box.

You can include a series of the switches detailed above and nest them to create the equation you want. For example, the field

{EQ \r(3,\f(81,16))

returns this equation:

$$\sqrt[3]{\frac{81}{16}}$$

FILENAME

See "INFO" in this section.

FILESIZE

See "INFO" and Bytes under "DOCPROPERTY" in this section.

FILLIN

The {FILLIN} field prompts the user to enter text that is inserted as the field's result. See "Mail Merge" for more information.

GOTOBUTTON

The {GOTOBUTTON} field displays text that, when double-clicked, moves to another location. Macros and interactive documents use this field to quickly move to another location. You can also select a {GOTOBUTTON} field by moving the insertion point to the text to be moved and pressing ALT+SHIFT+F9. This field takes the format

{GOTOBUTTON *destination DisplayText*}

where destination is the location you want to go to when you select the field. This destination can be anything you would specify after selecting Edit | Go To or pressing F5, such as a bookmark or page number. *DisplayText* is either the text or graphic to appear as the field. DisplayText can use another field such as {bookmark} or {INCLUDEPICTURE} when you want to put the contents of the bookmark or picture on the button.

A document using this feature might look like this:

Click the text for the information you want to see

Sales Report **Production Report** **Statements**

Clicking any of the phrases, such as Production Report, quickly moves you to the described location in the document.

IF

The {IF} field compares two values. The result of the comparison determines which of the two values is displayed in the document. See "Mail Merge" for more information on how to use the field with merges. You can also use it for other reasons. The format is

{IF *expression operator expression* "*TrueText*" "*FalseText*"}

where *expression* is what is being compared. This can be text, numbers, or a bookmark. The operator is the type of comparison being made (see the table of operators just below). "*TrueText*" is the field's result if the comparison is true. "*FalseText*" is the field's result if the comparison is false. As an example, the field code {If {Priority} = 1 "Important!" ""} looks at the value stored in the bookmark Priority. If it equals 1, this field code returns Important! Otherwise, it returns nothing.

Operator	Purpose
=	Equals
>	Greater than
<	Lesser than
>=	Equal to or greater than
<=	Equal to or lesser than
<>	Not equal to

INCLUDEPICTURE

The {INCLUDEPICTURE} field inserts a graphic image from another document into the document. You can let Word insert this field for you when you use the Insert | Picture command and select the Link to File check box. You will only see this field code if you display field codes in the document. This field takes the format

{INCLUDEPICTURE *filename*}

where *filename* is the name of the graphic that you want to insert.

After the filename, you can include a \c and the graphics converter you want Word to use. You can also include \d when you do not want the image stored within the document. If field results display as Error! instead of the picture, check that you have used the correct document name and that the graphics converter Word uses for the file is correct and installed.

INCLUDETEXT

The {INCLUDETEXT} field inserts text from another document into the document containing the field. This field's results will also include any graphics from the source document. You can insert either the entire document, or just the contents of a bookmark. This field uses the format

>   {INCLUDETEXT *filename* [*bookmark*] *switches*}

where *filename* is the name of the document to insert, and *bookmark* is the section of the document you want to insert. If you do not use a bookmark name, Word inserts the entire document as the field's results.

Use the \c switch with the converter you want Word to use to bring the inserted document into the current document.

Use the \! switch to limit the updating of fields within the text that this field brings from another location. When you use this switch, the fields that are within the text inserted by the {INCLUDETEXT}, {*bookmark*}, and {REF} fields are not updated until the document containing the original text updates them. Without the \! switch, fields that are part of the text inserted by the {INCLUDETEXT}, {bookmark}, or {REF} field are updated when you print that part of the document.

>   **TIP:**   *You can take changes that you have made in the field results of an {INCLUDETEXT} field and apply them to the source document. Either press CTRL+SHIFT+F7, or select Tools | Macro and select Word Commands from Macros Available in, then select UpdateSource in Macro Name, then select OK.*

INDEX

The {INDEX} field indicates where Word will put an index created from index entry fields ({XE}) in the document. For further description of creating an index, see "Index."

INFO

The {INFO} field inserts data from the Properties dialog box into your document. This field returns a subset of a document's properties. Use {INFO} in place of {DOCPROPERTY} when you want to change one of the document's properties. This field takes the format

>   {[INFO] *InfoType* ["*NewValue*"]}

INFO is optional, because the *InfoType* value is what Word actually needs in order to know the information you want the field replaced with.

InfoType is the kind of summary information that you want inserted, such as Author, Comments, CreateDate, EditTime, FileName, FileSize, Keywords, LastSavedBy, NumChars, NumPages, NumWords, PrintDate, RevNum, SaveDate,

Subject, Template, and Title. Note that these are also separate fields as well. These are shown in the Properties dialog box. Some of them can be set by you; others are set by Word.

NewValue, which should be enclosed in quotes if it is text, is the information you want copied back into the Properties dialog box. When you include *NewValue* as part of the INFO or one of the information type fields, the field both replaces the entry and displays the new entry. You can use *NewValue* for the Author, Comments, Keywords, Subject, and Title fields; other information type fields will ignore any entry for *NewValue*.

KEYWORDS

See "DOCPROPERTY" and "INFO" in this section.

LASTSAVEDBY

See "DOCPROPERTY" and "INFO" in this section.

LINK

The {LINK} field creates a link with a document created by another application. See "Object Linking and Embedding" in this chapter for more information.

MACROBUTTON

The {MACROBUTTON} field displays text that, when selected, starts a macro. For a full explanation of how this field works, see "Macros."

MERGEFIELD

The {MERGEFIELD} field inserts a field from a data document into the main document in a merge. See "Mail Merge."

MERGEREC

The {MERGEREC} field inserts the number of the current merge record. See "Mail Merge."

MERGESEQ

The {MERGESEQ} field inserts the number of the current merge record according to its order within the records merged. See "Mail Merge."

NEXT

The {NEXT} field moves the mail-merge process to the next record. See "Mail Merge."

NEXTIF

The {NEXTIF} field moves the mail-merge process to the next record, depending on a condition. See "Mail Merge."

NOTEREF

The {NOTEREF} field returns the footnote or endnote number of a footnote or endnote in the document. See "Footnotes and Endnotes."

NUMCHAR

See "INFO" and Characters under "DOCPROPERTY" in this section.

NUMPAGES

See "INFO" and Pages under "DOCPROPERTY" in this section.

NUMWORDS

See "INFO" and Words under "DOCPROPERTY" in this section.

PAGE

The {PAGE} field inserts the page number for the page containing the field. You can use the format switch (*) to control how the page number appears, as described in "Other Options" later in this section. In addition to inserting this field yourself, you can insert it using the Insert | Page Numbers command. See "Page Numbers" for an explanation of adding the current page number to a document.

PAGEREF

The {PAGEREF} field inserts the page number where a bookmark is located. You can use this field to create cross-references. The field code takes the format

    {PAGEREF *bookmark*}

where *bookmark* is the name of the bookmark being referenced. You can use the number picture switch (\#) or format switch (*) to control how the page number appears, as described in "Other Options" later in this section. Most of the time, you have this field in your document because you used the Insert | Cross-reference command and Word created this field for you.

PRINT

The {PRINT} field sends printer instructions to your printer. This field takes the format

    {PRINT "*PrinterInstructions*"}

where *PrinterInstructions* are the printer instructions. These instructions vary by printer, so you must use your printer's manuals to learn the code you want to use. This field works well with PostScript printers and Hewlett-Packard LaserJet Series II or III. Other printers may not be able to use this field.

PRINTDATE
See "INFO" and LastPrinted under "DOCPROPERTY" in this section.

PRIVATE
Word creates this field for you when you add a document in another format into Word for Windows. This field contains the information Word needs to convert it back to its previous format. Do not change this field.

QUOTE
The {QUOTE} field inserts text. This field interprets the text as a possible code, rather than as what appears when you type. For example, entries not in quotes are assumed to be code numbers for the ANSI character set or to be part of a hexadecimal value when preceded by 0x. The format for this field is {QUOTE *LiteralText*}. For example, the field code

{QUOTE Word" "for" "Windows 153}

produces the result

Word for Windows™

Word interprets the 153 as an ANSI code for ™.

RD
The {RD} field indicates a document to be inserted as part of the current document for the purpose of generating index entries, tables of contents, and tables of authorities. After RD is the name of the document to include. This field does not display any result, but rather causes the indexes, tables of contents, or tables of authorities to include entries from the named document. You use this field to combine several documents into one for index entries, tables of contents, and tables of authorities; see also "Master Documents."

REF
The {REF} field returns a reference to another location in the document. Word will add this field for you when you create certain types of cross-references (see "Cross-References"). See "Bookmarks" in this section for how this field appears and its switches.

REVNUM
See "INFO" and RevisionNumber under "DOCPROPERTY" in this section.

F

SAVEDATE

See "INFO" and LastSaved under "DOCPROPERTY" in this section.

SECTION

The {SECTION} field inserts the section number where the field is located.

SECTIONPAGES

The {SECTIONPAGES} field inserts the total number of pages in the section where the field is located.

SEQ

Use the {SEQ} field to number items or sections of text in your document. You can create sets of items, such as graphics, photographs, and tables, and track the correct number for each item in each set. You can also use this field to automatically number sections or chapters in your document, as well as create cross-references to items or objects numbered using this field.

This field takes the format

{SEQ *identifier* [*bookmark*]}

where *identifier* is the name you provide for the set of items you are sequencing. For example, in a document using the {SEQ} field to number chapters, graphics, and tables, you might use chapter, figs, and table for the identifiers. In this example, the first time you enter {SEQ figs}, the field result would be 1, representing the first figure. The second {SEQ figs} code would show a field result of 2, and so on throughout the document. If you inserted {SEQ chapter} between these two {SEQ figs} field codes, its field result would be 1, since it would be the first SEQ field code for the chapter sequence.

When you include a bookmark in a SEQ field, the field's result is the sequence number of the item marked by the bookmark. For example, in a table with the bookmark name of Sales_Table, the field {SEQ table Sales_Table} returns the number of the table at Sales_Table, rather than the next number in the table sequence.

Word offers several switches that you can use to further customize the text inserted using the {SEQ} field:

- When you use the \c switch, Word does not use the next number in the sequence for this field's result. Instead, the field result is the current sequence number, which is the last one that appeared in your document.

- When you use the \h switch, Word hides the field result of the {SEQ} field. Use this switch to advance the sequence list without displaying the incremented sequence number. You can refer to that item in the list in a cross-reference.

- When you use the \n switch, Word proceeds to the next number in the sequence. This is the default setting when you do not use any switches.

- When you use the \r switch, you are telling Word to restart the numbering in that specific sequence list, starting with the number after the \r. For example, if you enter {SEQ figs \r 14}, the field result is 14. The {SEQ} fields after this one that use the same identifier would increment normally, starting at this number.

SET

The {SET} field assigns a bookmark to defined text. Any field that references that bookmark will insert or use that text. The format is

   {SET *bookmark* "*text*"}

where *bookmark* is the name of the bookmark assigned to the text, and *text* is the text marked by the bookmark.

For example, in a rental contract, when you need an address repeated several times, enter the field

   {SET address "2006 Waterbury Rd. #3"}

Each time a field references the address bookmark, Word will insert 2006 Waterbury Rd. #3. This field is useful in forms and in mail merges.

SKIPIF

The {SKIPIF} field makes Word skip an item if a particular condition is TRUE. This field is often used in mail merges. See "Mail Merge."

STYLEREF

The {STYLEREF} field inserts text from the previous paragraph that uses a defined style. This field does not work with character format styles. This field takes the format

   {STYLEREF "*StyleIdentifier*" [*switches*]}

where *StyleIdentifier* is the name of the style you are looking for, already assigned to text within the document.

You can use the \l switch to find the last paragraph on the current page using the specified style, even if it comes after the field. You can also use the \n switch when you want the copy of the paragraph that this field returns to include the paragraph numbering from the original paragraph.

F

SUBJECT

See "DOCPROPERTY" and "INFO" in this section

SYMBOL

The {SYMBOL} field inserts a symbol or a string of characters. The format of this field is

{SYMBOL *CharNum* [*switches*]}

where *CharNum* is the decimal or hexadecimal code for the symbol you want to insert. You can define the symbol by specifying the ANSI code using decimal or hexadecimal numbers, or you can type a character. After *CharNum*, you can use these switches:

- The \f switch followed by a font name sets the font the symbol uses, which can change the characters available.

- The \s switch sets the size of the symbol that the field inserts. After \s is the number of points for the height of the character.

- You can use the \h switch to set the line height; after the \h is the number of points to set the height.

For example,

{SYMBOL 255 \f "Wingdings" \s24}

creates a small Windows logo that is 1/3-inch high. You can also change the font, size, and line height attributes for this symbol by selecting only the field code or its result and applying formatting with the Word menu commands, shortcuts, or toolbars. This field offers an alternative to using the Insert | Symbol command to add unusual symbols to a document. See "Special Characters" for more information.

TA

The {TA} field represents an entry to appear in a table of authorities. See "Table of Authorities" for instructions.

TC

The {TC} field represents an entry to appear in the table of contents. See "Table of Contents and Figures" for instructions.

TEMPLATE

See "DOCPROPERTY" and "INFO" in this section.

TIME

The {TIME} field inserts the current time (or the time when the field was last updated). You can use the date-time picture switch described under "Other Options" in this section to control the time's format. As a default, Word uses the default Windows time format. You can insert this information in a variety of ways other than by using this field; see "Date and Time" for more information.

TITLE

See "DOCPROPERTY" and "INFO" in this section.

TOA

The {TOA} field is replaced by a table of authorities using entries defined in other locations in the document. See "Table of Authorities" for instructions.

TOC

The {TOC} field is replaced by a table of contents that references the headings and other table of contents entries in the document. See "Table of Contents and Figures" for instructions.

USERADDRESS

The {USERADDRESS} field inserts the user address that appears under Mailing Address in the User Info options for the Tools | Options command. You can include text after USERADDRESS when you want something different to appear as the user address without changing the setting for the user address set with the Tools | Options command.

USERINITIALS

The {USERINITIALS} field inserts the user initials that appear under Initials in the User Info options for the Tools | Options command. You can include text after USERINITIALS when you want something different to appear as the user initials without changing the setting for the user initials set with the Tools | Options command.

USERNAME

The {USERNAME} field inserts the user name that appears under Name in the User Info options for the Tools | Options command. You can include text after USERNAME when you want something different to appear as the user name without changing the setting for the user name set with the Tools | Options command.

XE

The {XE} field marks entries to appear in an index. See "Index" for more information about creating index entries.

F

Other Options

Word has three general switches that can be used with most fields, described in the sections that follow.

Format Switch: *

You can use the * switch to set the format of a field result. You can designate character case, numeric format, and character formatting.

To set the case of the field's result when it is text, enter one of the following after the switch: *upper* to cause the entire field result to appear in uppercase, or *lower* for lowercase letters; *firstcap* to capitalize the first letter in the first word and leave the rest of the field in lowercase; or *caps* to capitalize the first letter in each word and leave the other letters in lowercase. Here are examples:

Field Entry	Result
{subject *upper}	SHOWS THE DIFFERENT FORMATTING FOR FIELD RESULTS
{subject *lower}	shows the different formatting for field results
{subject *firstcap}	Shows the different formatting for field results
{subject *caps}	Shows The Different Formatting For Field Results

You can also control how a number is presented. Using the * format switch, you can designate arabic numbers, cardinal or ordinal numbers, roman numbers, alphabetic numbers, hexadecimal numbers, or numbers as text. Examples of these settings are shown here:

Field Code Entry	Result
{ NUMPAGES * Arabic * MERGEFORMAT }	1
{ NUMPAGES * Ordinal * MERGEFORMAT }	1st
{ NUMPAGES * Roman * MERGEFORMAT }	I
{ NUMPAGES * Alphabetic * MERGEFORMAT }	A
{ NUMPAGES * Cardtext * MERGEFORMAT }	one
{ NUMPAGES * Ordtext * MERGEFORMAT }	first
{ NUMPAGES * Hex * MERGEFORMAT }	1
{ NUMPAGES * Dollartext * MERGEFORMAT }	one and 00/100

You can set character formatting using the * switch. The field switch * charformat causes the entire field result to use the character formatting applied to the first character after the {. For example, if you enter {Filename * charformat} in the document named Report, the field result is *Report*.

The field switch * mergeformat tells Word to combine new and old formats when you change or update the field. Any formatting applied to the prior field result will apply to an updated field result. If there is no previous result to the field, Word uses the format of the first character after the { to format the result.

For example, suppose you enter a {SUMMARY} field to display the document summary. If you enter {SUMMARY * charformat} and you make the first sentence boldface and then update the result, the entire summary will be in boldface. If you enter {SUMMARY * mergeformat}, only the first sentence is in bold and the rest is not. If you do not use either * charformat or * mergeformat, the formatting you apply to the field or field's result disappears the next time the field is updated.

Date-Time Picture Switch: \@

The \@ switch controls how fields that show a date or a time display their result. You use this switch to create a picture that you want the field result to match. This picture is composed of the elements shown in Table 4-7. Most fields that add dates and times display options to select one of several popular date and time formats. As an example, you can have the field code {SAVEDATE \@ "dddd', 'MMMM' 'dd', 'yyyy"} and if the document is last saved on 05/05/96, this field displays the result Thursday, May 5, 1996. The text in the single quotes tells Word to include the spaces and commas so Word knows it is not a code in the date and time format.

Do not include spaces in your date-time picture. If you want spaces between the date-time picture elements, you must enclose them in quotation marks as shown in the example above. Then you can include spaces or other characters in your date-time picture, and they will appear in the field results.

You can include a sequence value (such as the results of the {SEQ} field) in your date-time picture. To do this, enclose the identifier name in accents grave (`).

> **TIP:** *You can assign formats to the individual parts of a date, time, or number by formatting the characters in the date-time picture switch or number picture switch. Since the characters in the pictures have a one-to-one correspondence with the characters in the field result, Word matches the field result formatting with the formatting assigned to individual characters in the pictures.*

Number Picture Switch: \#

Use the \# switch to create a number picture that sets the appearance of the field's result when it is a number. Following the \# is a series of characters in quotes that represent the character positions in the field's result. This picture is composed of the elements shown in Table 4-8.

For example, using the switch \# "#,##0.00" for a field that returns 1642.6 will cause the field result to be displayed as 1,642.60.

Table 4-8 indicates that for the decimal point and thousands separator, the period and the comma are used. The characters for these two purposes are set by the

Character	Effect
m	Minutes without leading zeros
mm	Minutes with leading zeros
h	Hour of 12-hour clock without leading zeros
hh	Hour of 12-hour clock with leading zeros
H	Hour of 24-hour clock without leading zeros
HH	Hour of 24-hour clock with leading zeros
d	Day number
dd	Day number with leading zero for single-digit days
ddd	Three-letter abbreviation for day name
dddd	Day name
M	Month number
MM	Month number with leading zero for single-digit months
MMM	Three-letter abbreviation of month name
MMMM	Month name
yy	Last two digits of year
yyyy	Year number
AM/PM	Uppercase AM and PM indicate morning and afternoon hours
am/pm	Lowercase am and pm indicate morning and afternoon hours
A/P	Uppercase A and P indicate morning and afternoon hours
a/p	Lowercase a and p indicate morning and afternoon hours

Table 4-7.   *Date-Time Picture Elements*

Windows Control Panel. After the decimal point, you will want to use the # or 0 character to indicate how many digits you want after the decimal point.

You can also have more than one format after \# to tell Word to format positive numbers and negative numbers differently. Two formats separated with a semicolon tell Word that the first format applies to positive numbers and the second one applies to negative numbers. Three formats separated with a semicolon tell Word that the first format applies to positive numbers, the second one applies to negative numbers, and the third one applies to zero. For example,

```
\# "#,###;(#,###);zero"
```

Character	Effect
0	Displays the number in that place using 0 if a digit is not present
#	Leaves the number in that place blank if not needed
x	Truncates or rounds the digits on each side of the decimal point. When x is to left of decimal point, digits to left of x are truncated. When x is to right of decimal point, digits to right of x decide whether digit in x's position is rounded up or down, and the extra digits do not appear
.	Represents the decimal point
,	Represents the thousands separator
+	Displays + in front of positive numbers and – in front of negative ones
–	Displays = in front of negative numbers and nothing in front of positive ones

Table 4-8. *Numeric Picture Elements*

displays positive numbers with a comma separating the thousands and no digits after the decimal point, negative numbers the same way except they are enclosed in parentheses, and zeros as the text "zero".

You can include additional text in your number picture, such as the zero shown in the above example. The dollar sign, or other appropriate characters, can be included in a number picture and will be used in the field results. If you want to include spaces or other characters and you don't know if Word will understand that they are part of the number format, put the format in quotes. When you want to specify that text appears in the field result exactly as it appears in the number format, enclose it in accents grave (`). You will also use accents grave to enclose an identifier name used with a {SEQ} field used to produce the value of one of the identified sequences you are using in your document.

Figures

See "Graphics."

File Formats

Most applications use their own formats or document types, for storing their data. Since applications are designed to accomplish different tasks, they need to store your data in specific formats. Also, application developers have designed individual formats to handle the data their applications use.

Word can share data with many popular applications because it can read the various document types. When Word sees that a document you open is not in Word's own document type, it converts the file to Word's type. When you save a document in Word, the Save as Type drop-down list box offers you a choice of file types; your selection determines the format for saving your file. Word can also use graphics document types, so you can put pictures in your documents. When you add the picture, Word converts it from one of many popular graphics image types into Word's own type for graphics.

Related Topics

Graphics
Opening Documents
Saving Documents

File Location Options

See "Document Location Options."

File Management

See "Document Management."

File|Add Routing Slip

See "Electronic Mail."

File|Close

See "Closing Documents."

File|Exit

See "Exiting Word."

File|List of Last Open Files

See "Opening Documents."

File|New

See "New Document."

File|Open

See "Opening Documents."

File|Page Setup

This command displays a dialog box with four page tabs that change settings on how the document is laid out on a page. These options are further described under "Margins," "Page Size and Orientation," "Sections," and "Paper Source."

File|Post to Exchange Folder

See "Electronic Mail."

File|Print

See "Printing."

File|Print Preview

See "Viewing Documents."

File|Print Setup

See "Printing."

File|Properties

See "Document Properties."

File|Save

See "Saving Documents."

File|Save All

See "Saving Documents."

File|Save As

See "Saving Documents."

File|Templates

See "Templates."

FILENAME Field

The FILENAME field displays the current document's name. Look at the INFO field under "Fields" for more information.

Filenames

See "Saving Documents."

Files

Windows 95 refers to files as documents, so features for working with files are described under topics such as "Document Management," "Document Properties," and "Opening Documents."

Fillin Fields

See "Fields."

Filling in Text and Graphics

See "Borders and Shading" and "Highlighting."

Filtering

See "Mail Merge" for information on filter records that are included in the mail merge process; see "Sorting" to filter the data that Word sorts. You can also filter which documents you look at as described under "Document Management."

Find and Replace

Use the Find feature to locate specific instances of text or formatting in your document. Use the Replace feature to locate specific text or formatting and replace it with other text or formatting.

Procedures

Using Word's Find or Replace feature, you can: search for text, including special characters; search for text with certain formatting applied; search for certain formatting without specifying text. When you search for text with formatting, you define both the text and the formatting that you want to find, and Word finds only instances of that text with that formatting.

With the Replace feature, you can also specify text or formatting to replace the text or formatting that you find. You specify text, formatting, or both, to replace the text, formatting, or both that you find. If you find text and replace it with formatting, the text is not deleted; the formats you specify are applied to it.

F

Finding Text or Formatting

1. Select <u>E</u>dit | <u>F</u>ind or press CTRL+F to open the Find dialog box (Figure 4-19).

NOTE: *If you have used Find during the current session, the dialog box displays your old settings. You have to delete them before entering new ones.*

2. Specify the text or formatting you want to find, using the options described under "Options" in this section.

3. Select the direction in which you want Word to search through the document. Choose from All, Up, or Down in the <u>S</u>earch drop-down list box. Up or Down starts from the insertion point's position. The All option searches the entire document, starting from the insertion point and returning to the top of the document if necessary.

4. Set any other criteria you want, as described in "Options."

5. Select <u>F</u>ind Next to locate the first occurrence of the specified text or formatting. Word highlights the first occurrence, but the Find dialog box does not close.

6. You can continue searching in two ways. Select <u>F</u>ind Next again; or select Close, closing the Find dialog box, and then press SHIFT+F4. This key combination repeats the last Find command, and Word finds the next occurrence of the search text or formatting.

Figure 4-19. *Find dialog box*

Replacing Text or Formatting

1. Select Edit | Replace or press CTRL+H to open the Replace dialog box. (If you are starting from the Find dialog box, you can switch to the Replace dialog box by selecting the Replace button; you cannot then switch back to the Find dialog box.) The Replace dialog box looks just like the Find dialog box in Figure 4-19, except that you can now make an entry for the replacement.

NOTE: *If you have used the Replace feature during the current Word session, your old settings still appear in the dialog box. You have to delete these settings before entering new ones.*

2. Specify the text or formatting you want to replace, using the options described under "Options" in this section.

3. Specify the replacement text or formatting. Enter the text after Replace With, and use the buttons along the bottom of the dialog box to select the formatting.

4. Select Find Next to locate the first occurrence of the text or formatting. Word highlights the first occurrence, and the Replace dialog box remains open. Select Replace to replace that occurrence with the substitute text or formatting you specified. Word finds the next occurrence of the text to find so you can continue selecting Replace to make the next replacement or Find Next to skip the current occurrence and find the next one. To replace all occurrences of the search text or formatting, select Replace All, and Word moves through the

document and does all the replacements at once, leaving the Replace dialog box open.

5. Select Close to close the Replace dialog box.

Options

Word has many options in the Find/Replace dialog box. These options help you to only find the text and/or formatting you want without having to look at more of the document than intended.

Find What/Replace With

In Find What, enter the text you want to locate, and in Replace With enter any text you want to use as a replacement. (If you want to find or replace formatting instead of or as well as text, look at the "Format" section just below.) You can enter up to 255 characters in both Find What and Replace With. Below these boxes will be descriptions of any formatting you have designated for the text you have entered there. You can use the shortcut keys to set character and paragraph formatting for the text you enter in these boxes. This formatting appears below the text boxes as if you used other options in the dialog box to set the formatting you want to find or replace. If you want to use one of the last four entries you searched for, open the drop-down list box and select the one you want from the list.

When you search for formatting only without entering any text for Find What, Word finds any text with the specified combination of formats. If you do enter text for Find What and then specify formats to find, Word only finds instances of the formatting when it is applied to the specified text; Word will not find the formatting when it is applied to other text. If you do not specify a format for Word to find but you do enter text in Find What, Word finds the specified text regardless of its format.

SEARCHING FOR AND REPLACING SPECIAL CHARACTERS   Besides entering the exact characters you want to find, you can enter other types of characters in the Find What and Replace With boxes. You can search for and replace special characters such as paragraph markers, tabs, and hard page returns. In your entry for Find What or Replace With, enter your choice of the character codes shown in Table 4-9. Most of the codes require that the characters be entered using the upper or lowercase characters you see in Table 4-9. You can add these special characters by typing them into the Find What or Replace With text box or by selecting the Special button and the description of the special character. Also, notice how some special characters can only be used in the text to search for or in its replacement.

Find Whole Words Only

Select the Find Whole Words Only check box when you want to find only occurrences of the complete word—nothing more and nothing less—that you entered in the Find What. With this option enabled, Word does not find instances of the Find What text

Characters to Enter	Matches
^?	Any character in the Find What text box only
^#	Any digit (0-9) in the Find What text box only
^$	Any letter (A-Z, a-z) in the Find What text box only
^&	Contents of the Find What text box in the Replace With text box only
^a	Annotation mark in the Find What text box only
^b	Section break in the Find What text box only
^c	Clipboard contents in the Replace With text box only
^d	Any field in the Find What text box only
^e	Endnote mark in the Find What text box only
^f	Footnote mark in the Find What text box only
^g	Graphic in the Find What text box only
^l	End-of-line character created by SHIFT+ENTER
^m	Manual page break created by CTRL+ENTER
^n	Column break
^p	Paragraph mark
^s	Nonbreaking space
^t	Tab character
^w	White spaces (nonbreaking spaces; paragraph, section, and hard page breaks; tab, end-of-line, and end-of-cell characters)
^-	Optional hyphens
^~	Nonbreaking hyphens
^	Caret
^+	Em dash
^=	En dash
^0nnn	ANSI character, where nnn is ANSI character code
^nnn	ASCII character, where nnn is ASCII character code

Table 4-9. *Entries to Find Special Characters*

that are part of another word. For example, if you type the word **real** after Find What and then turn on Find Whole Words Only, Word finds every instance of the word *real* in your document, but skips words like really, arboreal, and surreal.

Match Case

Select the Match Case check box when you want to find only text whose case exactly matches what you have entered in Find What. With this option enabled, Word only finds instances of the word with the same pattern of capitalization as the one you entered. For example, if you enter **Pre-Raphaelite** for the Find What and then turn on Match Case, Word will find Pre-Raphaelite but not *pre-raphaelite, Pre-raphaelite,* or *pre-Raphaelite.*

Sounds Like

Select the Sounds Like check box if you want Word to find text that sounds like your entry in the Find What box. For example, if you turn on Sounds Like and enter **ther** in Find What, Word will find *their, there,* and *they're.* Use this technique when you want to find a word and you're not sure how it is spelled.

Find All Word Forms

If you are looking for a word like choose, you may also want to find this word as it appears in other grammatical forms. If you select the Find All Word Forms check box, Word looks for the word and its variations. For example, when you look for *choose* with this check box selected, Word also locates *chooses, choosing,* and *chosen.*

Use Pattern Matching

Word can use *pattern matching* to look for text that has the same pattern as the pattern you enter in the Find What box. To use pattern matching, select its check box, then enter the patterns in the Find What and Replace with boxes.

Pattern matching has even more choices for selecting the types of characters you are looking for. These additional choices are listed in Table 4-10. They also appear when you select the Special button to add them to the Find What or Replace With boxes.

No Formatting

To clear any of the formatting settings you have made for Find What or Replace With entries, select No Formatting. In the Replace dialog box, when you select this button, you only clear either the formatting for the text to find or its replacement—depending on the last text box or drop-down box you used. You can see which formatting this button will clear by looking at the text that appears to the left of this button.

Format

The Format option selects the formatting you want to find or replace. Once you select the formatting, it appears beneath Find What or Replace With, depending on which was active when you selected Format. You can see where the formatting applies by looking at the text that appears above and to the left of the No Formatting, Format, and Special buttons.

Characters to Enter	Effect
?	Matches any character in that position
*	Matches zero or more characters in that position
[x-y]	Matches any character in that position in the range x to y, where x to y are characters
[...]	Matches any character in the brackets, so [abc] matches the character a, b, or c
[!...]	Matches any character that does not appear in the brackets, so [!abc] matches any character except a, b, or c
[!x-y]	Matches any character that is not in the range from x to y, so [!a-c] matches any character except a, b, or c
{n}	Matches n occurrences of the previous character, so Michel{2}e matches *Michelle* but not *Michele*
{n,}	Matches n or more occurrences of the previous character so Michel{1}e matches *Michelle* and *Michele*
{n,m}	Matches between n and m occurrences of the previous character, so 50{1,3} matches *50*, *500*, and *5000* but not *50000*
@	Matches one or more occurrences of the previous character, so 50@ matches *50*, *50000*, and *5000000*
<(*characters*)	Matches words that start with *characters*, as in <cab to match *cab*, *cable*, and *cabinet*
>(*characters*)	Matches words that end with *characters*, as in tion > to match *action* and *elocution*
\	Matches the next character as it appears, so \@ matches @
( )	Groups the entries in the parentheses so they are evaluated before other parts of the expression in the Find What or Replace With boxes or groups the entry in the Find What box so you can rearrange the entry using /n
/n	Selects an expression in the Find What box, such as using **(time) (managing)** and **/2 /1** in the Replace With box to change time managing into managing time

Table 4-10. *Special Entries for Pattern Matching*

Once you select Format, you can choose from Font, Paragraph, Tabs, Border, Language, Frame, Style, or Highlight. All but the last two display dialog boxes that look and behave just like the dialog boxes you use when you are setting the font, paragraph formatting, and language of text. The only difference you will notice is that check boxes are grayed out, and list boxes do not show their selections. Only the formatting selections you make are remembered as formatting you want to find or replace. For example, you can select Format, Font, and 10 for Size to find any text 10 points high, regardless of the font. The Find Style dialog box only has a list box containing the available styles and a description of the highlighted style to select the style to find. Highlight adds Highlight to the formatting you want to find without showing a dialog box.

TIP: You can use the toolbars and keyboard shortcuts described in "Shortcut Keys" to apply formatting to entries in the Find What and Replace With boxes. For example, while the Find and Replace dialog boxes are displayed, choosing a font from the Formatting toolbar adds that font to the format you are finding or replacing, as if you had selected Format and Font. You can use the Formatting toolbar buttons for style, font, font size, bold, underline, italic, and paragraph alignment, and their keyboard shortcuts, as well as keyboard shortcuts for all caps, subscript, superscript, underline, double-underline, hidden, small caps, and for removing character formatting. Word also accepts keyboard shortcuts for single-, double-, and 1 1/2 spacing, and for removing paragraph formatting.

F

Hints

Use Word to find and replace all sorts of formatting and text. This feature can easily fix your most commonly made mistakes. You can also have Word replace text with graphics to quickly add frequently used graphics to a document.

Use Find and Replace to Fix Common Mistakes

If you frequently make the same mistakes, you can use Word's find and replace tools to fix them. For example, if you use the wrong homonym, you can use Word to find the ones you frequently misuse and select the ones you want Word to replace. The box "Problem Homonyms to Watch For" lists the most commonly misused homonyms.

Problem Homonyms to Watch For

Homonyms are words that sound the same but have a different spelling and meaning. Even when you know the correct use for each word in a homonym group, your brain can play tricks as you are hurrying to complete an important document. Word's spell checker will not find these errors in usage as long as each one is correctly spelled. Word's grammar checker will find some but not all of them. Even when grammar checker does find one of these errors, Word may think it is a grammatical error for a reason other than an incorrect homonym. In addition to using Word's tools, you will need to proof your documents carefully to find homonym errors; consider using the Search function, too, if you have a recurring problem with one or two.

Here are ten homonym groups that frequently cause problems.

by, buy	I walk *by* his house each day.
	I need to stop at the store to *buy* milk.
chord, cord	If you play the first *chord* of the song, I will try to guess the tune.
	Do you have a piece of *cord* with which to tie the package?
cue, queue	Without the *cue* card, she couldn't remember her lines.
	Fans began to *queue* up hours before the ticket booths opened.
feat, feet	It was a *feat* of daring to jump from the cliff.
	How many *feet* are in one yard?
flair, flare	She has a *flair* for decorating.
	The police helped light a *flare* to mark the accident.
in, inn	John is *in* the dining room.
	We would like to stay at a cozy *inn* this weekend.
its, it's	The group wants to renew *its* vendor's license.
	It's too late to go to the movies.
led, lead	He *led* the horse to water.
	Lead poisoning can come from exposure to some paint.
their, there, they're	*Their* luggage was lost.
	There are five houses on the street.
	They're not here yet.
to, too, two	He went *to* the meeting.
	She asked for a raise, *too*.
	The *two* boys went to the office picnic.
whole, hole	I can't believe he ate the *whole* pie.
	You have a *hole* in your glove.

Word can also find extraneous phrases. As you look over documents you have written, you may find that you have unnecessarily used certain phrases, or overused others. The box "Rules for Correcting Wordiness and Redundancy" lists some common phrases that can be shortened to clarify your writing.

Undoing Replacements

Before doing extensive replacements, save your document. If you replace text or formatting incorrectly, you can always close the window without saving, open the unchanged copy of your document, and try again.

Rules for Correcting Wordiness and Redundancy

When you are working against a tight deadline, you might find it difficult to take sufficient time rewriting your initial draft. When you are short on time, sometimes you miss opportunities to remove unnecessary words and redundant phrases. Each of us has a personal set of problem phrases that can appear in our writing; following are some typical examples. Once you identify the phrases that cause you problems, you can use Word's search and replace features to eliminate them from your writing.

Problem	Correction
He plans to call at 3:00 P.M. *in the afternoon.*	He plans to call at 3:00 P.M.
Always call 911 *in the event of* an emergency.	Always call 911 if there is an emergency.
We would like *to call your attention* to our special 50%-off sale.	We would like to notify you of our special 50%-off sale.
A salad *can be used for* a quick meal.	A salad is a quick meal.
She *is a woman who* is always on time.	She is always on time. *or* She is always punctual.
We need to discuss wages, benefits, retention rates, *and so forth.*	We need to discuss wages, benefits, and retention rates.
Silicon *can be used for* repairing the window track.	Silicon can repair the window track.
Pollution *is a topic that* interests me.	Pollution interests me.
She proceeded down the aisle *in a quiet manner.*	She proceeded quietly down the aisle.
John *is able to* go to school.	John can go to school.

TIP: *You can still use Undo to remove the effect of one of your replacements. When you use Undo, it only affects one choice at a time. Using Undo after* <u>R</u>*eplace only restores one replacement at a time while using Undo after Replace* <u>A</u>*ll affects all of the replacements made.*

Replacing Text with Graphics

You may have a small piece of clip art, such as an icon, that you plan to use frequently in your document. Rather than inserting the art repeatedly as you create your

F

document, enter some special text instead as a placeholder, such as Art1. After you are finished editing, you can replace the placeholder with the art automatically. First, copy the art to the Clipboard. Then open the Replace dialog box, and enter the placeholder text in the Find What box, and type ^c for Replace With. Then select Replace or Replace All. Word replaces placeholder text with the graphic from the Clipboard. Of course, if you want to have the change from text to graphics made automatically, make the graphics an AutoCorrect entry.

Another option is to insert the graphic in the document once, and name the graphic with a bookmark. When you want the same graphic to appear in other locations, use the {bookmark} field code. (See "Fields" for more information.) Using a field instead of using Edit | Replace to insert multiple copies of the graphic makes the document size smaller; also, any edits, such as changes made with Format | Picture, apply to each appearance of the icon.

Searching from the Middle of a Document

When Word reaches the end or beginning of the document while searching, it does not stop searching. Instead, it displays a message box asking you if you want to continue searching at the beginning (if you're searching down) or end (if you're searching up) of the document. Select Yes, and Word continues until it has searched the entire document. Select No, and Word stops the find or replace operation.

Searching for Multiple Formats

When you specify a combination of formats to find, Word only locates text that has all those formats. For example, if you are searching for bold text in a double-spaced paragraph, Word will not find bold text in a paragraph with single spacing. Be careful that you do not define formatting that may not be appropriate.

Deleting Text

Here's a technique for deleting all instances of some particular text. Put the text you want to delete in the Find What box, and leave Replace With empty. Select Replace (or Replace All), and the next occurrence of the text (or all occurrences) will be deleted. Word has smart deletion, so if the text appears at the end of the sentence or has some punctuation mark, Word removes the extra space after deleting the text.

Related Topics

ASCII Text Files
ANSI Codes
Character Formats
Grammar Checking
Paragraph Formats
Spelling

Find File

See "Document Management."

Finding and Replacing Text, Formatting, and Special Characters

See "Find and Replace."

First Pages

In some documents, you may want to treat the first page differently. This includes giving the first page an odd page number (in many books, each chapter starts on an odd page so the first page is on the right side). Word has several features that you may want to employ for creating the first page of a document.

When you want the first page to start with an odd page, use Layout features, described under "Sections." When you want a specific page to start on the right side, use the Insert | Break command described under "Pagination." "Page Numbers" describes how you can designate the page number appearance, the starting page number, and whether you want the page number to appear on the first page. "Headers and Footers" tells you how to specify a different header and footer for the first page.

Floating Toolbars

See "Toolbars."

Flush Left and Flush Right

See "Alignment" and "Tabs."

Folders

You can use folders to organize the documents on your disk in a logical fashion. Folders can contain other folders as well as documents.

The sequence of folders between the drive letter and a specific document is called a *path*. Folder names in a path statement are separated by backslashes (\). For example, in C:\Word for Windows\Data\Financial Statements\1995 Statements, the document 1995 Statements is found in the Financial Statements folder, which is in the Data folder, which is in the Word for Windows folder, which is on the C drive.

You should organize your Word documents and other documents in folders to make them easier to find. For example, you could put all of your Word documents in

F

one folder, and all of your Excel documents in another folder. Alternatively, you can organize all of your documents by purpose, putting all of your personal documents, from whatever application, in one folder, all of your financial documents in a second, and all of your sales information in a third. A third option is to put shortcuts to the documents that you use every day into your Favorites Folder as described under "Favorites Folder" and organize other documents less frequently used according to application or purpose.

For more information about folders and how to create them or use them, see your Windows documentation. See "Document Location Options" for setting the folders Word uses.

Fonts

Fonts are a set of characters in a particular style. Figure 4-20 shows several fonts in use. You can set both the font and the size of that font. Windows offers you a variety of fonts that can be scaled to any size, and your printer probably offers additional fonts. You can also buy and install additional fonts to expand the available font selections on your system.

Before you can use a font in Word, you must have the font installed in Windows. Word includes several fonts that the installation program will install for you. Fonts can

Figure 4-20.   *Use different fonts to make a document look more attractive*

be enhanced with various features such as bold, italic, and underline (see "Bold," "Italics," and "Underline").

Procedures

A font can be selected to take effect as you are typing or after the text is typed. To choose the font while typing, select the font and then type the text; when you are ready, select a different font or revert to the default font. To choose a font for typed text, select the text to format and then select the font.

Selecting a Font/Font Size with the Formatting Toolbar

1. Open the Font drop-down list in the Formatting toolbar by clicking its down-arrow button or by pressing CTRL+SHIFT+F.
2. Select a font by clicking it, or by highlighting it and pressing ENTER.
3. Open the Font Size drop-down list in the Formatting toolbar by clicking its down-arrow button or by pressing CTRL+SHIFT+P.
4. Choose a font size by clicking it, by highlighting it and pressing ENTER, or by typing the size and pressing ENTER.

Selecting a Font/Font Size with the Menus

1. Select Format | Font to open the Font dialog box.
2. Select a font in the Font list box.
3. Select a font style in the Font Style list box.
4. Select a size for the font in the Size list box or type a size in this text box.
5. Select OK.

Hints

A document's normal font is set by the Normal style. To change the font for an entire document at once, modify this style. See "Styles" for more information.

Make the font's appearance fit the document. For example, Matura MT Script is inappropriate for most business correspondence, but it may be just what you need for printing invitations to a party.

Don't use too many fonts in the same document. Switching fonts frequently makes the document harder to read and distracts the reader from the content.

Font sizes measure the height of the font and are listed in points (1/72 inch). Some fonts are scalable to any size, from 1 to 1,638 points in half-point increments; others only have a limited number of sizes. The Points drop-down list box on the Formatting toolbar or in the Font dialog box shows the available point sizes. If the font is scalable,

F

you can also enter a value in this text box. You can even enter a size that is not listed, such as 11.5.

If you designate a size that does not appear in the Points drop-down list box, and the font is not scalable, then the font is displayed and printed in the closest available size of the font.

To help make font selection easier, the Font drop-down list in the Formatting toolbar shows you the fonts already in use in the document at the top of the list, as well as placing them alphabetically in their normal position in the list, as you can see here:

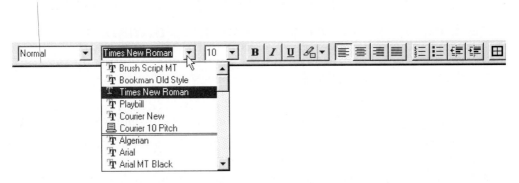

You can expand your font selection by installing soft fonts and add-on printer fonts. *Soft fonts* are installable programs that create fonts. *Printer fonts* can be cartridges or disks of fonts that you install directly to your printer. When you seek to expand your font selection, look for scalable fonts that can be enlarged or reduced to many sizes, because they add versatility. If your needs are simple, however, a few useful nonscalable fonts may suffice.

TrueType fonts have an advantage: on your screen they look just as they do when printed. The disadvantage is that printing with TrueType fonts may take longer than with other fonts, such as the fonts your printer provides. Word tells you which type of font you are selecting: TrueType fonts have double-T symbols next to them in the Font list, and printer fonts have a small printer next to them. Fonts available from other sources may have other icons. Fonts with no icons include plotter fonts, which are designed for working on plotters, and screen fonts, which are designed for displaying data on the screen.

The following key combinations are also available to change the size of text you will type or that you have selected:

Shortcut Key	Function
CTRL+SHIFT+>	Selects the next larger font size in the font size list
CTRL+SHIFT+<	Selects the next smaller font size in the font size list
CTRL+[	Decreases font size by one point
CTRL+]	Increases font size by one point

Related Topics

Character Formats
Styles

Footers

Footers are text that appears at the bottom of every page. See "Headers and Footers."

Footnotes and Endnotes

Footnotes and endnotes are references that describe the source of information in a document or provide ancillary information about an idea presented by the document. Footnotes appear at the bottom of a page or another location in your document. They provide commentary or documentation about your text. You can have both endnotes and footnotes in the same document.

F

Procedures

To effectively work with endnotes and footnotes, you must be able to create, delete, edit, and arrange them as described in the following procedures.

Creating a Note

To create a note, you must first insert a note reference mark in the text that identifies text with a related note. The second step is to enter the text of the note.

1. Position the insertion point where you want the note reference mark.

2. Select Insert | Footnote then select Footnote or Endnote to determine the type of note you are creating.

TIP: You can also quickly add a note by pressing ALT+CTRL+F or an endnote with ALT+CTRL+E.

3. If you want automatically numbered notes, select AutoNumber. Select Custom Mark and then enter your note reference mark in the text box, using up to ten characters (numbers, letters, or symbols). You can select Symbol to enter a nonkeyboard symbol. Select OK.

NOTE: When renumbering notes that are numbered automatically, Word skips notes with custom marks.

4. If you are in Normal view, Word opens the Notes pane, and you enter the note text in this pane. If you are in Page Layout view, Word moves the insertion point to where the note will print, and you enter the text there.

5. When you finish entering the note text, leave the Notes pane and return to the document:

■ In Normal view, click the Close button, press ALT+SHIFT+C, double-click the split bar, or select View | Footnotes. To return without closing the pane, click on the document or press F6.

■ In Page Layout view, either click the document or use the arrow keys to move into the document text. You can quickly return to the document location where you entered the note by pressing SHIFT+F5.

Editing a Note

In Page Layout view, move to the note text in the Notes pane and edit it. In Normal view, open the Notes pane by selecting View | Footnotes, and then edit the note.

Deleting a Note

To delete a note, delete its note reference mark in the document by selecting it and pressing DEL or BACKSPACE.

Moving a Note

To move a note, move its note reference mark using the Clipboard. Both the note reference mark and the note text are moved at the same time. (For instructions on changing where notes are printed, see "Specifying Note Locations and Numbering" in this section.)

1. Select the note reference mark for the note you want to move.

2. Cut the note reference mark to the Clipboard. You can cut to the Clipboard by selecting Edit | Cut, by clicking the Cut button on the toolbar, or by pressing CTRL+X.

3. Move the insertion point to the new location for the note.

4. Paste the note reference mark back into the document. You can paste from the Clipboard by selecting Edit | Paste, by clicking the Paste button on the toolbar, or by pressing CTRL+V.

TIP: *You can also move note references by selecting the reference then dragging and dropping it to its new location. Word handles renumbering any notes. This also works for copying notes.*

Copying a Note

To copy a note, copy the note reference mark to the Clipboard and then paste it back into your document. Both the note reference mark and the note text are copied.

1. Select the note reference mark for the note you want to copy.

2. Copy the note reference mark to the Clipboard. You can copy to the Clipboard by selecting Edit I Copy, by clicking the Copy button on the toolbar, or by pressing CTRL+C.

3. Move the insertion point to where you want the note.

4. Paste the note reference mark back into the document. You can paste from the Clipboard by selecting Edit I Paste, by clicking the Paste button on the toolbar, or by pressing CTRL+V.

Specifying Note Locations and Numbering

1. Select Insert I Footnote.

2. Select Options, then select the All Footnotes or All Endnotes tab, depending on the settings you want to change.

3. From the Place At drop-down list box, choose where you want the notes to appear.

4. Select a numbering method from the Number Format drop-down list box.

5. Enter the number of the first note in the Start At text box.

6. By default, Word numbers notes continuously throughout the document. To start numbering notes again after each section break in your document, select Restart Each Section. On the All Footnotes tab, you can select Restart Each Page to start numbering footnotes again on each page.

7. Select OK.

Designating Note Separators

Word uses three types of note separators: The *separator* appears above the notes, separating them from the body text. The *continuation notice* appears after the notes, indicating they are continued on the next page. The *continuation separator* appears above the continued notes on that page. Notes are continued onto the next page when one page has too many notes to fit comfortably and they can be fit onto the next page. You cannot change note separators until after you have added that type of note first.

The default separator is a 2-inch line starting at the left margin. The default continuation separator is a line extending from the left to right margins. Word does not use a default continuation notice, but you can add one.

1. Add a footnote or endnote to the document.

2. Open the note pane by selecting <u>V</u>iew | <u>F</u>ootnotes.

3. Select a type of note from the Notes drop-down list box in the Notes pane toolbar. The options in the list box depend on what notes you have added to your document. If you have inserted both footnotes and endnotes, you can choose All Footnotes or All Endnotes to display the appropriate set in the note pane. The Separator, Continuation Separator, and Continuation Notice options are for the set of notes currently displayed in the pane.

4. Select the continuation separator or notice you want to edit. For footnotes choose Footnote Separator, Footnote Continuation Separator, or Footnote Continuation. Endnotes have similar choices.

5. Edit or create the continuation separator or notice using any of the usual text or graphics editing tools. To delete a separator's line, highlight it and press DEL. You can return to the default by clicking the <u>R</u>eset button or pressing ALT+SHIFT+R.

TIP: *You can create lines as footnote or endnote separators by creating paragraph borders.*

6. Close the note pane by selecting <u>C</u>lose or pressing ALT+SHIFT+C.

Hints

Some of Word's features make working with endnotes and footnotes more useful, including: putting notes in columns, formatting notes, viewing notes, suppressing notes, referencing note numbers in another location, converting notes, and indexing notes.

Notes in Columns

When you add notes to text in columns, Word places the notes for that column's text at the bottom of the column. For the purpose of notes, Word essentially treats each column as a separate page.

Note Formatting

Notes and note reference marks are formatted using the Footnote Reference, Endnote Reference, Endnote Text, and Footnote Text styles. By default, the two note text styles use the Normal style's font in 10 point. The two note reference styles use the Normal style's font in 8 point and superscript. To change the formatting for all notes and reference marks, simply change these styles. The box "Footnote Forms" describes the format most commonly used for various source material.

You can also apply the usual formatting features and techniques for formatting text in your notes. For example, to apply italic to text in your note, you can use the Italic button on the toolbar or press CTRL+I.

Viewing Notes

How you view notes depends on the Word view you are using. In Page Layout view, the notes are displayed on the page where Word will print them. To edit them, you move the insertion point to their location and edit them as you do text. If you double-click a note reference mark, Word moves your insertion point to the note text. You can return to the note reference mark's location by pressing SHIFT+F5.

In Normal view, you have to open the Notes pane to view notes. You can do this in several ways: Select View | Footnotes, or double-click a note reference mark, or press SHIFT while dragging the split box down. You can drag the split up or down to change how much of the document window is devoted to the Notes pane. In Normal view, pressing F6 switches the insertion point between the Notes pane and the document without closing the Notes pane. As you move among notes in the Notes pane, the view of the document in the top of the window changes to show the part containing the note reference with the insertion point.

F

Suppressing Notes

You can choose to have notes print at the end of each section of your document or you can print all notes from every section at the end of the document. When you suppress notes for a section, they appear at the end of the next section, as if they were part of

---

Footnote Forms

Many professional societies have their own specialized style conventions for footnotes and endnotes. You will need to follow the style of the organization or group for whom you are writing. If you are writing an academic paper, you will probably be asked to follow the conventions of Turabean style, the Modern Language Association, or the Chicago Manual of Style. If you need a reference for your general business writing, you can use these general rules for the two most common types of references.

For books:

1. Author name, <u>book title</u> (place of publication: publisher name, publication year), page numbers if applicable.

1. John Smith, <u>Lazy Days of Summer</u> (New York: Wonder Press, 1993), 301-325.

For magazine articles:

1. Author name, "article title," <u>magazine name</u> (publication date): page numbers.

1. Emily Richards, "Watching Stars by Day," <u>Star Watcher Gazette</u> (July 1993): 57-59.

that second section. For example, let's say the first section of a document has three columns and the next section of the document has no column division; suppressing the endnotes in the three-column section puts the endnotes for the three-column section with the endnotes for the section that does not have the column division. Suppressing notes is done on a section-by-section basis rather than applying it to the entire document.

To suppress notes in a section, move the insertion point to that section, or select text in all the sections where you want to suppress notes. Select File | Page Setup and the Layout tab, select the Suppress Endnotes check box, and OK. This check box is only available if you have already formatted endnotes to appear at the end of sections instead of the end of the document. Select OK to return to your document.

Referencing Notes

You can create a cross-reference to another note using the Insert | Cross-reference command. When you select this command, you can choose Endnote or Footnote from the Reference Type list box. You can include the note's number or the page that the note is on by selecting Footnote Number, Endnote Number, or Page Number from the Insert Reference To list box. When you select the note you want to reference from the For Which Endnote/Footnote list box, you can select Insert and Close. When you add a reference with this command, Word adds a NOTEREF field type to your document. You can also directly enter this field. However, you must first insert a bookmark in the note you want to reference. Then enter a {NOTEREF} field in the note containing the reference. The NOTEREF field type takes the format

{NOTEREF "*bookmark*"}

where *bookmark* is the bookmark name in the note that you are referencing. The field's result is the number of the note containing the bookmark.

For more information on inserting fields and bookmarks, see "Bookmarks" and "Fields." For more information on cross-references, see "Cross-References."

Converting Notes

You can convert footnotes into endnotes and vice versa. To make this switch, select Insert | Footnote. Select Options and Convert. From here, you can select one of the three option buttons to change all footnotes to endnotes, change all endnotes to footnotes, or to change the endnotes to footnotes and the footnotes to endnotes.

Indexing Footnotes

You can index text that appears in footnotes or endnotes the same way that you index document text. See "Index" for more information.

Related Topics

Bookmarks
Cross-References
Fields
Index
Sections

Forcing Text to a Page

See "Sections."

Foreign Language Support

When you work with text in a language other than English, Word's proofing tools can use a different dictionary for that text. You can set the language either through Word or through Windows. You can also tell Word that you want to use a different language for documents created with a template.

Procedures

The following procedures set another language to use either in Word or in Windows.

Setting a Language in Word

1. Select the text in the other language.

2. Select Tools | Language, to open the Language dialog box.

3. Choose a language from the Mark Selected Text As list box, and select OK.

 NOTE: *If you want Word to skip over the selected text during grammar and spell checking, choose the no proofing option, which is the first item in the list box. Use this option for tables of abbreviations, sections of programming code, or other types of text that you want Word's proofing tools to skip over.*

If you want the language you are selecting to be the default language for documents created with a particular template, select Default from the Language dialog box. Word prompts you to confirm that you want that language to be the default for all new documents created using the same template as the one used in the document you are working on. If you select Yes, every document subsequently created using that template will be formatted for that language. If you select No, the default language is not changed.

Setting a Language in Windows

Once you have set Windows up to work with multiple languages, you can switch the language you are using in Windows and Windows tells Word what language is appropriate for the text that you are entering. When you install multiple languages in Windows, the task bar includes an indicator next to the time showing an abbreviation for the language currently selected. You can click the two letter abbreviation and select a language from the pop-up menu. Changing the language in this pop-up menu changes the language setting within <u>T</u>ools I <u>L</u>anguage as well.

Hints

When you are using a proofing tool, such as the spell checker, grammar checker, or thesaurus, Word automatically switches to the dictionary of the language the text is formatted as. If you do not have a dictionary for that language, Word displays a dialog box telling you that it cannot locate the dictionary. After you select OK from this dialog box, Word skips the formatted text and proceeds to the next text in the document.

To purchase alternate language dictionaries for use with Word, contact Microsoft through the phone numbers in your program documentation.

Related Topics

Grammar Checking
Spelling
Templates
Thesaurus

Form Letters

See "Mail Merge."

Format

See "Character Formats," "Paragraph Formats," "Sections," "Columns," "Borders and Shading," "Frames," or the name of a particular format you want to apply.

Fo<u>r</u>mat I <u>A</u>utoFormat

See "AutoFormat."

Format | Borders and Shading

See "Borders and Shading."

Format | Bullets and Numbering

See "Lists."

Format | Change Case

See "Capitalization."

Format | Columns

See "Columns."

Format | Drawing Object

See "Drawing on a Document."

Format | Drop Cap

See "Dropped Capitals."

Format | Font

See "Fonts."

Format | Frame

See "Frames."

Format | Heading Numbering

See "Outlines."

Format | Paragraph

See "Spacing," "Pagination," Indents," and "Alignment."

Format|Picture

See "Graphics."

Format|Style

See "Styles."

Format|Style Gallery

See "Styles."

Format|Tabs

See "Tabs."

Formatting an Index

See "Index."

Formatting Toolbar

The Formatting toolbar lets you quickly apply many of the most popular formatting changes to text in a document. Adding the Formatting toolbar to your display is done following the same steps as for any other toolbar. Select View | Toolbars, then the Formatting check box, and then OK. Like other toolbars, you can customize the Formatting toolbar, as described in "Toolbar Options." Once the Formatting toolbar appears, you can click its buttons (see the following table) to apply formatting to selected text or the text you are about to enter.

Toolbar Button	Name	Function	Described In
Normal	Style	Selects a style to apply	"Styles"
Times New Roman	Font	Selects a font to apply	"Fonts"
10	Font Size	Selects a point size to apply	"Fonts"
B	Bold	Applies boldface	"Bold"

I	Italic	Applies italic	"Italics"
U	Underline	Applies underlines	"Underline"
	Highlight	Applies highlighting	"Highlighting"
	Align Left	Left-aligns paragraph	"Alignment"
	Center	Centers paragraph	"Alignment"
	Align Right	Right-aligns paragraph	"Alignment"
	Justify	Aligns paragraph on left and right sides	"Alignment"
	Numbering	Adds sequential numbers to paragraph	"Lists"
	Bullets	Adds bullet characters to paragraph	"Lists"
	Decrease Indent	Indents paragraph to previous tab stop	"Indents"
	Increase Indent	Indents paragraph to next tab stop	"Indents"
	Borders	Displays the Borders toolbar	"Borders and Shading"

F

Procedures

The Formatting toolbar is intended for use with the mouse. However, some of the buttons in the Formatting toolbar can be used by the keyboard. Other features available through the Formatting toolbar have keyboard shortcuts to use when using the mouse is not convenient.

Using the Formatting Toolbar with the Mouse

1. Select the text to format, or move the insertion pointer to where you want to enter the formatted text.

2. Click the button for the formatting you want.

3. If the button requires further selection, such as selecting the font, size, or style to apply to the text, make your selection.

Using the Formatting Toolbar with the Keyboard

Most of the Formatting toolbar buttons have keyboard shortcuts. These shortcuts either activate the button in the toolbar or apply the formatting that the button provides. The buttons and their key combinations are listed in the following table.

 NOTE: The buttons that do not have a keyboard shortcut are Highlighting, Numbering, and Borders. Highlighting does require a mouse. You can apply the formatting that these other buttons provide by using the Format | Bullets and Numbering command and the Format | Borders and Shading command.

Toolbar Button	Key Combination
Style	CTRL+SHIFT+S
Font	CTRL+SHIFT+F
Font Size	CTRL+SHIFT+P
Bold	CTRL+B
Italic	CTRL+I
Underline	CTRL+U
Align Left	CTRL+L
Center	CTRL+E
Align Right	CTRL+R
Justify	CTRL+J
Bullets	CTRL+SHIFT+L
Decrease Indent	CTRL+SHIFT+M
Increase Indent	CTRL+M

Related Topics

Ruler
Toolbar Options
Toolbars

Forms

Use Word to created *printed forms* (forms to be printed and then filled out by hand or typewriter), or *online forms* (forms to be completed on a computer).

Printed forms are created using text editing commands, tables, borders, and symbols. Printed forms are not covered here in depth; however, see "Applications" in this section for an example form and the features used to create it.

Online forms use form fields and macros to prompt the user through the process of completing the form and to adapt the form to the information entered. Word includes specific online form features, such as the Forms toolbar and form fields. This section focuses on online forms using form features.

Procedures

Forms are created using standard formatting features, special form fields, and macros. The form fields let you add text boxes, check box fields, and drop-down list box fields to your form. The Forms toolbar has buttons for some of the more common tasks in creating a form.

Displaying the Forms Toolbar

To display the Forms toolbar, right-click on another toolbar, and select Forms from the shortcut menu. You can also select Insert | Form Field, and Show Toolbar. The Forms toolbar is shown below; for full descriptions of the buttons, see "Forms Toolbar."

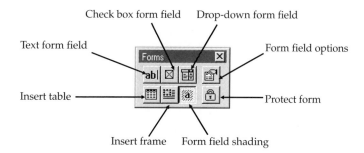

Adding Form Fields with the Menus

1. Lay out your form.

   Create the document to include the information other than the form fields you will be adding. You can add form fields as you create the form in a document since you can always move form fields if you rearrange your form.

F

2. Position the insertion point where you want a form field to appear, and select Insert | Form Field.

3. Select Text, Check Box, or Drop-Down, depending on the type of field you want to insert. The types of form fields are discussed later in "Options."

4. Select Options, and specify the options for this field, as described later in "Options."

5. When you're done, select OK twice.

TIP: *Another way to add form fields while the Forms toolbar is displayed is to click the Text, Check Box, or Drop-Down Form Field button from the toolbar.*

Specifying Options for Form Fields

1. Move the insertion point to the form field.

2. Open the Form Field Options dialog box by either double-clicking the field, right-clicking and selecting Form Field Options from the shortcut menu, or clicking the Form Field Options button in the Forms toolbar.

3. Make your settings, as described in the "Options" section.

4. Select OK.

Locking the Document

The form fields that you add to your document do not act as form fields until you have locked your document as a form. To do this, click the Protect Form button on the Forms toolbar. You can also select Tools | Protect Document, then Forms, and OK. When you protect a form with the Tools | Protect Document command, you can prevent anyone from unlocking the document by adding a password when you lock the document. This password will have to be provided before the document can be unlocked. To unlock a form, select Tools | Unprotect Document or click the Protect Form button on the Forms toolbar. If a password is used to protect the form, you must supply the password before the form is unlocked. While a form is locked, you can only move from field to field in the form so you skip over everything else in the form.

TIP: *If you lock a template, all documents created with that template are locked.*

To prevent a section of the document from being locked, select Tools | Protect Document, then Forms, and then Sections. Clear the check boxes for the sections you don't want to lock. When you're done, select OK twice.

Options

A form can use many different types of fields. These fields are often identical to the items you use in a dialog box to make a selection. These different fields have their own settings that let you select how an entry is made, its initial value, and any limits on the entries you make.

Types of Form Fields

You can insert three types of form fields: text, check box, and drop-down list fields. In addition, there are seven types of text fields, which you select by changing the options for that text field.

REGULAR TEXT FORM FIELD   Use a Regular text form field where any type of text might be inserted—letters, numbers, or symbols. You can set a default entry.

NUMBER TEXT FORM FIELD   Use a Number text form field when the entry is always going to be a number. Only numbers can be entered, and you can set a specific format for those numbers and a default value for the form field.

DATE TEXT FORM FIELD   Use a Date text form field when the entry is always going to be a date. Only valid dates can be entered, and you can set their display format. You can also set a default date.

CURRENT DATE OR TIME TEXT FORM FIELD   Use a Current Date or Current Time text form field to have Word supply the date or time the form is created or printed. You can set the format for the date or time, and choose whether these fields will be updated when the form is printed.

CALCULATION TEXT FORM FIELD   Use a Calculation text form field to total numbers or perform other calculations. You can enter a specific calculation in this field, and choose whether the total will be updated when the form is printed.

CHECK BOX FORM FIELD   Use a check box form field to get yes or no answers.

DROP-DOWN FORM FIELD   Use a drop-down form field to limit users' selection to a list of acceptable options for the field.

Options for Text Fields

The options for text fields include the type of text field, its initial value, the maximum length of the entry, any formatting, when a macro is run, the bookmark name for the field, and help text.

TYPE   Select one of the seven types of text form fields, described under "Types of Form Fields" above, from this drop-down list box.

F

DEFAULT/EXPRESSIONS   The title of this text box changes depending on the type of text form field selected for Type. In this box, enter the default entry for the field, whether it is a bookmark name, a date, or a value.

MAXIMUM LENGTH   Enter the field's maximum length in this spin box, or select Unlimited (the default).

FORMAT   The name of this drop-down list box, and the available formats, change depending on the type of text field selected for Type. Depending on the field, this list box offers date and time formats, capitalization formats, or number formats.

RUN MACRO ON   Word can run a macro when the insertion point enters or leaves the field. After Entry, select the macro to run when the insertion point enters this field; after Exit, enter the macro to run when leaving the field. These drop-down list boxes contain the macros you have in your document's template.

FIELD SETTINGS   In the Bookmark text box, enter a bookmark name that macros will use to reference the field. The default name is simply the field type and a sequential number. Turn off the Fill-in Enabled option if you want to make the text box read-only.

ADD HELP TEXT   Select Add Help Text to open the Form Field Help Text dialog box. Select Status Bar to designate help that will appear in the status bar when the insertion point is in the field, or Help Key to designate help that will appear when the user presses F1 from this field. Whichever tab you select, you can choose None to provide no help; AutoText Entry and an entry name to display the text of that entry; or Type Your Own, and type the help text into the text box. You can enter up to 255 characters of help text in the text box.

Options for Check Box Fields

The options for check box fields include the size of the check box, its initial value, when a macro is run, the bookmark name for the field, and help text.

CHECK BOX SIZE   Select Auto to make the text box the same size as the surrounding text, or Exactly to specify a check box size in points.

DEFAULT VALUE   Select Not Checked or Checked to specify the default setting for the check box form field.

RUN MACRO ON   Select the macro to run when the insertion point enters this field after Entry, and the macro to run when leaving after Exit. These drop-down list boxes contain the macros you have in your document or template.

FIELD SETTINGS   In the Bookmark text box enter a valid bookmark name that macros can use to reference the form field's value. Turn off the Check Box Enabled option to prevent users from selecting or clearing this field.

ADD HELP TEXT   Select Add Help Text to open the Form Field Help Text dialog box. Then select the Status Bar or Help Key tab. On the tabs, choose None to provide no help; AutoText Entry and an entry name to display the text of that AutoText entry; or Type Your Own and up to 255 characters of help text in the text box.

Options for Drop-Down Fields

The options for drop-down fields include the items available in a drop-down list box, when a macro is run, the bookmark name for the field, and help text.

DROP-DOWN ITEM   You can add items to the drop-down list, remove them, order the list, and edit items on it. Begin by entering items for the list in the Drop-Down Item text box, and select Add. The items then appear in the Items in Drop-Down List that lists all of the available choices for the drop-down list box in the form. Each item is added to the end of the list.

Sort the list by highlighting the item to move and selecting the Up or Down Move button beside the list. To remove an item from the list, highlight it and select Remove. To edit an item, highlight it, edit it in the Drop-Down Item text box, and select Add again.

RUN MACRO ON   After Entry, select the name of the macro to run when the insertion point enters this field; after Exit, select the macro to run when leaving the field. These drop-down list boxes contain the macros you have in your document or template.

FIELD SETTINGS   In the Bookmark text box, enter a valid bookmark name to use in macros. Turn off the Drop-Down Enabled option to prevent users from selecting this field.

ADD HELP TEXT   Select Add Help Text to open the Form Field Help Text dialog box. Then select the Status Bar or Help Key tab. On the tabs, choose None to provide no help; AutoText Entry and an entry name to display the text of that AutoText entry; or Type Your Own and up to 255 characters of help text in the text box.

Applications

You can use forms for several purposes. You can create printed forms using Word's formatting. You can combine forms and macros to have a macro guide you through providing the information you need in a document. Word takes advantage of the form capabilities so you can use the document as an interactive form.

F

Creating a Printed Form

Printed forms are meant to be filled out after they are printed. For example, the form shown in Figure 4-21 is printed, handed out to customers, and then returned after completion.

Gabrielle's
Wedding Invitations
212 Severn Way ♥ Akron, OH 44302
Tel: 216/722-3939 ♥ Fax. 216/722-4040

WEDDING INVITATION FORM

PERSON ORDERING

Name _____

Street Address _____

City, State, Zip _____

Phone (Day) _____ Phone (Evening) _____

Pick Up Date _____ Deposit _____

INVITATION

Paper Selected _____

Design Selected _____

Invitees (Parents) _____

Name of Bride _____

Name of Groom _____

Date and Time _____

Location (address) _____

RSVP AND RECEPTION INVITATION

RSVP Form _____

RSVP Address _____

City, State, Zip _____

Reception Address _____

State, City, Zip _____

Location _____

Time _____

FAX OR DROP OFF THIS FORM. CALL OUR MAIN OFFICE WITH ANY QUESTIONS.

Figure 4-21. *A printed form*

This form was very easy to create. The letterhead and the headings for each section are simply paragraphs. The sections that customers will complete are tables. A border was applied to the bottom of the cells in the second column of each table. In the first table, the second cell in the last two rows was split, making four cells in those two rows.

> **TIP:**   *To create attractive check boxes in a printed form, try inserting symbols such as circles, boxes, and diamonds. Using unfamiliar shapes can add a unique flair to your form.*

Creating an Online Form

You can easily create a form to be completed on the screen. For example, see Figure 4-22, which is a legal document. Each of the gray areas that you see is a form field. The current form field is a drop-down form field, and you can see the list of possible choices. Several of the form fields currently display their default settings. The drop-down list of the first field is displayed.

This document is locked, so pressing TAB or SPACEBAR moves you to the next field. Only form fields and sections of the document that were unprotected can be altered.

F

> **TIP:**   *If you want text in a document to change based on the value of a form field, use the {IF} field. This field can return one of two values based on the value of a bookmark. Form fields automatically have a bookmark assigned to their value.*

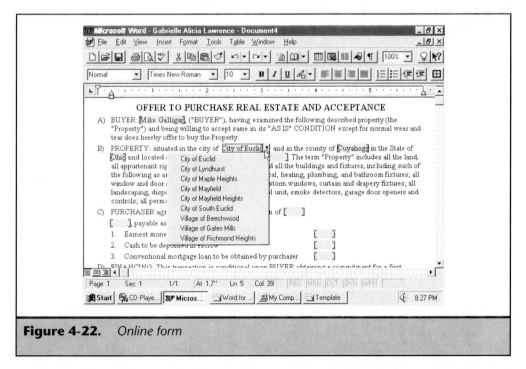

Figure 4-22.   *Online form*

Related Topics

Forms Toolbar
Locking and Protecting Documents

Forms Toolbar

The Forms toolbar offers shortcuts for features useful in creating online forms. The purpose of each button is explained in the table below.

Toolbar Button	Name	Function
ab|	Text Form Field	Inserts a text form field with default options
⊠	Check Box Form Field	Inserts a check box form field with default options
	Drop-Down Form Field	Inserts a drop-down form field with default options
	Form Field Options	Opens the Form Field Options dialog box for the current form field
	Insert Table	Inserts a table
	Insert Frame	Inserts a frame
	Form Field Shading	Toggles between shading and not shading form fields
	Protect Form	Toggles between locking and unlocking documents for forms

Related Topics

Forms
Frames
Locking and Protecting Documents
Tables
View Options

Formulas

See "Equation Editor" and the "EQ" field under "Fields." For formulas within a table and using values from the table, see "Tables."

FoxPro

FoxPro is a database management application designed for the Windows environment. Word can insert a FoxPro database, converting it into a Word table as it is opened. To work with this table, use Word's table features, described in "Tables." Each line in the table is a record, and each column is a field. The column widths are determined by the field widths in FoxPro. Word shows the entire table, even if it is wider than the current page width. You will need to modify the page size or edit the table if it is too wide to print on the current page.

You can also embed FoxPro databases into Word documents and link FoxPro databases into Word documents. Word lets you start FoxPro from within Word by clicking the Microsoft FoxPro button in the Microsoft toolbar. Once you start FoxPro, you are using FoxPro, not Word, and you must follow FoxPro's menu and features.

F

Related Topic

Databases

Fractions

You can create fractions with AutoFormat, by inserting a symbol, using the Equation Editor, or using the {EQ} field.

Type ½, ¼, ¾ with AutoFormat set to replace fractions as you type and Word will automatically replace the fraction with the ½, ¼, or ¾ fraction character.

The Insert | Symbol command can add symbols for ½, ¼, and ¾. These fractions appear the same size as the surrounding text.

You can also create fractions using the Equation Editor (see "Equation Editor").

The fourth option, using the {EQ} field, does not have as many complex options as the Equation Editor, but the fraction appears in line with other text. With the insertion point where you want the fraction, press CTRL+F9, and then type **EQ \f(x,y)** where x is the numerator of the fraction and y is the denominator of the fraction. Press F9. This last option lets you create simple fractions such as ⅞.

Related Topics

AutoFormat
Special Characters
Equation Editor
Fields

Frame-Positioned Object

See "Frames."

Frames

A *frame* is a box containing an object that appears in your document, such as a selection of text. You can move this frame to any position you want on the page. Use frames to position both text and graphics on your page. Putting text or graphics in a frame lets you wrap text around the contents of the frame.

Once a frame is added to a document, it can be moved and sized. Some items in Word are automatically in frames. For example, creating a dropped capital with the command Format | Drop Cap puts the dropped capital in a frame.

Procedures

To use a frame, you need to add it to a document, either to surround existing text or graphics or to place it and then add the contents you want inside the frame. Once you have the frame, you can move and size it to change how the framed contents appear in the document. You can also change the format of the frame so document text wraps around the frame's contents.

Inserting Frames

1. To frame objects that are already in your document, select them. You can select text, graphics, and tables. If you want to insert an empty frame, do not select anything; just move the insertion point where you want the frame placed.

2. Select Insert | Frame.

3. If you are in Normal view, Word prompts you to change to the Page Layout view so you can see where the frame appears on the page. Select Yes to do so, or No to remain in Normal view and cancel the command.

If you selected something before inserting the frame, Word now adds the frame around the selected objects, large enough to surround the objects. If you are inserting an empty frame, you have to indicate the size of the frame for Word.

When you insert an empty frame, Word changes the pointer to a plus sign, which you use to indicate the correct size and position of the frame.

■ With the mouse, point to where you want one corner of the frame, drag the mouse to the diagonally opposite corner, and release the mouse button.

■ With the keyboard, use the arrow keys to move the pointer to one corner of the frame, press ENTER, move to the diagonally opposite corner, and press ENTER again. You can move the pointer with the arrow keys, or by pressing SHIFT and the arrow keys to move larger distances.

TIP: When working with frames, use the Page Layout view. This view shows the frame and surrounding text in the same location where the text and frame contents will appear when you print the document. Normal view displays the frame and its contents separately from the text. Some features, such as wrapping text around a frame, do not appear unless you are in Page Layout view.

Moving a Frame

Follow these steps to move a frame with the mouse:

1. Switch to Page Layout view.

2. Position the mouse pointer on the frame. The pointer turns into a four-headed arrow plus the pointer.

3. Drag the frame to its new position. The dotted line around the frame moves with the mouse pointer, but the text won't move to the new location until you release the mouse button.

Follow these steps to move a frame with the keyboard:

1. Switch to Page Layout view.

2. Position the insertion point inside the frame using the arrow keys.

3. Select Format | Frame, to open this Frame dialog box:

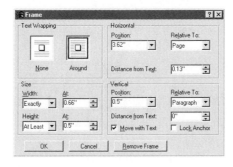

F

4. Under Horizontal and under Vertical, enter your choices determining the horizontal and vertical positions of the frame, as explained under "Options" in this section. Then select OK.

Sizing a Frame

Follow these steps to size a frame with the mouse:

1. Click on the frame to select it. Eight sizing handles appear on the frame, at each corner and in the middle of each side, as shown in Figure 4-23.

2. Move the insertion point to one of the sizing handles. When the mouse pointer is correctly positioned, the mouse pointer turns into a double-headed arrow.

3. Drag the sizing handle so that the frame is the size you want it.

Follow these steps to size a frame with the keyboard:

1. Using the arrow keys, position the insertion point inside the frame.

2. Select Format I Frame, to open the Frame dialog box shown earlier.

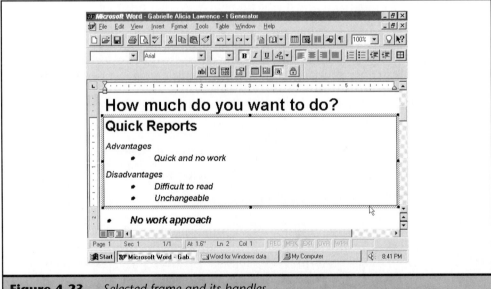

Figure 4-23.   *Selected frame and its handles*

3. Under Size, make selections and enter choices to set the size of the frame, as explained under "Options." Then select OK.

Wrapping Text Around a Frame

Move the insertion point to the frame. Then select Format | Frame, or select Format Frame from the shortcut menu when you right-click the frame, to open the Frame dialog box. Under Text Wrapping, make the selections to determine how the text wraps. These choices are explained under "Options" below. When you're done, select OK.

Options

There are variety of options in the Frame dialog box for formatting a frame. You can choose how text wraps around the frame, the size of the frame, and its position.

Text Wrapping

Choose None or Around. With None, the text will not appear beside the frame (as in Normal view). Choose Around, and if there is at least one inch of space between the edges of the frame and the margins of the document, Word will place text beside the frame's contents. Using the Vertical and Horizontal options, you can control how close to the frame the text is positioned. Figure 4-24 shows a frame with text wrapped around it.

Size

Set the size of the frame by defining its width and height:

■ Select Auto in the Width or Height drop-down list box to let Word determine the best size for the frame based on its contents.

■ Choose Exactly for either Width and Height and then enter a measurement in the At text box. When you choose Exactly, the frame's size does not change as the frame's contents shrink and expand.

■ Choose At Least in the Height drop-down list box and enter a value in the At text box. Word will not reduce the frame to less than this height, but it will increase the frame's height if needed.

Horizontal

The options under Horizontal set the horizontal position of the frame. You define the exact position of the upper-left corner of the frame in terms of distance from the margin or the edge of the paper. You can also specify how close the text can come to the edges of the frame when it is wrapped around the frame.

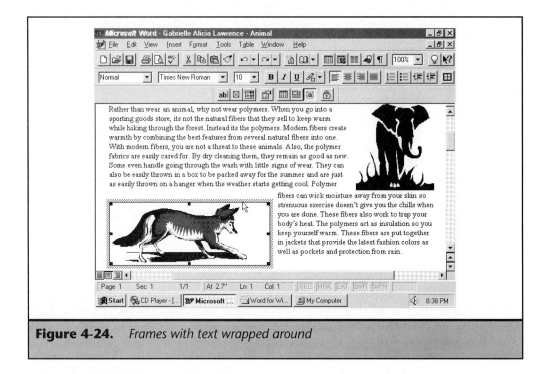

Figure 4-24. *Frames with text wrapped around*

First, select Page, Margin, or Column from the Relative To drop-down list box; this tells Word where to start measuring. Word measures from the left edge of the paper when you select Page, from the left margin when you select Margin, or from the left margin of the column when you select Column.

Next, select one of the distance choices in the Position drop-down list box or type in the measurement. The left side of the frame is placed at this distance from the object you select in the Relative To list box. For example, if you choose Page from the Relative To list box and enter **3"** in the Position text box, the left side of your frame is positioned at three inches from the left side of the paper. You will typically want to use Margin for Relative To, and an option such as Left or Right to put the frame against the left or right margin.

When you select Around, you can also control how close the text can come to the sides of the frame, by entering a measurement in the Distance from Text text box. The text will come no closer than that distance to the sides of the frame, giving you a margin around the frame.

Vertical

Using the Vertical options, you can set the vertical position of the frame, either by defining the vertical position of the upper edge of the frame or by keeping it with the text that surrounds it. You can also designate how close the text comes to the top and bottom of the frame.

Choose Paragraph, Margin, or Page from the Relative To drop-down list box to set the frame's relative placement to the top of the paragraph, the top margin, or the top of the page. Then select one of the position options from the Position drop-down list box, or type a measurement. When you position a frame relative to a paragraph, positive distances move the frame down from the top of the paragraph while negative distances move the frame above the top of the paragraph.

To control how close the text comes to the top and bottom edges of the frame, enter a measurement in the Distance from Text text box. You can use this text box to create a margin around the frame to make a graphic or other framed item stand away from the surrounding text.

Select the Move with Text check box to make the frame move up or down as you add text above or below the frame's position. Turn on Lock Anchor, and the frame remains with the current paragraph.

TIP: Dragging a frame changes the horizontal and vertical positions to Page so the frame is placed on the page relative to the page's dimensions rather than the margin or column edge. Word also changes the distances in the Position drop-down list boxes to the actual distance from the top or left side of the page to the top or left side of the frame. This also occurs when you move a frame's anchor.

Removing the Frame

Select Remove Frame from the Frame dialog box to remove the frame from the document. The frame's contents will appear just before the first paragraph the frame was in.

Hints

Use frames to precisely control the position of text and graphics on your page. When printing on forms, you need to determine exactly where your text is going to appear, so that it prints in the correct location on the page. Frames help you to ensure that your printed form looks professional.

F

You can also use frames to insert graphics and tables into newsletters, brochures, and other documents in an interesting way. You can wrap text around a frame, allowing you to include graphics, as shown in Figure 4-24, that stretch across columns.

Remember that frames are not the same as borders. If you want a visual frame around the contents of a framed object, select the frame and add a border with the Format | Borders and Shading command or the Borders toolbar. The Borders command has options that also set the distance between the border and the contents of the frame. The distance between the frame's border and the surrounding text is set with the Format | Frame command.

A frame's size and position do not determine the size and position of the frame's contents. To change the portion of a graphic that appears within a frame, or to enlarge it or reduce it, do not try to do it by moving or sizing the frame. Instead, change the graphics scaling, using the Format | Picture command. This command also can crop the graphic from the sides, top, or bottom, when you want to change the section of the graphic that appears in the frame.

Text contents inside a frame can have formats different from those of the surrounding text. Text inside a frame can use most of the formatting you apply to a document. The frame gives the effect of having a miniature document inside another.

If you plan to spend time formatting the contents of a frame, you may want to create the frame's contents in another document, frame it, copy it to the Clipboard, and then paste both the frame and its contents into the other document. This way, you can apply the formatting you want to the frame's contents without worrying that you are including other document contents you do not want.

To move a frame, you can just drag it. However, if you want to change which paragraph a frame is attached to, you need to move the frame's anchor. To see frame anchors and anchors for other objects, select Tools | Options and the View tab. Select the Object Anchors check box and OK. When you select a frame, you will see a small anchor character next to the top of the paragraph where the frame is attached. You can drag the anchor to a new location.

Related Topics

Borders and Shading
Captions
Graphics
Margins

Function Keys

The function keys are the keys labeled F1 through F12. These keys provide shortcuts for carrying out Word commands. They can be combined with the ALT, CTRL, and SHIFT keys to expand the range of choices. The keys and the commands they execute are shown in the following table.

Function Key	Action
F1	Open a Help topic regarding the Word operation you are currently doing
SHIFT+F1	Change the mouse pointer so you can click the part of the screen about which you want more information
F2	Move the selected text and graphics to the location you select before pressing ENTER
CTRL+F2	Preview the current document
SHIFT+F2	Copy the selected text and graphics to the location you select before pressing ENTER
F3	Make an AutoText replacement
CTRL+F3	Cut text or graphics to Word's Spike
SHIFT+F3	Cycle the selected text through lowercase, uppercase, and proper case (initial cap)
CTRL+SHIFT+F3	Insert the Spike's contents and clear the Spike
F4	Repeat previous action
ALT+F4	Close application window, exiting Word
CTRL+F4	Close the current document window
SHIFT+F4	Repeat the last Find or Go To command
F5	Go to an annotation, bookmark, endnote, equation, field, footnote, graphic, line, object, page, section, or table
ALT+F5	Restore application window to its previous size
CTRL+F5	Restore document window to its previous size
SHIFT+F5	Go to a prior insertion point position
CTRL+SHIFT+F5	Open the Bookmark dialog box
F6	Go to the next pane

F

CTRL+F6	Go to the next document window
SHIFT+F6	Go to the previous pane
CTRL+SHIFT+F6	Go to the previous document window
F7	Check the selected text's spelling
CTRL+F7	Move a document window if it is not maximized
SHIFT+F7	Open the Thesaurus dialog box
CTRL+SHIFT+F7	Update all links
F8	Extend a selection in extend mode
CTRL+F8	Size a document window
SHIFT+F8	Shrink a selection in extend mode
CTRL+SHIFT+F8	Select a column of text
F9	Update the selected fields
ALT+F9	Toggle between showing field codes or field results
CTRL+F9	Insert an empty field
SHIFT+F9	Toggle between showing one field code or field results
ALT+SHIFT+F9	Select a field as if you double-clicked it
CTRL+SHIFT+F9	Replace a field with its last result
F10	Activate the menu bar
ALT+F10	Maximize application window
CTRL+F10	Maximize current document window
SHIFT+F10	Display shortcut menu for the selected object
F11	Go to the next field
CTRL+F11	Lock a field
SHIFT+F11	Go to the previous field
CTRL+SHIFT+F11	Unlock a field
F12	Open the Save As dialog box
CTRL+F12	Open the Open dialog box
SHIFT+F12	Save the current document
CTRL+SHIFT+F12	Open the Print dialog box

Related Topic

Keyboard Options

General Options

You can set some general default options for Word.

Procedures

1. Select Tools | Options.
2. Select the General tab.
3. Select or clear the check boxes or select a new unit in the Measurement Units drop-down list box to make the default settings. The options are explained under "Options" next.
4. Select OK.

Options

The General options set features that affect the overall operation of Word.

Background Repagination

Clearing this check box means that Word does not repaginate when you pause. Background repagination is always on in Page Layout view and Print Preview, no matter what this setting is. Select this check box to have Word recalculate page breaks whenever you pause typing or editing. Pages are always repaginated when you switch to Page Layout view or Print Preview.

Help for WordPerfect Users

With this check box selected, each time you press a function key, Word interprets it as a WordPerfect 5.1 command, and offers help on how to carry out the same procedure with Word.

Navigation Keys for WordPerfect Users

When this check box is selected, Word reacts the same way WordPerfect does to the keys used for moving the insertion point. When this is cleared, these keys react as explained in this book.

Blue Background, White Text

Select this check box to have Word display your document as white on blue. This does not affect any other color assignments in Windows, as changing the colors in the Windows Control Panel would do.

Beep on Error Actions

Clear this check box to stop Word from beeping whenever an error occurs. Select the check box to have it beep again.

Confirm Conversion at Open

Select this check box when you want to confirm the format when opening documents saved in a non-Word format. When it is cleared, Word converts the document based on its document type without prompting for confirmation. When the document type and the actual format do not match, the document either does not convert at all, or converts incorrectly.

Update Automatic Links at Open

Clear this box to prevent Word from automatically updating any links to other documents in a document when it is opened. When selected, Word will update those links in the process of opening the document. See "Object Linking and Embedding" for an explanation of how linked documents work.

Mail as Attachment

Clear the check box to have Word use your documents as the text of messages sent using an electronic mail system from Word rather than attaching your document as a separate file.

Recently Used File List

Clear this check box to stop displaying recently used documents at the bottom of the File menu. The value in the Entries text box indicates how many documents are displayed. Nine is the maximum.

TipWizard Active

This check box activates and deactivates the Word TipWizard. Clear this check box and you disable it. Select it and you turn the TipWizard on and reset it. Resetting the TipWizard causes the TipWizard to forget the tips it has shown up to this point. This means that you may see some suggestions for a second time.

Measurement Units

The unit chosen in the Measurement Units drop-down list box is the one Word assumes is used in dialog boxes and uses to display the ruler. You can enter measurements in other units when you add the unit's code after the measurement.

Related Topics

Edit Options

Generating Lists and Tables

See "Table of Contents and Figures," "Index," or "Table of Authorities."

Global Search

See "Find and Replace."

Global Templates

See "Templates."

Glossary

Glossary is a term describing an older Word feature that has been replaced by Word's AutoText feature. See "AutoText" to learn how you can create AutoText entries. The glossary was one method of copying text and graphics to new locations. You can also perform the same function using the Clipboard, Spike, and Scrap, all described further in their respective sections.

Glossary Entries

See "AutoText."

Go To

See "Moving the Insertion Point."

GOTOBUTTON Field

See "Fields."

Grammar Checking

You can use Word's grammar feature to check your document for grammatical errors, spelling mistakes, and poor grammatical style. You can control which grammar rules are checked by changing the options for this command.

Procedures

1. Put the insertion point at the beginning of the document. To check only a section of the text, select it instead.
2. Select Tools | Grammar. Word immediately begins checking your document, one sentence at a time.

3. When Word finds a sentence that violates the rules of grammar and style it is checking for, it displays the Grammar dialog box. The sentence containing the possible error appears in the Sentence text box. The words of the error are bold. The possible corrections appear in the Suggestions list box.

4. If you do not understand the error that Word is pointing out, select Explain. Word provides an explanation of the rule of grammar the sentence may violate.

5. Select a change from the Suggestions list box, or highlight it and select Change to change the sentence. You can also edit the sentence in the Sentence text box to fix the sentence in another way and then select Change.

   Select Ignore to have Word skip the current problem and continue checking the grammar. Select Ignore Rule to have Word ignore the grammar rule it is using for the remainder of the grammar check. Select Next Sentence to have Word skip the current sentence and move to the next grammar problem.

6. When Word finishes the grammar check, it displays a set of *readability statistics* about the document. Select OK to close this dialog box.

Unless you select text beforehand, Word checks the grammar of your document from the insertion point to the end of the document. If the insertion point was not at the beginning of the document, when Word reaches the end of the document, it asks you if you want to start checking from the beginning of the document. When you select No, the Readability Statistics dialog box appears. When you select Yes, Word continues checking the document from the beginning, and finishes when it returns to where it originally started before showing readability statistics.

Options

You have several options for what action you can take when Word flags text as grammatically incorrect.

Ignore

Select this button to have Word skip the problem it found in the sentence. Only this specific error is ignored. Any other errors in the sentence are flagged, and any other violations of the same rule of grammar are flagged.

Change

First highlight a suggested change in the Suggestions list box. Next, select Change to have Word change the text of your document as described in the Suggestions list box, removing the error. You can also select Change after selecting Sentence and changing the sentence with the grammar error.

Remember that Word does not actually understand English, and will mark some correct text as wrong. If you do not understand why Word has flagged some text, select Explain to find out how Word thinks your document is incorrect. You may find that Word did not accurately interpret the construction of your sentence. For example, users of English seem to use adverbs and adjectives interchangeably at times, because of where the word appears in the sentence. Word may misinterpret what word the adjective or adverb modifies, and therefore tell you to change to a different modifier. See the box "Rules for Adjectives and Adverbs" to find rules that will help you determine whether Word's advice is right or wrong.

Rules for Adjectives and Adverbs

Adjectives always modify nouns, and adverbs always modify verbs. Although these rules can never be broken, there are many instances in English when it is easy to confuse the modifier needed. The following rules will help you make the right choices:

- When the form of the verb "to be" is followed by a word describing the sentence subject, an adjective is used. For example, "He is tired." When you substitute another descriptive verb such as looks or feels, an adjective is still used. For example, "He looks tired."

- Adjectives and adverbs have more than one form, depending on whether they are used to refer to one item or action, to compare two, or to differentiate when more than two are referred to in the comparison. The three forms are called positive, comparative, and superlative. Many adjectives form their comparative form with *er* ("bigger") and their superlative with *est* ("biggest"). Comparative is used to compare one thing or person against another, and superlative is used to compare one person or thing against a group. These forms should never be interchanged.

- Never use adverbs that do not add additional meaning to the verb. For example, "We will unite together to fight this problem" should be written as "We will unite to fight this problem."

- *Good* and *well* are frequently used incorrectly. *Well* is the adverb, and *good* is the adjective. For example, compare "Sharon stayed home from school since she was not feeling *well*" and "The new secretary received a *good* grade in the computer class."

- Some adjectives and adverbs have irregular forms. Be especially careful when using the comparative and superlative forms. For example: *good, better, best*.

- *Latter* and *last* are frequently confused. *Latter* is used when discussing two objects, and *last*, when there are more than two. "Of the two desserts you mentioned, I will have the *latter*." "The *last* dessert on our menu is the most popular."

G

- Adverbs can normally be formed by adding *ly* to an adjective, although there are some adjectives that end in *ly*. For example, "He was a lowly servant in the household."

- Adjectives and adverbs with many syllables normally form their comparative and superlative forms with *more, most, less,* and *least*. For example, "He was the *most* troublesome lad at the school."

- Do not use two negative adverbs together. For example, "We never hardly planted in the garden before" is wrong. It should be "We hardly planted in the garden before" or "We never planted in the garden before."

- Keep adjectives and adverbs as close as possible to the word they modify.

Next Sentence

You may have a sentence that you know Word will find several errors in, but do not want to change. Select Next Sentence when the first error in the sentence is flagged. Word then skips to the next sentence, ignoring any further errors.

Use this command when checking elements in a table, since the table entries probably are not complete sentences. Also, this command is useful when you use quotations that do not conform to Word's grammar rules, or when intentionally creating an ungrammatical sentence for emphasis.

Ignore Rule

Word checks your document using many grammatical rules. At times, you may not want to apply all the rules to your document. For example, a personal letter does not need to be as grammatically accurate as a business proposal.

When Word uses a grammar rule you do not want to apply to your document, select Ignore Rule. Word no longer applies that rule of grammar to your document.

Explain

When you select Explain, Word displays a dialog box containing an explanation of the error currently flagged. Word does not explain how your sentence is incorrect. Instead, Word explains the rule of grammar your sentence supposedly violates and includes examples. Press ESC or click the Close button to return to the Grammar dialog box.

Options

Selecting Options opens the Grammar Options dialog box, from which you can select the set of grammar rules you want applied to your document, and whether you want readability statistics to appear when you are done. These features are described fully under "Grammar Options."

Undo **L**ast

This option undoes the effect of your last selection in the Grammar dialog box. It can undo a change you made to a sentence or return you to the previous grammar error that you chose to ignore. You can select this button repeatedly to undo multiple selections.

Hints

Remember that Word is only a computer program, not an English professor. A sentence or phrase flagged as incorrect isn't necessarily incorrect. Word has difficulty understanding unusual phrasing or odd sentence construction. Sometimes, its corrections will seem nonsensical to you. Remember to use the grammar checker as a guide to potential errors, but not as the final arbiter of what is correct.

For example, Word might run into difficulty with pronouns. See the box "Rules for Using Pronouns Correctly" to see some rules that govern how pronouns should be used. Word may not catch all of your violations of these rules, or it may flag as incorrect a usage that fits these rules. Remember to consider Word's suggestions carefully, but in light of your own grammatical understanding.

Rules for Using Pronouns Correctly

Pronouns are tricky because they come in several forms. You first need to decide whether to use first, second, or third person (I, you, he/she). You also need to decide whether you want the singular or plural form of that person (I/we, you/you, he/she/it/they). The last decision is which case to use depending on the pronouns within the sentence. The subject of a sentence uses nominative case, objects of the sentence or of a preposition use objective case, and ownership is denoted by use of possessive case. There are also different types of pronouns: personal pronouns, relative pronouns, and possessive pronouns. The rules are too numerous to list here, but these are some of the important ones:

- A plural pronoun should be used when it refers to more than one word. For example, "*Dave* and *I* propose *we* begin to write the book immediately" or "*Dave* and *Carol* think *they* will be able to join us on Thanksgiving."

- If the pronoun is intended to reference only one of the words, the singular form will be used: "*John, Dave,* or *Mark* will give up *his* day off to ensure that we have adequate staffing on Saturday."

- Pronouns used in comparisons are tricky and are best determined by pretending to finish the sentence with extra words. For example, "Dave writes better than *I*." When you change the sentence to "...than *I* write," it is clear that the pronoun cannot be *me*.

G

- The form of the pronoun is the object form when the pronoun is the object of a sentence or the object of a preposition. For example, "John invited *Karen* and *me* to the opera on Saturday" and "Let's keep the secret between *you* and *me.*"

- Possessive pronouns and similar contractions are sometimes confused, but are very different words. For example, "The cat is washing *its* paws." You cannot substitute *it's*, which means *it is.*

- Use *which* and *that* to refer to things. Use *that* when the clause it introduces is required for a meaningful sentence and *which* when the sentence is meaningful without the clause. For example, "The house *that* sold last week was on the market for three weeks." Compare that to "Karen's new listing, *which* I saw last Thursday, may be just the right house for you."

- Use *who* and *that* when referring to people. These words parallel the use of *which* and *that* for required and nonrequired clauses in the preceding rule.

- The relative pronoun *whose* and the contraction *who's* meaning *who is* are often confused. For example, "*Whose* coat is this?" versus "*Who's* the better writer?"

- The indefinite pronouns, *everyone* and *anyone*, are always singular and require a singular verb. For example, "*Everyone* at the office tries to please the new director."

- For clarity, pronouns such as *it* or *they* may have to be replaced by a noun. For example, "Money, security, and pleasant working conditions are important to most employees; *they* are important to a productive workplace." It is unclear whether the employees or the rewards are important. You could rewrite that part of the sentence to read, "these *conditions* are important to a productive workplace."

Besides making changes to words by checking the grammar, you can also use Edit | Find or Edit | Replace. When you use either command and select the Find All Word Forms check box, Word searches for word forms of the word you have entered in the Find What text box. This means that if you enter **purchase** in the Find What text box and **buy** in the Replace With text box, Word will replace purchase with buy, purchasing with buying, and purchased with bought. This feature is describe further under "Find and Replace."

Related Topics

Grammar Options
Spelling
Thesaurus

Grammar Options

You can set options for Word's grammar checking using the Grammar Options dialog box.

Procedures

You can open this box in two ways.

Setting Options While Grammar Checking

1. To open the Grammar dialog box, start checking grammar.

2. Select Options.

3. Change the settings described next under "Options" as you prefer.

4. Select OK.

Setting Options with the Menus

1. Select Tools | Options.

2. Select the Grammar tab.

3. Change the settings described next under "Options" as you prefer.

4. Select OK.

Options

The grammar options set the types of checks that Word will perform on your document.

Use Grammar and Style Rules

Select the set of grammar rules you want to enforce from this list box. The preset options include Strictly (all rules), For Business Writing, and For Casual Writing. There are three potential custom settings, which are initially set to enforce all rules.

Check Spelling

You can clear this check box to prevent Word from checking spelling as it checks the grammar in your document.

Show Readability Statistics

Clear this check box to prevent Word from displaying the Readability Statistics dialog box when it finishes checking the grammar in your document.

Customize Settings

You can customize the sets of grammar rules to fit your own needs, as described previously. To begin customizing, you select Customize Settings, to open a new dialog box. Start by selecting the set of rules you want to customize from the Use Grammar and Style Rules drop-down list box. The other dialog box elements then display the current settings for that set of rules.

- Word divides the rules into two sets, Grammar and Style. You must select the Grammar or Style option button to display those rules in the list box. The list box contains check boxes for each of the rules that can be applied. Select the check boxes for the rules you want to enforce and clear the check boxes for those you do not want to use.

- When you find a grammar or style rule that you do not understand, select Explain. Word displays a dialog box that explains the currently highlighted rule. Press ESC to close this dialog box, or click the Close button.

- Select the number of words that can come between "to" and an infinitive verb in the Split Infinitives drop-down list box. If more words than you specify come between "to" and an infinitive verb, Word flags the text as an error. You can choose to allow up to three words. You can skip this check by choosing Never or strictly enforce it by choosing Always.

- Select the number of nouns that can follow each other in the Consecutive Nouns drop-down list box. You can allow up to four in a row before Word will flag the nouns as an error. Select the number of prepositional phrases that can follow each other in the Prepositional Phrases drop-down list box. You can allow up to four in a row. For both consecutive nouns and prepositional phrases, you can skip this type of grammar checking by selecting Never.

- You can have Word flag as an error any sentence that has more than a set number of words by entering the maximum number in the Sentences Containing More Words Than text box.

- If you decide that you don't like the set of rules you have created, or if you change settings accidentally, select Reset All, restoring the default settings for all the sets of rules.

Hints

The following is an explanation of the grammar options and readability statistics that may help you decide how to use these features.

Grammar Options

You want to flag split infinitives because they can make sentences difficult to understand. They can, however, be used in casual writing to make a point. You will want to flag consecutive nouns because when several nouns appear in a row, the first ones are usually being used to modify the last one. Your reader may not understand how the modifying nouns interrelate. Use adjectives to modify nouns instead of other nouns.

Graph *273*

Avoid using many prepositional phrases in a row because they are also confusing. Unless the sentence is very well constructed, your readers will quickly lose track of which noun is being modified by each of the prepositional phrases.

Readability Statistics

The Readability Statistics dialog box displays three types of statistics: counts, averages, and readability indexes. The Counts area shows the number of words, characters, paragraphs, and sentences in the document. The Averages area shows the average number of sentences per paragraph, words per sentence, or characters per word.

The Readability area shows a set of standard statistical indexes used to determine the readability of your document including the percentage of sentences with passive verbs, and several indexes. Word displays the Flesch Reading Ease, Flesch-Kincaid Grade Level, Coleman-Liau Grade Level, and Bormuth Grade Level indexes.

The Flesch-Kincaid index uses the word length in syllables and the sentence length to calculate the reading skill, expressed in grades, necessary to read the document. The Coleman-Liau and Bormuth Grade Level indexes use word length in characters and sentence length to calculate a grade level. The Flesch Reading Ease index provides a percentage score indicating how easy the text is to read.

Related Topics

G

Grammar Checking
Spelling
Thesaurus

Graph

When you want to create graphs to include in Word for Windows, you can create them using Word's supplementary application, Microsoft Graph. These graphs are included in your Word document as embedded objects.

There are two parts to Microsoft Graph: the datasheet and the chart. The datasheet displays your data, while the Chart displays the chart created from that data. The datasheet appears in a separate window, while the chart appears as an embedded object in your document. Word's menu changes as it is replaced by the menu for Microsoft Graph.

Procedures

You can use Microsoft Graph to create a graph using data in a Word table, data you enter into Microsoft Graph, or data saved with another program that you can import into Microsoft Graph. After creating the first graph, you can change the type of graph, and add or remove elements such as arrows and text, legends, data labels, and labels along the axes.

Creating a Graph from a Word Table

1. Select the table containing the information you want to graph in Word for Windows. Use the Table | Select Table command to select an entire table quickly.

2. Select Edit | Copy to copy the information to the Clipboard.

3. Move the insertion point to where you want the chart.

4. Select Insert | Object, highlight Microsoft Graph in the Object Type list box, and select OK. You may need to select the Create New tab in the Object dialog box.

   Word now opens Microsoft Graph and creates a graph using the data in the table you selected. Microsoft Graph starts a ChartWizard to help you create your graph.

5. Respond to the ChartWizard's prompts about creating the chart. Some of your choices include the chart type, format, how the values in the table are organized on the chart, and the chart's titles.

6. Select Edit | Paste to copy the table's data into the datasheet.

7. Edit or format your graph so that it looks the way you want it.

8. Click outside of your graph to leave the Microsoft Graph application.

The graph appears in your document as an embedded object. You can add a frame, delete or relocate the graph just as you would any other embedded object. For more information on embedded objects—what they are and how they work—see "Object Linking and Embedding."

Editing a Graph

Editing a graph is just like editing any other embedded object. You can open Microsoft Graph from within Word, edit it, and then close Microsoft Graph when you are done. To edit a graph:

- Double-click on the graph in your Word document.
- Highlight the graph and select Edit | Chart Object | Edit.

As with other embedded objects created by separate applications, you can choose to edit the graph in the Word document or in a separate application window. When you edit the graph by double-clicking the graph, selecting Edit | Chart Object | Edit, or right-clicking the graph and selecting Edit Chart, the chart is edited in your Word document. You can also edit the chart in its own window by opening Microsoft Graph as a separate application. To do this, right-click the graph and select Open Chart, or select the graph and the Edit | Chart Object | Open command. To leave Microsoft Graph in its own window, you will use the File | Exit command.

Microsoft Graph has its own toolbar. The buttons, similar commands that perform the same features, and a description are included in Table 4-11.

Graph 275

Button	Button Name	Similar Microsoft Graph Command	Effect
	Import Data	Edit I Import Data	Imports data to graph from another document into the datasheet
	Import Chart	Edit I Import Chart	Imports the chart from another document into the graph
	View Datasheet	View I Datasheet	Displays the datasheet
	Cut	Edit I Cut	Cuts the selected item to the Clipboard
	Copy	Edit I Copy	Copies the selected item to the Clipboard
	Paste	Edit I Paste	Pastes the Clipboard's contents into the graph or datasheet
	Undo	Edit I Undo	Removes the effect of the last change you made
	By Row	Data I Series in Rows	Organizes the data in the graph so each series represents a different row in the datasheet
	By Column	Data I Series in Columns	Organizes the data in the graph so each series represents a different column in the datasheet
	Chart Type	Format I Chart Type	Sets the overall chart type
	Vertical Gridlines	Insert I Gridlines	Adds gridlines in a vertical direction

Table 4-11. *Microsoft Graph Default Toolbar Buttons*

G

Button	Button Name	Similar Microsoft Graph Command	Effect
	Horizontal Gridlines	Insert I Gridlines	Adds gridlines in a horizontal direction
	Legend	Insert I Legend	Displays or hides a legend on the graph
	Text Box	View I Toolbars	Adds a text box to the graph
	Drawing	View I Toolbars	Opens the Drawing toolbar to add drawn objects to the graph
	Color	Format I Selected *Object*	Sets the color of the selected item
	Pattern	Format I Selected *Object*	Sets the fill color of the selected item

Table 4-11.   *Microsoft Graph Default Toolbar Buttons* (continued)

TIP: *Microsoft Graph has shortcut menus. You can right-click any object and see a list of possible options for that object. This is in addition to the menu commands described in this section.*

Options

The preceding steps explain how to create a simple graph, but Graph offers some other options which can customize your graph, or create it in a different way.

Creating a Graph Without a Word Table

You can enter your data directly into Graph, or you can retrieve data from a document saved with Excel, Works, Multiplan, 1-2-3, or Symphony, or one that has been saved in a format compatible with one of those programs.

1. Open Graph without selecting a table of data.

2. You can type data into the datasheet window, which will be used to create the chart. Entering data into the datasheet is done the same way you enter data into a Word table.

Graph *277*

3. You can import data by moving to where you want the imported data placed and selecting Insert | Import Data. Select the document to import and, for some document types, you can select whether you will import the entire document or just a range. You may need to respond OK to the prompt about the imported data overwriting the data already on the Datasheet.

You can open any ASCII file that uses either comma or tab characters to separate fields, or any Excel or Lotus 1-2-3 spreadsheet document.

TIP: *When you import data, you can import up to 4,000 columns and rows of data. If your spreadsheet is larger, name a range containing the section of data that you want to chart, and then select that range when you import the data.*

4. Format and insert your graph as usual.

Changing Graph Types

You can change the type of graph that displays your data. Graph offers a variety of two- and three-dimensional graph styles. To change a graph type, select Format | Chart Type, then 2-D or 3-D for the overall appearance type of the chart. For example, selecting 3-D Column displays the dialog box in Figure 4-25.

Select the specific type of graph you want to use and select OK to change the chart. You can further enhance the chart by setting that chart type's options. To change the

G

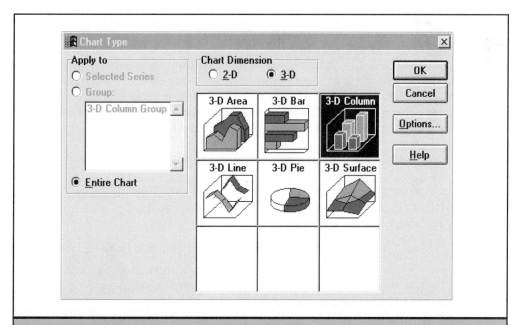

Figure 4-25. *Dialog box for setting the chart type for your graph*

options, select the chart type from the Format menu, as in Format | 3-D Column Group. From here, you will see options about the overall changes you can make to the chart. Since there are so many options, they are divided between tabs that vary depending on the overall chart type. You can also switch between setting the overall chart type and setting options for a specific type with the Options button from the Chart Type dialog box and the Chart Type button in the Format *Chart Type* dialog box. As an example of the Format *Chart Type* dialog box, the following shows the dialog box for a 3-D Column Group chart type:

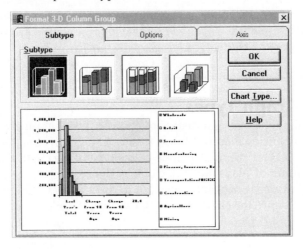

Rearranging Data Series

You can manipulate how your numbers are displayed and used in your graph by making selections from the Data menu. From this menu you can choose data to use as labels for the X axis in an XY (Scatter) graph, include or exclude specific rows or columns of data from the chart, have the graph treat rows or columns as the shape of a series of related data, and, in combination graphs, assign specific series of data to the main chart or the overlay.

TIP: It is often difficult to visualize what is meant by a data series in a graph. Remember that the contents of the legend are each a label of one data series. So if North appears in the legend, and all the information for North appears in a single row, then your data series is arranged in rows.

Some of these options will not be available, depending on the graph type you are using and what is selected when you open the menu. You must select a column or row before you include or exclude it or plot it on the X axis, and you must select a data series before you add it to a main or overlay chart.

Graph 279

Adding Graph Elements

You can add more to your chart than just the data you are charting. You can add elements to your graph, such as arrows, lines, pictures, and other drawn objects. These elements are added by displaying the Drawing toolbar and using the buttons on this toolbar. Drawing objects on a chart is just like drawing objects on a Word document. You can also add other items such as data labels, a legend, titles, gridlines, and axis labels. These are added by selecting them from the Insert menu and responding to the dialog boxes. The chart in Figure 4-26 uses these table elements and labels them.

Unattached text is entered differently than chart or axis titles. Instead of selecting a menu command, just make sure that Chart is the active window, and that no text is selected, and start typing. You can move this text to a new location when you are finished.

Formatting Graph Elements

Each element of the graph has many features that you can format. To format these elements, first select them, and then select an available option from the Format menu. The options available depend on the element currently selected, since some options are simply not appropriate to certain elements. For example, you can change the number format for the numbers along your axes, but it would be useless to try changing the number format for the text in your legend.

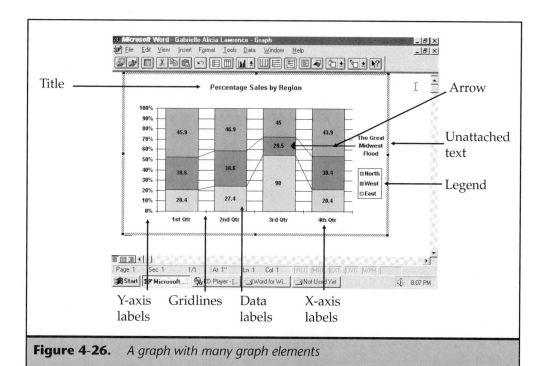

Figure 4-26. *A graph with many graph elements*

TIP: *You can tell an element is selected when handles appear around it.*

Working with Single Data Points

You can work with a single data point in your chart by clicking it twice. After it is selected, you can format it, just as you can format other graph elements. In certain chart types, when you select a single data point, you can move to one of the handles and the mouse pointer changes to a double arrow or cross. When the mouse looks like this, you can drag the handle to another location. As you drag this black handle, you change the value of the data point, changing the entry in the datasheet as well.

TIP: *If the datasheet is not visible, you can display it with the View | Datasheet command.*

Hints

Charts can make it easier to spot trends in sets of numeric data. They also allow you to create a great impact with very few words, because the relationship between the factors being graphed is intuitively clear. However, in most business or professional settings, the actual numbers used to create the graph are also very important and should be included in an easy-to-read table along with the chart.

Use arrows and unattached text together to create callouts to refer to unusual situations in your graph. For example, your readers may not instantly remember when major flooding occurred in the Midwest, which means they probably won't understand sudden sales drops in that period, unless you provide an explanation. Adding this explanation to the graph makes the impact immediate.

Related Topics

Drawing on the Document
Drawing Toolbar
Tables

Graphics

Graphics are pictures or other images that you bring into Word. You can add graphics to provide visual interest to a wide variety of documents.

Procedures

You can insert graphic images into your Word documents. Once they are inserted you can adjust their sizes or crop them to focus on a single element of the image.

Inserting Graphics

Use the following steps to insert a graphic using the Insert | Picture command. You can also insert graphics using the Clipboard, as described under "Clipboard."

1. Put the insertion point where you want the graphic to appear.

2. Select Insert | Picture to open the Picture dialog box.

3. Use the Look In boxes to find the document for the graphic you want to insert. The Insert Picture dialog box is just like the Open dialog box, so if you cannot find the graphic you want, look at how to find documents as described under "Document Management."

TIP: As mentioned in "Document Management," you can click the Preview button to see a picture of the graphic you select in the list. You can also use the List, Details, and Properties buttons to look at other information on the graphics documents.

4. If you want to import the graphic as a linked object, select the Link To File check box.

   When you import and link the graphic, you choose whether to save the picture with the document by selecting Save Picture in Document. If this is not selected, the link must be renewed each time you open the document.

5. Select Insert to insert the graphic.

Selecting Graphics

Before you can work with a graphic in Word, you need to select it. Click on the graphic, put the insertion point before the graphic, and press SHIFT+RIGHT ARROW. You can tell when the graphic is selected because it is marked with eight handles.

Sizing Graphics with the Mouse

To size a graphic, select the graphic, and drag a handle until the box is the right size and release it. When you size a graphic, it maintains the same relative distance from the margin. If you resize a graphic using one of the corner handles, the height-to-width proportion of the graphic stays the same. If you resize it using one of the handles in the middle of a side, you change the height-to-width proportion.

TIP: Watch the status bar to see the percentage of change in the size of the picture as you resize it.

Cropping Graphics with the Mouse

Select the graphic, press SHIFT, and drag a handle. The mouse will change shape when you are cropping instead of sizing.

If you crop outwards, you add white space around the image in the picture. This is negative cropping. If you are creating the graphic yourself, with Microsoft Word or another program, try to do any cropping there.

Figure 4-27 shows the difference between sizing and cropping a figure.

Sizing and Cropping Graphics with the Menus

1. Select the picture.

2. Select Format | Picture. Word tells you the original height and width of the graphic under Original Size. Use this as a comparison as you make changes.

3. Crop a graphic by entering measurements in the text boxes under Crop From. You can crop from the Top, Bottom, Left, or Right.

4. Size a graphic either by percentages of the original size or by specific measurements. Change the percentages in the Width and Height text boxes, or specify measurements in the Width and Height text boxes.

5. Select Reset to return the graphic to its original settings.

6. Select OK to apply your changes.

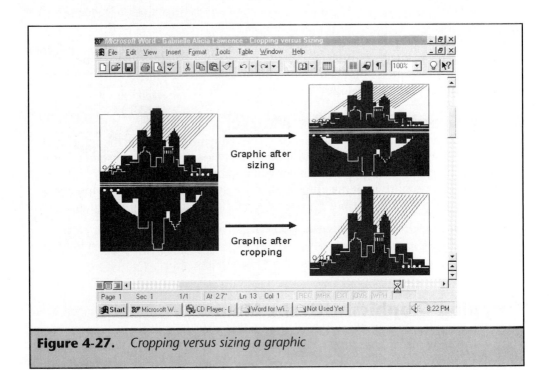

Figure 4-27. *Cropping versus sizing a graphic*

Hints

The following hints on editing, positioning, framing, and converting imported graphics may help make your work with graphics images easier.

Editing Imported Graphics

Your ability to edit imported graphics depends on whether your graphic is in a raster (bitmapped) or a vector format. *Raster* images are recorded as many dots of color. Each dot is recorded individually. *Vector* images are recorded as lines, using mathematical formulas to represent each line that is in the image.

Raster images are commonly available. However, raster images are larger than vector images and are more difficult to edit. Vector images are smaller and much easier to edit. You can use Word's drawing feature to change many of these types of graphics.

If you have raster images and want to edit them, you may be able to do it by editing the original imported graphics document in Microsoft Paint, then reimporting the graphic. Another possibility is using a trace feature which is available in some graphics programs to convert a raster image into a vector format.

Supported Graphics Formats

Word can import any graphic for which it has the correct graphic import filter installed. The graphic import filter tells Word how to read the format. You can see which filters Word has available because they are listed in the Files of Type drop-down list box when you select Insert | Picture. If you have the application that created the graphics that you want to import and that filter is not available, you may be able to link or embed it using the Clipboard as described under "Object Linking and Embedding."

Applying Borders to Graphics

You can apply borders to graphics, to surround them with a box or to add a line to one side of the graphic. See "Borders and Shading" for a full explanation of how to apply borders.

Positioning Graphics

When you first insert a graphic, it appears on the line of text just like another character. This means that you can position the graphic just like text. You have all the character and paragraph formatting at your disposal for placing the graphic. If you want to have more control of the graphic's exact position, insert a frame around it, and then position the frame using the methods described under "Frames."

Related Topics

Drawing on a Document
Frames
Object Linking and Embedding

Gridlines

Table gridlines let you see which cell you are working in. For more information on showing or hiding table gridlines, see "Tables." Drawing on a document also uses a grid to help you place drawn objects on your document. "Drawing on a Document" and "Drawing Toolbar" describe Word's features for drawing, which include turning on or off a grid.

Hand Feeding Pages

See "Printing."

Hanging Indents

See "Indents."

Hard Hyphen

A hard hyphen is a hyphen that causes a word not to break at the end of the line.

Procedures

1. Put the insertion point where you want a hard hyphen.
2. Press CTRL+SHIFT+HYPHEN. You will see a regular hyphen or a long hyphen depending on whether or not you are displaying nonprinting characters.

Hints

You can control how hard hyphens are displayed by setting Word's options for displaying nonprinting characters. If you choose to show optional hyphens, hard hyphens are displayed as longer than normal hyphens, marking them as hard hyphens. If you choose not to display optional hyphens, hard hyphens are shown as regular hyphens, so that, visually, there is no way to distinguish between hard and normal hyphens in your document.

To change the default determining whether optional hyphens are displayed, select Tools | Options, and then select the View tab. Select or clear the Optional Hyphens check box. To change this setting temporarily, select the Show/Hide button to display all nonprinting characters.

Related Topics

Hyphenation

Hard Page Break

A hard page break forces Word to start the following text at the top of a new page. You can insert a hard page break by pressing CTRL+ENTER. See "Pagination" for more information.

Hard Space

Insert a hard space between two words you do not want separated when Word wraps the line. The hard space keeps the words from being separated.

Procedures

1. Put the insertion point where you want the hard space.
2. Press CTRL+SHIFT+SPACEBAR.

Hints

Use hard spaces when you have two words that should not be separated, such as elements of a name, or a title and a name. For example, you would want to keep *Ms. Brown* together on one line, rather than splitting the words between two lines.

Displaying Hard Spaces

You can set how hard spaces are displayed by setting Word's options for displaying nonprinting characters. If you choose to show spaces, hard spaces are displayed as degree signs. Regular spaces are shown with a small dot. If you choose not to display spaces, there is no way visually to distinguish between hard and normal spaces in your document.

To change the default determining whether spaces are displayed, select Tools | Options, and then select View. Select or clear the Spaces check box. To change this setting temporarily, select the Show/Hide¶ button to display all nonprinting characters.

Header and Footer Toolbar

See "Headers and Footers."

H

Headers and Footers

Headers and footers are text and/or graphics that appear at the top or bottom of every page. Headers and footers are good ways to include page numbers or identify information for pages in your document.

Procedures

The following procedures describe how to create, edit, delete, position, and link headers and footers.

Creating or Editing Headers and Footers

1. Select View | Header and Footer. Word switches to Page Layout view, if necessary, to display a header in a nonprinting box of dotted lines, and displays the floating Header and Footer toolbar, shown next.

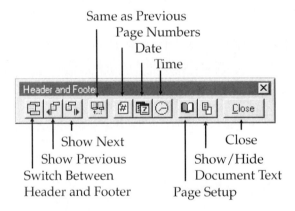

Same as Previous
Page Numbers
Date
Time

Show Next
Show Previous
Switch Between
Header and Footer

Close
Show/Hide
Document Text
Page Setup

TIP: If you are in Page Layout view and you want to edit an existing header or footer, you can double-click on the header or footer area to activate it and open the Header and Footer toolbar.

2. When you want to create or edit a footer on the current page, select the Switch Between Header and Footer button.

3. When you want to edit a header or footer that starts on a previous or later page, select the Show Next or Show Previous button in the toolbar.

4. Create the header or footer using the same techniques for creating and formatting text or graphics that you would use in the main document.

   You can also insert a field for the page number, the time, or the date by using the Page Numbers, Time, or Date button in the toolbar.

5. To have the current header or footer appear only on specific pages, select the Page Setup button, and then the Layout tab. Select Different Odd and Even and then OK.

The current header or footer will appear on only odd or even pages, depending on the type of page it is on now. Use the Show Next or Show Previous button to move to the next kind of page, and create the header or footer for that.

6. Select Different First Page on the Layout tab if you want no header or a unique header or footer for the first page of the document or section. If the current header or footer is not on the first page of the section or document, use the Show Next or Show Previous button to move to the header or footer area on that page, and create it there.

7. Select Close or double-click in the document area.

When you divide your document into sections, the header and footer carry over into each section by default, so that you only need to create one header and footer for the entire document.

Deleting Headers and Footers

1. Select View | Header and Footer or, in Page Layout view, double-click on the header or footer area.

2. Select the contents of the header or footer.

3. Press DEL or BACKSPACE.

4. Select Close or double-click on the document area.

If the header or footer that you deleted is linked to appear in several sections, you delete that header or footer in all sections where it appears. If you want the header or footer to remain in one of the sections, move to that section and click the Same as Previous button to deselect the button and break the link between the section's header or footer and the sections before it.

Vertically Positioning Headers or Footers

Headers and footers appear respectively in the top and bottom margins of your document. If your header or footer is very long, Word readjusts the top or bottom margin to allow enough room for it. You can adjust the position of the header and footer with the File | Page Setup option or follow the next steps to make these changes visually:

1. Select View | Header and Footer, or double-click in the header or footer area in Page Layout view.

2. Move to the header or footer you want to reposition, using the Show Previous or Show Next button, if necessary.

H

3. Drag the margin markers in the vertical ruler to adjust the size of the header or footer box. If you move the header down, or the footer up, into the area used by the document text, Word readjusts the document's margins so that it does not print on top of the document text.

4. Select Close.

TIP: *You can also increase or reduce the space between headers or footers and body text by changing the margins of the body text. If you make the top margin smaller, for example, the body text comes much closer to the header text.*

Horizontally Positioning Headers or Footers

Headers and footers use all the space from the left to the right margin, just like body text. Headers and footers have two preset tab stops—a center tab in the center of the page and a right-aligned tab at the right margin—which you can use for aligning text. You can also align the paragraphs in the header or footer by creating new tab stops or by using indentation.

NOTE: *Word's paragraph formatting can also affect header and footer positioning. This includes space before and after paragraphs, spacing, and indents.*

Linking and Unlinking Headers and Footers

If your document is divided into sections, you do not need to create new headers and footers for each section. Instead, Word creates links so that you only need to create one header or footer for the entire document. Even if you use different headers or footers for odd and even pages, you only need to define one odd header for the entire document, no matter how many sections there are.

If you *want* different headers or footers for separate sections, you need to unlink the headers or footers between the sections. You can unlink headers and footers by moving to a header or footer in a section, and selecting the Same as Previous button so it does not appear depressed. The nonprinting text "Same as Previous," which appeared at the top of the header or footer, disappears but the text of the header or footer remains. You can then edit the header or footer to customize it for that section of the document and any later sections. When you have different headers for first, odd, and even pages, you can unlink one of these types of headers or footers while leaving the others linked. For example, in this book the even header continually shows the book's title, while the odd header changes to show the chapter name.

To reestablish the link between a header and footer and that of the previous section, select the Same as Previous button again, while editing the header or footer. You will be prompted about losing the current text, and using that of the previous section. Select Yes.

Options

The Header and Footer toolbar offers shortcuts to several useful features.

Button	Action
Switch Between Header and Footer	Switches the insertion point between the header and footer of the current page
Show Previous	Shows the header or footer of the previous page
Show Next	Shows the header or footer of the next page
Same as Previous	Deletes the current header or footer and links to the one in previous section or removes the existing link
Page Numbers	Adds a field inserting the page number at the insertion point
Date	Adds a field inserting the current date at the insertion point
Time	Adds a field inserting the current time at the insertion point
Page Setup	Opens the Page Setup dialog box for the current section
Show/Hide Document Text	Switches between showing and hiding the text of the document while you edit the header or footer
Close	Closes the header and footer pane

Formatting Page Numbers in Headers and Footers

You can quickly change the format of the page numbers that you insert in headers or footers. The steps for setting the format of page numbers are described under "Page Numbers."

Applications

Creative use of headers and footers can help you produce unique documents. You can use headers or footers that appear on the side instead of the top or bottom of the page, or create watermarks which appear in the background of the main text.

Headers at the Side

Headers and footers contain text or graphics that appear at the top or bottom of each page. However, you can change a header or footer so that the text or graphic appears at the side of the page, rather than at the top or bottom. You can use this feature to create special effects in your document.

For example, see Figure 4-28, which shows the Print Preview of a letterhead. The large *Gabrielle Fox* down the left side of the letterhead is actually part of the header. Using this feature you can create exciting letterheads, and other documents.

Create this letterhead by adding a WordArt object with your name at the beginning of the footer, and then your address. Then close the header/footer pane and switch to Page Layout view. Select the WordArt object, and insert a frame to contain it. Size and

Figure 4-28.   *Using headers in different ways*

move the object along the left side of the page, since it is no longer confined to the footer area. Change the margins of the document so that the WordArt object fits entirely inside the margin. In this letter, the address remains at the bottom of the page.

Watermarks

Watermarks, which are graphics or text appearing in the background of a document, usually in a light color or gray, can be created as headers and footers. To create a watermark, first insert a frame around a graphic or text in a header or footer. Then use the Send Behind Text button in the Drawing toolbar to move the graphic or text behind the main body of the document. You can position the frame containing the text or image to use as a watermark at any point on the page, instead of just within the header or footer boundaries. The advantage of creating a watermark as part of a header or footer is that it then appears on every page.

Related Topics

Drawing on the Document
Frames

Page Numbers
Sections
Watermarks

Headings

See "Outlines."

Help

You can use Help to get information on all aspects of Word. You will find that the onscreen help is complete and extremely useful. Word's Help behaves just like help for other Windows applications, so once you learn how to get the help you want for one application, you know how to get it anywhere.

Procedures

There are many ways for you to access Help.

Opening the Help Index

You can open Help for Word by using the following methods:

- Press F1 to open the Help window to the initial help topic for Microsoft Word or to the one appropriate for the task you were completing.

- Select Help | Microsoft Word Help Topics to open the Help Topics: Microsoft Word dialog box. This dialog box has four tabs to match the four ways you can look for the help information you want. Contents behaves like a table of contents or an outline where you can select major topics, then select subtopics below to see the exact information you want. Index behaves like the index at the back of a book. Find searches the text in help topics to find a phrase or word anywhere in a help topic. Answer Wizard finds help topics that answer the question that you ask.

 TIP: *If you want to know more about a particular feature in a dialog box, click on the ? button at the top of the dialog box and click on part of the dialog box. You will see a description of that item. This help is called* QuickTips.

- Press SHIFT+F1 or click the Help button and then choose a menu command, press a key or key combination, or click on a region or object on the Word window to open the Help window on the Word feature you selected.

H

Options

Help is a separate application with its own menus, commands, and toolbar. When you open it, one topic of information is displayed. You can move from that one topic to other topics to find the topic that fully answers your questions.

Switching Topics with Hotspots

Hotspots are the green, underlined text in a help topic. Use hotspots to move to other topics or to display definitions of terms. When the hotspot's underline is solid, selecting it displays the topic referred to. These hotspots also appear as a button containing >>. Other hotspots may be boxed text that has a button that turns red when you point to it. When the hotspot's underline is dotted, selecting it displays a definition of the term, as you can see here:

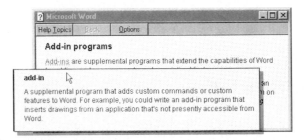

You select a hotspot by clicking it, or pressing TAB until the hotspot is highlighted and then press ENTER.

TIP: *The mouse pointer becomes a hand when it is pointing to a hotspot.*

Selecting a Topic with Help's Table of Contents

The Contents tab in the Help Topics: Microsoft Word dialog box behaves like a table of contents with the available topics organized in a hierarchy.

1. In Help, select Help Topics, to open the Help Topics: Microsoft Word dialog box. You may need to click on the Contents tab if another tab is selected.

2. Move to an entry and press ENTER or double-click it to open up that section of the outline. You can repeat this step to close that section as well. Each of the entries that can be further expanded or contracted shows a book icon next to the concept.

3. Open the entries until you find the topic you want. Topics have a help document icon in front of the concept. This icon is a blue ? (question mark) on a small document.

4. Double-click the help topic, or highlight the topic and select Display. The new topic appears in Help.

Selecting a Topic from the Index

You can search for topics by providing Help a keyword. Help displays a range of possibly related topics that you can explore to find the answers to your questions.

1. In Help, select Help Topics to open the Help Topics: Microsoft Word dialog box. You may need to click on the Index tab if another tab is selected.

2. Type a word in the first text box or highlight an option from the list box. If you cannot find the word you are looking for, try again with a related word.

3. Select Display. The Topics Found dialog box now displays a series of topics.

4. Highlight the topic you want to see, and select Display. The new topic appears in Help.

Selecting a Topic with a Word or Phrase

You search for topics by providing Help with a word or phrase that you want the text for a help topic to contain.

1. In Help, select Help Topics to open the Help Topics: Microsoft Word dialog box, and then select the Find tab. When you use Find, Help uses a word list that includes all the words used in the help topics. If you have not used this feature before, you will answer several prompts as the word list is created.

2. Type a word or phrase that you want to find. As you type, the possible words and help topics change to match what you have typed.

3. Select the word or phrase in the middle list box that matches what you want to find.

4. Select the help topic name that you want to see from the list box at the bottom of the dialog box and select Display.

TIP: You can limit which topics appear in the list. Click the Options and Files buttons, then click the topics that you want to include before you select OK twice.

Selecting a Topic with the Answer Wizard

1. In Help, select Help Topics to open the Help Topics: Microsoft Word dialog box. You may need to click on the Answer Wizard tab if another tab is selected. You can also select Answer Wizard from the Help menu in Word.

2. Type a description of what you want to find. Examples include **Print my document sideways** or **Create a form letter**.

3. Select Search to find the topics that might answer your question. The list box in the middle of the dialog box now shows topics arranged by steps, by explanatory text, and by programming topics.

4. Move to any one of the topics and select Display to switch the Help window to that topic. You can return to the same list of topics by selecting the Help Topics button. When you select this button, you return to the same tab you were at the last time with the same topics listed.

Viewing Topics While Using Word

Help often provides step-by-step instructions that you may want to view while working with Word. Depending on the Help setting, you may be able to keep these on top. When a Help window is on top, it appears on top of any other window you are working with, even though it is not the current application window. The Keep Help on Top setting determines which Help windows remain on top. This setting is available from the Options button. By choosing On Top, Help windows are on top. By choosing Not On Top, when you switch to another application, the help window no longer is on top. You can return to the default by choosing Default. This only keeps windows that have Microsoft Word in the title bar on top and others are treated as regular windows.

TIP: *Help windows can be sized and moved just like other application windows. To size and move windows, look at "Sizing Windows" in Chapter 1 and "Document Window" in this chapter.*

Printing Topics

Another way to view the step-by-step instructions while working with Word is to print the topic. That way, you have a hard copy of the instructions for reference.

To print a topic, follow these steps:

1. Display the topic.

2. Select the Options button and select Print Topic.

Moving Back to Topics

While in Help, you can move back through the topics you looked at. To look at the previous topic, select Back.

Getting Help on Help

Window's Help provides help about itself. Press F1 in the Help window to display help on Windows.

Help I About Microsoft Word

This command displays the About Microsoft Word dialog box, which tells you which release of Word and its supplementary programs you are using. From here, you can select OK to put the dialog box away, or Tech Support to open Help showing information on how to contact Microsoft Corporation for information on using Word. You can also select System Info, which starts a program that lets you see many details about Word and your computer.

To use System Info, highlight the category of information you want to see in the left hand side. The right hand side shows the current settings for that category. You can choose File I Run to open a program that will allow you to make changes to this information, File I Print to print the settings, or File I Save to save the information in a text file. Select Edit I Select All to select all of the settings then select Edit I Copy if you want the selected settings saved to the Clipboard so you can paste the information into another location. The View menu contains commands to show the toolbars and status bar. Select Help I About to see information about the version of Microsoft System Info you are running. Select View I Refresh to update the settings in the Microsoft System Info window. Select File I Exit to close this window when you are finished.

Related Topics

Help

Help I Answer Wizard

See "Answer Wizard" and "Help."

Help I Microsoft Word Help Topics

See "Help."

Help I The Microsoft Network

See "Help."

H

Help | WordPerfect Help

This command provides help to people who have already mastered WordPerfect. Appendix B, "Switching from WordPerfect to Word for Windows," contains more information on the Word features to help WordPerfect users.

Hidden Text

Hidden is a character format that produces text that (by default) will not appear when your document is printed or in the Page Layout view. You may use hidden text to include notes about your document that are meant for you, or for a coauthor, or to hide text that you are considering deleting.

Procedures

The Hidden character style can be applied as the text is being typed or after it is typed. To apply it while typing, select the feature, type the text to be affected, and then remove the feature. To apply the format to typed text, select the text, and then add the style.

1. Select Format | Font or right-click the text and select Font.
2. Select the Hidden check box. Clear it to remove the hidden format. Select OK.

Hints

Use the following hints to change whether hidden text displays or prints as well as removing this formatting from text.

Displaying Hidden Text

You can hide or display hidden text by setting whether nonprinting characters are displayed or hidden. To change the setting, select Tools | Options, and then View. Select or clear the Hidden Text check box and select OK. When you display all nonprinting characters, hidden text also displays. This can be done either with Tools | Options or with the Show/Hide ¶ button in the Standard toolbar.

Printing Hidden Text

While hidden text is considered to be nonprinting characters, you can actually print hidden text as part of your document. To change whether hidden text prints, select Tools | Options, and Print. Select or clear the Hidden Text check box under Include With Document and select OK. This setting remains in effect until you change it.

Hidden Paragraph Characters

If the paragraph character at the end of a paragraph of hidden text is not also formatted with the Hidden text style, the extra line appears in your document even though the hidden text does not. Remember to format both the paragraph you want to hide and its paragraph character.

Removing Formatting

Another procedure for removing the Hidden style from text is to select the text and press CTRL+SPACEBAR. This removes all character formatting from the selected text.

Applications

The hidden text format may not appear useful at first glance, but as you work with Word more, you will find many uses for the feature.

For Updating Your Document

Some documents you create may need to be re-created periodically. Monthly or quarterly reports, project completion reports, or sales memos may use mostly the same text with only a few changes each time. Use hidden text to include notes in your document telling you, or another person, where to get the information.

For Collaborating on Documents

You may find yourself working with another person in creating a document. Many large reports are not created by one person, but by a group of people working together on a document. Use the hidden text format to include text you want added to the document or for notes. This may include reminders to yourself for the details that need to be completed on a newsletter you are creating.

Related Topics

Character Formats

Hide Text

See "Hidden Text."

Highlighting

Highlighting in Word behaves like a highlighting pen—it changes the background color of the text. You can add this feature to your text to emphasize any points or changes in the document.

Procedures

To use Highlighting, you can set the color of the text and then apply it to the text. You can also hide it or make it visible.

H

Set the Highlight Color

You can set the highlight color with either method:

- Select <u>T</u>ools | <u>O</u>ptions and the Revisions tab. Select the color for the highlight from the Hig<u>h</u>light Color drop-down list box and select OK.
- Click on the down arrow at the end of the Highlight button on the Formatting toolbar, and then click on one of the available colors.

Highlight Text

Click on the Highlight button shown on the side and drag the mouse over the text you want highlighted. The Highlight button remains selected until you remove its selection, so you can repeat selecting more text to highlight before you click the Highlight button again to stop highlighting text. If you just want one section of text highlighted, select the text before selecting the Highlight button, so that once the highlighting is applied, the Highlight button is no longer selected.

Viewing and Hiding Highlighting

To turn on or off display of the highlighting, select <u>T</u>ools | <u>O</u>ptions and the View tab. Select the Hig<u>h</u>light check box to have the highlighting appear, or clear it to not show highlighting. When you select OK, the highlighting appears or disappears as you have chosen. This setting applies for all open documents.

Related Topics

Comparing Versions

Highlighting Text

See "Selecting Text."

Horizontal Lines

See "Borders and Shading."

Horizontal Ruler

See "Ruler."

Horizontal Scroll Bar

See "Scroll Bars."

HTML Codes

HTML codes allow you to create hypertext documents for use with the World Wide Web. They allow you to code links to other documents. You also use these codes to supply all formatting to allow all Internet users with a Web Browser that supports HTML 2.0 codes to view the text and graphics they contain. See Chapter 9 for more information on how to use Microsoft's Internet Assistant to painlessly add these codes to Word documents.

Hyphenation

You can use hyphens between words to combine them, as in *forget-me-not*. You can also put hyphens in words so they can be broken by the end of a line. You can add hyphens in your document or let Word add hyphens to words for you, after appropriate settings have been selected.

See the box "Rules for Hyphenation" for instructions on how words should be hyphenated in English. Word will be using these rules for hyphenating, but you will want to know them when you manually hyphenate.

Procedures

You can let Word hyphenate documents automatically, or you can have Word prompt you for where to hyphenate words.

H

Rules for Hyphenation

When you turn on hyphenation in Word, you can have Word add hyphens automatically where they are appropriate. You can also elect to approve their location and insert them manually. Although this latter approach provides an additional measure of control, you will want to follow some basic rules if you choose the manual approach. Let these simple rules guide you in deciding where hyphens should go:

- Always use the syllable marks provided by Word in choosing a location. Words should never be split anywhere other than a syllable break.

- Divide words after prefixes or before suffixes rather than within them.

- Limit the number of lines that end in hyphens to no more than 20-25 percent of the lines on the page.

- Three consecutive lines should never end in hyphens.

- Hyphens should not be used in the last line of a paragraph or page.

- Syllables should always have at least two and preferably three letters divided from the rest of the word.

- Contractions should not be hyphenated.
- Abbreviations such as AICPA, ASCII, and *indef.* should never be hyphenated.
- Long numbers can be split after a comma if you need to break them.
- Choose divisions that do not make real words that might be confusing. For example, *be-atific* (*be* is a word) would be better hyphenated as *bea-tific*.

Hyphenating Automatically

1. Put the insertion point at the beginning of the document or select the text to hyphenate.
2. Select Tools | Hyphenation.
3. Select the Automatically Hyphenate Document check box.
4. Clear the Hyphenate Words in CAPS check box to prevent Word from hyphenating words that are all capitals.
5. Enter a measurement in the Hyphenation Zone text box setting how much white space is allowed at the end of each line.
6. Enter a value in Limit Consecutive Hyphens To, to limit the number of consecutive lines that can be hyphenated. Select OK.

Word now proceeds to repaginate the document and hyphenate the text in the document automatically.

Hyphenating Manually

1. Move to the beginning of your document or select the text to hyphenate.
2. Select Tools | Hyphenation.
3. Make the setting selections you want regarding hyphenating words in capitals, the size of the hyphenation zone, and the number of consecutive hyphenated lines as described in the previous procedure.
4. Select Manual.
5. Word displays a word in the Hyphenate At text box, with hyphens at each place the word can be hyphenated using the rules of the current language. The highlighted hyphen is the one Word wants to insert. Move the highlighted hyphen to change where the word is hyphenated.

6. Select <u>Y</u>es when the hyphen is placed correctly. Word inserts the hyphen and continues checking the document. Select <u>N</u>o to leave the word unhyphenated and continue checking the document.

7. When Word finishes hyphenating text, a message box saying "Hyphenation Complete" is displayed. Select OK to return to the document.

Hints

The following are some hints that explain how hyphenation works in Word, which may help you work with hyphenation more effectively.

Hyphenation or Hot Zone

The *hyphenation (or "hot") zone* is a percentage of the length of the line running along the right end of the line. Word attempts to have some text in the hyphenation zone of every line. If the hyphenation zone of one line is empty, Word hyphenates the first word of the following line so there is text in the hyphenation zone. For example, in Figure 4-29, Word will hyphenate the word "Hyphenation," since the hyphenation zone on the prior line is empty.

The narrower your hot zone is, the more hyphenated words you have. When you increase the width of the hot zone, you have fewer hyphenated words, but the right margin of your page is more ragged.

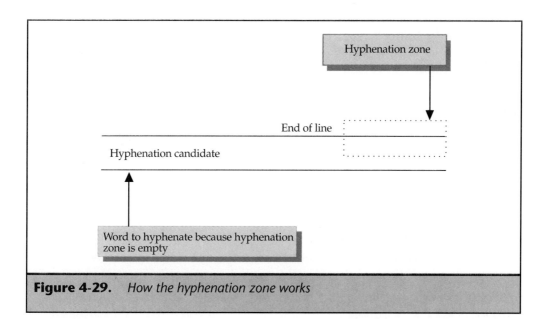

Figure 4-29. *How the hyphenation zone works*

Types of Hyphens

Word uses three types of hyphens: regular hyphens, hard or nonbreaking hyphens, and optional hyphens. Regular hyphens are inserted using the - key on your keyboard. These hyphens always appear and always print. If one appears in a word near the end of a line, Word automatically breaks the word after the hyphen and wraps the second part down to the next line.

Hard, or nonbreaking, hyphens, are inserted by pressing CTRL+SHIFT+- (hyphen). When you have inserted a hard hyphen in a word, or between two words, they are not broken apart by word wrapping, unless Word breaks them at some other location in the word. Nonbreaking hyphens print as normal hyphens, but when you display optional hyphens or nonprinting characters, they appear as longer than normal hyphens.

Optional hyphens are inserted to tell Word where a word can be broken if it needs to be. You can insert these optional hyphens by pressing CTRL+- (hyphen). Optional hyphens do not print unless the word is broken at the optional hyphen at the end of the line, when they are printed as normal hyphens. If you display nonprinting characters or optional hyphens, you will see these hyphens as longer than usual hyphens.

When to Hyphenate

Do not hyphenate immediately after entering text. As a rule, it is better to write and edit all of your text, and then lay out your page before hyphenating. This is because if you change column width, or add or remove words from a paragraph, you have to rehyphenate the document to have the hyphenation complete. Hyphenation should be one of the very last things that you do in creating a document.

You can disable hyphenation for individual paragraphs by changing their paragraph format. When you select Format | Paragraph or right-click the selected paragraphs and select Paragraph, you can select the Don't Hyphenate check box on the Text Flow tab. Selecting this check box disables automatic and manual hyphenation.

IF Field

See "Fields" and "Mail Merge."

Importing Graphics

See "Graphics."

INCLUDEPICTURE Field

See "Fields" for how you can use this field to add a picture stored in another document into your current document.

INCLUDETEXT Field

See "Fields" for how you can use this field to add another document into the current one.

Indents

When you change the indent for paragraphs, you are effectively adding extra margin settings for that paragraph. You can set indentation for the entire paragraph and a separate indent for the first line only.

Procedures

Indents are paragraph formats. When an indent is changed, it affects the paragraph containing the insertion point, or all selected paragraphs. If you press ENTER in a paragraph, creating a new paragraph, the new paragraph has the same indentation as the original.

Changing Indents with the Dialog Box

1. Mark the paragraphs you want to format by selecting text in each or by putting the insertion point in one.
2. Select Format | Paragraph or right-click the selected text and select Paragraph.
3. Select the Indents and Spacing tab if necessary.
4. Enter a measurement in the Left text box to set the left indent. Enter a positive number to move the paragraph in from the margin. Enter a negative number to move the paragraph out into the margin area.
5. Enter a measurement in the Right text box to set the right indent.
6. Set any special indents by selecting First Line or Hanging from the Special drop-down list box, and enter the indent in the By text box.
7. Select OK.

Changing Indents with the Ruler

1. Mark the paragraph(s) you want to format by selecting text in each one or by putting the insertion point in a single paragraph.
2. Click the symbols on the ruler that indicate paragraph indents as shown here.

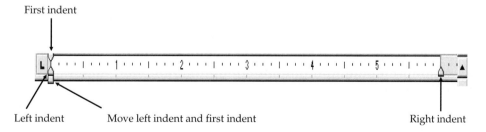

First indent

Left indent   Move left indent and first indent   Right indent

3. Drag the indent markers to where you want the paragraph indented.

Changing Indents with Shortcut Keys

1. Mark the paragraph(s) you want to format by selecting text in each one or by placing the insertion point in a single paragraph.

2. Press the shortcut keys shown next to format the selected paragraphs.

Shortcut	Result
CTRL+M	Changes left and first line indent to the next tab stop to the right
CTRL+SHIFT+M	Changes left and first line indent to the next tab stop to the left
CTRL+T	Changes only the left indent one tab stop to the right (hanging indent)
CTRL+SHIFT+T	Changes only the left indent one tab stop to the left

Changing the Indents with the TAB Key

1. Move to the beginning of the paragraph that you want to change.

2. Press TAB to move the first line indent to the next tab stop to the right. If you overestimate, you can press SHIFT+TAB to return the first line indent one tab stop to the left.

3. Move the beginning of the second line of the paragraph that you want to change. Being at the beginning of any line except the first will make this work.

4. Press TAB to move the left indent to the next tab stop to the right. If you overestimate, you can press SHIFT+TAB to return the left indent one tab stop to the left.

Changing Indents with the Formatting Toolbar

 Click either of the two buttons shown here from the Formatting toolbar to change the left indent of a paragraph. Select the one on the left to move your left indent one tab stop to the left and the one on the right to move your left indent one tab stop to the right.

Hints

The following hints on using negative indents and applications may help you work with indents better.

Negative Indents

You can move the indent of a paragraph into the margins of your document. If you are using the menus, you would do this by entering a negative number in the indent text boxes instead of a positive number. With the ruler, simply move the indent markers outside the margins. You might do this to provide emphasis for headings or introductory paragraphs.

Hanging Indents

Hanging indents are commonly used in bibliographies to emphasize the authors of the works cited and separate each entry. In a hanging indent the first line of a paragraph starts at the left margin, but the rest of the paragraph is indented one tab stop (usually 0.5 inch) to the right. You can create these hanging indents by selecting Hanging Indent from the Special drop-down list box and entering the amount you want the text indented from the first line in the By text box.

TIP: *If you want to see the indents for the paragraphs in a document's Page Layout view, show the text boundaries. To display them, select Tools | Options, select the View tab, and select Text Boundaries.*

Related Topics

Margins
Paragraph Formats

Index

An index is a list of items marked in the text and the page number on which they appear. An index is created using a combination of Index and Index Entry fields, in which Index Entry fields mark text or objects to include, and the Index field marks where the collected index entries are to appear. Figure 4-30 shows a sample index showing how Word can handle cross-references and page ranges.

Procedures

In addition to the procedures described here, you can insert the Index and Index Entry field codes directly into your document. When you do that, you have further customization options. See "Options" about entering fields.

Marking an Index Entry

1. Select the text to include as the entry in the index, or put your insertion point where you want an entry.

2. Press ALT+SHIFT+X or select Insert | Index and Tables | Index | Mark Entry. Pressing ALT+SHIFT+X picks up any text that you have selected as the main index entry.

3. If necessary, enter the text to appear in the index in the Main Entry text box.

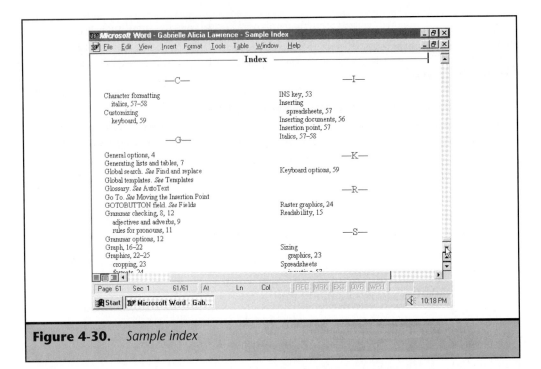

Figure 4-30. *Sample index*

4. To create a subentry, enter the parent entry in the Main Entry text box, and the subentry in the Subentry text box.

5. Select the page reference to appear in the index. You have several options:

   ■ To have the index reference the current page, select the Current Page option button.

   ■ You can have the index refer to a range of pages. Select the Page Range option button, then the bookmark for those pages in the Bookmark drop-down list box.

   ■ You can also choose to create an index entry to serve as only a cross-reference by selecting the Cross-reference option button and entering the other index entry this should reference in the text box.

6. Select the Bold check box to boldface the entry's page number in the index.

7. Select the Italics check box to italicize the entry's page number in the index.

8. Select Mark to create the entry.

9. Select Close to put the Mark Index Entry dialog box away.

Index entries are automatically formatted as hidden text. When you create an index entry, Word displays nonprinting characters in the document, including hidden text. You can hide the index entries by hiding nonprinting characters when you are done adding entries.

Automatically Marking Index Entries

Word can automatically insert index entries when you create and use a *concordance file*. A concordance file contains both words or phrases you want referred to in the index, and the text to appear in the index for those references. For example, you can use a concordance file to create index entries whenever "whale" appears in the document. You can then have Word automatically go through your document and mark the text for entry in the index.

1. Select Insert | Index and Tables, and, if necessary, the Index tab.
2. Select AutoMark.
3. Select the concordance file. Select OK.

Word will now mark index entries in your document, using the concordance file entries. You only have to perform these steps once, since the index entries remain in the document.

Creating a Concordance File

A concordance file can automatically mark text for indexes as just described.

1. Open a new file.
2. Create a two-column table by selecting Table | Insert Table and selecting OK.
3. In the first column, type text you want referenced in the index, using the capitalization used in the document. Since Word can only find exact matches, you may have multiple entries to match when the word or phrase appears in the middle of the sentence (*whale*), at the beginning of a sentence (*Whale*), or as a plural (*whales, Whales*).
4. Press TAB to move to the second column.
5. Type the entry to appear in the index. You may have multiple words you want referenced under the same index entry. For example, *orca, dolphin, cetacean,* and *whale* might all appear under *whale* in your index. If the entry you want created is a subentry, type the main entry, a colon, and the subentry as in *Whale:great*.
6. Repeat steps 3 through 5 until you have included all the text and index entries.
7. Save the document.

Inserting an Index

1. Put your insertion point where you want the index.

TIP: *Insert the index at the end of your document so that it does not affect pagination and on a new page so it stands out clearly. Often indexes are formatted as two columns, even when the main document is not, to fit more of the short entries in less space.*

2. Select Insert | Index and Tables, and then the Index tab, if necessary.

3. To have subentries below the parent entry and indented, select Indented. To have subentries on the same line as the parent entry, select Run-in. The effect of any of your formatting selections for the index is shown using the sample index in the Preview list box.

4. Select a format from the Formats drop-down list box to choose a set of styles to use with the index.

5. To move the page numbers for index entries to the right margin, select Right Align Page Numbers. After selecting this check box, you can select a style of line to run from the index entry to the page number from the Tab Leader drop-down list box.

6. To format your index with multiple columns, enter the number in the Columns text box.

7. Select OK to add the index to the document.

To Update an Index

■ Move to the index and press F9.

Options

Indexes are created with Index and Index Entry ({XE}) fields. They are entered with all of the coding when you mark index entries and insert your index using the steps just described. When you enter the field codes directly, without using the menus, you have some further options for customizing your index. You can add these options to an index that you added with Insert | Index and Tables by displaying field codes and modifying the {Index} field. The {XE} field also has its own switches that you can add to the fields when you add the index entry or afterwards.

Index

The Index field type collects the text and page numbers from Index Entry fields in the document and creates an index using those entries. Word offers a number of switches you can use to control the index's format.

The Index field takes the format

{INDEX [*switches***]}**   where *switches* are the switches that control the format of the index, and are described next. When the index does not use switches, subentries are indented beneath entries, and page numbers are separated from text by a space and from each other by commas.

\B   The \b switch collects index entries only from pages marked with a bookmark. For example, {**INDEX \b chap1**} will create an index for the pages marked with the bookmark chap1.

\C   The \c switch formats the index in columns. For example, {**INDEX \c 3**} would create a three-column index.

\D   The \d switch, always used with the \s switch, sets the characters that separate sequence numbers from page numbers. You can use up to three characters. Remember to enclose the separator character in quote marks.

\E   The \e switch lets you set up to three characters to separate index entries from page numbers. For example, enter {**INDEX \e "..."**} to separate index entries and page numbers with ellipses.

\F   The \f switch creates an index using the specified entries only. For example, enter {**INDEX \f "a"**} to index only entries that include \f "a" in the index entry field. The "a" is an identifier included in the index entry field and the index field specifically so you can create an index from a subset of all index entries.

\G   The \g switch lets you set the character to separate pages in a range. For example, {**INDEX \g -**} separates the first and last pages in a range with a hyphen.

\H   The \h switch lets you set characters that are inserted as headings for the letter groups in the index, such as an A that appears before the list of index entries that start with A. You can use any alphabet character, any other character, or a space. These must be enclosed in quotation marks.

TIP: If you include a letter of the alphabet as part of a heading, Word advances to the next letter in the alphabet automatically when it reaches a new letter group in the index.

\L   The \l switch lets you set the character that separates page numbers in the index. You must enter the character separator and any spaces in quote marks. For example, enter {**INDEX \l "; "**} to separate page numbers by a semicolon and a space.

\P   The \p switch creates a partial index covering only part of the alphabet. Use this switch with a very large document or index so you do not run out of memory while creating the index. For example, {**INDEX \p a-b**} creates an index for the *a* and *b* letter groups of entries.

\R   The \r switch creates an index in which subentries are on the same line as their parent entries. A colon follows parent entries, while subentries are separated by semicolons. The line wraps around if necessary.

\S   The \s switch lets you use sequence numbers in your index. Sequence numbers, defined using the Sequence field type described under "Fields," separate your document into parts that are used with indexes, tables of contents, and other referencing fields. With the \s switch, your index entries display a sequence number, a separator, and a page number. For example, enter **{INDEX \s section}** to use sequence numbers using the sequence named *section*.

Index Entry

The Index Entry field marks entries to include in an index. You must specify the text to appear in the index.

The Index Entry field uses the field code format {XE "*text*" [*switches*]}. *Text* is the text that actually appears in the index. *Switches* are the switches that let you control the index entry, and are described next.

Indexes can have up to seven levels of subentries. You indicate a subentry in text by separating each level of entry with a colon, for example, Whales:carnivorous:orca.

TIP: *To use a colon in the text of an index entry, put a \ (backslash) before it.*

\B   The \b switch bolds a page number of this index entry only. You could boldface page numbers referring to graphics or tables to distinguish them. If your index page numbers are already formatted bold, this switch removes the bold.

\F   The \f switch defines the index entry as being of a specific type. An example is {XE \f "a"}. You can create an index of only one type of index entries.

\I   The \i switch italicizes the page number of this index entry only. Again, use this to distinguish between references to different types of entries in your document. If your index's page numbers are already formatted as italics, this switch removes that format from the page numbers of the entry.

\R   Use the \r switch to mark ranges of pages, by following it with a bookmark name that refers to those pages, for example, {XE "Copying Disks" \r "diskcopy"}.

\T   Use the \t switch to give Word text to use in place of page numbers for this entry. For example, enter {XE "DISKCOPY" \t "*See* Copying Disks"} to create a cross-reference in the index.

Hints

Indexes normally start on a new page at the end of the document, so that they are set apart from the body of the text and do not affect the text's formatting. Since the entries in an index are usually quite short, it is common to use multiple columns, letting you fit more index on fewer pages with much less wasted space.

You can index text found in the body of your document or in footnotes or endnotes.

When you create an index, look over it to find missing bookmarks for ranges used by the index that are not properly defined.

You can delete indexes or index entries by deleting the {INDEX} or {XE} field.

When you want to set the character format of a specific index entry, format the text within the {XE} entry. When you want to set the format of all index entries, modify the Index styles.

Related Topics

Bookmarks
Table of Authorities
Table of Contents and Figures

INFO Field

See "Fields" for how you can add the contents of your document's properties to your document.

Initial Caps

See "Capitalization" or "Dropped Capitals."

INS Key

The INS key switches Word between insert and overtype modes, which affects what happens when you type with the insertion point before characters. In insert mode, Word moves text after the insertion point right, making space for the new text. In overtype mode, what you type replaces the existing text to the right of the insertion point. When you are in overtype mode, the status bar displays "OVR." You can also switch between insert and overtype modes by double-clicking on the OVR indicator in the status bar.

In overtype mode, hidden characters and graphics are treated just like other characters. For example, if the insertion point is just before a graphic in overtype mode, and you type a character, the graphic is replaced by the character. Overtype mode has no effect when revision marks are on.

Insert Mode

See "INS Key."

Insert | Annotation
See "Annotations."

Insert | Break
See "Pagination," "Columns," or "Sections."

Insert | Caption
See "Captions."

Insert | Cross-reference
See "Cross-References."

Insert | Database
See "Databases."

Insert | Date and Time
See "Date and Time."

Insert | Field
See "Fields."

Insert | File
See "Inserting Documents."

Insert | Footnote
See "Footnotes and Endnotes."

Insert | Form Field
See "Forms."

Insert | Frame

See "Frames."

Insert | Index and Tables

See "Index."

Insert | Object

See "Object Linking and Embedding."

Insert | Page Numbers

See "Page Numbers."

Insert | Picture

See "Graphics."

Insert | Symbol

See "Special Characters."

Inserting a Date

See "Date and Time."

Inserting Documents

Use the Insert | File command to import all or part of another document into the current one.

Procedures

1. Move to the location in the document where you want the other document to appear.

2. Select Insert | File to open the Insert File dialog box.

3. Using the File Name and Look In boxes, select the document you want to insert in your document. You can select any type of document that Word can

open. This dialog box resembles Word's Open dialog box, so you can try all the document management techniques described under "Document Management."

4. If you want to insert only part of the document, enter what selects that part of the document in the Range text box. You can enter a bookmark, a range name, a range, or another identifier in this text box.

TIP: *The bookmark, range, or identifier is created in the program the document was originally created in and depends on what that program is.*

5. To create a link to the document, select the Link to File check box. For a full explanation of what a link is, see "Object Linking and Embedding."

6. Select Insert.

Hints

You can use the Insert | File command to insert the contents of a spreadsheet, as described here. However, you may also want to see "Databases" for other methods of inserting information from a spreadsheet.

Inserting Spreadsheets

Inserting a spreadsheet is just like inserting any other document into a Word document. However, since the organization of a spreadsheet is somewhat different from that of another word processing document, there are some variations.

In step 4, you can select to insert the entire document, or part of the document. To select part of a spreadsheet, you must know which range of cells in the spreadsheet you want to use. The easiest method is to name a range of cells in the spreadsheet. You can enter the range (specified the same way you specify the range in the spreadsheet program) in the Range text box, or enter the range name, making sure to match the spelling and punctuation of the name you assigned that range in the spreadsheet.

If you do not specify a range in step 4, a dialog box appears after you select OK that lets you select a named range from the spreadsheet or specify a range. The advantage of waiting to this point to select the range is that you can choose the named range, making sure that the name is correct. You also have other options, such as selecting the sheet to insert and whether the data is inserted in such a way that you can easily use the inserted data as the data source for a mail merge.

The process of naming a range of cells in your spreadsheet depends on which program you are using to create the spreadsheet, so you will want to consult that spreadsheet's documentation.

Related Topics

Object Linking and Embedding
Opening Documents

Inserting Spreadsheets

You can insert or open spreadsheets for which you have a valid converter. Word for Windows ships with converters for Lotus 1-2-3 and Microsoft Excel documents, but you can get others. See "Opening Documents," "Inserting Documents," or "Object Linking and Embedding" for a further explanation of how to insert spreadsheets into your Word document.

Insertion Point

The *insertion point* is the blinking upright line that appears in your document. This line indicates where you are in the document at the moment. When you type text, it appears at the insertion point's location. The insertion point may also be called the *cursor*. If you are unfamiliar with the insertion point, or how to move it, see Chapter 1.

Install

Installing Word, or any of its ancillary features, is done using the Word Setup program. A full explanation of how to install Word, and how to use the Setup program to install further components, is given in Appendix A.

Internet Assistant

The Internet Assistant is an add-in for Word that allows you to view Web pages if you are using a computer connected to the Internet. It also offers an easy way to add the necessary HTML codes to Web pages using the Word template and style features that you may already be familiar with. See Chapter 9 for more information on how to use the Internet Assistant to add HTML codes to your Web documents.

I

Italics

Italics is a character format that produces slanted text. You may use italicized text to provide emphasis for new terms or for explanatory text.

Procedures

The Italics formatting is applied either as text is typed, or after it is typed. To apply it while typing, add the format, type the text, and then remove the format. To apply it to typed text, select the text and add the formatting.

Adding and Removing Italics with the Menu

1. Select Format | Font or right-click the document area and select Font.
2. Select a font style that includes the word *Italic* from the Font Style list box to

   add italics. Select a font style that does not include *Italic* to remove the format. Select OK.

Adding and Removing Italics with the Mouse

Select the Italic button, the one with the *I*, from the Formatting toolbar, to toggle the Italics format on or off.

Adding and Removing Italics with the Keyboard

Press CTRL+I to add or remove the Italics format.

Hints

You can also remove italics from text by selecting the text and pressing CTRL+SPACEBAR. This removes all character formatting from the selected text.

Related Topics

Character Formats
Fonts

Justification

See "Alignment."

Keeping Paragraphs Together

See "Pagination."

Kerning

See "Spacing Characters."

Keyboard Options

You can change the assignment of macros or commands to various key combinations.

Procedures

1. Select Tools | Customize.

2. Select the Keyboard tab if necessary.

3. Select a category of things you want to assign shortcut keys to from the Categories list box. You can choose to assign shortcut keys to commands, macros, fonts, AutoText entries, styles, or common symbols.

4. Select the specific item you want to assign a shortcut key to from the Commands (Macros, Fonts, AutoText, Styles, or Common Symbols) list box. The Current Keys list box displays the keys currently assigned to this item.

5. In the Press New Shortcut Key text box, press the key combination you want to use for the currently highlighted item. The keys' current assignment displays beneath this text box when you press them.

6. Select or enter a template in the Save Changes In drop-down list box to indicate which template these keyboard assignments are saved with.

   If they are saved with the Normal template, they will be available for all documents. Otherwise, they are only available for documents created with the template they are saved in.

7. Select Assign, to assign the shortcut key displayed in the Press New Shortcut Key text box to the selected item.

8. Move to the Current Key list box and select Remove to unassign the shortcut key highlighted in the Current Key list box.

9. Select Reset All to return to the default key assignments.

10. Select Close to return to the document and save your key assignments.

Related Topics

Shortcut Keys

Keywords

See "Document Properties."

KEYWORDS Field

See "Fields" for how you can add a document's Keywords property to your document.

K

Labels

You can easily create mailing labels two ways in Word: You can create mailing labels using the Mail Merge feature as described in "Mail Merge." You can also create mailing labels without a merge operation. The address for the labels can come from several locations: the document, a direct entry, your Word address, or from one of your address books. You can print a whole page of labels or just one label at a specific location on the page of label stock.

Use this feature to create custom mailing labels for yourself and for the people to whom you mail items. You can also use this feature to print other types of repetitive labels such as folder tags or disk labels. Since Word can print a label at the location of the next available label, you won't waste label stock when you print a single label.

Procedures

1. Select the address in your document if the document contains the address you want printed on a label.

2. Select Tools | Envelopes and Labels. Word opens the Envelopes and Labels dialog box. You may need to select the Labels tab.

3. Check the address in the Address text box. The text box currently contains the address you selected or the address Word picked up from the document. You can enter new text, edit it, or delete it. You can also click on the Address button to select an address out of one of your address books. If you want to create labels with your own address, click the Use Return Address check box. Then, the Address text box contains the address entered as your address in the User Info tab of the Options dialog box.

4. Indicate the number of labels you want printed. With Full Page of the Same Label selected, Word prints an entire page full of the same label. If you only want one printed, select Single Label. Then select the position on the page where you want the label printed in the Row and Column text boxes. When you provide this information, Word places the label at the correct location.

5. Select the Delivery Point Bar Code check box if you want this bar code added. You only want the bar code printed if you are using the labels for the delivery address. Do not use them for mailing labels used as the return address. This check box is not available for all label sizes.

6. Change the options described in the next section. These options do not appear until you select the Options button.

7. Select Print or New Document. When you select Print, Word immediately prints the label. When you select New Document, Word creates a document containing a page's worth of the selected labels.

If you are printing return address labels and you changed the return address, when you complete the dialog box, Word prompts to see if you want to save the new address as the default mailing address. Select Yes to save the modified address or No to leave the return address unchanged.

Options

The following options are available when you select Options from the Labels tab of the Envelopes and Labels dialog box.

Printer Information

The options under Printer Information ensure that Word makes the correct choices for the type of printer it will use. Select your printer type (Laser or Dot Matrix) and how the paper is fed to the printer (Tray).

Label Size

The Label Products drop-down list box selects the size of the label using one of several standard size selections. Most labels have an Avery equivalent number, if they are not made by Avery, so you can choose Avery Standard from this drop-down list box. The choice you make here determines which label sizes are listed in the Product Number list box.

Once you have chosen the appropriate entry for Label Products, you can select the label size from the Product Number list box. Once you choose a label size, the information that Word has on that label size appears below Label Information. You can see further details about the label size by selecting Details. Then you see a diagram of how the labels are laid out for that label number. If you select Custom in the Product Number list box, you will want to select Details and enter the appropriate distances for each of the text boxes in the diagram.

Related Topics

Address Book
Envelopes
Mail Merge
Printing
Styles

Landscape Printing

Landscape printing prints the page with the widest side of the paper at the top. See "Printing."

Language

See "Foreign Language Support."

LASTSAVEDBY field

See "Fields."

Layering Text and Graphics

When you look at a document, you can visualize one sheet of paper on which your text and graphics are placed. Although everything appears to be integrated on one sheet, Word actually has three "layers," with one layer over the text and one layer under it. Think of these layers as sheets of plastic through which the entries on all three layers are visible.

Procedure

When you draw on a document with the Draw feature, the object you create is automatically placed on the layer over your text. These steps explain how to move a drawing object you have drawn using the Drawing toolbar to the layer over or under your document text.

1. Select the object.

2. Click the Drawing button in the Standard toolbar.

3. Select the Send Behind Text button from the Drawing toolbar to move the object behind your text. You can also select the Bring in Front of Text button when you want the selected drawn objects moved from behind text to in front of it. These buttons are shown in the margin (Send Behind text is on the right). The appropriate command also appears on the shortcut menu when you right-click a drawing object.

Figure 4-31 shows a document with a drawing of a cat and a feeding dish behind the text. The feeding dish was drawn using the Line, Arc, and Ellipse buttons on the Drawing toolbar. The cat came from the Cat.wmf document in the Clipart folder. The cat is added as the contents of a text box that was drawn using the Text Box button on the Drawing toolbar. Once the feeding dish was drawn and the cat added, these objects were selected; then the Send Behind Text button was selected to put them behind the document text. Notice that you do not need to put the letter's text in a text box. When you move a drawn object behind text, you are putting it behind the main text of the document.

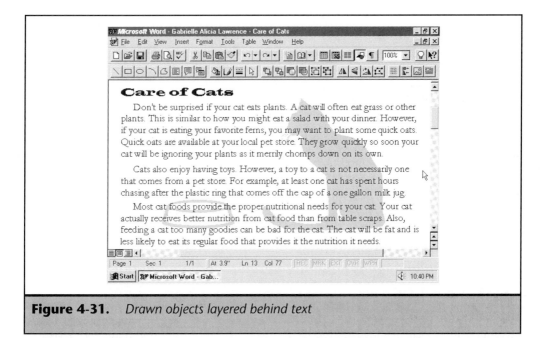

Figure 4-31. *Drawn objects layered behind text*

NOTE: *You may also need to use the Send Behind Text and Bring in Front of Text buttons to make drawn objects appear on top of embedded objects.*

Hints

Imported graphics are always placed on the layer with the text and cannot be moved behind or in front of text. If you want to create a watermark logo with an imported graphic, or you want to put an imported graphic behind text, you will need to put it in a text box using the Text Box button in the Drawing toolbar, rather than putting the imported graphic in a frame.

Related Topics

Drawing on a Document
Drawing Toolbar
Frames
Watermarks

Layout

See "Margins," "Page Size and Orientation," "Paper Source," and "Sections."

Leading

See "Spacing."

Left-Alignment

See "Alignment."

Left Justification

See "Alignment."

Legal Documents

Word provides a Wizard for creating legal pleadings. To use it, all you need to do is select File | New and choose the Pleading Wizard on the Other Documents tab. Use the dialog boxes for your entries. Word also will help you create a table of authorities for your legal documents, as described under "Table of Authorities."

Letter Spacing

See "Spacing Characters."

Line Draw

With WordPerfect, you use Line Draw to draw lines and other shapes on your page. With Word, you can use Draw features, or borders and frames for the same effects. See "Drawing on a Document" and "Borders and Shading."

Line Numbers

Word can print line numbers in the left margin of your documents. This feature is often used in legal documents and is also useful, for example, in a document that will be discussed in a meeting. Word assigns a number to each line of text, but not to any extra spacing between lines that is achieved by changing the paragraph formatting.

Header and footer lines are not numbered. Word also does not number lines containing headers, footers, footnotes, and endnotes. The page numbers appear in Page Layout view and Print Preview. Since the line numbers are in the left margin, you may need to shift the document display in Page Layout view to the left to see the numbers.

Line numbering is a format that you assign to sections of your document. When you select the parts of your document to assign line numbers, follow these guidelines:

- When your document is not divided into sections, line numbers will be added to the whole document.

- When your document is divided into sections, move the insertion point to the section, or select text in each of several sections, that you want to have line numbers.

- To number just a few lines of your document, select those lines only. Word will add section breaks before and after them when you apply this format.

Procedures

1. Select the section of the document to be numbered.
2. Select File | Page Setup, the Layout tab, and the Line Numbers button.
3. Select the Add Line Numbering check box.
4. Designate any options you want to use for line numbers, as described next in "Options."
5. Select OK twice. Figure 4-32 shows a document with line numbers.

Options

Following are the options Word offers for customizing a document's line numbers.

STARTING WITH A NUMBER OTHER THAN 1   You can enter a number in the Start At text box to assign it as the number of the first line. This number starts the line numbering for the entire section. Whether this number displays depends on the increment that you choose. For example, if you enter **2**, then set the increment as **3**, the numbering works like this:

Actual Line Number	Line Number Displayed
1	
2	3
3	
4	
5	6

6

7

8   9

9

10

USING AN INCREMENT OTHER THAN 1   You can choose to number every other line, every third line, and so on. Set the numbering increment in the Count By text box. For example, if you enter **3** in this text box, Word numbers lines with 3, 6, 9, 12, and so on.

THE DISTANCE BETWEEN NUMBERS AND THE TEXT   You can designate the amount of space between the right side of the line numbers and the left side of the text, by entering a distance measurement in the From Text text box. The default of Auto is 0.25 inch, unless you are using newspaper-style columns, where the default is 0.13 inch. This setting does not change the margins for the text; rather, the line numbers appear within the margin. If you set this distance at more than the margin width, the line numbers will not appear.

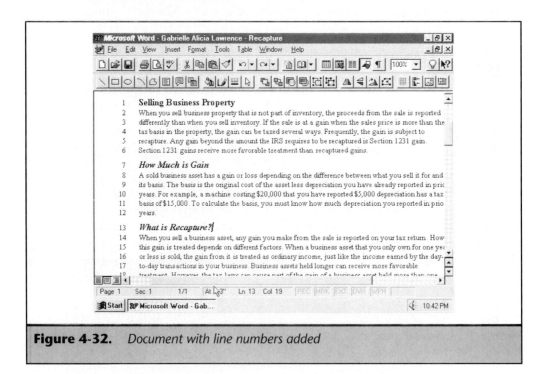

Figure 4-32.   *Document with line numbers added*

THE LOCATION TO START NUMBERING   Word can start line numbering on each new page, at each new section, or from the beginning to the end of the document. Designate this by selecting Restart Each Page, Restart Each Section, or Continuous.

Hints

You can quickly number paragraphs rather than individual lines, using the Numbering button in the Formatting toolbar that adds paragraph numbers. See "Lists" for more information about numbering paragraphs.

You can suppress line numbering for specific paragraphs. When you suppress line numbering in a paragraph, Word skips the paragraph when numbering lines, as if the paragraph were not there. To do this, move the insertion point to the paragraph (or select text in several paragraphs) that you don't want to be numbered, and select Format | Paragraph and the Text Flow tab. Then select the Suppress Line Numbers option.

Numbering lines this way is different than adding numbers to the paragraph format. See "Lists" for how to add numbering to a paragraph format.

Related Topics

Page Numbers

Line Spacing

See "Spacing."

LINK Field

See "Fields."

Linking

See "Object Linking and Embedding."

L

Lists

You can easily create numbered or bulleted lists with Word. These lists are useful for listing steps in a procedure or highlighting important points or agenda topics.

Procedures

You can create numbered or bulleted lists by using the menu or toolbar as described in these procedures.

Creating a Bulleted or Numbered List

1. Select the paragraphs to which you want to add bullets or numbers.

2. Select Format | Bullets and Numbering. You can also right-click the selected paragraphs and select Bullets and Numbering from the shortcut menu.

3. Select the Bulleted, Numbered, or Multilevel tab, depending on what you want to put in front of the list items.

   When you select the Multilevel tab, the level added to the paragraphs will depend on the indentation of the paragraph or the tabs at the beginning of the paragraph. The paragraphs with the least indentation or fewest tabs will have the highest level numbering.

4. Select the type of bullet, number, or multilevel labeling that you want in your list, and then select OK.

NOTE: *If you do not see a list option that you want, you can create one as described later under "Options." You can choose the character used for the bullets or numbers, as well as their size and placement. If you want to set levels using styles, use the Outline features described under "Outlines."*

Figure 4-33 shows a document with bullets added to several paragraphs, to create lists.

Creating Numbered or Bulleted Lists with the Toolbar

Select the paragraphs you want to format as a bulleted or numbered list. Then click the Bullets or Numbering button on the toolbar. These buttons are shown in the margin.

When you select these buttons, Word automatically creates a list with a hanging indent of 0.25 inch. If the paragraphs you selected were already formatted as a numbered or bulleted list, Word prompts you to confirm that you want to replace the current numbers or bullets. Select Yes to replace them.

Removing Bullets and Numbers

If you want to convert paragraphs from a list back to regular text, select the paragraphs, then select Format | Bullets and Numbering, and then the Remove button. You can also remove bullets and numbers by clicking the Bullets or the Numbering button on the toolbar a second time.

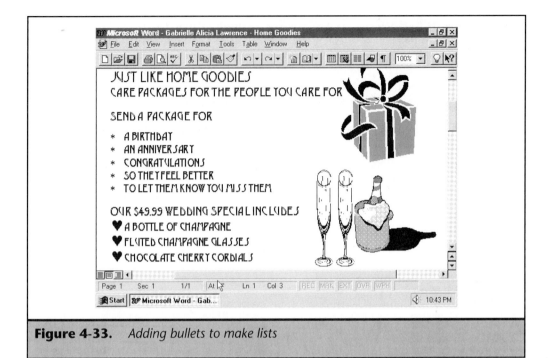

Figure 4-33. *Adding bullets to make lists*

Options

When you select <u>M</u>odify from the Bullets and Numbering dialog box, you can change the characters used for the bullets or numbers, their size, and their position. The dialog box changes to offer appropriate options for bullets or numbers.

When you select the M<u>u</u>ltilevel tab before you select <u>M</u>odify, the options presented are slightly different. Since you can choose the identification of each level, you must first select the level you want to change from the <u>L</u>evel list box. You can also select a level by clicking on that level in the Preview box. The other settings match the current settings for the selected level. You can also have a level adapt the number and position options from the prior level, by selecting Nothing, Numbers, or Numbers and Position from the Include from <u>P</u>revious Level drop-down list box.

SPECIFYING THE APPEARANCE OF BULLETS OR MULTILEVEL BULLETS The Bullet Character area selects the actual character of the bullet. Select from the characters shown, or select <u>B</u>ullet and choose a symbol from the Symbol dialog box. <u>P</u>oint Size sets the size of the bullet or number. The default is Auto, rather than an actual point size, which lets Word determine the bullet or number size depending on the size of the adjacent text. Use the <u>C</u>olor drop-down list box to choose the color of the bullet or number.

SETTING THE APPEARANCE OF NUMBERS   Under Number Format, enter any text you want to appear before and after the number in the Text Before and Text After text boxes. Remember to include any blank spaces you want in this text. Set the style of the number to one of the choices listed in the Number drop-down box. To change the font of the number and text, select Font and choose a font. You can also set the starting number of the series with the Start At text box.

CHOOSING THE POSITION OF THE NUMBER OR BULLET   In the Bullet Position or Number Position section of the dialog box, you select the position of the bullet/number Word will add. Choose the alignment from the Alignment of List Text drop-down list box; designate the amount of space between the left margin and the bullet/number with Distance from Indent to Text, and the amount of space between the bullet/number and the heading text with Distance from Number to Text; and specify the indentation of the rest of the paragraph by turning the Hanging Indent check box on or off.

Hints

Arrange your list with the most important entries first.

AutoFormat can automatically set paragraphs to start with a number or a bullet. Just start a paragraph with a number and a period or *, o, >, –, or a symbol character. When you press ENTER to finish the paragraph, Word sets the paragraph formatting to include a number or bullet using the number style or bullet appearance that you provided. For this feature to work, the AutoFormat Automatic Bulleted Lists and Automatic Numbered Lists check boxes must be selected. The subsequent paragraphs continue to have the same formatting until you press ENTER twice or you press ENTER to start a new paragraph and then BACKSPACE.

TIP: *You can also make a paragraph start with a bullet by pressing SHIFT+CTRL+L.*

Related Topics

AutoFormat
Outlines

Locate

See "Find and Replace."

Lock Documents or Files

You can lock a document using a password when you save the document, or lock a document so that only its original author can edit it. See "Locking and Protecting Documents," "Saving Documents," and "Annotations" for explanations of these features.

Locking and Protecting Documents

There will be times when you do not want your documents edited. To prevent editing, you can lock your document, protecting it against changes. You can use a password to prevent unauthorized users from accessing a document, and to lock a master or subdocument to prevent changes. There are several ways to lock your document, and each method has a slightly different effect on how your document can be edited. You can protect a document for annotations, revisions, or forms. Protect a document for annotations, and only annotations can be added to the document. No other changes can be made. Protect a document for revisions, and all changes made to the text are marked. Protect a document as a form, and you can only move between form fields in the document, not change any other text. When you protect a document, you can use a password so that it cannot be unprotected by a user.

Procedures

Word offers two ways to lock a document, depending on the type of protection you are looking for. You can lock a document when you save it. The other method, for annotations, merge revisions, forms, and master documents, is set separately on the Tools menu.

Saving a Document with Passwords

1. Select File | Save or Save As.
2. Select the location where you want to save the document using the Look In boxes.
3. Enter the name for the document in the File Name text box.
4. Select Options.
5. Set the save options for passwords which include

   Protection Password   Enter a password in this text box, and the document cannot be opened unless the person attempting to open it can supply the correct password.

L

Write Reservation Password   Type a password in this text box, and the person opening the document can either provide the password and open the document normally, or open the document without the password as read-only. Read-only documents cannot be saved using the same name.

Read-Only Recommended   Select this check box to have Word display a message when the user attempts to open this document recommending that they open it read-only. However, the user can still choose, without using a password, to open the document normally.

6. Select OK to close the Options dialog box. If you entered a protection password or write reservation password, you must retype the password and select OK.

7. Select OK to save the document with the document protection settings you have set.

Protecting for Annotations, Revisions, or Forms

1. Select Tools | Protect Document.

2. Select what you want to protect the document for:

Revisions   Select this option button, and Word lets you edit the document, but marks all changes made. You can change how revisions are marked using the Tools | Revisions command.

Annotations   Select this option button, and you cannot edit your document. However, you can insert annotations.

Forms   Select this option button, and you cannot edit or move to text in your document. You can move between and make selections or entries to form fields. When this option button is selected, the Sections button is selectable. (This button is used as described in step 4.)

TIP: *You cannot protect your document in more than one way at one time.*

3. To ensure that your document stays protected, enter a password in the Password text box. Before the document can be unprotected, this password has to be supplied.

4. Select Sections, when the Forms option button is selected, if you want to let users edit certain sections of your document. Clear the check boxes for the sections you want unprotected from the Protect list box. Then select OK.

REMEMBER: *Sections are divided using section breaks.*

5. Select OK to protect the document.

Removing Document Protection

You can remove document protection by selecting Tools | Unprotect Document. If you supplied a password when protecting the document, Word now prompts you for the password. If you do not supply the correct password, the document is not unprotected.

Locking and Unlocking Master and Subdocuments

Master documents are documents that contain field references to other Word documents, called *subdocuments*. Subdocuments appear in the master documents, as if they were portions of the master document. When you open a master document that you created, it and all the subdocuments that you created are unlocked, while any subdocuments in it that you did not create are locked. You can also choose to lock the master document or the subdocuments, even if you did create them. Locked documents cannot be edited until they are unlocked. Word determines the user name based on your Word session and the Author document property.

To lock or unlock a master or subdocument:

1. Put the insertion point in the master document outside any subdocuments, or in the subdocument you want to lock or unlock.
2. Click the Lock Document button on the Master Document toolbar.

Hints

As you can tell by reviewing the steps just given, protecting a document is of little use for maintaining security unless you include a password. These non-password protection features are not used to protect against unauthorized changes so much as against accidental changes. These protection features are a tool to let you work with documents, without having to worry that you will accidentally delete or change text beyond revision. This is particularly important when you are reviewing technical or legal documents, or when you are reviewing a document shared among several people.

When security is an issue, and you are attempting to protect documents against unauthorized access or changes, you need to use passwords. The downside to using passwords is that if you forget your passwords, those documents are no longer available to you. If you use passwords, be sure to record them in a secure location. Another alternative is to keep copies of the document, saved without a password, as backups on a disk kept in a secure location. Windows 95 and networks have their own features for protecting your computer from unwanted access.

The terms *read-only* and *read-write* refer to how you can open documents. Documents opened with read-write, which is the usual way of opening documents, can be edited and saved. Documents opened read-only can be edited, but if you want to save the document, you must use a different name.

L

Related Topics

Annotations
Compare Versions
Forms
Master Documents
Opening Documents
Saving Documents
Sections

Logical Operators

See "Equation Editor."

Lotus

The Lotus Development Corporation publishes the 1-2-3 spreadsheet program. Word can open spreadsheet files created in 1-2-3, as described in "Opening Documents." You can also embed 1-2-3 objects in Word files; see "Object Linking and Embedding."

Lowercase

See "Capitalization."

Macintosh

Word can open files that you have created on a Macintosh computer if you have put the document on a disk with Apple File Exchange. Word for either Windows or the Macintosh can read each other's files.

Macro Toolbar

The Macro toolbar has buttons for running and recording macros, but most of its buttons are to help you edit your macros. Here are descriptions of the Macro toolbar buttons:

Toolbar Button	Name	Task Performed
FixNumberSteps	Active Macro	Selects the macro to be active and affected by the buttons on the Macro toolbar

Toolbar Button	Name	Task Performed
●	Record	Records your commands and actions and adds them to a new macro
●1	Record Next Command	Records the next command you select and adds it to the macro
▶	Start	Runs the macro
▷	Trace	Runs the macro and highlights each statement as it is performed
‖	Continue	Continues macro execution after a pause
■	Stop	Halts macro execution
⥁	Step	Steps through the macro one statement at a time
⥁	Step Subs	Steps through the macro one subroutine at a time
👓	Show Variables	Shows the variables in a macro when you are running it, so you can see their current value
≣	Add/Remove REM	Adds and removes REM from the selected lines, converting them to either remarks (Add) or statements (Remove)
⬡	Macro	Displays the Tools	Macro command's dialog box
🖳	Dialog Editor	Starts the Dialog Editor application to create a dialog box for the macro to use

M

Word also has a Macro Record toolbar that has a Stop and Pause button to use when recording a macro. Stop halts recording a macro and Pause temporarily stops (and toggles to resume) adding instructions to the macro you are recording.

NOTE: *For more details on working with macros, and the functions of these toolbar buttons, see Chapter 7, "Macros."*

Related Topics

Macros

MACROBUTTON Field

The MACROBUTTON field displays text that, when selected, starts a macro. For a full explanation of how this field works, see "Macros" in this chapter.

Macros

A *macro* is a set of instructions that tell Word how to perform a task. You can tell Word to record the selections you make from Word menus and store them as a macro, and then replay this macro when you want to quickly perform the task.

When you record a macro, Word converts your menu selections to WordBasic commands. With some additional technical guidance and practice, you can also write your own WordBasic instructions that extend macro capabilities even further. If you take this approach, you can add *logic* to your commands to test for specific conditions, or create your own dialog boxes and process user input.

Macros are stored with the normal template that is accessible to all documents, or with another template attached to your current document. After you finish recording a macro, you will need to choose File | Save All to save the template along with any macros that you have stored in it.

This section focuses on the macro recorder feature of Word. Chapter 7 provides some additional macro examples as well as a discussion of some more advanced techniques for creating and testing macros.

Procedures

The basic steps in creating and using a macro are recording it, editing it, and running it. You can also stop and restart the macro recording, rename the macro, and assign it to a toolbar, menu, shortcut key, or button in the document.

Recording a Macro

1. Set up a document so it has the conditions you plan to have in effect when you use the macro.

2. Start recording and activate the macro recorder by double-clicking the status bar button REC, or choosing Tools | Macro and selecting the Record button.

3. Type a name for the macro in the Record Macro Name box, or accept the name Word suggests. Do not include spaces, periods, or commas in your macro name. When your macro name is acceptable, the OK button will become available.

4. Type up to 255 characters in the Description box as an optional description of the macro.

5. Set how you want the macro to run in the future. Select Toolbars, Menus, or Keyboard, depending on where you want the macro assigned. Then specify how you want the macro assigned.

If you selected Toolbars, drag the macro from the list box containing the macro name to the desired position on any of the available toolbars. Then, from the Custom Button dialog box, choose one of the buttons and select Assign. (You can also select Edit to create a new custom button.) If you select Text Button, enter the text you want to appear on the button in the Text Button Name text box. Select Assign.

If you selected Menus, select where the macro appears as a menu command. From the Change What Menu drop-down list box, select the menu where the macro will appear as a command. From the Position on Menu drop-down list box, select the position for the macro in the menu; the default is Auto, to let Word decide where it is placed. You can also use this drop-down list box to see the underlined letters of the menu commands already in the menu; the underlined letters have an ampersand (&) in front of them. In the Name on Menu text box, you can alter the macro name to what you want to appear on the menu; this includes putting an & in front of the character you want underlined. You can also select Menu Bar and add another menu to the menu system, and then add the macro to that menu. Select Add to add the macro to the menu.

If you selected Keyboard, press the key combination you want to use for the macro while in the Press New Shortcut Key text box. Examine the text under Currently Assigned To to see if some other macro or Word function is assigned to the key combination you chose. If another function uses the key combination, press BACKSPACE to remove the key combination and enter a different one. Select Assign to assign the key combination.

TIP: *If you do not assign a keyboard, menu, or toolbar shortcut when you record the macro, you can add the shortcut later. The steps for adding a shortcut for an existing macro are in the "Toolbar Options," "Menu Options," and "Keyboard Options" sections.*

M

6. When you are satisfied with your choices, select Close.

7. Perform the actions you want recorded. Notice that the mouse pointer now has a cassette tape next to it, and your workspace now contains a Macro Record toolbar with buttons for Stop (the one with the square) and Pause (the one with the two lines and a circle).

CAUTION: When performing these actions, you will want to work carefully, avoiding mistakes and mistyping. Though you can correct any errors by editing the macro, the process of creating it is easier when there are no mistakes to correct.

You can pause while recording a macro—for instance, to add data to your document so your macro will have the entries it needs to work on, or if you just want to check out a few Word features without recording them. Just click Pause in the Macro Record toolbar, perform the actions that you do not want recorded, and click Pause again to restart the recording process.

8. When you have performed all the steps of your task, click the Stop button in the Macro Record toolbar or double-click REC on the status bar. The Macro Record toolbar disappears.

CAUTION: Word does not record mouse clicks, except for clicks to select menu commands and dialog box options. Most of the time, Word will beep when you try doing something with the mouse that the macro cannot record.

Running a Macro

Macros are often attached to a key, toolbar button, or menu; however, if this is not the case, you will need to run the macro from the Macro dialog box.

NOTE: Word offers buttons in the Macro toolbar that you can use when running a macro to control how quickly it runs. These are used when you are testing a macro to make sure there are no mistakes. You will find more information about the Step, Step Subs, Trace, and Show Variables buttons on this toolbar in Chapter 7 "Adding Sophistication to Merge and Macro Features."

1. Select Tools | Macro.
2. If you don't see the macro you want, select a different macro source from the Macros Available In drop-down list box.
3. Select the macro to run in the Macro Name box, and then select OK.

Assigning a Macro to a Button in the Document

Another option for executing a macro is to assign it to a "button" in your document.

1. Move to the position in your document where you want the macro button, and select Insert | Field.

2. Select the MACROBUTTON field from the Field Names list box. It now appears in the Field Codes text box.

3. Select Options.

4. In the Macro Name list box, select the macro to run when the button is clicked. This list box contains macro instructions for most Word commands, as well as the macro names you see in the Macro dialog box (displayed with the Tools | Macro command).

5. Select Add to Field. The macro name appears in the Field Codes text box as part of the Macro button field.

6. In the Field Codes text box, type the text you want to see as the macro button. For example, the final entry in the Field Codes text box might be something like this:

    MACROBUTTON TotalAllNumbers [Double-click here to calculate the totals]

7. Select OK twice.

At this point, you can run the macro by double-clicking the button, or by moving to the button and pressing ALT+SHIFT+F9. For example, the result of assigning the TotalAllNumbers macro to a button, as described in step 6, will look like this in the finished document:

Summary Report   [Double-click here to calculate the totals]

NOTE: *If you see the field code instead of the assigned macro text, press ALT+F9 to switch from displaying field codes to field results.*

Moving or Copying Macros to Another Template

Word automatically stores new macros in the Normal template, making the macros available in all documents. Macros that you only need for specialized applications can be copied or moved to other templates.

1. Select Tools | Macro.

2. Choose the Organizer button.

3. In the Macros Available In box on the left side of the dialog box, select the template where the macro is now stored.

M

NOTE: *You may need to use the Close File button under the Macros Available In box if another template is open. Then select the Open File button and open the desired template.*

4. In the Macros Available In box on the right side of the dialog box, select the template to which you want to move or copy the macro.

NOTE: *You may need to use the Close File button if you have another template open. Then use the Open File button to open the desired template.*

5. In the In or To list box of macro names, select the macro you want to move or copy. When you select a macro from either list box, that list box becomes the In list box and the other list box becomes the To list box. This lets you copy from either source of macros to the other.

6. Select the Copy button.

7. If you are removing the original macro, select the Delete button; if you are copying the macro, you can skip this step.

8. Select the Close button.

Renaming a Macro

1. Select Tools | Macro.

2. Choose the Organizer button.

3. In the Macros Available In box on the *left* side of the dialog box, select the template where the macro is stored.

NOTE: *You may need to use the Close File button under the Macros Available In box if another template is open. Then select the Open File button and open the desired template.*

4. Select the macro name you want to change.

5. Choose the Rename button, type the new name, and select OK.

6. Select the Close button.

Editing a Macro

1. Select Tools | Macro.

2. If the macro you want is not displayed, select the source of macros you want to edit from the Macros Available In box.

3. Select the macro to edit in the Macro Name box, and then select Edit.

4. Make your changes to the macro.

Figure 4-34 shows a macro opened for editing. Most of the macro instructions in this case are for menu commands, so the macro statement for the Format | Drawing Object command includes all of the possible settings that can be made for the text box the command is formatting. When you edit a macro, Word gives you the Macro toolbar, which provides many of the features you will need when you are editing a macro.

5. Close the macro window just as you would close a document window.

6. When prompted, select Yes to save the edited macro.

Using Macros Supplied with Word as Models

Word provides a number of existing macros. These macros are stored in the Convert7, Layout7, Macro7, and Tables7 templates. If you load one of these templates as a global template (see "Templates"), you can use its macros in your document. You can also use the Organizer to copy any of these macros from its template to the Normal template, or to a template of your own.

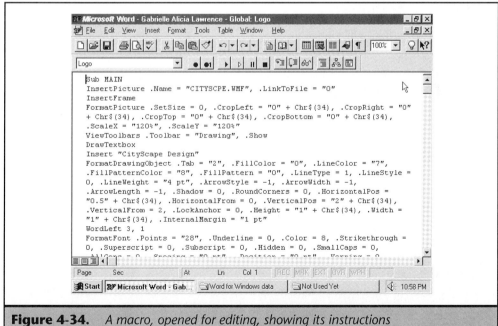

Figure 4-34. *A macro, opened for editing, showing its instructions*

M

NOTE: *If you did not do a complete Word for Windows installation, you may need to run the setup program again to copy these templates to your disk.*

Hints

Macros recorded with the macro recorder require conditions while they are recorded to be the same as the conditions under which they will work. This is because the task is actually performed as the macro is recorded. For instance, if you are creating a macro to copy the two paragraphs following the insertion point, when you record the macro, you must actually have two paragraphs following the insertion point in your current document.

If you hear a beep when you are recording a macro, it may be that Word does not record actions performed with a mouse (except for clicking to select menu commands and dialog box options). You may want to move the mouse out of reach while recording the macro, in case you forget and reach for it out of habit.

To make a macro from another template available in the document you are using, add the macro's template as a global template. See "Templates" for complete instructions.

Related Topics

Fields
Keyboard Options
Macro Toolbar
Menu Options
Templates
Toolbar Options

Mail

See "Electronic Mail."

Mail Merge

Word's mail merge feature lets you combine text in a main document with variable data stored in a data source. Mail merge can dramatically accelerate and simplify the process of creating many similar copies of a document. Your *data source* can have hundreds or thousands of entries—typically names and addresses—that are combined with unchanging text in the main document to create customized letters, mailing labels, or advertisements. The data source provides the variable information to be inserted into a main document during a mail merge operation. Figure 4-35 illustrates the

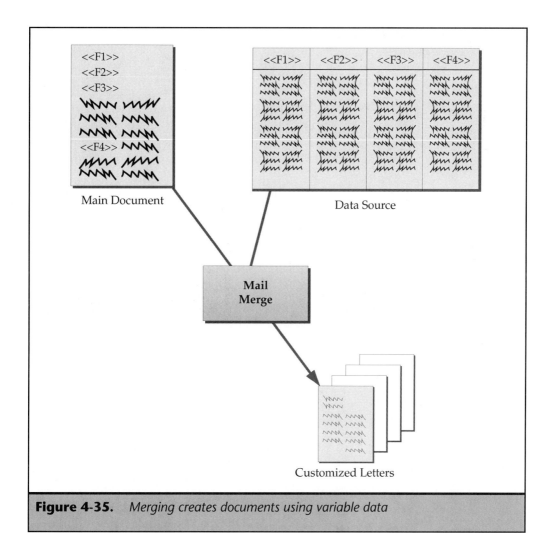

Figure 4-35. *Merging creates documents using variable data*

process of merging records in a data source with a form letter to create many customized letters.

Normally, the data source is organized into a table, with each type of variable information in a column. Each column is known as a *data field*. Each row in the table contains one entry for each data field in the table and is called a *data record*. You can enter values directly into the table or use a form for your entries.

You can add fields to your main document to control how your merge will occur. *Merge fields* indicate where contents of the data source are inserted into your final documents. *Word fields* can prompt you to enter data to include in your merge document,

M

or can process information from your data source in a particular way, for instance, skipping records or displaying certain text.

Procedures

Many of the mail merge procedures take advantage of the Mail Merge Helper dialog box, a Wizard-like helper that guides you through the required steps, is shown in Figure 4-36. This helper provides options for each step in the merge. You cannot select the final merge step until you have defined a main document and a data source with entries in this dialog box.

Creating the Main Document

The main document for a merge can be an existing document or a document you create from the Mail Merge Helper. To use an existing document, be sure to open it before activating the Mail Merge Helper.

1. Choose Tools | Mail Merge, opening the Mail Merge Helper dialog box.

2. Select Create.

3. Select the type of main document you want to set up from the Create drop-down list. You can create a main document that uses one of these formats: Form Letters, Mailing Labels, Envelopes, or Catalog (for catalogs or other lists).

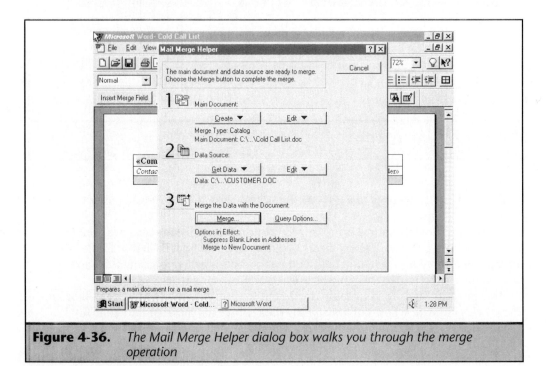

Figure 4-36.   *The Mail Merge Helper dialog box walks you through the merge operation*

Alternatively, select Restore to Normal Word Document to have Word break the connection between this document, assuming it is an existing main document, and the data source, making it a normal document again.

4. Choose the Active Window button to create the main document in the active window, or the New Main Document button to open a new window for creating the main document.

   The Active Window button is the Change Document Type button if the current document is already a main document.

5. Select the Get Data button to select the source of the variable information as described in the next sections.

6. Select Edit under Main Document in the Mail Merge Helper dialog box; then select the name of the document, and create your main document.

   The Mail Merge toolbar appears while you are creating or editing a mail merge main document or data source. As you edit the main document, you are adding text and other Word features that you want to see on every copy of the final document, as well as fields that represent where Word places variable information.

7. Select the Mail Merge Helper button (shown in the margin) from the Mail Merge toolbar to return to the Mail Merge Helper dialog box.

Creating the Data Source

1. Select the Get Data button in the Mail Merge Helper dialog box and select Create Data Source.

2. Word displays field names in the Field Names in Header Row box in the Create Data Source dialog box shown next. These field names identify the fields that occur in each record of the data source. You want the list of field names to match the entries and the order that you will enter data into this source.

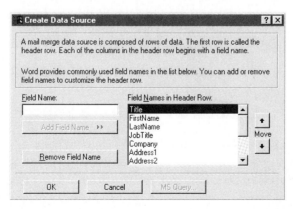

M

■ To add a field, type the field name in the Field Name text box and select Add Field Name. A field name can be up to 40 characters long; you may use only letters, numbers, or the underscore character. The first character must be a letter, and spaces are not allowed.

■ To remove a field, highlight the field name in the list box and select Remove Field Name.

■ To move a field in the list, highlight the field and reposition it using the Move arrow buttons beside the list box.

3. When the Field Names in Header Row list box shows the field names you want in the correct order, select OK. The Save As box appears. Type a new name for the document in the File Name box, and select OK.

4. Word now allows you to edit the data source or edit the main merge document. Select Edit Data Source to enter the variable information for the merge. You enter this data in a Data Form dialog box. If you selected Edit Main Document, the dialog boxes would disappear and you could start adding text and fields to the main merge document.

5. Enter the variable information for this record into the text boxes labeled with the field names. Use TAB or SHIFT+TAB to move between the fields. Select Add New to enter the record and move to the next one. More information about using this form appears under "Database toolbar."

6. Select OK when you are finished entering variable data. You can always return to the data source to enter further variable data later.

Using an Existing Document as the Data Source

1. Select the Get Data button in the Mail Merge Helper dialog box and choose Open Data Source.

2. Select the document that contains the variable information from the Open Data Source dialog box. This dialog box is just like the Open one, so you can use all the features described under "Document Management" to find the document you want.

3. Select Open.

Using an Address Book as the Data Source

1. Select the Get Data button in the Mail Merge Helper dialog box and select Use Address Book.

2. Select the address book to use from the list box and select OK.

3. Select the profile to use from the Profile drop-down list box and select OK. Depending on how you have set up your address book, you may need to respond to additional prompts to access the address book.

Adding a Header for the Data Source

Some possible sources of data for mail merge do not include the field names as header information. When you want to use data that is missing the field names, you need to include the field names and their order in a separate document called a *header document*. You can create one with these steps:

1. Select the Get Data button in the Mail Merge Helper dialog box.

2. Select Header Options and select Create.

3. The Create Header Source dialog box that you now see is identical to the Create Data Source dialog box described earlier.

4. Select the fields to be included in the header document and their order using steps 2 and 3 listed under "Creating the Data Source." The document that you save will include the header information, not the data.

At this point, you return to the Mail Merge Helper dialog box. Now you can select Get Data and Create Data Source to create the document containing just the variable information, not the field names. You will not select the field names because they are provided by the header document. You can also select Get Data and Open Data Source when the data is already in a document without the header information.

To use an existing header document:

1. Select Get Data from the Mail Merge Helper dialog box.

2. Select Header Options and Open.

3. Select the document containing the field names for the header information and select OK.

Just as with creating a header document, at this point, you can continue selecting an existing document to supply the variable information or create a new one.

Inserting Merge Fields

Merge fields allow you to place the variable data wherever you want it in the main document. When the merge is performed, the merge fields are converted to the values in the record being processed.

1. In the Mail Merge Helper dialog box, choose Edit under Main Document and select the main document you want to edit.

2. Position the insertion point where, in the main document, you want the variable information to be placed in the merged document.

M

3. Click the Insert Merge Field button in the Mail Merge toolbar.

> **REMEMBER:** *The Mail Merge toolbar appears when you are creating or editing a Mail Merge main document.*

4. Select a merge field from the list presented. Word inserts the field into your document surrounded by chevrons << >>. In Figure 4-37, fields have been added in the address block and salutation line. Merge fields are the fields that are in your data source.

5. Repeat steps 2 through 4 until you have added all the fields you need.

6. Select File | Save to save the document.

7. Click the Mail Merge Helper button in the Mail Merge toolbar.

INSERTING WORD FIELDS   You can select the following Word fields from the Mail Merge toolbar:

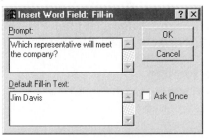

When you select a field from this list, Word displays a dialog box in which you provide the information needed to create the field. For example, the dialog box for the Fill-in field is shown here:

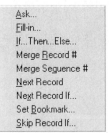

When you enter a Word field in the main document, you see the field's results rather than the field code. Or you can select Tools | Options and the View tab, and then the Field Codes check box under Show. When you change this setting, the field codes are displayed, as you can see in Figure 4-38. This main document uses only MERGEFIELD fields, which are inserted using the Insert Merge Field button in the Mail Merge toolbar and the FILLIN field which is inserted using the Insert Word Field button.

Figure 4-37.   *Merge fields are enclosed in chevrons << >>*

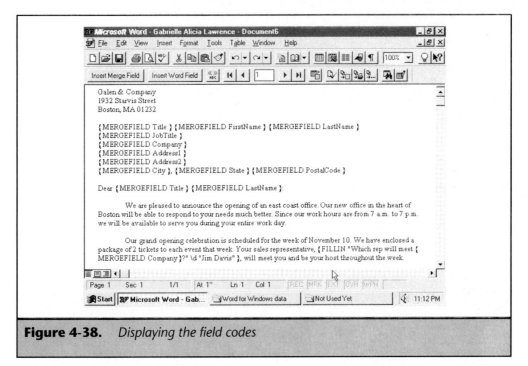

Figure 4-38.   *Displaying the field codes*

M

To insert Word fields, follow these general steps:

1. In the Mail Merge Helper dialog box, select Edit under Main Document and select the main document.
2. Position the insertion point where you want to insert the field.
3. Click the Insert Word Field button in the Mail Merge toolbar.
4. Choose the field you want to use.
5. Complete the dialog box for the field and select OK.
6. Click the Mail Merge Helper button in the Mail Merge toolbar to return to the Mail Merge Helper dialog box.

Executing the Merge

When you have entered all the records in the data source and created the final version of your main document, you are ready to complete the merge operation.

1. In the Mail Merge Helper dialog box, select the Merge button, opening the Merge dialog box.
2. Select the location for the merge output in the Merge To drop-down list box. You can choose New Document or Printer. You may also have Electronic Mail and Electronic Fax if these systems are set up on your system.
3. To specify which records are to be merged, you can select the All option button under Records to be Merged, or you can select From and enter the first and last record to merge in the From and To text boxes.

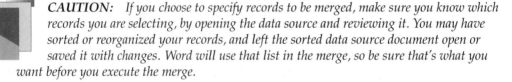

CAUTION: If you choose to specify records to be merged, make sure you know which records you are selecting, by opening the data source and reviewing it. You may have sorted or reorganized your records, and left the sorted data source document open or saved it with changes. Word will use that list in the merge, so be sure that's what you want before you execute the merge.

4. If you don't want Word to print lines that are empty because a field is empty, select "Don't print blank lines when data fields are empty," under When Merging Record to Print. To have Word print the blank lines, select "Print blank lines when data fields are empty."
5. To specify how Word handles a merge error, select Check Errors and choose a new option, then OK.
6. Choose Query Options to select which records are merged by designating criteria for the records to match. See "Specifying Query Options to Choose Records" later in this section for more information.

7. Select <u>M</u>erge to execute the merge.

If you chose to merge to a new document (step 2), the merged document will appear. Review the merged records before printing the documents. Figure 4-39 shows one of the mail merge letters.

Options

Word provides many ways to customize your mail merges.

Word Fields

When creating the main document, you can add Word fields to the main document by selecting one of them from the Insert Word Field button's drop-down list box. The fields you insert with this button let you alter the merge in various ways. The names of the Word fields for mail merges that appear in this list are not the names you would

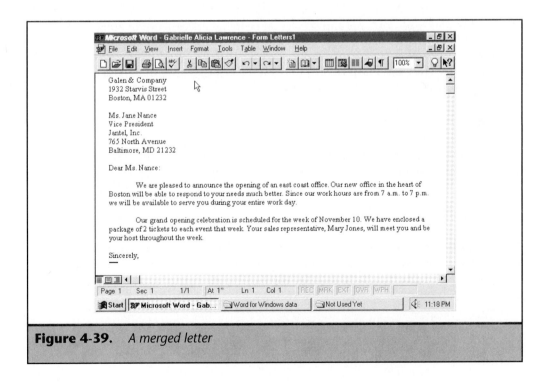

Figure 4-39.   *A merged letter*

M

look up in your documentation, or that appear in your document when the field codes are displayed. The following table explains the Word fields and their results:

Word Field	Field Code Inserted
Ask...	ASK field
Fill-in...	FILLIN field
If...Then...Else	IF field
Merge Record #	MERGEREC field
Merge Sequence #	MERGESEQ field
Next Record	NEXT field
Next Record If...	NEXTIF field
Set Bookmark...	SET field
Skip Record If...	SKIPIF field

The following paragraphs describe the Word fields and switches as if you were actually typing the fields, rather than the dialog box elements you can use when inserting them from the Insert Word Field button in the Mail Merge toolbar. The relationships between the dialog box options and the actual switches are self-explanatory.

ASK FIELD   The ASK field is used to prompt the user for input while Word is merging documents. The input is used to control the merge program, or is inserted into the document. This field takes the format

{ASK *bookmark* "*prompt*"}

where *bookmark* is the bookmark assigned to the text the user inputs, and *prompt* is the text that appears on the screen asking the user for the input.

You can use this field with the \o switch, to have Word prompt you only once when the merge begins, rather than for each record in the merge. Use the \d switch to specify the default text that is used when no input is provided.

FILLIN FIELD   The FILLIN field prompts the user for data, which will be displayed as the result of the field. Since this data is not assigned a bookmark, it is not available for use by other fields. This field uses the format

{FILLIN "*prompt*"}

where *prompt* is the text that prompts the user to enter the text that will be displayed.

Use the \d switch to specify the default data that is used when no input is provided. You can also use the \o switch to have Word prompt you only once in the merge, rather than for each iteration of the main document.

IF FIELD   Use the IF field to compare two expressions and then insert text depending on the results of that comparison. The format is

{IF *expression operator expression* "*TrueText*" "*FalseText*"}

where *expression* is what is being compared. This can be text, numbers, another field, or a bookmark. The *operator* is the type of comparison being made (see the table of operators that follows). "*TrueText*" is the field's result if the comparison is true. "*FalseText*" is the field's result if the comparison is false.

Operator	Purpose
=	Equals
>	Greater than
<	Less than
>=	Greater than or equal to
<=	Less than or equal to
<>	Not equal to

The following shows the dialog box for the IF field:

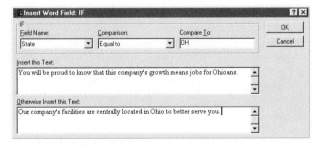

MERGEREC AND MERGESEQ FIELDS   The MERGEREC field result is the number of the current data source record. You can use this field to number the documents you create with the merge, or use it for further merge programming. This field uses no switches.

The result of the MERGESEQ field, which is very similar to MERGEREC, is the number of the current data record among the records actually being used. If you have chosen to skip some records, or limited the number of records being used, this number will be different from the one inserted with the MERGEREC field.

M

NEXT FIELD   The NEXT field advances the merge to the next record in the data source, but displays no result of its own. It uses no switches.

NEXTIF FIELD   The NEXTIF field advances the merge to the next record if a comparison is true. It combines the features of the NEXT and IF fields. It uses the format

> {NEXTIF *expression operator expression*}

where *expression* is the text, number, or bookmark to be compared. The operators used are described under the IF field just discussed.

SET FIELD   The SET field is used to assign a bookmark to data, which can then be inserted at any point in the document. This field uses the format

> {SET *bookmark "data"*}

where *bookmark* is the name of the bookmark to which the data is going to be assigned, and which will be used to insert that text throughout the document. The *data* argument is the data to be assigned to the bookmark.

SKIPIF FIELD   The SKIPIF field is used to skip records while merging, thus creating no merged information for the skipped records. This field takes the format

> {SKIPIF *expression operator expression*}

where *expression* is the text, numbers, or bookmarks to be compared, and *operator* specifies the comparison to be made. All the operators listed for the IF field can be used. When the comparison is true, Word does cancel the merged document created for the current record. It starts the merge again at the beginning of the main document, using the next record. Therefore, no document is created for the data record that was skipped, and a complete document is created for the next data record.

Specifying Query Options to Choose Records

Word lets you select the data source records to be used in the merge, using *query options*. The Query Options dialog box allows you to base your specifications on values in multiple fields.

1. In the Mail Merge Helper, select Query Options under Merge the Data with the Document.

2. Select the Filter Records tab if it is not on top. It looks like this:

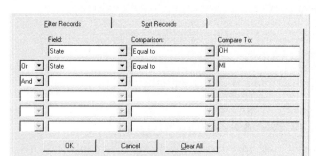

3. Open the drop-down list for Field, and select a field name from the data source.

4. Open the drop-down list for Comparison, and select from the comparison operators presented.

5. In the Compare To box, type an entry to be used with the Comparison operator.

6. To look at another entry, choose And or Or, using the drop-down arrow at the left of the next line of text boxes. This sets the relationship between the current rule and the next.

7. Repeat steps 3 through 6 for the next field you want to query.

8. When you have finished your specifications for record selection, choose OK.

Organizing the Data Source

You can choose to sort the data source records by the values in from one to three fields. These fields are called *sort keys*. The first one is specified as Sort By; the second, as Then By; and the third, as Then By. Word only looks at the second sort key when there are duplicate entries for the first Sort By field and looks at the third key when there are duplicate entries in the first and second. Specifying extra sort keys allows you to have tiebreakers.

1. From the Mail Merge Helper, select Query Options under Merge the Data with the Document.

2. Select the Sort Records tab.

3. Open the drop-down list in the Sort By box to display the list of fields in the data source, and choose the field you want to use for the primary sort key.

4. Choose Ascending to sort from A to Z and 1 to 9, or choose Descending to sort from Z to A and 9 to 1.

M

5. If you want to sort by a second field, repeat steps 3 and 4, using the Then By field. Repeat step 3 again, with the Then By field, if you need to specify a third key.

Hints

There are some hints to make working with the mail merge feature easier and more productive.

Using Data from Another Source

You may already have data in a document that is acceptable to Word as a data source for a merge. Word supports Microsoft Access databases and Microsoft Excel documents as data sources. Also, you can use databases for which you have an ODBC (open database connectivity) driver set up. Word supplies these drivers for Paradox, FoxPro, and Access. You can also use other documents for which Word has a converter. This includes the types of documents that you can open with the File | Open command. To use data from one of these sources, just select the document containing the data in the Open Data Source dialog box.

Using E-Mail to Distribute Merged Documents

If you plan to distribute merged documents via fax or e-mail, you will want to use the Query Options dialog box to choose only those records that have an entry in the fax number or e-mail address fields. See "Specifying Query Options to Choose Records" earlier in this section.

Organizing Data in a Different Way

Data source tables are limited to 31 data fields. When you need to create records with more fields, you can create a document that includes the header row entries and the records beneath them as paragraphs. *Delimiters* are used to mark the end of each field in these records. Your delimiter can be either a tab character or a comma.

It is important to use the same delimiter in all records in your data source. Make sure that the fields appear in the same order for each record. You need the same number of fields in each record, although a field can be left empty as long as the delimiters are correctly positioned. If your field contains a punctuation mark such as a comma or period, make sure that you enclose the field in quotation marks.

Ensuring That Non-Variable Text Is Correct

An important part of creating your main document is making sure that it reads correctly when merged. An important part of creating a data source is making sure that it contains *all* of the data that needs to be varied. While names and addresses are obvious forms of data that can vary, there are some other issues that are not so obvious.

For example, many people new to merges forget to include a title to use in salutations in the data source files and main documents. Consider the response to your letter, however, if you send out seven letters in which the salutation reads "Mr. *Name*," but three of the letters should be sent to "Ms. *Name*." Three of your recipients will develop a bad opinion of you or your company.

Do not limit yourself to Mr. and Ms. in your titles. Many officials and special professions have specific forms of address which are correct. Addressing people appropriately makes them more likely to give your message a fair hearing. See the box "Forms of Address" for some forms of address you will want to remember to use.

Nobody enjoys being the recipient of a "form letter." By using the merge process creatively, you make your documents look more personal, without taking more time to create the documents. The trick is taking the time originally, when creating the data

Forms of Address

If you are writing to Mr. Smith, it is easy to tell how to address your letter. If you are writing to an important official, a member of the clergy, or a dignitary, you might not be as certain how you should address your letter. The entry that you use in the address block sometimes matches the salutation, but at other times it is different. The list that follows provides an acceptable alternative for many of these special situations. The address form is used in the address block at the top of the letter. The salutation form is preceded by the word *Dear.*

Individual	Address Form	Salutation Form
Ambassador to the U.S.	His/Her Excellency ... Ambassador of ...	Ambassador
U.S. Ambassador	The Honorable ...	Ambassador
Rear Admiral	Rear Admiral ...	Admiral ...
Lieutenant General	Lieutenant General ...	General ...
U.S. President	The President	Mr. President
Former U.S. President	The Honorable ...	Mr. ...
U.S. Senator	The Honorable ...	Senator ...
Court Judge	The Honorable ...	Judge ...
Mayor	The Honorable ...	Mayor
Catholic Bishop	The Most Reverend ... Bishop of ...	Bishop
Catholic Priest	The Reverend ...	Father ...
Episcopal Bishop	The Right Reverend ... Bishop of ...	Bishop
Minister without Ph.D.	The Reverend ...	Mr. ...
Rabbi	Rabbi ...	Rabbi ...

M

source, or the main document, to record all possible bits of information, and then to use them effectively in the merge document. For example, a travel company might want to record clients' last vacation spot, and use that text in writing letters about scheduling their next year's vacation.

One thing you should be extremely careful about is making sure that the data source is correct. Nothing causes a worse impression than misspelling a person's name, or incorrectly identifying his or her company in a merge document. This adds to the reader's feeling of being treated impersonally. This is most important with merge documents because the printed copy is normally not proofread again. You should regularly proofread data sources that you use often, to check for incorrect or multiple entries. Make sure that people's names and titles are spelled correctly. If you are using abbreviations for degree and professional associations in your mail merge, make sure that these are correct, so that you do not present a sloppy image. The box "Rules for Abbreviating Degrees and Professional Associations" will help you keep these correct.

Rules for Abbreviating Degrees and Professional Associations

When you are creating a mailing list, you will want to be certain that you use the correct abbreviations for academic degrees and professional associations that you reference. These rules can guide you to the correct entries:

- Academic degrees use periods but no spaces in the abbreviations. For example B.A., Ph.D., J.D., L.L.M., M.D., and M.B.A.

- M.B.A. is written without periods when it is used generally to refer to a specific type of training, as in "the job market for MBAs is much better this year."

- Abbreviations for religious orders such as the Jesuits use the same form as academic degrees, as in S.J.

- Professional credentials are normally recorded in all capitals without periods, as in CPA representing Certified Public Accountant and CFP representing Certified Financial Planner.

When degree abbreviations follow a name, you do not use titles such as Mr., Ms., or Mrs. For example, you can use George P. Jones, Ph.D., or Mr. George P. Jones, but you would not use Mr. George P. Jones, Ph.D. Other more specific titles such as President, Chancellor, or Provost can be used along with the degree abbreviation.

Related Topics

Database Toolbar
Fields
Mail Merge Toolbar

Mail Merge Toolbar

The Mail Merge toolbar provides access to many of the special mail merge options
while you are working with a Mail Merge main document or data source. You can
use its buttons for inserting fields in a main document, for moving among fields
when working with a data source, and so forth. Here is a list of the Mail Merge
toolbar buttons:

Button	Button Name	Purpose
Insert Merge Field	Insert Merge Field	Lets you select a merge field from your data source to insert into the main merge document
Insert Word Field	Insert Word Field	Lets you select a Word field to insert into the main merge document
« » ABC	View Merged Data	Toggles between showing codes and data from the data source
◄|	First Record	Displays the first record
◄	Previous Record	Displays the previous record
	Go to Record	Lets you enter the record to display
►	Next Record	Displays the next record
►|	Last Record	Displays the last record
	Mail Merge Helper	Opens the Mail Merge Helper dialog box

M

Button	Button Name	Purpose
	Check for Errors	Runs the merge, checking for errors and creating no output
	Merge to New Document	Runs the merge, storing the merged document to a new document window
	Merge to Printer	Runs the merge, sending the merged document to the printer
	Mail Merge	Opens the Merge dialog box letting you set merge options
	Find Records	Finds a record in the data source that contains the specified data
	Edit Data Source	Displays the Data Form dialog box for editing the data source

Managing Documents

See "Document Management."

Margins

With Word, you can set the top, bottom, left, and right margins of a page all at the same time. You can create mirror margins for double-sided documents, and add a gutter when you plan to bind the document.

Procedures

Margins are an element of page formatting; you can change them using the menus or the ruler.

Changing Margins with the Menus

You can set the margins for a whole document, from a specific page to the end of the document, or for a section. If you select text before changing margins, you can specify the margin settings for that selected text only; Word will make the selected text a section and set the margins for that section.

1. Select File | Page Setup.

2. Select the <u>M</u>argins tab, if necessary.

3. Enter your margin settings in the <u>T</u>op, <u>B</u>ottom, Le<u>f</u>t, and Right text boxes.

■ To create mirror margins that you would use for a document that you will print on both sides of the page, select the M<u>i</u>rror Margins check box. The Le<u>f</u>t and Right text boxes change, becoming the <u>I</u>nside and <u>O</u>utside text boxes. The inside margin is the right margin for even-numbered pages, and the left margin for odd-numbered pages; the outside margin represents the other side margins.

■ To reserve part of the page for binding your document, enter the width of the binding area in the G<u>u</u>tter text box. This value will be added to the inside or left margin value.

4. Select the part of the document to which you want to apply these margins, from the <u>A</u>pply To drop-down list box.

5. Enter the minimum distance between headers or footers and the page edge, in the H<u>e</u>ader and Foote<u>r</u> text boxes. (Headers and footers appear between the document margin and the page edge. This setting effectively sets a margin for the headers and footers.)

6. Select OK.

Changing Margins with the Ruler

Margins changed with the ruler affect the selected section of the document, or the entire document if no section breaks have been inserted.

Switch to Page Layout view by selecting <u>V</u>iew | <u>P</u>age Layout or clicking the Page Layout button. Then drag the margin to its new location on either the vertical or horizontal ruler. The margin is the division between the gray and white areas on the ruler. When the mouse is positioned over it, it becomes a two-headed arrow. To position the mouse, assuming you have not created indents, point at the spot between the left and first line indent markers. There is no separate visual indicator, such as the arrows, of the margin location. Changing the margins this way also works from Print Preview when you display the ruler.

Hints

When you want to change the margins for a single paragraph, use the Indent paragraph format. This lets you establish what are effectively temporary margins for the paragraph.

Don't use margins to center text vertically on a page. Instead, change the vertical alignment for the section as described under "Sections."

M

Related Topics

Indents
Page Size and Orientation
Ruler
Sections
Viewing Documents

Master Document Toolbar

When you select the Master Document view, Word displays the Outline and Master Document toolbars. The outlining buttons let you change the outline you are creating for the master document, altering the levels of entries in the outline or expanding and collapsing the outline branches, setting which text you actually see. The right side of the toolbar is the Master Document toolbar. It contains the buttons for working with subdocuments. You can use these buttons to merge a subdocument or to split or join subdocuments. See "Master Documents" for more information.

The following table explains the function of each button:

Button	Button Name	Purpose
	Create Subdocument	Makes the selected headings into a subdocument
	Remove Subdocument	Makes the selected subdocument part of the main document
	Insert Subdocument	Opens a document and inserts it as a subdocument
	Merge Subdocument	Combines the selected subdocuments into a single subdocument
	Split Subdocument	Splits the current subdocument into two documents at the insertion point location
	Lock Document	Locks or unlocks the document for editing

Related Topics

Master Documents
Outline Toolbar

Master Documents

The master document feature is the ideal solution for working with large documents. Master documents help you take projects that might be unwieldy because of their length and organize them into smaller pieces, called *subdocuments*. You can control the formatting for the entire project by setting format options in the master document, but you can also work on the individual subdocuments. For example, you can use a master document to split a writing project into subdocuments among several individuals, yet ensure the consistent overall appearance of the combined project.

Since master documents work with outline features, it is easy to organize the final document after all the subdocuments have been written.

Procedures

There are several procedures for working with master documents that are unique to master documents, and some, though similar to those used in working with normal documents, that need to be modified when working with master documents.

Creating a Master Document

1. Select <u>F</u>ile | <u>N</u>ew.

2. Select <u>V</u>iew | <u>M</u>aster Document.

   The next three steps create subdocuments out of your entries in the master document. You can also have an existing document become the subdocument of a master document. These steps are described later under "Adding an Existing Word Document as a Subdocument."

3. Create an outline, using the heading styles 1 though 9.

NOTE: *See "Outlines" for the procedures used to create outlines.*

M

4. Select the outline headings and text to be used in creating the subdocuments. The first heading level (highest level heading) selected should be the heading level that marks the beginning of subdocuments. When you create subdocuments, as described in the following steps, each occurrence of this heading level is the beginning of a new subdocument, and headings and text that are part of a branch begun by a heading of this level are part of the subdocument.

5. Click the Create Subdocument icon on the Outline and Master Document toolbar. Figure 4-40 shows a master document after subdocuments have been created for the outline.

6. Select File | Save As, specify a name for the master document, and click OK to save the master document and all of its subdocuments.

Word creates a unique name for each subdocument, using the text in the heading that started the subdocument. For example, if the headings were Article 11, Article 12, and Article 13, the subdocument names would be Article 11, Article 12, and Article 13. If a document with that name already exists, Word adds numbers to make it unique.

Formatting a Master Document

Master documents and subdocuments rely on styles to set the overall document appearance. Master documents and their subdocuments often share the same styles.

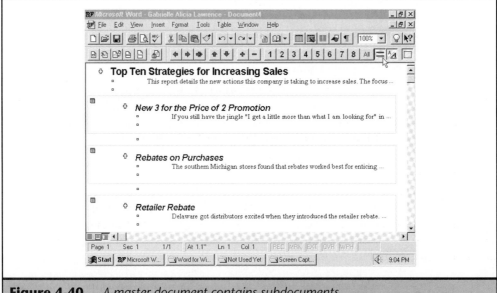

Figure 4-40.   *A master document contains subdocuments*

Styles ensure that the formatting remains consistent between the subdocuments. The style formatting set by the master document will override the style formatting set in the subdocument. This means that a subdocument opened up separately may look different if its style definitions differ from its master document. When you insert an existing document as a subdocument, you will see a message reminding you that the master document's styles will replace the styles with the same names from the subdocument. You can still use non-style formatting to change the appearance of characters and paragraphs in subdocuments.

Printing a Master Document

If you want to see all the detail of your master document, print the document in Normal view. If you want to see just an outline of the document, print from the Master Document view, first using the Expand and Collapse buttons on the toolbar to control the level of detail. After selecting the desired view, choose File | Print, select the desired options, and then OK.

Opening a Subdocument

You can open subdocuments by choosing File | Open. You can also open subdocuments from within a master document, and you should use this approach whenever you plan to rename a subdocument; otherwise, the link to the master document will be broken. Double-clicking the document icon opens the subdocument. This is the icon that appears at the top of any subdocument in Master Document view.

Renaming a Subdocument

1. Open the subdocument by double-clicking its icon in the master document.

CAUTION: *It is important that you open the subdocument from within the master document, or the link between the master document and subdocument will be destroyed.*

2. Choose File | Save As, type the new subdocument name, and click OK.
3. Close the subdocument.

Reorganizing Master Documents

You must have the master document open to reorganize it. You will probably find it easiest to work in Master Document view. You can move, combine, and join subdocuments, incorporate other Word documents, change a subdocument into a master document, and delete subdocuments.

MOVING A SUBDOCUMENT   Click the subdocument icon in the master document, and drag it to the new location to reorganize the master document.

M

TIP: *Set the outline level shown to the initial level used by all subdocuments to make reorganizing subdocuments easier.*

ADDING AN EXISTING WORD DOCUMENT AS A SUBDOCUMENT

1. Move the insertion point to the place in the master document where you want to insert the existing document as a subdocument.

2. Click the Insert Subdocument button, opening the Insert Subdocument dialog box. This dialog box is just like the Open dialog box, so you can use all the features described in "Document Management" to find the document you want.

3. Select the name of the document you want to insert, and then Open.

4. If needed, change the outline level of the new subdocument entry.

SPLITTING A SUBDOCUMENT   It's easy to divide a subdocument into two documents, to enable different people to work on the two sections. Just move the insertion point to the location where you want to make the split, and click the Split Subdocuments button. Choose File | Save As to save the new subdocuments and the changed master documents.

MERGING SUBDOCUMENTS   To combine subdocuments, they must be adjacent. Reposition them, if necessary, and then follow these steps:

1. Click the subdocument icon of the first subdocument to be merged.

2. Press SHIFT, and click the subdocument icons of any other adjacent subdocuments to be merged.

3. Click the Merge Subdocument button on the toolbar.

DELETING A SUBDOCUMENT   Select the subdocument icon, and press DEL or BACKSPACE. Since the subdocument is deleted, the subdocument icon no longer appears. When you delete a subdocument, you delete the link between the master document and subdocument. The subdocument is replaced by the text of the subdocument. Deleting a subdocument does not delete the contents of that subdocument nor does removing it from the master document.

Hints

Here are some hints to help you work with master documents and subdocuments.

Page Numbering

If you want to sequentially number all the pages in a master document, Word will handle the task for you automatically. If you want some sections to have numbers that do not follow the sequence of the rest of the master document, you can change the numbering within the subdocument. You will find it easier to modify the header and footer from the main document rather than work with the separate subdocuments.

Access to Subdocuments

When you open a master document, Word only opens the subdocuments for which you are the author with read/write access. Subdocuments authored by someone else are opened as read-only. To make changes to a subdocument that you did not author, you will need to click the Lock Document button on the Master Document toolbar before you can make a change. Word determines whether you are the author by comparing the document's Author property (see "Document Properties") with the user name entered on the User Info tab in the Options dialog box.

NOTE: If you want to lock your subdocuments more effectively, you will need to use different methods. See "Locking and Protecting Documents" in this chapter for procedures for locking your document in different ways.

Applications

Master documents are typically used for long reports or books; the subdocuments contain large sections of the report or chapters of the book. Master document features make it easy to ensure a consistent look to the completed document—even when your work on it is not all done at the same time, or when the sections are written by several individuals.

Math Calculations

Word will perform math calculations in your documents. You can perform the calculation with numbers entered in tables, by inserting formulas in other cells of the table, as explained in "Tables" in this chapter. Or you can use the = (expression) field and insert the results into the document, as described under "Fields."

TIP: If you have a one-time calculation to perform, remember that you have a calculator as one of Windows' accessory programs.

M

Maximize

Maximize a window to make it as large as possible in your screen. A maximized window takes the entire screen for an application window, or the entire application window for a document window.

Procedures

There are three ways to maximize:

■ Click on the Maximize button, shown here in the margin.

■ Open the program icon's or document icon's menu by clicking on the icon at the left end of the title bar (or press ALT+SPACEBAR for the application window or ALT+– (minus) for the document window), and select Ma<u>x</u>imize.

■ Press ALT+F10 for an application window or CTRL+F10 for a document window.

Related Topics

Document Window
Minimize
Windows

Menu Options

You can customize Word's menus to suit your own needs, or to accommodate a particular template, by assigning macros and commands to the menus. You can also create menu options to assign AutoText entries, styles, and fonts. For example, you might add a custom menu to a template, providing the specific commands useful in that document, like the <u>S</u>hortcuts menu shown in Figure 4-41.

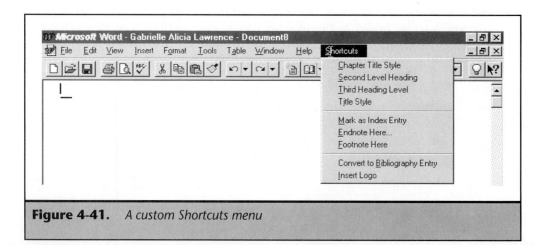

Figure 4-41. *A custom Shortcuts menu*

Procedure

1. Select Tools | Customize, and the Menus tab if necessary.

2. In the Categories list box, choose the category of elements you want to assign to menus: shortcut keys to commands, macros, fonts, AutoText entries, or styles.

3. From the Commands (Macros, Fonts, AutoText or Styles) list box, choose the specific item you want to assign to a menu.

4. From the Change What Menu drop-down list box, choose the menu to which you want to assign this item.

5. In the Position on Menu drop-down list box, specify where you want the item to appear.

6. In Name on Menu, enter the text to appear on the menu for this item.

    TIP: *Enter an & before a letter to underline it in the menu option.*

7. To change the menus available, select Menu Bar:

   ■ To add a new menu, enter its name in the Name on Menu Bar text box, choose a position in the Position on Menu Bar list box, and select Add.

   ■ To change the name of a menu, enter its new name in the Name on Menu Bar text box, select the menu in the Position on Menu Bar list box, and select Rename.

   ■ To remove a menu, highlight it and select Remove.

   ■ Select Close when you are done.

8. In the Save Changes In drop-down list box, select the template that this menu is to be saved in. If it is saved with the Normal template, the menu is available for all documents. Otherwise, the menu is only available for documents created with the template that the menu is saved in. Only the Normal template and other templates attached to the current document are shown in this list box.

9. Select Add to add the item to the menu. (Or select Remove to remove the selected item, or Reset All to return to the default menu.)

10. Select Close to return to the document and save your menu assignments.

Remember to save your changes to the template to make these menu changes available the next time you use Word.

M

TIP: *You can create separators in a menu by selecting the Separator in the Commands list box, the menu item in the Position on Menu drop-down list box, and Add.*

Related Topics

Keyboard Options
Toolbar Options

Merge

See "Mail Merge."

MERGEFIELD Field

See "Mail Merge" for how you can add this field to a main document to represent where you want variable data placed in a mail merge document.

MERGEREC Field

See "Mail Merge" for how to include a record number from the data source in the results of a mail merge.

MERGESEQ Field

See "Mail Merge" for how to add the sequence number of a record within the group of records used in a mail merge.

Microsoft Exchange

See "Electronic Mail" for how you can share documents with Microsoft Exchange.

Microsoft Paint

Microsoft Paint is the basic graphics package that comes with Windows. It replaces Paintbrush. You can create drawings in Microsoft Paint and then embed or insert them into your Word documents. You can also create graphics for your Word document by drawing on the document. See "Drawing on a Document," "Graphics," "Inserting Documents," and "Object Linking and Embedding."

Minimize

When you minimize a window, you reduce it to an icon. This clears space on the desktop and saves some memory.

Procedures

There are two ways to minimize:

■ Click the Minimize button, shown here in the margin.

■ Open the program icon's or document icon's menu by clicking the icon at the left end of the title bar, or press ALT+SPACEBAR for an application window or ALT+– for a document window, and select Minimize.

Related Topics

Document Window
Maximize
Windows

Mouse Installation and Customization

You need a mouse to use Windows 95. If you purchase a new one, you will need to install it before use. After you attach it to your computer as described in the mouse manufacturer's instructions, you can change the settings for the mouse in Windows. You can also customize some mouse setup features to make them work better for you.

M

Procedures

1. Select Settings from the Start menu and then select Control Panel.

2. Double-click the Mouse icon.

3. Select Right-handed or Left-handed to match the hand that will use the mouse.

4. Move the scroll box in the Double Click Speed scroll bar, to determine how quickly you have to click the mouse in order for the computer to interpret it as a double-click.

   A slower double-click speed can help new users as well as a person with arthritis or other mobility problems, because the two clicks that make a double-click can be further apart. Otherwise, setting a faster double-click helps prevent two single clicks from being mistakenly recognized as a double-click.

 TIP: *Test the double-click speed you've selected by trying to double-click in the Test area box. The jack-in-the-box will either pop-up or be put away when Windows recognizes the two clicks as a double-click.*

5. Select the Pointers tab and select the mouse pointer appearances for the different occasions when Word can change the mouse pointer.

6. Select the Motion tab, then move the scroll box under Pointer speed to set the speed for the movement of the mouse pointer on the screen as you move the mouse across your desktop.

   A slower tracking speed means you can place the mouse more precisely, because the pointer moves a little while the mouse moves a lot. A faster tracking speed makes the mouse pointer move faster, requiring less desk space for rolling the mouse.

7. Select the Show pointer trails check box to have Windows display mouse pointers trailing behind the main mouse pointer when you move the mouse. This feature does not affect the mouse's operation, but can help you find the mouse on the screen, especially on laptop computers. You can set by how much the pointer trails appear by adjusting the scroll box under Pointer trail.

8. Switch to the General tab and check the setting for the mouse. If it is not correct, select Change, then select your mouse from the list and select OK.

9. Select OK when all the settings are what you want.

10. Click the Close button or press ALT+F4 to put the Control Panel window away.

Related Topics

Mouse Pointer
Mouse Techniques

Mouse Pointer

The *mouse pointer* indicates the location of the next mouse action on the screen. The mouse pointer may change its shape, to tell you what the program is expecting you to do next. Table 4-12 explains some of the mouse pointer's appearances and tells you what you can do with the mouse when it has that shape.

Mouse Pointer	Function
↖	Selects objects
↖?	Gets help on the next command or object selected
⧗	Tells you to wait while the computer finishes a command
↔	Sizes a frame, object, or window
+	Creates a frame
I	Moves the insertion point to a location that you select

Table 4-12.   *Mouse Pointer Shapes and Their Actions*

M

Related Topics

Mouse Techniques

Mouse Techniques

The mouse is a device used for pointing at elements on the screen and selecting them. A mouse is the most common type of pointing device, but you can also use a trackball, stylus, or other device for the same purposes. A mouse makes using Windows and Word for Windows easier, because you can make selections without typing. Your selections can be based on what is on the screen, rather than what you know about the program.

Procedures

When you move the mouse device, the *mouse pointer,* which is the small icon on the screen, moves around the Word window. When an instruction in this book says to move the mouse to or point to a certain location, it means use the hand-held mouse to move the mouse pointer to that location on the screen.

Dragging

Use dragging to move an object around on the screen, or to select text.

1. Point the mouse at an object you want to move (drag). When you are selecting text, point the mouse at the beginning of the text you want to select.

2. Press the left mouse button and hold it down.

3. Without releasing the left mouse button, move the mouse pointer to where you want the object dragged or to the end of the text that you want to select.

4. Release the mouse button.

 TIP: *When you drag across text, you are dragging from the beginning to the end of the text to select it, rather than moving an object to another location. You can also drag text that is already selected, to move or copy it as described under "Drag and Drop" in this chapter.*

Clicking

Clicking is most often used to highlight or select an object. Simply point the mouse pointer at the button or other object you want to select, and press and quickly release the left mouse button once.

Right-Clicking

Right-clicking is the same procedure as clicking, except that you use the right mouse button instead of the left one. Right-clicking a toolbar or the document area opens a shortcut menu.

Double-Clicking

Double-clicking is most often used to execute a menu command or select an option in a menu or dialog box. Point the mouse pointer at the item you want to select or execute, and click and release the left mouse button twice, quickly. You can use the Control Panel to change how close two clicks must be to register as a double-click.

Related Topics

Mouse Installation and Customization
Mouse Pointer

Keys	Moves Insertion Point To
UP ARROW	The line above
DOWN ARROW	The line below
RIGHT ARROW	The character to the right
LEFT ARROW	The character to the left
CTRL+RIGHT ARROW	The word to the right
CTRL+LEFT ARROW	The word to the left
HOME	The beginning of a line
END	The end of a line
CTRL+UP ARROW	The paragraph above
CTRL+DOWN ARROW	The paragraph below
PAGE UP	Text one window above
PAGE DOWN	Text one window below
CTRL+PAGE UP	The text at the top of the window
CTRL+PAGE DOWN	The text at the bottom of the window
CTRL+HOME	The beginning of the document
CTRL+END	The end of the document

Table 4-13.   *Keyboard Methods for Moving the Insertion Point*

N

Move

See "Clipboard," "Drag and Drop," and "Spike" for moving text. See "Document Window" for moving windows. See other Word features for how to move the items that they create.

Moving the Insertion Point

The insertion point marks your location in your document. Whatever actions you take in Word occur at the insertion point's location. When you type text, it appears at the insertion point; if you change format settings, it affects the text at the insertion point. Therefore, it is important that you be able to easily move the insertion point where you want.

Procedures

You can move the insertion point in several ways: with the keyboard, the mouse, and the Go To command.

Moving with the Keyboard

The available keys and key combinations for moving the insertion point are listed in Table 4-13.

Moving with the Mouse

If necessary, use the scroll bars to display the position in the document where you want to move the insertion point. Using the scroll bar changes what part of the document is displayed, but does not actually move the insertion point itself. Use the scroll bar by clicking the scroll bar on either side of the scroll box, or dragging the scroll box along the scroll bar. Then click on the location onscreen where you want the insertion point to appear.

Moving with the Go To Command

1. Select Edit | Go To or press F5.

2. Indicate where you want to go by selecting the type of item you want to move to in the Go To What list box, such as page, annotation, or footnote. Then select

the specific item in the <u>E</u>nter drop-down list box. The name of this box changes depending on the item type you chose.

3. Select Go <u>T</u>o.

TIP: You can move to the next or previous one of any item by selecting the <u>N</u>ext or <u>P</u>revious button.

Hint

Usually, the destinations you specify with the Go To command are counted from the beginning of the document. You can use + (plus sign) and – (minus sign) to specify destinations relative to your current position. For example, to move to the 21st page after the insertion point's current location, enter **+21**. To move to the 21st page of the document, no matter where you start from, enter **21**.

Related Topics

Scroll Bars

Multiple Copies

You can print multiple copies of your document at once. See "Printing."

Naming Documents

See "Saving Documents."

Negative Indents

Negative indents move text closer to the edge of the paper and are used to create hanging indents, or to move entire paragraphs into the margin. See "Indents."

N

New Document

When you open a new document in Word, you choose a template to define the document's default settings and formats.

Procedures

1. Select File | New.

2. To open a new Word document, leave Document selected. To open a new template, select Template.

3. Select a template from one of the Template tabs. Each tab contains a group of templates as you can see in Figure 4-42. Templates contain option settings, formatting, and macros that help you create a certain type of document.

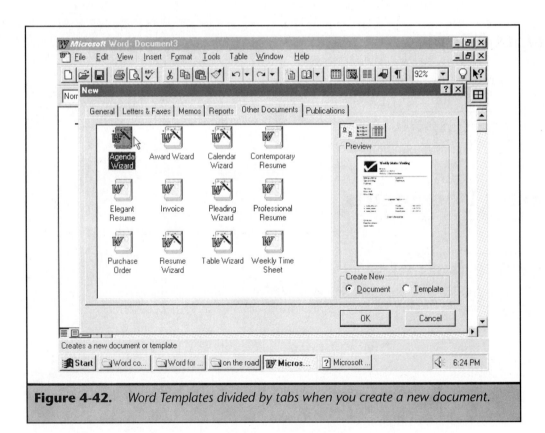

Figure 4-42.   *Word Templates divided by tabs when you create a new document.*

> **TIP:** *Templates that include the word "Wizard" will help you create your new document with a set of specific features.*

4. Select OK.

Hints

You can open a document using the Normal template by clicking on the New button on the Standard toolbar, shown here in the margin.

Some templates have macros that begin when the new document is created, such as the Wizards. When you select a new document using these templates, you are prompted by dialog boxes to enter certain information about your document, such as an author name, a fax number, or a date, before you are able to edit the new document directly.

Related Topics

Templates
Wizards

New Page

See "Pagination."

New Page Number

At any point in your document, you can restart the page numbering at any number you choose. See "Page Numbers."

Newspaper-Style Columns

See "Columns."

NEXT Field

The NEXT field merges data from the next data record in a mail merge without starting a new document. See "Mail Merge."

N

NEXTIF Field

The NEXTIF field decides whether to create a mail merge document for a data record based on a condition. See "Mail Merge."

Nonbreaking Hyphen

See "Hard Hyphen."

Nonbreaking Spaces

See "Hard Space."

Nonprinting Characters

Nonprinting characters are characters that you can see on your screen, but which do not appear in your document when it is printed. Word can display the nonprinting characters with the symbols shown in Table 4-14. You can choose to display or hide these nonprinting characters. Figure 4-43 shows many nonprinting characters displayed in a document.

Item	Displays As
Space	Small dot
Hard space	Degree symbol
Tab	Right-pointing arrow
Paragraph	Paragraph symbol
Optional hyphen	Long hyphen (em dash)
Nonbreaking hyphen	Double hyphen
Hidden text	Dotted underline
New line	Left-pointing arrow

Table 4-14. *Nonprinting Character Display Codes*

NOTE: Hidden text, while considered a nonprinting character, can actually be printed by following steps described under "Hidden Text."

Procedures

You can choose whether to display nonprinting characters. You can also change the default display to include or exclude these characters.

Displaying Nonprinting Characters

You can toggle between showing and hiding all nonprinting characters. Click the Show/Hide ¶ button on the Standard toolbar, shown here in the margin.

Displaying and Hiding Nonprinting Characters

1. Select <u>T</u>ools | <u>O</u>ptions, and the View tab or icon.

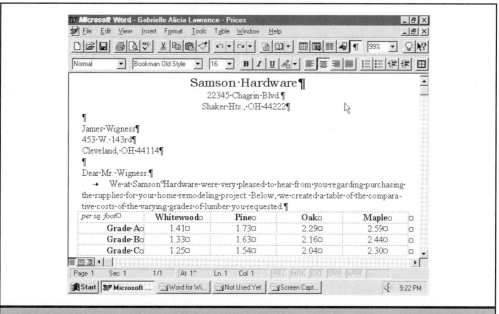

Figure 4-43.   *Displaying nonprinting characters*

2. Select or clear the appropriate check boxes under Nonprinting Characters that you want to see on your document. You can select from the ones listed in Table 4-14.

3. Select OK.

TIP: *Selecting All from the Options dialog box has the same effect as clicking the Show/Hide ¶ button and vice versa.*

Hints

Whether you want to see the nonprinting characters depends on personal preference and whether you are looking at the effects of these characters. Showing these characters helps you see where you have used spaces, tabs, and other features to create your document.

Related Topics

View Options

Normal

Normal is the default style assigned to text. Changing the formatting of this style, as described under "Styles," changes the format of all text not otherwise formatted.

Normal View

See "Viewing Documents."

NOTEREF Field

The NOTEREF field returns the number for a footnote or endnote reference mark or bookmark. See "Footnotes and Endnotes."

Notes

To learn about footnotes and endnotes, see "Footnotes and Endnotes." Look at "Annotations" to see how you can add notes to the document. You can also add notes to a document by adding the note as hidden text.

Numbered Lists

See "Lists."

Numbering

See "Line Numbers" and "Page Numbers."

Numbering Across Documents

See "Master Documents" and "Page Numbers."

NUMCHARS Field

This field returns the number of characters in a document—the same number displayed after Characters when you select Tools | Word Count or select File | Properties and switch to the Statistics tab.

NUMPAGES Field

This field returns the number of pages in a document—the same number displayed after Pages when you select Tools | Word Count or select File | Properties and switch to the Statistics tab.

NUMWORDS Field

This field returns the number of words in a document—the same number displayed after Words when you select Tools | Word Count or select File | Properties and switch to the Statistics tab.

Object Linking and Embedding

Object Linking and Embedding (OLE) is a technology used by Windows and Windows applications to share data, through either linking or embedding. OLE lets you add pictures, charts, and other data objects created in another application to your Word document, as well as put Word documents into other application's documents. With OLE, you can effectively add the functionality of other software to the program you are using. Dynamic Data Exchange (DDE) is also used by Windows applications to allow one application to run another.

Linking vs. Embedding

Using OLE, you embed or link data objects into your Word document, and embed or link Word data objects into the data of other applications. You decide whether to link or embed the object; the difference is based on the location of the data that you are sharing and whether you plan to use the data in one or many documents or applications.

When you *link* an object, the *data object* you are sharing is stored in its own document using the format of the application that created it. That application, the *source application*, is used to edit the data. Word and other applications can include the data in their own documents by linking to that document. When you see a data object in a Word document, you are seeing a picture of data stored in another document that uses a different format. You edit the data object from the Word document it is linked into, by opening the source application (which opens the document), making your changes, and saving the edited data into the same document. Then the data object in the Word document is updated to reflect the new contents of the linked document. You can still use the source application to work with the data document separately from Word. For example, you can link a Paint document containing a company logo into a Word document. This image can be edited in the Paint application or by starting the Paint application from Word. The same document, containing a copy of the logo, can be linked into many different Word documents, or into Excel worksheets and Access database reports.

When you *embed* a data object into a Word document, the data object is actually stored in the Word document. You still use the source application to edit the data; however, the data is provided to the source application from the Word document, rather than the source application opening a separate document that contains the data. You cannot use other applications to edit the data, nor can you include the data in other documents unless you link or embed the Word document containing the embedded data object. The object in the Word document is the original copy of the data. For example, when you embed an Excel worksheet into a Word document, the worksheet is edited using Excel, but the data is stored as part of (embedded in) a Word document. Other applications cannot edit the Excel spreadsheet.

If you plan to use a data object only in a single Word document, embed it in that document. An embedded data object is stored in the document that uses it, even though the data is saved in the format of another application. When you plan to use the data in many different documents, you want to link (instead of embed) the object. When the linked object is edited and saved in its original document, all documents or applications that have a link to that document use the updated version in their data links.

Before you can share data between applications, the applications must have embedding or linking capability. Some applications can only provide data, some applications can only accept data, some can do both, and some can do neither. Applications that can accept data to embed or link are called *client applications.* Applications that can provide data to embed or link are called *server applications.* Word for Windows can be both client and server. Word also provides some applications that can supply objects you embed into Word documents: Microsoft Graph creates graphs, WordArt creates enhanced text, and Equation Editor creates equations.

Special Fields Used to Share Documents

When you embed or link data objects in Word, you may see the LINK and EMBED fields in your documents. Most fields insert something into the Word document that contains them, and these fields are no exception. These fields insert the data object displayed in the field's location. You do not have to be concerned with the switches in these fields. The Word commands that modify embedded or linked objects make the necessary changes to these fields.

TIP: As mentioned in the "Fields" section earlier in this chapter, you can switch between displaying field codes and field contents in your documents. Press ALT+F9, or select Tools | Options, and then turn on or off the Field Codes check box option in the View tab.

Procedures

The following procedures will tell you how to link or embed an existing document or part of an existing document into your Word document, as well as how to create and insert an embedded object without leaving Word. You will also learn how to set the format of an object when it is linked or embedded into your Word document, and how to change the format in which an embedded object is stored.

Creating an Embedded Object

You can create and insert an embedded object without ever leaving Word.

1. Move the insertion point to where you want the object to start.

2. Select Insert | Object.

3. From the Object Type list box, choose the application for the type of data you want to add, and select OK. The application opens. The applications available in this list box are all the registered server applications.

O

4. At this point, you can proceed to create the data you want to appear in the embedded object, using the application you selected in step 3.

5. Choose Exit from the File menu to close the application you are using to create the embedded object. In some applications, this command may appear as Exit and Update.

Depending on how the application appears when you open it, there may not be a File menu to select Exit from. For example, some applications change Word's toolbars and menus. In these cases, you can leave the source application by clicking a part of the document that is not part of the embedded object. You return to your document, and the embedded object appears in the document.

Inserting an Embedded or Linked Object

You can insert a document as an embedded or linked object, without opening the application used to create the document.

1. Move the insertion point to where you want the object to start.

2. Select Insert | Object and the Create from File tab.

3. Select the document you want, using the File Name text box. You can also click Browse to open a Browse dialog box to help you select the document. This dialog box is just like the Open dialog box, so you can use the features described under "Document Management" to find the document you want.

4. If you want the inserted object to be linked to the Word document, select the Link to File check box; if you want the object embedded into the current document, clear the check box.

5. Select OK to add the object to the document. The object is linked if the Link to File option is on, or embedded if the option is off.

If you decide you want to be more selective about the part of the linked document that appears in the Word document, use the Edit | Links command and change the contents of the Item text box (see "Changing Settings for Linked Objects" later in this section).

Embedding or Linking Data Using the Clipboard

You can embed or link data objects by starting the application used with the data and copying the data to the Clipboard.

1. In the source application, display and select the data that you want to share.

2. Choose Copy from the source application's Edit menu to copy the selection to the Clipboard.

3. Switch to Word, and move the insertion point to where you want to insert the data from the Clipboard.

4. Choose Edit | Paste Special to display the Paste Special dialog box like the one shown here:

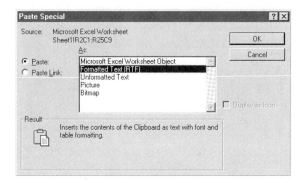

Select the format to use when pasting the Clipboard data into Word from the As list box. The formats listed depend on the source of the data, since they are the formats the source application can support. Select either the Paste or the Paste Link option button. Choose Paste, and Word either embeds or copies the data into your document. The data on the Clipboard will be embedded when the selection in the As list box includes the word *Object* and the Paste option button is selected. Paste Link links the data using the selected format. Paste Link is only available if you can link to the source document.

5. Select the format you want the data object to use.

6. Select OK to add the object.

Figure 4-44 shows several objects added to a Word document. They look different because we have selected different formats for pasting them.

 TIP: *When you are creating the data to link, save the document before creating the link. Word needs to know the name of the linked document so that it can update the data object using the document.*

Embedding Part of an Existing Document

1. Display and select the portion of data that you want to embed in the source application.

2. Choose Copy from the source application's Edit menu to copy the selection to the Clipboard.

3. Switch to Word, and move the insertion point to where you want to embed the data.

4. Choose Edit | Paste Special and then OK. The data from the source application is embedded, assuming the application is a server and Word can accept the format.

O

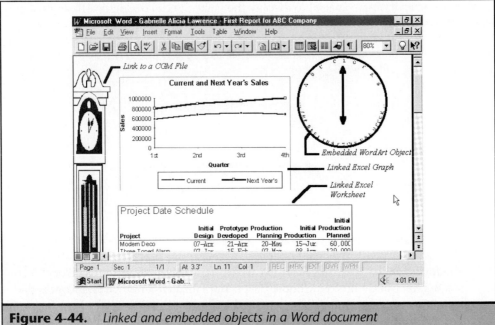

Figure 4-44.   *Linked and embedded objects in a Word document*

Editing an Embedded or Linked Object from Word

The following are several ways to edit linked or embedded objects from within Word.

- Double-click the object. (Note: Sound and video-clip objects cannot be edited this way, because double-clicking them will play them.)

- Select the object, and then select Edit | *ObjectName* Object, where *ObjectName* is the name of the object's source, such as Microsoft Graph. If the object is a linked object, the command will be Edit | Linked *ObjectName* Object. Some objects do not include their name in the command. Then, select Edit to edit the object while remaining in Word, or Open to open the other application and work with the object there; Edit is only available for some types of objects.

- Open the source document containing the linked object, using the creating application. For example, to edit an Excel spreadsheet object that appears in a Word document, open Excel and the spreadsheet. When you return to the document in Word, the document with the link to the spreadsheet will display the modified version of the spreadsheet.

- Select the object, and then Edit or Open from the object's shortcut menu. Select Edit to edit the object in Word, or Open to open the other application and work with the object there. Edit is only available for some types of objects.

Figure 4-45 shows an embedded object being edited from Word. Excel can provide in-place editing, which is why the Word menus and toolbars are replaced with Excel's. Depending on the application that provided the embedded data, you may see the application in a separate window with the embedded data appearing shaded in Word while you edit it.

Changing the Format of an Embedded Object

You can change the format of an embedded object.

1. Select the object whose format you want to convert, or any object using the format you want to change.

2. Select Edit | *ObjectName* Object | Convert, where *ObjectName* is the name of the object's source.

3. You can choose to convert the current object to another format, or you can choose a new application to use for editing or opening all objects in the document that use the format of the selected object. While theConvert To option button is selected, choose the type of object you want the selected object converted to from the Object Type list box. Change the application used to edit all objects with the same format as the currently selected object by selecting the

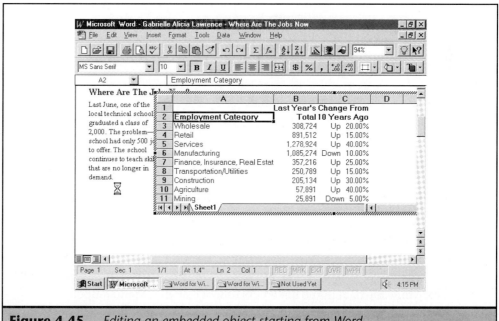

Figure 4-45.   *Editing an embedded object starting from Word*

Activate As option button and choosing the object type from the Object Type list box that normally uses the application you want to use.

For example, if you want an embedded Excel worksheet to appear in a Word document and you don't plan to make any changes to it, you can select Microsoft Word Picture as the object type for the embedded object. Word converts the embedded Excel worksheet object into a picture of the data. After making this type of conversion, you cannot revert to the previous object type.

4. Select OK to make the change.

TIP: *You can convert an embedded object into a picture by selecting the object and pressing CTRL+SHIFT+F9.*

Changing Settings for Linked Objects

When you change the settings for linked objects, you can change the nature of the link itself. You can choose when to update the link, break the link, or change what the link is to.

1. Select Edit | Links to open this Links dialog box:

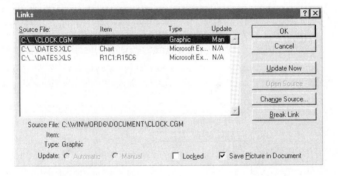

2. From the Source File list box, select the linked object to change.

3. Select the link options that you want to change, as described next. Then select OK to return to the document (if necessary).

Here are the link settings you can specify:

■ The Automatic or Manual option buttons let you control when Word checks the linked data to include any changes. With Automatic, Word updates every time the data in the linked document changes. Manual updates the linked data only when you use the Edit | Links command and select Update Now, when you move to the field and press F9, or when you select Update Link from the field's shortcut menu. To prevent subsequent updates to the linked data, select the Locked check box. The linked data will not change until you use Edit I Links again and clear this check box.

■ To convert the contents of the link into the text or picture as it appears in Word, select Break Link. This breaks the link between the data in Word and the source data document. Select Yes to confirm that you indeed want to break this link, and the Word document will then contain either the text or a picture of the data in the source document. Another way to do this is to move to the field code for the linked data and press CTRL+SHIFT+F9.

■ To work with the data in the linked document, select Open Source. This is the same as double-clicking the object, selecting Edit I Linked *ObjectName* Object I Open, or selecting Open from the field's shortcut menu.

■ If you want to change the document or the part of the document from which the linked object comes, select Change Source. In the Change Source dialog box, use the File Name and all of the other features in this dialog box to select a document to provide the data of the link. This dialog box is just like the Open one, which is further described in "Document Management." In the Item text box, you can enter or modify the location of the document the object is linked to. The entry depends on the application you use to work with the data. For a linked Word document, you can enter a bookmark name. For an Excel spreadsheet, you can enter a range address or name.

■ You can make the document containing the linked data smaller by not saving a picture of what the linked data looks like in the document. To do this, clear the Save Picture in Document check box so Word only stores the link information in the document, not a picture of the data that the link represents.

Options

You can display the embedded or linked object as an icon, rather than display the actual data. To do this, select the Display as Icon check box in the Paste Special dialog box. The icon for the inserted object is usually the icon of the application that created it. Just double-click the icon to edit the data that the icon represents. This icon makes the data always available without having it displayed on the screen. For some types of objects, such as sounds, you expect to see the icon rather than the data that the icon represents.

You can also change the icon that Word uses for the embedded or linked object. When you use the Edit I Paste Special or the Insert I Object command and select the Display as Icon check box, Word shows you the Change Icon button. Select this button and you see another dialog box where you can select the icon to represent the embedded or linked object. Choose one of the displayed icons in the Icon list box, or select Browse to see another document containing icons. You can also enter your own special caption to appear below the icon by entering new text after Caption.

O

If you change your mind about whether to display an object as an icon, use the Edit | *ObjectName* Object | Convert command again and change the setting of the Display as Icon check box.

Hints

If you want to have some position options for the embedded or linked object, add a frame around it. Frames and their options are described under "Frames."

To make the embedded or linked object smaller or larger, the usual method is to select Format | Picture and change the percentage of scaling. "Graphics" in this chapter explains several features for Word pictures that you can use on the pictures of embedded and linked objects that appear in your Word documents.

Embedding and linking does not increase the number of applications installed on your computer. Word can only work with embedded and linked objects created with applications you have installed.

You can format the results of linked or embedded text if the object type allows it. If you are allowed to select individual characters, words, and paragraphs, you can use Word's formatting features to enhance the appearance of the text. For example, in a linked worksheet, you might want to format the table's headings. The "* mergeformat" that you may see as part of the field code for the linked or embedded data tells Word to keep the formatting applied to embedded data or to linked data.

To make Word data available in another application, you need to copy it to the Clipboard, as described under "Clipboard" in this chapter. Several Microsoft applications can work with Word data. You can also click buttons on the Microsoft toolbar to quickly switch to other Microsoft applications. By selecting buttons in this toolbar, you can start Microsoft Excel, PowerPoint, Mail, Access, FoxPro, Project, Schedule+, and Publisher, assuming these applications are installed.

TIP: *Word provides several applications that create embedded objects. The Equation Editor, Graph, and WordArt all create embedded objects.*

Related Topics

Clipboard
Drawing on a Document
Equations
Frames
Graph
Graphics
Inserting Documents
Scrap
WordArt

Office Binder

See "Binder."

OLE

See "Object Linking and Embedding."

Online Forms

Online forms are forms meant to be filled out on the screen and then printed. See "Forms" for more information.

Online Help

Word has online help as described under "Help."

Opening Documents

You can open documents in Word without closing documents that are already open. You may open as many documents as your computer's memory can accommodate.

Procedures

The following procedures explain how to open a Word document or one created in another application.

Opening a Word for Windows Document

1. To open the Open dialog box, select File | Open, or press CTRL+F12, or select the Open toolbar button, or press CTRL+O.

2. Choose the location of the document you want to open.

   The Look In list box shows the documents available in the specified folder. The list only includes folders and documents of the type selected by the Files of Type drop-down list box. You can change to another location by selecting folders in the Look In list box or by selecting a new location from the Look In drop-down list box. Another option is to click the Up One Level button to the right of the Look In drop-down list box to switch to the folder that contains the folder you are currently looking at. You can also click on the Look In Favorites button to show the shortcuts to the documents that you have added to your Favorites folder. When you change the folder where you are working from in

O

Word, you are setting a new *working folder.* Word continues to use that new location as the working folder until you choose another one or leave Word.

3. Select the document you want to open from the Look In list box, or type its name in the File Name text box.

Another way to open a document from another location is to enter the full path and name of the document you want to open in the File Name text box. This way you can open a document in another drive or folder without changing the working folder.

4. In the Files of Type drop-down list box, select the type of documents you want to see. Your selection here determines what documents will be listed in the Look In list box. The default is to list Word documents. To list a different type of document, choose that document type from this drop-down list box.

5. Select OK to open the document. You also select OK when you double-click a document in the Look In list box.

Opening a Non-Word for Windows Document

You can also open a document that is not a Word for Windows document type. To do so, follow the steps described earlier. Once you select OK, Word will look at the document and realize that the document is not a Word for Windows document type. At this point, either Word converts it for you, or you see a prompt for how you want Word to convert it for you, depending on the Confirm Conversion at Open General option setting.

When this check box is selected, the Convert File dialog box lists the possible document types that Word will accept, and Word's guess for the appropriate type will be highlighted. Select OK if the selection is correct, or make another selection before you select OK. When the Confirm Conversion at Open check box is cleared, Word automatically selects the type of the document without your input. You will not see the prompt for a document type unless Word is not sure of the type of the document you are opening.

After the document type is selected by you or Word, Word converts the document from its original type to Word for Windows's type. If Word requires any further information to assist in the conversion, it prompts for that information. A message appears on the status line telling you the percentage of the ongoing conversion process Word has completed.

Hints

The following are some tips that may make opening documents faster or more accurate.

Shortcuts to Opening Documents

At the bottom of the File menu, Word displays the names of the last four documents you saved, as shown here:

```
1 First Report for ABC Company
2 C:\...\Where Are The Jobs Now
3 C:\...\First Report for ABC Company
4 C:\...\Miscellaneous comments to keep...

Exit
```

To reopen one of those four documents, select it from the menu. You can select one of these menu options either by clicking it, or by highlighting it and pressing ENTER, or by typing the number that precedes the document name.

You can designate how many documents—up to nine—Word will remember for displaying at the bottom of the File menu. Select Tools | Options, then the General tab, and enter a new number after Recently Used File List.

Other Ways to Open Documents

In the Open dialog box, you can right-click a document to see its shortcut menu. From this menu, you can select Open to open documents just as if you selected the Open button in the Open dialog box. You can also select Open Read-Only. This opens the document, but if you want to save the document, you must save it with a different name.

You can also use Windows to open Word documents. Select File | Open when you highlight any Word document in a folder window to open that document in Word. The most recently used files for Windows are available through the Start menu under Documents.

Finding Documents

The Open dialog box has options you can use to locate a document that you want to open. "Document Management" describes how you can search your computer for the document that matches criteria that you provide.

Opening Multiple Documents

If you have several documents selected when you select the Open button or Open from a shortcut menu, you will open all of the selected documents. You can select a group of documents by clicking the first one, holding down SHIFT, and clicking the last one in the group. You can add and remove individual documents from the selection by holding down CTRL while you click them.

Default Document Location

Word assumes that the next document you want to open is in the working folder. This folder is set to the last folder you specified for a document-selection command. When you first start Word, it assumes your documents are in the folder set with Tools | Options, the File Locations tab, and Documents. These options are described in "Document Location Options" in this chapter.

Designating How Word Converts Documents

If you want to change the settings for how Word converts documents that are a different type than Word, these options are described under "Compatibility Options."

Using Documents on a Network

When you are working on a network and want to open a document, you select it just like any other document. This probably will include selecting the location of the network's folders in the Look In drop-down list box. You can only save the document to a network drive if you have the network's permission—as set by the network administrator, rather than in Word. To protect your documents from other users' changes, assign a password or use Word's annotation features. See "Saving Documents" and "Annotations."

Related Topics

Annotations
Closing Documents
Compatibility Options
Document Location Options
Document Management
Favorites Folder
Saving Documents

Optional Hyphens

See "Hyphenation."

Options

Word has many settings that you can change to make Word operate the way you want it. Most of these options are set with the Tools | Options command. Since there are so many options, they are categorized and described individually in this chapter as shown in the following table.

See This:	**About Customizing This:**
AutoFormat	How AutoFormat works with your document
Comparing Versions	How revisions are marked
Compatibility Options	How Word converts documents of other document types
Edit Options	How you edit documents
File Location Options	Where Word expects to find documents
General Options	General features
Grammar Options	How Word checks the grammar in your documents
Keyboard Options	The shortcut keys
Menu Options	Word's menus
Print Options	How Word prints documents
Save Options	How Word saves documents
Spelling Options	How Word checks spelling in your document
Toolbar Options	The toolbars
User Info Options	The information Word maintains about you
View Options	The screen display for Word

Ordinal Numbers

When you enter ordinal numbers, like 1st, you can have Word automatically change it to 1st. To let Word make this change, select Tools | Options, select the AutoFormat tab, and then select the AutoFormat As You Type option button. Select the Ordinals (1st) with Superscript option button and select OK. When you type an ordinal number, Word will superscript the text after the number.

Organizer

Word's Organizer lets you transfer styles, AutoText, toolbars, and macros among templates and documents. You can also delete these items and rename them with the Organizer. Rather than create these items, the Organizer lets you share them among your Word documents and templates. Use the Organizer to copy these items among the templates you use, so that documents based on the templates will have these items available. You can also copy these items from the current document to its template, for the use of other documents using the same template.

O

Procedures

1. Open the Organizer. You can do it one of these ways:

   ■ Select Format | Style and then Organizer.

   ■ Select Tools | Macro and then Organizer.

   ■ Select File | Templates and then Organizer.

Word displays a dialog box that looks like this:

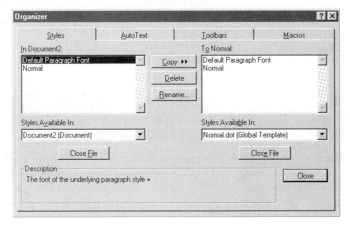

2. Use the Organizer to work with the styles, AutoText entries, toolbars, and macros, as described next.

3. Select Close to leave the Organizer.

Your activities in step 2 will depend on what you want to do. The tabs all have the same elements, since they are only changing the Word feature you are working with. Select the styles, AutoText entries, toolbars, or macros you want to work with from either the In list box or the To list box. You can change the template that appears in either list by using the Close File button below the list box. Once you select Close File, it changes to Open File.

When you select Open File, you can choose a template or document whose items you want to work with. For example, the Look In list box can show the contents of a template or a document when you want to copy one particular document's styles for use in other documents created with a template. When Normal is not the selected file, you can also choose from the Available In drop-down list box and switch between Normal and the template or document that is currently open.

   ■ To delete a style, AutoText entry, toolbar, or macro, choose it in the list and then select Delete. You will be asked to confirm that you want to delete the selected item. Select Yes to delete it, Yes to All to delete all selected items without further confirmation, <u>N</u>o to skip over deleting the listed item, or Cancel to stop deleting styles, AutoText entries, macros, or toolbars.

■ To rename a style, AutoText entry, toolbar, or macro, select it in the list and then select <u>R</u>ename. Type a new name and select OK.

■ To copy a style, AutoText entry, toolbar, or macro, select it in the <u>I</u>n list box and then select <u>C</u>opy. The selected item is copied into the template in the <u>T</u>o list box.

Related Topics

AutoText
Macros
Styles
Templates
Toolbars

Organizing Data and Documents

Word has several organization features you can use for your documents. "Document Management" describes how you can use the <u>F</u>ile | <u>O</u>pen command to locate and work with specific documents. "Sorting" covers sorting data within a document, including how to organize the data you will use for Mail Merge. For large documents, look at "Master Documents."

Orientation

See "Page Size and Orientation" and "Sections."

Orphans

See "Pagination."

Outlines

Word's Outline feature provides a hierarchical format to a document, letting you work with the headings in the outline to organize and rearrange the document. By displaying only the headings, you can quickly move to a specific part of the document. You can also use outline headings to rearrange the document's text, and to quickly execute formatting tasks. Word's Outline view shows the different levels of headings and the text that belongs to each one. By applying outline headings to your document and using the Outline view, you have a new way of working with your document.

Procedures

When you create an outline, all paragraphs are marked as either headings or as body text. Word offers you nine levels of headings styles. Any paragraph that is not a heading is body text. The following procedures tell you how to create, edit, or print an outline.

Switching to Outline View

Select View | Outline, or click the Outline View button at the left of the horizontal scroll bar. To switch back to Normal view, select View | Normal or click the Normal View button at the left of the horizontal scroll bar.

Creating a New Outline

1. Open a new document.
2. Switch to Outline view by selecting View | Outline. The Outline toolbar appears as shown here:

3. Type a heading. Word assigns the Heading 1 format automatically.
4. Press ENTER to end the first paragraph, and type another heading or a few lines of text. Note that paragraphs are automatically formatted at the same level as the paragraph that precedes them.
5. Change the level of the heading you just typed, or convert the paragraph text to body text, using either the mouse or the keyboard. The buttons and key combinations you can use to do this are shown in Table 4-15.
6. Repeat steps 3 through 5 until you have created your entire outline document. You can have up to nine levels of headings in your document. Figure 4-46 illustrates an outline, without body text.

Outlining an Existing Document

1. Open the document you want to outline.
2. Switch to Outline view by selecting View | Outline.
3. Move to the paragraphs you want to use as headings, and change them to the appropriate heading level. You can do this by selecting buttons on the Outline

toolbar or by pressing the keys shown in Table 4-15. Another way to do this is to drag the bullet character in front of a paragraph to the appropriate indentation for the level you want to use.

Toolbar Button	Key Combination	Result
	ALT+SHIFT+LEFT ARROW	Switches to next higher level
	ALT+SHIFT+RIGHT ARROW	Switches to next lower level
	ALT+SHIFT+5 (the 5 on numeric keypad)	Converts to body text
	ALT+SHIFT+UP ARROW	Moves up one position in the outline
	ALT+SHIFT+DOWN ARROW	Moves down one position in the outline
	ALT+SHIFT+– or – on numeric keypad	Expands to next higher level
	ALT+SHIFT+– or – on numeric keypad	Collapses to next lower level
1 to 8	ALT+SHIFT+*level number*	Displays outline only through level number specified
All	ALT+SHIFT+A or ALT+SHIFT+*	Expands or collapses the entire outline
	ALT+SHIFT+L	Shows either all text or just the first line
A/A	/ (on numeric keypad)	Shows or hides character formatting

Table 4-15.   *The Outline Toolbar*

TIP: When AutoFormat is on, Word automatically assigns a paragraph to the Heading 1 style when you press ENTER three times to end a new paragraph if the Headings check box is selected. Word will change to Heading 2 any new paragraph that you end by pressing ENTER three times if you start the paragraph with a tab. See "AutoFormat" for the other automatic format changes that Word can make.

Collapsing and Expanding Heading Levels

To *collapse* or *expand* the branches of the outline means to hide or show the body text and headings under the current heading. *Branch* is a term used in outlines which refers to the body text and headings under a specific heading. Collapsing and expanding do not affect the headings and text elsewhere in the outline that are not subordinate to the heading you collapse or expand.

1. Switch to Outline view. If you have not yet added body text to your document, it may look something like Figure 4-46.

2. Move to the last heading in a branch. For example, in Figure 4-46 you could move to the first third-level heading, "Applicant Testing."

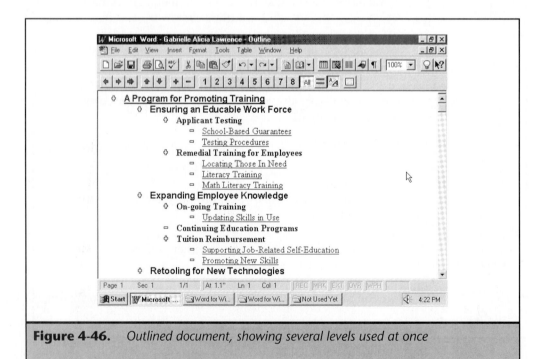

Figure 4-46. *Outlined document, showing several levels used at once*

3. Click the Collapse button in the Outline toolbar, or press ALT+SHIFT+–, or press the – key on the numeric keypad. The body text that is lower than the current one disappears. Each time you click the Collapse button (or press either key combination), the next higher level of heading disappears. You cannot collapse the current paragraph. When you collapse the entire branch, nothing appears on the level under the current paragraph, as shown here:

     ⊕ <u>A Program for Promoting Training</u>
          ⊕ <u>Ensuring an Educable Work</u> Force
          ⊕ <u>Expanding Employee Knowledge</u>
          ⊕ <u>Retooling for New Technologies</u>
     —

4. Move to one of the collapsed headings.

5. Click the Expand button in the Outline toolbar, or press ALT+SHIFT++, or press the + key on the numeric keypad. The highest level of headings under the current paragraph reappears. Keep clicking the Expand button (or pressing either key combination) until you see all the levels you want.

Collapsing or Expanding Heading Levels

To expand all collapsed headings and body text under a heading, double-click the + in front of the heading or press ALT+SHIFT++. If all headings and text under that heading are already expanded, your double-click or pressing ALT+SHIFT+– will collapse them all.

Displaying Selected Heading Levels

Instead of individually collapsing or expanding branches, you may want to display only through a particular level heading in your document. You can do this with either the mouse or the keyboard:

■ Click on the numbered button in the Outline toolbar to display only headings through that level.

■ Press ALT+SHIFT followed by the level number, to display only headings through that level; for example, ALT+SHIFT+3 shows only the first three levels.

Selecting Outline Branches

When you want to select text in Outline view, you can use most of the usual selection methods. Also, keep the following guidelines in mind:

■ You cannot select part of two paragraphs. When your selection extends from one paragraph to another, both complete paragraphs are selected. For example, if you drag to select the last sentence in one paragraph and the first sentence in the next paragraph, when you release the mouse button, the entire contents of both paragraphs will be selected.

■ When you click in the selection bar, you select the paragraph beside the mouse pointer, as usual. When you double-click in the selection bar in Outline view, however, the heading and all its subordinate headings and body text are selected.

■ When you click on the + in front of a paragraph, you select that paragraph as well as all the headings and body text paragraphs under it.

Moving Outline Branches

In Outline view, you can easily move a heading, and all of its subheadings and body text, within the document. You can change the level of the headings in the branch up or down just as easily.

Begin by moving to the highest-level heading in the branch you want to move, and then select it. If the heading's subheadings and body text are displayed, and you want to move them as well, click the + before the heading to select them all. Only the part of the outline that is selected is moved. If subheadings are collapsed, selecting the heading automatically selects the subheadings.

■ To move the branch up in the outline, click on the Move Up button in the Outline toolbar or press ALT+SHIFT+UP ARROW.

■ To move the branch down in the outline, click on the Move Down button in the Outline toolbar, or press ALT+SHIFT+DOWN ARROW.

■ You can also move a heading, along with its subheadings and text, up or down by dragging the + or − at the beginning of the heading. Word displays a line with an angle bracket (>) marking where the branch will move when you release the mouse, as shown in the following:

      + Windows
            □ Windows is not actually an operating system by itself since it enhances the ...
      ✧ OS/2
            □ OS/2 is an operating system designed to overcome many of the limitations in ...
    ✧ Applications
       □ The real powerhouse of a computer is the applications you use.
      ✧ Games
           □ If you have a computer at home, you probably have played several games. ...
      ✧ Business
           □ Business software is like ice cream—it comes in many different flavors and ...

Promoting or Demoting Branches to Other Levels

Move to the highest-level heading in the branch you want to promote or demote. If the heading's subheadings are displayed and you want them promoted as well, click the + before the heading to select them, too.

■ To increase the heading and its subheadings by one level, click the Promote button in the Outline toolbar or press ALT+SHIFT+LEFT ARROW.

■ To decrease the heading and its subheadings by one level, click the Demote button in the Outline toolbar or press ALT+SHIFT+RIGHT ARROW.

Subheadings that are not selected are not changed. When you have hidden subheadings, selecting the heading automatically selects the subheadings.

 TIP: *You can also promote and demote branches by dragging the symbol in front of a heading to the left or right. When you drag body text to the left, you change it into a heading. When you drag the symbol for a heading level all the way to the right, it changes the heading to body text.*

Deleting Branches

Move to the highest-level heading in the branch that you want to delete, and select the part of the outline to delete. If the heading's subheadings and body text are displayed and you want them deleted as well, click the + before the heading to select them, too. Only the part of the outline that is selected will be deleted. When you collapse subheadings, selecting the heading automatically selects the subheadings.

When you're ready, delete the entire heading, including its paragraph character and selected subheadings and body text, by pressing DEL or BACKSPACE.

Reducing the Body Text Display

This is a useful feature that makes reorganizing a document easier and lets you quickly find the text you want. Switch to Outline view. Then press ALT+SHIFT+L or click the Show First Line Only button on the outline toolbar. Your document will look like Figure 4-47. The ellipses at the end of the lines of body text indicate that the document has more text for each paragraph.

Adding Outline Numbers

1. Select the part of the outline you want numbered. (To select the entire outline, you can press CTRL+5 using the 5 key on the numeric keypad.)

2. Select Format | Heading Numbering to open the Heading Numbering dialog box.

3. Choose the style of outline numbering you want from one of the boxes, and select OK.

Figure 4-48 shows an outline that has numbers added.

To remove outline numbers, select the part of the outline from which you want outline numbers removed, select Format | Heading Numbering, and select Remove.

O

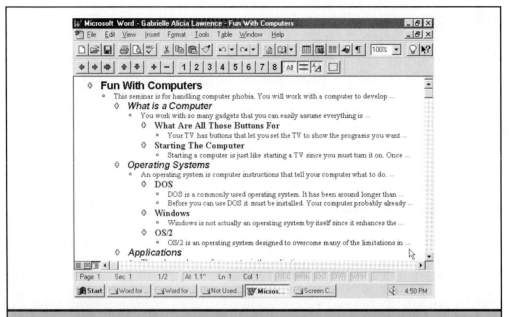

Figure 4-47. *Displaying only one line of body text*

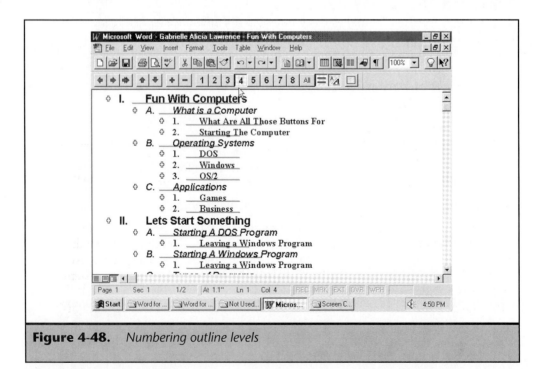

Figure 4-48. *Numbering outline levels*

Printing an Outline

When you print a document from Outline view, only the displayed elements of the outline are printed.

NOTE: *Print Preview, of course, still shows the entire outline.*

1. Switch to Outline view.
2. Collapse or expand branches to display only the paragraphs you want to print.
3. Select File | Print, and select the print options you want to use.
4. Select OK to print the outline.

Hints

When you need to have an outline as well as a document (for instance, when you are submitting an academic paper or an outline of a speech for a conference), switch to Outline view after finishing the document, and collapse branches so that only the headings show. Then print the outline. This is much easier than creating an outline as a separate document.

Using Outlines to Create Documents

Create an outline of your document first, and then fill in the document with the body text. By creating the outline first, you can be sure that you have covered all of the major topics you want to deal with, and you will avoid spending time writing text that you have to eventually remove as irrelevant.

Moving Around in Long Documents

Use the Outline view to move quickly through large documents. Switch to Outline view, display only high-level headings, move to the heading closest to the text you want to work with, and then either expand that text or switch back to Normal view.

Using Styles and Headings

When you set the heading levels for an outline, you are assigning styles to the paragraphs containing the headings. The heading styles are Heading 1 to Heading 9, to match the heading level. You can quickly format all headings of a specific level by changing the formatting applied with that style. This lets you maintain consistent formatting for headings throughout the document.

Use outlining to add headings to a document even when you do not necessarily need the other Outline view features. The same Heading 1 through Heading 9 styles that Word uses for outline headings can be helpful in headings for documents. If you later want to change the headings' appearance, just change the styles.

O

TIP: *Using text marked with heading styles, you can use your outline to create the document's table of contents. See "Table of Contents with Headings" for more information.*

Changing Outline Numbering Styles

You can modify the outline's styles so that they supply exactly the features you want. To create an outline style, select Modify from the Heading Numbering dialog box (opened by selecting Format | Heading Numbering). From the Level list box, select each outline level that you will use for the outline style you are creating, or click each outline level in the Preview box. Then, for the selected outline level, change the other options in the dialog box to change how the outline will appear.

Under Number Format, enter any text to appear before the number in the Text Before and Text After text boxes. Remember to include any blank spaces you want in the entry. You can also choose a style of numbering from the choices listed in the Bullet or Number drop-down box. To change the font of these entries, select Font and choose a font. You can also set the starting number of the series, with the Start At text box. If you want this level of outline heading to include the number or number and position of the previous heading, select an option from the Include From Previous Level list box.

In the Number Position section of the dialog box, select the position of the number Word will add. Choose from these options: use the Alignment of List Text drop-down list box to control the alignment; designate the amount of space from the left margin to the number with the Distance from Indent to Text option; designate the amount of space between the heading number and the text in the Distance from Number to Text option; and use the Hanging Indent check box to set whether the rest of the paragraph at the heading level is indented. You can also select the Restart Numbering at Each New Section option when you want Word to restart counting after each higher-level heading.

Once you have finished changing the outline style, select OK, and Word uses the new style you have created. You can modify the style by selecting Format | Heading Numbering and Modify again without selecting one of the boxes displaying outline styles. If you select one of the outline style boxes, that style replaces the style you have created.

Related Topics

Lists
Printing
Styles

Outline Numbering

See "Outlines."

Outline Toolbar

The Outline toolbar lets you quickly set the outline levels in a document in Outline view, and determine the parts of the outlined document that you see. This toolbar appears when you switch to Outline view (by selecting View | Outline or clicking the Outline View button to the left of the document's horizontal scroll bar). As with other toolbars, you can customize the toolbar to change the buttons available on it, as described in "Toolbar Options." The buttons of the Outline toolbar are listed in Table 4-15.

The Master Document View button switches to Master Document view and uses the unused portion of the Outline toolbar for the Master Document toolbar.

Outline View

When you switch to Outline view, the Outline toolbar appears and the text in your document is arranged in an outline. If the ruler was visible, it disappears. Some paragraphs are headings, which means that one of the nine headings styles has been applied. Other paragraphs are body text. In Outline view, you can control what levels of text are displayed, reposition entire sections or branches of the outline, and promote or demote them as you reorganize your document. For a full explanation of the Outline view features, see "Outlines."

Overtype Mode

See "INS Key."

Padlock

See "Master Documents."

Page Break

See "Pagination."

PAGE Field

The PAGE field inserts the page number for the page containing the field. For more information, see "Fields."

Page Formats

See "Margins," "Page Size and Orientation," "Paper Source," and "Sections."

Page Layout

See "Margins," "Page Size and Orientation," "Paper Source," and "Sections."

Page Layout View

See "Viewing Documents."

Page Numbers

You can add page numbers to your document, specify the first page number, and designate the format of page numbers.

Procedures

You can add page numbers by themselves, or you can add them to headers and footers.

Inserting Page Numbers Alone

1. Select Insert | Page Numbers, opening the Page Numbers dialog box.

2. Select an option under Position to set the position of the page number. With Top of Page (Header), the header contains the page number; with Bottom of Page (Footer), the footer contains the page number.

3. Select an Alignment option to set how the page number is aligned in the header or footer. The choices include Right, Center, and Left, as well as Inside and Outside, to put the page number on different sides of the page for odd and even pages. The page number is aligned using tab characters.

4. Select the Show Number on First Page check box if you want the page number to appear on the first page.

5. Select Format to open the Page Number Format dialog box and specify the format of the page number.

   ■ Select a format from the Number Format drop-down list box. You can use Arabic numbers, upper- or lowercase letters, or upper- or lowercase roman numbers.

   ■ Select the Include Chapter Number check box and choose the style that marks when a new chapter begins from the Chapter Starts with Style drop-down list box. Then, select the character that separates the chapter number from the page number in the Use Separator drop-down list box.

   ■ Select the initial page number for the current section under Page Numbering. Choose the Continue from Previous Section option button to have the first page in the current section use the page number following the last page of the previous section. To use a specific page number, select the Start <u>A</u>t option button and enter the first page number for the section in the adjoining text box.

6. Select OK twice to return to the document.

When you return to the document, Word adds the page number to the header or footer. The page number is added to any other entries already in the header or footer.

TIP: *You can also add a page number at any location by pressing ALT+SHIFT+P. This key combination adds the PAGE field to the document. Word substitutes this field with the current page number. You can also use the <u>I</u>nsert | Fi<u>e</u>ld command when you want to set the format of the page number.*

Adding Page Numbers to Headers or Footers

1. Select <u>V</u>iew | <u>H</u>eader and Footer or, in Page Layout view, you can double-click any existing header or footer.

2. Enter the text or graphics you want to appear in the header or footer.

3. Move the insertion point to where you want the page number, and click the Page Numbers button on the Header and Footer toolbar or press ALT+SHIFT+P. Word inserts a PAGE field code. (Unless you have turned on the display of field codes, however, you see the current page number.)

4. If you want the page number to have a different format, select <u>I</u>nsert | Page N<u>u</u>mbers and <u>F</u>ormat. Once you select the page number's format, select OK and Close.

5. Select <u>C</u>lose to finish editing the header or footer, or select one of the views from the <u>V</u>iew menu.

TIP: *The difference between adding a page number with the Page Numbers button and the <u>I</u>nsert | Page N<u>u</u>mbers command is that the page number added with the command is in a frame, which may give you more options for positioning and appearance.*

Hints

You can also insert page numbers in a document by inserting the PAGE field code yourself. For a full explanation of adding fields, see "Fields."

Related Topics

Fields
Headers and Footers

Page Orientation

See "Page Size and Orientation."

Page Setup

See "Margins," "Page Size and Orientation," "Paper Source," and "Sections."

Page Size and Orientation

When setting the size and orientation of your page, you can choose from certain standard paper sizes or specify a custom size. You can set the page size and orientation for a whole document, from a particular page forward to the end of the document, or for a section.

Procedure

1. Select File | Page Setup and the Paper Size tab.

2. If the paper you are going to use is a standard size, select it from the Paper Size drop-down list box. The height and width of that paper size will appear in the Height and Width text boxes. If your paper is a not a standard size, enter its width and height in the Width and Height text boxes.

3. Select either the Portrait or Landscape option button, depending on how you want to feed your paper into your printer. Portrait mode uses the narrow side of the paper as the top; Landscape mode uses the long side of the paper as the top. Figure 4-49 shows an example of both portrait and landscape orientations.

4. Select the part of the document in which you want to use the new page size or orientation, from the Apply To drop-down list box. Then select OK.

   ■ With Whole Document, the entire document uses the designated page size and orientation.

   ■ With This Section or Selected Sections, the section containing the insertion point or the sections included in the selected text use the designated settings.

   ■ With This Point Forward or Selected Text, Word inserts a section break just before the insertion point or before and after the selected text, and the new section uses the new settings.

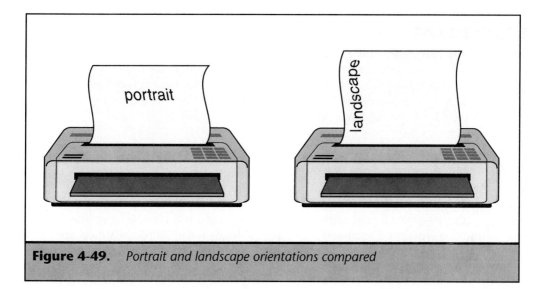

Figure 4-49. *Portrait and landscape orientations compared*

Hints

Word uses the defined paper size to format your document and repaginate it. You can mix page sizes and orientations: For example, you can write a letter and include an envelope for it in the same document, by changing the page size and orientation of the last page and entering the information for the envelope in this last page. Also, if you are creating a report that includes wide tables or graphics, you can switch to landscape for a single page to accommodate the wide table, and then return to portrait for the remainder of the document.

Related Topics

Envelopes
Margins
Pagination
Paper Source
Printing
Sections

PAGEREF Field

The PAGEREF field inserts the page number that a bookmark is on. Usually, Word adds this field to your document when you create a page reference with the Insert | Cross-reference command. See "Cross-References" for how you can add page references to headings and other items in your document. See "Fields" for more information on how this field and others operate.

Pagination

Word automatically breaks your document into pages, based on the page size and margin settings. You can also add manual page breaks, keep lines or paragraphs together on a page, start a page with a specific paragraph, and allow or disallow widow and orphan lines. Page breaks are *soft page breaks* when Word adds them for you, or *hard page breaks* when you add them yourself. These page breaks look different in Normal view, as you can see from this document:

Soft page break is above the text and a hard page break is below the text
Page Break

Procedures

The following procedures will explain how to turn automatic pagination on and off, and how to insert and remove hard page breaks. These procedures also explain how to keep text together on one page and prevent awkward or unattractive page breaks.

Turning Off Automatic Pagination

By default, Word automatically breaks your document into pages by inserting soft page breaks as you are typing. You can turn this on and off for all views except Print Preview and Page Layout, which always have automatic pagination. Turning it off can accelerate Word's performance, depending on the size of the document and the editing changes you are making.

To turn off automatic pagination, select Tools | Options and select the General tab. Then turn off the Background Repagination check box option, and select OK. If you want to restart automatic pagination, just check this box again.

Inserting and Removing Hard Page Breaks

■   Press CTRL+ENTER, or select Insert | Break and select OK.

Hard page breaks do not move as a page contains more or less text. In Normal view, these page breaks look different from the soft page breaks that Word displays to show where text is split between pages.

■ Move to the page break character in Normal view, and press DEL or BACKSPACE.

If the page break exists because the paragraph has a page break before it as part of its formatting, the only way to remove the page break is by using the Format | Paragraph command and clearing the Page Break Before check box.

Keeping a Paragraph at the Top of a Page

You can apply a paragraph format that keeps a hard page break just before that paragraph, so that it always starts a new page. When this format is enabled, it affects the paragraph the insertion point is in, or all selected paragraphs.

■ Select Format | Paragraph, and the Text Flow tab. Select the Page Break Before check box, or clear this box to remove the format. Then select OK.

TIP: *When you add paragraph formatting and then move to the end of the line and press* ENTER *to start a new paragraph, the new paragraph has the same paragraph formatting as the old. However, if instead you assign the paragraph formatting to a style and assign that style to a paragraph, creating a new paragraph from that one adopts the style set up for the following paragraph. This style may have entirely different paragraph formatting.*

Keeping Paragraphs Together on the Page

You can apply a paragraph format that keeps the formatted paragraph on the same page as the next paragraph. Word moves any soft page break that exists between these two paragraphs to a position before both of them, to prevent them from being separated. When this format is enabled, it affects the paragraph the insertion point is in, or all selected paragraphs. You might use this feature for a title for a paragraph, so that the page does not break between the title and the subsequent text.

■ Select Format | Paragraph, and the Text Flow tab. Select the Keep with Next check box, or clear this box to remove the format. Then select OK.

Keeping Lines on the Same Page

You can apply a paragraph format which prevents a paragraph from being broken in two by a page break. Word moves the soft page break to before the formatted paragraph to prevent it from being split. When this format is set, it affects the paragraph the insertion point is in, or all selected paragraphs.

■ Select Format | Paragraph, and the Text Flow tab. Select the Keep Lines Together check box, or clear this box to remove the format. Then select OK.

Allowing Widows and Orphans

As a default, Word places page breaks to avoid leaving the first line of a paragraph alone at the bottom of a page (orphan) or the last line of a paragraph alone at the top of a page (widow). You may need to change this with the following steps if you need to print a specific number of lines on a page or reduce the number of pages you need to use.

1. Select Format | Paragraph, and make sure the Text Flow tab is selected.
2. Clear the Widow/Orphan Control check box. If you do not want to allow widow and orphan lines, select this check box. Then select OK.

Hints

Automatic pagination makes it easier for you to see how your document is laid out. On the other hand, you can work with long documents more quickly when this feature is turned off. When editing and entering long documents, turn it off and then restart it when you are ready to edit the pages. You will also find that Word performs faster when you edit and enter lengthy documents using Normal view versus Page Layout or Print Preview.

As you are reviewing a document for page breaks, you are better off changing the paragraph formatting to include the Keep With Next, Page Break Before, and Keep Lines Together formats than adding hard page breaks. As your document is edited further, you will discover that in large documents, you are frequently rearranging hard page breaks, but the paragraph formats naturally keep the lines together when you want them.

When a paragraph is the start of a new section of your document, keep the paragraph at the top of a page. You can keep the paragraphs of a table together, to prevent the table from being split across pages.

Keeping the lines of a paragraph together whenever possible will prevent your readers from losing the train of thought because the page has to be turned.

Avoid widow and orphan lines whenever possible; they make your document look less professional and make it much less readable.

Page Break Displays

In Normal view, soft page breaks, which Word inserts, appear as a light dotted line. Hard page breaks, which you insert, appear as a heavy dotted line. The words "Page Break" also appear in the middle of a hard page break line.

In Page Layout view and Print Preview, Word does not distinguish between soft and hard page breaks. These views represent each page of the document as it will appear when printed.

Related Topics

Margins
Page Size and Orientation

Panes

See "Viewing Documents."

Paper Source

You can designate the source of the paper used to print a document. This option is effective only if your printer has multiple bins or trays, or both a single tray and a manual feeder for paper. For example, in a document that contains both an envelope and a letter, you can have Word print the envelope using paper from a manual feeder and then use the regular sheet feeder for the letter.

You can set the paper source for a whole document, or for a particular section. If you select text before changing the paper source, you can choose to change the paper source for the selected text only, in which case the selected text is turned into a specific section.

Procedure

1. Select File | Page Setup and the Paper Source tab.

2. In the First Page list box, select the source of paper for the first page of the section. The available options depend on the printer selected. Most printers that Windows supports have at least a single tray and can also be fed manually. Other printers may have multiple trays or may not have a manual feeder. Some printers have an envelope feeder.

3. In the Other Pages list box, select the source of paper for the remainder of the pages in the section.

4. Select the part of the document you want the paper source settings to affect by choosing an option from the Apply To drop-down list box, and then select OK.

   ■ With Whole Document, the first page of the document uses the paper source chosen in the First Page list box, and the remainder of the document uses the setting of the Other Pages list box.

   ■ With Selected Text or This Point Forward, Word inserts a section break before the insertion point, or before and after the selected text, creating a new section. The first page of the new section uses the paper source specified in the First Page list box, and the rest use the setting in the Other Pages list box.

   ■ With This Section or Selected Sections, the current or selected sections use these settings.

5. Select OK to apply the page size setting to the document or sections.

Hints

Most letters today use letterhead for the first page only, and then blank sheets after that. You can use two separate trays of paper, one loaded with letterhead and the other with blank sheets, or you can manually feed the letterhead and then use the default tray for the blank paper.

Related Topics

Printing
Sections

Paragraph Formats

With Word, you can specify many formats that affect a paragraph of text, including its indentation, how page breaks affect it, and the spacing before, within, or after the paragraph.

See "Alignment," "Indents," "Pagination," "Spacing," and "Tabs" for detailed information on these paragraph formats.

Paragraph Marks

See "Nonprinting Characters."

Parallel Columns

See "Columns."

Passwords

See "Locking and Protecting Documents" and "Saving Documents."

Pasting

See "Clipboard" and "Object Linking and Embedding."

Personal Address Book

A personal address book created with your electronic mail package or Microsoft Schedule+ can supply addresses for mail merges, envelopes, labels, and the document. See "Mail Merge" for how to use your personal address book as the source of variable data for a merge. See "Envelopes" and "Labels" for how you can create envelopes and labels out of the contents of your personal address book. The procedure below describes how to add an address from your personal address book to the current document.

Procedure

1. Move to where you want the address label placed.
2. Click the Insert Address button on the Standard toolbar.
3. Select the source of the address from the Show Names From drop-down list box if you do not want an address from the source shown.
4. Select the person whose address you want to insert from the list box and select OK.

Once you have performed these steps, every time you want to add an address that you have previously used, just click the down arrow at the end of the Address button and select one from the list.

PICT Files

PICT files, a Macintosh graphics format, are one of the document types Word accepts for graphic images. You can add these images as pictures to your Word documents. Look under "Graphics" for more information about bringing images such as these into a Word document.

Picture Command to Import Graphics

See "Graphics."

Pictures

See "Graphics."

Pie Charts

The pie chart is one of the graph types available in Microsoft Graph. See "Graph" for more information.

Pitch

Word for Windows measures font size using points rather than pitch. *Pitch* is used to describe font size by how many characters fit across a one-inch space. *Points* represent the height of the characters, with one point equaling 1/72 inch.

Placeholders

Placeholders can mark where a graphic will appear. Displaying placeholders instead of their contents makes moving through a document containing graphics faster. To show placeholders, select Tools | Options, select the View tab, select Picture Placeholders, and select OK. When you want to see the final version, with the contents instead of the placeholders, repeat these steps and clear the Picture Placeholders check box.

Placing Text Around a Framed Object

See "Frames."

Playing Macros

Macros perform a series of steps for you, such as typing or selecting Word features to apply to a document. See Chapter 7 for information on how macros are developed. "Macros" in this chapter describes how you run a macro in Word.

Point Size

See "Fonts."

Positioning

See "Equations" and "Frames," as well as ADVANCE under "Fields."

Positioning Equations

See "Frames."

Positioning Graphics and Charts

See "Frames."

Positioning Objects

See "Frames."

Positioning Tables and Spreadsheets

See "Frames."

Positioning Text

See "Frames."

PostScript

Word accepts graphic images in Encapsulated PostScript format (EPS) files. You can add these images as pictures to your Word documents. However, you cannot print these images as Encapsulated PostScript unless you are using a PostScript printer. Depending on the file, you may not be able to display it, either. If the file is saved with an embedded WMF or TIFF format image, that image is used to display the EPS graphic. If there is no attached graphic, you cannot even display the EPS file without a PostScript printer. Look under "Graphics" for more information about bringing image files such as these into a Word document.

PowerPoint

Microsoft PowerPoint is a Windows application that can share data with Word. You can embed and link PowerPoint data in Word documents, as described in "Object Linking and Embedding." You can start PowerPoint from within Word, by clicking the Microsoft PowerPoint button in the Microsoft toolbar. Once you start Microsoft PowerPoint, you are using PowerPoint, not Word, and you must follow PowerPoint's menu and features.

Preferences

Word has many settings that you can change to make Word operate the way you want it. Most of these options are set with the Tools I Options command. Since there are so

ma... ...ns, they are categorized an... ...escribed individually in this chapter as
sh... ...e following table.

...s:	**About ustomizing This:**
...mat	How A... ...oFormat works with your document
...g Versions	How re... ions are marked
...ility Options	How W... d converts documents
...ns	How yo... edit documents
... Location	Where ... rd expects to find documents
...ptions	General features
... Options	How Word checks the grammar in your documents
... Options	The shortcut keys
...ions	Word's menus
...ns	How Word prints documents
...ns	How Word saves documents
...ptions	How Word checks spelling in your document
...tions	The toolbars
...Options	The information Word maintains about you
...ons	The screen display for Word

Previ... Print

See ... ...Documents."

Prima... Documents

See "... ...Merge" and "Master Docume... "

PRINT ... ...eld

The PR...NT field sends instructions to y... ...r printer. For more information, see "Fields."

Print Merge

See "Mail Merge."

Print Options

Word lets you define certain default settings for print operations.

Procedure

1. Select <u>T</u>ools | <u>O</u>ptions or the <u>O</u>ptions button from the Print dialog box.
2. Select the Print tab, displaying the dialog box shown here:

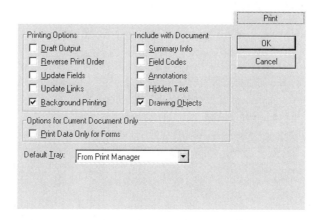

3. Select the options you want to change, as described in the following section, and select OK.

Options

The options that you can set for printing include settings for how Windows and Word interact to print your document, what Word includes in the document, and the location of the paper for the printing.

Printing Options

The check boxes under Printing Options control general features which affect the printing process.

D<u>R</u>AFT OUTPUT   When you enable the <u>D</u>raft Output option, Word prints the document's text without any formatting, and prints pictures or other graphics as blank frames. Depending on your printer, formatted text may print with underlining. Turn on this option when you simply want to proof your document faster and without formatting. Turn this option off again when you are ready to print the document with all of the selected formatting.

REVERSE PRINT ORDER   When you turn on Reverse Print Order, Word prints the document starting with the last page. (By default, Word prints from first to last.)

UPDATE FIELDS   Select the Update Fields check box when you want Word to update all fields in your document before it begins printing. This avoids printing a document with outdated information if you forgot to update all of your fields.

UPDATE LINKS   Select the Update Links check box when you want Word to update all links in your document before it begins printing. This ensures that the linked data in a document uses the latest version available.

BACKGROUND PRINTING   When you select Background Printing, Word prints the document in the background so you can continue to work with Word while Windows prints the document. Turning off this option frees up memory and may accelerate the printing of your document.

Include with Document

The options under Include with Document let you control the types of ancillary information printed with the document.

SUMMARY INFO   Select the Summary Info check box to have Word print the summary information about your documents on a separate page after the document.

FIELD CODES   When you select the Field Codes check box, Word prints the field codes rather than the results of the fields. If a document is not printing correctly, printing the document's field codes can help you figure out why.

ANNOTATIONS   Select the Annotations check box to have Word print all annotations, and the document pages they reference, on a separate page. You can use this list of annotations while reviewing a document, to help you correct or clarify it.

HIDDEN TEXT   When you select the Hidden Text check box, Word prints any text that is formatted as hidden. Usually, hidden text is not intended to print; it provides commentary or documentation within a document.

DRAWING OBJECTS   Select the Drawing Objects check box to print drawn objects, including objects added to your document such as clip art, graphics, and charts. Turn the option off to omit these objects from the printed document.

Print Data Only for Forms

When this check box is selected, Word prints only the data from the form. Select this check box when you are printing data on preprinted forms such as invoices or insurance forms. For other types of documents, leave this check box cleared. This option is only in effect for the document in which you select it. To use these settings for another document, you have to reselect them for that document.

Default Tray

You can select the source of paper for the document sections that are not set separately with the File | Page Setup command. The available options depend on the printer selected.

> *TIP:*   *If you see the option "From Print Manager" in this list box, it means Word is going to use the default setting made as part of the printer's properties.*

Related Topics

Printing

Print Preview

See "Viewing Documents."

PRINTDATE Field

The PRINTDATE field returns the date a document was last printed. For more information, see "Document Properties" and "Fields."

Printer Fonts

Printer fonts are fonts that are installed in your printer's memory. See "Fonts."

Printing

The last step in creating a document with a word processor is usually to print it on paper. Printing, in Windows, involves sending what the final document will look like to the printer folder. From there, Window's Print Manager will send the document to the printer with the information that the printer needs, while you continue working in Word or another application. The formatting and placement features you can use with a specific printer are controlled by the capabilities of that printer.

Procedures

The following procedures explain how to print your document, and how to change the default settings for the printer.

Printing Documents

1. From the document you want to print, select File | Print, to open the Print dialog box. You can also press CTRL+P or CTRL+SHIFT+F12.

2. If you need to change the printer you are using, select the printer from the Name drop-down list box. If you need to change the settings for this printer, select the Properties button and make the necessary changes. This opens the Properties dialog box set up by Windows so your changes affect all printing you do on that printer, not just printing from Word. Select OK when you are done. If you want to send the output to a permanent file, select the Print to File check box. Word will prompt you for the file name and location after you select OK.

NOTE: Selecting Print to File prints the document to a permanent file. You can then move this file to a printer folder and print it. You might do this to create a document on one system and then print it on another system that has a better printer but not the Word software.

3. Select one of the Print Range option buttons to specify the portion of the document you want to print:

   ■ All prints the complete document.

   ■ Current Page prints the page the insertion point is on.

   ■ Selection prints the selected text as if it were the complete document.

   ■ Select Pages to print a range of pages from the document. Type the range to print in the adjoining text box, using a hyphen between the first and last pages in the range and commas between individual pages. For example, type **1,5-7,10** to print pages 1, 5, 6, 7, and 10.

4. In the Number of Copies text box, enter the number of copies you want to print. If you are printing more than one copy and you want Word to automatically collate your copies, select the Collate Copies check box. You can see the diagram showing how the pages in your copies will be organized to the left of this check box.

5. In the Print What drop-down list box, select what you want to print. You can print the document, the document's summary information, the document's annotations, descriptions of the styles the document uses, the AutoText entries used by the document's template, or the key assignments and macros used by the document's template.

6. Select the part of the range to print from the Print drop-down list box. You can print all the pages in the selected range, just the odd pages, or just the even pages.

7. You can select the Options button to change some of the default printing options in Word. See "Print Options."

8. Select OK to begin printing the document.

Figure 4-50 shows the beginning of a document printed several times, with different Print What settings. The header for each page describes the Print What setting for the page.

 TIP: *To print a document using the default settings, you can click the Print button in the Standard toolbar. Word immediately prints the document without displaying the Print dialog box.*

Hints

The following hints will help you to print more effectively and create better documents, and tell you what to do when common printer errors occur.

Handling Printer Problems

When you select OK to start your print job, and your document does not print, check the following possible problems:

■ Is the printer turned on? (This may sound stupid, but it's one of the two most common printer problems.)

■ Does the printer have paper? (This is the other most common problem.)

■ Is the printer ready to accept information? Most printers have a button that turns them on line. Usually, pressing this button when the printer is off line will begin the flow of information from the computer to your printer.

■ When you select File | Print, are the printer and the entries below it correct?

If the wrong printer is selected, simply select the correct printer from the Name drop-down list box.

If the printer connection is wrong, select the Properties button and change the printer's properties there.

■ Is the printer paused? Switch to the Printers folder and right-click the printer's icon. If "Pause Printing" is selected, select it again to remove the check mark.

■ Are you using a printer switch box? If so, check that the printer switch box is turned to the setting for your computer.

■ Is your computer connected to the printer? This problem normally occurs when you are first setting up your printer or when you have moved furniture.

nected print
h the cable u
co nputer.

ge on your p
d I P+, you i

ng on a netwo
eue, or someo
ent.

forma
the c

ple,
to |

ou
ue

Fun With

This seminar is f
compu ter to dev
start a new applic
compu ter can pr
package. The co
packages that ma
skills you will de
using the compu

ou
wil
ess
nin
se
ou
u

What is a Co

You work with so
s computerized

What Are All T

Your TV has butto
want to watch. A

y

w t
art

Starting The C

Starting a comput
Once you turn it o

Su

Funwit~1
C:\WORDB
C:\OFFICE
Fun With C
Class Semi
Mary Cam
Computers
Handouts f
the Adult E

:   9/29/95 05
ber: 4
:   9/29/95 06:

ted documen sum

Annotations

Page: 1
[MC1]Sue, let's try stressing what the course is good for, rather than what
it won't do for them.
Page:1
[MC2]Missing period here.
Page1
[MC3]Sue, what's this sentence about?

Styles

Annotation Reference
Default Paragraph Font + Font: 8pt

Annotation Text
Normal +

Default Paragraph Font
The font of the underlying paragraph style +

Head Topics
Font: Bookman Old Style, 18 pt, English (US), Kern at 16 pt, Flush
left, Line Spacing Single, Space Before 6 pt, Widow/Orphan Control

Heading 1
Style for Next Paragraph: Normal

Normal + Font: Arial, 14 pt, Bold, Kern at 14 pt, Space Before 12 pt
After 3 pt, Keep With Next

Heading 2
Style for Next Paragraph: Normal

Normal + Font: Arial, 12 pt, Bold, Italic, Space Before 12 pt After
3 pt, Keep With Next

Figure 4-50. *Printed document, summary, annotations, and styles* (continued)

As you can see, most printing problems are easily solved. In most situations, you
will see a message telling you why your document is not being printed. You will need
to correct the error before you can print the document.

Preview Before Printing

You can avoid having to reprint a document by previewing the document or by using the
Print Preview or Page Layout view of the document. These options show the document
as it will appear when printed. See "Viewing Documents" for more information.

Confirming the Selected Printer

Look at the printer name that appears in the top of the Print dialog box. This is the printer Word will use when printing your document. The printer selection will determine how the printed document appears, because printers have their own individual features.

Printing Drafts

You can print a draft version of your document by selecting the Draft Output check box in the Printer Options dialog box. Draft output prints faster because formatted text and graphics, which take longer to print, are not sent to the printer. What is not printed in draft mode will vary based on the type of printer you have. For example, when you print draft output with a PostScript printer, both graphics and formatted text do print, because there is no gain in time by not doing so. On a laser printer, such as a Hewlett-Packard LaserJet III, formatted text will print, but not graphics. On a dot-matrix printer, graphics will not print, and text is printed without formatting.

Printing Multiple Documents

You can print several documents at one time, without opening and printing each one separately, using the File | Open command. Begin by selecting File | Open, to display the Open dialog box. Select the documents to print in the Look In list box. Then, select Print from the menu displayed when you click the Commands and Settings button or right-click one of the selected documents. Choose the printing options and settings you want to use, and then select OK. Word prints each document consecutively.

For more information on using the File | Open command, see "Document Management."

Printing Merged Documents

In Word, you can create form letters that, when printed, can be combined with data source documents containing information that changes in each version of the letter. You can also use mail merge to create and print envelopes and labels. See "Mail Merge" for details.

Printing Envelopes and Labels

Printing an envelope or label is like printing any other document. You define, within a document, a page size that conforms to the envelope's measurements, and print the document normally. Word can create an envelope or label for printing quickly, using addresses you provide or that are found in your document. See "Envelopes" to learn how to create envelopes, "Labels" to learn how to create labels, and "Paper Source" for how to make sure that the envelope page of your document is actually printed on an envelope.

Printing Outside of Word

You can print documents that are not necessarily loaded in Word or while Word is not running. Just drag the document's icon to the Printer folder or icon. The document is printed with Word's standard printing choices.

Related Topics

Document Management
Mail Merge
Print Options
Viewing Documents

Printing the Current Page

See "Printing."

Printing Multiple Copies

See "Printing."

PRIVATE Field

Word creates this field for you when you add a document of another format into Word for Windows. This field contains the information Word needs to convert the document back to its previous format. Do not change this field.

Programs

You can add the functionality of other programs to Word. These add-in programs provide commands that can extend the features available to you. You can use add-in programs created by software publishers, and you can also write your own.

Procedures

- ■ To add-in a program, select File | Templates, then Add and the document name for the add-in, and then the OK button.

- ■ To unload an add-in when you're finished using it, select the File | Templates command, clearing the check box next to the add-in program name.

- ■ To remove an add-in program, select Remove after selecting the add-in program.

Remeber that an add-in might have its own commands for adding, unloading and removing the add-in. Use the instructions that accompany the add-in whenever they are provided.

Project

Microsoft Project is a Windows application that can share data with Word. You can embed and link Project data in Word documents, as described in "Object Linking and Embedding." You can start Project from within Word by clicking the Microsoft Project button in the Microsoft toolbar. Once you start Microsoft Project, you are using Project, not Word, and you must follow Project's menu and features.

Proofing

Word has several proofing tools, described in this chapter, to help improve your documents. Word can check the spelling in a document, as described under "Spelling." You can review your document for incorrect grammar, as described under "Grammar Checking." Word will look for synonyms, antonyms, and so forth, for the words in your document, as described under "Thesaurus." You can also display various statistics about your document, including the number of words, paragraphs, and pages, as described under "Document Properties" and "Word Count." AutoCorrect and AutoFormat can also make proofing corrections for you automatically, as described under those topics.

Properties

Properties are descriptions of an item the same way that adjectives describe nouns. Items in Word have properties: These items include documents, paragraphs, and characters. To learn about a specific property, look up the item that it belongs to such as "Paragraph Formats" and "Character Formats."

Protecting Documents

See "Annotations," "Locking and Protecting Documents," and "Saving Documents."

Publisher

Microsoft Publisher is a Windows desktop publishing application that can share data with Word. You can embed and link Publisher data in Word documents, as described in "Object Linking and Embedding." You can start Publisher from within Word by clicking the Microsoft Publisher button in the Microsoft toolbar. Once you start Microsoft Publisher, you are using Publisher, not Word, and you must follow Publisher's menu and features.

Queries

Word can use queries to select data. You can create queries when you insert a database as described in "Databases." Mail merges can also use queries to select which records are used to create form letters, envelopes, labels, and other documents. Creating queries for mail merges is described under "Mail Merge." You can also use the Find Record button on the Database toolbar to locate records in a table. This toolbar is described under "Database Toolbar."

Quick Keys

See "Shortcut Keys."

QuickTips

Word's help for dialog boxes can show quick information on the different parts of a dialog box. To see these QuickTips, click the ? button in the upper-right corner of the dialog box, then click on the area in the dialog box where you want more information.

Quitting Word

See "Exiting Word."

Quotation Marks

Word can work with various types of quotation marks. When you check a document's grammar, Word verifies that you have both beginning and ending quotation marks. See "Grammar Checking" for instructions on turning this feature on and off. You can use the Insert I Symbol command to add specific quotation marks; for instance, you might need to use " " instead of " ". In "Special Characters" you can read about using this command. Word can make smart quote replacements, so "text" becomes "text." To accomplish this, you turn on the 'Straight Quotes' with "Smart Quotes" check box in the AutoFormat options. More information about this AutoFormat feature is described in "AutoFormat" and "Smart Quotes."

QUOTE Field

The QUOTE field inserts literal text in a merged document. See "Mail Merge."

RD Field

The RD field indicates a d   ient for
generating index entries, t   is" and
"Master Documents" for n

Readability

See "Grammar Checking."

Read-Only

See "Document Management   ning
Documents," and "Save Optio   ts in
read-only status, so they cann   er
Documents" for information a   ents and
subdocuments so they are read

Recompiling

You can *recompile* indexes, tables   bles of figures.
Recompiling updates these docu   id out more
about recompiling them, look at "I   ble of Contents
and Figures."

Redlining

See "Comparing Versions" and "Revisic

Redoing an Action

Word can redo actions you have executed, just as   ee "Undoing and
Redoing Actions" for more information.

REF Field

The REF field inserts the contents of a bookmark that has the same name as a particular field type, or creates a cross-reference. See "Cross-references" and "Fields."

References

See "Cross-references" and "Footnotes and Endnotes."

Registry

Word can store many of its settings in the Windows registry. This registry allows many people using the same computer to create their own set of settings which they can use when they work on the computer. The registry also allows for network-wide settings so that your settings are available when you work on different computers on the network.

Removing Features

Just as you can add an option, element, attribute, or other feature to a Word document, you can also remove it. The steps for removing a feature depend on the feature, and are explained with the particular feature's description in this chapter. For example, to find out how to remove a footnote, consult "Footnotes and Endnotes."

Removing Formatting

The formatting you add to text can be removed. Word has several shortcuts to make removing formatting easier.

Procedures

The following sections explain the shortcuts for removing character formatting and paragraph formatting.

Removing Character Formatting

Word offers four easy ways to remove character formatting from your text. You can remove specific features, or you can remove all of the formatting at once. Before removing character formatting, select the characters from which you want to remove formatting. Then choose one of these techniques:

- Press the key-combination for the formatting you want to remove, such as CTRL+B to remove boldfacing. (Remember, most key combinations switch between applying and removing the format.)
- Open the Font dialog box, and clear the settings you want to remove.
- Press CTRL+SPACEBAR to revert to the default character formatting of the style currently in effect for the text.
- Assign the Normal style to the text, using the Style button in the Formatting toolbar or by pressing CTRL+SHIFT+N. This removes all prior formatting and applies the Normal style's formatting.

Removing Paragraph Formatting

First select the paragraph or paragraphs from which you want to remove formatting. Then do one of the following:

- Press CTRL+Q to remove the manual paragraph formatting and revert to the default paragraph formatting of the style currently in effect for the paragraphs.
- Assign the Normal style to the text, using the Style button in the Formatting toolbar or by pressing CTRL+SHIFT+N. This removes prior formatting and assigns the Normal style's formatting.

Related Topics

Character Formats
Paragraph Formats

Renaming Documents

You can rename documents from the Open dialog box, described under "Document Management." You can also save a document with a new name using the File|Save As command, as described under "Saving Documents."

Renumbering

See "Lists."

Reorganizing an Outline

See "Outlines."

Repagination

See "Pagination."

Repeating Actions

You can easily repeat the last action you performed in your document, such as reapplying formatting to several passages of text, or inserting some text in several locations.

Procedures

You can repeat a command, or repeat the typing of text.

Repeating Commands

Choose one of these techniques:

- Press F4.
- Press CTRL+Y.
- Select Edit | Repeat. The Repeat command changes to match the action you can repeat—for instance, Repeat Formatting or Repeat Insertion. It changes to Can't Repeat when the last action you performed is one that cannot be repeated.

REPEATING GO TO OR FIND The Go To and Find commands are repeated differently than other commands: Press SHIFT+F4.

Repeating Text

Move your insertion point to where you want to insert another occurrence of the text you just typed, and press F4 or select Edit | Repeat.

Hints

When Word repeats text, it inserts the text you entered before you moved the insertion point. The text you type—not the action of moving the insertion point—is the action that Word repeats.

When you repeat formatting, you must first select the text to which you want to apply the identical formatting.

Often, you will have to move the insertion point, or select text, paragraphs, or sections, before you repeat the last action. For example, if you want to repeat the action of entering an address, you need to move to where you want the second address before you choose to repeat the action.

Related Topics

Copying Formats
Undoing and Redoing Actions

Repeating Formats

See "Copying Formats."

Replacement Typing

See "INS Key."

Replacing Text in a Document

See "Find and Replace."

Replacing Text and Formats

See "Find and Replace."

Resizing

Several features of Word documents can have their size adjusted, including columns, frames, graphics, tables, toolbars displayed in boxes, and windows. The steps for resizing depend on the feature, and are explained with the particular feature in this chapter. For example, to find out how to change the size of a frame, see the section "Frames."

Restoring

Word can restore the original version of something you have changed. See "Undoing and Redoing Actions" for more information. If you need to restore the original formatting to edited text or paragraphs, see "Removing Formatting."

Retrieve

See "Opening Documents" or "Inserting Documents" for how you can open existing documents in a new document window or the document window of an existing document.

Return Characters

See "Nonprinting Characters" to see how you can display the special characters that end paragraphs in Word.

Return to a Prior Editing Location

You can return to one of the three previous locations where you did some editing. Press SHIFT+F5, and Word cycles through the three prior editing locations and the current one. An "editing location" is where the insertion point was located when you made a change.

Reusing Entries

See "AutoText" for creating reusable entries.

Reversing Print Order

See "Printing."

Revision and Annotation Merging

When you share the same document with several people and they make their comments separately, you need some way to combine the different annotations and revision marks. Word lets you take one version of a document that contains annotation and revision marks and merge it with the current document. This feature lets you combine the revision marks from several documents into one that you can use to analyze and decide what revisions you want to keep. To use this feature, the changes in the other documents must be marked using Word's annotations and revision marks. You can make sure that other people add their changes using annotations or revision marks by protecting the document you give them.

Procedures

Merging revision marks combines the revision marks and annotations that you have in multiple documents.

Merging Current Revision Marks

1. Open the version of the document containing the revision marks you want to merge with another document.

2. Select Tools | Revisions and then the Merge Revisions button from the Revisions dialog box. You can also select Tools | Revisions by double-clicking the MRK indicator in the status bar.

3. Select the document that you want to receive the revision marks, and then OK. Selecting a document in this dialog box works just like selecting a document to open.

Word opens the document you selected in step 3 and merges into it the revision marks from the document you opened in step 1. Figure 4-51 shows a document with revision marks incorporated from several other documents.

 NOTE: When you are merging revision marks from subdocuments into the master document, you open the subdocuments in step 1 and select the master document in step 3.

Once the revisions marks are combined into one document, you can apply the revisions using the Tools | Revisions command, as described in "Comparing Versions." Each person's revision marks are tracked separately so as you review revisions, you can see which person made the revision.

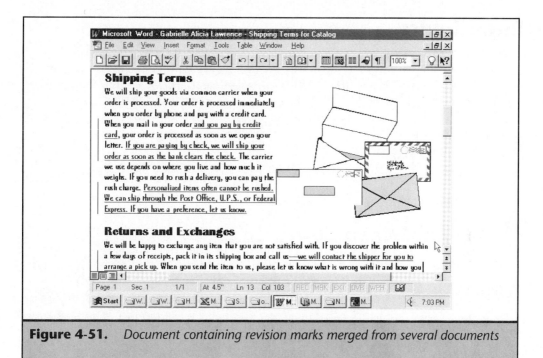

Figure 4-51. *Document containing revision marks merged from several documents*

MERGING REVISIONS TO MAILED DOCUMENTS   If you have routed the document using Microsoft Mail to other Word users, when you receive the edited documents there will be a document icon in the returned mail message. When you double-click this icon, Word will ask if you want to merge the revision marks. When you select Yes, you can select OK again since the original document name is already selected. If you want to merge the revision marks with a different document, specify the document before selecting OK. You can double-click the document icons repeatedly to merge the other routed documents.

Compiling All the Revisions

Repeat the merge process for each document whose revision marks you want to merge. For example, suppose you have several copies of a document called Propose stored in different locations. Open one copy of Propose, and follow the steps above for selecting another version of the Propose document. Once the newly opened "control" document contains the revision marks, repeat the steps for another version of the revised Propose document. Once you merge all versions of the Propose document, the current version will contain the revision marks from all versions of the document. At this point, you can close the revision versions.

Related Topics

Annotations
Comparing Versions
Locking and Protecting Documents

Revision Marks

See "Annotations," "Comparing Versions" and "Revision and Annotation Merging."

REVNUM Field

This field returns the revision number of a document. Each time you save a document, the revision number increases by one. This is the same revision number you see when you select File | Properties and choose the Statistics tab. See "Fields" and "Document Properties."

RFT-DCA

RFT-DCA is a format used by IBM 5520 and DisplayWrite. See "Opening Documents" and "Saving Documents" for information on opening documents saved in this format or saving documents in this format.

Rich Text Format (RTF)

RTF, or *Rich Text Format*, is a format that most Microsoft applications can use for sharing data. Word can open and save documents in an RTF format, as described under "Opening Documents" and "Saving Documents." You can also embed and link data that's in RTF format, to keep the formatting of the data as it is in its original location. RTF is one of the possible formats displayed with the Edit | Paste Special command; see "Object Linking and Embedding."

Right-Align Text

See "Alignment" and "Tabs."

Rotating

You can rotate text using WordArt, as described under "WordArt," and drawn objects as described under "Drawing on a Document." If you want to rotate graphics that are not drawn in Word, you must use a graphics package that can work with the picture to rotate it. Then you save the rotated version in a graphics document and insert it as a picture, or copy it via the Clipboard into the Word document.

Routing

See "Electronic Mail" for instructions on routing a document from one Word user to another, to let other Word users make comments to the same document.

Rows

See "Tables."

RTF

See "Rich Text Format (RTF)."

Ruler

Word's ruler is a bar on the screen that shows the position of margins, indents, tabs, columns, and table boundaries. In the horizontal ruler, you can change left and right margins, tabs, indents, and column and table boundaries. The vertical ruler, which appears in Page Layout view and Print Preview, lets you set top and bottom margins, header and footer position, and row heights in tables. The rulers appear at the top and left side of the document. When the document window is not maximized, the rulers are inside the document's window, rather than appearing below the menu bar and toolbars. The ruler does not appear in Master Document view or in Outline view.

Procedures

You can choose to show or hide the ruler, depending on what you are doing. You can also use the ruler to open dialog boxes as described in the following procedures.

Hiding and Displaying the Ruler

■   Use the <u>V</u>iew | <u>R</u>uler command to toggle between showing and hiding the ruler.

In Normal view, selecting <u>V</u>iew | <u>R</u>uler to display the ruler will show the horizontal ruler but not the vertical one. In Print Preview you always see both the horizontal and the vertical rulers. In Page Layout view, you see the horizontal ruler and the vertical ruler if it is selected. To select whether the vertical ruler appears in Page Layout view, select <u>T</u>ools | <u>O</u>ptions while in Page Layout view, select the View tab, select or clear the Vertical R<u>u</u>ler, and select OK.

The ruler uses the measuring system set by Word's General options. The section of the ruler that appears above a document matches the part of the document that is displayed. When you zoom to make the document look larger or smaller, the ruler proportionally increases or decreases, so an inch on the ruler is as wide as an inch on the document when it is printed, even if on the display it looks smaller or larger than an inch.

Using the Ruler

The symbols for the ruler and the information they provide are labeled below:

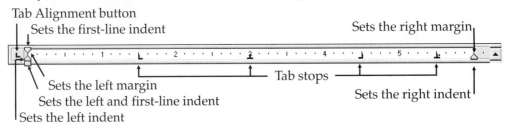

The ruler dynamically changes to match the paragraph, column, or table column containing the insertion point. A vertical ruler contains only the margin indicators that apply to the document, the table row, or to the header or footer. When you change margins, they apply to the entire section containing the insertion point; when you change indents and tabs, they only apply to the paragraph with the insertion point. If you want to set indents and tabs for multiple paragraphs, select the paragraphs before changing the indents and tabs with the ruler.

You can make the following changes using the mouse with the ruler:

■   *To change the margins* for the selected page, column, or table column, drag the appropriate margin symbols to a new location on the ruler. Remember that for columns and table columns, you can set the margins for both the columns and for the spaces between the columns.

■ *To change the indents* for the selected paragraphs or current paragraph, drag the indent triangles to new locations on the ruler. You can change the first-line indent independently of the left indent by dragging the first-line indent triangle. To change both the first-line and left indents by the same amounts, drag the little box below the left indent triangle. The indents are relative to the margin, so when you change the margins, the indents will change as well.

■ *To set a tab,* click the Tab Alignment button for the type of tab you want to add. Each time you click the Tab Alignment button, the symbol on the button cycles among left-aligned, centered, right-aligned, and decimal tabs. When you insert a tab symbol, all default tabs before that tab symbol are deleted.

TIP: *You can clear a tab stop by dragging the tab stop symbol down off the ruler. You can move a tab stop by dragging the tab stop symbol to a new location.*

Opening Dialog Boxes with the Ruler

■ Double-clicking a tab stop in the ruler displays the Tabs dialog box, as if you selected the Format I Tabs command. If there is no tab stop at the location where you double-click, Word adds one and then opens the Tabs dialog box.

■ Double-clicking an indent marker in the ruler displays the Paragraph dialog box, as if you selected the Format I Paragraph command.

■ Double-clicking a part of the ruler that is not used for margins, indents, or tabs displays the Page Setup dialog box, as if you selected the File I Page Setup command.

Rules

See "Grammar Options" for instructions on changing the grammar rules Word uses when it proofs your documents. See "Columns," "Footnotes and Endnotes," and "Tables" when you want to set the lines and borders Word uses in columns, footnotes and endnotes, and tables. See "Mail Merge" for information about the changes you can make to selection rules when you are creating a mail merge document.

Running Macros

Macros can execute a series of steps for you, such as typing or selecting Word features to apply to a document. Chapter 7 explains how to create macros. "Macros" in this chapter tells how to run a macro in Word.

Save Options

You can set the Save options, the default options that affect the document saving process.

Procedure

You can open the Options dialog box for the default save options from the Tools menu or from the Save As dialog box.

From the Tools Menu

1. Select Tools | Options.

2. Select the Save tab.

3. Set the options as you want them. For information on these options, see the following "Options" section.

4. Select OK.

From the Save As Dialog Box

Select Options from the Save As dialog box as you save a document. Word opens the Options dialog box with the Save tab displayed. Select your options, described under "Options" next, and then select OK.

Options

The Save options change how Word saves your documents.

ALWAYS CREATE BACKUP COPY   Select Always Create Backup Copy to have Word create a copy of your document each time you save it. The backup copy is named **Backup of** *Document Name* where *Document Name* is the original document name. For example, if your document is named Budget Report, the backup will be named Backup of Budget Report. The backup copy is the previous version of your document before your latest save request.

ALLOW FAST SAVES   Select Allow Fast Saves to have Word save only your changes to a document, rather than reformatting and saving the entire document each time. Fast saves save only the document changes you have made, so they are faster than normal saves. Fast save is the default setting.

Use a normal save before carrying out certain tasks. When you use a normal save, Word saves more complete information about your document. Use a normal save before compiling an index, converting your document to a new type, or transferring it to another application. You can use a normal save by clearing the Allow Fast Saves text box and then saving the document again.

PROMPT FOR DOCUMENT PROPERTIES   Document properties store information about your document that you can use to help organize your documents and for other purposes. Select Prompt for Document Properties to have Word prompt you for document properties when you first save each document.

See "Document Properties" for a description of the document properties that Word tracks.

PROMPT TO SAVE NORMAL TEMPLATE   Select Prompt to Save Normal template to have Word prompt you about saving changes to default settings for macros, AutoText entries, menus, shortcut keys, and toolbars in the Normal template each time you exit Word and have made changes to this template.

SAVE NATIVE PICTURE FORMATS ONLY   Select Save Native Picture Formats Only to have Word save all graphics in your document as a Windows Metafile type only (assuming they originally were a different type of graphic document). This saves space.

EMBED TRUETYPE FONTS   Select Embed TrueType Fonts to have Word save TrueType fonts with the document they are used in, so that readers of the document can see it as you designed it, even if their system does not have those fonts installed.

SAVE DATA ONLY FOR FORMS   Select Save Data Only for Forms to have Word save only the data from form documents so that you can use the information as a database. By default, the data and the form features are saved together.

AUTOMATIC SAVE EVERY   Most computer users know they should save often to prevent losing information when there is a power surge or program error. Very few users, however, actually do so, because it is easy to forget to save documents while working. Select Automatic Save Every to have Word save your document for you regularly. The interval between saves is the number of minutes you enter in the Minutes text box.

This feature does not replace saving the document as you normally would. The automatic save option saves documents as temporary files that can be opened only if Word was unloaded without exiting (such as when the power is interrupted or your system crashes) and you have to reboot. When you exit Word properly, these temporary files are deleted. If Word was unloaded without exiting, the next time you open Word, it will recover those files.

FILE SHARING OPTIONS FOR CURRENT DOCUMENT   If your document is going to be shared with other users, you may want to control their access to it. Enter a password in the Protection Password text box to prevent the current document from being opened by someone who does not know the password. Enter a password in the Write Reservation Password text box to prevent other users from saving an edited version of your document with the same name, though they can still open the document. Select Read-Only Recommended to have Word suggest to users that they open your document as a read-only document, unless they have actual changes to make.

Related Topics

Saving Documents
Forms

SAVEDATE Field

The SAVEDATE field returns the date a document was saved last. See "Fields" for information on using this and other fields, and "Document Properties" for the type of properties Word saves for a document.

Saving Documents

One of the most important features of a word processor is that a document you create and save can be opened again and edited later. This fundamental advantage of a word processor over a typewriter or other method of recording text is so basic that its importance is often unappreciated.

Procedures

Saving a document has different steps when you are saving it the first time, saving it subsequent times, saving it using new settings, and saving all open documents at once.

Saving a Document for the First Time

1. Select File | Save, click the Save button on the Standard toolbar, or press SHIFT+F12 or CTRL+S. Doing any of these opens the Save As dialog box.

2. Type the document's name in the File Name text box.

   Your entry must be an acceptable document name. Its name may be up to 255 characters, and can include any character except for /, \, :, *, ?, ", <, >, or | .

TIP: *Don't set a DOS file extension. Word sets the document type based on the choice in the Save As Type drop-down list box. If you will later use that file in DOS, you can rely on Word assigning a default file extension based on the document type.*

3. Use the Save In boxes to select another folder, if desired.

    The list box below Save In displays the documents in the selected folder. The Save In drop-down list box shows the currently selected folder. You can select another folder from this drop-down list box or the list box below to change to another folder. You can also change to a higher level folder by clicking the Up One Level button at the top of the dialog box.

    Move to an undisplayed folder by selecting a folder above the open folder, closing the open folder, and opening the one above it. The folders in the newly opened folder are displayed.

    When you open the folder where you want to save the document, check the list box to ensure that the name given for the current document is not already used in the folder.

4. Select a document type from the Save as Type drop-down list box to set the type that the document is saved in. The default is Word Document.

5. Select Options to open the Options dialog box for the Save category. In this dialog box, you can change Word's default options relating to saving. You can also define passwords for the current document with this option. These settings are explained under "Save Options."

6. Select OK to save the document.

 TIP: Once you save a document, Word adds it to the bottom of the File menu to make it easier to open at a later point. Windows also adds it to its Most Recently Used list of documents so you can reopen that document by selecting Documents from the Start menu and selecting the document.

Resaving a Document with the Same Name and Type

Resaving a document with the same name and type is done using the same commands you used to save it originally.

- Click the Save button on the Standard toolbar.
- Press SHIFT+F12.
- Press CTRL+S.
- Select File | Save.

    Word saves the document to the same name, without requiring any further information from you.

Resaving a Document with a New Name or Type

You can save a document with a new name or type by selecting File | Save As or pressing F12. The Save As dialog box is the same dialog box just explained. Make the appropriate selections from the dialog box options and select OK.

CAUTION: *You can have two files with the same name only when they have different types.*

Saving Multiple Documents at Once

When you have multiple documents open at one time, you may find it difficult to remember which of these opened documents you have saved. To save them all at one time, select File | Save All. Word saves each document to its previously set name and type. If a document was not previously saved, Word opens the Save As dialog box, letting you assign a name and type.

Related Topics

Closing Documents
Compatibility Options
Exiting Word
Locking and Protecting Documents
Opening Documents
Save Options

Scaling Graphics

See "Graphics."

Scrap

Windows' scrap feature stores data temporarily to give you an opportunity to place copies of that data or embed that data into other applications.

Procedure

While this procedure focuses on Word, the procedure is similar when you use the scrap in other applications.

1. Select the text, graphics, and other Word features that you want copied.

2. Change the Word application window so it no longer uses the entire desktop—so you can see part of your desktop background.

3. Drag the selected text to the desktop. When you release the mouse, you will see a new icon on your desktop like this:

Document
Scrap 'Yes_ it
really i...'

Windows automatically provides the label Document Scrap and adds to it the first few characters from the text that created the scrap: in this situation "Yes _it really i...".

4. Move to where you want the contents of the document placed—in Word or another application. You may need to size that application's window to see the icon for the scrap on the desktop.

5. Drag the scrap icon onto the location where you want the contents of the scrap placed. The selected data is placed into that location. If the final destination is not Word, the scrap may become an embedded object.

The scrap remains on the desktop until you delete it. Therefore, when you are done with the scrap, right-click the scrap's icon and select Delete or drag the scrap's icon to the Recycling Bin.

TIP: *Since you can have more than one scrap, you can use the Scrap in place of the Clipboard when you have more than one item that you want to share between documents.*

Screen Fonts

Screen fonts are fonts for displaying text onscreen. See "Fonts."

Scroll Bars

Scroll bars are used to move through a document or list box. You can choose to display or to hide them on a document.

Procedures

Horizontal and vertical scroll bars work in the same way, except that horizontal scroll bars move you left to right in the document, while vertical scroll bars move from top to bottom.

- Click the arrow at either end of the scroll bar to move in small increments in that direction. The vertical scroll bar moves you one line at a time, and the horizontal scroll bar moves you a small distance to the left or right.

- Click the scroll bar between the arrow and the scroll box to move one window in that direction.

- Drag the scroll box to a place on the scroll bar to move to approximately the same location in the document. The page number will appear next to the scroll box showing the page number that will be displayed when you release the mouse.

- Page Layout has an extra set of buttons at the bottom of the vertical scroll bar. Clicking these buttons moves backwards or forwards by one page.

Options

Scroll bars consist of the scroll bar itself, the scroll arrows, and a scroll box, as shown here:

Scroll box   Scroll bar

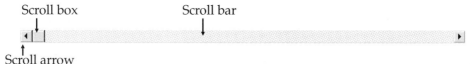

Scroll arrow

You can choose to hide or display the scroll bars by selecting Tools | Options and selecting the View tab. Clear or select the Horizontal Scroll Bar or Vertical Scroll Bar check boxes to set whether these features appear.

Related Topics

View Options

Scrolling

Scrolling is the process of moving through a document to view the document and move the insertion point. You can do this using movement keys or the scroll bars. See "Scroll Bars" or "Moving the Insertion Point" to learn how to move in your document.

Searching a Document

See "Find and Replace."

Searching for a Document

See "Document Management."

Secondary Files

Secondary files, called *data sources* in Word, are used during merges to provide text to be merged into a main, or primary, document. See "Mail Merge."

Section Breaks

See "Sections."

SECTION Field

The SECTION field returns the section number of the current section. See "Fields."

Section Formats

See "Sections."

SECTIONPAGES Field

The SECTIONPAGES field returns the total number of pages of the current section. See "Fields."

Sections

Sections break your Word document into smaller segments, which usually contain various formats. Some formats must be the same throughout a single section, so you must break the document into sections used just for these formats. Each section can have different margins, columns, page size and orientation, line numbering, page numbering, headers and footers, and endnote settings. For example, the newsletter shown in Figure 4-52 uses several different sections in order to have different columns.

Procedures

You can add section breaks where you want them. Changes to such features as margins, page size, page orientation, and number of columns are made using the File | Page Setup command. When you make these changes using this command, you have the choice of applying the change to the entire document, to the current section, or to the rest of the sections in the document in the Apply To drop-down list box.

Inserting Section Breaks

1. Put your insertion point where the new section will begin.

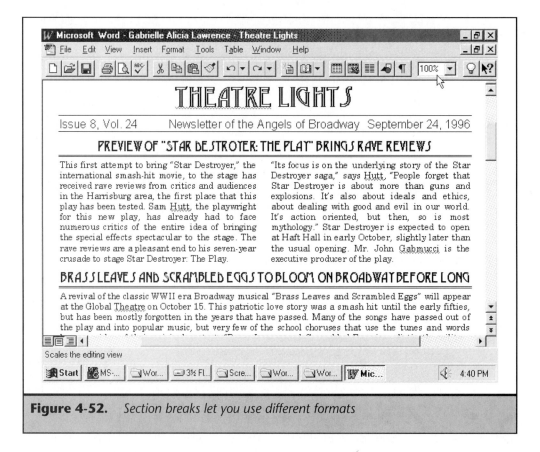

Figure 4-52. *Section breaks let you use different formats*

2. Select Insert | Break.

3. Select an option button in the Section Breaks area of the dialog box. These selections set where the first page of the section will be.

   ■ Select Next Page to start the next section on a new page.

   ■ Select Even Page to start the next section with the next even-numbered page, or select Odd Page to start with the next odd-numbered page (you may end up with an extra blank page).

   ■ Select Continuous to start the new section on the current page.

4. Select OK.

Apply Layout Formats to a Section

1. Put your insertion point in the section to format or select the text to format.

2. Select File | Page Setup and the Layout tab. The Apply To drop-down list box indicates which sections will be affected by the changes you make.

3. Change where you want the section to start from the Section Start drop-down list box. It will have the current starting point for the section. Selecting a different option changes the section's starting location just as if you had selected the new option when you inserted the section break. You have the same starting location choices that you have when you insert a section break.

4. Select how you want the text vertically aligned on the page by choosing an option from the Vertical Alignment drop-down list box. Select Top to start the text at the top margin, Center to center it between the top and bottom margins, or Justified to have Word add space between paragraphs to make the text start at the top margin and end at the bottom.

5. When a document has endnotes that are placed at the end of each section, the Suppress Endnotes check box is available. Select this check box and the endnotes appear after the next section instead.

6. Select Line Numbers to add line numbers to the section and to set how they appear. Information on all the line numbering features is provided under "Line Numbers."

7. Select OK.

Deleting Section Breaks
Move to the section break you want to delete and press DEL. The section above adopts the section formatting of the section below it.

Hints
Section formats control how the pages of the section appear when printed. The effect of some of these formats, such as vertical alignment, is not apparent unless you use Print Preview or Page Layout view to view them.

Vertical Alignment
Do not use different vertical alignments for sections that occur on the same page. When you choose to start sections continuously, multiple sections occur on a single page. If the sections have different vertical alignments, your text prints oddly, with each section laid out separately on the page and often overlapping other sections.

Forcing Odd Pages
When you start a section on the next odd page, this forces Word to put that first page of that section on an odd page. Chapters and sections of a report usually start on an odd page as a visual organizational signal. You force page breaks with the Insert | Break command in the same way as for dividing the document into sections.

Copying Section Breaks

Section breaks can be copied to other locations in the document to apply the formatting specific to the section to another section in the document. Copy it to the Clipboard as described under "Clipboard." All of the settings made with File | Page Setup, Format | Columns, and View | Header and Footer are copied. Pasting the section breaks pastes all of those section settings to the new location. You can also copy and move section breaks with drag and drop.

Finding Section Breaks

To find section breaks, you can select Edit | Go To, select Section in the Go To What list box, and select Next or Previous. You can also select Edit | Find or Edit | Replace and look for ^b to find the next section break.

Sections and Master Documents

When you add a document as a subdocument of a master document, Word adds a section break before and after the subdocument.

Related Topics

Columns
Drag and Drop
Footnotes
Line Numbers
Margins
Page Numbers
Page Setup

Selecting Text

Selecting text is the process of telling Word that you want to do something with that text.

Procedures

You can select text using your mouse or keyboard. The way you select text depends on the method that you find convenient and the text that you want to select.

Selecting Text with the Mouse

You can select text quickly with the mouse. Table 4-16 shows how you can use the mouse to select different amounts of text. Some of these possibilities use the selection bar. The selection bar is the area to the left of the paragraph. When you point here, you will notice that the mouse points upwards and to the right.

Do This	To Select
Drag mouse across text	The text you drag across
Press SHIFT and click text	The text from the insertion point to where you click
Double-click a word	The word you click
Press CTRL and click	The sentence you click
Drag in the selection bar	The lines beside where you dragged
Click in the selection bar	The line beside where you clicked
Double-click in the selection bar	The paragraph beside where you clicked
Press CTRL and click in the selection bar	The entire paragraph
Drag with the right mouse button	A column of text

Table 4-16. *Using the Mouse to Select Text*

Selecting Text with the Extend Key

1. Press F8. *EXT* appears in the status bar to indicate you are in extend mode. You can also turn on EXT by double-clicking the EXT placeholder in the status bar.

2. Select text by using one of these key combinations:

   ■ Press the arrows and other movement keys to extend and contract the selection.

   ■ Press F8 (the Extend key) repeatedly to extend the selection, as shown in Table 4-17.

   ■ Press a character key to extend the selection to that character. Pressing the key again extends the selection to the next occurrence of that character.

3. Press ESC to end extend mode.

Selecting Text with the Keyboard

Table 4-18 shows the keypresses used to select text and the text that they select. You can combine these keypresses. For example, you can press CTRL+SHIFT+DOWN ARROW to select to the end of the current paragraph and then press SHIFT+LEFT ARROW to keep from selecting the paragraph mark at the end.

Press F8	To Select
Once	Current word
Twice	Current sentence
Three times	Current paragraph
Four times	Current section
Five times	Entire document

Table 4-17. *Using Extend to Select Text*

Keypress	Selects
SHIFT+RIGHT ARROW	One character to the right
SHIFT+LEFT ARROW	One character to the left
SHIFT+UP ARROW	To the same position in the previous line
SHIFT+DOWN ARROW	To the same position in the next line
CTRL+SHIFT+RIGHT ARROW	To the beginning of the next word
CTRL+SHIFT+LEFT ARROW	To the beginning of the current or previous word
SHIFT+END	To the end of the current line
SHIFT+HOME	To the beginning of the current line
CTRL+SHIFT+UP ARROW	To the beginning of the current or previous paragraph
CTRL+SHIFT+DOWN ARROW	To the beginning of the next paragraph
SHIFT+PAGE UP	One screen up from the current position
SHIFT+PAGE DOWN	One screen down from the current position
CTRL+SHIFT+HOME	To the beginning of the document
CTRL+SHIFT+END	To the end of the document
CTRL+5 (num. keypad)	The entire document

Table 4-18. *Selecting with Keys*

Selecting Columns of Text

You can select columns or rectangles of text. This can be useful for selecting numbers arranged in a tabular column, as shown in Figure 4-53.

1. Press CTRL+SHIFT+F8. The status bar shows COL to indicate that you are in column mode.

2. Use the movement keys to extend your column selection.

3. Press ESC when you wish to leave column extend mode.

Hints

In extend mode, you can use the Edit | Go To and Find commands to extend the selection. The selection extends from the insertion point's location to the text that you go to or find.

Other ways to select all of the text in the document are to select Edit | Select All or press CTRL+A.

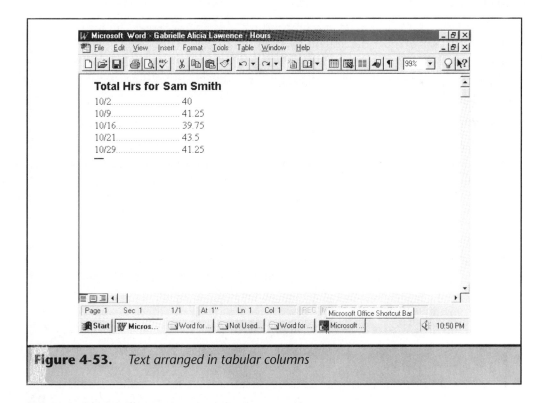

Figure 4-53.   *Text arranged in tabular columns*

SEQ Field

The SEQ field numbers items or sections of text in your document. See "Fields."

SET Field

The SET field assigns a bookmark to defined text. See "Fields."

Shading

See "Borders and Shading."

Shadowed Text

See "WordArt."

Sharing Data

See "Clipboard," "Object Linking and Embedding," "Scrap," or "Spike" for information on sharing data with other documents or applications. See "Saving Documents" for information on security for documents shared with other Word users. See "Object Linking and Embedding" for information on sharing data with other applications.

Shortcut Keys

Shortcut keys are used to activate commands with the keyboard without having to use the menus. Word has many shortcut keys for different features. The features and the topics that describe the shortcut keys for these features are shown next.

Shortcut Keys For	See
Adding and updating fields	Fields
Adding special characters	Special Characters
Applying and removing font styles	All Caps, Bold, Italics, Small Capitals, Spacing Characters, Strikethrough, Super/Subscript, Text Color, Underline
Assigning styles	Styles
Changing the size and font	Fonts

Function keys	Function Keys
Moving in a document	Moving the Insertion Point
Moving in a table	Tables
Outlines	Outlines
Paragraph formatting	Alignment, Indents, Pagination, Spacing
Selecting text	Selecting Text

Besides the shortcut keys for the features just described, Word also has shortcut keys for many of its commands. The following table shows the shortcut keys you can use to select various menu commands.

Command	**Press**
File | New	CTRL+N
File | Open	CTRL+O or CTRL+F12
File | Close	CTRL+W
File | Save	CTRL+S or CTRL+F12
File | Save As	F12
File | Print Preview	CTRL+F2
File | Print	CTRL+P or CTRL+SHIFT+F12
File | Exit	ALT+F4
Edit | Undo	CTRL+Z or ALT+BACKSPACE
Edit | Repeat	CTRL+Y or F4
Edit | Clear	DEL
Edit | Cut	CTRL+X or SHIFT+DEL
Edit | Copy	CTRL+C or CTRL+INS
Edit | Paste	CTRL+V or SHIFT+INS
Edit | Select All	CTRL+A or CTRL+5
Edit | Find	CTRL+F
Edit | Replace	CTRL+H
Edit | Go To	CTRL+G OR F5
Edit | Bookmark	CTRL+SHIFT+F5
Edit | Links | Update Now	F9
View | Normal	ALT+CTRL+N

S

View | Outline	ALT+CTRL+O
View | Page Layout	ALT+CTRL+P
Insert | Page Numbers	ALT+SHIFT+P
Insert | Annotation	ALT+CTRL+A
Insert | Date And Time	ALT+SHIFT+D or ALT+SHIFT+T
Insert | Footnote | Footnote	ALT+CTRL+F
Insert | Footnote | Endnote	ALT+CTRL+E
Insert | Index and Tables | Index | Mark Entry	ALT+SHIFT+X
Insert | Index and Tables | Tables of Authorities | Mark Citation	ALT+SHIFT+I
Insert | Field | TC Field	ALT+SHIFT+O
Format | Font	CTRL+D
Format | Change Case	SHIFT+F3
Format | AutoFormat	CTRL+K
Format | Style	CTRL+SHIFT+S
Tools | Spelling	F7
Tools | Thesaurus	SHIFT+F7
Table | Select Table	ALT+5
Table | Table AutoFormat	ALT+CTRL+U
Window | Split	ALT+CTRL+S
Help | Contents	F1
Context-sensitive Help	SHIFT+F1

See "Keyboard Options" for information on changing existing shortcut keys or adding new ones.

Shortcut Menus

You can right-click or press SHIFT+F10 to display a pop-up menu. This menu contains the most popular commands for the item that you are pointing at. The contents of the menu change according to what you are pointing at. Selecting an item from the shortcut menu is the same as selecting the appropriate command from Word's regular menu. The features provided through these menus are described with the commands and features using Word's regular commands.

Shortcuts

You can create shortcuts to your most commonly used documents. See "Favorites Folder."

Sizing Windows

See "Document Window."

SKIPIF Field

The SKIPIF field makes Word skip a record during a mail merge when a particular condition is true. See "Mail Merge."

Small Capitals

Small Caps is a character format that produces text in which letters typed as lowercase appear as capitals in a smaller font size. Small caps are often used in titles and headings and in scripts and speeches.

Procedures

The Small Caps style can be applied as the text is being typed or after it is typed. To apply the style while typing, first add the format, then type the text, and then remove the format. To apply it to typed text, select the text to be formatted and then add the style.

Adding and Removing Small Caps with the Menu

1. Select Format | Font or right-click the selected text or insertion point location and select Font from the shortcut menu.
2. Select the Small Caps check box. Clear this box to remove the Small Caps format.
3. Select OK.

Adding and Removing Small Caps with the Keyboard

Press CTRL+SHIFT+K to add or remove the Small Caps format.

Removing Formatting

Another method for removing Small Caps from text is to select the text and press CTRL+SPACEBAR, removing all character formatting from the selected text.

Related Topics

Character Formats
Fonts

Smart Cut and Paste

Smart cut and paste, or smart deletion, is the feature that decides whether to insert or remove a space as you insert and delete text in a document. When this feature is on, Word adds spaces or removes them as necessary. For example, when you move to the end of a sentence and delete the last word, Smart Cut and Paste also removes the space after the last word. Conversely, when you paste text at the end of the sentence, Word adds a space between what was the last word and the phrase that you just pasted into place. Once this feature is on, you do not have to do anything to take advantage of its effects.

Procedure

1. Select Tools | Options and the Edit tab.
2. Select or clear the Use Smart Cut and Paste check box to turn this feature on or off.
3. Select OK when done.

Smart Quotes

Word can automatically change single quotes, double quotes, and apostrophes to become angled like these:

Before

I thought my computer "crashed" but it was just my foot hitting the reset button.
Today's special is cherry pie 'a la mode.'

After

I thought my computer "crashed" but it was just my foot hitting the reset button.
Today's special is cherry pie 'a la mode.'

This type of change can be made as an AutoFormat change. Once you turn on Smart Quotes, the quotes are changed automatically. However, Smart Quotes only improves the looks of the quotation marks. It does not set them to the grammatically appropriate ones. To see which ones you should use, see the box "Rules for Quotes."

Rules for Quotes

Quotation marks are always used around direct quotes but are never used for indirect quotes or paraphrased remarks. There are some additional rules that cause the following elements to be enclosed in quotes:

- Unfamiliar jargon, as in: Our network guru even managed to "crash" the system.

- Misspelled words and slang, as in: Tommy's first-grade teacher has been correcting his use of "ain't."

- Words that indicate stamping or marking, as in: The package was marked "Undeliverable."

- The definition of a word in italics, as in: *Multimedia* is "the creative combination of text, graphics, audio, and animation."

- Chapter titles and magazine articles.

- Use single quotes within a quotation to mark text normally in quotation marks, as in: Sally said, "I just finished reading 'Sailing on the Great Lakes' in the *Forever Sailing* magazine and wondered if you would like to borrow it."

- Alternate between single and double quotes when quotes are nested, as in: Tonya said, "I was offended when Jim said, 'You have been wasting too much time repackaging parcels marked "Undeliverable"' and decided not to work late any more this week."

Procedure

1. Select Tools | Options and the AutoFormat tab.
2. Select the AutoFormat As You Type option button.
3. Select or clear the Straight Quotes With 'Smart Quotes' check box to turn this feature on or off.
4. Select OK when done.

Snaking Columns

See "Columns."

Sorting

You can quickly sort tables or paragraphs in alphabetic order. You can sort using up to three fields, using the second and third ones to break ties. For example, if you have two people named Campbell in your list, you can use a second key to sort the Campbells by their first name. Each field is a column in the table or text in the paragraph divided by some specific character.

Procedures

1. Select the text you want to sort. If you don't select the text to sort, Word selects the entire table if you are in a table, or the entire document if you are not.

2. Select Table | Sort Text. When the insertion point is in a table, this command is Table | Sort Table.

3. Specify the sort field in the Sort By drop-down list box. This list box will list the available fields you can use to sort using entries such as Column 1 and Column 2. If you have a header row in the table you are sorting, this drop-down list box will contain the column heading entries.

4. Select the type of sorting to do from the Type drop-down list box:

   ■ Select Date to have Word sort using text in a standard date format, ignoring any other text.

   ■ Select Number to have Word sort using numbers, ignoring dates and other text.

   ■ Select Text and Word sorts both alphabetically and numerically, putting numbers and special characters before letters.

5. Select Ascending or Descending to choose how Word sorts your text, as shown here:

   Ascending Sort
   A . . . Z 1 2 3

   Descending Sort
   Z . . . A 3 2 1

6. If you want to select tiebreakers, select a second or third field using the Then By and Then By drop-down list boxes. Repeat steps 3 through 5 to set up these sort keys.

7. Word may assume that your table or list has a header row that should not be sorted. If you want the top row sorted along with the rest of the rows, select the No Header Row option button rather than the Header Row option button.

8. Change any sort options by selecting Options and then changing the entries for any of the following:

   ■ Select how the entries to sort are divided into fields by choosing one of the options under Separate Fields At. Select Commas to have Word treat commas as marking the ends of fields. Select Tabs to have Word treat tabs as marking the ends of fields. Select Other and enter another character used to mark the ends of fields in the text to sort.

■ Select Sort Column Only when you select a tabular or table column, and want to sort that column without affecting any other columns.

■ Select Case Sensitive to have Word separate lower- and uppercase when sorting text. Uppercase letters will come before lowercase letters.

9. Select OK twice to sort the text.

Hints

Word has several features that make sorting easier. These features include using different fields for sorting, undoing a sort if the data is not sorted the way you want, and using acceptable date and time formats when you sort by date.

Fields

In ordinary sorting, only the first word in a paragraph or line may be used to determine the sort order. When you want to sort using a word other than the first word, the words in a line or paragraph must be separated into fields by a comma, by a tab, or by a character specified after selecting the Other option button in the Sort Options dialog box. Fields may also be created by using Word's Table feature. Then you can select which column in the table you want to use for sorting.

Undoing Sorts

You can undo a sort by selecting Edit | Undo Sort or by using the Undo button in the Standard toolbar to undo the sort and everything done since the sort.

If you save your document before sorting it, you can be assured of being able to restore your document if the sort does not work the way that you thought it would, even if you do some editing before realizing that the sort is incorrect. Simply close the current sorted document without saving it, and then open the original unsorted document again.

Date and Time Formats

When you choose to sort according to Date, Word sorts only those paragraphs or cells containing dates in certain recognizable formats like the ones shown next. If Word cannot find a date, that paragraph, row, or cell is sorted as if it contains nothing.

11/6/95

11-6-95

11 6 95

November 6, 1995

Nov. 6, 1995

Nov 6

06-Nov-95

November-95

11/06/95 3:30 PM

Related Topics

Tables

Sorting the File List

See "Document Management."

Sorting Tables

See "Sorting."

Sorting Text

See "Sorting."

Sound

You can add sound to your Word documents. To add the sound, your computer needs sound capabilities available with a sound card. Sounds can either be part of a document or part of the annotations in a document.

Procedures

Sounds can be added to a document as an embedded object or as voice annotations. Voice annotations are an alternative to using written annotations. Voice annotations are usually created by one user and heard by another.

Adding an Embedded Sound Object

1. Move the insertion point to where you want the icon for the sound placed.

2. Select Insert | Object.

   You can add a sound object two ways.

   ■ Choose Sound from the Object Type list box with the Create New tab selected and OK. Depending on your computer, your choice from the Object

Type list box may be different. Word and Windows opens the Sound Recorder application. You can use the Edit | Insert File command to insert a sound file as well as using other Sound Recorder application features to add the sound you want. When you have the sound you want, select File | Exit and Yes when prompted about updating the object.

■ Choose Sound from the Object Type list box with the Create from File tab, select the sound file to add as an object, and then select OK.

Word and Windows adds an icon for the sound object you have embedded into your document. To hear the sound, double-click the icon or select the icon and press ALT+SHIFT+F9.

Creating Voice Annotations

Creating a voice annotation lets a user make comments about a document. To create voice annotations, you must have a microphone installed as well as a sound board.

1. Position the insertion point on the text the voice annotation will belong to.

2. Select Insert | Annotation, and click the Insert Sound Object button in the annotations pane's toolbar.

3. Record your voice annotation, using the instructions for recording that came with your sound board.

4. If, when you finish recording, Word displays a message asking if you want to update the sound object, select Yes. The document will have a icon for the sound object you just recorded.

5. Select Close or return to the document window.

When you want to listen to the voice annotations, look at the document's annotations. Double-clicking the sound icons will replay the recorded voice annotations.

Spacing

You can set two kinds of spacing for your paragraph with Word—line spacing and paragraph spacing. Line spacing controls the space between the lines within the paragraph. Paragraph spacing controls the spacing between paragraphs. You can see these spacings marked in Figure 4-54.

Procedures

Both line spacing and paragraph spacing are paragraph formats. When these are set, the setting affects the paragraph the insertion point is in or all selected paragraphs. If

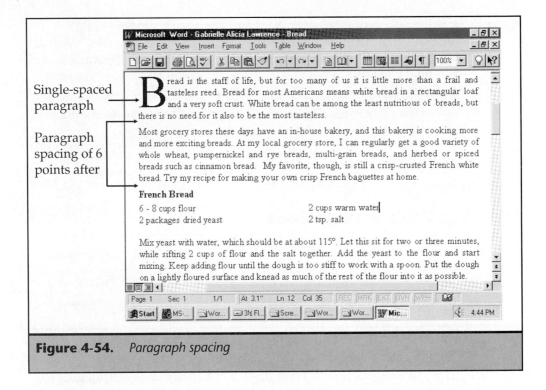

Single-spaced
paragraph

Paragraph
spacing of 6
points after

Figure 4-54.   *Paragraph spacing*

you press ENTER in a paragraph, creating a new paragraph, the new paragraph uses
the same spacing formats as the previous paragraph.

Setting Line Spacing

1. Select Format | Paragraph or right-click the document area and select
   Paragraph.

2. Select the Indents and Spacing tab, if necessary.

3. In the Line Spacing drop-down list box, select Single, 1.5 Lines, Double, At
   Least, Exactly, or Multiple to set the line spacing. For more information on
   these choices, see "Options."

4. If you selected either At Least or Exactly in the Line Spacing box, enter the
   number of points in the At text box for these settings to use. If you selected
   Multiple in the Line Spacing box, enter the multiple of the single line size you
   want the paragraphs to use.

5. Select OK.

Setting Paragraph Spacing

1. Select Format | Paragraph, or right-click the document area and select Paragraph.
2. Select the Indents and Spacing tab, if necessary.
3. To leave space before the paragraph, enter a measurement in the Before text box. Enter a measurement in the After text box to leave space after the paragraph.

   Word defines the space before or after paragraphs in terms of points, which are 1/72 inch. Each click of the arrows that are part of this text box changes the value by 6 points.
4. Select OK.

Options

There are options for spacing lines within a paragraph:

- *Single, 1.5 Lines, Double*   Sets one of these standard line spacings for the formatted paragraph.

- *At Least*   Sets a minimum line spacing for Word to use. Word can expand the lines if necessary, but cannot decrease the line spacing below this measurement. You need to specify the line spacing in the At text box when you select this option.

- *Exactly*   Sets an exact line spacing for Word to use. Word cannot expand or shrink the line spacing you specify in the At text box.

- *Multiple*   Sets the spacing for the lines in the formatted paragraph based on a multiple of the font and font size. For example, 1 is the same as Single, but you can also use decimals such as 1.2 to have line spacing 120 percent larger than Single.

Hints

Double-spacing is often required for academic papers. It is also useful for drafts that you (or a proofreader) are reviewing, because changes can be marked in the space between the lines.

Related Topics

Paragraph Formats

Spacing Characters

With Word, you can control the spacing between the characters in your document by adding extra space to the right of a character. For example, the text in Figure 4-55 uses expanded spacing to make an attractive flyer.

Procedures

The spacing between characters can be applied either as the text is being typed or after it is typed. You can add the format, type the text to affect, then remove the format, or you can select the text to format and then add the format.

1. Select Format | Font or right-click the selected text or insertion point location and select Font.

2. Select the Character Spacing tab.

3. Select Expanded or Condensed from the Spacing drop-down list box to add or remove space between characters. Select Normal to return to the default spacing.

4. Specify the distance to add or remove between characters in the By text box. You can enter between 0 and 1584 points.

Figure 4-55. *Expanded character spaces make interesting effects*

5. Select the <u>K</u>erning for Fonts check box to have Word automatically kern text, adding and removing space between individual pairs of letters to make them fit together better. Enter the smallest font size you want kerned in the P<u>o</u>ints and Above text box.

6. Select OK.

Hints

You can change the spacing between characters for a special effect in a brochure or newsletter. This feature may work well if you are planning to superimpose the text on a graphic.

You can change the spacing between specific letter pairs throughout your document by using the <u>E</u>dit I <u>R</u>eplace command, and replacing those character pairs with the same characters, but with different character spacing. You may need to change the character spacing of character pairs in camera-ready copy to make the text read more smoothly by taking out oddly placed gaps.

Related Topics

Character Formats
Find and Replace
Super/Subscript

Special Characters

Word can insert special characters or symbols. Special characters are those that print, and are part of normal fonts, but that do not have their own key on the keyboard, such as an é and a copyright mark. Symbols are usually selected from special decorative fonts, such as Wingdings or Zapf Dingbats. When you insert a symbol, you cannot change the font that it is in.

Procedures

You can insert special characters and symbols using a menu command. With frequently used special characters and symbols, you may want to assign a shortcut key so you can press the shortcut key to add the special character or symbol.

Inserting Symbols

1. Select <u>I</u>nsert I <u>S</u>ymbol and select the <u>S</u>ymbols tab, if necessary.

2. Select the font you want to use in the <u>F</u>ont drop-down list box. If you want to insert a standard character that cannot be typed at the keyboard, without defining a particular font, select Normal Text. Look for fonts with names like

Symbol, Wingdings, or Dingbats to find a set of different characters, such as those in Figure 4-56.

3. Highlight the character you want to use. As you highlight characters, a box displays them in a larger size. Note that any shortcut keys for this character are displayed in the upper-right corner of the dialog box.

4. Select Insert. You can continue inserting more characters or select Close.

Inserting Special Characters

1. Select Insert | Symbol.

2. Select the Special Characters tab, if necessary.

3. Highlight the character you want to insert in the Character list box.

NOTE: *The shortcut key for the character appears in this list box as well.*

4. Select Insert. You can continue inserting more characters or select Close.

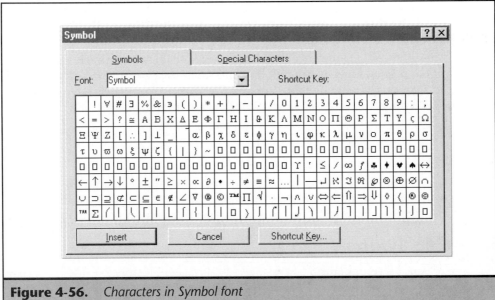

Figure 4-56. *Characters in Symbol font*

Automatically Inserting Special Characters

1. Select Tools | Auto Correct.
2. Select the Replace Text As You Type check box.
3. Select OK.

Now when you type one of the symbols shown on the left side of the following table, Word automatically replaces it with the symbol on the right. If you want the automatic replacement to stop, repeat the preceding steps and clear the Replace Text As You Type check box.

Type	To Replace with This Symbol
:) or :-) or (: or (-:	☺
:| or :-| or |: or |-:	☻
:(or :-(or): or)-:	☹
<-- or <- - -	←
--> or -> - -	→
<== or <=	⬅
==> or =>	➡
<=> or <==>	⇔
(c)	©
(r)	®
(tm)	™
-	–
--	—
... or . . .	…

Changing Shortcut Keys

1. Select Insert | Symbol.
2. Highlight the symbol or character associated with the shortcut key you want to assign or edit.
3. Select Shortcut Key.
4. Press the keys to use as shortcut keys with the insertion point in the Press New Shortcut Key text box.

S

5. Select OK.

6. Select Insert or Close.

Once the shortcut key is assigned, you can add it to any location in the document by pressing the key combination you pressed in step 4.

Hints

When you use special characters in Word, the special character appearance depends on the font. Symbols do not change when you change the font. When you insert symbols, these symbols are protected from changes in font. That is, although you can apply a new font size, position, or even (depending on the symbol or font) a format such as italics or underlining, you cannot change the font. The characters you insert as symbols are usually part of special fonts that do not include the usual letters and symbols that are part of standard font sets. If you were to change the font, you might change your "smiley face" (Wingdings) into a J (normal text).

Special characters, on the other hand, are characters that appear in most normal font sets, but that cannot be typed from the keyboard, such as ¶, ÷, or smart (curly) quotes. You can insert these characters from the Special Characters tab or from the Symbols tab, if you have selected normal text as the font. These characters can change fonts, since most font sets have the same characters. Your "smiley face" will not turn into a J when you switch to the next font.

Related Topics

Fields
Keyboard Options
Nonprinting Characters

Spell It

See "Spelling."

Spelling

Word's Spelling feature enables you to locate misspelled words in your document, and to replace them with correct ones. The Spelling feature also flags incorrectly capitalized words and repeated words.

Procedures

You can check spelling two ways: by displaying the Spelling dialog box and reviewing the misspellings all at once, or by letting Word mark potentially misspelled words and fixing them individually.

Checking Spelling Through the Spelling Dialog Box

1. Select the section of the document to check, or move to the beginning of the text that you want checked.

2. To activate the Spelling feature, select Tools | Spelling, select the Spelling button from the Standard toolbar, or press F7.

   The first word in the document or selected text that Word cannot locate in its dictionaries is highlighted, and the Spelling dialog box appears. You may also notice how these misspelled words show a wavy line under them.

   The highlighted word also appears in the Not in Dictionary text box. The suggested replacement words appear in the Suggestions list box. Your next action will depend on whether you agree with Word's suggestions.

3. You can either correct the word that is flagged as misspelled or ignore it. You can also choose to add the word to a custom dictionary, correct all instances of the word, or ignore all instances of the word, depending on the option you select.

   ■ When the flagged word is wrong and the correct word is suggested, highlight the correct word in the Suggestions list box and select Change.

   ■ When the flagged word is wrong, and the correct word is not suggested, type the correct word in the Change To text box and select Change. You can click on the word in the Not in Dictionary text box to change the Change To text box to contain the flagged entry, if it makes entering the correct replacement easier. Select Change All if the word is consistently misspelled to have Word correct it each time it is encountered.

   ■ When the flagged word is correct, select Ignore. Select Ignore All to avoid flagging the word when it occurs again. Select Add to add the word to a custom dictionary so it is not flagged in other documents. You can change which dictionary the word is added to by selecting a dictionary from the Add Words To drop-down list box.

   ■ When the flagged word is one that is repeated, such as "the the," select Delete and Word will delete the second instance of the word.

   For a fuller explanation of each of these choices, see "Options" in this section.

S

4. After you select one of the preceding options, Word continues checking the document, highlighting the next word that cannot be found in the dictionary. Make a selection regarding the newly flagged word as described in step 3.

5. When Word finishes, it displays a message box saying "The spelling check is complete." Select OK to return to your document.

Turn On Automatic Marking of Misspelled Words

1. Select Tools | Options and the Spelling tab.

2. Select the Automatic Spell Checking check box.

3. Select OK.

   You will also turn on this feature when you display the Spelling dialog box, with the steps described earlier.

   While this feature is turned on, when Word finds a word that is not in the dictionary, it puts a wavy line beneath it, as you can see in Figure 4-57. Once this feature is turned on, it remains in effect unless you shut it off. At this point, you can correct any misspellings at your own pace.

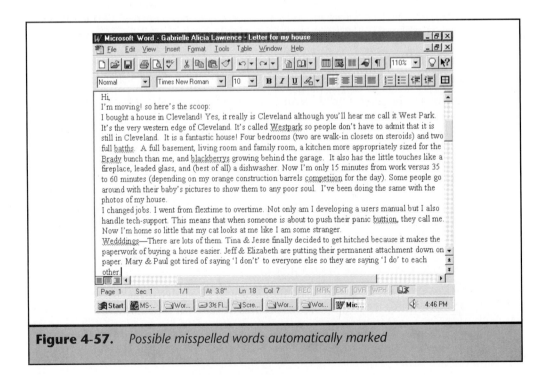

Figure 4-57. *Possible misspelled words automatically marked*

Fixing Marked Misspellings

■ Right-click any word with a wavy line underneath to display a pop-up menu like the one here:

From here, you can select one of the suggestions to replace the misspelled word with the one correctly spelled. You can also choose Ignore All to have Word not flag that instance or all instances of the word. You can choose Add to add the word to the last dictionary chosen when you added a word. You can also click the misspelled word to edit it or just to leave the pop-up menu and continue with other edits in the document. You may also notice that marked words include duplicates so you can select Delete from the pop-up menu to remove the second of the two repeated words.

 TIP: *You can move to the next possible misspellings, even if the misspelled markings are hidden, by pressing* ALT+F7, *pressing* SHIFT+BACKSPACE, *or double-clicking the dictionary at the right end of the status bar. Word moves to the next word that Word believes is misspelled.*

 TIP: *You can tell when a document has no misspellings when Word has been set to automatically mark misspellings. When a document has perfect spelling, the little dictionary icon in the status bar includes a check mark. When it includes an X, the document has a misspelling. When you do not see this dictionary icon, Word is not marking misspelled words.*

Options

When you are checking the spelling of a document using the Spelling dialog box and Word encounters a word that does not appear in its dictionaries, it highlights the word in your document and shows it in the Not in Dictionary text box. Word's suggested spelling appears in the Change To text box, and some alternate spellings appear in the Suggestions list box. You have a number of choices about what to do with the word in question.

CHANGE To insert the correct word in place of the flagged word, make sure that the correctly spelled word appears in the Change To text box. You can select the correct spelling from the Suggestions list box or type it into the Change To text box yourself. Then select the Change button.

When Word flags an improperly capitalized word, selecting Change corrects the capitalization but does not change the spelling.

CHANGE ALL   When you know that a flagged misspelling appears frequently in your document, select Change All instead of Change. Word will correct that word each time it finds it. However, Word does not correct the subsequent instances of the word until it reaches them. If you cancel the Spelling feature before reaching the end of your document, the later appearances of the misspelled word are not changed to the correct spelling.

DELETE   This option is only available when the misspelling that Word located is actually a word repeated, as in "the the." Delete removes the second instance of the two.

IGNORE   When Word flags a word that is spelled correctly, select Ignore and Word skips the word in question. If the word appears again in your document, Word flags it again.

IGNORE ALL   When Word flags a correctly spelled word that reappears in your document, select Ignore All instead of Ignore. Word then ignores every appearance of the word, treating the word as though it occurred in the Word dictionaries. However, in other documents, the word is flagged as usual.

ADD   Select Add to add the flagged word in the Not in Dictionary text box to the custom dictionary, letting you create a personalized dictionary for use in Word. For more information on custom dictionaries, see "Custom Dictionaries" under "Spelling Options."

UNDO LAST   Select Undo Last to undo your last correction. You can select it more than once to remove the effect of more than one selection.

SUGGEST   Select Suggest to have suggestions provided for a word in the Change To text box. You can type the word in the Change To text and request suggestions as well as request suggestions for a flagged word.

ADD WORDS TO   When you select Add, Word adds the word to the custom dictionary you selected in the Add Words To drop-down box. Creating and working with dictionaries are described under "Spelling Options."

OPTIONS   Select Options to open the Options dialog box, in which you can set the defaults that the Spelling feature uses. These options are fully described under "Spelling Options."

AUTOCORRECT   Select AutoCorrect to replace the flagged word with the word appearing in the Change To text box, and to record the correction as an AutoCorrect entry. AutoCorrect can replace the word automatically when you type the word incorrectly. This feature is described under "AutoCorrect."

Hints

Spelling in Word checks your document against dictionary files to find misspelled words. With documents that include such things as invoices and ones containing acronyms (words formed from the initial letters of a name), you can add these words to your dictionaries. You can create your own custom dictionaries as well as use ones from other sources such as dictionaries containing medical or legal terms. Word can suggest words when you use wildcard characters in the Change To text box. If a document contains foreign text, you can mark the language the text uses so Word can switch the language to check the spelling of the text.

How Spell Works

When you use the Spelling feature, Word compares words in your document with the words in its dictionary files. If a word is not found in a dictionary file, Word flags it as potentially incorrect. Word also flags words when the capitalization appears improper or if the same word occurs twice in sequence.

Word makes suggestions for flagged words by searching for words in its dictionaries that are similar in spelling or sound to the flagged word. You can select a suggested word to replace the incorrect one, or type the correct word in the Change To text box.

Invoices and Acronyms

Word normally checks all words in your document that are not entirely composed of numbers. This means that Word checks words with some numbers, such as invoice numbers or IRS tax form titles. Word also flags acronyms, such as NAFTA or CINC-PAC, since they are usually not in the dictionary. You can set Word to ignore words containing numbers or words all in capitals (which includes most acronyms) by changing the Spelling options.

You can add acronyms you use regularly to your custom dictionary. If a word with numbers is one that you have to use frequently, such as an ID number or street address, such as 25th St., add it to the custom dictionary, too.

Using Wildcard Characters

You can use wildcard characters when entering a word in the Change To text box to see Word's suggested spellings. Wildcard characters take the place of letters in the word you type, letting you look for related words. The ? character takes the place of any one letter. The * character takes the place of any number of characters.

For example, if you know the word starts with *pred*, but aren't sure how the rest of the word is written, type **pred*** and select Suggest. Word suggests a series of words starting with *pred*.

Spell Checking Foreign Text

You can use Word's spelling feature for a foreign language, as long as you have the dictionary for the language. First, you need to mark the text as being in a specific language with Tools | Language. When the Spelling feature reaches text marked for another language, Word switches to the dictionary for that language. If you do not have the dictionary for a language, you cannot check the spelling of that language. You can call Microsoft to check on the availability of foreign language dictionaries.

To format a section of text as a different language, select the text first. Then use Tools | Language and select the new language from the Mark Selected Text As list box.

Related Topics

Find and Replace
Foreign Language Support
Grammar Checking

Spelling Options

You can set the Spelling options, the default options which control how Word checks the spelling in your document.

Procedures

1. Select Tools | Options and select the Spelling tab.

2. Make your settings as described under "Options" next.

3. Select OK.

TIP: *Another way to set the Spelling options is to select Options from the Spelling dialog box.*

Options

The following options are available in the Spelling tab in the Options dialog box.

Automatic Spell Checking

Select this check box to have Word place red wavy lines under words that are not in one of the loaded dictionaries. Clear this check box to remove the lines.

Hide Spelling Errors in Current Document

Select this check box to not show the red wavy lines. The misspelled words are still marked so you can move to the next misspelling by double-clicking the dictionary icon at the end of the status bar, pressing ALT+F7 or SHIFT+BACKSPACE.

Always Suggest

Clear the Always Suggest check box to prevent Word from suggesting correct spellings for flagged words. You can still request suggestions by selecting Suggest in the Spelling dialog box.

From Main Dictionary Only

Clear the From Main Dictionary Only check box when you want Word to check your custom dictionaries to see if a word might be correctly spelled.

Words in UPPERCASE

Select the Words in UPPERCASE check box to have Word ignore words all in capitals when checking spelling in your documents.

Words with Numbers

Select the Words with Numbers check box to have Word ignore words with numbers in them while checking spelling in your document.

Reset Ignore All

Select Reset Ignore All and Yes to remove all entries from the Ignore All list that Word creates when you select Ignore All from the Spelling dialog box in response to a flagged word. After you select this, all the words Word had been ignoring in the current session are now flagged again.

Custom Dictionaries

Select this button to work with your custom dictionaries. The dialog box that this button displays includes a list of the custom dictionaries that Word can use. Dictionaries with selected check boxes are opened and used to check spelling.

> *TIP:*   *You can open a custom dictionary by clicking it or by highlighting it and selecting Edit.*

ADD Select Add to add a dictionary to the Custom Dictionaries list box. Next, select the dictionary to add by locating the file the same way you locate a document that you will open from the Open dialog box.

NEW Select New to create a new custom dictionary. You will need to supply a name for this new dictionary and select OK.

REMOVE Select Remove to remove the highlighted custom dictionary from the list. This does not actually remove the document from your disk so it is still available to add later.

EDIT Select Edit to have Word open the highlighted dictionary as a Word document that you can edit. If automatic spell checking is on, you will see a message about disabling the feature. The dictionary is displayed as a single column list of words. When you are finished editing the dictionary, simply select File | Close and then select Yes when asked if you wish to save the changed file. At this point, you can turn the automatic spell checking on as described under "Spelling."

Recheck Document

Select this button to have Word check the document to mark misspelled words and "Reset Ignore All."

Hints

Knowing more about the dictionaries that Word uses will help you create and maintain your own custom ones.

Custom Dictionaries

Word automatically uses the main dictionary when checking your text's spelling. As a default, Word also uses a custom dictionary file called CUSTOM, which is created when you first install Word. The CUSTOM dictionary is initially empty. You will add words to this dictionary when you select the Add button while Add Words To is set to CUSTOM.DIC. You can create or purchase any number of other dictionary files to use as well as the CUSTOM dictionary. You can have only ten custom dictionaries open at one time for checking the text of your document.

Word uses the open custom dictionaries when proofing your document's spelling. All of the dictionaries that Word knows about are listed in the Custom Dictionaries list box in the Custom Dictionaries dialog box. It includes the dictionary files in the default folder and any you have added to the list box. The ones that are open have a check mark. These dictionaries also appear in the Add Words To drop-down list box in the Spelling dialog box.

Creating Custom Dictionaries

You can create custom dictionaries instead of simply using the Spelling dialog box to add words to an existing one. You may want to start out with all the acronyms or specialized terms that you use frequently. To do this, create a file that lists the words you want in your dictionary, with one word on each line and no extra spaces. Save the file with the filename extension .DIC, after selecting Text Only in the Save as Type drop-down list box. Open this file as you would open other custom dictionaries.

When creating a custom dictionary, be aware of capitalization. When your entry is all lowercase, Word will recognize and avoid flagging it regardless of capitalization. If you enter a word in the dictionary with an initial capital, Word recognizes the word only if you enter it in your document with an initial capital or all capitals; the word will be flagged if you enter it all lowercase. If your dictionary entry is all capitals, Word recognizes the word only if it is all capitals. If you make your dictionary entry using an irregular capitalization, such as PostScript, Word recognizes the word only with exactly the same irregular capitalization. See Table 4-19 for examples of these rules.

Exclude Dictionaries

An exclude dictionary is a special custom dictionary that lets you flag words you don't want in your documents. An exclude dictionary works the reverse of a normal dictionary. When Word finds a word in a regular dictionary, the word is not flagged. However, when Word finds a word in an exclude dictionary, Word flags the word.

An exclude dictionary consists of words you don't want in your documents even if they are correctly spelled. For example, Word recognizes and therefore does not flag most normal contractions. To ensure that you don't use those contractions, create an exclude dictionary containing them; the contractions will then be flagged. Another use is flagging mistyped words that are a correct spelling of another word. For example, in a book about databases, *field* is a commonly used word that might be regularly mistyped as *filed*. Add *filed* to an exclude dictionary to have all occurrences flagged so they are checked.

Create an exclude dictionary using the steps given above for creating a custom dictionary. However, save the file with the name MSSP2_EN.EXC and a file type of Text Only. MSSP2_EN is the same name as the main dictionary file (MSSP2_EN.LEX).

Professional or Technical Dictionaries

You may want to purchase professional dictionaries. These dictionaries can be used with Word and contain medical, legal, or other technical terms for a specific field. The

Dictionary	Word Flags	Word Ignores
tree	trEe	tree, Tree, TREE
Spanish	spanish	Spanish, SPANISH
AWOL	awol, Awol	AWOL
d'Arcy	d'arcy, D'Arcy, D'ARCY	d'Arcy

Table 4-19.   *Custom Dictionary Entries Affect Flags*

advantage is that you do not need to add words to a dictionary. These dictionaries have already been double-checked for correctness. Such dictionaries are created by Microsoft as well as by third-party software vendors.

Related Topics

Spelling

Spike

Word's Spike feature is somewhat like the Windows Clipboard, but offers some added advantages. You can cut text from your document and place it on the Spike, then insert it back into the document, just like the Clipboard. However, unlike the Clipboard, you can cut many selections to the Spike, without deleting the Spike's previous contents.

 CAUTION: You cannot copy text to the Spike, only cut it. However, once you cut text to the Spike, you can use Edit | Undo to restore your deleted text.

Procedures

1. Select the text or graphic to be cut.

2. Press CTRL+F3 and Word cuts the selection to the Spike.

3. To paste the Spike's contents into the document and remove them from the Spike, put the insertion point where you want the Spike's contents and press CTRL+SHIFT+F3.

4. To paste the Spike's contents into the document without removing them from the Spike, put the insertion point where you want the contents. Make sure there is a space, tab character, or paragraph mark before the insertion point. Type **spike** and press F3 or ALT+CTRL+V. Of course, you can always add this AutoText entry by selecting Edit | AutoText, selecting Spike in the Name list box, and selecting Insert.

Hints

The Spike is actually a special type of temporary AutoText entry and, like these features, uses the F3 key to carry out its operations. You can also see part or all of the Spike's contents by selecting Edit | AutoText and highlighting Spike in the Name list box. All or some of the contents appear in the Preview box.

When you cut several selections of text to the Spike, the selections are stored in the order you cut them. That is, the first text you cut to the Spike is the first entry within the Spike, and so on, so the last text in the Spike is the last selection of text you cut to the Spike. Each selection of text added to the Spike is separated with a paragraph mark.

Related Topics

AutoText
Clipboard

Split Table

See "Tables."

Splitting a Document Window

See "Viewing Documents."

Spreadsheets

Spreadsheet applications create documents, called worksheets, that are arranged like Word's tables. Worksheets can carry out calculations using cell entries. Word can open Lotus 1-2-3 and Excel worksheet files. You can use fields to create spreadsheet-like tables that perform limited math calculations.

See "Opening Documents" and "Tables" for more information on opening worksheet files and performing math calculations in a table.

Standard Toolbar

The Standard toolbar provides the most popular Word commands available as quickly as a mouse click. You can display this toolbar the same way that you display other toolbars--select View | Toolbars, select the Standard check box, and select OK. Once this toolbar appears, click its buttons to take advantage of its features.

Button	Button Name	Purpose
	New	Opens a new document using the Normal template
	Open	Displays the Open dialog box for opening documents

Button	Button Name	Purpose
	Save	Saves documents or displays the Save As dialog box
	Print	Prints the document with the default settings
	Print Preview	Switches to Print Preview view
	Spelling	Checks the spelling in the document
	Cut	Deletes the selected text after copying it to the Clipboard
	Copy	Copies the selected text to the Clipboard
	Paste	Copies the Clipboard's contents into the document
	Format Painter	Copies the format of the selected text to the next selected text
	Undo	Lets you select the actions to undo
	Redo	Lets you select the actions to redo
	AutoFormat	Automatically formats your document
	Address	Inserts an address from an address book into the document
	Insert Table	Inserts a table with the specified rows and columns
	Insert Microsoft Excel Worksheet	Inserts a worksheet created by Excel as a table
	Columns	Reformats the current section as the specified number of equal-width columns
	Drawing	Displays the Drawing toolbar

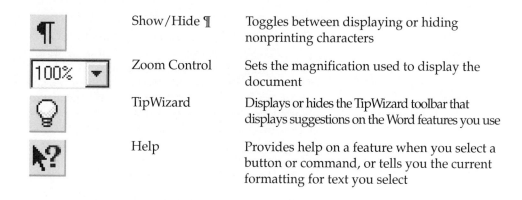

	Show/Hide ¶	Toggles between displaying or hiding nonprinting characters
	Zoom Control	Sets the magnification used to display the document
	TipWizard	Displays or hides the TipWizard toolbar that displays suggestions on the Word features you use
	Help	Provides help on a feature when you select a button or command, or tells you the current formatting for text you select

Standard Word Styles

Word has standard styles that are applied automatically, such as header and footer styles, footnote text and footnote reference styles, and index styles. You can change or remove these styles. See "Styles" for further information on what styles are and how they work.

Start a New Page

See "Hard Page Break" and "Pagination."

Startup Options

Startup options can be included with Word and other applications. Startup options change how Word performs as it is loaded or after it is loaded. You add startup options by changing the icon's properties that start Word.

Procedures

1. Locate the shortcut that you use to start Word. This may be an icon on your desktop or you may need to use the Windows Explorer's application to look at the contents of Windows\Start\Programs.

2. Right-click the Word shortcut and select Properties.

3. Select the Shortcut tab.

4. Move to the end of the Target entry and add, edit, or remove the startup options. Word's startup options are listed in the following table.

Startup Option	Effect
/a	Starts Word without loading any add-ins and global templates, including the Normal template, so you cannot use any predefined settings
/l *addinpath*	Starts Word and then loads the Word add-in you specify
/m	Starts Word without running any AutoExec macro
/m *macroname*	Starts Word and then runs the macro named macroname instead of running any AutoExec macro
/n	Starts Word without providing a new document as a starting point
/t *document*	Starts Word and then opens *document* as a template

5. Select OK to put the Microsoft Word Properties dialog box away.

Statistics

See "Grammar Checking" or "Summary Info."

Strikethrough

Strikethrough is a character format that produces text with a horizontal line through its middle. You may use text with the Strikethrough style to indicate deleted or proposed text.

Procedures

The Strikethrough style can be applied while text is being typed or after it is typed. To apply while typing, add the format, type the text, and then remove the format. To apply to typed text, select the text and then add the format.

1. Select Format | Font or right-click the insertion point's location area and select Font.

2. Select the Strikethrough check box to apply the format or clear it to remove the format.

3. Select OK.

Removing Formatting

Another procedure for removing Strikethrough from text is to select the text and press CTRL+SPACEBAR. This keystroke removes all character formatting from the selected text.

Related Topics

Character Formats
Comparing Versions
Fonts

Style Area

See "Styles."

Style Gallery

See "Styles."

Style Sheets

In Word for DOS all styles available for a document are stored in a separate document called a style sheet. In Word for Windows, styles can be stored in a template or in the document itself. See "Styles."

STYLEREF Field

The STYLEREF field inserts text from the previous paragraph that uses a defined style. See "Fields."

Styles

Styles are sets of formats that you can apply to text. The advantage to using styles instead of applying the formats directly is that you can easily change your entire document's formatting by changing the formatting assigned to a particular style. You can think of styles as the numbers in a paint-by-numbers set, as shown in Figure 4-58. This paint-by-numbers approach can apply to paragraphs (paragraph styles) or characters (character styles). *Paragraph styles* affect all of the text in a paragraph and can apply both paragraph and character formatting. *Character styles* apply only character formatting and can be applied only to the text you select, even if it is just a single word. Use styles any time you want to have a consistent look to text. For example, in a document that uses several long quotations, you would want these quotations to have the same paragraph formatting.

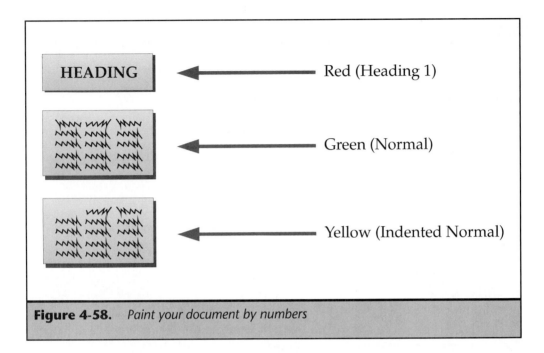

Figure 4-58.   *Paint your document by numbers*

Word's AutoFormat feature can automatically apply styles to your document. You can use this feature as a shortcut for formatting your document. For more details of AutoFormat, see "AutoFormat."

Procedures

To use styles effectively, you need to know how to apply them, how to create them, and how to work with the ones you have.

Applying Styles with the Formatting Toolbar

1. Select the text to apply the style to.
2. Click on the Style drop-down list box on the Formatting toolbar.

TIP: *Press CTRL+SHIFT+S to activate the Style drop-down list box.*

3. Select a style by clicking it or by highlighting it and pressing ENTER.

TIP: *Paragraph style names in the Style list box have a ¶ in front of their names, while character style names have an a.*

Applying Styles with the Menu

1. Select the text you want to format with the style.
2. Select Format | Style.
3. Select a style name from the Styles list box.
4. Select Apply.

Creating Paragraph Styles with the Formatting Toolbar

1. Select text with formatting you want to save as a style.
2. Click on the Style box in the Formatting toolbar.

TIP: *Press CTRL+SHIFT+S to activate the Style list box.*

3. Type a name for the style.
4. Click outside the Style list box, or press ENTER.

Creating Styles with the Menu

1. To create a paragraph style using formatting already applied to a paragraph, select that paragraph. When creating a character style, select that text.
2. Select Format | Style.
3. Select New and then type a name for the new style in the Name text box.
4. Select Character or Paragraph from the Style Type list box to set the type of style.
5. To use another style as the basis for this one, select the base style in the Based On drop-down list box.

   For example, to create a style named "Bibliography" that is the same as the Normal style, except that it has a shadow-box border and uses a larger font size, select Normal in the Based On drop-down list box and change those two formatting settings.

S

6. To apply a different style to paragraphs following paragraphs formatted with the style you are creating, select a style from the Style for Following Paragraph list box.

   For example, if you create a style called "Section Head," you know that the paragraph after each section head is to be formatted with the style First Text. Select First Text in the Style for Following Paragraph list box. When you press ENTER ending a paragraph formatted with Section Head, the new paragraph is automatically formatted with First Text.

7. Select an option from the Format menu to set the formats for the style. You can select Font, Paragraph, Tabs, Border, Language, Frame, and Numbering. Character styles have only Font and Language. The dialog boxes that are opened are the same ones you use when formatting text directly.

8. For styles you use frequently, assign a shortcut key combination you can use to apply that style. To do this, select Shortcut Key. With the insertion point in the Press New Shortcut Key text box, press the keys you want to use to apply the style and select Assign. Select Close to return to the New Style dialog box.

9. Select the Add to Template check box to add the style you are creating to the document's template. Adding the style to the template makes it available to all documents created using that template. Adding a style to the Normal template makes it available to all documents.

10. Select OK to add the style you just created to the document.

11. You can now create more styles by following steps 3 through 10.

12. Select Apply to close the dialog box and apply the highlighted style to the current paragraph. Select Close to close the dialog box and return to the document without applying a style to the text, and without losing the new style.

Editing Styles

1. Select Format | Style.

2. Highlight the style to edit in the Styles list box and select Modify.

3. Change the formatting for the style as if you were creating the style. (The steps for changing formatting assigned to a style were described earlier under "Creating Styles with the Menu.")

4. Select OK.

5. Create or edit additional styles, or select Apply to apply the current style to the selected text, or select Close to simply close the dialog box.

Removing Styles from a Document

1. Select Format | Style.

2. Highlight the style's name in the Styles list box.

3. Select Delete.

4. When Word prompts you asking whether you actually want to delete the style, select Yes. Text assigned to that style is now assigned to the Normal style.

5. Close the dialog box to return to the document, or continue creating or modifying other styles.

Renaming Styles

1. Select Format | Style, opening the Style dialog box.

2. Select the style's name in the Styles list box and select Modify.

3. Type the style's new name in the Name text box.

4. Select OK.

5. Close the Style dialog box to return to the document, or continue creating and modifying other styles.

Copying Styles Between Documents and Templates

To copy styles between documents and templates, use the Organizer feature. You can copy styles between any two documents or templates, regardless of which document is open when you open the Organizer.

1. Select Format | Style.

2. Select Organizer.

3. By default the In and To list boxes show the styles available in the current document and its template.

   When you want to copy styles between some other documents, select the Close File button under that list box, and then select the Open File button and select the file to use.

4. Highlight the styles to copy.

5. Select Copy.

6. Select OK.

TIP: *There are other uses for the Organizer. See "Organizer" for a full explanation of this feature.*

Copying Styles from a Template

The Style Gallery feature lets you preview what your current document would look like with styles from various templates and then copies styles from a specific template into the current document.

1. Format your document with styles. Use the styles included with your template.

2. Select Format | Style Gallery.

3. Highlight a template in the Template list box. The Preview box shows how your document would look, formatted with that template's styles.

   If you want to see an example document or a listing of the styles displaying their format, select Example or Style Samples instead of Document under Preview.

4. Select OK to copy the highlighted template's styles into the current document, or Cancel to close the dialog box without copying the styles.

Hints

To make working with styles easier, you can use style aliases or style families. Word automatically comes with several styles that it applies to certain texts, such as footnotes, for you. You can display the paragraph style names in the margin.

Style Names and Aliases

Style names can be up to 253 characters long, but cannot include a backslash(\), braces([]), or a semicolon(;). Word does not distinguish between uppercase and lowercase letters in style names. You can provide short names, or *aliases*, for styles by typing a comma and the short name following the full name in the Name text box. This short name will appear in the Style list box or in the Style bar at the side of your document. You can then type the alias in the Style drop-down box to invoke that style.

Style Families

You can create families of styles that are based on the same style. Creating families of styles makes it easy to keep your document looking organized.

For example, you could create a style for the body text of your document that uses the font Arial at 10 points. You can then create styles for figure captions, tables, sidebars, headings, the table of contents, and indexes that are based on this body text style. If you change the font of the body text style to Times Roman, then all of these other styles change to Times Roman. Doing this maintains a uniform appearance throughout your document.

Standard Styles

Word has some standard styles that it automatically applies to certain types of text, such as tables of contents and footnotes. When you look at the Style box on the

Formatting toolbar or the Styles list box in the Style dialog box, you do not normally see these styles. However, you can modify these styles just as you can modify styles that you create.

To display these additional styles, press SHIFT before clicking the arrow for the Style button in the Formatting toolbar, or select All Styles in the List drop-down list box in the Style dialog box.

Many of these styles are applied automatically, such as the styles for annotation text, captions, and index entries. Others, such as the Headings styles, you can apply.

Seeing Style Names in Your Document

When you use styles often, you may want an easier way to see which paragraph uses which styles. To do this, display the style names in a *style area* on the left side of your document in Normal view. To do this, select Tools | Options, select the View tab, and enter a measurement in the Style Area Width text box. A style area is shown in Figure 4-59. Reducing the Style Area Width to 0 removes the style names from view.

Switching from One Style to Another

You can change the style assigned to text by using the Edit | Replace command. Select the old style for the Find What text box and the new style for the Replace With text box. You can also assign new styles to text when the text includes distinguishing

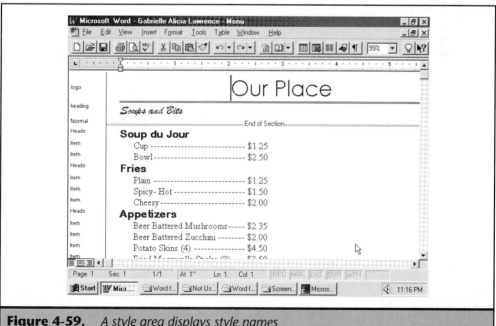

Figure 4-59. *A style area displays style names*

characters. For instance, if you want to assign text that contains *(1)* to Heading 1, enter **(1)** in the Find What text box, and then select Heading 1 for the formatting for the Replace With text box. Word will assign the style to paragraphs containing *(1)* without replacing the *(1)*.

Related Topics

AutoFormat
Organizer
Outlines

Subdocument

See "Master Documents."

SUBJECT Field

The SUBJECT field returns the contents of the Subject document property. See "Document Properties" and "Fields."

Subscript

See "Super/Subscript."

Summary Info

See "Document Properties."

Superscript

See "Super/Subscript."

Super/Subscript

Superscripted text appears above the line of the text and is used for marking footnotes and for exponents and other mathematical symbols. Subscript appears below the line of the text and is used in mathematical and scientific formulas. An example of superscript and subscript is shown here:

$$a^2 \times b^2 = c^2 \quad \text{or} \quad H_2O$$

Procedures

The Superscript or Subscript format can be applied as the text is being typed or after it is typed. To apply these formats while typing, add the format, type the text, then remove the format. To apply it to typed text, select the text and add the format.

Adding and Removing Superscript or Subscript with the Menus

1. Select Format | Font.
2. Select the Superscript or Subscript check box.

   By default, superscript or subscript text moves the baseline of the formatted text up or down 3 points.
3. Select the Character Spacing tab if you want to change how much of the text is superscript or subscript.
4. Select Raised (superscript) or Lowered (subscript) from the Position drop-down list box.

   Select Normal to return to the normal amount of superscripting or subscripting.
5. Enter the measurement in points in the By spin box. This measurement is how far the baseline of the formatted text is raised or lowered from the normal baseline.
6. Select OK.

Adding and Removing with Shortcut Keys

- Press CTRL+SHIFT++ to make text superscript.
- Press CTRL+= to make text subscript.

Related Topics

Equations
Spacing

Switches

See "Fields."

SYMBOL Field

The SYMBOL field inserts a symbol or a string of characters. See "Fields" and "Special Characters."

System Information

System Information is available through the Help | About Microsoft Word command. See "Help" for more information on Word's help as well as system information.

TA Field

See "Tables of Authorities."

Table of Authorities

Table of authorities are used in legal briefs to list all citations of court decisions. The citations are normally sorted by different sources of legal authority, such as the Supreme Court, federal courts, state courts, federal laws and regulations, state laws and regulations, and legal commentary. Each group of citations from the different authorities is a separate table. Figure 4-60 shows an example of a very brief table of authorities. You can easily create tables by marking the citations in the text, assigning them to a particular category, and then telling Word where to create the tables.

Procedures

The following procedures indicate how to create and update tables of authorities in your document. When creating tables of authorities, you must first mark all the citations you want to include in the tables, assigning each citation to the appropriate

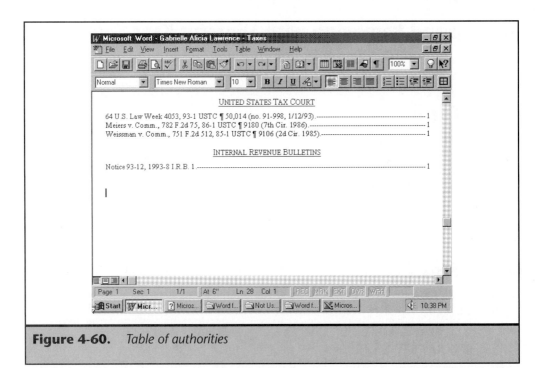

Figure 4-60.   *Table of authorities*

category. Then you insert the tables and update them. You can modify the available categories to customize this feature to your needs.

Marking Citations

1. Select the first citation in the document.

    The first time a particular case or authority is cited in the text of a brief, it should be cited in the long form, which includes all necessary information for a reader to locate the source. When the same case or authority is cited later in your brief, it should be in the short form, such as *Kramer v. Kramer,* which lets the reader know to which previously cited case or authority the reference is being made.

2. Press ALT+SHIFT+I, or select Insert | Index and Tables, the Table of Authorities tab, and Mark Citation. The selected text appears in the Selected Text box and the Short Citation text box.

3. Edit the text in the Selected Text box to match how you want the long citation to appear in your table.

TIP: *You can include formatting features such as bold and underlining by using the shortcut keys.*

4. Select Category and then the category you want to assign this citation to in the Category list box.

5. Edit the text in the Short Citation text box to match the short citations you have entered in the document.

6. Choose what you want Word to do with this citation.

    ■ Select Mark to mark this particular occurrence of the citation.

    ■ Select Mark All to have Word search for all appearances of the text in the Short Citation text box, and mark all of them as citations.

7. Either select Next Citation to have Word scan the document for the next citation, which Word recognizes because it contains "in re" or other terms usually found in citations, or select Close to quit marking citations.

    If you see the TA field, Word is displaying the field codes rather than their results. You can change the codes to show the results by selecting the field and pressing ALT+F9, or by changing the view options to not display field codes.

Modifying Categories

Word lets you use up to 16 categories of citations in a table of authorities. The first seven are already assigned names: Cases, Statutes, Other Authorities, Rules, Treatises, Regulations, and Constitutional Provisions, while the remaining ones are simply assigned numbers. You can change the names of any of the 16 categories to reflect the types of citations you need to include in your table of authorities.

1. In the Mark Citations dialog box, select Category.

2. Highlight the category in the Category list box.

3. Type a new name in the Replace With text box.

4. Select Replace.

5. Continue until you have renamed all of the categories you need to, and then select OK.

Inserting the Table of Authorities

1. Put the insertion point where you want to insert your table of authorities. If you are putting the table of authorities on the first page of a document, you may want a section break after the table of authorities so you can change the beginning number of the subsequent page to 1.

2. Select Insert | Index and Tables.

3. Select the Table of Authorities tab.

4. Select a format in the Formats list box. The effect of this format on a sample table is shown in the Preview box.

5. Clear the Use Passim check box if you do not want Word substituting "passim" for any citations with more than five page references.

6. Clear the Keep Original Formatting check box to allow Word to override the formatting in the citation with the formatting applied with this feature.

7. Select the category to show tables for in the Category drop-down list box. You can insert tables for all categories or for any one category.

8. Select a tab leader from the Tab Leader drop-down list box to set the type of line between the citation and the page references.

9. Select Modify with From Template in the Formats list box to create a new format.

   Word formats your table of authorities by applying one style (TOA Headings) to the headings for each table, and a second style (Table of Authorities) to the citation and page references. After selecting Modify, you can modify these styles just as you would any other style. See "Styles" for instructions on modifying styles.

10. Select OK to insert your tables.

Updating a Table of Authorities

1. Select <u>I</u>nsert | Inde<u>x</u> and Tables.

2. Select the Table of <u>A</u>uthorities tab.

3. Select OK.

4. When Word asks if you really want to replace the current table, select <u>Y</u>es.

TIP: *A shortcut for updating your table is to put your insertion point in the table and press F9.*

Hints

Always mark citations for your tables of authorities after finishing the editing on your document, so that you are sure you've included all citations. Also, this gives you one last check that the first citation is in fact the long citation.

When you mark citations, Word inserts a TA type field. If you delete the citation, make sure that you also delete this field. To change how a citation's long or short form will appear, edit the TA field in the document, as described under "Fields." When you insert a table of authorities in your document, Word inserts a TOA type field. You can edit your table directly, but you will have to reenter all of your corrections after updating the table.

TA Fields

Word marks text for tables of authorities with the {TA [*switches*]} field, which marks the text and sets the form of the table entry.

\B   The \b switch makes the page number in the table entry bold.

\C   The \c switch sets the category the entry belongs to.

\I   The \i switch makes the page number of the table entry italicized.

\L   The \l switch sets the text of the long form of the citation.

\R   The \r switch includes the range of pages marked with the given bookmark in the table entry.

\S   The \s switch sets the short citation form.

TOA Fields

TOA fields, which use the format {TOA [*switches*]}, insert a table of authorities in your document compiled from TA fields in your document. Each table has its own TOA field.

\B   The \b switch compiles the table from the part of the document marked with the given bookmark.

\C   The \c switch sets the categories of entries for which tables are inserted.

\D   The \d switch defines the characters separating a sequence number and a page number and is used with the \s switch.

\E   The \e switch sets the characters that separate a table entry and its page number.

\F   Use the \f switch to remove the formatting applied to table entries in the document, so that table entries use the formatting of the table styles only.

\G   The \g switch sets the characters with separate page numbers in a page range.

\H   Use the \h switch to include the category as a heading for the table.

\L   Use the \l switch to set the characters separating page numbers when the entry has several page references.

\P   The \p switch uses "passim" as the page reference when there are five or more page references for a single entry.

\S   Use the \s switch to include a sequence number with the page number.

Related Topics

Fields
Styles

Table Columns

See "Tables."

Table Commands

The Table commands all relate to working with tables. All of the table commands are described under "Tables," except for the Table | Sort command, which can be used to sort tables or text outside of a table. Table | Sort is described under "Sorting."

Table of Contents with Fields

See "Table of Contents and Figures."

Table of Contents and Figures

You can create tables of contents using text marked with styles or fields. You can create tables of figures or other objects in your document for which you inserted captions.

> **TIP:** *You can double-click a page number in a table of contents to quickly move to that referenced location in the document.*

Procedures

The following procedures explain how to create a table of contents, or how to create a table of figures using text marked with styles. The final procedure also explains how you can mark table of contents or table of figures entries with fields.

Creating a Table of Contents

1. Put your insertion point where you want the table of contents.

2. Select Insert | Index and Tables, and select the Table of Contents tab.

3. Select the options that determine how the table looks:

   ■ Select a format for the table of contents from the Formats list box. A sample table of contents using these styles appears in the Preview box. If you highlight From Template in this list box, you can select Modify and adjust the style formatting for each level in the table of contents.

   ■ Clear the Show Page Numbers check box if you don't want to include page numbers in your table of contents.

   ■ Clear the Right Align Page Numbers check box to have page numbers appear after the heading separated by a space.

   ■ Select the number of levels to appear in the table of contents in the Show Levels text box.

   ■ Choose a tab leader from the Tab Leader drop-down list box to stretch from the entry to the page number.

4. Select the source of the table of contents entries. To use text marked with TC type fields as entries in your table of contents, select Options and Table Entry

Fields. To use paragraphs formatted with specific styles as entries in your table of contents, select Options and Styles. You can use both.

Select a style to include by entering the level it uses in the table of contents in the TOC Level box after the style's name. All heading styles and all styles used in the document appear in this list.

5. Select OK twice.

Creating a Table of Figures

1. Put your insertion point where you want the table.

2. Select Insert | Index and Tables, and select the Tables of Figures tab.

3. Select the caption label you are creating a table for from the Caption Label list box.

4. Select the options that determine how the table looks:

   ■ Select a set of styles to use from the Formats list box. A sample table shows the effect of these styles in the Preview box. Highlight From Template and select Modify to change the style used by the text in the table of figures.

   ■ Clear the Show Page Numbers check box if you don't want to include page numbers in your table.

   ■ Clear the Right Align Page Numbers check box to have page numbers appear after the entry separated by a space.

   ■ Clear the Include Label and Number check box to keep Word from including the caption label and number in the table entry.

   ■ Choose a tab leader from the Tab Leader drop-down list box to stretch from the entry to the page number.

5. Select Options to set which entries the table is compiled from.

   ■ Select Style and then choose a style from the list box. The table is compiled using text marked with this style.

   ■ Select Table Entry Fields to compile the table from TC fields that use a specific identifier after the \f switch. Select a code that identifies the fields you want to use in this table from the Table Identifier list box. For example, if you leave the default of F, Word compiles the table of figures using TC fields that have the switch of \f F.

6. Select OK twice.

Adding Table of Contents Entries Using Fields

1. Select the text you want for the table of contents entry.
2. Press ALT+SHIFT+O. The dialog box shows the selected text as the table of contents entry.
3. Change the text to match the table of contents entry if you want something different than the current contents of the Entry text box.
4. Set the table identifier by selecting a letter from the Table Identifier drop-down list box. You can use different table identifiers to create separate tables of contents for different identifiers.
5. Set the table of contents level for the entry you are creating by selecting a number in the Level text box.
6. Select Mark to create the table of contents entry and Close to put the dialog box away.

Hints

You can mark text with a TC field to include it in a table of contents, or create your table of contents with certain text styles. The table of contents is created with the TOC field. For a table of figures, you add references to the table when you insert a caption which inserts a SEQ field.

TC

The TC field marks text for compiling into a table of contents or figures. It uses the format {TC "*text*" [*switches*]}. *Text* is the text to appear in the table. Nest an REF field in place of *Text* to actually include document text as it is modified.

\F   The \f switch marks the entry with a table identifier, which can be used to include the entry in only one table.

\L   The \l switch assigns a level to the table entry.

\N   The \n switch prevents the page number for this entry from appearing.

TOC

The TOC field type collects TC entries or text marked with a particular style for a table of contents or other list. The field uses the format {TOC "*switches*"}.

TIP: *Before updating a TOC field, hide your field codes so that the pagination is correct.*

\A   The \a switch compiles the table without using caption labels or numbers that are automatically included with the inserted caption.

\B   The \b switch compiles a table from entries in the part of your document marked with the bookmark.

\C   The \c switch compiles the table using SEQ fields with a specific table identifier. SEQ fields are inserted when you create a caption.

\D   The \d switch sets the characters used to separate sequence numbers and page numbers. Sequence numbers are added with the \s switch.

\F   The \f switch compiles a table using only TC entries with the given table identifier.

\L   The \l switch compiles a table using only TC entries with the levels given.

\O   The \o switch compiles a table using text formatted with the built-in heading styles given.

\P   The \p switch sets the character separating a table entry and its page number.

\S   The \s switch compiles a table using the sequence given, or a table that includes the sequence number.

\T   The \t switch creates a table using the styles given.

Related Topics

Fields
Outlines
Tables of Authorities

Table of Contents with Headings
See "Table of Contents and Figures."

Table of Figures
See "Table of Contents and Figures."

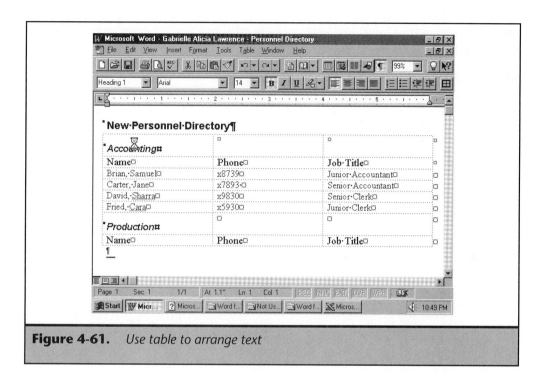

Figure 4-61. *Use table to arrange text*

Tables

Tables are ways to arrange text. They consist of cells arranged in rows and columns, as can be seen in Figure 4-61. Text, numbers, or graphics can be entered into the cells. You can carry out mathematical calculations with numbers entered into cells, very much as you do with spreadsheet programs. The Table AutoFormat feature can quickly format your tables.

In Figure 4-61 you can see how a table can arrange text in a readable fashion. You can also use tables when creating online or printed forms.

There is a long list of procedures for operations you can do with tables. The length of the list does not mean that tables are difficult to understand or use, just that there is a great deal of flexibility in how you use tables.

Procedures

The following procedures will explain how to work with a table. They include steps for inserting tables and converting between text and a table, as well as steps for moving and selecting in a table. There are also procedures for inserting formulas for doing math in a table. Steps for adding or removing cells from a table are explained, along with how to split and merge cells and tables. You will learn how to format the rows and columns of a table, to display or hide gridlines, and to apply a set table format.

Inserting a Table with the Menu

1. Put the insertion point where you want a table.

2. Select Table | Insert Table.

   You can skip the following steps by selecting Wizard and letting the Table Wizard help you create a formatted table by prompting you for information about how you want the table laid out. You can select Back or Next to move between the dialog boxes in the Wizard, and select Finish when you want it to insert the table.

3. Enter the number of columns you want for the table in the Number of Columns text box.

4. Enter the number of rows you want for the table in the Number of Rows text box. The default is 2. You can easily add more rows, so this number does not need to be final.

5. Enter the columns' width in the Column Width text box. With Auto, the default, Word spaces the columns across the page.

6. Select AutoFormat if you want the table formatted now. This feature is discussed later under "Using Table AutoFormat."

7. Select OK.

Inserting a Table with the Toolbar

1. Put the insertion point where you want a table.

2. Click the Insert Table button on the Standard toolbar, and Word displays a grid pattern, as shown here:

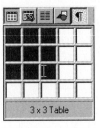

3. Drag across the grid so that the number of rows and columns you want in your table is highlighted, and then release the mouse button.

Press	To Move To
TAB	The next cell
SHIFT+TAB	The previous cell
ALT+HOME	The first cell of the current row
ALT+END	The last cell of the current row
UP ARROW	The previous row
DOWN ARROW	The following row
ALT+PAGE UP	The first cell in the current column
ALT+PAGE DOWN	The last cell in the current column

Table 4-20. *Keystrokes for Moving in a Table*

T

Moving in a Table

Moving in a table is a little different from moving in normal text. You can move through a table quickly by using the keypresses shown in Table 4-20, or by clicking in the cell you want to move to with the mouse.

Converting Text to a Table

1. Select the text to convert into a table, making sure there are no hard page breaks selected, as well as having tabs or commas separating the data you want in separate columns.

2. Select Table | Convert Text to Table, or click the Insert Table button in the Standard toolbar.

3. Tell Word how the text breaks into separate cells. Select Paragraphs, Tabs, or Commas to indicate where you want the information divided. You can also select Other and provide a character used to divide the text, such as a slash or quotes.

   You can set the total number of columns in your table and the column width as well as use the AutoFormat feature to format the table, as described later under "Using Table AutoFormat."

4. Select OK. The entry in each cell in the new table ends at the character selected in the dialog box.

Converting a Table to Text

1. Select the rows of the table you want to make into text. The Table | Select Table command, described later, quickly selects all of the table.

2. Select Table | Convert Table to Text.

3. Tell Word how you want to divide the separate cells. Select Paragraphs, Tabs, or Commas to divide cells with paragraph breaks, tabs, or commas. You can also select Other and provide a character used to divide the text, such as a slash or quotes.

4. Select OK. The entry in each cell now is separated by the character you selected in step 3.

Selecting in a Table

When you select a cell, row, column, or table, the entire table element is highlighted, not just the text or graphics within the cell.

SELECTING A CELL

■ Drag across the entire cell, including the end-of-cell character.

■ Click in the cell's selection bar at the left edge of the cell.

■ Move to the cell by pressing TAB, selecting all the text in the cell. Press SHIFT+RIGHT ARROW to include the end-of-cell character. When you display nonprinting characters, at the end of every cell is an end-of-cell character.

SELECTING A ROW

■ Click in the selection bar to the left of the row.

■ Double-click the selection bar of a cell in the row.

■ Select Table | Select Row with the insertion point in a cell of the row to select.

■ Drag the mouse across the entire row to include the end-of-row character to the right of the table's edge. When you display nonprinting characters, each cell has an end-of-cell character, and the same character appears at the end of the row as an end-of-row character.

SELECTING A COLUMN

■ Put the mouse above the column and click when the mouse pointer looks like a down-pointing arrow.

■ Drag the mouse across the entire column.

■ Select Table | Select Column with the insertion point in a cell in the column to select.

SELECTING A TABLE

- Drag across all the columns or rows in the table, including the end-of-row characters.

- Select Table | Select Table with the insertion point in the table.

- Press ALT+5 (on the numeric keypad with Num Lock off) with the insertion point inside the table you want to select.

Inserting Formulas in a Table

1. Move to the cell you want the formula in.

2. Select Table | Formula. Word analyzes your table and may present a formula. If not, the Formula text box displays only an equal sign (=). The = is for the = (Equation) field that you can use to create evaluated expressions (described under "Fields").

TIP: *Word automatically provides a SUM formula if Word decides you are in a cell which, given the table layout, would logically sum values above or on the side. This SUM formula is sometimes called AutoSum, since it automatically appears.*

3. Enter a formula using the four standard operators or by selecting a function in the Paste Function drop-down list box and inserting that function in the Formula text box. (The *standard operators* are + for addition, – for subtraction, * for multiplication, and / for division.) Functions added with the Paste Function drop-down list box are added to the Formula text box rather than replacing any existing function or operator. Cells can be referenced by cell names or bookmarks.

   Cell names are a combination of the number and letter assigned to each cell. Columns are labeled left to right starting with the letter *A*. Rows are numbered from the top starting with 1. For example, in a table with five rows and three columns, the bottom right cell has the cell name C5. When you have multiple cells that you want in a formula, separate the cell names with commas, as in B2,B3. When you want a range or block of cells in the table in a formula, enter the cell name of the cell in the first row and column, then a colon, and then the cell name of the cell in the last row and column. For example B3:D4 includes cells B3, C3, D3, B4, C4, and D4.

4. Select a format for the formula result in the Number Format drop-down list box.

5. Select OK to insert the formula. Unless you have Word set to display field codes, the result of your formula will appear in the cell.

Adding Cells to a Table

1. Mark where and how many cells you want to insert. Select a row or column below or to the right of where you want to insert another row or column. If you select multiple rows or columns, that is the number that will be inserted. To insert cells, select the number of cells to insert.

   TIP: *If you select nothing, you will insert rows.*

2. Select Table | Insert Cells/Rows/Columns, or click the Table button in the Standard toolbar.

   If you selected rows or columns, they are simply inserted. If you selected a cell or cells, you must now select how those cells are inserted.

3. Select Insert Entire Row or Insert Entire Column to insert complete rows or columns. Select Shift Cells Right to insert the cells to the left of the selected cells while leaving the cells in the other rows in place. Select Shift Cells Down to insert the cells above the selected cells while leaving the other cells in the other columns in place. You will insert as many rows or columns as you selected cells in.

4. Select OK.

   TIP: *Press TAB in the last cell of a table to add a new last row.*

Deleting Cells from a Table

1. Select the cell, row, or column you want to delete. To delete the entire table, select the entire table.

2. Select Delete Cells/Rows/Columns.

   If you selected rows, columns, or the entire table, they are now deleted. If you selected one or more cells, you must now tell Word how to delete them.

3. Select Shift Cells Left to delete only the selected cells and move those to the right into their place. Select Shift Cells Up to delete the selected cells, and move the ones below up into their place. Select Delete Entire Row or Delete Entire Column to delete complete rows or columns. You will delete as many rows or columns as you selected cells in.

4. Select OK.

Setting Row Options

1. Select the row or rows to format.

2. Select Table | Cell Height and Width, and select the Row tab if necessary.

3. Select an option in the Height drop-down list box to set how the row height is determined.

   With Auto, the default, Word varies the row height to match the row's contents. Select At Least to enter a minimum height for the cell in the At text box. Select Exactly to enter the exact row height in the At text box. If the contents cannot fit in this height cell, you will not see the part that doesn't fit.

4. Enter how far the row should be indented from the left margin in the Indent From Left text box. This sets the *cell's* position rather than the indentation of the text within the cell.

5. Select an alignment—Left, Center, or Right—to align the row with the page's margins.

6. To change settings for other rows, select Previous Row or Next Row. Select OK when you are finished changing settings.

Setting Column Width Options

1. Select the column or columns whose width you want to set.

2. Select Table | Cell Height and Width, and select the Column tab if necessary.

3. Enter the column's width in the Width for Column # text box. Select AutoFit to let Word select the column width based on the column's contents.

4. Enter a measurement in the Space Between Columns text box for how much space separates the column's entries.

5. Select Previous Column or Next Column to change these settings for other columns, or select OK when you are finished.

Setting Column Width with the Mouse

You can change the width of table columns using the mouse and the gridlines or the ruler.

- Drag the column gridline using the mouse.
- Drag the column marker on the ruler to a new location.
- Select just the cells in the column that you want to resize, and drag the column gridline with the mouse, or drag the column marker on the ruler to a new location.

Merging Cells

1. Select two or more cells on the same row to merge together.

2. Select Table | Merge Cells. Word merges the cells, as shown next. If the cells have contents, each cell's contents are separated with a paragraph mark. The merged cell is considered part of the column that the first selected cell is in.

Sam·Catering¶			
216/762-4039¶			
¤			
Name:¤		Phone:¤	¤
Address:¤			¤
¤			¤
Item¤	Quantity¤	Price¤	¤
¤	¤	¤	¤

Splitting Cells

1. Select the cells you want to split.

2. Select Table | Split Cell.

3. Enter how many columns you want the cell broken into and select OK.

Word breaks the text between the new cells at the paragraph mark. If there is only one paragraph in the cell, all the text appears in the first cell.

Merging Tables

Merge two tables by deleting any text or paragraph marks between the two tables.

Splitting a Table

1. Put the insertion point in the first cell of the planned second table.

2. Select Table | Split Table or press CTRL+SHIFT+ENTER. Word inserts a paragraph mark between the two tables.

Using Table AutoFormat

1. Select Table | Table AutoFormat with the insertion point within the table you want to format, or select Table AutoFormat from the shortcut menu.

   You can also start the Table AutoFormat feature by selecting AutoFormat in the Insert Table dialog box while inserting the table.

2. Select a set of formats from the Formats list box. These formats will be displayed in the Preview box with sample data.

3. Select the formatting features you want to use under Formats to Apply.

You can choose to remove the Border, Shading, Font, Color, or AutoFit format. For example, if you clear Font, your table is not specially formatted with the font saved with that format. AutoFit sizes the columns to match the widest text they contain.

4. Select where you want special formatting applied under Apply Special Formats To.

   Special formats are applied to Heading Rows, the First Column, the Last Row, or the Last Column. When you clear one of these check boxes, that row or column uses the same formatting as the other rows or columns in the table.

5. Select OK.

Displaying Gridlines

Select Table | Gridlines to display nonprinting gridlines around the table that indicate the current column width and row height settings. Select this command again to make the gridlines disappear. If you want the table's grid printed, add borders.

Hints

The following hints can help you work with tables effectively. They give you further guidance on how to format tables, how tables are constructed in Word, and how to make multipage tables easier to read.

Formatting Table Contents

The table contents can be formatted using the same Word features you use for formatting other types of text. This includes using the Format | Font and the Format | Paragraph commands to change features such as character appearance and alignment. The box "Aligning Entries in Tables" describes several of the alignment conventions you will use on your tables.

Aligning Entries in Tables

Table entries are difficult to read if they are not properly aligned. The following are some general conventions for aligning different types of entries:

Text	Left
Number without decimals	Right
Number with decimals	Decimal
Time with minutes	Colon
Beginning and ending time	Left
Percentages with decimals	Decimal
Percentages without decimals	Right
Money	Decimal
Text and numbers	Left

End-of-Cell or -Row Marks

End-of-cell or -row marks indicate where the cell or row ends. You can choose to display or not display these marks. They are important because features may work differently depending on whether these marks are selected.

- Select the Show/Hide ¶ button in the Standard toolbar to toggle between showing and hiding these marks.

- If you choose to show paragraph marks by selecting Tools | Options and the View tab, and then selecting Paragraph Marks, the end-of-cell and end-of-row marks will also be displayed.

Sorting in Tables

You can sort tables just as you can sort text. When you sort tables, each row is a record, and each column is usually considered a field. You can sort a single column, without affecting other text, by selecting only that column and selecting the Sort Column Only check box. See "Sorting" for a complete explanation of the Sorting feature.

Numbering Cells in Tables

You can number the cells in your table using the numbered or bulleted list feature. To do this, select the cells you plan to number, and click the Numbering button in the Formatting toolbar. In the Table Numbering dialog box, select whether you want to Number Across Rows or Number Down Columns.

If there are multiple paragraphs of text in a cell, Word will, by default, number each paragraph. If you want only one number in each cell, select the Number Each Cell Only Once check box. Select OK to number your table.

You can also include bullets or numbering in a table using AutoFormat features. You will need to press ENTER after starting a line with a number or a bullet character (*, o, >, or –) to automatically make this change. Then subsequent cells in the same column will already have this format.

Applying Borders and Shading

You can apply borders and shading to cells, rows, columns, or tables separately from the borders and shading you apply to the contents of those cells. See "Borders and Shading" for instructions on how to apply borders and shading. You can also use the Table AutoFormat feature to automatically apply many different formats to your table, including borders and shading.

Repeating Headings on Each Page

You can designate some rows, including the first row of the table, as *heading rows*. When a table breaks across pages, any heading rows are repeated at the top of each page. The advantage of using heading rows instead of copying that information over again is that when you change formatting features, such as margins, row height, or font sizes, you may change which row appears at the top of the next page. Using heading rows, you can be sure that the identifying information appears at the top of each page for ease of reading. Also, when you sort the table, Word automatically knows that the first row contains a header row with entries to use as field names.

To designate rows as heading rows, select the rows, which must include the first row of the table, and then select Table | Headings. If you ever want to remove this designation, select this command again. This feature does not work when you force a hard page break, such as by pressing CTRL+ENTER.

Entering Text and Formatting Inside Cells

You enter text and graphics inside cells normally. You can use any normal formatting features within a cell, such as paragraph and character formatting. For example, indentations in a cell measure distance from the edge of the cell.

TIP: *You cannot press TAB to enter a tab character in a cell. To enter a tab character, press CTRL+TAB.*

Controlling Page Breaks

You can set how page breaks are placed in tables. To prevent a row's contents from splitting between two pages, move to the table and select Table | Cell Height and Width, clear the Allow Row to Break Across Pages check box, and then select OK. You can also keep a row with the next one in the table. Select the row or rows involved, and then select Format | Paragraph. Select the Text Flow tab and the Keep With Next check box. This feature is useful when a table starts at the bottom of the page and you want to keep the first few lines of the table together.

Cell References

Before entering formulas, you need to know how to reference other cells. When you use numbers in other cells, you must refer to those cells according to their names. Since all cells are intersections of a column and row, cell names consist of the letter of the column and the number of the row. For example, a cell in the third row of the fourth column is called "D3."

When you want to reference a range, or set, of cells, you have two choices. You can assign a bookmark to that range of cells and insert the bookmark in the formula.. Alternatively, you can reference the range of cells by the name of the first and last cells in the range.

There are two ways to reference a range of cells using cell names, depending on whether you want the formula to take into account added columns or rows. The easiest way is to reference the first and last cell in the range that you want to refer to, separating the cell names with a colon, as in A1:B3. Alternatively, you can repeat the row number or column letter, separated by a colon, indicating you want to select the entire row or column. For example, use 1:1,2:2,3:3 instead of A1:B3 when you want to make sure that all of the cells in rows 1, 2, and 3 are included, rather than just A1 through B3.

Using a Table as a Database

Tables can also be operated on as if they were a database. This means that you can use the Database toolbar to work with the data in a table. From the Database toolbar, you can use buttons to see table information in a data form, sort the table, find records in the table, add rows to the table, remove rows from the table, and reorganize the columns in the table. Using the Database toolbar for these functions is described under "Database Toolbar" and "Data Form."

Related Topics

Borders and Shading
Columns
Data Form
Database Toolbar
Fields
View Options

Tabs

New documents in Word open with default tab stops. You can change the default tab stop interval, or create new tab stops in your document, by using one of four alignments.

Procedures

Set tabs using the Tabs dialog box or the ruler. Tabs are a paragraph format, so position the insertion point in the paragraph you want to format, or select text in all paragraphs you want to format. When you create a new paragraph by pressing ENTER, the new paragraph uses the same tab stops as the original.

Changing the Default Tab Interval

1. Select Format | Tabs. You can also double-click a tab marker in the ruler.

2. Set the interval between default tab stops in the Default Tab Stops text box. This number is between 0 and 22.

3. Select OK.

Settings Tabs with the Ruler

1. Select the alignment for the tab. The tab alignment options are left, centered, right, and decimal. Click the Tab Alignment button until it displays the alignment you want to use.

2. Click the tab stop's position on the ruler, and a tab indicator of the chosen alignment appears at that position.

TIP: You can also move a tab stop by dragging the tab stop symbol on the ruler to a new location. You can also delete a tab stop by dragging the tab stop off the ruler.

Setting Tabs with the Dialog Box

T

1. Select Format | Tabs. You can also double-click a tab marker in the ruler.

2. Enter the tab stop's distance from the left margin in the Tab Stop Position text box.

3. Select the Left, Right, Center, Decimal, or Bar option button. The effect of these tab alignments is explained in Table 4-21.

   When you enter more text than can fit to the right of the right and center tabs, the remaining text uses the paragraph alignment.

4. Select the type of line from the Leader area to appear between the tab and the character that precedes it.

5. Select Set to add the tab stop to the Tab Stop Position list box.

6. Remove a tab stop by highlighting it in the Tab Stop Position list box and selecting Clear. Remove all tab stops by selecting Clear All.

   The tab stops that you clear appear in the Tab Stops to be Cleared area. When you select OK to exit the dialog box, the tab stops are cleared.

7. Select OK.

Hints

All paragraphs are initially formatted with the default tab stops, all of which are left-aligned. When you create a tab stop, all default tabs between the left margin and that tab stop are cleared, so that the tab stop you create is the first one. To continue using the default tab stops between the left margin and the new tab stop, you need to set them yourself.

Tabs can also set paragraph formatting. When you press TAB at the beginning of an existing paragraph, Word sets the first line indent to the first tab stop. You can also

Alignment	Effect
Left	Left edge of text after tab aligned with tab stop.
Right	Right edge of text after tab aligned with tab stop.
Center	Center of text after tab aligned with tab stop.
Decimal	Decimal point with adjacent numbers aligned with tab stop. Other text is right-aligned.
Bar	Inserts a vertical bar at the tab stop.

Table 4-21.   *Effect of Tab Alignments*

press TAB at any line other than the first to shift the paragraph's left indent to the next tab stop.

Related Topics

Indents
Ruler

TC Fields

See "Table of Contents and Figures."

TEMPLATE Field

This field inserts the name of the template used as the basis for the current document. This field can include the /p field when you want the results to include the full system path to the template's document name. See "Fields" for how you can add this and other fields.

Templates

Templates are files that store text and graphics, AutoText entries, macros, styles, toolbars, keyboard assignments, menus, and page layout settings. These settings or features are the defaults for all documents created using that template. Templates are models for documents, as shown in Figure 4-62.

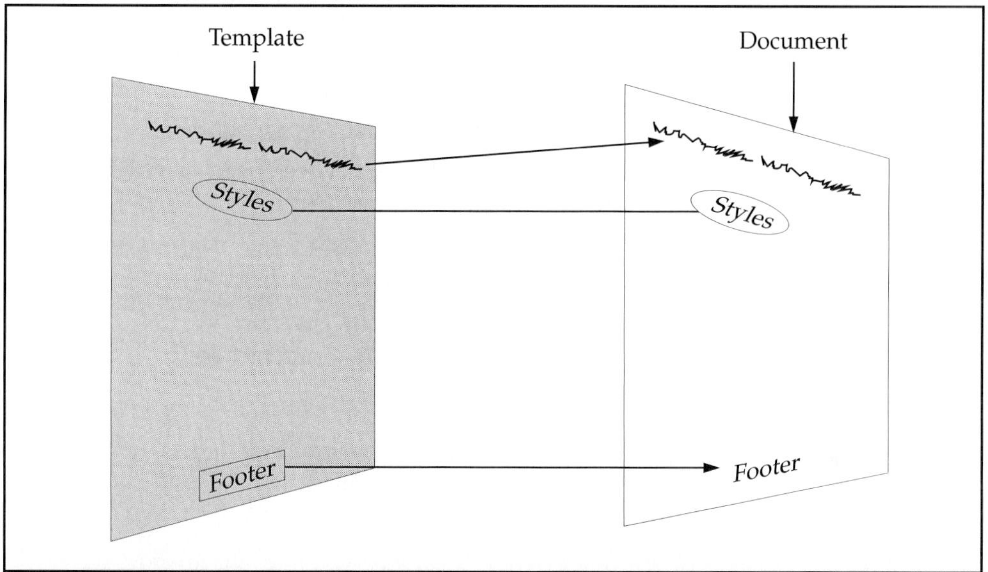

Figure 4-62.   *Templates are document models*

Procedures

The following procedures explain how to create a template, and how to attach a new template to a document.

Creating a Template

1. Select File | New to open a new document.
2. In the New dialog box, select the Template option button and select OK.
3. Add text or graphics or settings that every document created with this template is to use. This includes all of the document settings, such as styles that you want every document created with this template to use.
4. Select File | Save. Enter the template name in the File Name text box, and select Save to save the template. Word automatically saves the document as a Document Template type.

Attaching a New Template

You can switch the document template of the current document and add more than one global template. Then you can share template features such as styles and macros between documents.

1. Select File | Templates. The document's current template appears in the Document Template text box, and all open global templates appear in the Global Templates and Add-Ins list box.

2. Select Attach to select a new template. Select a template and OK.

3. Select the Automatically Update Document Styles check box to have the new template's styles override those currently applied to the document.

4. Select the check boxes of any templates in the Global Templates and Add-Ins list box that you want available. Clear the check boxes of those you do not want available.

   ■ Select Add to select any other templates to add to the list box.

   ■ Select Remove to remove the highlighted template from the list box.

5. Select Organizer, discussed under "Organizer," to copy or remove styles, toolbars, AutoText entries, or macros from the template.

6. Select OK.

TIP: You can also set a template for a document when you create it. When you select File | New, you can choose the template that is the basis for the document. The templates are organized into tabs to organize the templates according to function.

Hints

The following hints explain how to use templates, where they are stored, how conflicts involving multiple templates for a single document are resolved, and how you modify a template from one of the documents created using it.

Using Templates

You can create macros that, once saved with a template, will start as soon as you open a new document using that template. Any macro named AutoOpen automatically executes when you open the document. AutoNew automatically executes when you create a document using a template that contains a macro with this name.

Templates can help you create documents faster because in the template, you have all of the correct formatting and any text or graphics that always appear in these documents.

Another advantage of using templates is that you can ensure that your documents will have a standard appearance. By using the same template for all reports, for example, you can make sure that all of your reports have similar information arranged in a similar fashion, with little effort.

Conflicts

When you have multiple templates available, you may have conflicting settings such as multiple AutoText entries with the same name. The document templates settings override those of any global template, while the Normal template, which is always available but does not appear in the Global Templates and Add-Ins list box, overrides any other global templates. These other global templates override each other in alphabetical order, so that "ANNSTEMP" overrides settings in "YANSTEMP."

Template Locations

Word assumes that your templates are stored in one of the folders in the Templates folder of the folder that contains Word for Windows. The folder determines which tab that template appears on when you select a template for a new document. If you use a different location, change the File Locations options with the Tools | Options command. Select the new folder after selecting User Templates or Workgroup Templates from the File Types list box.

Modifying Templates from Documents

You can modify certain template items from documents. When you change font formatting, margins, page orientation or size, or languages, select Default to save those settings to the document's template. When you create toolbars, keyboard assignments, or menus, select which template they should be saved to. When you create styles, select Add to Template to include the style in the template that the current document is based on.

Special Features for Creating Templates

If you use the Style Gallery to select which template a document uses, you will want to create two AutoText entries in your templates. The first, named Gallery Example, contains what you want to see when you display a sample document for the selected template. The second is named Gallery Style Samples. This AutoText entry is what you see when you display style samples for the selected template. You do not want the sample document and sample styles left in the main document. The only entries you want in the main document are what you want every document created with that template to start off with.

As an example, suppose you are creating a template for the promotional flyers that you distribute for your home business. You can create an AutoText entry named Gallery Example that contains a sample flyer. You can create an AutoText entry named Gallery Style Samples that lists the styles in the document and the effect each has on your text. The body of the document is empty except for any initial text and graphics that you want each flyer to contain.

Another special feature that you will see in Word's templates that you may want to include in your own are the prompts that tell you where to click and the entry to make. If you open the document templates that Word supplies, you will notice that many of them have entries that tell you where to click and make entries. When you click there, the prompt is replaced by what you type. The template creates this effect using the MACROBUTTON field. This field would perform a macro when double-clicked, except that these fields are set to perform the contents of an empty macro. By using a MACROBUTTON field, the entire prompt is highlighted when you click it, and the entire field is replaced by what you type.

Related Topics

AutoText
Document Location Options
Macros
Margins
Organizer
Page Size and Orientation
Paper Source
Sections
Styles

Text Color

You can assign a color to text that will appear on color monitors and documents printed on color printers. Changing the text color changes the color of the letters, while changing the highlight changes the color of the area behind the text.

Procedures

Text color is a character format and is applied as the text is being typed or after it is typed. To apply while typing, add the format, type the text, and remove the format. To apply to typed text, select the text and add the format.

1. Select Format | Font, or right-click the text and select Font.

2. Select a color from the Color drop-down list box.

3. Select OK.

Hints

Remember that the text appears in color only if you use a color monitor or printer. If the printer is black-and-white, all colors except white print as black.

Related Topics

Character Formats
Highlighting
Printing

Text Files

A *text file* is a file that contains no formatting codes. Almost all programs can accept a text file. A text file is also known as an *ANSI* or *ASCII file,* since it contains only characters that represent ANSI or ASCII codes. For a full explanation of saving files as text files and opening text files, see "Opening Documents" and "Saving Documents."

Thesaurus

The Thesaurus shows you words with meanings similar or opposite to those of words in your document (synonyms/antonyms). You can use the Thesaurus to add variety to the vocabulary in your documents. If this feature is not available, use Word's setup program to install it.

T

Procedures

1. Put the insertion point in or beside the word to look up. To look up a phrase, select the phrase.

2. Select Tools | Thesaurus or press SHIFT+F7. The word or phrase you are looking up appears in the Looked Up text box. If the word does not appear in the Thesaurus dictionary, it appears in a Not Found text box.

3. Select the meaning for the word in the Meanings list box.

   Most words have more than one possible meaning. The meaning you select controls which synonyms appear. Select Related Words to see words that are related in meaning but not synonymous to your word, or select Antonyms to see words that are opposite in meaning. If the word being looked up does not appear in the dictionary, a list box called Alphabetical List displays words spelled like the looked up word.

4. Select an appropriate synonym in the Replace With Synonym list box.

   You can select a word in this list box, or type it in the Replace with Synonym text box and select Look Up to look up the word. If you look up multiple words in a single Thesaurus session, the Looked Up text box displays all the words looked up.

5. When the correct word appears in the Replace with Synonym text box, select Replace. This word replaces the selected word in the text.

Hints

If you are uncertain, check the spelling of a word before you look it up in the Thesaurus to prevent mistakes in meaning. Some of the more commonly misused verbs are described in the box "Problem Verbs." You can use the Thesaurus to find words close in meaning to these verbs and use the Grammar feature to find some of the misused verbs.

Foreign Languages

You can use a foreign language thesaurus to look up synonyms and antonyms of a word in a foreign language. Contact Microsoft at the number included in your Word for Windows documentation to ask about foreign language thesauruses.

Problem Verbs

Some verbs cause repeated problems as they are commonly substituted incorrectly for other verbs, or their irregular tenses are improperly formed. The following list shows some verbs that frequently cause problems, a definition of each verb, and the present, past, and past participle form of the verb.

Lay—To Place
lay   lay   laid

Lie—To Rest
lie   lay   lain

Raise—To Lift
raise   raised   raised

Rise—To Move up on Its Own
rise   rose   risen

Set—To Place an Object in a Location
set   set   set

Sit—To Rest on a Chair or Other Surface
sit   sat   sat

See—To Observe
see   saw   seen

Do—To Take an Action
do   did   done

Leave—To Depart
leave   left   left

> **Let—To Allow**
> let   let   let
>
> **Learn—To Absorb Knowledge**
> learn   learned   learned
>
> **Teach—To Share Knowledge with Others**
> teach   taught   taught

Related Topics

Grammar Checking
Spelling

Time

See "Date and Time."

TIME Field

See "Fields."

TipWizard

The TipWizard displays suggestions and alternative methods for how to perform the Word features that you use. The TipWizard appears as a separate toolbar that displays when you click the TipWizard button on the Standard toolbar.

Procedures

The TipWizard can display as a toolbar that you can use to look at other Word features.

Displaying the TipWizard

■ Click on the TipWizard button on the Standard toolbar. This button is the one that looks like a light bulb. Clicking on this button a second time removes the TipWizard toolbar.

Resetting the TipWizard

■ Hold down CTRL and click the TipWizard toolbar button on the Standard toolbar.

Working with the TipWizard Toolbar

While the TipWizard toolbar displays, you can switch between the tips it is displaying by clicking the up and down arrows at the end of the text. When you want to learn more about a particular feature that a toolbar describes, click on the Show Me button which is at the end of the TipWizard toolbar.

Turning On and Off TipWizard Suggestions

The TipWizard can track what you are doing and recommend more efficient methods—even when the TipWizard toolbar does not display. To turn this tracking on and off, select Tools | Options and the General tab, and then select or clear the TipWizard Active check box before you select OK.

TITLE Field

This field displays the document title that is part of a document's properties. See "Document Properties" and "Fields."

TOA Field

This field represents a table of authorities as described under "Tables of Authorities."

TOC Field

This field represents a table of contents as described under "Table of Contents and Figures."

Toolbar Options

You can modify any of the toolbars that come with Word or design new toolbars for use with the Normal template or other templates.

Procedures

1. Display the toolbar you want to modify (if you are editing an existing toolbar).

2. Open the Customize dialog box and select the Toolbars tab. You can open this dialog box by:

■ Right-clicking a toolbar and selecting Customize to modify an open toolbar.

■ Selecting View | Toolbars, then Customize or New. When you select New, enter a toolbar name and select a template from the Make Toolbar Available To drop-down list box to set where it is saved. Then select OK.

■ Selecting Tools | Customize and selecting the Toolbars tab to modify an open toolbar.

3. Select where you want to save changes to this toolbar by selecting a template from the Save Changes In drop-down list box.

4. Make the desired changes to any visible toolbar.

■ Select the category of buttons or features you want to add in the Categories list box. Depending on the option selected, the Buttons/Macros/Fonts/AutoText/Styles list box to the right displays buttons or other selections. Click a button or selection to see its description in the Description box at the bottom of the dialog box. Drag a button or other option to the place on the toolbar you want it to appear. When you drag a button to the toolbar, that button appears on the toolbar. When you select a command, macro, font, AutoText, or style, however, you need to select or create a button to use. After dragging a non-button to the toolbar, highlight one of the buttons displayed under Button, and then select Assign to use that button for that feature. When you select a text button which displays text rather than a picture, enter the text to appear on it in the Text Button Name text box. Select Edit to create a picture yourself to appear on the button. The button appears in the Picture box. You can select a color under Color and click a square in the Picture box, changing the square to that color. Use this method to draw your button picture, and then select OK to use that button.

■ To remove a button, drag the button off the toolbar.

■ To separate buttons, drag them apart. Spaces are always the same width.

■ To rearrange buttons, drag one on top of another. The moved button takes that space, while the others move apart to make room for it.

■ To modify a button's image, right-click it and select from the menu. You can choose Copy Button Image or Paste Button Image to transfer button images using the Clipboard. You can return a button to its original image based on

T

its function by selecting Reset Button Image. You can change the button's image to another available button appearance by selecting Change Button Image and choosing one of the listed buttons. You can also edit the graphic that appears as the button's face by selecting Edit Button Image.

5. When the toolbar looks the way you want it, select Close.

Hints

Toolbars belong to specific templates. This means that the same named toolbar may have different buttons depending on the template open at the time. You can return any toolbar to its default by selecting View | Toolbars, highlighting the toolbar name in the Toolbars list box, and selecting Reset. When you pull a custom toolbar away from the edge of the window, so it becomes a floating toolbar, the toolbar's title bar shows the name and includes the template name when the toolbar is not part of the Normal template.

You can also create new toolbars while the Customize dialog box is open by dragging a button or a name for an AutoText entry, command, font, macro, or style out of the Customize dialog box to an area where no toolbar appears. This toolbar initially has the name Toolbar # where # is the next unused number.

You can rename toolbars and copy them between templates using Word's Organizer. This feature works with toolbars just as if it were another macro, style, or AutoText entry. See "Organizer" for how to work with the toolbars available through a template.

Related Topics

Toolbars

Toolbars

Toolbars are sets of buttons that you can select to carry out a command or use Word's features. The advantage to toolbars is that they are fast and easy to use. Appendix C provides a complete list of the toolbars that Word supplies.

You can display several toolbars at once, as shown in Figure 4-63, and can create and modify any of them. You can also change where toolbars appear on the screen by dragging them. Some features work by opening a toolbar to make special commands available, such as headers and footnotes. Changing the features available through a toolbar is covered under "Toolbar Options."

Procedures

The following procedures explain how you can select buttons on toolbars, and control the display and location of toolbars.

Selecting Toolbar Buttons

■ Click the toolbar button with the mouse.

Keys can be assigned to the same features as buttons, as described in "Keyboard Options." In some cases, such as the Style box, pressing the key for a feature activates the toolbar element for the same feature.

Setting Toolbars to Display

1. Select View | Toolbars or right-click a toolbar and select Toolbars.
2. Select or clear the check boxes in the Toolbars list box to select which toolbars are displayed.

 TIP: *To display or hide a toolbar, right-click a displayed toolbar and select the toolbar you want to display or hide from the shortcut menu. You can also put floating toolbars away by clicking the Close button at the end of the toolbar's title bar.*

3. Clear the Color Buttons check box to have Word display the buttons in shades of gray instead of in color.
4. Select Large Buttons to have Word use a larger button that can be more easily seen. You may need to customize your toolbars if you plan to use this feature, so that you can see all the buttons on the toolbars.
5. Select Show ToolTips to have Word display a small box with the name of the button when you point the mouse at the button for a few seconds.
6. Select With Shortcut Keys to show any shortcut keys assigned to the button's feature as part of that button's ToolTip text.
7. Select New to create a new toolbar. The steps for actually adding buttons to the toolbar are described under "Toolbar Options."
8. Select Customize to edit the highlighted toolbar. The steps for editing a toolbar are described under "Toolbar Options."
9. Select OK.

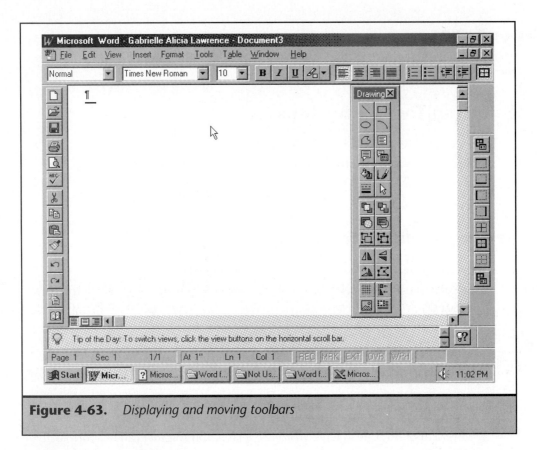

Figure 4-63.   *Displaying and moving toolbars*

Moving a Toolbar

To move a toolbar, click an empty spot of the toolbar, and drag it to the new location. A dotted gray line indicates where the toolbar appears when you release the mouse button. You can put toolbars at the top, bottom, right, or left edge of the screen, or you can display them within the document area, as you can with dialog boxes. See Figure 4-63 for all the positions where you can put a toolbar.

Related Topics

Formatting Toolbar
Toolbar Options

Tools | AutoCorrect

See "AutoCorrect."

Tools | Customize

See "Toolbar Options," "Keyboard Options," or "Menu Options."

Tools | Envelopes and Labels

See "Envelopes," "Labels," and "Mail Merge."

Tools | Grammar

See "Grammar Checking" or "Grammar Options."

Tools | Hyphenation

See "Hyphenation."

Tools | Language

See "Foreign Language Support."

Tools | Macro

See "Macros."

Tools | Mail Merge

See "Mail Merge."

Tools | Options

This command is used to set default options for many Word features. See "AutoFormat," "Comparing Versions," "Compatibility Options," "Edit Options," "Document Location Options," "General Options," "Grammar Options," "Keyboard Options," "Menu Options," "Print Options," "Save Options," "Spelling Options," "Toolbar Options," or "View Options."

Tools | Protect Document

See "Locking and Protecting Documents."

Tools | Revisions

See "Comparing Versions" and "Revision and Annotation Merging."

Tools | Spelling

See "Spelling."

Tools | Thesaurus

See "Thesaurus."

Tools | Word Count

See "Word Count."

ToolTips

ToolTips are Word's reminders of what any toolbar button does. See "Toolbars" to turn this feature on and off.

TrueType Fonts

See "Fonts."

Type

Windows describes the format for how the data is stored by its document type. When you save a document, you set its type—both to set how the data is saved, and as one of the document's properties. "Saving Documents" describes how to set a document type when you save a document. "Document Properties" describes how to look at the properties assigned to a document.

Type Style

See "Fonts."

Underline

Underlining is a character format that produces text with a line underneath. You can underline text to provide emphasis. You can underline words with a single line, double line, or dotted line; or you can underline characters only with a single line.

Procedures

You can apply the Underline style as text is being typed or after it is typed. Apply the Underline style while typing by adding the format, typing the text, and then removing the format. Apply the Underline style to typed text by selecting the text and then adding the style.

Adding and Removing Underlining with the Dialog Box

1. Select Format | Font or right-click the text and select Font.
2. Select a type of underlining from the Underline drop-down list box. To apply underlining, choose Single, Words Only, Double, or Dotted. Select None to remove underlining.
3. Select OK.

Adding and Removing Underlining with the Mouse

■ Select the Underline button, shown in the margin, in the Formatting toolbar to add or remove the Single Underline format.

Adding and Removing Underlining with Shortcut Keys

■ Press CTRL+SHIFT+U or CTRL+U to add or remove single underlining from the text.

■ Press CTRL+SHIFT+D to add or remove double underlining from the text.

■ Press CTRL+SHIFT+W to add or remove single underlining from words only in the text.

Hints

Another procedure for removing underlining from text is to select the text and press CTRL+SPACEBAR. This removes all character formatting from the selected text.

The difference between Single and Words Only underlining is whether spaces between words are underlined. Single underlines spaces as well as words while Words Only does not.

Related Topics

Character Formats
Fonts

Undoing and Redoing Actions

You can easily undo most actions you take in Word. After undoing them, you can choose to redo them. You can also redo actions to repeat the same Word feature on another selection of text.

Procedures

You can redo and undo actions by using the toolbar, menus, or shortcut keys. You can redo and undo as many actions as Word has room to store.

Using the Toolbar

■ Click the Undo button on the Standard toolbar.

You can also select the down arrow next to this button, to display a list of actions, and click the oldest action that you want undone to select a backup point.

■ Click the Redo button or display the list of actions and drag to select the ones you want to redo.

Using the Menus

■ Select Edit | Undo. The command changes to indicate the last action taken. For example, the command may change to Undo Typing or Undo Paste.

The Undo command indicates the last action taken. If you undo that action, Undo indicates the last action before the action that was undone. Each time you select Edit | Undo, you undo the next action.

Using the Shortcut Keys

■ Press CTRL+Z to undo the next action that Word has remembered.

Hints

The Undo command undoes most actions in Word, excluding those that change basic settings or have an effect beyond the program, such as saving a document. When you undo typing, Word removes all the text since the last command or other action was executed or since the last time the insertion point was moved.

Actions must be undone or redone in a series. Therefore, if you want to undo a formatting change, but there are four other actions between that change and the most recent action, you must undo all five actions. To redo that same formatting change, you must redo all five actions.

Related Topics

Repeating Actions

Unlocking Documents

See "Annotations," "Comparing Versions," "Forms," "Locking and Protecting Documents," and "Saving Documents."

Updating Links

See "Object Linking and Embedding."

Uppercase

See "Capitalization."

User Info Options

You can change the information about the user that you entered when you installed Word.

Procedures

1. Select Tools | Options.
2. Select the User Info tab.
3. Enter your name in the Name text box.

4. Enter your initials in the Initials text box.

5. Enter your name address in the Mailing Address text box.

6. Select OK.

Hints

The initials entered in the User Info Options box are used to set the initials used in annotation marks or to distinguish among different authors while marking revisions. The mailing address is used as the default return address for creating envelopes and labels.

Related Topics

Comparing Versions
Envelopes
Labels

USERADDRESS Field

This field returns the user address from the User Info tab of the Tools | Options command. See "Fields."

USER.DAT

This file stores all of the customizing settings that you make for Word and other Windows programs. You never modify this file directly—instead, make the change in Word and Word will change USER.DAT for you.

USERINITIALS Field

This field returns the user initials from the User Info tab of the Tools | Options command. See "Fields."

USERNAME Field

This field returns the user name from the User Info tab of the Tools | Options command. See "Fields."

Vertical Lines

See "Borders and Shading."

View Options

You can change what appears when you view your document, by changing which nonprinting characters or screen elements are displayed.

Procedures

1. Select <u>T</u>ools | <u>O</u>ptions.
2. Select the View tab.
3. Select from among the options described under "Options."
4. Select OK.

Options

The View options set what appears in the document as you are working on it. The available options under Show or Window depend on the current view. For example, a view option that only applies to Normal view only appears when you select <u>T</u>ools | <u>O</u>ptions from the Normal view. The options under Nonprinting Characters are the same for any view. For Full view, the view options set under Show and Nonprinting characters are the same as the current Normal, Outline, or Page Layout view. The choices under Window, however, can be set separately.

Show

The options under Show let you use some display features that can help you better edit your document.

DRAFT FONT (NORMAL AND OUTLINE VIEW)   Select the <u>D</u>raft Font check box to display all text using a draft font; character formatting appears as underlined and bold, and graphics appear as empty boxes. Draft font makes moving through large documents faster.

DRA<u>W</u>INGS (PAGE LAYOUT VIEW)   Select this check box to have Word display objects created using the Draw feature. Clearing this option lets your work with documents proceed more rapidly.

WRAP TO WINDOW (NORMAL AND OUTLINE VIEW)   Select this check box to have Word wrap text at the end of the window rather than the end of the line to make sure that you can see all of the text as you edit. When this option is in effect, the Status bar does not display the Line and At measurements which indicate the insertion point's location.

OBJECT ANCHORS (PAGE LAYOUT VIEW)   Select the Object Anchors check box to have Word display a small anchor at the beginning of the paragraph where a frame is anchored, as shown here:

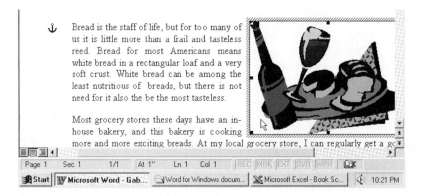

TEXT BOUNDARIES (PAGE LAYOUT VIEW)   Select the Text Boundaries check box to have Word display dotted lines indicating text boundaries at margins and around objects and frames.

PICTURE PLACEHOLDERS (NORMAL, OUTLINE, AND PAGE LAYOUT VIEWS) Select the Picture Placeholders check box to have Word display boxes in place of graphics inserted in your document, enabling the document to scroll and update the screen more quickly.

HIGHLIGHT (NORMAL, OUTLINE, AND PAGE LAYOUT VIEWS)   Select the Highlight check box to display highlighting applied to text or clear this check box to hide the highlighting colors.

FIELD CODES (NORMAL, OUTLINE, AND PAGE LAYOUT VIEWS)   Select the Field Codes check box to display field codes instead of field results. You can temporarily change the display for a document by pressing ALT+F9.

BOOKMARKS (NORMAL, OUTLINE, AND PAGE LAYOUT VIEWS)   Select the Bookmarks check box to display bookmarks in the document, enclosed in square gray brackets.

FIELD SHADING (NORMAL, OUTLINE, AND PAGE LAYOUT VIEWS)   You can select when nonprinting shading is applied to field results in your document. You can choose Never, Always, or When Selected, which is the default option, to never shade field results, to always do so, or to shade results only when part or all of the field is selected.

Window

The selections under Window let you set what elements appear in your document and application windows.

STATUS BAR (NORMAL, OUTLINE, AND PAGE LAYOUT VIEWS)   Clear the Status Bar check box to remove the status bar from the bottom of your application window.

HORIZONTAL SCROLL BAR (NORMAL, OUTLINE, AND PAGE LAYOUT VIEWS)
Clear the Horizontal Scroll Bar check box to remove the horizontal scroll bar from the bottom of your document windows as well as the buttons for switching between views.

VERTICAL SCROLL BAR (NORMAL, OUTLINE, AND PAGE LAYOUT VIEWS)
Clear the Vertical Scroll Bar check box to remove the vertical scroll bar on the right side of your document windows.

STYLE AREA WIDTH (NORMAL AND OUTLINE VIEWS)   Enter a measurement to open the style area at the left edge of your document window. The style area displays the style names for each paragraph.

VERTICAL RULER (PAGE LAYOUT VIEW)   Clear the Vertical Ruler check box to hide the vertical ruler that appears when you display the ruler.

Nonprinting Characters

Use this check box to set the nonprinting characters that are displayed.

TAB CHARACTERS   Select the Tab Characters check box to show tabs in text. Tab characters are right-pointing arrows.

SPACES   Select the Spaces check box to display spaces as small round dots in the document. Hard spaces, which are characters that print as a space but don't allow Word to break a line at that point, are indicated with the degree symbol.

PARAGRAPH MARKS   Select the Paragraph Marks check box to show paragraph marks in the text. Paragraph marks appear as the ¶ character.

OPTIONAL HYPHENS   Select the Optional Hyphens check box to show hard and optional hyphens. Optional hyphens appear in words, indicating where the word should be hyphenated when necessary; they look like normal hyphens. Hard hyphens stop Word from hyphenating a word in that position and are indicated by long hyphens.

HIDDEN TEXT   Select the Hidden Text check box to show text formatted as Hidden. Hidden text does not print, even when this check box is selected, unless the Print options have been set to print hidden text.

ALL   Select the All check box to show all nonprinting characters. The other check boxes are not selected, although Word displays all nonprinting characters as if the check boxes were selected. You can also click the Show/Hide ¶ button in the Standard toolbar to toggle between showing all nonprinting characters or just the ones that you select.

Related Topics

Fields
Frames
Nonprinting Characters
Styles
Tables
Viewing Documents

View I Annotations

See "Annotations."

View I Footnotes

See "Footnotes and Endnotes."

View I Full Screen

See "Viewing Documents."

View I Header and Footer

See "Headers and Footers."

View I Master Document

See "Master Documents."

View | Normal

See "Viewing Documents."

View | Outline

See "Outlines."

View | Page Layout

See "Viewing Documents."

View | Ruler

See "Ruler."

View | Toolbars

See "Toolbars."

View | Zoom

See "Viewing Documents."

Viewing Documents

Word offers several views of documents. Each view provides another method of both viewing and working with the document.

Procedures

Word offers several features that help you view your documents. These features include switching between Word's views, changing the magnification, working with the document in Print Preview, splitting a window into panes, and opening another window to the same document.

Switching Views

You can switch to another view of the same document using the menus by selecting the view you want to use from the View menu.

- Select View | Normal. The Normal view is the default document view. Columns of text appear after each other, instead of on the same page, and breaks are indicated by lines across the screen. You can also select the Normal View button which appears next to the horizontal scroll bar, to switch to the Normal view.

- Select <u>V</u>iew | <u>F</u>ull Screen. The Full Screen view removes all Word and other elements from the screen and displays the document using the entire area. You can use shortcut keys and menus or toolbars to format in this view. To return to the previous view, press ESC or click the Full Screen button on the Full Screen toolbar.

- Select <u>V</u>iew | <u>M</u>aster Document. In the Master Document view, you can see the overall organization of your master document on a single screen. See "Master Documents" for an explanation of how to work with master documents in this view.

- Select <u>V</u>iew | <u>P</u>age Layout. In Page Layout view, Word displays your document the way it will print. You can also select the Page Layout View button that is on the left side of the horizontal scroll bar to switch to this view.

- Select <u>V</u>iew | <u>O</u>utline. In the Outline view, you can manipulate the document by showing headings only or showing only headings of certain levels. In this view you can easily promote and demote outline items and reorganize the headings and text in the outline. The horizontal ruler is hidden and the Outline toolbar is displayed. You can also switch to this view by selecting the Outline View button to the left of the horizontal scroll bar.

- Select <u>F</u>ile | Print Pre<u>v</u>iew. Print Preview lets you see your document to review it before printing. You can also switch to Print Preview by clicking the Print Preview button on the Standard toolbar.

Zooming Your Document

You can change the magnification of your document in all views.

1. Select <u>V</u>iew | <u>Z</u>oom.

   TIP: You can also activate the Zoom drop-down list box in the Standard toolbar and select an option or type a percentage before pressing ENTER or clicking on another location.

2. Select a zoom option to size your document. You can choose a percentage of the document, and the screen will display the document at that size. Select <u>P</u>ercent and enter a specific percentage, to have the document displayed at that percentage.

   You can also have Word calculate the zoom percentage by indicating what part of the document you want to view. Select <u>P</u>age Width, <u>W</u>hole Page, or <u>M</u>any Pages and set the number of pages you want to see in the window. The last two selections are available only for the Page Layout view and Print Preview.

3. Select OK.

Working in Print Preview

In Print Preview, you can edit your document using most of the features available in normal text editing. This includes using keys and the scroll bar and the mouse to move through your document. To edit the document, click the Magnifier button on the Print Preview toolbar and click the now normal mouse pointer on the text you want to edit. When you are finished editing the document, click the Magnifier button again to return the mouse pointer to a magnifying glass. While the mouse looks like a magnifying glass, you can toggle between full page and 100% by clicking the document.

You can also use the Print Preview toolbar to change the amount of document displayed, to add rulers, or to shrink the document to fit on one page. The Print Preview toolbar buttons are shown and listed in Table 4-22. You can change the margins and indents using the ruler just as you can for the Page Layout view. See "Ruler" for more information on making these types of changes.

Splitting Windows into Panes

1. Select <u>W</u>indow I Split and a line with arrows appears.

2. Use UP ARROW or DOWN ARROW to move the line where you want the document split.

3. Press ENTER.

TIP: You can also drag the split box, at the top of the vertical scroll bar, to where you want the document split. You cannot split a document in Print Preview.

The document window is now split into two panes. This is like having two windows looking at the same landscape because the document is the same in both panes. The advantage to panes is that you can view two different parts of your document at the same time. For example, you can view the introduction to your document and the conclusion at the same time to make sure that all issues raised in the introduction are resolved in the conclusion. You can switch between panes by clicking them or pressing F6. When you are done, select <u>W</u>indow I Remove Split or drag the split box to the top or bottom of the document area.

Opening a Second Window on the Same Document

■ Select <u>W</u>indow I <u>N</u>ew Window and a line with arrows appears.

Word opens a second window to the same document. As you make changes in one window of the document, those changes will also appear in the other window of the same document.

Button	Name	Purpose
	Print	Prints the document using the default print settings
	Magnifier	Toggles being able to edit the document on and off
	One Page	Displays one full page at a time
	Multiple Pages	Displays the number of pages you select at a time
31% ▼	Zoom Control	Lets you set a zoom percentage
	View Ruler	Toggles the horizontal and vertical rulers on and off
	Shrink to Fit	Reformats the document to eliminate a last page with a small amount of text
	Full Screen	Displays the document on the full screen without other elements
Close	Close	Returns to the previous display
	Help	Turns on the Help feature

Table 4-22.   *Print Preview Toolbar Options*

Hints

Be sure to preview every document before you print it. Although the Page Layout view is a good way to check the appearance of your document, you may not have a correct screen font, or you may have difficulty displaying the page correctly. In Print Preview, Word displays the document graphically, so that even if you do not have the appropriate size of screen font, the text takes up the correct amount of room on the page.

Related Topics

Master Documents
Outlines
Ruler
View Options
Windows

Watermarks

You can create watermarks: designs or text that appear on each page. Watermarks were originally markings included in some papers to identify the maker or the user of the paper.

Procedures

1. Select View | Header and Footer.
2. Click the Drawing button on the Standard toolbar to open the Drawing toolbar.
3. You can create your own watermark or import a graphic to use as a watermark.

   ■ Draw or enter the drawing or text using the features described under "Drawing on a Document."

   ■ Create a text box. Then select Insert | Picture to import a graphic.

4. Select all elements of the watermark and select the Send Behind text button on the Drawing toolbar.
5. Select Close on the Header and Footer toolbar or select View | Header and Footer again.

The watermark will appear on every page that the header or footer appears on.

Hints

When you use a graphic or text as a watermark, try to make it pale—for instance, a light-colored graphic or light-colored text—so that it does not compete with the actual document text and make it difficult to read. Watermarks provide an easy way to add a border graphic to all pages of a document.

W

Related Topics

Drawing on a Document
Headers and Footers
Graphics

Widows and Orphans

Widows and orphans are single lines of paragraphs that appear at the top or bottom of pages while the rest of the paragraph appears on another page. You can prevent widows and orphans as described in "Pagination."

Window | Arrange All

See "Windows."

Window | List of Open Windows

See "Windows."

Window | New Window

See "Windows."

Window | Split

See "Viewing Documents."

Windows

You can move quickly between document windows or create or arrange the currently open document windows by using the Window menu.

Procedures

You can work with document windows several ways. You can open a second window to look at the same document two different ways. You can select which document window you want to work with. You can also have Word arrange your open document windows to see all of the documents you are working with.

Opening a Second Window for a Document

You can open multiple windows for the same document to compare text in different parts of a long document. You can also use separate windows to look at the same document in different views.

■ Select Window | New Window.

> **TIP:** *Changes made in one window for a document are reflected in all windows for that document.*

Moving to Another Document Window

You can move between document windows quickly.

■ Select Window and then the number of the window to which you want to move.

■ Press CTRL+F6 or SHIFT+CTRL+F6 to move forward or backward through the active document windows, in the order they appear on the Window menu.

■ Click on any visible part of the document window.

Arranging Open Document Windows

You can arrange open document windows so you can see into each document.

■ Select Window | Arrange All.

Word arranges the windows so that each one can be completely seen, as Figure 4-64 shows.

Wizards

Wizards are special Word templates that can help you create a new document. Wizards include macros that guide you through creating a document. They ask you questions and you respond based on your needs. Word uses your answers to create the document. Although Wizards are normally used when creating a document, Word also has a special Wizard that can help you create a table. You can even create Wizards by creating templates that have AutoNew macros which guide the user through the choices that the macro interprets to create a more complete document.

Procedures

1. Select File | New.
2. Select a template that includes "Wizard" in its name. You can select one from any tab of templates available.

W

3. Select OK.

4. Respond to the questions of the Wizard, using standard dialog box elements. Select Back or Next to move between the different dialog boxes' setting options.

5. Select Finish in the last dialog box.

Word Count

You can easily find out how many pages, words, characters, paragraphs, or lines are in your document. This feature is especially useful if you are writing for a publication with limited space, which can use only so many words or lines of text.

Procedures

1. Select Tools | Word Count.

2. Select the Include Footnote and Endnote check box to have Word count these when it counts words, lines, paragraphs, pages, and characters in your document.

3. Select Close.

Figure 4-64. *Arranged windows in Word for Windows*

Related Topics

Document Properties

Word for Windows 2.0 Toolbar

The Word for Windows 2.0 toolbar contains the same toolbar buttons as the toolbar in Word for Windows 2.0. Use this toolbar if you are making a transition from Word for Windows 2.0. The buttons and their functions, along with all of Word's toolbars, are listed in Appendix A.

WordArt

WordArt is a separate program that can be started in Word to enable you to create graphic images with text. Figure 4-65 shows a document that has the unusual word effects created with WordArt.

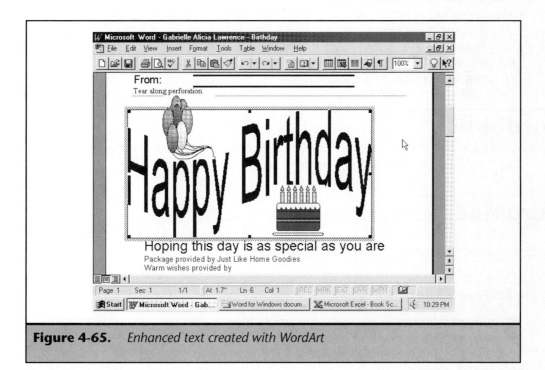

Figure 4-65.   *Enhanced text created with WordArt*

Procedures

1. Select Insert | Object.
2. Select Microsoft WordArt 2.0. Then select OK. Word's menu and toolbar are replaced by WordArt's.

 TIP: *Don't click in the document, because doing so closes WordArt.*

3. Type your text in the Enter Your Text Here dialog box. Select Insert Symbol to insert a special character. When you are finished, enter Update Display.
4. Select the effects, using the toolbar, as shown in Table 4-23. Several of these effects are also available as commands since WordArt's menu has replaced Word's.
5. Click on your document to exit WordArt.

You can edit your WordArt by double-clicking the existing WordArt, right-clicking it, and selecting Edit, or selecting Edit | WordArt Object | Edit. The toolbar and menu change just like they did in step 2. At this point, you can edit the text and the effects. You can also edit your WordArt by right-clicking it and selecting Open or selecting Edit | WordArt Object | Open. When you edit WordArt by opening it, the WordArt options display in a dialog box. When you select OK, you finish editing the WordArt and return to editing your document.

WordBasic

Word Basic is a programming language that you can use to create macros in Word. Chapter 7 has more information on how macros use WordBasic.

WordMail

Word can be your standard Exchange message editor. See Chapter 9 for more information on using Microsoft Word for your e-mail.

WordPerfect

WordPerfect is another word processing application. Word can open WordPerfect documents and save Word documents as a WordPerfect document type. Word supports WordPerfect types for WordPerfect Releases 4.1 through 6.

Button	Purpose
— Plain Text ▼	Lets you select a shape for the text to fill
Arial ▼	Lets you select a font to use for the text
Best Fit ▼	Lets you select a font size
B	Boldfaces the text
I	Italicizes the text
Ee	Makes all letters the same height
◁	Flips the text on its side
⊹A⊹	Stretches the text to fill the space you created
≡	Lets you select an alignment for the text
AV	Lets you adjust the spacing between letters
↻	Lets you rotate the text
▨	Lets you set a color or pattern to fill the text
⬚	Lets you choose a method of shadowing your text
≡	Lets you set a border for your WordArt box

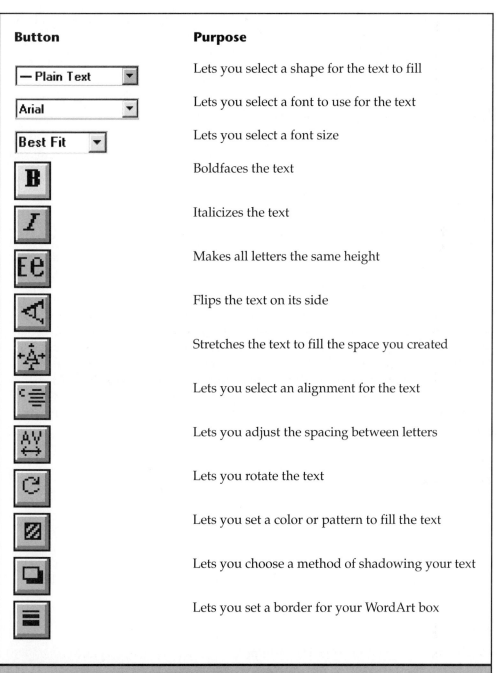

Table 4-23. *WordArt 2.0 Toolbar Buttons*

W

See "Opening Documents" and "Saving Documents" for a full explanation of how to open WordPerfect documents or save documents in a WordPerfect document type. See Appendix B, "Switching from WordPerfect to Word for Windows" for more information on Word features that make the transition easier.

Workgroup Features

Several of Word's features make working on a network easier. See "Master Documents," "Electronic Mail," "Annotations," "Comparing Versions," and "Forms" for information on those features.

Working Folder

This folder is the location where Word currently looks for and saves new documents. You can change the working folder by changing the folder that Word displays in any dialog box where you are selecting a document. This includes dialog boxes like Open and Save As.

Hint

Use one folder for all of your currently-in-use Word for Windows documents, so that they are easy to retrieve and save. If all of them are in the same directory, you won't need to change directories to save or retrieve documents. However, over time this folder may become quite crowded. To prevent this, set up a regular schedule for transferring documents that you are not using to another folder or to archival floppy disks. Remember that you can put shortcuts to your most commonly used documents into your Favorites Folder as described in "Favorites Folder."

Worksheet

Spreadsheet applications create documents, called *worksheets*, that are arranged like Word's tables. Worksheets can carry out calculations using cell entries. Word can open Lotus 1-2-3 and Excel worksheet documents. These worksheets appear in Word as tables. You can use fields to create spreadsheet-like tables that perform limited math calculations. See "Opening Documents," "Math Calculations," and "Tables" for more information on opening worksheets and performing math calculations in a table.

XE Fields

This field marks an index entry. See "Index."

Zoom

See "Viewing Documents."

PART THREE

Special Features

Chapter Five

Exchanging Data with Other Applications

W ord documents are not limited to being created and used with Word alone. Not only can you share your Word data with other applications, but you can take data that you have worked with in other applications—for instance, eye-catching graphics and complex spreadsheets—and incorporate them into your Word documents.

Word takes advantage of Windows' object linking and embedding (OLE) capabilities. The OLE technology lets Windows applications share data with one another, even if those applications cannot otherwise use one another's documents. Often, the initial problems you may have with OLE as you first start using these features occur because you are working with two applications at once.

Besides using the OLE features of Windows, you can share data among applications by *inserting* other documents into Word documents. This applies to documents containing text, spreadsheets, and graphics. Word can also share data with some applications by opening their documents and saving documents as other document types.

 NOTE: This chapter assumes that you have read the "Object Linking and Embedding" section in Chapter 4 and are comfortable using terms and ideas that were introduced in the section. If you need a reminder, the basic steps are described in the box "Linking and Embedding Data."

Linking and Embedding Data

Here is a summary of how to create linked and embedded objects. For complete procedures, see "Object Linking and Embedding" in Chapter 4.

Linking and Embedding Data with the Clipboard

1. Copy the data you want to link or embed to the Clipboard, starting from within Word or another server application.

2. Open the document that will receive the linked or embedded data in the client application, and move to where you want the data positioned.

3. Select Edit | Paste Special, and choose the appropriate options to specify how you want the data linked or embedded.

   ■ To embed the data, select the Paste option button, then the Object option in the As list box (usually the first one). If none of the As options include the word "Object," the data cannot be embedded.

   ■ To link the data and have the data's appearance set by its creating application, select the Paste Link option button and then the Object option in the As list box.

■ To link the data in Word and have the data's application (server application) initially set the data's appearance but allow you to change it within Word, select the Paste Link option button and then Rich Text Format in the As list box.

■ To link the data and have Word set the data's appearance, select the Paste Link option button and Unformatted Text in the As list box.

■ To link the data and display it as a Word picture or as a bitmapped image, select the Paste Link option button and then Picture or Bitmap in the As list box.

4. Select OK.

Linking and Embedding Existing Objects with Insert|Object

1. Move the insertion point to where you want the object to start.

2. Select Insert | Object and the Create From File tab.

3. Select the document using the File Name text box and the Look In list box, just as if you are opening a document.

4. Select the Link to File check box if you want the data linked to the Word document, or clear the check box if you want the document's contents embedded into the current document.

5. Select OK to add the object to the document.

Linking and Embedding New Objects with Insert|Object

1. Move the insertion point to where you want the object to start.

2. Select Insert | Object.

3. From the Object Type list box, select the application for the type of data you want to add, and select OK.

4. Create the data you want to appear as the embedded object, using the server application you have selected.

5. Leave the server application by selecting Exit from the File menu, OK from the dialog box, or by clicking another part of the Word document.

Why Use Embedding and Linking?

Data sharing among Windows applications means the data is still available to you even if it is created and stored in an application other than Word. For example, you can use your Excel data in your Word documents, and you can put Word documents into Excel worksheets. Word works with Windows and other Windows applications to establish a two-way communication that sends data between applications.

In this two-way communication, one Windows application requests data from another application, and the other application fills the request by sending the data. The data sent to another application can have its appearance set by the requesting application or by the application that sent the data. Because this two-way communication link remains in place, you can make changes in the original data, and the changes will also be made where the data appears.

Linking and embedding have an advantage over strictly copying data from one application to another. Copying adds the data to a document, but there is no updating after the copy operation. Linking, on the other hand, not only provides the contents of the data but also allows updates of the data: as the original data changes, so does the linked copy in the document. Embedding puts the original data in the document. When you want to change the embedded data, you edit it using the application that created it.

The difference between linking and embedding is where or how the data is stored in the new location.

Embedded objects are stored as part of the document that contains the embedded object. For example, when you embed an Excel worksheet in a Word document, as illustrated in Figure 5-1, the Excel worksheet *is stored with the Word document*. However, when you edit the worksheet data in the Word document, you will be using Excel, not Word. Word tells Windows to open Excel, and provides the Excel data to put in a worksheet. If you were to edit the data in a separate window, the separate window would have a different type of name than you normally see for Excel worksheet documents, indicating that the data is stored as part of another document rather than as an Excel worksheet.

Linked objects show data from another application that *is stored in the original application's data documents*. This data is not stored with the application that contains the link. For example, when you link an Excel worksheet into a Word document, as in Figure 5-2, the Excel worksheet is in its own document. When you edit the Excel worksheet, you will use Excel, not Word. You can start Excel from Word or you can start Excel separately. When you modify the worksheet, this link makes sure that the Word document contains the latest version of the Excel worksheet. When you tell Word you want to edit the linked data, Word tells Windows to open Excel with the selected worksheet.

Although the Excel worksheet data is displayed in the Word document, it is stored in an Excel worksheet document. You can see in Figure 5-2 that the Excel worksheet has a standard document name. With linked data, you can either have the application tell Word how the linked data appears in the Word document, or let Word format the

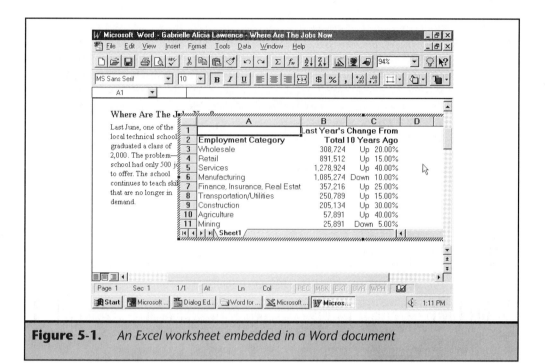

Figure 5-1.   *An Excel worksheet embedded in a Word document*

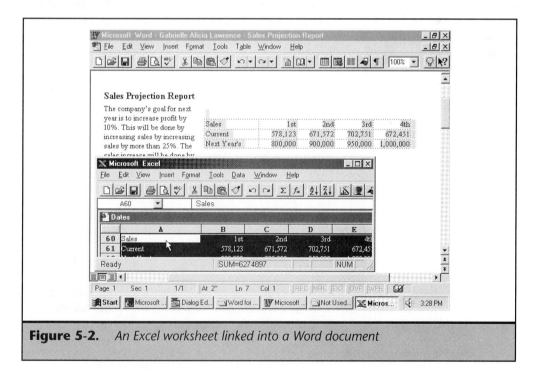

Figure 5-2.   *An Excel worksheet linked into a Word document*

linked data depending on the type of link. In our example, the linked data uses the Rich Text format, so Excel initially tells Word how the data appears, but you can still use Word features to change the data's appearance within Word. The linked Excel data appears shaded, because it is edited by starting Excel from within Word.

With either linked or embedded data, you are using another application within your Word document to include spreadsheet and database data and capabilities (for example) in your Word documents. For the two examples above to work, you need to have Excel installed. Linking and embedding adds the *capabilities* of the other applications you already have installed on your system, not the applications' software.

Word data can be linked or embedded into other applications as well. Figure 5-3 shows a Word document as a linked object in an Excel worksheet. (This worksheet also includes an embedded WordArt object.) Excel uses this linked object to give itself word processing capabilities.

TIP: *If you want to use data from a single document in two or more locations in a Word document, create a link to the document containing the desired data. If you only need to insert the data in one location, you can either link or embed the data.*

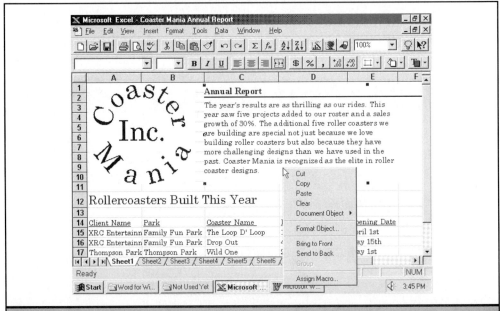

Figure 5-3. *A Word document embedded in an Excel worksheet*

Understanding Windows OLE

Object linking and embedding (OLE) is the technology Windows uses to share data among applications. OLE provides gateways for data to pass between applications. For applications to use OLE, they must be able to support this technology. Windows cannot provide OLE capabilities to applications that are not created to use them.

> **TIP:** *In earlier versions of Windows, Windows applications also used dynamic data exchange (DDE) technology to share data between applications. OLE now handles all of the features originally offered through DDE.*

An application may provide data for OLE, receive data for OLE, or both. The technical term for an application that can provide data is a *server application*, while an application that can accept data is a *client application*. Word is both, but not all other applications are. For example, you can use the Windows Paint accessory application as well as the supplementary applications that come with Word, such as WordArt and Graph, to create OLE objects in your Word documents, but these applications cannot contain OLE objects. The supplementary applications can only create embedded objects, because they cannot store the objects they create as separate documents. To see if linking and embedding will work with a particular application, you can consult its documentation or just try linking and embedding with the application and see if it works.

To share data between applications, you do not need to remember that you are using OLE. You only need to remember that you are using Windows to share the data among applications. Word handles communication to Windows and placement of the correct information in your document. You only need to select the data to share, tell Word where you want the data, and indicate whether you want it linked or embedded.

> **TIP:** *You can still use data from another application even if it does not support OLE, as long as you can copy the data to the Clipboard and then copy it from the Clipboard to Word. The disadvantage with this method is that if you change the data in the other application, you must then repeat the copying process to get the new results into your Word document.*

Working with Linked and Embedded Objects in Word

If you have not yet used linked and embedded objects in other applications, you will want to know something of how these objects work when you add them to your Word documents.

The data you want to link or embed must come from an application that supports linking or embedding. For example, you cannot select a .WK1 file for linking or embedding, because 1-2-3 Release 2.x does not support OLE. When you link or embed data using the Clipboard, the Edit | Paste Special command can tell you if the server application for the source of the data supports object linking and embedding. When the source of the data is from an application that does *not* support linking, Paste Link is not available. When the source of the data is an application that does *not* support embedding, the word "Object" will not be included in any of the formats available for adding the data.

When you link or embed the data into your Word document, a field is actually inserted. This field inserts the linked or embedded data into your Word document. If you show field codes instead of their results, you will see the fields used for linking or embedding, rather than the linked or embedded data. The fields used to link or embed data are the LINK and EMBED fields.

What Happens to Data When You Link or Embed It

When you bring data from other Windows applications into Word, the fonts do not change. Windows applications share fonts, so the fonts your system has in Word are the same fonts you have in Excel, Access, or other Windows applications.

Some formats of linked data can have their text altered, using the same Word features that you use on text stored in a normal Word document. Embedded data and some formats of linked data appear in Word documents as a picture. The formats available for linking objects include both linked objects and bitmapped or picture formats. You cannot use Word features to change the appearance of the text in the object when the linked or embedded object appears as a picture. You can, however, use the same Word features that you use to work with pictures.

Some Word features you can use are the Format | Picture command, which can enlarge or reduce the size of the data as well as crop it, and the Insert | Frame and Format | Frame commands, which can set the location of the object. For example, the picture in Figure 5-4 is acquired via a link to a graphics document. The graphic is in a text box, which allows it to appear behind the document text, and it is sized and cropped using the Format | Picture command. (The picture was created with CorelDRAW!, using a trumpet clip art image from Presentation Graphics. CorelDRAW! was used because it lets the user draw lines and subsequently modify them, to create the naturally flowing bands of color in the flag. Also, CorelDRAW! has more features for altering the look of text than does WordArt; and CorelDRAW! provides thousands of pieces of clip art, hundreds of fonts, and more graphic alterations than are offered by Paint or Word's drawing feature.) Also notice that the embedded Excel worksheet in the lower-right has a frame around it to make placement easier.

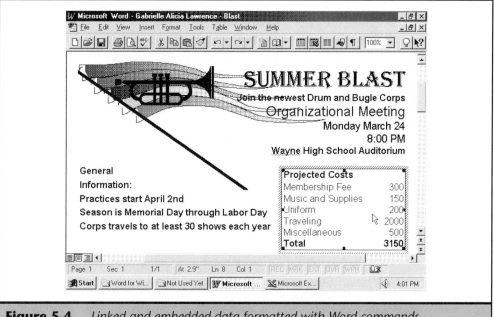

Figure 5-4. *Linked and embedded data formatted with Word commands*

TIP: *If you frequently use linked and embedded objects, you will want to invest in more memory (RAM) for your computer. The additional memory improves the performance of Word and other applications when working with linked and embedded objects.*

Linked or embedded objects remain linked or embedded until you unlink the object, delete all of the embedded data, or delete the field code for the embedded or linked data. A linked object is converted to the link's contents by selecting Edit | Links, then the link, the Break Link command button, then Yes, or by moving to the linked data and pressing CTRL+SHIFT+F9. When you do this, the link to the original document is broken, and the linked object is converted into text or a picture.

Updating Data from Linked and Embedded Objects

The primary advantage of linked and embedded objects is that when you change the data used by the linked or embedded object, the data that appears in the Word document changes. Word handles updating the linked and embedded data for you.

Data embedded in Word is updated when you edit the data in the source application and then return to Word. When you exit from the source application, you may see a prompt for updating the object in the document. Select Yes to update, and the data in the Word document is updated to match the changes you have made. Selecting No cancels the changes you have made while working in the other application. Since the Word document contains the original (not updated) data, Word does not have to verify that the data is up to date.

TIP: *Embedded data can often be updated with in-place editing. With in-place editing, the menus and toolbars of the embedded data's application replace Word's. To finish editing the embedded data, click outside of the area where the embedded data appears.*

You can set when linked data is updated by specifying how it is to be updated. When you add linked objects with Edit | Paste Special and Insert | Object, Word sets the links to be updated automatically. You can use the Edit | Links command to set the link to only be updated manually or to not be updated until you indicate otherwise. When you select the Manual option button from the Links dialog box, the link is updated only when you tell Word to do so and not when other links are automatically updated. Selecting the Locked check box freezes the locked data while still keeping the link available. Locked links cannot be updated until you select the Edit | Links command again and clear the Locked check box.

Word updates linked data at the following times:

- When you tell Word to update the data, by selecting Edit | Links, then the links to update, and then Update Now. You can also do this by moving to a linked object or selecting several linked objects and pressing F9. Or you can select Update Link from the linked object's shortcut menu.

- When you open a document containing automatically updated links. You may see a prompt; select Yes, and the links are updated.

- When you print a document containing linked objects. This assumes the Update Links check box is selected on the Print tab in the dialog box that the Tools | Options command displays, or when you select Options from the Print dialog box that the File | Print command displays.

When Word and Windows update linked data, in the background they open the source application, open the document containing the original version of the linked data, update the copy in Word, then close the source application and its documents. Since the linked data is replaced with an updated version, if you have made changes to the contents of a linked section, those changes are replaced. This is not necessarily true for formatting or picture settings you have made, however. Most linked objects keep the formatting you apply to the data in Word. If you want the formatting updated as well as the data, remove the * mergeformat statement that is part of the linked data's field code.

Word continues to update linked data until one of the following occurs:

- You tell Word you want to manually update links, by selecting Edit I Links, then the link, then Manual, and OK.

- You break the link by selecting Edit I Links, then the link, then Break Link, and then Yes to confirm that you want to break the link. This is the same as selecting the link and pressing CTRL+SHIFT+F9.

- You delete the link by deleting either the linked data's document or the field code within Word.

- You lock the link by selecting Edit I Links, then the link, then the Locked check box, and OK.

 TIP: Make sure that your computer's clock is correct. Word uses the computer's clock to determine whether linked documents need to be updated. Also, if you have several versions of a document, having the correct time and date makes it easier to determine which document version you want to use. You can see the time in the taskbar.

Changing the Data Shown in a Link

You can change the part of the linked item that appears in your Word document. One way is to change the field, but Word makes it easier with the Edit I Links command. This command opens the Links dialog box that lists the links in the current document and lets you change the section of the linked data.

When you select a link and the Change Source button, you can select the part of the document you want to show from the linked object by changing the contents in the Item text box. When this text box is empty, the entire document will appear as the linked data. The format of the Item text box entry depends on the source of the data. For example, to select part of an Excel worksheet, you supply the sheet as well as the range of rows and columns. Therefore, Sheet1!R1C1:R50C6 in the Item text box selects rows 1 through 50 and columns 1 through 6 from Sheet1.

Using this command changes the field code that represents the linked data. Although you can make the same changes directly in the field, using Word's dialog box prevents you from accidentally typing something that will corrupt the link.

Switching Between Linked and Embedded Objects

An object that is linked can be switched to be embedded, and vice versa. However, this switch does not involve just selecting the object and telling Word that you want it to be embedded into or linked to the document. Rather, you are transferring the data in the object to another source and using the new version to create a new link or embedded object. With an object that can only be embedded (such as those created with the supplementary applications Graph, Equation Editor, and WordArt), you cannot convert it to a linked object, because these applications do not save their results in a document.

If you want to transfer embedded data into linked data, edit the embedded data and copy it to a new document in the source application. For example, if you have an embedded Excel worksheet that you want to include in multiple Word documents, you can edit the Excel data, select it, and copy it to a new worksheet. Save the new worksheet and use the new version to link the data in all documents where you want to work with it—including the document that contained the original embedded object. After creating the new document, delete the embedded object and create a link to the new document.

If you want to transfer linked data into embedded data, edit the linked data and copy to the Clipboard the part you want to embed. For example, if you have a linked Excel worksheet in one Word document that you no longer want to be available to other documents, you can make an embedded object with the data. First, edit the Excel worksheet, select the part you want to embed in your document, and copy it to the Clipboard. Next, switch to the document, delete the linked data in your Word document (since you still have the data in a document, you will not lose it), and add the Clipboard data as an embedded object. Once you add the embedded object, try editing it. If it is now an embedded object, you can delete the document that the link used, assuming you no longer want the document.

Fields Used for Linked and Embedded Data

Word has several fields that you will see when you link and embed fields. Embedded data is represented by the EMBED field and linked data by the LINK field. The EMBED and LINK fields are used even when the source of the data is a Word document. These fields are just like the fields that Chapter 4 describes under "Fields." You can edit these fields directly, or you can use the Edit | Links command to change settings, which will change the fields. Usually, you will only see these field codes and let Word change them for you.

In the EMBED field:

- After EMBED is the *ClassName* that describes the application you use to modify the embedded data. This might be Excel.Sheet.5 for an Excel worksheet, or Equation.2 for the Word Equation Editor.

- After the *ClassName*, the \s switch may appear when you want the embedded object to remain the same size when you finish working on it, instead of letting the embedded object become larger or smaller as its data changes.

- The * mergeformat switch tells Word that any formatting changes you make to the embedded object should stay with the embedded object when you edit the embedded data. This includes the picture scaling and cropping set with Format | Picture.

In the LINK field:

- After LINK is the *ClassName*, as described just above for the EMBED field.
- After *ClassName* is the document name containing the linked data.
- Next comes *PlaceReference* for the part of the document to show, unless you are including the entire document in a link. *PlaceReference* is the same entry you see in the Item text box when you change a link's source with the Edit I Links command.
- Next is the \a switch if the linked data is automatically updated. When this switch is omitted, the link is manually updated.
- Other switches may include the \b for bitmap, \p for graphic or picture, \r for Rich Text format, and \t for unformatted text, which indicate the appearance of the linked data in the Word document. Linked objects often use the \p switch since they appear in the document as a picture. You can also include the \d switch to omit keeping the graphic image of the linked data in the Word document; this makes the Word document smaller.
- This field, like EMBED, can use the * mergeformat switch to keep the formatting when the linked data is updated.

Figure 5-5 shows several embedded and linked objects, and it also presents the same document showing the field codes instead.

Word also has INCLUDETEXT and INCLUDEPICTURE fields that include text and graphics from other documents. These linked objects are not the same type as the ones discussed so far; these fields are handled solely by Word, as described under "Linked and Inserted Documents" later in this chapter.

Word Documents as Linked and Embedded Data

Word documents can be linked or embedded into other documents. Several applications can take Word data that you put on the Clipboard and copy it or paste it into their own data documents as linked or embedded data. You must use the other application's commands to import the Word data.

When you use a Word document as the source for a linked object in another Word document or a client application's document, you can change which part of the Word document is shown in the linked object. A link to a Word document creates, in the source document, a bookmark of OLE_LINK*n*, where *n* is the next sequential number. To change what part of the Word document appears in the link, assign the OLE_LINK bookmark to a different part of the document. When you embed a Word document in another document, the embedded object shows all of the embedded data, not just a part.

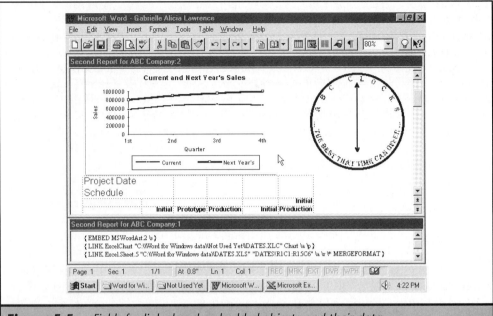

Figure 5-5. *Fields for linked and embedded objects and their data*

Working with Documents of Other Document Types

Word can work with documents that are stored in the format of another application. When you open one of these documents, Word can convert the document into Word's own document type. When you save the document, depending on the original document type, Word can save the data in a document type designed for another application. You can also insert documents when you want to add a document's contents into your documents.

A document can be copied into a Word document. Any changes you make to the original document do not get incorporated into the Word document.

Another possibility is to insert and link another document to the Word document. Then if the linked document changes, those changes appear in the Word document. It's important to understand that this document linking is different from the Windows OLE linking. This type of inserted and linked document is entirely handled by Word. Rather than using Windows to create a communication link with the other application, Word works directly with the document.

The advantage to the second method is that you do not need the other application installed. The disadvantage is that Word must be able to open documents of that document type. For example, if you have a document created with the application

VaporWare (not a real product name), and VaporWare can use OLE, you can link and embed its data. If VaporWare cannot use OLE, however, the only way you can insert the VaporWare document is if Word has text or graphics file converters that handle this type of document.

Graphics are inserted into Word documents using the Insert | Picture command, and other documents are added with the Insert | File command. Both commands have a Link to File check box. When this check box is selected, the Word document is linked to the inserted document, so as the other document changes, the version that appears in the document changes. After selecting the command, select the document and select OK.

Linked and Inserted Documents

Once you insert linked documents, they are treated just like the data you link using Windows' OLE. Linked and inserted Word documents can be automatically or manually updated; other types of linked and inserted documents can only be manually updated. Just like OLE linked data, you can change the settings for the links (except for how the link is updated) using the Edit | Links command.

Linked and inserted documents are represented by different fields than links created through Windows. As with Windows links, you normally do not enter the fields but let Word add them for you. When you insert and link another document that includes text, Word inserts the INCLUDETEXT field. When you insert and link a graphics document, Word inserts the INCLUDEPICTURE field.

After inserting these fields you will see the following:

- The document name to insert.
- After the document name for INCLUDETEXT is any bookmark name or description of the part of the document you want inserted. This is just like the Item selection with the Edit | Links command when you are changing a link.
- INCLUDETEXT and INCLUDEPICTURE can also use \c and a converter name to specify the converter to use with the picture. Omitting this switch lets Word use the default converter based on the document type.
- INCLUDEPICTURE can also use the same \d switch that the LINK field uses to omit storing a graphics image of the picture in the document, so only the link is stored.
- INCLUDETEXT can include \! to prevent Word from updating fields from the inserted document, so they are only updated when you update them in the document you are inserting.

Converting Documents

When you take a document that is not a Word for Windows document type and bring it into a Word for Windows document, or when you take a Word for Windows document and save it as a document type designed for another application, Word *converts* the document.

Document conversion does not usually have perfect results; to write a perfect conversion program, the programmer would have to consider every possible combination of features. When the conversion program overlooks some feature combination, the conversion process cannot provide the results you want. Also, how you want a feature of the document converted when the document is imported into Word may depend on what you plan to do with the data in Word.

For example, depending on the other application, you may get different fonts or very different text formatting from what you expected. This process also affects how a Word document appears when you save it in a format designed for another application.

Conversion is usually limited to the features both applications share in common. For example, when you save a Word for Windows document in Word for DOS format, you lose expanded or condensed character spacing, because Word for DOS cannot change this setting.

Conversion can be altered with compatibility options; these are on the Compatibility tab in the dialog box that the Tools | Options command displays. Compatibility options include the fonts Word uses. For example, when you bring a WordPerfect for DOS document into Word for Windows, you can have Word replace the document's fonts with the TrueType fonts you have installed in Windows. These options are further described under "Compatibility Options" in Chapter 4.

TIP: *The converter for the document type must be installed. If it is not, run the Word Setup program and install it.*

You can also edit the document converter, using the EditConversionOptions macro that is part of the Convert template. To use this macro, open the Convert template; then use the Tools | Macro command, run this macro, and follow the dialog boxes for setting the options.

You can convert multiple documents at once using the BatchConverter macro that is part of the Convert template. To use this macro, open the Convert template; then use the Tools | Macro command, run the BatchConverter macro, and follow the dialog boxes for selecting the documents to convert.

If you want to bring a Word document into an application with which Word is not compatible, find out in what other formats the other application can save its data. Often, applications can save their data in more than one format, and one of these may be one that Word will accept.

TIP: *When you import a document from a spreadsheet or database program such as Excel, 1-2-3, Quattro Pro, or dBASE, the data often appears in a table. You can use Word's table features to change the table's appearance and formatting features to improve the appearance of the data in the table's cells.*

ANSI vs. ASCII

You need to know the difference between ASCII and ANSI codes when converting documents between Windows applications and nonWindows applications. Your computer remembers every character by using a code. Word for Windows uses ANSI characters, but most programs that are not intended to run under Windows use ASCII characters. When you are using solely characters from the first half of either the ANSI or ASCII character set (characters, numbers, and common punctuation symbols), it doesn't matter which character set you are using, because the first halves of these character sets are the same. The characters in the second half of the ASCII or ANSI character set, however, are different. When you are working with a document that uses these characters, make sure that you are using the correct set; you want to prevent, for instance, a £ (ANSI 163) symbol from appearing as a ú (ASCII 163).

When you save a text file, Word has various format options that save text in an ASCII versus ANSI format. Text Only and Text Only with Line Breaks are text file formats that use the ANSI character set. MS-DOS Text and MS-DOS Text with Line Breaks are text file formats that use the ASCII character set.

Document Type Registrations

When you install Word for Windows, the installation program registers several document types with Word. Windows is informed that any document that is a Word Document type is used with Word for Windows. What this means is that you can start Word with methods other than starting the Word for Windows program icon. So if you open a Word document, Windows knows to open Word for Windows with the document opened. This is true whether you open a Word document from a folder through the Start menu or from a desktop shortcut. When you view documents using large icons, Word documents show the icons below:

ABC Clock
Report

Ad Astra -
February

Andrea
Johnson -
Letter

Animal

TIP: *Word also registers templates and wizards. You can create new documents using a template or wizard by starting the template or wizard document the same way you start a Word document.*

Chapter Six

Desktop Publishing in Word

When you first started using a word processor, you probably felt lucky being able to type error-free documents. After mastering the basics, though, you need to begin thinking about the most effective way to present your message. Most readers are bombarded daily with messages from many different sources. In order to get your reader's attention, your message must have an edge. This means you need to start focusing on document design more. You can then think of your task as publishing a document rather than just typing it. The term *desktop publishing* was coined because word processing programs like Word now let you perform tasks with the equipment on your desktop that once could only be accomplished by a professional printer.

You can use Word's desktop publishing features for a wide variety of tasks. You can create forms such as invoices or purchase orders with a company logo and shading to make them easy to read and fill out. You can create interesting and attractive reports that include graphics and charts. And you can use different fonts, graphics, and text arrangement features to easily create flyers, business cards, and other mailers.

In this chapter, you will be introduced to some key desktop publishing terms and concepts. You will need these terms and ideas when you get involved with professional printers and other desktop publishers. Examples of many of the most popular types of documents created with desktop publishing features are presented, along with an explanation of the procedures involved in creating them and some of the considerations involved in designing them.

How You Can Use Desktop Publishing

You may think that desktop publishing is something for professional graphic designers using advanced computer systems. However, much of the work that you do with Word falls within the category of desktop publishing. As you use different fonts and font styles, add borders and shading, and include drawing objects and clip art in your documents, you are actually using desktop publishing features. Even creating a sales report with charts and an opening graphic uses desktop publishing skills you didn't realize you had.

The big difference between "desktop publishing" and what you have done with Word is the time spent planning the visual design of the documents. Desktop publishers start a document by considering its design, while you probably just start typing and think about design later. By integrating the process of designing a document with the process of writing it, you too can become a desktop publisher.

Basic Steps in Desktop Publishing

The following are some general steps in desktop publishing, which will make creating visually interesting documents easier for you. You will find that these steps mirror the steps you already take to create the text of your document. They don't need to take much time, but even a few minutes of thought spent on design can result in significant improvements in your document.

1. Consider your audience. Make sure you know who you are sending this document to and what you want to tell them. Just as you would create different text for invitations to a child's birthday party and your company's reception, you should also create different designs.

2. Consider your message. Take a minute to make sure you have all the information that needs to appear in the document. If the document you are creating is primarily text, such as a report or paper, you probably want to finish creating the document, then start designing a format, since you will then know what kind of elements you need to include.

3. Sketch out your general design. Just grab a blank piece of paper and sketch out where you expect things to go, such as graphics, lines, or other elements. This gives you a quick idea of what you want to do and how it might look. Remember, this sketch isn't a rough draft, but it will guide you.

4. Apply the formatting you want to use, such as character formats, borders or shading, paragraph and page formats.

5. Preview it. Always look the document over. If you display multiple pages or small pages, you will get a better idea of the graphic impact of the document than if you view each page in full size on the screen. Use Print Preview to make sure you are viewing the document as it will print. You may need to go back and move figures or adjust some formatting if you don't like how it looks.

6. Print a preview copy of your document after previewing it on the screen. Because of the difference in resolution between the screen and a printer, some graphic effects will look very different.

7. Print it. You can either print the document yourself or take it to a service bureau and/or professional printer to have them print it using professional-quality printing equipment.

Learning About Design

The hardest step for a new desktop publisher is to figure out how to make documents look good. Very few people have professional training in graphic design or layout, so figuring out where to get started to create nice-looking documents is very difficult.

The first step in learning how to do graphic design is to remember that while you haven't created expertly laid-out documents yet, you've been reading them for years. Thousands of professionally trained graphic designers and publishers spend millions of dollars every year to present you with potential learning experiences.

Start by looking at the documents around you with a more careful eye. When you receive business cards, flyers, or brochures, make your own judgment. Do you like them? Do you know why? Try to break down the elements in a publication to see what you like. When you create a similar document, keep those ideas in mind. If you find documents you really like, keep them as examples of good graphic design. When you need to create a similar document, imitate the one you liked.

You should also invest in a good book on graphic design or desktop publishing if you are going to be doing a great deal of it. The best book will have plenty of examples, perhaps even before-and-after examples showing you how a document was improved.

Remember to trust your instincts. There are no final answers in publishing or graphic design. Your own taste and judgment is the final arbiter that decides if the document's design works or it doesn't. Educate yourself with books and by looking out for effective documents elsewhere—but your judgment still has to make the final call.

Specialized Terms and Ideas

When you step into the arena of desktop publishing, you are going to quickly find many new terms and ideas. How much of this you need to know depends on what you use Word to do. If you are creating a flyer for a school bake sale, your requirements are going to be less rigorous than if your boss just handed you the task of creating a regular newsletter for your clients.

Some of the terms explained below were originally used in professional printing, back when printing used metal type in trays. You may never have a need for them; desktop publishing has revolutionized how printing is done, and some terms just aren't used anymore. However, if you need to print your material professionally, your printer may use these terms.

- *Art*   In desktop publishing, this refers to all nontext material, including words that have been manipulated with WordArt or another package.

- *Bitmapped Images (Raster)*   Bitmapped or raster images are composed of many little dots. Raster image files are usually larger than vector files and cannot be manipulated in Word with the Draw feature. However, bitmapped images are often easier to obtain, since scanners save images as bitmapped, and they can be accepted by more programs.

- *Bleed*   This is text or art that extends to the very edge of the page, so that it can be seen on the side. This is very hard to do with most desktop systems, because most standard printers can't print right up to the edge.

- *Camera-Ready Material*   Camera-ready material is material that is ready to print. If you are photocopying your document, this means your final printout, but if you are planning to use a professional printer, you may need to find out about creating "negatives."

■ *Clip Art*   Clip art is a saved graphic image that you can use in Word. Packages of several images can be purchased from many different suppliers. Word itself comes with many images, but you may find the need or desire for different types of images. You can purchase these through the mail or from a local computer or software store. Some clip art is sold with the right to use them anywhere—as part of your logo, in a company report, or in your church newsletter. Other clip art requires the permission of developer before using it in any commercial endeavor.

■ *Copy-Fitting*   Copy-fitting is the process of adjusting the amount of text you have and the space you have to put it in. You need to make sure that the whole message is included in your publication, but you also want to keep to a readable layout. You may need to change your layout or adjust the text.

■ *Graphics Packages*   Graphics packages are programs designed to create and manipulate graphic images. Most come with a selection of fonts and clip art or previously saved graphic images.

■ While there are many graphics packages available, a common one is CorelDRAW!. You can see an example of CorelDRAW!'s work in the form in Figure 6-7 (CorelDRAW! was used to create the company's logo). While Paint and WordArt have some of the abilities of a graphics package, if you intend to do a lot of work with art and graphics, you will probably want to invest in a high-end product such as CorelDRAW!. CorelDRAW! also comes with hundreds of fonts and thousands of images.

■ *Gutter*   A gutter is the space between text, either the space between text on two facing pages, the space between columns, or the space between text and the bound edge of the document.

■ *Imagesetter*   An imagesetter is a printer with more features and much higher resolution than you have in your office or home. Imagesetters can cost up to $100,000, so only service bureaus and professional publishers usually have one.

■ *Kerning*   Kerning is the trick of removing or adding space between characters. Some pairs of characters look better if they are slightly closer together. You can let Word do automatic kerning or you can kern letters manually. Kerning is most important in high-quality publications.

See "Spacing Characters" in Chapter 4 to learn more about kerning.

■ *Offset Printing*   Offset printing is what many of us think of as "real" printing. Offset printing uses a system in which a film or metal plate of your document is created. The image from the plate or film directs where the image is printed on paper.

- *Optical Center*   The optical center of a page is where the reader's eyes naturally and immediately go. The optical center is usually located at the horizontal center of the page approximately 3/5 of the way up, assuming your document is arranged in a rectangle. Use this idea in your layout plan.

- *Pica/Point/Em/En*   Publishers use an entirely different set of measurements than the rest of us. These measurements may be used when you submit ads to newspapers or magazines or when you talk to a printer. A point, which you've already encountered in learning about font sizes, is 1/72 of an inch. A pica is twelve points.

  An em or en is a horizontal measurement based on the height of the text around it. An em is the same height as the font (such as 6 points), while an en is half of an em. These are used to described certain spaces and dashes. See the "Rules for Using Specialized Characters" box for an explanation of these dashes and what they are used for.

- *Print Shop*   A company with the ability to print your document using advanced printing techniques, which is usually useful for printing quantities in the hundreds and up. Make sure you talk to your print shop so you know what you need to provide them with. Many print shops use offset printing.

- *Resolution*   Resolution indicates how many dots per inch (dpi) are used to create your document. The higher the resolution, the less your document's text and graphics will suffer from jagged edges, which look unprofessional. Most laser printers can print text at about 600 or 300 dpi, which is fine for most purposes. For creating documents such as a slick annual report for your corporation, consider printing your document at higher dpi to create a better look. Consult a service bureau about doing this.

- *Rules*   Rules are lines used to separate text, like those created with borders or between columns.

- *Screens*   Screens are blocks of a color or black. You can use a light block with regular text or a dark block with reversed text to create emphasis. Screens are often used as headings.

- *Serif and Sans Serif Fonts*   Serif fonts have little lines (serifs) at the corners and ends of characters; sans serif fonts don't. As a rule, use serif fonts for body text; use sans serif fonts for headings, since they are harder to read in long sections of text. Serif fonts usually have a more traditional feel, while sans serif fonts are more "techy." The types of fonts you use can have a great effect on how your document is perceived by the reader.

- *Service Bureau*   A company that can print out your document using a high-quality imagesetter, making it ready for printing by an offset printer. Most service bureaus can also do your desktop publishing or provide training or equipment and software.

◼ *Vector Images* (Algorithm)   Vector images are images composed of objects represented by mathematical formulas or algorithms. They are easier to edit in many ways, and, in Word, can be manipulated using the Drawing toolbar. Vector image files are usually smaller than comparable bitmapped image files. When you size your graphic, these images will maintain a fine line with very little jaggedness.

NOTE: *For a different graphic look, you might try some of the images offered by small companies to supplement your collection. Many of the graphics used in this chapter were provided by A. J. Graphics.*

Rules for Using Specialized Characters

There are some characters that were used in printing but not in everyday typing, until the advent of computer desktop publishing. While these characters are available, few people know when or how to use them. You may have already encountered some of these special characters, while others may be new to you.

Many of these special characters can be inserted by selecting Insert | Symbol and selecting them from the Special Characters tab. Other characters automatically replace your entries when the AutoCorrect or AutoFormat feature is turned on to automatically make these replacements.

Smart/Curly Quotes   Many people are still using the straight inches mark (") rather than actual quote marks (" "), because the inches mark is entered from the keyboard and the quote marks involve extra steps. You do not have to worry about this, since Word's AutoFormat feature will automatically convert these quotes as you type, assuming you've turned the feature on.

Hyphen   The hyphen is the minus sign on the keyboard, and it is commonly used as both a hyphen and a dash. Hyphens should be used between noninclusive numbers (e.g., your phone number) or between compound words. Hyphens are the shortest of the dashes. Word includes other types of dashes.

Em Dash   The em dash, also called the dash, is used when there is a break in the line of thought in a sentence. Em dashes are the longest of the hyphen-like characters. AutoFormat will automatically replace two hyphens with a single dash when you have this feature turned on.

En Dash   The en dash, which is half the length of an em dash but longer than a hyphen, is used to combine numbers that are inclusive, as in 2-6 P.M.

Ligatures   Ligatures are two characters combined into one. These letters are no longer used in English, but they are still appropriate when writing Old English or foreign words, since they represent a sound that the letter alone does not. You can approximate ligatures by radically changing the kerning between the two letters.

Frequently used ligatures, like Œ and æ are included in the normal character set, however, and they can be entered as characters using the Insert | Symbol command.

Ellipsis   An ellipsis is the three dots used to indicate missing text in quotes or faltering conversation. An ellipsis is not actually three periods; it is a single character all of its own, which you can enter using the Insert | Symbol command or by typing three periods when AutoFormat is set to automatically replace symbols.

Em and En Space   Em and en spaces are spaces of a set width. There are no set rules for when you should use these special spaces. You would use the differing spaces when you felt they were appropriate to create attractive documents.

Copyright/Registered Trademark Symbols   The copyright symbol is a ©, while a ® is the registered symbol, and ™ is the trademark symbol (©, ®, ™). These are all special characters that can be inserted using Insert | Symbol. Also, if you have one of the AutoFormat settings on, Word will automatically replace (C), (R), and (TM) with these characters.

Creating Sample Documents

In the following section, you will see samples of several different kinds of documents you may want to create and an explanation of how they were created. Use these as a guide for creating your own documents or as the start of developing your own ideas. The general steps used to create the sample documents are explained as well as some of the considerations that went into the design.

Business Cards

You can create your own business cards using paper that can be divided into standard-size business cards. Creating your own business cards is useful, because you only print the ones that you need, making the cost cheaper than if you went to a professional printer and had a thousand made up. You also have more control over how the cards look, and you can quickly make changes for new numbers, names, or other information.

Figure 6-1 shows the business card for Howard Robinson of Robinson and Nichols, a law firm.

Designing Business Cards

Business cards create a strong impression about yourself and your company. Make sure that your business cards give other people a good impression.

The primary factor to consider in designing a business card is size. You have very little space, and you have very definite information that must be on the card. Therefore, you must allocate space on the card carefully.

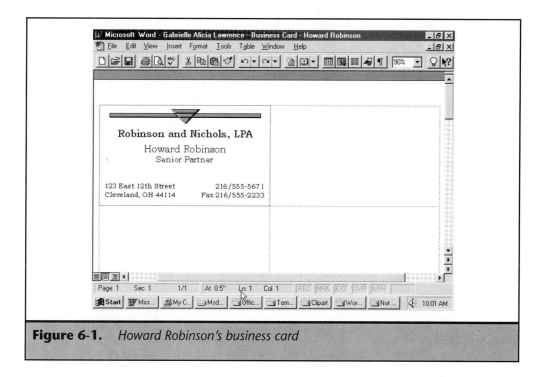

Figure 6-1. *Howard Robinson's business card*

Keep your art simple and relatively small. Rarely is there ever a good reason for a graphic to dominate a business card. Often, stylized text that is visually interesting and conveys information is the best choice. Simple line art or geometric designs are the best art, because they print clearly. Complicated designs will seem blurry and hard to read since they are so small on the card. The sample card in Figure 6-1 uses a simple logo at the top, without much detail.

Everyone should find your card easy to read, so don't reduce your font size too much. Fonts smaller than 10 points are going to be very hard to read and should be avoided. On the sample card, the address is 10 points, while Howard Robinson's name is 14 and his title is 12. The larger point sizes provide emphasis for the more important information.

Note that only one font, Bookman Old Style, is used on this card. Generally, you shouldn't use multiple fonts on a business card, because too many fonts will make the card look very busy. Stick to one font in slightly different sizes or use, sparingly, font styles such as italics. Remember that a business card is seen as a single image, and that image must look coordinated and professional.

Creating Business Cards

To create a business card, follow these steps:

1. Select Tools | Envelopes and Labels. In the Envelopes and Labels dialog box:

   a. Select the Labels tab.

   b. Select Options, and choose the label layout you want to use. The labels provided are standard formats that many different companies use to set up their sheets of labels. For business cards, you probably want Avery 5371 - Business Card, but check the package of paper you are using to make sure. After choosing the setup, select OK.

   c. Select New Document to create a new, unnamed document, which contains a table. Each cell of the table is the precise size of the business cards on the form you are using. If you selected Avery 5371, ten cells are arranged in two columns.

   Each cell of this table matches the location of one business card on the paper; you can create ten individual cards, or you can copy one card to each of the cells.

 Usually, this feature is used with the Mail Merge feature to create mailing labels or other sets of labels. See "Labels" and "Mail Merge" in Chapter 4 to learn how to create a new document with these features.

2. Insert or draw any graphic images you want to use. Because a table is used to divide the page into the business cards, you cannot insert a frame around the graphic image. You have three choices:

   ■ Use an imported graphic that you do not want to put text beside. Figure 6-1 uses this option.

   ■ Split the cell, and add an imported graphic to one cell and the text to the other.

   ■ Draw the graphic using Word's drawing features, then send it behind the text. You can either make the text avoid appearing over this drawing object, or you can use it as a watermark like a background figure. Do not make this graphic a picture, or you will have the same problems as with an imported graphic.

In Chapter 4, see "Drawing on a Document" and "Graphics" for more information on working with graphic images in Word, and see "Tables" for more information on working with tables.

3. Add the text. You can include text formatting as usual.

4. Copy the business card to each of the other cells in the table to print the ten business cards available on the sheet.

Letterheads

Figure 6-2 shows the letterhead for Kensington Designs, which was created as a template in Word. By creating a letterhead as a template, you can simply open a document using that template, and the letterhead is right there.

Designing Letterheads

Letterheads originally contained just the name and address of the sender, appearing at the top of the page, usually centered. Now, you can add a lot more to your letterhead. Your clients will see more of your letterhead than they will of any other single document you put out. Therefore, you should be very careful about your letterhead design, because it will do a lot to set the image of your company in other people's minds.

When you design letterhead, remember that while it is supposed to convey information and an image of your company, it is not supposed to overwhelm the actual message, which is the letter, proposal, or other document. It's supposed to function as a frame—attractive, but not the center of attention.

You can create a letterhead without graphics that appears only at the top of the page. This is a traditional format, which is good for companies with a conservative image, such as accounting firms and banks. Companies that need to project a more creative and up-to-date impression can use letterhead that is less traditional, using graphics, unfamiliar fonts, or unique placement of information.

The sample letterhead in Figure 6-2 is for an interior design company, a company that wants to convey a sense of style and a creative image. The company name and slogan are at the top, in a font chosen to convey the image of being creative. The company name is large enough to catch attention. The graphic was chosen because it is simple enough not to steal the reader's attention, but suitable for the company. These graphics are fairly large for a letterhead, and while they are appropriate for a creative service firm, they probably are not for a professional company.

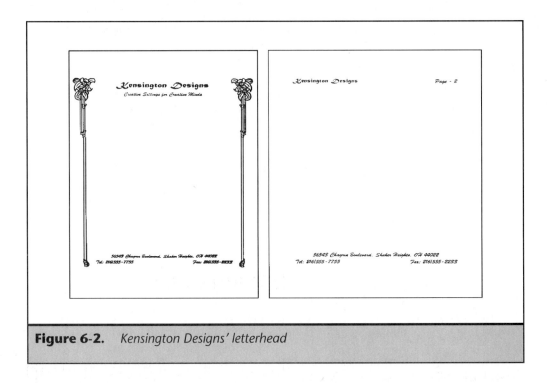

Figure 6-2. *Kensington Designs' letterhead*

Splitting the information, that is, putting the company name at the top and address at the bottom, is easily done and conveys a contemporary image. In this letterhead, it helps to balance the page, since the company name and slogan are so "heavy." You will want to consider the comparative weight of text and graphics on a page when designing a letterhead.

Creating Letterheads

To create a letterhead template, follow these steps:

1. Open a new template file.

See "Templates" in Chapter 4 to learn more about templates and how they work.

2. Press CTRL+ENTER to add a hard page break. Now the document has two pages—one for where the first page header will appear and one for where the header used by the rest of the document will appear.

3. Press UP ARROW to move back to page 1 of the document.

4. Select <u>V</u>iew | <u>H</u>eader and Footer. You want to create your letterhead as a header or footer so that it appears on every page.

See "Headers and Footers" in Chapter 4 for more information on creating headers and footers.

5. Change the Header and Footer options to use a different header and footer for the first page than the rest of the document. Select <u>F</u>ile | Page Set<u>u</u>p and the <u>L</u>ayout tab, select the Different <u>F</u>irst Page check box, then select OK.

6. Add the graphics and text of the first page of the letterhead to the header or footer.

   In Figure 6-2, the company name and slogan appear in the header and the address and phone information appear in the footer. You can include these elements of the letterhead in either.

   You can add graphics to a header or footer, which can appear either in the header or footer area, or elsewhere on the page. An interesting effect for some letterheads is to add the company name as a WordArt image and arrange it down one side of the page rather than across the top.

   In Figure 6-2, bitmapped graphics were added to the first page header. The graphic is inserted in a text box created with the Draw feature. After the graphic was sized to fit down the entire page, Draw's Send Behind Text button was selected, so that the text of the letter would appear "on top of" the graphic.

In Chapter 4, see "Graphics" and "Drawing on a Document" to learn how to work with imported graphic images; see "Watermarks" for more detailed steps on inserting a graphic image in a header or footer.

7. Move to the header of the second and subsequent pages.

   You will not want the letterhead on the first page to appear on all the pages of the letter or document. Instead, you should create a simpler header and footer, like the second page in Figure 6-2, for subsequent pages, so that more information can be included on them.

8. Create the header and footer for the remaining pages.

   The address and telephone number are the only information that appears in the footer of the subsequent pages. While dividing a document into sections and using different headers and footers might seem like another solution for creating a letterhead like this one, it will not work well as you edit the document and the page breaks within the document move.

In Chapter 4, see "Sections" for an explanation of what sections are and how they work; see "Headers and Footers" to learn about creating headers and footers.

9. Close the Header and Footer view.

10. Remove the extra page break created in step 2. The document still contains the settings for what prints as the header and footer on pages after the first one.

11. Save the document as a template.

Brochures

Figure 6-3 shows two sides of a brochure (mailer) created in Word using columns and frames. Brochures are normally designed around a standard-size paper, which is then folded. Legal paper (8 1/3 by 14 inches) can be folded four ways, while 8 1/2-by-11-inch paper is normally folded three ways.

Designing a Brochure

A brochure like the example shown in Figure 6-3 is one of the more difficult documents to design. You are working with very limited space and a very confined layout.

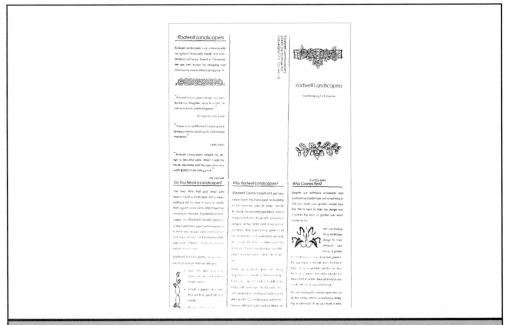

Figure 6-3.   *Rodwell Landscapers' mailing brochure*

Keep in mind the process of reading a brochure. The reader will either read the front or the back, then open the brochure and read the inside. You have to make both the front and the back interesting enough to get the reader to open the brochure. The inside three panels have to work together to create an attractive look.

Consider your front and back panels as individual pages, since that is how a reader will view them. The front panel should usually include a title and enough text to get people to open the brochure. This is a good location for catchy graphics, which will grab their attention before they throw the brochure out.

The back panel should also be attractive and catchy. A selection of endorsements or effective quotes is a good way to catch a reader's interest.

When you format the inside, make sure that all three panels work well together. The inside of a brochure is often primarily text, but you will want to make sure that there is plenty of white space and graphics to keep the interest of readers. Lines of tightly packed text with no relief provided by white space and graphics make the text hard to follow, presenting an unpleasant appearance that turns readers away.

Creating a Brochure

Follow these steps to create a similar brochure:

1. Use the File | Setup command. You need to change the page orientation to landscape to create a brochure. In the sample brochure, the page alignment was changed to justified so that the text would stretch from the top to the bottom margin, even though the text didn't quite fill the space.

2. Use the Format | Columns command to evenly divide the page into three newspaper-style columns.

See "Columns" in Chapter 4 for more information about creating columns. Word also has a Brochure template to perform these first two steps as well as set up styles for this document.

3. Enter the text of the document. If you type the text first, you just have to worry about fitting the text to the size of the panels in the brochure.

You can use styles to format headings in your brochure to keep them consistent. For example, in this document, the headings on the outside of the brochure are formatted with a Heading 1 style.

The return address on the center panel of the outside page was included as a WordArt object rather than as text. WordArt makes it easy to rotate sections of text.

See "WordArt" in Chapter 4 for more instructions on using the WordArt program.

4. Insert or create the graphic images. You want to add the graphic images after the text so that you don't add more graphic images than there is room on the page. If the image is important, you can delete text to make room for it, but why play around with your message if you don't have to?

In Figure 6-3, the graphic images are included in frames so that they can appear alongside the text, as you can see on the first panel of the inside page.

Flyers or Announcements

Figure 6-4 shows a flyer created in Word for the Cleveland Wine Festival. Flyers are basically small posters that you can mail or post for people to read. While you can make flyers of any size, creating them in a standard size like 8 1/2 by 11 makes copying or printing them easy and inexpensive.

Designing a Flyer

The difficulty with flyers, as with posters, is that they depend more than most documents on their layout or graphic design. Flyers usually need to catch someone's attention immediately, since they are probably only seen in passing. You will see many

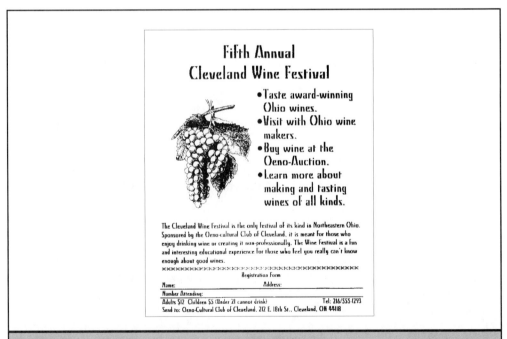

Figure 6-4. *Flyer for the Cleveland Wine Festival*

ineffective flyers created by people who have placed the text and graphics on the page without any thought about the overall design.

It is even more important with flyers than with other documents that you take the time to consider the effect of the fonts and graphics that you are using on your intended audience.

Remember to consider how your flyer will be seen. If it's to be posted, make very certain that the text is large enough to be read from a distance. If it's going to be distributed by hand, you can afford to use a smaller font. Never include so much text on a flyer that it's like reading a book, because readers will just drop the document off in the nearest waste can.

Designing flyers is a great test of your personal sense of style. Since they can be used for so many different purposes, you will need to determine which elements are most important, based on your needs. Don't be afraid to spend a fair amount of time on a flyer. Once you find the art and text you want, spend some time playing with different fonts and placement until it looks right.

A flyer is a good place to use large, complicated graphics, like the cluster of grapes in Figure 6-4. In a smaller document, the fine lines in this graphic might blur or disappear, but in a document like this flyer, it's perfect. This old-style line drawing was chosen over other possible selections because it fits the style of the event, which is meant to be fun, but elegant. The same decision went into the font, which is meant to convey an elegant but "artsy" feeling.

Creating a Flyer

Flyers are remarkably easy to create. There are only two steps to actually putting a flyer together:

1. Enter and format the text.

2. Insert or create the graphics.

Greeting Cards

You can create a greeting card for your business or personal use, like the one shown in Figure 6-5. Use Word to create individualized cards for friends or family or effective low-cost cards for your company.

Designing a Greeting Card

Greeting cards can differ, according to why you are creating them. The elements of design and format you choose can vary greatly. However, the format of a standard greeting card is very simple. You will have a panel or graphic and an inside message, or, more rarely, another graphic.

The greeting card in Figure 6-5 is an 8 1/2-by-5 1/2-inch sheet folded, with a message or graphic on the front outside flap and a message or signature on the inside. This size is useful because it uses a standard paper and a fairly standard envelope (A-2).

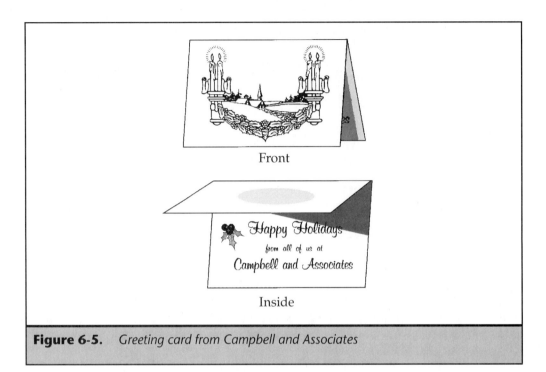

Front

Inside

Figure 6-5. *Greeting card from Campbell and Associates*

Choose your graphic according to the feeling you are trying to convey. For the greeting card in Figure 6-5, a traditional winter scene has been chosen, suitable for a traditional company. Any message in a greeting card should be kept very short and fairly generic, unless you are making the card for only one person. Keep it short, because there isn't a lot of space on a greeting card. Choose a font that reflects the same mood as the outside message—in our example, a traditional feeling is exemplified by the calligraphic-type font.

Creating a Greeting Card

To create a greeting card, follow these steps:

1. Use the File | Page Setup command to set landscape orientation.

2. Change the top margin to 4.5 inches.

   If you fold the page in half with a horizontal crease, the fold is at 4.25 inches. You've added .25 inch to the top margin to allow for a margin from the fold. Adjust this measurement depending on the size of paper you are using.

In Chapter 4, see "Page Size and Orientation" for details on changing page orientation; see "Margins" for information on changing margins.

3. Insert or create your outside message or art on the first page.

The outside message on the greeting card in Figure 6-5 is the graphic with the candles. You could also use WordArt to create a message or just use a nice font to include a message.

4. On the second page, enter the message that will appear on the inside.

In the greeting card in Figure 6-5, this is the "Happy Holidays" message. Not all greeting cards need to have an inside message. For example, a thank you card created in this way might have "Thank You" on the outside flap, with space left on the inside flap for a message.

Unless you have a two-sided printer or copier, you will need to print twice on the same sheet of paper. The second time, you want to reverse the page from top to bottom to get the inside and outside art in the correct locations. To envision this, imagine you are holding the paper with the outside message at the bottom. The inside message should appear on the back of that page, at the top and upside down.

Cards created in this way fit into A-2 size envelopes. You should be able to get these envelopes in a paper that matches what the cards are printed on at most paper supply stores.

Reports

You may not think of creating a report as a graphic design feature, but it can be. Most reports have a purpose beyond simply making data available; they involve trying to persuade a boss or group of people to decide to do something. You want to make that report as persuasive as possible. Careful graphic design will help you make your point. Figure 6-6 shows a multiple-page view of a report created in Word, showing how the careful use of graphic design can help your report look better.

Designing a Report

Designing a report depends less on the use of graphics and more on the layout and formatting of text, unlike the previous sample documents. Reports are not the place to show off all the new desktop publishing tricks you have learned, since this will detract from the message of the text. The point in designing a report is to keep it simple, give it a professional look, and make it easy to read and enjoy.

In the sample report, the design elements are kept to a minimum. The cover page is very simple: it includes the title, a copy of the company's logo, and the authors' names. This page means to attract with simplicity, a style that reinforces the streamline appearance of the logo.

The text of the report is formatted into two columns, because two columns are easier for most people to read—the lines are shorter, and the gutter between columns allows for a fair amount of white space to break up the page. Despite the added white space, the text actually takes fewer pages when you use columns.

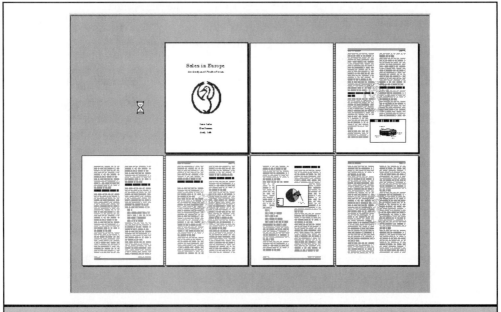

Figure 6-6. *Thumbnail sketch of a report*

The header and footer are kept simple, serving as frames for the text. They include a double line, the report's title, and the page number. When the reader opens this document, which is meant to be printed double-sided and bound, the lines will frame the text.

A watermark of the company's logo is repeated on every odd-numbered page to provide a visual continuity to this report. Since there are so few graphics in this report, the watermark adds a graphic element that would otherwise be lacking.

One problem with using the watermark graphic is that it looks odd if your charts or other graphics overlay it. Graphs in this report either appear on the page without the watermark or are carefully placed away from the watermark.

Choose the fonts for your headings and text carefully. You want to select fonts that do not stand out but reinforce your document's impression. A technical paper might use a sans serif font primarily, since sans serif fonts often convey a feeling of technology. However, they are hard to read for long stretches of text. Using them in headings, when the body text is in a serif font, contrasts the headings to the body text further and introduces a similar feel without making the document difficult to read.

Creating a Report

To create a similar report, follow these steps:

1. Use File | Page Setup to make Word use a different header and footer for odd and even pages and the first page.

For more information on headers and footers see "Headers and Footers" in Chapter 4.

2. Enter the cover page information on the first page, inserting the graphic into a frame.

3. Enter an odd page section break at the end of the first page, so that the actual text of this report will appear on the next odd page.

For more information on sections and how they work, see "Sections" in Chapter 4.

4. Create a header on the first odd page using a border line across the top and a watermark, which, in this case, is the company's logo.

   The watermark is included in the odd page's header within a text box added with the Draw feature. It is then sent behind the text so that it never overwrites the text.

For more information on inserting a watermark, see "Watermarks" in Chapter 4.

5. Create an even page footer using a border line and text.

6. Format the second section with two columns.

For more information on creating columns, see "Columns" in Chapter 4.

7. Add graphics or charts to the text. The charts used in this report were created using Word's Graph program.

See "Graph" in Chapter 4 to learn about creating charts with this supplementary program.

8. Use styles to format headings in the text.

See "Styles" in Chapter 4 for an explanation of how styles work in Word.

Forms

Figure 6-7 is an invoice form created using Word. A form is any type of document meant to be filled in by hand or on a computer. Creating form fields for completion on the computer is described under "Forms" in Chapter 4. An effective form, whether it will be completed with pen or keystrokes, requires that you spend the time planning its design.

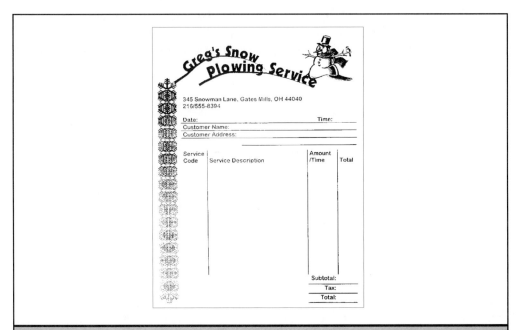

Figure 6-7. *An invoice for Greg's Snow Plowing Service*

Designing a Form

A primary consideration in designing a form is how it will be filled out. The sample form was designed to be filled out by hand, so it needs to allow plenty of space for people to write in.

Another important consideration is that information has to be arranged in an easy to follow fashion, and those places that need to be filled out have to be marked carefully so that users don't miss a piece of information.

Since the sample form in Figure 6-7 is handed back to customers, it also needs to serve as advertisement for Greg's Snow Plowing Service. The comparatively large amount of space dedicated to the graphic is meant to help Greg's company advertise. Almost anybody who sees this form will take a second look.

The information is arranged in tables, making alignment of the different pieces of text easy. The comparatively large font size makes the form easier to read, even if it is filled out by customers standing out in the snow after having their driveway plowed.

The row heights are set to 20 points. Again, this is in consideration of how the form is likely to be used. Since it is going to be filled in by hand, the rows are high to let anyone's handwriting fit. Since it is probably not going to be filled out at a desk but rather on a clipboard outside, these rows are even higher than usual. A form meant to be used in an office would probably have rows only 14 or 15 points high.

The alternating rows of gray and white where the items in the invoice are listed are used to make it easier to follow a single line across the form. It is very easy while filling out a form to skip down a line, making the form much harder to figure out later. This light shading not only makes it easier to follow single lines across the form but also provides further graphic interest.

Creating a Form

To create a form like the sample invoice, follow these steps:

1. Insert the art, then use the Draw feature to send it to the back.

   This piece of art does not need to be inserted into a text box or frame, because the document will not have text wrap around it. To create a form like this, you want to insert your art first, because the art limits the text area of the document. If your art is meant to appear as a watermark or as part of a heading in the document, it may not need to be inserted first.

See "Graphics" and "Drawing on a Document" in Chapter 4 for information on working with imported graphics.

The graphic in Figure 6-7 was created using the CorelDRAW! graphics package, and it was saved in the .CGM format. The snowman and snowflake are pieces of clip art that come with that package. The text was formatted with the "Align with Line" format to make it match the drawn lines. The snowflake was inserted in two places in two different colors, then blended, creating those overlapping snowflakes. Being able to create graphics like this is why you may want to purchase a graphics package.

2. Adjust your margins so that the text area is limited to inside the art.

See "Margins" in Chapter 4 for information on adjusting margins.

3. Add any text that won't appear in a table, such as the address in this form.

4. Add the tables you are going to use to create the form. In this document, there are two tables, one for the customer information, and the second for the invoice data.

See "Tables" in Chapter 4 for further information on creating tables.

5. Enter the form's text.

6. Use the F̲ormat | B̲orders and Shading command to add lines and screen to your tables. In this form, every other row in the invoice area is formatted with 20% shading. This makes it easier to follow text across the lines when the text is written in. The row height is 20 points, which is fairly high, to make it easy for someone to write in information.

Newsletters

Creating a newsletter—for a social group, business, or charity—is the first step many people take into the realm of desktop publishing. Many different groups use newsletters to keep their members aware of current information, and if you have access to a computer and some skill in using it, you are very likely to be corralled into serving as the editor. Figure 6-8 shows a newsletter created for just such a group.

Designing a Newsletter

Designing a newsletter can be difficult. You first need to know what kind of information is to go into it. You will have a different type of newsletter if you can expect two or three four-page articles every issue or two pages of short snippets of information.

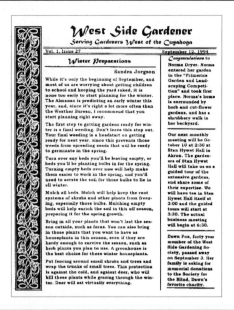

Figure 6-8.   *A newsletter for the West Side Gardening Club*

When you create the newsletter design, remember that you want to create a flexible design that can be used without significant change for many issues. Readers will feel more comfortable with your newsletter if they know what it's going to look like and where to find regular features. A familiar layout also lets the publishing group—and editor—look more professional.

TIP: You can save the newsletter as a template to make it easier to re-create. Another possibility is to simply save individual elements, such as the masthead, as AutoText items to make creating them easier.

Start with your masthead or flag, which is the title and other publishing information for the newsletter. This appears in every single issue and sets the tone for your group and the publication. Make sure that the masthead contains all the necessary information, such as the group your newsletter is for, the date the newsletter is published, and any other information you deem necessary.

The masthead should be fairly large, just as the masthead of your local newspaper is large. As a quick rule of thumb, make your total masthead use a little less than a quarter of the page. Font sizes of 24 to 36 points are appropriate for the title, depending on the font and how you've laid your masthead out. While having a masthead at the top of the first page isn't required, it is traditional and it makes sure that readers know from the beginning what they are reading.

Choose the column structure of your newsletter. A two-column structure is traditional and can be easily formatted. A three-column structure also conveys an attractive and balanced look to the page. Uneven columns, like those used in the sample, are less traditional, but they can be effective. Selecting the column structure is a personal choice, without any particularly strong arguments in favor of one direction. Do, however, stay away from single-column newsletters. Long stretches of text leave little room for graphic development and are actually harder to read than columns. Also, with columns you can fit more text in the same amount of space.

Make sure you use standard styles for article titles, author bylines, and other regular text features. This helps make your newsletter look more consistent and will speed up the layout time.

To the extent feasible, avoid jumping stories across pages. The "continued on page 4" message frustrates readers and makes them more likely to just stop reading at that point. Also, this tends to leave short ends of stories all gathered on the back page of your newsletter. Since the reader is as likely to see the back of the newsletter as the front when it is picked up, an unattractive back page may decrease readership.

Limit the use of rules, or lines, in your newsletter. Used indiscriminately, they can confuse rather than help the reader separate individual stories and determine where sections fall.

Never go gung-ho on the fonts in your newsletter. Many first-time publishers will use a different font for every element in their newsletter. Instead of looking professional, the newsletter ends up looking messy. As a rule of thumb, don't use more than three fonts on a single page.

Also, make sure that your fonts all go together. The following illustration shows how poorly selected fonts detract from the message in your document. You should contrast text that you want to stand out, such as headings and the masthead, but not enough so that it looks like two different people designed the elements of the newsletter.

Creating a Newsletter

Word provides a shortcut for creating a newsletter—the Newsletter Wizard. The Wizard can guide you through several steps for creating a newsletter. Newsletters created this way are quite functional and attractive, and they take advantage of the time and experience of the professional graphic designers who put the designs together. However, the sample newsletter shown in Figure 6-8 was created without this tool. Follow these steps to create a newsletter:

1. Design and insert your masthead. As explained above, your masthead is vital to the effect of your document. Usually, a masthead extends across the whole page of a newsletter, and the text is divided into columns. A useful thing to do is to create your masthead, then save it as an AutoText entry so you never have to create it from scratch again. You can also create a template to store the masthead as well as styles and section formatting.

In Chapter 4, see "AutoText" for more information on saving your masthead as an AutoText entry; see "Templates" for more information on creating templates.

2. Enter your text. You are likely to receive articles for your newsletter on disk, in which case you can use the File | Insert command to bring them into the newsletter. You can also type your own articles or short bits of information, such as those in the second column of the sample newsletter. This is also the stage in which you should proofread or edit the text you have been given. It helps to edit text you receive on disk before inserting it. However, you may find after bringing it into your newsletter that you need to edit it again so that it uses less space.

See "Inserting Documents" in Chapter 4 for an explanation of inserting text from other files into a Word document. You may also need to convert the document, in which case see "Opening Documents" in Chapter 4 for information on document conversion.

3. Format your text. You should create styles that apply the formatting, then apply the style to various elements. Styles will speed up the formatting stage and keep your document consistent. For example, in the sample newsletter, the article title and author byline are saved as paragraph styles. The format applied to "Congratulations" is saved as a character style, to be used for emphasizing text.

See "Styles" in Chapter 4 for more information on creating and using styles.

4. Insert or create any art you want to use. You will want to use a fair amount of art in a newsletter, because it helps to make the newsletter more interesting to readers. You will want to edit and format the text first, so that you can select your clip art based on the room that you have available after the text is

inserted and to make sure that it is appropriately placed. You can also have photos scanned or converted into disk files and put those scanned images into the newsletter.

5. Adjust the text and art. You probably need to adjust how the document is formatted to make everything fit comfortably. You can size or move the art to fit the text more accurately. You may also want to remove a word or line of text in an article to make it fit better in the space you have allotted for it. Little things, like a single extra line or lines with just a single word, may need to be corrected to make your newsletter look its best.

6. Proofread your document.

Chapter Seven

Adding Sophistication to Merge and Macro Features

This chapter is for the user who wants to take macro and merge features beyond the basics presented in Chapter 4. It is important that you have mastered the basics presented in Chapter 4 first. In this chapter you will add to your knowledge of those features. You will also learn how to plan your macros and establish strategies for merge operations.

The information here is not comprehensive; it is designed to get you started with these topics, which are complex enough to merit several books—the Microsoft Developer's Documentation on macros alone spans two volumes. After absorbing the highlights presented here, you can decide if you would like to order the Microsoft Word Developer's Kit to get all the details.

What you will learn in this chapter are the important first steps in creating more sophisticated macros and merges. You will see how to extend macros beyond Word's basic macro recorder functions, by examining some of the WordBasic commands that allow you to add logic to menu selections. You will also learn how to take full advantage of the Word fields available to you while you are performing a merge operation.

Macros and merges are completely different functions in Word. However, users who are eager to work with advanced merge features are likely to also explore sophisticated macro capabilities.

Macros

Macros are sets of WordBasic instructions that tell Word how to complete a task. WordBasic, like its predecessor, QBasic, is a programming language. It has the commands you find in other versions of Basic, plus additional commands tailored to completing Word tasks. Word has hundreds of different functions and commands, allowing you to create or modify existing Word commands, create dialog boxes and process a user's input, and perform tasks usually handled by the menus.

Using the Macro Recorder

You have probably already experimented with Word's macro recorder, described under "Macros" in Chapter 4. Using the macro recorder, you can create a macro while you perform a task. As you work, the recorder creates WordBasic commands that duplicate the task you are executing.

In summary, the process of recording a macro is started with the Tools|Macro command. You supply a name or description for the macro, as well as assign the macro to a toolbar button, menu command, or key combination. These steps are all spelled out for you in Chapter 4.

Using the Macro Toolbar to Edit and Test a Macro

To change how a macro works, you edit it by selecting Tools|Macro, highlighting the macro name, and selecting Edit. While you are editing a macro, the Macro toolbar is displayed. This toolbar appears even when you are working in other windows in

Word. This way, you can edit a macro, make changes, switch to a document window, and use the Macro toolbar to run the macro from any document window. For example, suppose you have the Logo macro, shown in Figure 7-1, for adding a logo to a document. Let's say this macro is not perfect yet, and you want to test it and edit it using the Macro toolbar.

Before testing a macro, switch to where you plan to use it. For example, since you would run the macro in Figure 7-1 from a document, either open a new document or retrieve an existing one. The Macro toolbar continues to display in this document window, so you can use the Macro toolbar to run the macro instead of the Tools|Macro command.

TIP: *If your macro will work on both new and existing documents, test it first on a new document. When it works correctly on the new document, test it on an existing one.*

Next, make sure the macro appears in the Active Macro button (the only drop-down list box in the Macro toolbar, at the far left), and click the Start button. Word will execute the macro until it reaches either the end of the macro or an error.

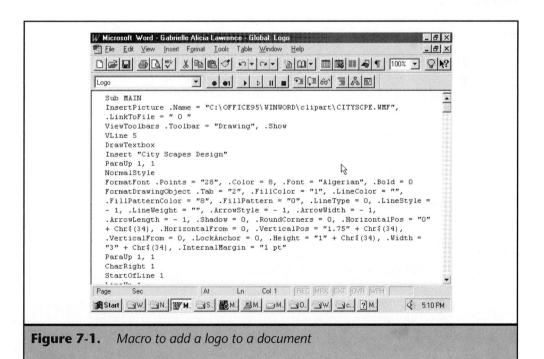

Figure 7-1. *Macro to add a logo to a document*

In a fast-running macro, it is difficult to see the actions the macro performs, because the actions are happening so fast. The Macro toolbar has options for running a macro more slowly. Click one of these buttons on the Macro toolbar instead of the Start button:

- The Step button runs a macro one command at a time. You must click the Step button to perform each subsequent command in the macro.

- The Step Subs button performs the macro one step at a time, with subroutines treated as a single step.

- The Trace button highlights the macro's commands as they are performed, one at a time.

If you freeze a macro while it is running with either the Stop, Step, or Step Subs button, you can later continue the macro's execution at normal speed by clicking the Continue button.

When you use Step or Step Subs to examine a macro more closely, you may want to also use the Window|Arrange All button and show the macro and the affected document in their own windows. In Figure 7-2, a macro is being executed using the Step button; you can see one of the steps highlighted as Word performs it.

You can see in Figure 7-1 that menu commands in a macro include many statements and settings. Rather than having to remember them, or copying them from another macro, you can perform the command and have Word insert it in the macro

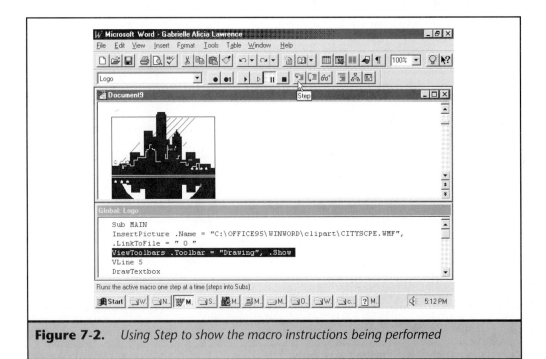

Figure 7-2. *Using Step to show the macro instructions being performed*

for you, using buttons in the Macro toolbar. When you need to insert a command, move to the position where you want the commands inserted in the macro and switch to where the macro command will be performed, such as a document window. Then click Record Next Command in the toolbar and perform the command to record. You can continue to select the Record Next Command toolbar button as many times as you need to record another command. When you return to the macro, the commands you performed will have been inserted at the proper location in the macro. The Record button in the toolbar also records macro commands, but it puts the recorded command in a new macro.

 TIP: *If you have a problem reading the macro text, select Format|Style and change the Macro Text style. You can change this style to use a different font and different tab stops when you look at and edit macros. Changing this style has no effect on how a macro performs.*

Using the WordBasic Programming Language to Create Macros

If you stick with the macro recorder method, your macros will not be any more difficult to create than the one in the example just above. Using the recorder is easy to do, since there is no need to learn the syntax of the commands or even how to spell the command names. The recorder automatically enters the correct WordBasic command for you. The downside of this method is that you cannot add logic and conditions to your macro. To use these extras, you need to enter the WordBasic instructions yourself.

The following sections cover some suggestions, guidelines, and basic instructions that you will need as you work with WordBasic to enhance your ability to create successful macros.

Planning Macros Can Actually Save Time

You may feel that you are not making progress on your computer tasks unless you are actually at the keyboard making entries. This is not true: You may actually accomplish your task more quickly if you first spend some time planning how to attack it. Well-planned macros are likely to have fewer errors ("bugs") to fix. Preventing these problems usually takes less time than finding and fixing them.

The most important planning step is deciding exactly what you need to accomplish. Think this through in detail. Make sure that you consider who the macro's users will be. If you will be the only one to use your macro, you can assume more about when and where it will be used than if others will use it. If the macro is meant to be used by others, you will want to list your assumptions and have the macro verify that the user is entering the correct information, to ensure the macro is always successful. For example, if you assume that the macro will be used after a paragraph of text is selected, the macro should check for that circumstance and display a message if a paragraph has not yet been selected.

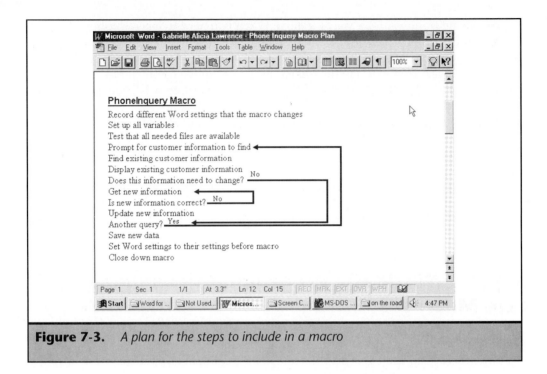

Figure 7-3. *A plan for the steps to include in a macro*

MAPPING YOUR LOGIC   For planning the logic of your macro, a brief sketch of what you want to accomplish and the steps required to get there are sufficient. You can write the steps in phrases or, if you want to get fancier, use some of the tools of the programming trade, such as flowcharts or diagrams, to map out the logic.

Flowchart templates use symbols such as a diamond to represent condition checks and a rectangle to show a formula or procedure. Writing down the logical processing you plan to accomplish is helpful even if your diagram or list is not neat. Its purpose is to help you consider all conditions. Figure 7-3 shows the design for a macro entered in a document.

The Building Blocks of Your Macro

No matter what project you attempt, you need to use the correct materials, and building a Word macro is no exception. Here are the components of the WordBasic language that you will use:

- A *statement* carries out a specific action.

- A *function* performs a computation or other action to provide information. Functions are predefined expressions where you provide the information a function works with and the function calculates the result.

- *Variables* are special storage locations for numeric or string values.

- *Expressions* perform computations. They are not predefined like functions, and you are free to create whatever you need.

- You will use all of these components as you create *logical structures* to control the order in which macro instructions are executed.

Figure 7-4 illustrates several of these building blocks in a macro.

TIP: *If you need help for a macro, don't forget the help that is available with F1. When you press F1 while working on a macro, you see the WordBasic Help, which includes descriptions for all of the WordBasic statements and functions you can use as well as other topics that can help you create your own macros.*

Statements

Statements provide a way to duplicate the actions of Word commands within your macro. Most of the entries recorded by the macro recorder are statements. These statements are executed one after another, starting at the top and going to the bottom of the macro. Since you may not always want the statements to execute sequentially, some statements are used to alter the processing flow, to create a macro with a logical structure.

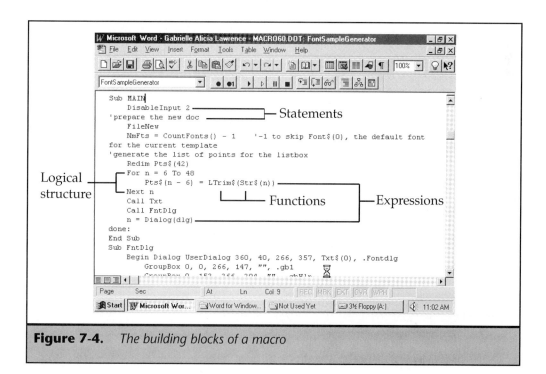

Figure 7-4. *The building blocks of a macro*

Most statements have arguments that further define the action to take. For statements that are equivalent to Word commands, the arguments are the options in the dialog box for the command. Arguments start with a period and are separated from one another by commas. For example, the following statement has four arguments:

```
EditFind .Find = "Mary", .Direction = 1, .MatchCase = 1, \
.WholeWord = 1
```

Notice that Mary is enclosed in quotes; this is because Mary is text and is therefore considered a string. Strings are always enclosed in quotes. The backslash (\) at the end of the statement's first line is a line break and makes the line more readable by continuing the statement on the next line. This statement is long because of the arguments, but even short statements must have a paragraph mark at the end. In other words, each statement is a separate paragraph.

It is easy to make mistakes when you first start writing macros with WordBasic. The "Things to Watch Out for When Writing Macros" box contains some mistakes you should avoid when creating your macros.

There are many different categories of Word statements in WordBasic. Every statement will be in one of these categories:

Address Book
Application Control
AutoCorrect
AutoText
Basic File Input/Output
Bookmarks
Borders and Frames
Branching and Control
Bullets and Numbering
Character Formatting
Customization
Date and Time
Definitions and Declarations
Dialog Box Definition and Control
Disk Access and Management
Document Properties
Documents, Templates, and Add-Ins
Drawing
Dynamic Data Exchange (DDE)
Editing
Electronic Mail and Routing

Environment
Fields
Finding and Replacing
Footnotes, Endnotes, and Annotations
Forms
Help
Macros
Mail Merge
Moving the Insertion Point
Object Linking and Embedding
Outlining and Master Documents
Paragraph Formatting
Proofing
Section and Document Formatting
Strings and Numbers
Style Formatting
Tables
Tools
View
Window

Functions

Functions return information about the current Word document or the actions of Word. They also convert one type of data to another type. Functions are organized into the same categories as statements. Functions are distinguished from statements by the parentheses at the end. There are many statements with the same name as functions. The difference is that the statement sets a value, and the function returns a value. For example, the AppMinimize statement minimizes an application window, and the AppMinimize() function returns a 1 or 0 depending on whether an application window is minimized. Some functions, such as Files$(), contain a $ in their name. The $ indicates that the function returns a string.

Data Values

Macro statements often contain data values, such as the name of a document, the number of copies, or the value to search for. Depending on the argument the value is supplying, it must be either a string or a number. If it is a string, it must be enclosed in quotation marks and cannot exceed 65,280 characters. A number can be a whole number, or it can include decimal digits. Its length cannot exceed 14 digits. Do not use a comma separator in numbers, because WordBasic uses commas to separate different values or strings.

Things to Watch Out for When Writing Macros

Mistakes come easily when you are first writing macros using WordBasic. After you write a few, you will become more careful. Here is a list of some things that can cause problems. Watch out for them when you are writing your code:

- Quotation marks missing from string values
- A reserved word used as a string variable name
- Two subroutines with the same name
- A statement that requires multiple reserved words, such as If...Then missing a reserved word
- A missing closing parenthesis in a function
- A dialog box option argument that does not have the initial period, a missing comma separator when there are multiple arguments, or an extra comma after the last argument
- A misplaced commas separator or extra comma
- A misspelled statement or function name
- A data type that is incorrect for an argument

Variables

Variables are memory locations to which you assign a name and use to hold either numbers or strings. Variables add flexibility to macros that use data values in statements and functions, because you can use a new data value for a variable each time you use the macro. You can create string variables with names that have a $ at the end, such as MYDOC$ or THISMANY$. The $ lets Word know the variable contains a string (or text) as compared to a number.

Variable names are limited to 40 characters. Numbers and the underscore character are allowed, but the first character must be a letter. Never use any of WordBasic's reserved words as variable names; this includes the names of functions, statements, arguments, and operators.

You assign a value to a variable by following the variable name with an equal sign. The value is entered to the right of the equal sign. Remember to use the quotes for string values. The following are valid examples of variable assignments:

```
MyDoc$ = "Letter9"
Copies = 2
MyState$ = "Ohio"
```

Expressions

Expressions are either string or numeric formulas. Numeric formulas use the following operators: addition (+), subtraction (–), multiplication (*), division (/), and modular division (MOD). String expressions use only the concatenation operator to join strings (+). You can use variables or data values in expressions; for example:

```
Whole – 10
Some + More
```

Logical Structures

The commands you capture with the macro recorder represent a list of steps to execute sequentially. There is no way to skip or repeat steps. You can use Word statements and the other building blocks to create logical constructs like those you use daily to process data and make decisions. These include If...Then statements, loops, and subroutines.

When you use If...Then, a condition is tested and evaluated as true or false. Depending on the outcome, one of two paths is followed. For example, you may test to see if data is selected. If it is, the macro can proceed to process it. If data is not selected, the macro can display a message box asking the user to make a selection. There is no way to handle this type of situation with the macro recorder; you must enter the If condition yourself.

A While loop is an extension of the condition. It continues to execute a series of instructions while a condition is true. A second statement, Wend, marks the end of the statements to be repeated.

A subroutine is a self-contained unit of WordBasic code that carries out a specific task. You can call a subroutine from within a macro and then return to the next statement in the macro after executing the instructions in the subroutine. Subroutines offer organizational advantages, because you can remove many of the details from the main routine, making it easier to follow. You can use a single subroutine in a number of different macros, increasing your productivity.

Some Macro Examples

Word contains a number of macro examples that are stored as part of the Macros7 template. If you do not have this template in your Macros folder, you can always go back to Setup and install the Wizards, Templates, and Letters option. Looking at these examples is a good way to see some of the WordBasic commands in action, as well as some common logic constructs that you can use when you create your own macros. Following are several examples of the most popular logical structures. If you have ever programmed with another language, these logical structures will be familiar to you, although the exact format of the logical structure varies by language.

Goto

The Goto logical structure, shown in the OrganizationChartMaker macro in Figure 7-5, changes the next direction that Word performs. The two Goto statements are after the Then in the If...Then logical structure. Combining If...Then with Goto means the Goto statements are only performed when the condition after If is true. In this case, Word only goes to Bye when A equals 0, and it only goes to DisplayDialog when A equals 1. Both Bye and DisplayDialog are labels identified elsewhere in the same subroutine.

With WordBasic's extensive subroutine and function features, you can create better working macros using subroutines and functions rather than Goto statements. However, Goto is a fundamental element for changing the order in which Word performs the statements in a macro.

If...Then...Else

The If...Then...Else logical structure in Figure 7-6 determines which one of two sets of steps is performed. These statements are from the FontSampleGenerator macro in the Macro7 template. When you run this macro, Word prompts you for the point size of the sample fonts. Since 48 is the largest size font size that the FontSampleGenerator can generate, the If...Then...Else logical structure handles what happens when you enter a larger number.

The DlgText$() function returns the point size selected, and the Val() function converts the result of the DlgText$() function from a string to a value. Word uses the result of these two functions to compare to 48. When this value is more than 48, Word performs the three statements between Then and Else. When the value is 48 or less, the macro performs the Do_It subroutine and ends the If...Then...Else logical structure.

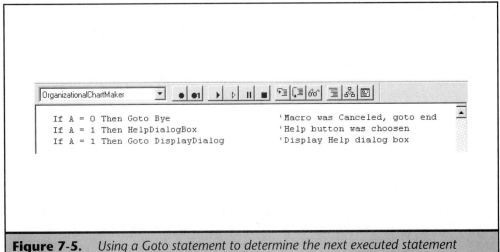

Figure 7-5. Using a Goto statement to determine the next executed statement

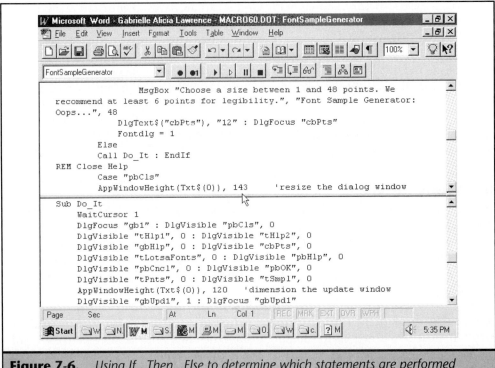

Figure 7-6. Using If...Then...Else to determine which statements are performed

Select Case

The macro statements from the MindBender macro shown in Figure 7-7 use the Select Case statement to select the parameters for the DlgValue() function. This function selects or clears dialog box controls such as check boxes and options.

The Select Case statement looks at the value of CMPSPEED. When it equals 3000, Word evaluates the statement below Case 3000... and so on down to the statement below Case 200. When it equals anything else, Word evaluates the statements below Case Else.

For...Next

The For...Next logical structure in Figure 7-8 performs a set of steps a specific number of times. These statements are from the FontSampleGenerator macro in MACRO60.DOT, which creates samples of each of the fonts you have installed. The (NmFts) equals the number of fonts you have installed on your system. This macro repeats the statements between For and Next for each of the installed fonts. The statements between For and Next use the value of X to select the font the macro is currently working with. When Word reaches the Next X statement, Word increases the value of X and repeats the statements until X equals the number of installed fonts.

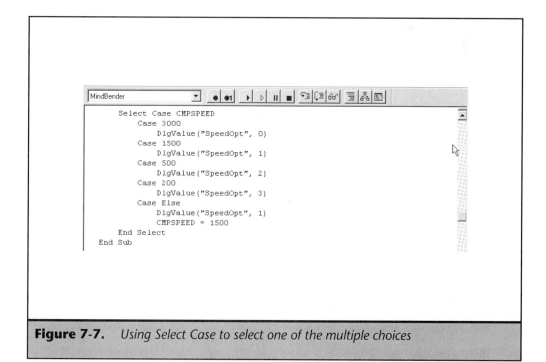

```
        Select Case CMPSPEED
            Case 3000
                DlgValue("SpeedOpt", 0)
            Case 1500
                DlgValue("SpeedOpt", 1)
            Case 500
                DlgValue("SpeedOpt", 2)
            Case 200
                DlgValue("SpeedOpt", 3)
            Case Else
                DlgValue("SpeedOpt", 1)
                CMPSPEED = 1500
        End Select
End Sub
```

Figure 7-7. *Using Select Case to select one of the multiple choices*

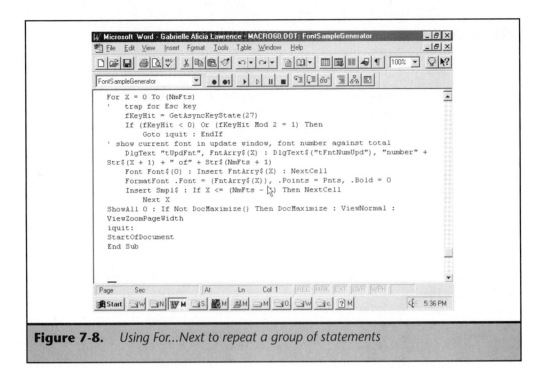

```
For X = 0 To (NmFts)
'    trap for Esc key
     fKeyHit = GetAsyncKeyState(27)
     If (fKeyHit < 0) Or (fKeyHit Mod 2 = 1) Then
          Goto iquit : EndIf
' show current font in update window, font number against total
     DlgText "tUpdFnt", FntArry$(X) : DlgText$("tFntNumUpd"), "number" +
Str$(X + 1) + " of" + Str$(NmFts + 1)
     Font Font$(0) : Insert FntArry$(X) : NextCell
     FormatFont .Font = (FntArry$(X)), .Points = Pnts, .Bold = 0
     Insert Smpl$ : If X <= (NmFts - 1) Then NextCell
        Next X
ShowAll 0 : If Not DocMaximize() Then DocMaximize : ViewNormal :
ViewZoomPageWidth
iquit:
StartOfDocument
End Sub
```

Figure 7-8.   *Using For...Next to repeat a group of statements*

MsgBox

The statements that illustrate the If...Then...Else logical structure in Figure 7-6 also use the MsgBox statement. This MsgBox statement makes the macro tell you that you have entered a number that is too large. When Word executes this statement, Word displays the dialog box shown below. You can see how the text in the MsgBox statement is repeated in the dialog box. The exclamation mark appears next to the message because the MsgBox uses a Type (the third argument in the MsgBox command) of 48, which creates an attention symbol—an exclamation mark. Word executes the next macro statement when you select the OK button in the dialog box.

InputBox

When you run the MindBender macro and get a higher score than the current posted high score, the macro prompts you for your name, like this:

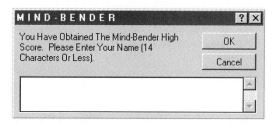

If you look at the MindBender macro, you'll find this statement:

```
name$ = InputBox$(HighScore$, UCase$(appName$) + " " +
HighScoreTitle$)
```

This statement uses the InputBox function to return the user's name. The macro uses the InputBox function rather than a dialog box, because only one piece of information is needed. The statement sets the value of Name to the entry you make in the dialog box. If the macro needs more information than you can get from the one input box, you would create a dialog box.

Subroutines

The section of the FontSampleGenerator macro shown in Figure 7-6 verifies whether you have entered a valid point size and then generates the list of fonts. When you enter a number below 48 in the dialog box that prompts for the point size to use in the generated samples, the Else part of If...Then...Else is true. The statement after Else,

```
Call Do_It : EndIf
```

starts the Do_It subroutine. When the Do_It subroutine is finished, Word performs the EndIf statement and continues with the next statement.

Remarks

A macro like those in Figures 7-5 through 7-8 needs some explanations, or *remarks*, to describe what it does; these remarks are the *macro documentation*. Documentation lets you or another user know what the macro does; a macro is useless if you forget why you created it or another user can't determine its role. Documentation also helps you understand the roles of the macro's statements when it is necessary to modify the macro. In Word macros, the lines that start with an apostrophe (') are the documentation comments or remarks.

NOTE: *Remarks must be created by editing an existing macro, because Word does not create them for you when you record a macro.*

The Word Dialog Editor

When your macro needs a dialog box, you want to create it with Word's Dialog Editor. The Word Dialog Editor is a separate program that lets you create custom dialog boxes to use with your macros. From the Dialog Editor, you create what you want the dialog box to look like, then use the Dialog Editor to copy the WordBasic statements that create the dialog box into your macro. A full installation of Word creates a Word Dialog Editor program item. If this program item is not available, you can return to the Word Setup procedure to modify your installation.

The Dialog Editor is an advanced feature, but it is useful if you want to create an interactive macro that accepts user input. Since the dialog boxes you can create have the look and feel of other Word dialog boxes, you can feel comfortable using them to define your needs. Although this section provides only a brief introduction to creating your own dialog boxes, you can learn more information about the Word Dialog Editor in the Microsoft Word Developer's Kit.

Creating a Dialog Box

Although you can create a dialog box by adding WordBasic commands directly to a macro, the Word Dialog Editor is a more practical approach. The Word Dialog Editor displays the dialog box to show you that it is what you want. As you make changes, these modifications are also visible. When the dialog box is complete, you use the Clipboard to copy the dialog box from the Word Dialog Editor into your Word macro. The dialog box appears in a Word macro as the WordBasic commands that create the dialog box.

When you start the Word Dialog Editor application, you have an empty dialog box. You can alter the size of the dialog box and where it appears on the screen. Change the size by dragging a side of the dialog box, just as you would size a document or application window. Change a dialog box's placement by dragging the dialog box's title bar to a new location. Word records the changes you make as commands that will later become part of your Word macro.

A dialog box contains *items* such as text, text boxes, check boxes, list boxes, option buttons, and other buttons such as OK and Cancel. You add these items with the Item pull-down menu. After selecting Item and the type of item to add, you may be prompted for further clarification of the type of item to add. Each item has its own settings that you can change by double-clicking the item or by selecting the item and selecting Edit|Info. You can select an item by clicking it or pressing TAB until the item has an extra outline. The settings include the size and position of the item.

Figure 7-9 shows a dialog box created with the Word Dialog Editor. This dialog box is designed to be used in a macro that adds data to a table in Word. The table data is then used to create form letters. In this dialog box, several text boxes, a picture item (the clip art document ARTIST.WMF), check boxes, option buttons, and other items are displayed.

As you add items to the dialog box, they will not appear in their final form. For example, text items initially have text of "Text" and check boxes initially have text of "Check Box." The initial text is replaced by the text that you see in Figure 7-9. Most of the text includes an ampersand (&) in the text. This & indicates that the letter that follows is underlined. For example, the Gallery Name text item actually has the text "Gallery &Name."

The items are then placed and sized by dragging the item or item's borders to the desired location in the dialog box. By double-clicking the item, you can type numbers for the placement and size that will position and size the item in small increments. The dialog box title is added by selecting the Edit|Select Dialog and Edit|Info commands.

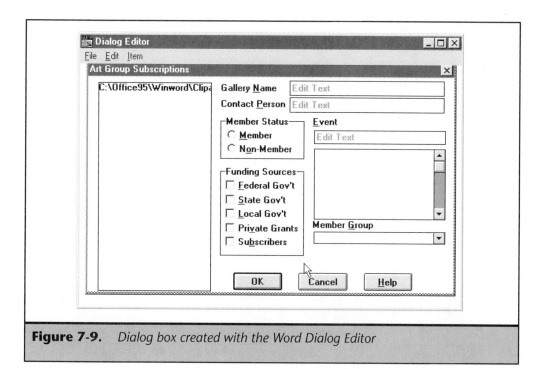

Figure 7-9.   *Dialog box created with the Word Dialog Editor*

When the dialog box is complete, select the Edit|Select Dialog and Edit|Copy commands to copy the dialog box to the Clipboard. Next, switch to the macro editing window and move the insertion point to where you want the macro statements that create the dialog box. Select Edit|Paste. The WordBasic instructions to create the dialog box are pasted from the Clipboard to the location of the insertion point in the macro code. Figure 7-10 shows the WordBasic statements Word pastes for the dialog box in Figure 7-9. When you run the macro in Word, you get a dialog box like the one in Figure 7-11.

TIP: If you add items to a dialog box in a different order than you will use them, you might notice that pressing ALT and the underlined letter does not select the dialog box item. You can fix this problem by editing the order of the statements in the macro. Make sure that Text statements for text items are before the statements for the dialog box item described by the text item. Selecting a text item actually selects the dialog box item described immediately after the Text statement. For example, a Text statement that displays Name in a dialog box must be the statement immediately before the TextBox statement to store the name.

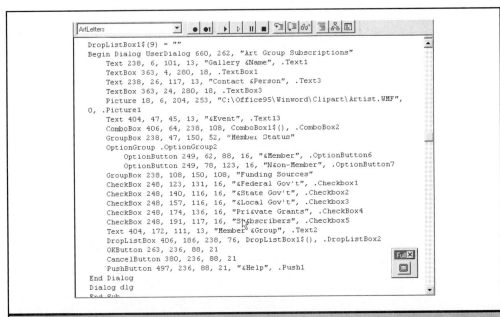

Figure 7-10.   *Macro statements created by the Word Dialog Editor*

At the end of each WordBasic statement that creates an item in the dialog box is an *identifier* that starts after the period. This identifier is the text that other WordBasic statements use to set the value of an item. Other statements can use this identifier to return the value of the item when the macro user makes an entry. For example, a macro can have a statement that sets the identifier "TextBox1$" to "Letters." Assuming TextBox1$ is for a text box, this text box will initially contain the string "Letters." When the user finishes with the dialog box, TextBox1$ contains either "Letters" or what the user typed as a replacement. After the macro's user finishes with the dialog box, another statement can use the identifier to determine this text box's value. The identifier names can be set by you or the Word Dialog Editor. When you double-click an item in the Word Dialog Editor, one of the settings is .Field. *.Field* sets the identifier of the item. Once the WordBasic statements for a dialog box are in a Word macro, you can rename an identifier by changing the existing identifier in the WordBasic statement that creates that dialog box item.

Besides the statements that set up a dialog box like the ones shown in Figure 7-10, the macro must also have other statements to use the dialog box. For instance, in the dialog box shown in Figure 7-11, the text that appears in the drop-down list boxes and list boxes must be added. This text is added to the macro before the Begin Dialog

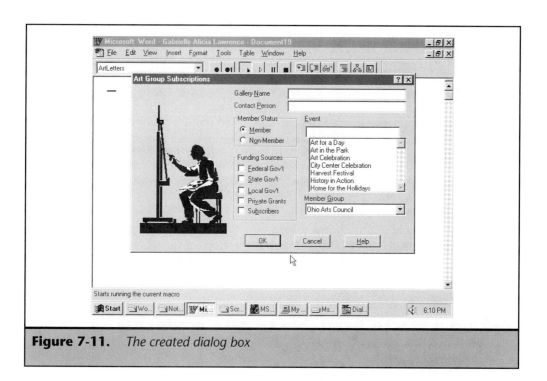

Figure 7-11. *The created dialog box*

statement that creates the dialog box. To add "Art for a Day" as you see in Figure 7-11, the macro has the statement **ComboBox1$(0) = "Art for a Day"**. In this example, ComboBox1$ is the array variable containing the items that the list box displays.

The macro in Figure 7-10 also includes two other required statements to use the dialog box. Below the macro statements you see in Figure 7-10 are the following statements:

```
Dim dlg As UserDialog
Dialog dlg
```

The first statement tells Word that you are working with a user-defined dialog box. The second statement activates the dialog box. After the Dim statement, which describes the dialog box name (dlg in this case), is a Dialog statement or function. It is the Dialog statement or function that tells Word to take the statements like the ones in Figure 7-10 and display a dialog box like the one in Figure 7-11. If you want to return a value based on how the user leaves the dialog box, such as when you want to test whether they selected OK or Cancel, use the Dialog() function. Otherwise, use the Dialog statement. After these two statements shown above are the macro statements to perform when the user finishes using the dialog box.

> **TIP:** *If you need to modify a dialog box you already have in a macro, select the statements from the Begin Dialog to End Dialog statements. Copy them to the Clipboard then paste them to the Word Dialog Editor. The dialog box defined by the copied statements appears in the dialog box in the Word Dialog Editor.*

Where Macros Are Stored

In Word, macros are always stored in a template. When you create or record the macro, it is stored automatically in the Normal template. When a macro is stored in the Normal template, it is available no matter which document you are working in. If you want to store the macro in another template, you will need to select that template when you record the macro.

Select the template to contain the macro from the Macros Available In drop-down list box, *before* selecting Record and performing the steps of the macro. The Macros Available In list box displays only attached templates, so you may also have to attach the template to the current document, using File|Templates, before you start to record the macro.

Making a Macro Available to All Documents

As stated just above, macros in the Normal template are *global*—they are automatically available in all documents. You can arrange for other macros, to also be global. When you want to edit global macros in a template besides Normal, you must be working in a document that uses that template; open the template with File|Open, or make the other template globally available with the File|Templates command.

Priority of Macros with the Same Names

If all of your macros are stored in the Normal template, you will not have name conflicts, because Word does not let you create macros with the same name in a particular template. You can, however, have the same macro name in two *different* templates. If you do this, the macros will be assigned the following execution priority whenever both templates are active:

1. Macros in the template attached to the active document

2. Macros in the Normal template

3. Macros in other global templates, in alphabetical sequence of template names from A to Z

Copying and Moving Macros Among Templates

To transfer a macro from one template to another, use the Organizer, described under "Organizer" in Chapter 4, which lets you copy macros from one template to another.

Automatic Macros

You can create macros with special names that will execute automatically when a certain condition occurs in the templates to which they are attached. What makes these macros special are their names, which determine when they start executing. Automatic macro names and the conditions that trigger their execution are listed in the following table:

Automatic Macro Name	Executed
AutoExec	When you start Word
AutoOpen	When you open a document
AutoNew	When you create a new document
AutoClose	When you close a document
AutoExit	When you exit Word

NOTE: All automatic macros function globally if stored in the Normal template. If stored in another template, all automatic macros function only on the document that uses the other template.

What to Do When Your Macros Don't Work

If all your macros work correctly the first time you use them, you will be very lucky. Unfortunately, this kind of luck is highly unlikely. Nearly everyone who creates more than a few macros or programs gets stumped occasionally by a mysterious problem of one sort or another. Though it may be obvious that the task isn't being completed correctly, the actual cause of the problem can be difficult to identify. We have found the following strategies to be helpful when wrestling with stubborn bugs in macros or programs:

- Work on something else for a while—you will come back to the problem with a fresh perspective.

- Explain the problem to a coworker or friend. Even if neither of you is an expert, frequently the process of simply explaining what is supposed to be happening will turn on the light that illuminates the problem.

- Add message boxes to your macro temporarily, to help you track your progress, using the MsgBox statement. Remove them when you've fixed the bug.

- On the Macro toolbar, use the Trace button to have Word highlight the macro instructions as they are performed. Or use the Step button and step through the instructions one by one as slowly as you like.

- If you have subroutines, use the Step Subs button to have Word walk through the main routine a step at a time and perform a correctly functioning subroutine without interruption as if it is one statement.

- Use the Show Variables button to display variable values while the macro is paused or stopped, so you can track the values currently in the variables.

- Use the Rem statement to treat an instruction as a remark. Selecting the Add/Remove REM button adds a REM to the beginning of the selected statements. Select it again to remove the REM so Word performs the statement in the macro.

- Test your code one section at a time, by saving the entire macro under a new name and deleting everything except what you want to test.

- Limit the amount of data you are testing with. First try simple data that is unlikely to "break" your code. You can then progress to real-life data, and then potential-problem data.

Mail Merge

Merging is easier than ever with Word's wizardlike feature, the Mail Merge Helper dialog box. This dialog box makes it easy to create exactly what you need in your first attempt. But beware: the Mail Merge Helper looks so inviting that you may be tempted to start making selections without thinking through the full process of your merge.

If you have never performed a merge operation, be sure to review the fundamentals in "Mail Merge" in Chapter 4. The following text describes how to set up mail merge documents. Once they are set up, they need to be merged when you want the variable data inserted into the document. The steps for merging the document are described under "Mail Merge" in Chapter 4.

Putting Together a Long-Term Merge Strategy

Although you can create a new data source for every merge you perform, the creation of this data source is the most time-consuming part of the merge operation. It's a good idea to take some additional time when you first create your data source to ensure that it is suited for future merge needs as well as current ones.

For example, if you are creating mailing labels for clients, you may think that you do not need to have phone numbers in the data source. Although it may save a few seconds not to have to enter them on each record, these numbers would be useful if you later need to create a customer contact list. If you have left them out of the data source records, you will later have to look up and add a phone number for each client, spending minutes rather than seconds on each record.

As you extend the scope of your merge goals to a longer time frame, have other users who work with the data review the contents of a planned data source. Explain the merge concept, and ask if they can think of any other information that would be useful to add.

TIP: *If you already have the data in another application's document, find out which of the application's features you can use to provide Word with a document containing the data you want merged.*

TIP: *When you create a main document for a merge, consider how you want the merge performed when one of the data fields is empty. You can use Word fields to create different merged results based on a field's contents or whether the field has any contents.*

Merge Documents Other Than Form Letters

Certainly, form letters are the most typical products of a merge operation, but Word can easily create other types of merge documents, as described here. Word will automatically adjust the page layout, depending on the type of document you select when creating your main document.

Envelopes

In a merge to print envelopes, Word will help you set up layout and print options specific to envelopes. You specify the envelope size and the font used for the return and sending addresses. You can even print a POSTNET delivery point bar code.

The steps for creating an envelope-type merge operation start with setting up the main document. You can create a new data source for the envelopes, but you will likely be using an existing one, such as the one you use for form letters. Here are the steps:

1. Select Tools|Mail Merge.

2. Under Main Document, select Create.

3. Select Envelopes.

4. Select Active Window or New Main Document.

TIP: *Active Window becomes Change Document Type if the current document is already a main document.*

5. In the Mail Merge Helper, select Get Data, and then open or create the data source. Word has many options for how to set up and get the data that the mail merge will use. These methods are detailed in Chapter 4 under "Mail Merge."

6. When Word prompts you, select Set Up Main Document. (Word will prompt you after you select a data source or finish entering data in the new data source.) The Envelope Options dialog box appears, which has two tabs: Envelope Options and Printing Options.

7. Select the Envelope Options tab, if necessary. On this tab, specify the following options about what Word will print on your envelopes:

TIP: *The options under the If Mailed in the USA heading are dimmed out because they are not currently available. You can enter the bar code options in the next dialog box, but not here.*

■ Select the size of envelope from the Envelope Size list box. If the size you want is not listed, select Custom Size, enter the height and width of the envelopes, and select OK.

■ To set the font for the addresses, select Font under Delivery Address or Font under Return Address.

■ To set the location of the addresses, enter measurements in the From Left or From Top text boxes under Delivery Address or the From Left or From Top text boxes under Return Address. The Default is Auto, which changes depending on the envelope size selected.

8. Select the Printing Options tab and specify any of the following options for how your envelopes will be printed:

   ■ Select one of the icons under Feed Method to designate how your printer will be fed the envelopes.

   ■ Select Face Up or Face Down to designate whether envelopes will be sent into the printer with the printing side up or down.

   ■ Select Clockwise Rotation if you want to reverse which edge of your envelope is fed into the printer first.

   ■ Select one of the options in the Feed From list box to specify where your printer will get the envelopes. The available sources depend on the printer you have selected.

9. Select OK when you have set all the needed envelope and printing options.

10. Using the Envelope Address dialog box options, enter the merge fields and text to use as the delivery address:

   a. Enter the address in the Sample Envelope Address box.

   b. Insert merge fields at the insertion point's location by selecting the Insert Merge Field button, and then the field name to insert.

   c. Add a postal bar code by selecting Insert Postal Bar Code. In this dialog box, choose the field containing the zip code in the Merge Field with ZIP Code drop-down list box, and the field containing the street address in the Merge Field with Street Address drop-down list box. Word will then include the delivery point postal bar code at the top of the address. This code can help your mail reach its destination faster. When you are finished with the Insert Postal Bar Code dialog box, select OK.

> **TIP:** *Select the FIM-A Courtesy Reply Mail check box to include a facing identification mark on your documents. This mark is often used with courtesy reply mail and can get you a discount from the Postal Service.*

11. When you are finished creating the address, select OK.

Using the options you have specified, Word sets up the main document, which appears behind the Mail Merge Helper dialog box. If you select Edit under Main Document and this document, or Close, Word removes the Mail Merge Helper dialog box so the document looks like Figure 7-12.

> **NOTE:** *You will see "Zip code not valid" where the bar code should appear, because you have not entered any real zip codes in this document; you have entered just the merge field for zip codes. This message will be replaced by the actual bar code when you start the merge.*

Mailing Labels

You can easily create mailing labels with the Mail Merge feature, using a variety of standard label formats. Once you define the format of a label and the type of label stock you want to use, the merge operation automatically arranges labels across and down the page. Follow these steps:

1. Select Tools|Mail Merge.

2. Under Main Document, select Create.

3. Select Mailing Labels.

4. Select Active Window or New Main Document.

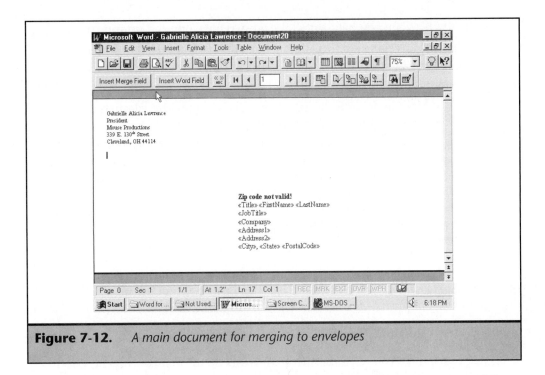

Figure 7-12. *A main document for merging to envelopes*

5. In the Mail Merge Helper, select <u>G</u>et Data, and then open or create the data source. Word has many options for how to set up and get the data that the mail merge will use. These methods are detailed in Chapter 4 under "Mail Merge."

6. When Word prompts you, select <u>S</u>et Up Main Document. (Word will prompt you after you select a data source or finish entering data in the new data source.)

7. The Label Options dialog box appears, where you choose options for your labels:

   a. Specify your printer: Dot <u>M</u>atrix or <u>L</u>aser. This determines which label formats are available. When you select <u>L</u>aser, specify the source of the labels in the <u>T</u>ray list box.

   b. From the Label <u>P</u>roducts list box, choose which set of label formats you need to select. These may include Avery Standard, Avery Pan-European, and Other, depending on what type of printer you have selected.

   c. In the Product <u>N</u>umber list box, choose the labels you are using. These selections are standard label layouts. For example, Avery's 5160 label format is used by many companies, so these labels can be used interchangeably. Your labels will be marked with the equivalent standard size, no matter who manufactured them.

d. If needed, select Details to open another dialog box and set other label options, such as the margins inside and outside the label boundaries. You can use the Details options to create custom-sized labels.

8. When all label options are specified, select OK, and Word displays the Create Labels dialog box.

a. Enter the address in the Sample Label box.

b. Insert merge fields at the insertion point's location, by selecting the Insert Merge Field button, then the field name to insert.

c. Add a postal bar code by selecting Insert Postal Bar Code. In this dialog box, choose the field containing the zip code in the Merge Field with ZIP Code drop-down list box, and the field containing the street address in the Merge Field with Street Address drop-down list box. Word will then include the delivery point postal bar code at the top of the address. This code can help your mail reach its destination faster. When you are finished with the Insert Postal Bar Code dialog box, select OK.

TIP: *Select the FIM-A Courtesy Reply Mail check box to include a facing identification mark on your documents. This mark is often used with courtesy reply mail and can get you a discount from the Postal Service.*

9. Select OK after entering the label text.

Using the options you have specified, Word sets up the main document, which appears behind the Mail Merge Helper dialog box. If you select Edit under Main Document and this document, or Close, Word removes the Mail Merge Helper dialog box so the document looks like Figure 7-13.

Catalogs

The Catalog option for the main document of a mail merge is like the Form Letter option, in that the document itself is not formatted in any way. In contrast to form letters, however, catalogs are not designed to create a series of individual documents; rather, they draw information from the data source together into one document. Each copy of the main document, instead of being separated by section breaks, is part of the same section, creating a single document. Instead of one record on each letter, envelope, or label, you want as many records as will fit on one page.

Since the only difference between form letters and catalogs is the final product of the merge, the steps to creating a catalog are identical to those or creating a form letter main document, except that you select Catalog from the Create list box under Main Document in the Mail Merge Helper. See "Mail Merge" in Chapter 4 for the steps to create a form letter merge.

The Catalog main document type is useful for creating documents such as product catalogs and lists, in which you want all of the information extracted from the data source and stored together.

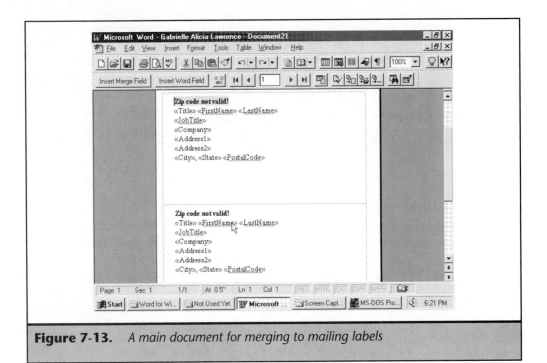

Figure 7-13.   *A main document for merging to mailing labels*

Combine the Catalog main document type with the Query Options, and select exactly the records you need to create lists of specific clients that you may want to call back or send correspondence to. For example, the merged document shown in Figure 7-14 was created using a very large database. The merge operation document selected only those customers who had not placed an order since 1994 and extracted only the information necessary for a salesperson to contact these companies. The main document used for this merge is shown in Figure 7-15; you can see that it is very much like the one you might create for a form letter.

REMEMBER: Query options are set by selecting Query Options from the Mail Merge Helper dialog box.

Utilizing the Full Potential of Word Fields

By now you are probably a pro at inserting merge fields from the data source into your main document. Now you will want to explore the Word fields to ensure that you are utilizing these fields, too. In this section, you will have an opportunity to take a closer look at these fields as well as explore some situations where they might be just what you need.

ABC Company		216\762-1212	
Contact:	Jane Nichols	*Last Order In:*	5/2/94
XYZ Company		216\762-4541	
Contact:	Sam Jones	*Last Order In:*	11/4/94
Maple Street Supply		216\790-7309	
Contact:	Jeffrey Fein	*Last Order In:*	12/1/94
Sam's Supply		216\983-4920	
Contact:	Susan Knettel	*Last Order In:*	10/3/94
Rimber & Associates		217\931-3985	
Contact:	George Forester	*Last Order In:*	9/6/94
March Inc.		216\783-3920	
Contact:	Kristin Estep	*Last Order In:*	9/4/94
Otlowski Company		216\392-9304	
Contact:	Darren Horan	*Last Order In:*	10/16/94
Elegil & Associates		216\943-9203	
Contact:	Isabella Wade	*Last Order In:*	9/28/94
Manzuk Supply		216\839-2034	
Contact:	Tobias Walters	*Last Order In:*	10/8/94
Matthew Company		217\983-3924	

Figure 7-14. *A document created by merging to a catalog main document*

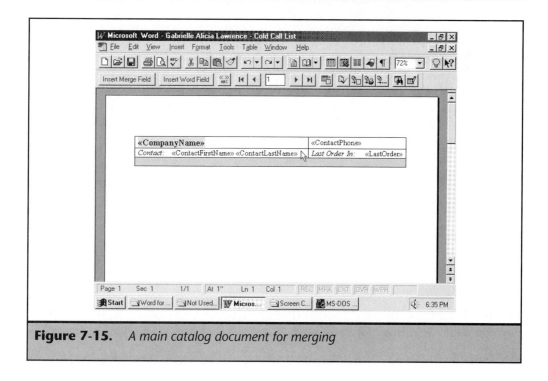

Figure 7-15. *A main catalog document for merging*

TIP: See "Mail Merge" and "Fields" in Chapter 4 for explanations of merging and the fundamentals of inserting and using Word fields.

Displaying Field Codes

How you edit merge fields depends on how they are displayed, so it is important to know about their display. You can choose to either display or hide field codes.

- When you hide field codes, merge field codes are displayed between chevrons, << >>, and you'll see only the name of the field that will be inserted. All other fields, such as those explained in the following sections, show their results. Some fields do not display results so they do not appear at all.

- When you display field codes, the fields appear in curly brackets. They begin with a field code, followed by the arguments or switches that create settings for the field. To display field codes, select Tools|Options and the View tab, and turn on the Field Codes check box option.

TIP: See "Fields" and "View Options" in Chapter 4 for more details on displaying field codes.

ASK

Use the ASK field when your main document requires information that needs to change for each merge but that cannot be saved in a data source.

When you merge a document containing an ASK field, a dialog box is displayed for this field, showing a prompt you have assigned. Users enter the response in the dialog box and select OK, and the text that is assigned to a bookmark. You can then use that data in an IF field to determine what happens next with the merge, or insert it into a document using another field.

A good use for ASK fields is to make a form letter seem less of a form. For example, form letters are often used by salespeople to contact clients about new offers or products. However, sales figures often improve when clients believe the letter is personally written to them. Using ASK, various names and other information can be inserted into these letters. Instead of using the title and last name of the client in the salutation and body of a letter, you use an ASK field to prompt for the correct way to refer to this person. Each salesperson can customize letters by using a nickname or other familiar term of address for clients with whom this is appropriate.

An ASK field for this purpose might read as follows:

```
{ASK Nickname "What is {MERGEFIELD FirstName}
{MERGEFIELD LastName}'s nickname, if you use one?"
\d {MERGEFIELD Title} {MERGEFIELD LastName}}
```

When the merge process encounters this ASK field, it prompts the user for the nickname of the client and assigns that nickname to the Nickname bookmark. Notice that the embedded merge fields in the prompt let the user know which client is being discussed. The default, when the user selects OK without entering a nickname, is to use the title and last name.

When you select ASK from the list box that appears when you click the Insert Word Field button in the Mail Merge toolbar, a dialog box appears where you can insert the bookmark name, prompt, default text, and whether you want to be prompted for this text only once for the entire merge.

TIP: *If you want to insert a merge field into a prompt used by an ASK field, add the ASK field as described above. Then edit the ASK field code and insert the merge field code. For example, after inserting the merge field into an ASK field code, your document may contain the code {ASK Numb_Encl "How many copies do you want to send to {MERGEFIELD Name}?" \D "1"}.*

To insert the text assigned to this bookmark, move to where you want the text in the main document, press CTRL+F9, and type the bookmark name.

FILLIN

The FILLIN field is similar to the ASK field because it prompts the user for input. However, where the ASK field assigns the text requested by a prompt to a bookmark, the FILLIN field inserts that text as the field result. Since it is not assigned a bookmark, the response text can only be used once in the merge document.

For example, Misty Rivers Boating uses the same response letter to all people who call and request a pamphlet about boating trips, and that letter is saved as read-only to prevent it from being altered. The information gathered by phone about the client goes into a data source, but each response letter must be personalized for the person who took the call. In the read-only main document, the code

```
{FILLIN "Who took these calls?" \d Misty Travel Boating \o}
```

appears for the signature line. The \o switch means the user (the company employee) is only prompted the first time that the document is merged, and all remaining documents in the merge use the same text entered initially. The \d switch provides the default text, to be used when no name is provided.

IF

Sometimes it seems that for every rule there are ten exceptions. Dealing with all the exceptions is made easier by the IF...THEN...ELSE merge field. Without this field, you would have to select subsets of records and perform separate merges with altered main documents. With the IF field, however, you can test for any condition in merge fields and provide text depending on the situation. You can also use other fields, such as INCLUDETEXT, to place text from another document into the merge document, depending on the condition test.

You can choose a variety of comparison operators for use in the If dialog box:

=	Equal
<>	Not equal
<	Less than
<=	Less than or equal to
>	Greater than
>=	Greater than or equal to
=""	Is blank
<>""	Is not blank

You can create simple or complex conditions within the IF statement. You can compare a merge field to a string or value or the contents of another merge field. The entire expression is displayed within brackets, and merge fields are enclosed in their own set of braces. Any strings are enclosed in quotation marks. Consider the following examples:

```
{IF {MERGEFIELD MiddleName} <> "" " " ""}

{IF {MERGEFIELD Thisyear} <= {MERGEFIELD Lastyear} "Your sales
performance is lower than last year. We would like to help you
improve your sales performance and income and have enrolled you
in the seminar, Doubling Your Sales Potential on Friday October
10 at 9 a.m.. You will receive more information in the next few
weeks." "Economic times have caused our overall sales to decrease
```

```
significantly. Since you have been able to exceed your sales level
from last year you should feel proud of your accomplishment."}
```

The first example tests if a field has an entry to decide whether to include a space to separate the field from the next one. The second example returns different text based on whether a current record's Thisyear field is greater or less than the Last year field value.

You can join conditions with "and" or "or." When conditions are joined with "and," all conditions must be met. To create an IF statement that requires a second condition, place another IF statement where you would normally enter text for the THEN, which is the text to use when the first IF statement is true. To create an IF statement in which text is used when *either* of two conditions is true, create a second IF statement where you would normally place the ELSE text, which is used when the IF statement is false. An IF statement requiring that both conditions be met might look like the following:

```
{IF {MERGEFIELD State} = "MD" {IF {MERGEFIELD City} = "Towson"
"We are having an open house in our Towson location we would
like you to attend from 8 a.m. to 5 p.m. on Tuesday, August 14."
""} ""}
```

Next Record

The NEXT field lets you use data from several records in one copy of the main document. When Word encounters the field in your Word document, it immediately advances to the next data record and uses that record for filling in merge fields in the main document. When you create mail merge documents for envelopes, labels, and catalogs, these documents include the NEXT field to tell Word to advance to the next record.

Next Record If

The NEXTIF field combines the features of the NEXT and IF fields. In response to NEXTIF, Word tests the condition just as if it were evaluating an IF field. However, instead of entering text depending on the result of this evaluation, Word does nothing if the evaluation is false, and moves to the next data record if it is true.

As with NEXT, you can use NEXTIF to create lists. The advantage here is that you can choose which lists you want to use by testing against some criteria. For example, you could create a list of your first 25 customers who ordered over $50,000 of goods last year. You can also create limits like this through the mail merge query options to select which records are potentially included from the data source.

MERGEREC and MERGESEQ

The MERGEREC field inserts the number of the current data record into your final merged document. The MERGESEQ field inserts the number of the current data record as a subset of the total data records. You can use these fields in other fields to control the merge or to label your documents.

MERGESEQ inserts a number that is different from what MERGEREC inserts only if you are using some of the data records in the data source. If you were to open the data source and count down the records, the number MERGEREC inserts is always the number of the data record. MERGESEQ inserts the number of the data record in the list of records used in this merge. In a merge that only includes data records from a specific zip code, for example, MERGEREC will leave gaps in the numbers of the records used, as in 1, 4, 7, 10, 14, 16, 20, 30, 39, 40, and so on. MERGESEQ, on the other hand, would use one run of numbers, for instance, from 1 to 10.

Set Bookmark

A bookmark is used as a variable within a merge document. You can place a value in a bookmark once and then use it throughout your merge document by placing the bookmark field within your document. For example, you might set the term of a loan to 30 years, and refer to the loan term in three locations within the main document. You would have a statement like this:

```
{SET Loanterm "30 years"}
```

When you need this value within the main document, you use the bookmark name. Just press CTRL+F9 and type the bookmark name.

Skip Record If

The SKIPIF field is used to skip records in your document, based on Word's evaluation of a comparative statement you include in this field. When SKIPIF is encountered in a merge, Word evaluates the statement. If it is false, Word ignores this field. If the statement is true, Word skips the current data record. SKIPIF is different from NEXTIF because the copy of the main document created for this data record is completely erased and a new copy is started for the next data record. Many times, you don't need SKIPIF—you can use query options to select which records you want merged.

You can use the SKIPIF field to help restrict your merge. For example, if you include the field

```
{SKIPIF zipcode <> 44302}
```

Word will only merge data records with a zip code field not equal to 44302.

Solving Merge Problems

Merge problems can be frustrating to solve, because there are several components involved in the merge operation. If you are having difficulty with a merge, check out the following sections—your problem may be here, and you can try the suggested solutions.

Printed Data Is Not Correct

If you find an address in your merged documents where you expect to see a name, the problem is in your data source document. If you used a table for the data entries, you may have placed the first and last name in the same column, putting the address in the last name column by mistake. This problem occurs most frequently with delimited data, where it is easy to forget to put in an extra delimiter when a field is empty.

The Field Names Print Instead of the Data

This problem occurs often for first-time users, since it is easy to accidentally type the field name you want rather than have Word insert it. The only way to insert fields is to have Word do it; you cannot type the field name even if you enclose what you type in curly braces or chevrons. You will need to return to the main document and replace the field names with field codes that insert the field names.

Blank Lines Appear in the Merged Document

The display of blank lines that represent a missing field can be turned on and off. To change the setting, select the Merge button in the Mail Merge Helper dialog box. Then check to be sure the Don't Print Blank Lines When Data Fields Are Empty option button is selected.

Labels or Envelopes Have Entries in the Wrong Location

You have probably chosen the wrong size for your labels or envelopes. Edit the document to have the setting you want.

You Get an Out of Memory Message

The first thing to do in this situation is try closing other applications and other unneeded Word windows. By reducing the operations that are using your computer's memory, you may free up enough to continue the merge. If the problem persists, you can use Query Options to select a subset of the data records and try the merge again. The last option is to check and see if you are using TrueType fonts. If so, try switching to built-in printer fonts, which require less memory.

Merge Does Not Produce All the Documents You Expect

Look in the Mail Merge Helper, and check to see if the message "Query Options have been set" is displayed under Merge Data with the Document. If it is, you have defined a selection criteria or specified that the records will be sorted. If you are not getting all of the records you expect, there is likely to be a mistake in the selection criteria. Select Query Options, and to make sure your criteria are correct.

Inserted Data Has the Wrong Font

The inserted data is probably using the font set by the Normal style, while the text in the main document has had its font changed. You can solve this problem by changing the font of the Normal style to match the font you set for the document.

Chapter Eight

Using Word in a Workgroup Environment

W ord has the features you need, whether you are working by yourself to complete a memo or collaborating with a group of people to produce a project report. In addition to typing text and formatting, which work the same on individual or collaborative projects, other Word for Windows features are designed especially for group projects.

Word provides complete support for network activities when your group is linked through a local area network (LAN). For example, you can place shared documents on the file server to allow group members to review and modify appropriate sections of the document. Windows 95 also allows file sharing to allow you to directly work with files on other workstations.

You can also interface directly with electronic mail (e-mail) systems to route documents to each member of your workgroup. Even when the various users are not on the same network, Word provides support for group efforts. Features that support large documents, such as master and subdocuments, annotations, and document revisions, can expedite shared contributions on a project even without the benefits of network connections. The ability to annotate documents and mark revisions lets you elicit the contributions of many group members and track the contributions of each. E-mail extends document routing capabilities to employees who are traveling, and to clients that are not on the network.

Workgroup Options

A *workgroup* is simply a group of people working together to complete a project. Thanks to the advantages of technology, workgroup members do not need to be in the same physical department or office to work together effectively. Individual workgroup participants can be selected for the set of skills they bring to the project—regardless of their location.

Workgroup members who work in the same office often have face-to-face meetings about a project before creating the Word documents they will ultimately share. With Word's workgroup features, they may be able to reduce the number of these meetings before completing all the work involved, because of the ease with which they can share their work in progress. Workgroup users may work in different locations and discuss the project by phone before going off to do their own part of the project. Notes can then be placed in the documents shared by these users, reducing the need to schedule meetings to discuss the project. This can be especially helpful when all of the participants are not in the same time zone or on the same working schedule. Sometimes the shared information in Word is the sole communication among workgroup members.

Workgroup members can share in the creation of information in Word documents, or data can be placed in templates by one individual and used by the others. Shared templates are a practical way to share forms for proposals, budget data, purchase orders, and in other areas where consistency is important.

Some Workgroup Scenarios

Each of the following scenarios describes workgroup activities in which Word's features make the task of completing collaborative projects easier.

Scenario #1

John works for a large manufacturing company, and he is collaborating with individuals in several departments on a competitive bid for a large government contract. All the workgroup members are connected by the same LAN, although they are members of three different Microsoft Mail post offices, as shown in Figure 8-1. After a meeting on the project and a discussion of the tight time schedule for the project, the four team members divided the proposal into several segments that need to be written. John agrees to create a master document on the network file server to provide the introductory information in the proposal. Each team member, including John, will write a separate section.

John creates an outline for the proposal and has Word create a subdocument for each level-one heading in the outline. This lets each person work on a subdocument component and still allows John to access the master document to review the subdocuments—all of which use the same formatting and styles John has placed in the master document. When the subdocuments are complete, John will work with the master document in Normal view, making the final formatting and reorganizing changes. Workgroup members can also route messages to one another using Microsoft Mail, even though they use different post offices. (Microsoft Mail allows you to establish a global address list with entries in address books for both local and remote Microsoft Mail users.) With the efficient use of Word, the company is able to meet the deadline for the project.

Scenario #2

A large publishing company needs to update a best-selling book within a short time frame without compromising the quality of the final product. The author is asked to use revision marks within Word to the mark the changes in each chapter. This document is zipped to achieve a compressed format and is then routed electronically to a technical reviewer. The technical reviewer checks the accuracy of the chapter, with special attention paid to the updated material—using as guidance the revision marks noting changes—before routing the document to the publisher's copy editor. The copy editor checks the material for grammatical accuracy. Figure 8-2 provides an overview of the connections. By focusing special attention on the manuscript revisions, the publisher is able to meet a tight deadline. The revision marks also make it easy to track changes throughout the process and to consult with the author before finalizing each chapter.

Scenario #3

Several consultants who live in different cities are pooling their talents to provide training for a Fortune 500 company on the use of Microsoft Access. They develop their

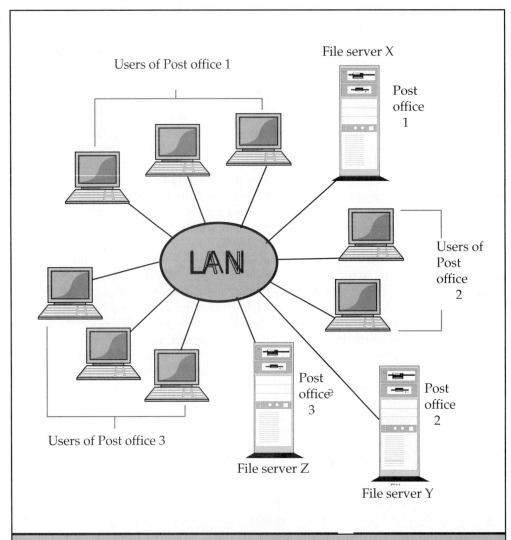

Figure 8-1. *A local workgroup can access Word documents on the network as well as route electronic mail messages*

training materials with Word and share documents in process, with revision marks, eventually developing the final version of the training materials. Once the training sessions start, each consultant works with several instructors to complete the training in a timely manner. They have developed a template for the instructors' billings; a second template is used for client-reimbursable travel and living expenses during the training. Despite the remote locations of the consultants, with the help of Word they are able to present a consistent, professional image in both the delivered material and

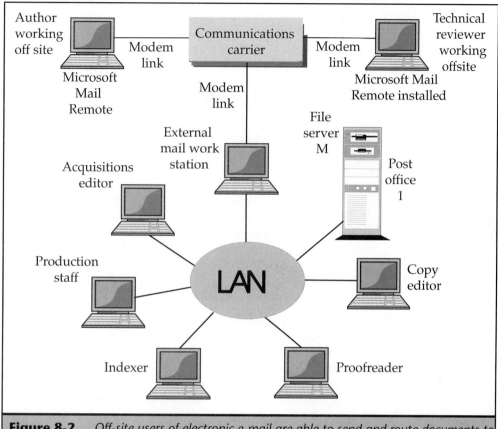

Figure 8-2. *Off-site users of electronic e-mail are able to send and route documents to the publishing company's staff on the LAN*

the billing data. Because their client has Word for Windows and electronic mail installed on a network, all concerned parties are able to utilize electronic mail to maintain communication with instructors during the on-site teaching.

Network Options

Most of what users do with Word on a network is no different from what users do with Word on a stand-alone PC. Documents are created and revised in the same way. The differences are in the way Word is installed and the fact that documents are often stored on the network file server rather than the hard disks built into individual PCs. The central storage capability makes sharing documents easier.

NOTE: *Whether or not you are a network user, you will be able to use the Word commands discussed throughout this book. The rest of this section, however, focuses on some of the tasks and features of special interest to users on a network.*

Routing Documents to Network Users

You can use electronic mail to route a document to a group of users, either to one user after another or to all at once. When the setting for Mail as Attachment, under the General tab in Tools | Options, is checked, Word uses the current document as an attachment to your e-mail transmission. Otherwise, when you select Send from Word's File menu, Word assumes the current document should be an e-mail message.

E-mail has become very popular, because it eliminates the telephone tag games that often occur when busy people are trying to communicate. If e-mail seems a little impersonal to you, consider spicing up your messages with emoters; a few examples are shown in the box "Adding Emotional Impact to Your E-mail Messages."

Adding Emotional Impact to Your E-mail Messages

With the increased use of e-mail in corporations, symbols have been invented for adding to the end of e-mail messages, to give a personal touch to these messages. The word *emoters* was coined to refer to these symbols. It is a bit easier to interpret these emoters if you turn your head to the side as you look at them. Many of them are already AutoCorrect entries to automatically convert the characters into symbols. Here are a few to get you started, but feel free to create your own:

Emoter	Meaning
:-)	Smiley face
:-(	Frowning face
;-)	Winking face
(:-&	Angry face
|-)	Sleepyhead
=:-)	Punk rocker
=|:-)>	Uncle Sam
:-X	Kissey face
@>-->--	A rose

After creating and saving a Word document for routing, follow these steps to add a routing slip for sending the document to multiple users:

1. Choose Add Routing Slip from the File menu.
2. Click the Address button, and then select the names of all the users to whom you want to route the document.
3. Choose Add, and select OK.
4. Select the desired routing method: One After Another or All at Once.
5. Select the Route button to send the document.

Users will be able to review the document and then use annotations, revision marks, or normal editing features to make their changes. The first two methods are preferred, because they maintain the integrity of the original document. Recipients use the Send command on the File menu in Microsoft Mail when they are ready to send the document back.

Using Word's Protection Features

When you are working on a network, you will have access to all the file-protection features of the network. In addition, Word's file-locking capability prevents conflicting changes from being made to a document, yet allows more than one user to read a document at the same time. When you open a document, other users who attempt to open the same document will be informed that it is in use. They can open the document as read-only, but they cannot save the document using the same name. You can also choose to open documents as read-only. If you open a document as read-only and decide you want to save your changes, you will need to choose File|Save As and specify a different document name.

Word's Support of Local and Remote Workgroup Activities

Some Word features are available whether you are working with a group of local network users or with individuals to whom you mail or hand-deliver documents. These features make it easy to solicit the input of all group members and to have each member involved in the final product. For example, you can turn on Word's revision marks feature so that each user's changes to a shared document will be marked, as described under "Comparing Versions" in Chapter 4. With the annotations feature, the user can make comments without altering the document. To work more efficiently with long documents, you will want to consider the use of Word's master document feature.

Several of Word's features are mentioned in this section's overview of features that support workgroups. You will find detailed explanations of these features in Chapter 4.

Revision Marks

Revision marks allow each user in a group to review a document and make alterations. Both newly added text and text to be deleted will be marked in the document, with underlines or other marks, distinct from the other text. The project leader or other individual who is in charge of the report can then elect to accept revision marks or to delete them.

See "Comparing Versions" in Chapter 4 for an explanation of these procedures.

To begin recording revision marks in an existing document, follow these steps:

1. Select File|Open and open the document you want to revise.
2. Select Tools|Revisions.
3. Select Mark Revisions While Editing under Document Revisions.
4. Select OK.

Another way to turn on the mark revisions feature is to double-click MRK in the status bar. Word displays each reviewer's revisions in a different color, which makes it easier to determine whose revisions you are reading after you have circulated the document to several people for their input.

TIP: *If someone makes revisions without turning on the revision marks feature, you can still identify changes that were made by using the document compare feature. To use this feature, select the Compare Versions button in the Revisions dialog box.*

You can accept or reject revisions all at once, or you can use the Review Revisions feature to look at each revision and make an individual decision. Figure 8-3 shows a document with this dialog box active (choose Tools|Revisions and select Review). Word can distinguish 16 different reviewers with the use of different colors before it begins reusing the colors again. In Figure 8-3, you cannot see that the underlined text is shown in a different color, but the color difference is visible on your monitor. All of Elizabeth Reinhardt's revisions will be displayed in blue.

See "Revision Marks" in Chapter 4 for additional information on using the revision marks feature. You can also protect revisions and annotations, as discussed in "Annotations" in Chapter 4.

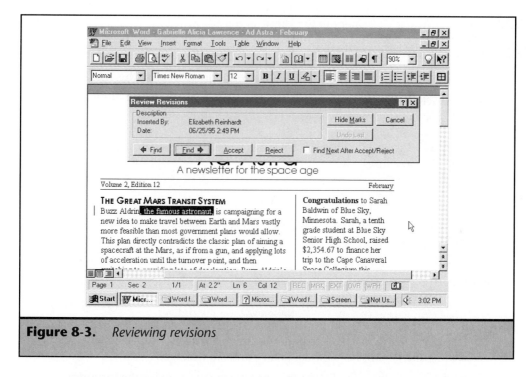

Figure 8-3.   *Reviewing revisions*

Master Documents and Subdocuments

If you need to work with long documents, the Word for Windows *master document* feature offers excellent organizing capabilities. A master document is nothing more than a sequence of *subdocuments* that divide the long document into manageable segments. The special Master Document view gives you an outline-style overview of the document, or you can use Normal view to show the detail in the subdocuments. You can also work in an individual subdocument.

Master documents let you move quickly from one section of a long document to another. It is also easy to restructure the document by moving the various subdocument sections to new locations within the master document. You can create a master document as large as 32MB, with as many as 80 subdocuments.

You will also find that it is much easier to create references from master documents. Indexes, tables of authorities, and cross-references are all maintained in the master document for the entire document. It is also easier to keep track of all the subdocuments; since you create them directly from headings within the master document, you do not have to scan the file server looking for all the pieces.

Creating a New Master Document

Creating a new master document is easy. All you need to do is open a new document in Word and follow these steps:

1. Select Master Document in the View menu.

2. Type the master document using headings in place of each subdocument you will want to insert. You can create all the subdocuments at once if they use the same heading level in the master document and you select this level first.

3. Select the first heading that is to become a subdocument, and all the entries between it and the last heading to become a subdocument.

REMEMBER: All headings in this selection that start each subdocument must be at the same level.

4. Select the Create Subdocument button from the Master Document toolbar; it looks like this:

In Figure 8-4, the master document is Green Earth. You can see the subdocument icons beside the History and Advantages headings.

5. Select Save As from the File menu, and enter the name for the master document.

Working in Master and Subdocuments

You can work in either the master document or subdocuments. Most often, you will work in each subdocument to complete it. You might then return to working in the master document for tasks such as reorganization. Normally the work of setting up and finalizing the master document's organization is the responsibility of one individual, even though the subdocuments might be divided among the members of the workgroup.

To work in a subdocument, use the File|Open command just as you would with any other document. Make any editing changes you want, and print the subdocument as needed.

If you decide you need to rename or move a subdocument, do so after opening the master document. Use the Master Document view for reorganizing the structure or opening a subdocument. Use the Normal view when you want to make detailed changes within subdocuments. Double-click the icon for the subdocument you need to rename, choose Save As from the File menu, type a new name, and close the subdocument. To move the subdocument to a new position in the master document, click its icon and drag it to a new location.

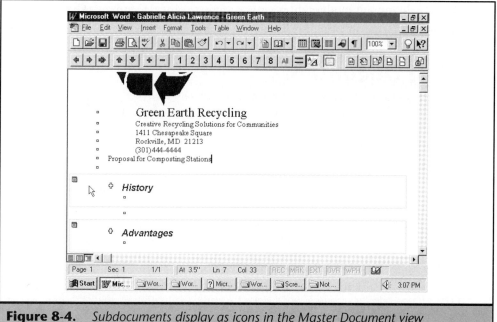

Figure 8-4.   *Subdocuments display as icons in the Master Document view*

To move passages of text or graphics among subdocuments, you will need to have the master document open in Normal view. You can then proceed to make changes just as you would in any other document.

CAUTION: Never rename or delete subdocuments using Windows commands. Because of the links from the subdocuments to the master document, this approach will cause problems the next time you attempt to open the master document. Subdocument naming and deletion must always be accomplished from within the master document.

See "Master Documents" in Chapter 4.

Special File-Locking Features for Network Users

If you are sharing a master document with other network users, you will want to utilize Word's file-locking features. Although anyone can unlock any subdocument for use, Word automatically opens subdocuments for read-write access only by their creator, and it restricts other users to read-only access. The Unlock Document button on the Master Document toolbar allows you to unlock other documents that you must update. You also have the option of adding a password or other file-protection capabilities.

Annotating Documents

Earlier in this chapter, you read about how multiple users can revise a document and keep track of changes using revision marks. When you need to enter comments about a document without actually making any changes to it, use Word's *annotations* feature. You can attach annotations to any selected text, perhaps to note that a passage is unclear, to suggest a specific revision, or to indicate disagreement with a particular point. Each annotation is numbered and shows the initials of the person who created it.

Annotations are a better choice than revision marks when you are seeking the comments of others, whereas revision marks might be more appropriate when a group has joint responsibilities for the creation of a report or proposal.

To annotate a document, follow these steps:

1. Move to the location in the document where you want to insert an annotation.

 TIP: *If you select a section of text before inserting an annotation, that text will automatically be selected when someone views or goes to that annotation. This helps the reader of the annotations to easily refer to the text about which you are commenting.*

2. Select Insert|Annotation to insert the annotation mark and open the Annotations pane.

3. Type the text of your comment, as shown in Figure 8-5.

4. Close the Annotations pane, by clicking Close or pressing ALT+SHIFT+C.

   If you prefer, you can switch back to the document window without closing the Annotations pane by clicking on the document text or by pressing F6. To return again to the open Annotations pane, click on it, or press F6.

5. When you are done making annotations, save the annotated document; if appropriate, you can then route it to another user for additional review and comments.

When you want to review all the annotations in a document or focus on the input of a single reviewer, select View|Annotations. The default choice is All Reviewers, but you can specify the name of a specific reviewer if you want. Select the Close button when you are finished reviewing the annotations. Another way to review annotations is to use the Go To option in the Edit menu to locate an annotation. Select Annotation and the reviewer's name if you are looking for a particular reviewer's comment, and select Next until you locate the comment you are looking for.

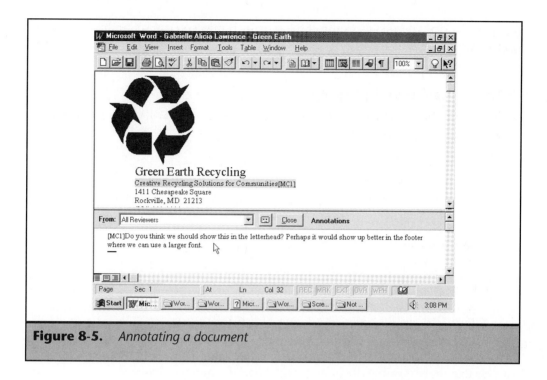

Figure 8-5.   *Annotating a document*

 READY *Chapter 4 provides specific information on topics such as creating and reviewing audio* **for** *annotations, editing annotations, deleting annotations, and printing annotations (see* **MORE** *"Annotations"). If you have circulated several copies of a document and want to merge annotations and revisions, see also "Comparing Versions" in Chapter 4 for more information.*

Templates

A *template* is a model for the creation of documents; use a template when you want to have consistent-looking documents created by several members of a workgroup. Templates can provide preset formats, graphics, styles, macros, customized settings, and AutoText entries. Word provides templates for many common types of documents, but you can create your own or modify existing ones to improve productivity as well as consistency.

What Templates Offer

In most manufacturing operations, a mold or template is used to create parts that are needed to complete the items being produced. Using the mold ensures uniformity and is much faster than fashioning each piece by hand. The same is true for documents created with Word templates. Some of the specific things you can set up in a template are listed here:

- Document margins
- A specialized header or footer
- A customized toolbar, containing buttons needed for the tasks in the document
- Macros
- A letter closing, or letterhead with a logo
- Columns with graphics in specific locations
- Custom styles for level-one and level-two headings or other elements
- Special keyboard settings
- AutoText entries

Using or Modifying Existing Word Templates

Every time you open a new document without selecting a specific template, the document will automatically use Word's Normal template. If you create macros and styles while using this template, they will be available in all documents using the template. This general-purpose template can be used to create a short report or menu, but you may find that some of the specialized templates have special settings or features that make creating documents with special requirements easier.

To use an existing template, select File|New, select the Document option button, and then choose a template from the Template box and select OK. If the template uses a Word wizard, a series of dialog boxes will prompt you for the information needed to complete the document. Otherwise, the template will be available for entries directly in the document editing window. You can make your entries and save the document under any name you wish.

You might find a Word template that comes close to meeting your needs—but wish you could change a few features. This is easy to do. Just retrieve the document template, make your changes, and save the template again. If you want to keep the original template available, be sure to save the modified one with the File|Save As command and specify a new name. Follow these steps to retrieve and modify an existing template:

1. Choose Open from the File menu.
2. Select Document Templates from the Files of Type drop-down list box.
3. From the Look In list box, choose the folder for the templates.

   In the default Word installation, the templates are in the Templates folder in the folder where you installed Word. If you have changed the location for the templates, you will need to revise the folder name accordingly.

4. Select the name of the template from the File Name list box and select Open.

5. Make your modifications to the template, adding formatting, creating macros, adding text, or otherwise customizing the template.

6. Select File|Save As and type a new name for the template before pressing ENTER.

Figure 8-6 shows the Emprl03 template provided by Word, saved as Smith - Thanks But No Position and with modifications made to the company name and address, as well as the letter closing. Making this change in the template will save time for Mr. Smith's secretary, who will then not need to make these modifications when using the template to create future letters. Some templates have macros attached to them that create dialog boxes and step the user through needed responses. Others, such as the one in Figure 8-6, require the user to select each variable item and type new text to replace it.

 NOTE: *The Options dialog box, opened by selecting Tools|Options, contains the File Locations tab where you specify a location for both User Templates and Workgroup Templates.*

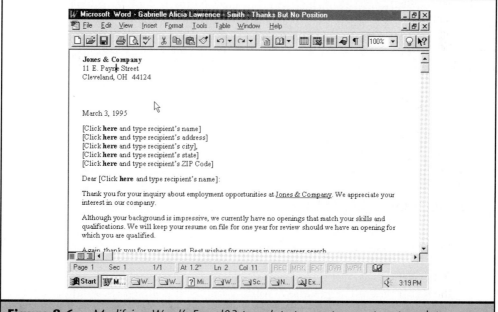

Figure 8-6. *Modifying Word's Emprl03 template to create a custom template*

Creating Your Own Word Templates

You may have a newsletter heading or a proposal outline that you feel would make a good template. To create a template from the current document, all you need to do is select File|Save As, type a name for the template, and select Document Template in the Save as Type text box. Select the folder where you want the template saved. Choose the Templates folder to have the template appear on the General tab, or select a folder within the Templates folder to have the template appear on the same tab name as the folder where you save the template. Select OK, and Word will save the document as a document template. When you select File|New, the template appears on one of the tabs if the template has been saved in the Templates folder or in one of the folders within the Templates folder.

Routing Documents with Microsoft Mail

You can route documents among network users and remote users who have a copy of Microsoft Mail Remote installed on their machines. For more information on routing a document with Microsoft Mail, see the discussion under "Network Options" earlier in this chapter.

Binder

Microsoft Office includes a Microsoft Binder application, which you can take advantage of when you are working on a group of documents. This application combines documents from multiple applications into a larger document. The purpose of a binder is to group documents according to function. This means that as you are working on a proposal, you can put all of your documents together into a binder regardless of whether you work on the documents in Word, Excel, PowerPoint, or another Microsoft Office application. Figure 8-7 shows a binder that includes Word documents along with documents using other applications.

You can switch between documents in the binder by clicking the document icon in the Binder pane on the left. As you change documents, you may also be changing the application you use to work with the document. While you work in each document, you are working with the application that creates that document. The document that you see in Figure 8-7 is using Word; the menu bar, toolbars, and other screen features are Word's. You will also notice that the File and Help menus have changed. Other than that, working with the Word document in a binder is the same as working with the Word document when it is not part of a binder.

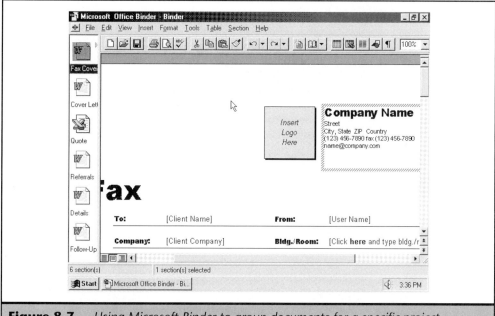

Figure 8-7.   *Using Microsoft Binder to group documents for a specific project*

When you share a binder with your coworkers, each person copies the binder to their local briefcase. Before and after you modify documents in a binder, you want to go to your Briefcase icon and select Briefcase|Update All. This command updates the documents in the binder on your local copy as well as updating the network's copy with changes that you have made in your version.

Chapter Nine

Using the Internet Assistant with Word

The Internet Assistant was first introduced in January 1995 to help Word users create documents that could be used as pages on the World Wide Web. If you have a connection to the Internet, the Internet Assistant can also serve as a browser, allowing you to navigate the many Web pages stored at locations around the world. You can obtain a copy of the Internet Assistant from Microsoft's World Wide Web site (www.microsoft.com) if you have a connectin to the Internet. The only version of the Internet Assistant available at the time of this writing is compativle with Word 6 for Windows. This version has been used throughout this chapter. It is likely that the new Internet Assistant for Word will function in an identical fashion to this release.

Even if you don't have an Internet connection from the system on which you use Word, you can still use the Internet Assistant to create Web pages. It allows you to add the cumbersome HTML (Hypertext Markup Language) codes used with Web pages directly from Word's style capabilities. The Web documents you create are simply coded with styles. They remain in their same readable state unless you decide that you want to see the actual HTML codes and perform a few extra steps.

TIP: *If you want to get connected to the Internet, you have lots of options, including the Microsoft Network and other services such as NetCom, Prodigy, and Delphi.*

This chapter introduces you to the basic options needed to create Web pages from within Word. It also explains some of the basic features of Web and the special codes needed to create Web documents. It is not designed to provide a complete set of information about the Web or HTML codes. For additional information, consult a comprehensive guide to the Internet, such as Osborne's *The Internet Complete Reference* (Osborne McGraw-Hill, 1994).

World Wide Web

The World Wide Web is the newest resource for accessing the Internet. It has experienced phenomenal interest and growth. It is the first Internet resource that allows users to make their way through a series of interconnected pages. These pages can be stored on the same computer as the original page or any other computer at locations around the world. Information on a page that provides a link to another document is highlighted. Once this highlighted area is clicked, the user is presented the information on the new page. This a quite a deviation from the beginning-to-end progression that other Internet resources allow, since you can develop your own path through available information based on entries that trigger your interest. This capability of marking text and attaching a link to a new page is called *hypertext*. The related capability supported by the Web allowing links to graphics, audio, and video clips is known as *hypermedia,* making the Web an exciting environment for both education and business.

To give text the attributes that allow effective presentation on the computer screen and links to other pages of information, a special coding language known as HTML is used. The special codes can be added to documents by typing the codes, creating your own styles or macros to add them, or using the Internet Assistant. After learning a little more about HTML codes in the next section, you will learn that the Internet Assistant is the easiest and quickest approach to creating Web pages. The browsers that are used to view Web pages interpret the HTML codes and effect the display or linkage capabilities you want to use. Figure 9-1 shows a simple Web page that offers a graphic image and links to various options. You will notice that you only see the effect of the codes and not any special codes when you use a browser to look at a Web page.

HTML Codes

HTML stands for the Hypertext Markup Language. This language is continuing to undergo change to offer more sophisticated options to the creators of Web pages. Although there is no complete uniformity in the codes that various browsers can handle, most of the newer versions can support the text and graphics coding discussed in this chapter. The codes that make up the HTML language can be divided into groups based on their function: page structure and character formatting, hypertext links, and graphics. Taking a brief look at what the HTML codes look like will give you a better appreciation for what the Internet Assistant can do for you as

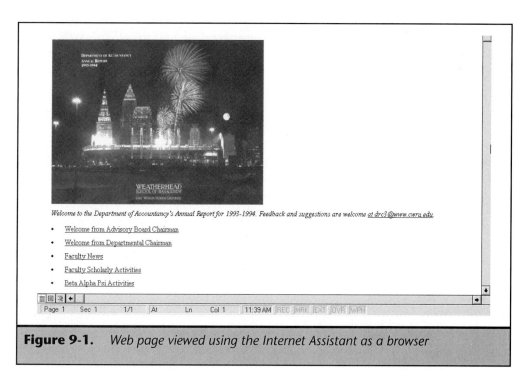

Figure 9-1. *Web page viewed using the Internet Assistant as a browser*

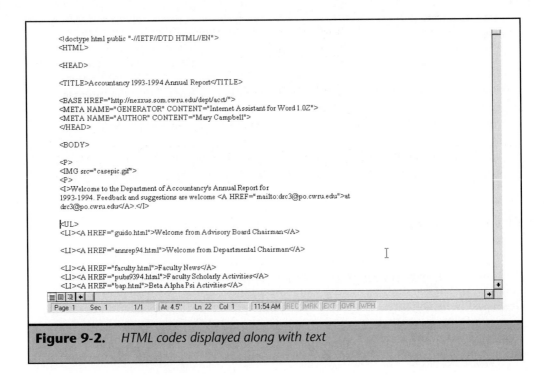

Figure 9-2.   *HTML codes displayed along with text*

well as indicate the importance of making the correct selections to get your Web pages to look and act as you want them to. Figure 9-2 shows part of the file used to create the Web page shown in Figure 9-1, including the HTML codes for inserting the graphic image and other features.

Page Structure and Character Formatting

Page structure and character formatting codes are used to define the structure and appearance of a page as well as to indicate to the browser displaying the page that it contains HTML codes. The commands are typically entered in all uppercase characters and are enclosed in angle brackets <> to distinguish them from surrounding text. For most commands in this category, they begin where inserted and end at the location where a second command appears. The end code repeats the original command preceded by a forward slash (/). For example, the command for a title for the current World Wide Web page is <TITLE>. This command ends with an entry of </TITLE> as shown here:

```
<TITLE>Favorite Web Sites</TITLE>
```

Table 9-1 shows some of the other popular codes in this category.

Code	Effect
<HTML>	Indicates the beginning of an HTML file
<H1>	Indicates the beginning of a level-one heading
<P>	Indicates the end of a paragraph
<UL>	Begins an unordered (bulleted) list
<U>	Indicates the beginning of underlined text

Table 9-1. *Page Layout and Character Formatting Codes*

Hypertext Links

The HTML codes for hypertext links are a little different than the previous category of codes, since the linking options supported offer more variations. They use anchors to describe the text that appears and the link that it attaches to when selected. The command used for anchors is <A> but there are many different parameters that can be used to indicate the type of link established.

If you want to link to a location on the current Web page, you must first use an anchor command to name that location on the page. An entry something like this will appear:

```
<A NAME=here>Names the current location "here"</A>
```

At the location on the page that can be clicked to jump to the location "here" you might see an HTML command like this:

```
<A HREF="#here">Click this text to jump to "here"</A>
```

Anchors are also used to jump to documents at any other location on the Web. To create this type of anchor, a URL (Uniform Resource Locator) is needed to specify the exact location of the page you want to jump to. As you look at Web pages, you might see an entry something like this to indicate this type of jump:

```
<A HREF="http://www.cwru.edu/acctrept/activity/faculty.htm">Click here to see
faculty activities</A>
```

Graphics

One of the glamorous aspects of Web pages is the ability to display graphics. HTML codes let you add inline or external graphics to a Web page. An inline graphic will display automatically if the user's browser supports graphics. External graphics are added with the <A> link option discussed earlier and display only when the user clicks the text or graphic representing the link.

Inline graphics are embedded images of graphic images that are normally in a JPEG or GIF format. The following entry will display the file STUDENT.GIF at the location of the code:

```
<IMG SRC = "student.gif">
```

TIP: *GIF is a better format than JPEG, as a larger number of browsers can display these images.*

You can use the ALT parameter with the command if you want to display text in the event that the user's browser does not support graphics. The HTML command might look like this:

```
<IMG SRC = "student.gif" ALT="Picture of student receiving award">
```

Using the Internet Assistant to Create Web Pages

Now that you have seen how cumbersome HTML codes can be, you will appreciate the time savings offered by the Internet Assistant. You can focus on how you want your Web pages to look and forget about the required coding. All you need to do is select the button, style, or menu option that gives your text and graphics the features you want, and the Internet Assistant adds the necessary codes behind the scenes. You can type new text as you do this or add the needed styles to an existing document to make it available for Web use. You can save a Web document and then reopen it to look at the codes (if you feel you must see them), or you can just test out your document and its links without ever seeing the codes. You can create informational pages, with as many links as you need, or you can create forms, which return data to you from those looking at your Web materials.

Starting the Internet Assistant

Once the Internet Assistant is installed on your system, all you need to do is select File | Browse Web to start it. You will see the informational page shown in Figure 9-3 when you first start it. You can use this page for links to information on creating Web pages or to look at the more detailed Internet Assistant for Word Help, which is added to the Help menu once you start the Internet Assistant. You can switch between HTML Edit and Web Browse using the View menu to give you the needed toolbar buttons to facilitate visiting Web sites or creating new Web documents. The HTML edit toolbar looks like this:

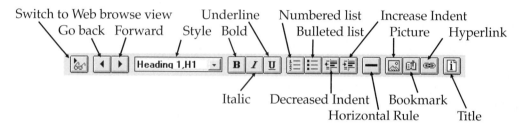

This toolbar lets you add the necessary styles to create a Web page.
If you choose View | Web Browse this toolbar will display:

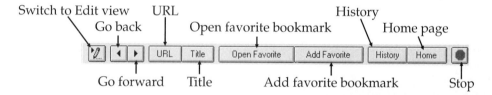

This toolbar provides buttons that let you look at documents at other Web sites if you have an Internet connection.

Creating a New Web Document

Once you start the Internet Assistant, you will have access to the toolbar options that make creating a Web file quite easy. To start a new Web document, just follow these steps:

1. Select File | New.
2. Select HTML for the Template, then select OK.
3. Create all your entries.

Since the HTML.DOT template is attached, the Internet Assistant limits editing selections to valid HTML options and provides easy-to-use buttons for tasks, such as creating a hyperlink.

4. Select File | Save and choose HyperText Markup Language (HTML) for the Save File As Type.

5. Type a name for the file in the File Name box and select OK.

TIP: *If you are already an HTML pro, you might find it easier to type certain codes yourself. Press CTRL+SHIFT+S, type your HTML code, and press ENTER..*

Converting a Word Document for Use on the Web

You can convert existing word documents into an HTML document for the Web. This means you can take an annual report or other document and quickly extract sections that will allow you to share highlights with Internet users with a minimum time investment. Word features that are not a part of the HTML options provided by the Internet Assistant's HTML editing features will be lost. These include options such as annotations, borders, captions, character formatting such as font selection, footnotes, headers, indented paragraph styles, page breaks, revision marks, and Table of Contents

Figure 9-3. *Initial informational screen when the Internet Assistant is started*

and Index entries. You can still keep your original document and use it for other applications, so you don't need to worry about losing all the formatting and special options in the original document if you save the Web file under a different name.

To convert an existing document to an HTML document for the Web, follow these steps:

1. Select File | Open.

2. Select the file you want to open, and select OK.

3. Select File | Save As.

4. Select HyperText Markup Language (HTML) from the Save File As Type box.

5. Type the name for the file in the File Name box with an .HTM extension and select OK.

NOTE: If the Internet Assistant was not active before starting these steps, it will automatically be started for you and the document will be displayed with the HTML Edit toolbar active.

Word Styles and Commands for Adding HTML Codes to a Web Document

Even if you are experienced with HTML codes, the Internet Assistant can be a big help. Commands such as <HEAD> and <BODY> are automatically added by the converter without your having to remember to add anything. Also, for commands you request such as a link, all the syntax details are handled by the Internet Assistant. It adds symbols such as <, &, ", and > in the correct location. Table 9-2 shows some of the most popular HTML tags, how they are added to Web documents, and the type of effect that they have on the document. You can use menu commands, toolbar buttons, and styles to add the needed HTML codes and yet never see them if you don't want to get bogged down with the details.

There are two basic approaches that you can use for creating your Web document. You can type the text and go back and add styles and other options once the focus on content is complete, or you can add these options as you go along.

We will look at some of the entries used to create a Web page with some of the authors' favorite Web sites listed. The text to indicate the authors favorite Web sites was entered first. This information is descriptive and will allow the reader of the Web page to locate topics of interest. The label for each category of entries was selected and an appropriate heading level was assigned. To keep text for each group of favorite site headings the same size, it is appropriate to choose the same level for each of these headings. Text indicating the name of the site can serve as a hyperlink to the URL that connects the user with this site. After selecting one of these hypertext entries, a style for hypertext was selected from the style box, as shown in Figure 9-4. You can select

HTML 2.0 Tag	Word Button or Action to Add the Code	Description of Code
`<A>`		Hyperlink with type of link defined by dialog box options
`<A HREF=...>`	or select Insert | Hyperlink then select URL	Links to a Web page at a remote location
`<A HREF="#...>`	or select Insert | Hyperlink then select Bookmark	Links to a local document
`<A NAME=...>`		Creates an anchor address from a bookmark
`<ADDRESS>`	Address style	Paragraph style
`<B>`	**B**	Turns on bold or encloses selected text between `<B>` and `</B>`. Must be turned off by repeating the command
`<BLOCKQUOTE>`	Block quote style	Paragraph style
`<BODY>`	Automatically added by the Internet Assistant	Indicates the beginning of the body of the page. Ends with `<?BODY>`, which is also added automatically
` `	SHIFT+ENTER	Adds a line break
`<CITE>`	Cite style	Character format
`<CODE>`	Code style	Character format
`<DFN>`	Definition style	Character format
`<DIR>`	Directory list style	Paragraph format
`<DL>`	Definition list style	Paragraph format

Table 9-2. *HTML Codes*

<DL COMPACT>	Definition compact style	Paragraph format
<DT>...<DD>	Definition term style	Character format
<EM>	Emphasis style	Character format
<FORM>	Insert I Form field	Used in creating a form
<H1>, <H2>, ... <H6>	Heading 1....Heading 6 styles	Paragraph format
<HEAD>	Automatically added by the Internet Assistant	Indicates the head area within the Web document
<HR>		Inserts a horizontal rule
<HTML>	Automatically added by the Internet Assistant	Indicates the file is an HTML document
<I>		Formats as italics
<IMG>		Allows you to add a graphic
<INPUT NAME=...>		Adds a text input box to a form
<INPUT TYPE-"CHECKBOX" NAME=...>		Adds a check box to a form
<KBD>	Keyboard style	Character style
<LI>	Automatically added by the Internet Assistant when you mark items as part of a list	Indicates the beginning of a numbered or bulleted list. Ends with </LI>, which is also inserted automatically
<MENU>	Menu style	Paragraph style
<META>	File I HTML Document Info I Advanced	Allows you to add advanced HTML codes yourself
<OL>		Paragraph style used to create a numbered list

Table 9-2.   *HTML Codes* (continued)

the Hyperlink button to display a Hyperlink dialog box that lets you define the location of the document you are linking to. The tab chosen defines the type of link you are creating. Since all of the favorite Web sites are at remote locations this is a link to a remote URL rather than a bookmark or local file. The tab shown in Figure 9-5 to link to a URL is selected since this is used for a remote site link. The selected text appears as the hypertext entry, a URL address is either typed or selected from the list, and OK is selected to finalize the entry. The text on the page will appear underlined and in a contrasting color when viewed from most browsers. Each hypertext entry is entered, and a similar process is used to provide links to each of the favorite sites. At no time is it necessary to worry about the correct syntax for the links, as the Internet Assistant enters everything for you. Be sure to save the newly created document as an HTML file when you are finished.

<P>	Normal style	Paragraph style for a Normal style; has <P> at the end of each paragraph
<PRE>	Preformatted style	Paragraph style
<PRE WIDTH=...>	Preformatted—wide style	Paragraph style
<SAMP>	Sample style	Character style
<SELECT NAME="Dropdown1" ...>		Adds a drop-down field to a form
<STRIKE>	Strikethrough style	Character style
<STRONG>	Strong style	Character style
<TITLE>	or added automatically; uses the first text entered	Defines the title for the Web page
<TT>	Typewriter style	Character style
<U>		Character style
<UL>		Paragraph style for a bulleted list
<VAR>	Variable style	Character style

Table 9-2. *HTML Codes* (continued)

Viewing the HTML Codes in a Web Document

Most people will feel that ignorance is bliss and will avoid looking at all the behind-the-scenes HTML codes. Those who have already mastered the language might want to make their own little tweaks to the coding and will have a need to see the HTML source. Follow these steps to take a look:

1. Select File | Save As then select HyperText Markup Language (HTML) as the File Type.

2. Type a name for the file in the File Name box.

3. Select OK.

4. Select File | Close.

5. Select File | Open. Select the Confirm Conversion box if it is not already checked.

6. Select the desired filename.

7. Select Text Only from the Convert File from box, then select OK.

The HTML codes will appear along with the other text you have entered. Figure 9-6 shows the code for some of the links established for Figure 9-4.

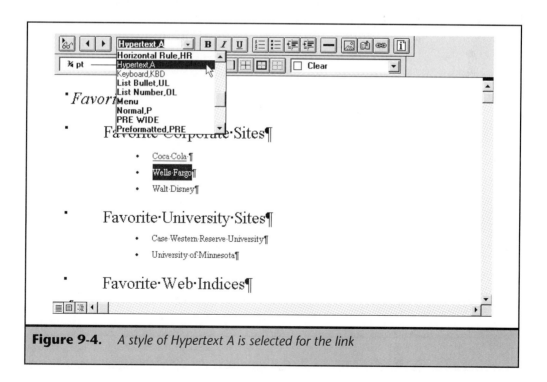

Figure 9-4.   *A style of Hypertext A is selected for the link*

Adding Graphics to Web Documents

You can add graphics at any location in a Web document. Although the change in appearance in your Web document can be spectacular, like the skyline and fireworks display from the annual report cover in Figure 9-1, there are also drawbacks. Each graphic that you include must be downloaded to the user's location. Depending on the size of the graphic, this can represent a significant increase in transmission time. Having many small graphics or a very large one is disastrous if the individual is connected to the Internet with a 14,400 dial-up connection and cannot turn off graphics with their browser. You should try to keep graphics files at less than 50K when you scan them for inclusion. When the picture in Figure 9-1 was originally scanned at a higher resolution, it was 400K. Although the image now shown is around the recommended size, much of the crisp resolution is lost by this change, yet the trade-off is appropriate.

You can use the Picture button in the toolbar while in HTML Edit view to insert a graphic. If you are in <u>W</u>eb Browse view, first select View | HTML <u>E</u>dit to change the view. You need to specify the filename and location; the Internet Assistant will add an HTML <IMG> command with the appropriate parameters.

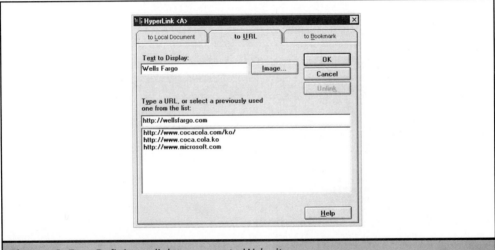

Figure 9-5. *Defining a link to a remote Web site*

Using the Internet Assistant to Create Forms

In addition to providing information to those reviewing your Web documents, you can solicit information from these same people. The Internet Assistant allows you to create forms for this purpose. Although the Internet Assistant provides all the capabilities you will need for text fields, drop-down list boxes, and check boxes, you need to have special software running on your Web server to process this information as it is sent back. You will need to work with your system administrator to get the proper software installed and to get some of the parameters that will control how the completed form is returned to your server. This special information is provided after creating your form fields. Once you have jointly defined your server requirements, select the Form Submit button options to define the Action, Method, and Enctype. You can look for these options under Submission Information in the Submit Button dialog box. You can also create a custom submission button for your form using the options in this dialog box.

```
<!doctype html public "-//IETF//DTD HTML//EN">¶
<HTML>¶
¶
<HEAD>¶
¶
<TITLE>Favorite Web Sites</TITLE>¶
¶
<META NAME="GENERATOR" CONTENT="Internet Assistant for Word 1.0Z">¶
<META NAME="AUTHOR" CONTENT="Mary Campbell">¶
</HEAD>¶
¶
<BODY>¶
¶
<H1><EM>Favorite Web Sites</EM> </H1>¶
¶
<H3>Favorite Corporate Sites</H3>¶
¶
<UL>¶
<LI><A HREF="http://www.cocacola.com/ko/">Coca Cola </A>¶
<LI><A HREF="http://wellsfargo.com">Wells Fargo</A> ¶
<LI><A HREF="http://www.disney.com">Walt Disney</A> ¶
```

Figure 9-6.   *HTML code can be viewed if you want to take a look at all the details*

Creating a good form requires some planning, to work out the best layout for information. Once you have decided on what your final product will look like, follow these steps to create your form:

1. Select <u>I</u>nsert | For<u>m</u> Field with the Internet Assistant active. Choose <u>C</u>ontinue when prompted about the creation of a new form.

This one step creates the entire form and displays the top and bottom form indicators on your screen. It also displays along with the Forms dialog box shown below and displays the Form Field dialog box ready to automatically add a text field for you.

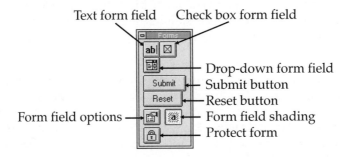

2. Insert the fields you want using the Forms dialog box. Figure 9-7 shows a form being created. You type the text that you want to precede the field first, then

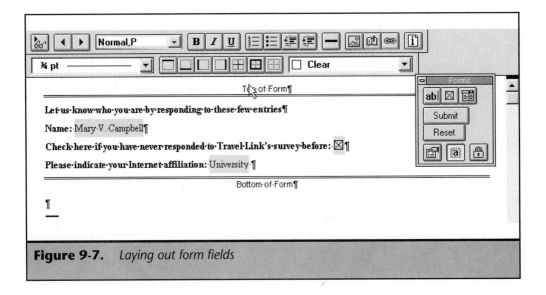

Figure 9-7.   *Laying out form fields*

insert the proper type of field using the three buttons at the top of the Forms dialog box. Your field choice depends upon whether you want the user to type a single or multiple-line response or choose an option by checking a box or picking an option from a list. The icons at the top of the special toolbar box are used to select the desired field type. From left to right, they represent these options:

- *Text field* Once you select this field type, the text form field appears in your document. You can double-click this field if you want a text area rather than a single line of entry. You can then define the rows and columns allocated to this field and assign a name to it or enter text that will appear as a default entry. For a single-line field, the double-click will allow you to enter a maximum length if you prefer as well as a name and default.

- *Check Box* This field type creates a check box that the user can click to select or unselect.

- *Drop-Down* This option allows you to provide the user with as many as 25 options from a drop-down list. You can double-click the field to enter the items in the list and add help text that will identify the item selected to your server when it is returned to your server. Don't confuse this with help text that will appear to the user of the form, since only your server will see this information.

3. When you are finished entering all fields, choose the Submit button from the Forms toolbar. You will need to work with your system administrator to determine the correct entries to conform with your Web server.

4. Choose the Reset button from the Forms toolbar to provide the reader an option to reset all fields to their default.

5. Choose Protect to prevent changes to the form once you are convinced you have the final product.

6. To view the form as it will appear, you will need to save it first, then reopen it. Figure 9-8 shows a simple form with a text box, a check box, and a drop-down list field. After finishing the design and saving the form, you will notice that the Submit and Reset buttons are no longer options in the Forms dialog box.

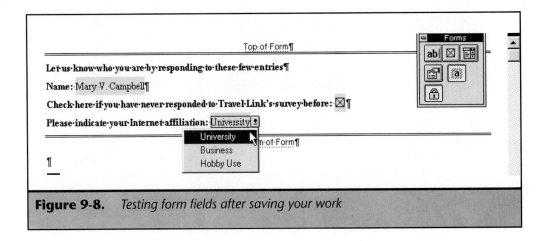

Figure 9-8. Testing form fields after saving your work

Although this chapter provided some information on the basic Internet Assistant options, there is a lot more to learn about the Web and HTML coding. If you are a novice you might want to consider taking a look at a comprehensive guide to the Internet, such as Osborne's *The Internet Complete Reference* (Osborne McGraw-Hill, 1994). Once you become more familiar with the requirements of creating Web pages, you will appreciate the time savings that the Internet Assistant can provide you.

PART FOUR

Appendixes

Appendix A

Installing Word for Windows 95

Installing Word for Windows 95 is a very easy process. The Microsoft Setup program takes care of most of the questions that might come up when installing Word. However, Setup does offer several variations that let you customize how Word is installed on your system. Right now you need to make a best guess on how to install Word on your system. You can later restart Word to reinstall updated sections, to install features you did not originally install, or to remove features.

Hardware Requirements

Before you can install Word for Windows, you need to make sure that you can use it on your computer. Word's minimum requirements are given in the table below. While you need at least the minimum requirements, there is no restriction about having more than the minimum. The better your computer and its resources, the better Word will run for you.

Microprocessor	An 80386 or higher compatible chip
Disks	A 1.2MB or higher floppy disk drive and a hard drive
Operating software	Windows 95
RAM	4MB
Monitor	EGA
Other	Mouse

While a printer is not actually required, having one available makes it easier for you to get the most from the package. You can print your documents to a file, then take these files to another computer that has a printer available to get a printout of your work.

Hard Disk Space Requirements

You can customize which aspects and features of Word you want to install to make the maximum use of the disk space you have available. If you have no reason to use a feature, simply do not install it, and save that hard disk space for other purposes. As you choose which components of Word that you will install, the Setup program indicates how much disk space is required.

Installing Word

1. Use the My Computer icon or the Windows Explorer to look at the contents of the disk containing the Word or Microsoft Office disk.

2. Double-click the icon for the Setup program.

3. Microsoft Setup prompts you to close all other applications before selecting OK. You need to close other applications because Setup restarts Windows later,

and because Setup changes settings that may be in use by other applications. To close other applications, switch to the other application by pressing CTRL+ESC and selecting it or by pressing ALT+TAB until you move to it. Close the application as you would normally. When you are done, only the Program Manager and Setup should be open.

4. Enter your name and your company's name and select OK. Select OK again to confirm that the name and company name are correct.

5. Setup displays your serial number. Before selecting OK, copy it down somewhere for easy retrieval later (for example, inside your User's Manual).

6. Setup asks you to confirm the directory Word is installed into, C:\WINWORD. Select OK to use this directory.

   To use another directory, select Change Folder, then select a directory, and then select OK. If you select a nonexistent directory, Word asks if you want to create it. Select Yes, then OK.

7. Setup offers you three choices for installing Word.

   - *Typical*   Takes 13MBs of hard disk space and includes the more commonly used Word features.

   - *Custom*   Takes up to 35MBs of hard disk space and lets you install any features you select.

   - *Compact*   *Takes 6MBs of hard disk space and includes only Word, the spell checker, and the Readme Help file.*

   - If you do not select Custom, skip to step 9.

8. After selecting Custom, you can choose the features to install. Select or clear feature check boxes in the Options list box. When you are finished, select Continue.

   You can include some features by highlighting the check box, selecting Change Option, then selecting or clearing check boxes for the specific features and selecting OK.

9. Exchange disks when Setup prompts you to.

10. When Setup is done, select Exit Setup to leave the program or Online Registration to register Word or Microsoft Office using your modem.

Updating Word

You can restart Setup in order to change which features are installed. You can also update features if Microsoft sends you update disks, install features you did not originally install, or remove features you've found you never use.

To use Setup again:

1. Select Settings from the Start menu. Then select the Control Panel.

2. Select Add/Remove Programs.

3. Select Microsoft Office or Microsoft Word from the list box on the Install/Uninstall tab.

4. Select Add/Remove.

5. Select the option that matches what you need to do with Word.

   ■ *Add/Remove*   Opens the dialog box for selecting Word components. Select the options you want to install or clear those you want to remove, and select Continue.

   ■ *Reinstall Again*   Reinstalls Word using the same settings you used originally. Replaces files that were accidentally deleted or altered.

   ■ *Remove All*   Uninstalls Word, deleting all files and changing the Windows default settings back. Setup asks you to confirm that you want to do this.

Appendix B

Switching from WordPerfect to Word for Windows

W ordPerfect is one of the most widely used word processors. If you have been using WordPerfect 5.1 or 6 for DOS and are upgrading to Word for Windows, you will find many differences. This appendix outlines some of the major differences and also provides a feature conversion list to make it easy to locate the Word command that you can use to complete a familiar WordPerfect task.

One of the major differences between WordPerfect and Word is that Word does not have a Reveal Codes screen. WordPerfect is a *text-based* word processor, which means that if you look at a WordPerfect file, it is basically a long string of words, interspersed with codes. Codes indicate exactly where different formats are supposed to be turned on and off. You can basically think of codes as special-purpose characters and work with them that way in the Reveal Codes screen.

TIP: Word for Windows provides some special help for WordPerfect users to make the transition easier. You can choose WordPerfect Help from the Help menu when you need assistance.

Word is a *paragraph-based* word processor. You never see codes for formatting, because formatting is not applied as part of the text. In a sense, the text of your Word document is saved in once place, and the map indicating where all of the formats are applied is stored in another. You never directly move or change the "codes" that apply formatting. For an old WordPerfect user, this is confusing because you cannot simply open Reveal Codes and see where all the formatting is applied in Word. However, in Word you do not have to worry about where your insertion point is when you change a formatting setting. For example, if you want to change margins for your entire document, you don't need to go back to the beginning of your document, delete the old margins code, and insert a new one. Instead, you just change the setting—Word knows to apply it to the entire document.

Codes are selected somewhat differently in Word for Windows than in WordPerfect. In WordPerfect, the primary method of accessing commands is to use the function keys. In Word for Windows, like most other Windows applications, you use the menu bar and the toolbars. Also, though Word offers all the same features as WordPerfect, you may have difficulty finding them since many have different names. The following chart indicates the equivalent Word commands for most WordPerfect (WP) features.

TIP: If you are very familiar with the WordPerfect function keys and don't want to have to change, consider creating a new keyboard that will assign the equivalent commands to those keys. This is one way in which Word is more flexible than WordPerfect.

WP Feature	WP Key	Word Menu Command
Block	ALT+F4	Select text by pressing SHIFT and the movement keys or dragging across.
Bold	F6	Format	Font	Font	Font Style	Bold
Cancel	F1	ESC

WP Feature	WP Key	Word Menu Command
Center	SHIFT+F6	Format	Paragraph	Indents and Spacing	Alignment	Center
Columns/Table	ALT+F7	Format	Columns or Table	Insert Table
Copy	CTRL+F4	Edit	Copy and Edit	Paste or drag selected text while holding the CTRL key
Date/Outline	SHIFT+F5	View	Outline or Insert	Date and Time
End Field	F9	Data sources are set up differently in Word: there is no equivalent command because there is no end field code
Exit	F7	File	Exit
Flush Right	ALT+F6	Format	Paragraph	Alignment	Right
Font	CTRL+F8	Format	Font	Font	Font
Footnotes	CTRL+F7	Insert	Footnote
Format	SHIFT+F8	Any of the options on the Format toolbar and File	Page Setup
Graphics	ALT+F9	Insert	Picture
Help	F3	F1
Indent Left & Right	SHIFT+F4	Format	Paragraph	Indents and Spacing	Left and Right
Indent Right	F4	Format	Paragraph	Indents and Spacing	Right
List	F5	File	Find File
Macro	ALT+F10	Tools	M ro
Macro Define	CTRL+F10	Tools	Macro	Record
Margin Release	SHIFT+TAB	Format	Paragraphs	Indents and Spacing	Right
Mark Text	ALT+F5	Edit	Index and Tables	select a tab	Mark Text
Merge Codes	SHIFT+F9	Tools	Mail Merge
Merge/Sort	CTRL+F9	Tools	Mail Merge or Table	Sort Text or Table
Move	CTRL+F4	Edit	Cut and Edit	Paste or drag selected text
Print	SHIFT+F7	File	Print
Replace	ALT+F2	Edit	Replace
Retrieve	SHIFT+F10	File	Open, Insert	File or Insert	Database
Reveal Codes	ALT+F3	Since Word does not use codes, there is no equivalent
Save	F10	File	Save or Save As
Screen	CTRL+F3	Any option on the View menu
Search Backwards	SHIFT+F2	Edit	Find
Search Forward	F2	Edit	Find
Setup	SHIFT+F1	Tools	Customize or Tools	Options

WP Feature	WP Key	Word Menu Command
Shell	CTRL+F1	CTRL+ESC for the Task Manager or ALT+TAB to move to another application
Spell	CTRL+F2	Tools	Spelling
Style	ALT+F8	Format	Style
Switch	SHIFT+F3	Window	*and a number for the correct window*
Tab Align	CTRL+F6	Format	Tabs
Text In/Out	CTRL+F5	Insert	File or File	Open and File	Save or Save As
Thesaurus	ALT+F1	Tools	Thesaurus
Underline	F8	Format	Font	Font	Underline

WordPerfect Help in Word

When you switch from WordPerfect to Word, you will learn new key combinations that perform the same features as WordPerfect. To help you learn these new procedures, Word provides special help features. To use help that is customized for WordPerfect users, you can choose Tools | Options and the General tab. When you select the Help for WordPerfect Users check box, anytime you request help, it will be the WordPerfect Users help instead of Word's standard help. This means that if you press F1, Word assumes that you want help on the WordPerfect feature that is available by pressing F1.

You can also see an overall help feature with the Help | WordPerfect Help command. The Help for WordPerfect Users window focuses on the WordPerfect features that you already know and how you do them in Word. In the Help for WordPerfect Users window, you can select the feature you want to use from the Command Keys list box. Then select Help Text to see text on that feature or Demo to have the help facility show you how that feature is done in Word.

Here's another feature you can turn on to assist with your transition to Word: make some of the navigation keys behave in Word in the same way that they did in WordPerfect. To turn this feature on, choose Tools | Options, the General tab, and select the Navigation Keys for WordPerfect Users check box. When this feature is on, keys such as PGUP, PGDN, ESC, HOME, and END behave the same way in Word that they behave in WordPerfect.

In the General tab of Tools | Options, if you have selected both the Help for WordPerfect Users and Navigation Keys for WordPerfect Users check boxes, then, when you press a WordPerfect for DOS key combination, Word assumes that you are pressing a key combination for a WordPerfect feature. You will also see a description for how to perform the same feature in Word and have the opportunity to let Word demonstrate how the feature is performed. The status bar shows which WordPerfect assist features you have turned on. WPH in the status bar means that the Help for WordPerfect Users check box is selected. WPN in the status bar means that the Navigation Keys for WordPerfect Users check box is selected. WP in the status bar means that both of these check boxes are selected.

Appendix C

Word for Windows Buttons

Word for Windows offers many different toolbars that serve as shortcuts for creating your documents. You will find it easy to become confused about why you should use a specific toolbar, or what that toolbar offers. Tables C-1 through C-20 list all of the available toolbar buttons, including those which do not appear on any of the default toolbars, but which can be used to create your own toolbars.

Button	Button Name	Purpose
	New	Opens a new document using the Normal template
	Open	Displays the Open dialog box for opening documents
	Save	Saves files or displays the Save As dialog box
	Print	Prints the document with the default settings
	Print Preview	Switches to Print Preview view
	Spelling	Opens the Spelling dialog box to check the spelling in the document
	Cut	Deletes the selected text after copying it to the Clipboard
	Copy	Copies the selected text to the Clipboard
	Paste	Copies the Clipboard's contents into the document
	Format Painter	Copies the format of the selected text to the next selected text

Table C-1. *Standard Toolbar*

Button	Button Name	Purpose
	Undo	Lets you select the actions to undo
	Redo	Lets you select the actions to redo
	AutoFormat	Automatically formats your document
	Address	Adds an address to the document from an address book
	Insert Table	Inserts a table with the specified rows and columns
	Insert Microsoft Excel Worksheet	Inserts a worksheet created by Excel as a table
	Columns	Reformats the current section as the specified number of equal-width columns
	Drawing	Displays the Drawing toolbar
	Show/Hide¶	Toggles between displaying or hiding nonprinting characters
100%	Zoom Control	Sets the magnification used to display the document
	TipWizard	Displays or hides the Tip Wizard toolbar that displays suggestions on the Word features you use
	Help	Provides help on a feature when you select a button or command, or tells you the current formatting for text you select

Table C-1.   *Standard Toolbar* (continued)

Button	Button Name	Purpose
Normal ▼	Style	Applies a style to the selected text
Times New Roman ▼	Font	Applies a font to the selected text
10 ▼	Font Size	Applies a font size to the selected text
B	Bold	Boldfaces the selected text
I	Italic	Italicizes the selected text
U	Underline	Underlines the selected text
✎ ▼	Highlight	Changes the background color of the selected text
≡	Align Left	Aligns the selected paragraphs with the left margin
≡	Center	Centers the selected paragraphs between the margins
≡	Align Right	Aligns the selected paragraphs with the right margin
≡	Justify	Aligns the selected paragraphs with the left and right margins
≟	Numbering	Makes the selected paragraphs a numbered list
≔	Bullets	Makes the selected paragraphs a bulleted list
≔	Decrease Indent	Moves the left indent of the selected paragraphs one tab stop to the left

Table C-2. *Formatting Toolbar*

Button	Button Name	Purpose
	Increase Indent	Moves the left indent of the selected paragraphs one tab stop to the right
	Borders	Displays the Borders toolbar

Table C-2.   *Formatting Toolbar* (continued)

Button	Button Name	Purpose
¾ pt	Line Style	Selects the style of line to apply
	Top Border	Toggles a top border for the selection on and off
	Bottom Border	Toggles a bottom border for the selection on and off
	Left Border	Toggles a border on the left of the selection on and off
	Right Border	Toggles a border on the right of the selection on and off
	Inside Border	Toggles a border between cells or paragraphs on and off
	Outside Border	Toggles a border outside the table, selected cells, or paragraphs on and off
	No Border	Removes all borders
Clear	Shading	Selects a shading to apply to the selected paragraphs or cells

Table C-3.   *Borders Toolbar*

Button	Button Name	Purpose
	Data Form	Lets you update a delimited list or table using a Data Form dialog box
	Manage Fields	Lets you add or delete a field from a database or a column from a table
	Add New Record	Adds a new record to the database or a new row to a table
	Delete Record	Removes a record from the database or removes the row from a table
	Sort Ascending	Sorts the database or table from A to Z or 1 to 9 according to the current field or column
	Sort Descending	Sorts the database or table from Z to A or 9 to 1 according to the current field or column
	Insert Database	Inserts data from another file into the current document
	Update Fields	Updates all fields in the text that you select
	Find Records	Finds a record containing specified data in one of the database's or table's fields
	Mail Merge Main Document	In mail merge, switches to the main document to which the current document is assigned

Table C-4. *Database Toolbar*

Button	**Button Name**	**Purpose**
	Line	Creates a line drawing object
	Rectangle	Creates a rectangle drawing object
	Ellipse	Creates an ellipse (oval or circle) drawing object
	Arc	Creates an arc drawing object
	Freeform	Creates a freeform drawing object
	Text Box	Creates a text box drawing object
	Callout	Creates a callout drawing object
	Format Callout	Formats a callout drawing object
	Fill Color	Sets the color of a drawing object's fill
	Line Color	Sets the color of a drawing object's lines
	Line Style	Sets the style of a drawing object's lines
	Select Drawing Objects	Changes the mouse pointer so you can select drawing objects

Table C-5.   *Drawing Toolbar*

Button	Button Name	Purpose
	Bring to Front	Places the selected object over other objects
	Send to Back	Places the selected object behind other objects
	Bring in Front of Text	Places the selected object over the document text
	Send Behind Text	Places the selected object behind the document text
	Group	Groups the selected objects into one object
	Ungroup	Breaks the selected objects back into their component objects
	Flip Horizontal	Flips the right and left of the selected object
	Flip Vertical	Flips the top and bottom of the selected object
	Rotate Right	Rotates the selected object so its right side becomes its bottom
	Reshape	Lets you reshape a freeform object
	Snap to Grid	Lets you set a grid for aligning objects
	Align Drawing Objects	Aligns the selected objects with the grid

Table C-5. *Drawing Toolbar* (continued)

Button	Button Name	Purpose
	Create Picture	Opens a window and lets you create a picture
	Insert Frame	Inserts a frame

Table C-5.   _Drawing Toolbar_ (continued)

Button	Button Name	Purpose
ab|	Text Form Field	Inserts a Text form field
	Check Box Form Field	Inserts a Check Box form field
	Drop-Down Form Field	Inserts a Drop-Down form field
	Form Field Options	Lets you set the options for the selected form field
	Insert Table	Inserts a table with the specified rows and columns
	Insert Frame	Inserts an empty frame or frames the selected data
	Form Field Shading	Toggles between shading and not shading the form fields
	Protect Form	Protects the document against changes except to form fields

Table C-6.   _Forms Toolbar_

Button	Button Name	Purpose
	Microsoft Excel	Starts or switches to Microsoft Excel
	Microsoft PowerPoint	Starts or switches to Microsoft PowerPoint
	Microsoft Mail	Starts or switches to Microsoft Mail
	Microsoft Access	Starts or switches to Microsoft Access
	Microsoft FoxPro	Starts or switches to Microsoft FoxPro
	Microsoft Project	Starts or switches to Microsoft Project
	Microsoft Schedule+	Starts or switches to Microsoft Schedule+
	Microsoft Publisher	Starts or switches to Microsoft Publisher

Table C-7. *Microsoft Toolbar*

Button	Button Name	Purpose
	New	Opens a new document using the Normal template
	Open	Displays the Open dialog box for opening files

Table C-8. *Word for Windows 2 Toolbar*

Button	Button Name	Purpose
	Save	Saves files or displays the Save As dialog box
	Cut	Deletes the selected text after copying it to the Clipboard
	Copy	Copies the selected text to the Clipboard
	Paste	Copies the Clipboard's contents into the document
	Undo	Lets you select the actions to undo
	Numbering	Makes the selected paragraphs a numbered list
	Bullets	Makes the selected paragraphs a bulleted list
	Decrease Indent	Moves the left indent of the selected paragraphs one tab stop to the left
	Increase Indent	Moves the left indent of the selected paragraphs one tab stop to the right
	Insert Table	Inserts a table with the specified rows and columns
	Columns	Reformats the current section as the specified number of equal-width columns
	Insert Frame	Inserts a frame

Table C-8.   *Word for Windows 2 Toolbar* (continued)

Button	Button Name	Purpose
	Drawing	Displays the Drawing toolbar
	Insert Chart	Opens the Graph application so you can create and embed a chart
	Create Envelope	Sets up an envelope for the current document
	Spelling	Checks the spelling in the document
	Print	Prints the document with the default settings
	One Page	Changes the view to Page Layout, showing the entire page
	Zoom 100%	Displays the document at full size
	Zoom Page Width	Zooms the document so you can see both sides of the page

Table C-8. *Word for Windows 2 Toolbar* (continued)

Button	Button Name	Purpose
	Promote	Makes the selected heading one level higher
	Demote	Makes the selected heading one level lower
	Demote to Body Text	Makes the selected heading body text

Table C-9. *Outline Toolbar*

Button	**Button Name**	**Purpose**
⬆	Move Up	Moves the selected heading up in the outline
⬇	Move Down	Moves the selected heading down in the outline
✚	Expand	Shows lower level headings and body text under the current heading
➖	Collapse	Hides lower level headings and body text under the current heading
1	Show Heading 1	Shows only level-one headings in the document
2	Show Heading 2	Shows through second-level headings in the document
3	Show Heading 3	Shows through third-level headings in the document
4	Show Heading 4	Shows through fourth-level headings in the document
5	Show Heading 5	Shows through fifth-level headings in the document
6	Show Heading 6	Shows through sixth-level headings in the document
7	Show Heading 7	Shows through seventh-level headings in the document
8	Show Heading 8	Shows through eighth-level headings in the document
All	All	Shows all headings and text in the outline

Table C-9.   *Outline Toolbar* (continued)

Button	Button Name	Purpose
	Show First Line Only	Toggles between showing all body text and only the first line
	Show Formatting	Toggles between showing formatting or using a draft font
	Master Document View	Opens the Master Document toolbar

Table C-9. *Outline Toolbar* (continued)

Button	Button Name	Purpose
	Print	Prints the document with the default settings
	Magnifier	Toggles the mouse between zoom in/out and normal mode
	One Page	Zooms the document to show the entire page
	Multiple Pages	Zooms the document to show the specified number of pages
29%	Zoom Control	Sets the magnification used to display the document
	View Ruler	Shows or hides the vertical and horizontal rulers
	Shrink to Fit	Changes formatting slightly to use one less page
	Full Screen	Displays the document using the full screen

Table C-10. *Print Preview Toolbar*

Button	Button Name	Purpose
Close	Close	Returns to the previous view
	Help	Provides help on a feature when you select a button or command, or tells you the current formatting for text you select

Table C-10. *Print Preview Toolbar* (continued)

Button	Button Name	Purpose
	Switch Between Header and Footer	Moves between the current header and footer
	Show Previous	Moves to the header or footer of the previous section
	Show Next	Moves to the header or footer of the next section
	Same as Previous	Links the current header or footer to the previous section's header and footer
	Page Numbers	Inserts a field that displays the page number
	Date	Inserts a field that displays the current date
	Time	Inserts a field that displays the current time
	Page Setup	Opens the Page Setup dialog box

Table C-11. *Header and Footer Toolbar*

Button	Button Name	Purpose
	Show/Hide Document Text	Displays or hides document text
Close	Close	Returns to the document text

Table C-11. *Header and Footer Toolbar* (continued)

Button	Button Name	Purpose
Insert Merge Field	Insert Merge Field	Lets you select a merge field to insert
Insert Word Field	Insert Word Field	Lets you select a Word field to insert
« » ABC	View Merged Data	Toggles between showing codes and data from the data source
⏮	First Record	Displays the first record
◀	Previous Record	Displays the previous record
	Go to Record	Lets you enter the record to display
▶	Next Record	Displays the next record
⏭	Last Record	Displays the last record
	Mail Merge Helper	Opens the Mail Merge Helper dialog box
	Check for Errors	Runs the merge, checking for errors and creating no output

Table C-12. *Mail Merge Toolbar*

Button	Button Name	Purpose
	Merge to New Document	Runs the merge, storing the merged document in a new document
	Merge to Printer	Runs the merge, sending the merged document to the printer
	Mail Merge	Opens the Merge dialog box, letting you set merge options
	Find Records	Finds a record in the data source that contains the specified data
	Edit Data Source	Displays the Data Form dialog box for editing the data source

Table C-12. *Mail Merge Toolbar* (continued)

Button	Button Name	Purpose
	Create Subdocument	Makes the selected text into a subdocument
	Remove Subdocument	Makes the selected subdocument part of the main document
	Insert Subdocument	Opens a file and inserts it as a subdocument
	Merge Subdocument	Combines the selected subdocuments into a single subdocument
	Split Subdocument	Splits the current subdocument into two subdocuments at the insertion point location
	Lock Document	Locks or unlocks the subdocument for editing

Table C-13. *Master Document Toolbar*

Button	Button Name	Purpose
`FigureCaption ▼`	Active Macro	Selects which macro is the active macro that is controlled by the buttons on the Macro toolbar
●	Record	Records the commands you select and adds them to a new macro
●1	Record Next Command	Records the next command you select and adds it to the macro
▶	Start	Runs the macro
▷	Trace	Runs the macro and highlights each statement as the statement is performed
▌▌	Continue	Continues macro execution
■	Stop	Halts macro execution
🔲	Step	Goes through the macro one statement at a time
🔲	Step Subs	Goes through the macro one subroutine at a time
👓	Show Variables	Shows the variables in a macro when you are running a macro so you can see their current value
☰	Add/Remove REM	Adds and removes REM from the selected lines to convert statements into remarks
🔳	Macro	Displays the Macro dialog box that the Tools|Macro command displays
🖻	Dialog Editor	Starts the Dialog Editor application to create a dialog box that the macro uses

Table C-14.   *Macro Toolbar*

Button	Button Name	Purpose
💡	1) To see only the document, click Full Screen on the View menu. Press ESC to close the full screen view.	
	TipWizard Box	Describes a shortcut that performs the same or similar steps to what you are doing
▣	Change	Removes effect of AutoFormat or other change performed automatically by Word. This button often is replaced by other Word buttons that perform the same feature as what is described in the TipWizard box
💡?	Show Me	Performs a mini-demonstration of how the tip described in the TipWizard Box is performed

Table C-15. *TipWizard Toolbar*

The following buttons can be used to create new toolbars, but they do not actually appear in any of the default toolbars. These are buttons you will see when you select Tools|Customize and the Toolbars tab.

Button	Button Name	Purpose
📁	Close	Closes all copies of the current document
📧	Send Mail	Sends an electronic mail message
🗐	Routing Slip	Adds an electronic mail routing slip to your document
↺	Repeat	Repeats your last action
🔍	Find	Finds text or formatting in your document

Table C-16. *Miscellaneous Buttons*

Button	Button Name	Purpose
	Zoom Control	Lets you select the zoom for your document
{a}	View Field Codes	Toggles between showing field codes or results
	Full Screen	Displays the document without a title bar, menu, or status bar
AB¹	Insert Footnote	Inserts a footnote reference at the insertion point
	Insert AutoText	Inserts an AutoText entry for the name in the document
	Insert Chart	Opens the Graph application so you can create and embed a chart
	WordArt	Starts WordArt
√α	Equation	Starts the Equation Editor
	Insert Sound Object	Inserts a sound stored in a file or that you create by recording
	Pen Annotation	Inserts a text annotation at the current location
D	Double Underline	Double underlines the selected text
W	Word Underline	Underlines text but not spaces
ABC	Strikethrough	Applies strikethrough to the selected text

Table C-16. *Miscellaneous Buttons* (continued)

Button	Button Name	Purpose
ABC	Small Caps	Makes the selected text small capitals
aA	All Caps	Makes the selected text all capitals
=	Single Space	Single spaces the selected paragraphs
=	1.5 Space	One and a half spaces the selected paragraphs
=	Double Space	Double spaces the selected paragraphs
A≡	Drop Cap	Makes the first letter of the paragraph a dropped capital
x^2	Superscript	Superscripts the selected text
x_2	Subscript	Subscripts the selected text
	Compare Versions	Compares the current document to a previous version
	Review Revisions	Lets you accept or reject revisions made to your document
	Insert Cells	Adds cells to a table
	Insert Rows	Adds rows to a table
	Insert Columns	Adds columns to a table

Table C-16. *Miscellaneous Buttons* (continued)

Button	Button Name	Purpose
	Delete Cells	Removes cells from a table
	Delete Rows	Removes rows from a table
	Delete Columns	Removes columns from a table
	Table Gridlines	Toggles displaying table gridlines on and off
	Table AutoFormat	Applies a standard format to the table
	AutoSum	Inserts a formula field that sums a row or column
	New Window	Opens a new window for the current document
	Arrange All	Arranges all open documents so you can see all of them
	Open Subdocument	Opens a subdocument from a master document
	Split Window	Splits the window into two panes
	Rounded Rectangle	Creates a rounded rectangle drawing object
	Bring Forward	Puts the selected object on top of the object above it
	Send Backward	Puts the selected object behind the object just behind it

Table C-16. *Miscellaneous Buttons* (continued)

Button	Button Name	Purpose
	Rotate Left	Rotates the selected object so its left becomes its bottom
	Reset Picture Boundary	Eliminates white space in a picture
	Disassemble Picture	Splits a metafile into its component drawing objects

Table C-16. *Miscellaneous Buttons* (continued)

The following are buttons that are not assigned any particular task. When creating your own toolbars, you can assign any task to these buttons.

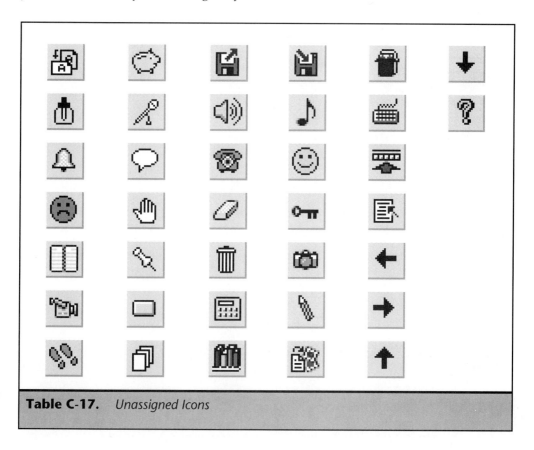

Table C-17. *Unassigned Icons*

Word's secondary applications use toolbars for their features. In the Equation Editor, the toolbar buttons have no names, but they insert different mathematical symbols and templates. In WordArt, the toolbar buttons format how the text appears. In Microsoft Graph, the toolbar buttons provide easy ways of formatting the chart and working with the data represented in the chart.

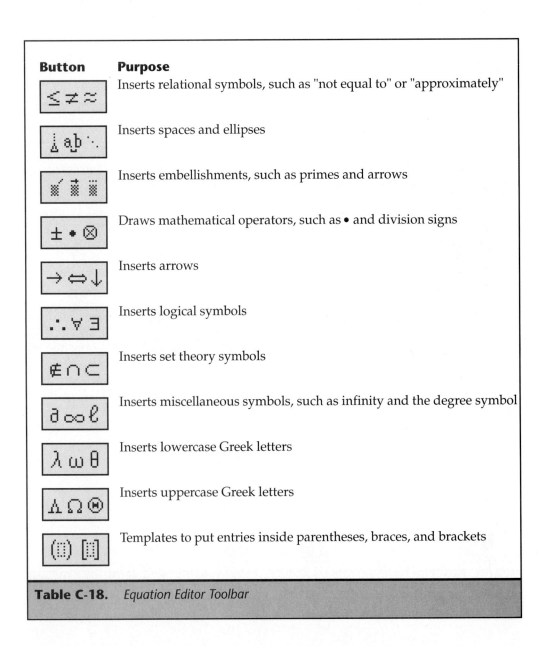

Button	Purpose
	Inserts relational symbols, such as "not equal to" or "approximately"
	Inserts spaces and ellipses
	Inserts embellishments, such as primes and arrows
	Draws mathematical operators, such as • and division signs
	Inserts arrows
	Inserts logical symbols
	Inserts set theory symbols
	Inserts miscellaneous symbols, such as infinity and the degree symbol
	Inserts lowercase Greek letters
	Inserts uppercase Greek letters
	Templates to put entries inside parentheses, braces, and brackets

Table C-18. *Equation Editor Toolbar*

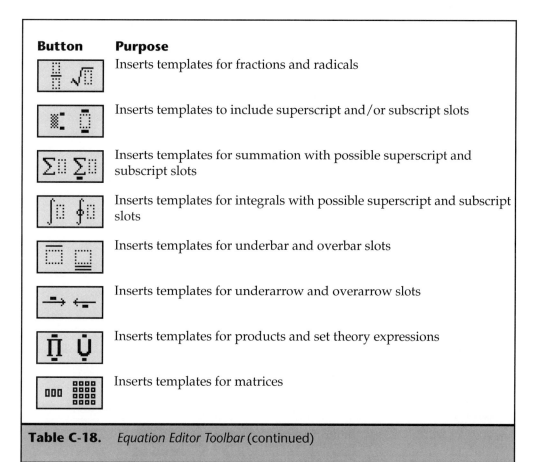

Button	Purpose
	Inserts templates for fractions and radicals
	Inserts templates to include superscript and/or subscript slots
	Inserts templates for summation with possible superscript and subscript slots
	Inserts templates for integrals with possible superscript and subscript slots
	Inserts templates for underbar and overbar slots
	Inserts templates for underarrow and overarrow slots
	Inserts templates for products and set theory expressions
	Inserts templates for matrices

Table C-18. *Equation Editor Toolbar* (continued)

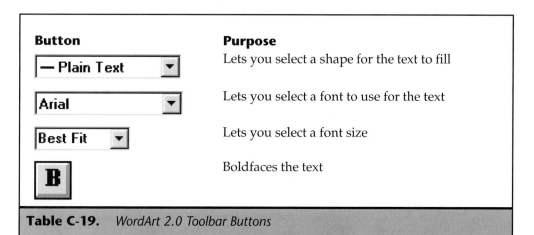

Button	Purpose
— Plain Text	Lets you select a shape for the text to fill
Arial	Lets you select a font to use for the text
Best Fit	Lets you select a font size
B	Boldfaces the text

Table C-19. *WordArt 2.0 Toolbar Buttons*

Button	Purpose
I	Italicizes the text
Ee	Makes all letters the same height
	Flips the text on its side
	Stretches the text to fill the space you created
	Selects an alignment for the text
AV	Lets you adjust the spacing between letters
	Lets you rotate the text
	Lets you set a color or pattern to fill the text
	Lets you choose a method of shadowing your text
	Lets you set a border for your WordArt box

Table C-19. *WordArt 2.0 Toolbar Buttons* (continued)

Button	Button Name	Purpose
	Import Data	Imports data to graph from another document into the datasheet
	Import Chart	Imports the chart from another document into the graph
	View Datasheet	Displays the datasheet
	Cut	Cuts the selected item to the Clipboard
	Copy	Copies the selected item to the Clipboard
	Paste	Pastes the Clipboard's contents into the graph or datasheet
	Undo	Removes the effect of the last change you made
	By Row	Organizes the data in the graph so each series represents a different row in the datasheet
	By Column	Organizes the data in the graph so each series represents a different column in the datasheet
	Chart Type	Sets the overall chart type
	Vertical Gridlines	Adds gridlines in a vertical direction

Table C-20. *Microsoft Graph Toolbar Buttons*

	Horizontal Gridlines	Adds gridlines in a horizontal direction
	Legend	Displays or hides a legend on the graph
	Text Box	Adds a text box to the graph
	Drawing	Opens the Drawing toolbar to add drawn objects to the graph
	Color	Sets the color of the selected item
	Pattern	Sets the fill color of the selected item

Table C-20.   *Microsoft Graph Toolbar Buttons* (continued)

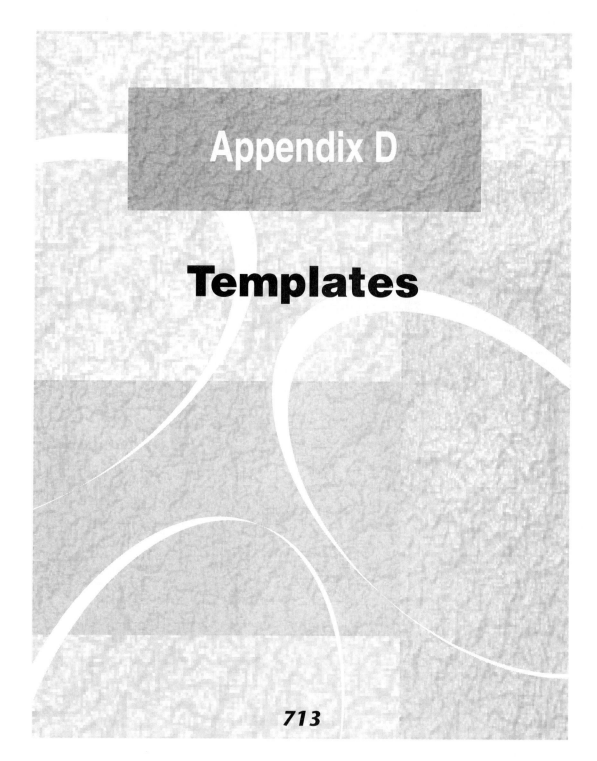

Appendix D

Templates

713

Templates are molds for creating documents. They were made part of Word for Windows to allow you to create frequently used documents quickly. Templates give you a head start by providing a defined appearance. Some may even have some text already in them. You are, of course, free to add your own text and change any of the formatting that you want; the changes you make will affect the document but will not alter the template from which it was created.

Word has 37 different templates. Some of these templates function as wizards and guide you through the needed entries.

The default template used for new documents is Normal (also called a blank document) if you do not select another one. The Normal template does not offer much in the way of formatting, with only the basics in styles, margins, and character appearance, and it does not contain any text. You can enhance it by adding your own macros, styles, toolbars, and AutoText entries. In this appendix, you will learn about each of the other templates offered by Word. You will learn which text is already stored in the template and which formatting is part of the template.

Creating a Document from a Template

To use a template for a document, you merely select the template from the list of available ones when you open a new document.

1. Select File | New, opening the New dialog box.

   The templates are divided into tabs according to purpose.

2. Select the tab containing the template that you want to use.

3. Select the icon for the template that you want to use.

4. Select OK.

At this point, Word opens a new document using the template you have selected. This template provides the styles, macros, toolbars, and AutoText entries initially available in a document. If the template you select is a wizard, the template has macros that display dialog boxes. You can use the dialog boxes displayed by the wizard to control exactly how the document is created. When the macros and the wizard finish executing, the newly created document is active on your screen. Most wizards will set the template of the document created to Normal when completed, so you will have the toolbar, macro, styles, and AutoText entries as most of your documents.

If you later change your mind about the template you want the document to use, you can change it by following these steps:

1. Select File | Templates.

2. Select Attach to select a new template file.

3. Select a template file and <u>O</u>pen.

4. Select OK.

A Look at Each of the Templates

Word includes all of the templates listed in this section. For each template listed below is a description of why you would use it and some of the styles and macros it offers. Most of the templates include many of the same style names as the styles in the Normal template, although they are given different appearances by the template. This includes styles like Normal and Heading 1 through Heading 9. Many of the templates start off with a sample document. The sample document frequently includes instructions on how to use the specific template. When you create a new document using a template that initially inserts text and includes instructions, print the document you created with the template and then modify the document to suit your needs.

 TIP: *If you want help using the wizards, you can select help in the last Wizards dialog box. The help information you will see depends on the selected wizard.*

Agenda Wizard

This template is a wizard that creates an agenda for a meeting. Figure D-1 shows a document created with this wizard. Some of the customizing you can do through this wizard includes:

- Selecting the style of the agenda
- Inserting the date and time of the meeting
- Inserting the title and location of the meeting
- Setting headings for sections of the agenda
- Inserting names for people performing various duties at the meeting
- Setting a table of topics, who is responsible, and expected length
- Adding a form for recording minutes

Award Wizard

This template is a wizard that creates awards that you can use for anything from the employee of the month or top sales performer to the top average on your bowling team or the winner of the spelling bee at your son's school. Some of the customization options include:

- Selecting the style of text and border

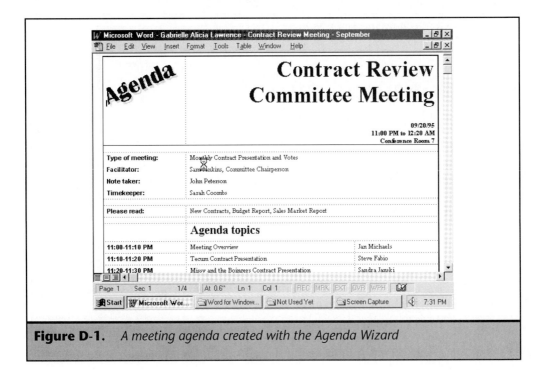

Figure D-1. *A meeting agenda created with the Agenda Wizard*

- Selecting the orientation and whether the paper has its own border
- Inserting the recipient and title of award
- Inserting signatories and presenters
- Inserting date and reason for award

Brochure Template

This template is used to create a folded brochure. The brochure can be printed on one sheet and folded in thirds. Figure D-2 shows one side of a brochure created with this template. When you use the template, replace the text in the sample brochure with your own. Here are some things to keep in mind:

- The template divides the document into three columns and assumes that you will fold the paper into thirds. The first three columns appear on one side of the paper, and the other three appear on the back. The column that appears in the front will be in the third column.

- You can purchase specialty paper just for brochures, which is scored where the paper is folded. This paper may have designs where your brochure has empty

Figure D-2. *A brochure created using the Brochure template*

space. Check your local paper suppliers for some of the different paper options available.

Calendar Wizard

This template is a wizard that creates monthly calendars. Some of the customization options include:

- Selecting the style of the calendar and placement of the days and months
- Selecting whether you want to include a picture (Word inserts CITYSCPE.WMF, but you can change it to another picture)
- Selecting a portrait or landscape orientation for the calendar
- Setting the starting and ending month and year for the calendar so each month has its own page

Directory Template

This template is used to create directories. Word provides you with a sample directory for you to modify and fill with your own entries. Each entry uses a combination of

Name, List, and List Last styles. Name is for the first entry for each directory entry. List is for the lines below Name, except for the last one, which uses List Last. Heading 3 divides the directory entries into groups, and Section Title divides the directory entries further, such as by letter.

Fax Wizard

This template is a wizard that creates a fax cover sheet like the one shown in Figure D-3. Some of the changes you can make while using the wizard include:

■ Setting page orientation

■ Selecting the style of text and placement of fax cover sheet items

■ Inserting your name, company, address, and phone numbers, or selecting an entry from an address book

Once you create the fax cover sheet, you only need to enter the addressee's information, the number of pages, and any comments. This document is a form, so you will notice that you can move to the check boxes in the form and press the SPACEBAR to select the ones you want.

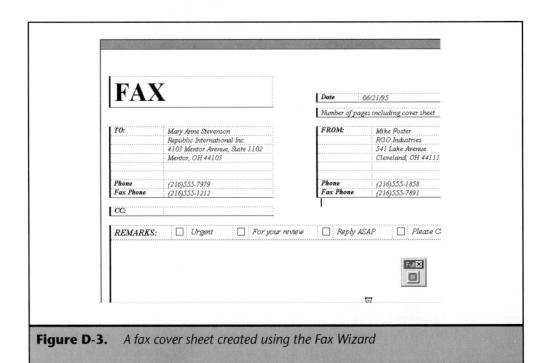

Figure D-3.   *A fax cover sheet created using the Fax Wizard*

Fax Cover Sheet Templates

The Contemporary Fax, Elegant Fax, and Professional Fax templates create fax cover sheets using a contemporary, elegant, or professional style. These are the same templates that the Fax Wizard uses when you select a style for the fax cover sheet's appearance. When you use the template, here are some things to keep in mind:

- When you open a document using this template, the document has text enclosed in brackets ([ ]) to remind you to supply information in that spot. Click there and type the replacement text.

- Alter the document template for the fax cover sheet so it automatically contains the information that remains the same every time you fax. For example, replace the fields where you enter your name, company name, address, and phone numbers with your own information. Then, you only need to enter the information that changes with each fax sheet that you create.

Invoice Template

This template creates an invoice form. It will do many of the basic computations, such as multiplying the amount of each item ordered by its price and adding the amounts for all items for the invoice's subtotal. When you use the template, here are some things to keep in mind:

- When you open a document using this template, the invoice has fields already set up for the shipping and ordering information as well as the items ordered. All you have to do is move to each form field and enter the appropriate information. When you are finished, print the invoice just like printing another document and save it if you want.

- If you are planning to use this invoice form, open the Invoice template, unprotect the document, make changes such as altering the company information, protect the document for forms, and save the document template. Then the next time you use the template, it will include the customized version with such specifics as your company name in place of the generic information. Another change you may want to make is to add a computation for sales tax based on your locality's tax rate.

Letter Wizard

This template is a wizard that creates various types of letters. Some of the customization options include:

- Selecting one of several standard business letters that you can modify to fit your own purposes. (These letters are stored in the files in the Letters folder in Word's folder.)

- Setting up a document to use a layout appropriate for a standard business or personal letter. This includes adding locations for the page number, date, initials, and other information that frequently appears in business and personal correspondence.

- Selecting whether the letter uses stationery. (You may want to select Yes if you are going to add graphics to print as a letterhead.)

- Providing the recipient's and return address.

- Selecting a professional, contemporary, or elegant style for the letter.

- Creating an envelope or mailing label for the letter.

Letter Templates

The Contemporary Letter, Elegant Letter, and Professional Letter templates create letters using a contemporary, elegant, or professional style. These are the same templates that the Letter Wizard uses when you select a style for the letter's appearance. When you use the template, here are some things to keep in mind:

- When you open a document using this template, the document has text enclosed in brackets ([ ]) to remind you to supply information in that spot. Click there and type the replacement text.

- You can alter the form letter so it contains the information that remains the same every time, such as the return address and your name. After you save the modified version of Contemporary Letter, Elegant Letter, or Professional Letter, the next letter you create with the modified template will already contain the correct return address and name.

Manual Template

This template is for creating manuals with a table of contents, body text, and index. This template includes so many predefined styles that are specific to creating manuals that you will want to print the eight pages of the document and follow its instructions that appear as the sample text.

Memo Wizard

This template is a wizard that creates an interoffice memo. Some of the customization options include:

- Adding a title to the memo
- Using a separate page for the distribution list

- Inserting items in the memo's heading, such as To, From, Date, CC, Subject, and Priority

- Inserting other text, such as writer's initials, typist's initials, number of enclosures, and whether any attachments are included

- Inserting text for a header, including a title, date, and page number, and text for a footer, including the date, page number, and the word "Confidential"

- Setting the style of text and placement of items

Memo Templates

The Contemporary Memo, Elegant Memo, and Professional Memo templates create memos using a contemporary, elegant, or professional style. These are the same templates that the Memo Wizard uses when you select a style for the memo's appearance. When you use the template, here are some things to keep in mind:

- When you open a document using this template, the document has text enclosed in brackets ([ ]) to remind you to supply information in that spot. Click there and type the replacement text.

- When you work with the Memo Wizard, you will see more prompts than you see in the documents created with these templates. These prompts include the typist's initials, the author's initials, the number of enclosures, and an attachment notice. If you want these in your memo that you create by using one of these templates, you will have to type them yourself. This also applies to entering a header and footer.

- You can alter these templates to change the [Names] prompt after From to your name since this is probably the same every time. After you save the modified version of these templates, the next memo you create with the modified template will already contain the correct author.

Newsletter Wizard

This template is a wizard that creates newsletters like the one shown in Figure D-4. Some of the customization options include:

- Setting the classic or modern style of the newsletter
- Selecting the number of columns in the newsletter
- Inserting the newsletter name
- Setting the number of pages in the newsletter
- Selecting whether the newsletter includes a table of contents, dropped capitals, the date, and volume and issue numbers

Figure D-4. *A newsletter created with the Newsletter Wizard*

Newsletter Template

This template offers a sophisticated three-column newsletter. It includes lots of tips for creating your newsletters, so creating a document from this template and printing it is worthwhile just for the suggestions it contains. You can replace its sample text with your own to create your newsletter.

Normal Template

This template is the default template. It includes many styles to fit varying tasks. These named styles include:

- ■ Normal style, which is used for paragraphs unless you select another one.

- ■ Styles for headers, footers, endnotes, and footnotes.

- ■ Styles named Heading 1 through Heading 9 that automatically label headings in a document for outline levels and entries for a table of contents. The styles named TOC 1 through TOC 9 set the format of the entries in the table of contents. If a document has an index, Index 1 through Index 9 sets the format of index entries.

- Three styles for lists: List through List 5, List Bullet through List Bullet 5, and List Number through List Number 5. If you have list text you want indented the same amount, use List Continue through List Continue 5. The five levels of the lists indicate how much the text is indented; the higher numbers are indented more.

- Named styles for addresses, including Closing and Signature.

- Other styles for title pages, such as Title and Subtitle.

- The Macro Text style, which sets the appearance of macros when you open a macro editing window.

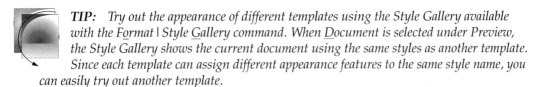

TIP: *Try out the appearance of different templates using the Style Gallery available with the Format | Style Gallery command. When Document is selected under Preview, the Style Gallery shows the current document using the same styles as another template. Since each template can assign different appearance features to the same style name, you can easily try out another template.*

Pleading Wizard

This template is a wizard that creates pleadings that are legal documents submitted to a court. Some of the customization options include:

- Setting the font, line spacing, and margins
- Adding a line on the sides of the pages
- Adding page numbers and line numbers
- Adding the attorney's name and address as well as setting the position
- Adding the name of the court
- Adding the locations for the plaintiff's name, defendant's name, case number, and pleading title.

Press Release Templates

The Contemporary Press Release, Elegant Press Release, and Professional Press Release templates create press releases using a contemporary, elegant, or professional style. When you use the template, you create a document with a sample press release. Replace the text with your own information.

Purchase Order Template

This template creates a purchase order form. This form performs many of the basic computations, such as multiplying the amount of each item ordered by its price and adding the amounts for all items for the subtotal. When you use the template, here are some things to keep in mind:

■ When you open a document using this template, the document is already set up as a form, with fields for the shipping and ordering information as well as the items you are ordering. For each field, move to the field and type the information. When you are finished, print the invoice just like printing another document and save it if you want.

■ If you are planning to use this purchase order frequently, open the Purchase Order template, unprotect the document, make changes (such as to the company information), protect the document for forms, and save the document template. Then the next time you use the template, the purchase order will include the customized information with such specifics as your company name.

Report Templates

The Contemporary Report, Elegant Report, and Professional Report templates create reports using a contemporary, elegant, or professional style similar to the styles that other templates use. The documents initially contain a sample report that you can replace with your own text.

Resume Wizard

This template is a wizard that creates resumés like the one shown in Figure D-5. Some of the customization options include:

■ Creating a resumé based on chronological experience, function, professional credentials, or for an entry-level position

■ Adding the name, address, and phone number

■ Adding headings for objective, education, awards, interests, hobbies, languages, work experience, volunteer experience, hobbies, references, extracurricular activities, summer jobs, summary of qualifications, community activities, professional memberships, accreditations and licenses, patents and publications, civil service grades, and security clearance

■ Arranging headings

■ Selecting a contemporary, elegant, or professional style for the resumé

■ Creating a cover letter by starting the Letter Wizard with Resume cover letter selected as the letter you want to create

Once the Resume Wizard creates the basis for your resume, click the different items and type the replacement text.

Figure D-5. *A resume created with the Resume Wizard*

Resume Templates

The Contemporary Resume, Elegant Resume, and Professional Resume templates are for creating a resumé using a contemporary, elegant, or professional style. These are the same templates that the Resume Wizard uses when you select a style for the appearance. When you use the template, here are some things to keep in mind:

- When you open a document using this template, the document has text enclosed in brackets ([ ]) to remind you to supply information in that spot. Click the reminder text and type the replacement text.

- The templates do not offer all of the choices you have when you use the Resume Wizard. For example, the Resume Wizard has more choices for sections within a resumé and lets you change the order of the sections. When you want to have the most options, use the Resume Wizard instead.

Table Wizard

This template is a wizard that creates a table like the one shown in Figure D-6. The Table Wizard can also be started by selecting Wizard from the Insert Table dialog box

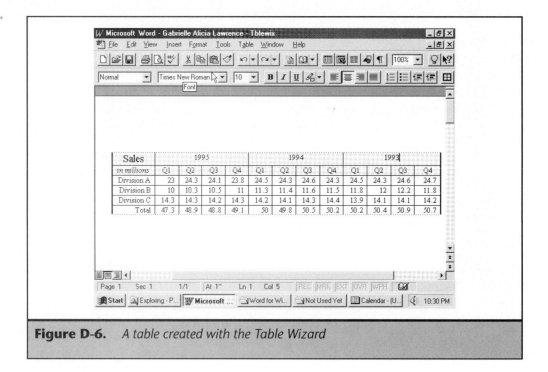

Figure D-6. *A table created with the Table Wizard*

that the Table | Insert Table command displays. Some of the customization options include:

- Selecting the line style for the table
- Selecting whether you have one or more rows used as table headings
- Selecting the number of columns
- Aligning the table headings and table entries
- Repeating table headings
- Adding column and row headings based on a regular series such as months, quarters, or years
- Setting the orientation of the table to portrait or landscape
- Displaying the Table AutoFormat dialog box so you can select character and paragraph formatting styles for the table

Thesis Template

This template is for creating a thesis. The difference between this template and the Normal template is the settings match the most common settings for theses. Use this template in place of Normal when you are creating a thesis. The document initially contains reminders for where you make entries. Click on the reminders and type the replacement text.

Weekly Time Sheet Template

This template creates a weekly time sheet form, which calculates total regular and overtime hours. When you use the template, here are some things to keep in mind:

- When you open a document using this template, the document is a form. Thus, you can move from field to field, supplying the appropriate information. When you are finished, print the invoice just as you would any other document and save it if you want.

- If you are planning to frequently use this form, open the Weekly Time Sheet template, unprotect the document, make changes (such as to the company information), protect the document for forms, and save the document template. Then the next time you use the template, it will show the customized version with such specifics as your company name in place of the generic information.

Altering a Template

Several of the templates mentioned in this chapter can be customized to fit your needs. For example, the fax cover sheet templates can be modified to include your name, address, and phone number. You can modify templates to assign different formatting to the styles a template provides. To change a template, follow these steps:

1. Select File | Open.
2. Select Document Templates under Files of Type.
3. Switch to the folder where the template is stored.
4. Select the template file to open and OK.

 NOTE: Remember that the document templates mentioned above are in the Templates folder in the folder containing your Word program or in the Microsoft Office folder. The document templates in tabs other than General are stored in folders inside the Templates one according to the name that appears on the tab.

5. Make the changes you want.

   If you modify the styles in a template, the modified style only changes documents you create afterwards. Documents that you created before using the template do not adopt the latest modifications.

6. Select File | Save to save the changes you have made to the template.

Creating Your Own Templates

You can create your own templates for specialized documents that you use repeatedly. To create a template, follow these steps:

1. Select File | New.

2. Select the template you want to use as the basis for the template you are creating. The template you are creating will have the same styles, toolbars, macros, and AutoText entries as the template you select in this step.

3. Select the Template option button, and select OK.

4. Make the changes you want, such as:

   ■ Use Format | Style to create new styles, modify existing ones, and delete the ones you do not want.

   ■ Add text to the document template that you want to be in every document created with the template. For example, if you want every document created with the template to have the same header, add the header to the template.

   ■ Create an AutoText entry named Gallery Example that shows what a document created with the template will look like.

5. Select File | Save to save the changes you have made to the template.

   You will want to save the template file in the same Templates folder where Word's templates are stored.

6. Type the name for the template in the File Name text box and select OK.

When you create your own templates, you can select which tab the template appears in by selecting the folder where you save the template. Templates saved in the Templates folder appear on the General tab, while templates saved in other folders within the Templates folder appear on the tab with the same name as the folder containing the template.

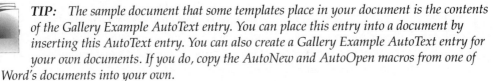 ***TIP:*** *The sample document that some templates place in your document is the contents of the Gallery Example AutoText entry. You can place this entry into a document by inserting this AutoText entry. You can also create a Gallery Example AutoText entry for your own documents. If you do, copy the AutoNew and AutoOpen macros from one of Word's documents into your own.*

Index

+ operator, in {=} field, 194
+ key, on the numeric keypad, 401
+ (plus sign) for specifying relative
    destinations, 374
- operator, in {=} field, 194
- key, on the numeric keypad, 401
- (minus sign), for specifying relative
    destination, 374
= operator, in {=} field, 194
= field, 193-195
* character, 479-480
* operator, in {=} field, 194
> operator, in {=} field, 194
>, in outlines, 402
>= operator, in {=} field, 194
< operator, in {=} field, 194
<= operator, in {=} field, 194
<> operator, in {=} field, 194
<>, in HTML, 660
^ operator, in {=} field, 194
$, in macros, 611, 612
% operator, in {=} field, 194
&, in dialog box text, 619

', in macros, 618
? button, 22, 291, 431
? character, 479
\#, 213-215
*, 212-213
* mergeformat statement, 566
* mergeformat switch, 213, 568, 569
    for preserving formatting, 191
\@, 213, 214
{}, in fields, 187
1.5 Space button, 705

A

Abbreviations, 62-63
    for states, 171
About Microsoft Word dialog box, 295
ABS function, allowed in {=} field, 194
Accelerator keys. *See* Shortcut keys
Actions, repeating, 435-436
Active document, 64
Active Macro button, 605

on the Macro toolbar, 332, 702
Active window, 6
Add New Record button, 126, 690
Add to Favorites button, 186
Add-in programs, 64, 429-430
Add/Remove REM button, 333, 624, 702
Address, forms of, 355
Address books, 65-66
    as the data source, 344-345
Address button, on the Standard toolbar, 65, 486, 687
Addresses
    checking for envelopes, 168
    inserting, 417
    selecting for labels, 318
Adjectives, rules for, 267-268
Advance feature, 66
ADVANCE field, 66, 195
Adverbs, rules for, 267-268
Agenda Wizard, 715, 716
Algorithms, 581
Aliases, 494
Align Drawing Objects button, in the Drawing toolbar, 157, 692
Align Left button, in the Formatting toolbar, 243, 688
Align Right button, in the Formatting toolbar, 243, 688
Aligning, frames, 66
Alignment, 66-69
Alignment buttons, 53
Alignment settings, for paragraphs, 52-53
All Caps button, 705
All Caps character format, 100
All Caps character formatting, 69-70
All Caps character style, 50
All check box, 542
Allow Accented Uppercase check box, 161
Allow Fast Saves option, 444
Alphabetizing. *See* sorting
ALT, 70-71
    activating the menu bar with, 5, 7
ALT+5, 460
ALT+-, 369
ALT+- (hyphen), 17
ALT+-(minus), 366
ALT+BACKSPACE, 35, 459
ALT+CTRL+A, 460
ALT+CTRL+E, 233, 460
ALT+CTRL+F, 233, 460
ALT+CTRL+N, 459
ALT+CTRL+O, 460
ALT+CTRL+P, 460
ALT+CTRL+U, 460
ALT+CTRL+V, 484
ALT+END, 509
ALT+F4, 185, 261, 459
ALT+F5, 18, 261
ALT+F9, 124, 190, 261, 540

ALT+F10, 18, 262
ALT+HOME, 509
ALT+PAGE DOWN, 509
ALT+PAGE UP, 509
ALT+SHIFT+*, 399
ALT+SHIFT++, 401
ALT+SHIFT++or+, 399
ALT+SHIFT+-, 401
ALT+SHIFT+-or-, 399
ALT+SHIFT+5, 399
ALT+SHIFT+A, 399
ALT+SHIFT+D, 131, 460
ALT+SHIFT+DOWN ARROW, 399, 402
ALT+SHIFT+F9, 261, 467
ALT+SHIFT+I, 460, 499
ALT+SHIFT+L, 399, 403-404
ALT+SHIFT+LEFT ARROW, 399, 402
ALT+SHIFT+O, 460, 505
ALT+SHIFT+P, 413, 460
ALT+SHIFT+R, 74
ALT+SHIFT+RIGHT ARROW, 399, 403
ALT+SHIFT+T, 131, 460
ALT+SHIFT+UP ARROW, 399, 402
ALT+SHIFT+X, 305, 460
ALT+SPACEBAR, 17, 366, 369
Always Create Backup Copy option, 444
Always Suggest check box, 481
Ampersand (&), in dialog box text, 619
Anchoring, 71
Anchors, displaying at the beginning of, 540
AND function, allowed in {=} field, 194
Angle bracket (>) marking, in outlines, 402
Angle brackets <>, in HTML, 660
Annotation marks, 71, 72
    displaying, 73
Annotations, 71-76, 650-651
    combining, 438
    deleting, 74
    editing, 74
    going to, 74
    inserting, 72-73
    pasting into text, 75
    printing, 75, 422, 427
    protecting documents for, 330
    reviewing, 650-651
    viewing, 73-74
Annotations pane, 73, 650
Announcements. *See* Flyers
ANSI characters, 207
ANSI codes, 76-77
ANSI file, 525
ANSI format, 573
Answer Wizard, 20, 22, 77, 294
Antonyms, 77, 525
Apostrophe ('), in macros, 618
Append. *See* Spike
Application window, 5-10
    sizing, 17
Arc button, on the Drawing toolbar, 155, 691

Arguments, in macro statements, 610
Arithmetic. *See* Math Calculations
Arrange All button, 706
Arrow, in graphs, 279
Arrow keys, 78
Art, in desktop publishing, 578
Ascending sort, 127, 353, 464
ASCII file, 525
ASCII format, 151, 573
ASCII text files, 78
ASK field, 78, 195, 350, 632-633
Attributes, 78-79
Audio, recording, 79
AUTHOR field, 79
Authorities, 79
AutoCaption, creating captions with, 101-102
AutoCorrect, 40, 79-83
    creating entries in, 81
    editing entries in, 81-82
    exception list in, 83
    replacing errors or abbreviations, 81
    turning on and off, 81, 83
AutoFormat, 83-86
AutoFormat button, on the Standard toolbar,
    84, 486, 687
Automatic Bulleted Lists check box, in the
    Options dialog box, 85
Automatic font substitution, 86-87
Automatic macros, 623
Automatic marking, of misspelled words, 476
Automatic Numbered Lists check box, in the
    Options dialog box, 85
Automatic pagination, 412, 414
Automatic Save Every option, 445
Automatic Save feature, 109
Automatic Spell Checking check box, 476, 481
Automatic updates, of links, 388
Automatic Word Selection check box, 160
Automatically Hyphenate Document check
    box, 300
AUTONUM field, 87, 195
AUTONUMLGL field, 87, 195-196
AUTONUMOUT field, 87, 196
AutoSum button, 706
AutoText feature, 87-89
    creating entries in, 88
    replacing or deleting entries, 88-89
AUTOTEXT field, 90, 196
AVERAGE function, allowed in {=} field, 194
Avery equivalent number, for labels, 319
Award Wizard, 715-716

B

Background Printing option, 422
Background Repagination check box, 263
Backnotes. *See* Endnotes
Backslashes (\)

in macros, 610
    separating folder names, 229
BACKSPACE, 30, 90, 134
Backup copies, of documents, 444
Bar codes, adding to addresses, 318
Bar tab alignment, 520
BARCODE field, 90, 196
BatchConverter macro, 572
Beep on Error Actions check box, 263
Bending Text. *See* WordArt
Binder, 90, 654-655
Binding area, entering the width of, 359
Bitmapped images, 578
Blank Document. *See* Normal template
Blank lines, in merged documents, 293, 348, 637
Bleed, 578
Block protection, 91
Blue Background, White Text check box, 263
Body text, displaying one line in outlines, 403
Bold, adding or removing, 91-92
Bold button, in the Formatting toolbar, 50, 242,
    688
Bold character style, 49, 51, 91-92
Book icons, in the Help Topics window, 20-21
Bookmark dialog box, opening, 92
BOOKMARK field, 92, 196-197
Bookmark indicators, 93
Bookmarks, 92-94, 196-197
    assigning to defined text, 209
    displaying, 540
    inserting the page number of the
        location of, 206
    naming, 92
    setting within merge documents, 636
Bookmarks check box, 540
Border graphics, adding to all pages, 547
Borders
    applying, 94-95
    applying in tables, 516
    applying to graphics, 283
    applying to paragraphs and frames,
        96-97
    applying to pictures, 97-98
    applying to tables, 98, 99
    and frames, 259
    removing, 95
Borders button, in the Formatting toolbar, 243,
    689
Borders check box, in the Options dialog box, 85
Borders toolbar, 94, 689
Bormuth Grade Level index, 273
Bottom Border button, on the Borders toolbar,
    689
Bottom margins, setting, 359
Branches, 400
    deleting, 403
    moving, 402
    promoting or demoting to other levels,
        402-403

selecting, 401-402
Break Link, setting, 389
Break Link command button, 565, 567
Breaks, 98
Bring Forward button, 706
Bring in Front of Text button, in the Drawing
toolbar, 156, 320,
692
Bring to Front button, in the Drawing toolbar,
156, 692
Brochure template, 716-717
Brochures, 588-590
Bulleted lists, 98, 326
Bullets, 98-99
adding automatically, 85
appearance of, 327
positioning, 328
removing, 326
Bullets button, 326
in the Formatting toolbar, 243, 688
on the Word for Windows 2 toolbar, 695
Business cards, 582-585
Buttons
assigning macros to, 336-337
displaying name/description of, 8
listing of miscellaneous, 703-707
listing of, 686-712
transferring images of, 529
By Column button, in the Microsoft Graph
toolbar, 275, 711
By Row button, in the Microsoft Graph toolbar,
275, 711

C

Calculation text form field, 247
Calculations. *See* Math calculations
Calendar Wizard, 717
Callout button, on the Drawing toolbar, 155, 691
Callouts, 99, 280
Camera-ready material, 578
Cancel command button, 14, 137
Cancel. *See* Close button
Capitalization, 100
Capitalize First Letter of Sentences option, in
AutoCorrect, 82
Capitalize Names of Days option, in
AutoCorrect, 82
Capitals, correcting errors beginning with two,
82
CAPS LOCK key, 26, 70, 100
correcting accidental usage of, 82
Captions, 100-103
creating with AutoCaption, 101-102
creating individual, 100-101, 102
deleting, 102
Cartridges. *See* Printer cartridges
Case

finding matching, 223
matching in document searches, 144
Catalogs, 629-630, 631
Cell names, in tables, 511
Cells
adding to tables, 512
deleting from tables, 512-513
formatting inside, 517
merging in tables, 514
numbering in tables, 516
referencing in tables, 517-518
selecting in tables, 510
splitting in tables, 514
Center button, in the Formatting toolbar, 243,
688
Center tab alignment, 520
Center-aligned paragraphs, 52, 53
Centered paragraphs, 68, 71
Centimeters, 103
Change button, on the TipWizard toolbar, 703
Change Case command, 100
Change Source dialog box, 389
Chapter numbers, 104
Character formats, 104-105
Character formatting
removing, 434, 535
setting with the * switch, 212
Character formatting codes, in HTML, 660-661
Character Spacing tab, 470
Character styles, 489
applying, 49-50, 51
guidelines for using, 50, 51
Characters
composing, 119
counting in documents, 550
deleting, 134
formatting, 46-51
inserting a string of, 210
returning the number in a document, 381
spacing between, 470-471. *See also*
Nonprinting characters
Characters per inch (cpi), 105
Chart Type button, in the Microsoft Graph
toolbar, 275, 711
Charts. *See* Graphs
Check Box fields, options for, 248-249
Check box form field, 247
Check Box Form Field button, in the Forms
toolbar, 245, 252, 693
Check boxes, 15, 16, 136
Check for Errors button, on the Mail Merge
toolbar, 358, 700
Check spelling. *See* Spelling
Chevrons <<>>
around field codes, 632
surrounding merge fields, 346, 347
Circle, drawing, 155
Citations
categories of, 500

marking for a table of authorities, 499
Clearing tabs. *See* Tabs
Clicking, 11, 372
Clicking speed, changing, 11
Client applications, 383, 563
Clip art, 105, 579
Clipboard, 105-108
copying with, 106, 107
cutting text to, 33-34
cutting with, 107
embedding data with, 384-385
linking data with, 384-385
linking and embedding data with,
558-559
moving with, 107
Close box, in windows, 19
Close button, 5, 6, 108, 703
in dialog boxes, 19
on the Header and Footer toolbar, 286,
289, 700
in the Print Preview toolbar, 546, 699
Close command, 37, 38
COL, on the status bar, 457
Coleman-Liau Grade Level index, 273
Collapse button, in the Outline toolbar, 401, 697
Collapsing heading levels, in outlines, 400-401
Collate Copies check box, 424
Color, setting for highlighting, 298
Color button, in the Microsoft Graph toolbar,
276, 712
Colors, assigning to text, 524
Column breaks, inserting, 113
Column widths
adjusting with the ruler, 112
changing, 111
setting options for in tables, 513
Columns, 109-113
balancing, 112-113
creating with menus, 111-112
creating with the Standard toolbar,
110-111
editing with menus, 111-112
endnotes in, 236
entering the number of, 111
footnotes in, 236
inserting breaks for, 111
selecting, 457
selecting in tables, 510-511
Columns button
on the Standard toolbar, 111, 486, 687
on the Word for Windows 2 toolbar, 695
Command buttons, 14-15, 137
Commands
for adding HTML codes to Web
documents, 665, 668
repeating, 435
Commands and Settings button, 141
Commas, rules for the placement of, 42
COMMENTS field, 114

Comments. *See* Annotations; Hidden text
Common abbreviations, 62-63
Comparative form, of adjectives and adverbs,
267
COMPARE field, 114, 197
Compare Versions button, 705
Comparison operators
for filtering merge records, 353
in the If dialog box, 634
Compatibility options, 117-118, 572
Compose, 119
Concatenation operator, in macros, 612
Concordance files, 307
Concordances, 119
Condensed character spacing, 470
Conditional end of page, 119
Confirm Conversion at Open check box, 264
Contemporary Fax template, 719
Contemporary Letter template, 720
Contemporary Memo template, 721
Contemporary Press Release template, 723
Contemporary Report template, 724
Contemporary Resume template, 725
Contents tab
in the Help Topics: Microsoft Word
dialog box, 292-293
in the Properties dialog box, 146
Context-sensitive help, 19-20
Continuation notices, in footnotes and
endnotes, 119, 235, 236
Continuation separator, 235, 236
Continue button, on the Macro toolbar, 333,
606, 702
Control Panel, 119
for changing mouse settings, 11
Conversion, of documents, 572
Convert File dialog box, 392
Convert template, 572
Copies, for printing, 424
Copy button
in the Microsoft Graph toolbar, 275, 711
on the Standard toolbar, 107, 486, 686
on the Word for Windows 2 toolbar, 695
Copy command, 35
Copy-fitting, 578
Copying, compared to linking and embedding,
560
Copyright symbol, 582
CorelDRAW!, 579
embedded graphics from, 564-565
Correct Accidental Usage of CAPS lOCK key, 82
Correct TWo INitial CApitals option, in
AutoCorrect, 82
Corrections, making, 30-31
COUNT function, allowed in {=} field, 194
Court decisions, listing citations for, 498
Create Data Source dialog box, 343-344
Create Envelope button, on the Word for
Windows 2 toolbar, 696

Create Labels dialog box, 629
Create Picture button, in the Drawing toolbar, 157, 693
Create Subdocument button, in the Master Document toolbar, 360, 648, 701
CREATEDATE field, 123
Criteria, 123
       for searching documents, 144
Cropping, graphics, 123
Cross-references, 123-124
CTRL+5, 32, 403, 456, 459
CTRL+[, 232
CTRL+], 232
CTRL+=, 497
CTRL+A, 457, 459
CTRL+B, 91, 244
CTRL+BACKSPACE, 30, 134
CTRL+C, 107, 459
CTRL+D, 460
CTRL+DEL, 30, 134
CTRL+DOWN ARROW, 29, 373
CTRL+E, 67, 244
CTRL+END, 29, 373
CTRL+ENTER, 285
CTRL+F2, 260, 459
CTRL+F3, 34, 261, 484
CTRL+F4, 19, 37, 261
CTRL+F5, 18, 261
CTRL+F6, 25, 149, 261, 549
CTRL+F7, 19, 150, 261
CTRL+F8, 18, 150, 261
CTRL+F9, 189, 190, 261
CTRL+F10, 18, 150, 262
CTRL+F11, 192, 262
CTRL+F12, 37, 262, 391, 459
CTRL+F, 219, 459
CTRL+G, 459
CTRL+H, 220, 459
CTRL+HOME, 29, 373
CTRL+(hyphen), 302
CTRL+I, 237, 244, 316
CTRL+INS, 459
CTRL+J, 67, 244
CTRL+K, 460
CTRL+L, 67, 244
CTRL+LEFT ARROW, 29, 373
CTRL+M, 244, 304
CTRL+N, 37, 459
CTRL+O, 37, 391, 459
CTRL+P, 41, 424, 459
CTRL+PAGE DOWN, 373
CTRL+PAGE UP, 373
CTRL+Q, 67, 434
CTRL+R, 67, 244
CTRL+RIGHT ARROW, 29, 373
CTRL+S, 37, 446, 459
CTRL+SHIFT++, 497
CTRL+SHIFT+<, 232

CTRL+SHIFT+>, 232
CTRL+SHIFT+A, 70
CTRL+SHIFT+C, 121
CTRL+SHIFT+D, 535
CTRL+SHIFT+DOWN ARROW, 455, 456
CTRL+SHIFT+END, 456
CTRL+SHIFT+ENTER, 113
CTRL+SHIFT+F3, 34, 261, 484
CTRL+SHIFT+F5, 92, 261, 459
CTRL+SHIFT+F6, 261
CTRL+SHIFT+F7, 204, 261
CTRL+SHIFT+F8, 113, 261, 457
CTRL+SHIFT+F9, 193, 261, 389, 397, 565, 567
CTRL+SHIFT+F11, 262
CTRL+SHIFT+F12, 262, 424, 459
CTRL+SHIFT+F, 231, 244
CTRL+SHIFT+HOME, 456
CTRL+SHIFT+HYPHEN, 284, 302
CTRL+SHIFT+K, 521
CTRL+SHIFT+L, 244
CTRL+SHIFT+LEFT ARROW, 456
CTRL+SHIFT+M, 244, 304
CTRL+SHIFT+N, 434
CTRL+SHIFT+P, 231, 244
CTRL+SHIFT+RIGHT ARROW, 456
CTRL+SHIFT+S, 244, 460, 490, 491
CTRL+SHIFT+SPACEBAR, 285
CTRL+SHIFT+T, 304
CTRL+SHIFT+U, 535
CTRL+SHIFT+UP ARROW, 456
CTRL+SHIFT+V, 121
CTRL+SHIFT+W, 535
CTRL+SHIFT, drawing with, 154, 156
CTRL+SPACEBAR, 434, 535
       for removing Small Caps, 461
       for removing Strikethrough, 488
CTRL+T, 304
CTRL+TAB, 137
CTRL+U, 244, 535
CTRL+UP ARROW, 29, 373
CTRL+V, 107, 459
CTRL+W, 19, 37, 459
CTRL+X, 107, 459
CTRL+Y, 459
CTRL+Z, 35, 459, 536
Curly braces {}, in fields, 187, 632
Current Date text form field, 247
Current time, inserting, 211
Current Time text form field, 247
Cursor. *See* Insertion point
Custom dictionaries, 481-483
Custom properties, 147
Custom tab, in the Properties dialog box, 147
Cut button
       in the Microsoft Graph toolbar, 275, 711
       on the Standard toolbar, 107, 486, 686
       on the Word for Windows 2 toolbar, 695
Cut command, selecting, 34

D

Dashes, 126
Data
    changing linked, 567
    embedded from other applications, 564
    embedding, 564-565
    embedding with the Clipboard, 384-385, 558
    inserting as a field, 129-130
    linked from other applications, 564
    linking, 564-565
    linking with the Clipboard, 384-385, 558-559
    updating in embedded objects, 565-567
    updating in linked objects, 565-567
Data field, 341
Data Form button, 126, 127, 128, 690
Data Form dialog box, displaying, 358
Data labels, in graphs, 279
Data object, 382
Data points, working with single, 280
Data record, 341
Data series, rearranging, 278
Data sources, 340
    adding headers for, 345
    address books as, 344
    creating for merges, 343-344
    existing documents as, 344
    from outside of Word, 354
    organizing, 353-354
Data Values, in macros, 611
DATABASE field, 126, 198
Database queries, inserting into documents, 198
Database toolbar, 126-127
    with data in tables, 518
    listing of buttons on, 690
Databases, 127-130
    importing documents from, 572
    inserting external, 127
    tables as, 518
Datasheets
    displaying, 275, 280
    in Microsoft Graph, 273
Date, 133
    formatting the display of, 213, 214
    inserting into documents, 130-133
    sorting by, 464, 465-466
Date button, on the Header and Footer toolbar, 286, 289, 699
DATE field, 132, 133, 198
Date formats, rules for using, 131-132
Date text form field, 247
Date and Time dialog box, 130
Date-time picture switch (\@), 213, 214
Days, capitalizing the names of, 82
DCA/RFT. *See* Rich Text Format (RFT)
DDE. *See* OLE
Decimal tab alignment, 520

Decorative fonts, 48
Decrease Indent button
    in the Formatting toolbar, 243, 688
    on the Word for Windows 2 toolbar, 695
Default folder, for documents, 133
Default options, setting, 533
Default settings. *See* Options
Default style, 380
Default tab stops, 27-28
Default tabs, changing the interval for, 518
Default Toolbar. *See* Standard toolbar
Default tray, selecting, 423
DEFINED function, allowed in {=} field, 194
Degrees, rules for abbreviating, 356
DEL, 30, 134, 459
Delete Cells button, 706
Delete Columns button, 706
Delete Documents. *See* Document Management
Delete Record button, 126, 690
Delete Rows button, 706
Delimiters, 354
Delivery Address text box, 168
Delivery addresses
    printing bar codes for, 318
    setting the style and position of, 170
Delivery Point Bar Code check box, 170
Demote button, in the Outline toolbar, 403, 696
Demote to Body Text button, on the Outline toolbar, 696
Descending order, sorting database records in, 127
Descending sort, 353, 464
Desktop publishing, 576-578
Details button, in the Open dialog box, 141
Dialog boxes, 13-14, 15, 135-137
    Close button in, 19
    creating, 618-622
    opening with the ruler, 443
    question mark (?) button in, 22
Dialog Editor, 618-622
Dialog Editor button, on the Macro toolbar, 333, 702
Dialog statement, 622
.DIC filename extension, 483
Dictionaries
    adding words to, 40
    custom, 481-483. *See also* Spelling
Dictionary icon, in the status bar, 477
DigValue function, 615
Directories
    creating, 717-718. *See also* Folders
Directory template, 717-718
Disassemble Picture button, 707
Display codes, for nonprinting characters, 378
Displaying, hidden text, 296
DOCPROPERTY field, 138, 199
Document conversion, 572
Document converter, editing, 572
Document icon, 6

Document icons, displaying menus for, 17
Document management, 140-145
Document margins. *See* Margins
Document numbers, 24
Document properties, prompting for, 445
Document Scrap label, 449
Document templates. *See* Templates
Document types
    converting to Word's, 570-572
    registering, 573
Document windows, 6-7
    148-151,. *See also* Windows
    arranging, 149
    maximized appearance of, 150
    moving, 150
    moving between, 149
    opening, 149
    sizing, 17
    sizing the active, 150
    typing in, 25-26
Document1 name, 24
Documentation. *See* Macro documentation
Documents, 71-72
    adding from another format, 207
    adding line numbers to, 322-325
    adding PAGE field to, 409
    annotating, 650-651
    attaching as separate files, 264
    attaching to electronic mail, 163-164
    automatically formatting, 84
    closing, 38, 108-109
    combining, 207
    comparing versions of, 114
    converting, 571-573
    converting non-Word, 264
    converting to the Word document type,
      570-572
    copying, 142
    creating, 24-25
    creating backup copies of, 444
    creating from outlines, 405
    creating from templates, 714-715
    creating properties for, 147
    default locations for, 394
    deleting, 142
    displaying recently used, 264
    distributing merged with e-mail, 354
    drawing in, 153-154
    editing, 28-36, 163
    embedding part of, 385-386
    faxing, 186-187
    fields for sharing, 383
    finding, 140-141, 393
    first pages in, 229
    formatting, 46-57
    inserting, 313-314
    inserting current date into, 198
    inserting database queries into, 198
    inserting date or time in, 130-133

inserting property values into, 147
linking to other applications, 560, 561
locating, 138-139
locking, 246, 329-332
making corrections in, 30-31
managing, 140-145
merging revisions to mailed, 439
modifying templates from, 523
moving around in with Outline view,
    405
naming, 37, 446
navigating within, 28-30
on a Network, 394
opening, 36, 142, 391-394
opening existing, 38-39
opening multiple, 393
opening new, 376-377
opening non-Word for Windows, 392
options for editing, 159-161
organizing by function, 90
of other document types, 570-573
outlining existing, 398-399
printing, 41, 142, 424-425, 428
properties of, 142, 145-148
protecting, 71-72, 329-332
removing protection from, 331
removing styles from, 493
renaming, 142, 434
resaving, 447-448
routing, 164-165, 644-645, 654
saving, 36-37, 329-330, 446-448
searching for, 143-145
searching from the middle of, 228
selecting entire, 32
sending to Microsoft Exchange
    members, 166
sharing, 148
shortcuts to opening, 393
sorting in the Open dialog box, 143
statistics of, 146
storing embedded objects in, 560, 561
switching among, 25
unprotecting, 71-72
viewing, 543-547
zooming, 544
DOS filename, for documents, 37
DOS text format, 151
Dot leaders. *See* Tabs
Dots per inch (dpi), 580
Double Space button, 705
Double spacing, 55, 469
Double Underline button, 704
Double underlining, adding/removing, 535
Double-clicking, 11, 373
    adjusting the speed of, 370
    for selecting words, 31
Double-diagonal arrow pointer, 18
Double-headed arrow pointer, 12, 18
Double-sided printing, 151-152

DOWN ARROW
    moving the insertion point with, 373
    moving in a table with, 509
Dpi, 580
Draft font, displaying all text as, 539
Draft Output option, 421
Drafts, printing, 428
Drag and Drop, 152-153
    copying text with, 153
    moving text with, 153
Drag and Drop Text Editing check box, 160
Dragging, 11, 372
    frames, 259
Dragging and dropping, moving and copying
    text by, 32-33
Draw feature, displaying objects created with,
    539
Drawing, on documents, 153-154, 157
Drawing button
    on the Microsoft Graph toolbar, 276, 712
    on the Standard toolbar, 153-154, 486, 687
    on the Word for Windows 2 toolbar, 696
Drawing objects
    moving in document layers, 320
    selecting, 157
Drawing toolbar, 155-157
    listing of buttons on, 691-693
Drawn objects
    aligning, 158
    printing, 422
Drop Cap button, 705
Drop-down fields, options for, 249
Drop-down form field, 247
Drop-Down Form Field button, in the Forms
    toolbar, 245, 252, 693
Drop-down list boxes, 15, 16, 136
Drop-down lists, 157
Dropped capitals, creating, 158-159
Dynamic data exchange (DDE). *See* OLE

E

E-mail messages, 644
Edit Data Source button, on the Mail Merge
    toolbar, 358, 701
Edit options, 159-161
EditConversionOptions macro, 572
Editing
    documents, 163
    embedded objects, 386-387
    fields, 191
    linked objects, 386-387
    styles, 492
Editing locations
    cycling through the last three, 30
    returning to prior, 437
Edits, undoing, 35-36
EDITTIME field, 163

Electronic mail, 163-166
Elegant Fax template, 719
Elegant Letter template, 720
Elegant Memo template, 721
Elegant Press Release template, 723
Elegant Report template, 724
Elegant Resume template, 725
Ellipse button, on the Drawing toolbar, 155, 691
Ellipses, 582
    in dialog boxes, 14
em, 580
em dash, 126, 581
em space, 582
EMBED field, 199, 383, 564, 568
Embed TrueType Fonts option, 445
Embedded objects, 166, 560
    altering in Word, 564-565
    changing the format of, 387-388
    creating, 383-384
    displaying as icons, 389
    editing, 386-387
    inserting, 384
    switching to be linked, 567-568
    updating, 565-567
    in Word documents, 563-570
Embedded sound objects, adding, 466-467
Embedding, 166, 382-383, 560-562
    data with the Clipboard, 558
    existing objects, 559
    new objects, 559
    part of a document, 385-386
    versus linking, 383-383
Embellishments
    selecting in Equation Editor, 175
    shortcut keys for popular, 178, 182
Emoters, for e-mail messages, 644
en, 580
en dash, 126, 581
en space, 582
Encapsulated PostScript (EPS) files. *See* EPS files
Enclosures, 167
END, 29
    moving the insertion point with, 373
End-of-cell character, 510
End-of-cell marks, 516
End-of-row character, 510
End-of-row marks, 516
Endnotes, 167, 233
    automatically numbered, 233
    in columns, 236
    converting, 238
    copying, 235
    creating, 233-234
    deleting, 234
    editing, 234
    formatting, 236
    indexing, 238
    moving, 234
    numbering, 235

referencing, 238
returning the number of, 206
specifying location of, 235
suppressing, 237-238
viewing, 237
ENTER key, 26, 27
Envelope Options dialog box, 169
Envelopes
    adding at the beginning of documents,
        168
    creating, 168-172
    inserting into the printer, 170
    printing, 168, 428
    printing in a merge, 625-627
    selecting the size of, 169
Envelopes and Labels dialog box, 318
Envelopes tab, in the Envelopes and Labels
    dialog box, 168-169
Environment defaults, WordPerfect's compared
    to Word, 172
EPS files, 167
EPS format, 172-173
EQ field, 173, 199-201
Equal Column Width check box, 112
Equation button, 704
Equation Editor, 173-183
    formatting with, 177-178
    listing of palettes in, 176-177
    opening as a separate application, 174
    shortcut keys for, 178-180, 181-182
    starting, 174
Equation Editor toolbar, 708-709
Equations
    creating, 199-201
    editing, 174
    entering, 173-183
Error messages, 183
Excel, 183-184
Excel worksheets, linked Word documents in,
    562
Exception list, in AutoCorrect, 83
Exchange Folder command, 166
Exchange. *See* Microsoft Exchange
Exclude dictionaries, 483. *See also* Spelling
Exiting, Word, 185
Expand button, in the Outline toolbar, 401, 697
Expanded character spacing, 470
Expanding heading levels, in outlines, 400-401
Exporting, Word documents, 185
EXPRESSION = field, 185
Expressions, in WordBasic, 609, 612
EXT indicator, 32
Extend key (F8), 32, 261
    selecting text with, 455, 456
External graphics, in HTML, 662

F

F1, 19-20, 260, 460
F2, 260
F3, 261
F4, 261, 459
F5, 261, 459
F6, 261
F7, 261, 460, 475
F8, 32, 261, 455
F9, 189, 261, 459
F10, 262
F11, 192, 262
F12, 37, 262, 459
Facing identification, including on documents,
    627, 629
FALSE function, allowed in {=} field, 194
Fast saves, 444
Favorites folder, 186
Fax cover sheet, creating, 718-719
Fax template, 186
Fax Wizard, 186, 718
Faxes, 186-187
Features, removing, 433
Field codes
    displaying, 540, 632
    editing, 191
    hiding, 632
    hiding/showing, 124
    inserted for Word fields, 350
    printing, 192, 422
    toggling with results, 190
Field Codes text, 188-189
Field command, 188
Field names, adding to data sources, 344
Field Names list box, 188
Field results
    applying, 541
    formatting, 191
Field shading selections, nonprinting shading
    to, 541
Fields, 187-215, 630, 632-636
    adding with shortcut keys, 189-190
    editing, 191
    for embedded data, 568-569, 570
    entering with menus, 188-189
    inserting with AutoText, 89
    for linked data, 568-569, 570
    locking, 192
    moving among in a document, 191
    nesting, 190
    preserving the formatting of, 189
    selecting for databases, 129
    shading, 190
    for sharing documents, 383
    sorting by, 465
    switches for, 212-215
    unlinking, 192-193
    unlocking, 192

updating, 190-191
Figures. *See* Graphics
File formats, 215-216
File management. *See* Document management
File menu, 7, 8
    recently used documents om, 39
File Name drop-down list box, 143
File-locking, 645
    for network users, 649
FILENAME field, 218
Files. *See* Documents
Files of Type drop-down list box, 143
Fill Color button, on the Drawing toolbar, 155, 691
FILLIN field, 202, 350, 633-634
Filter Records, selecting, 129
Filter Records tab, in the Mail Merge Helper
    dialog box, 353
Filtering, 218
Filters, for importing graphics, 283
FIM-A Courtesy Reply Mail check box, 170, 627
Find, 219-228
Find All Word Forms check box, 223
Find button, 703
Find dialog box, 219, 220
Find Records button
    on the Database toolbar, 127, 690
    on the Mail Merge toolbar, 358, 701
Find tab, in the Help Topics window, 22
Find What/Replace With option, 221
Find Whole Words Only check box, 221-222
First pages, in documents, 229
First Record button, on the Mail Merge toolbar, 357, 700
Flesch Reading Ease index, 273
Flesch-Kincaid index, 273
Flip Horizontal button, in the Drawing toolbar, 156, 692
Flip Vertical button, in the Drawing toolbar, 156, 692
Floating toolbars. *See* Toolbars
Flush Left/Right. *See* Alignment; Tabs
Flyers, 590-591
Folders, 229-230
    changing, 103
    creating new, 122-123
    deleting, 134
    looking in, 391-392
Font button, in the Formatting toolbar, 242, 688
Font cartridges, 103
Font dialog box
    for adding and removing All Caps, 70
    adding or removing bold with, 91
Font drop-down list, in the Formatting toolbar, 232
Font Size button, in the Formatting toolbar, 242, 688
Font substitution, automatic, 86-87
Font Substitution dialog box, 87, 118

Fonts, 47, 230-233
Footers, 233, 286
    adding page numbers to, 409
    at the side of the page, 289-290
    creating, 286
    creating watermarks as, 290
    deleting, 287
    editing, 286
    formatting page numbers in, 289
    horizontally positioning, 288
    inserting date or time in, 132
    letterheads in, 587
    linking, 288
    unlinking, 288
    vertically positioning, 287-288
Footnotes, 233
    automatically numbered, 233
    in columns, 236
    converting, 238
    copying, 235
    creating, 233-234
    deleting, 234
    editing, 234
    formatting, 236
    forms of, 237
    indexing, 238
    moving, 234
    numbering, 235
    referencing, 238
    returning the number of, 206
    specifying location of, 235
    viewing, 237
Foreign Language Support, 239-240. *See also*
    Language
Foreign language text, spell checking, 480
Foreign language thesauruses, 526
Form Field Options button, in the Forms
    toolbar, 245, 252, 693
Form Field Shading button, in the Forms
    toolbar, 245, 252, 693
Form fields, 245-246, 247
Form Letters. *See* Mail Merge
Format Callout button, on the Drawing toolbar, 155, 691
Format Painter button
    copying formatting with, 120
    on the Standard toolbar, 486, 686
Format switch (*), 212-213
Formats
    assigning to individual parts of
        dates/times/numbers, 213
    copying, 120-121
    searching for multiple, 228
Formatting
    characters, 46-51
    documents, 46-57
    with the Equation Editor, 177-178
    field results, 191
    finding, 223-225

footnotes, 236
frames, 257-259
graph elements, 279-280
inside cells, 517
master documents, 362-363
negative numbers, 214-215
note reference marks, 236
pages, 55-57
paragraphs, 46, 51-55
positive numbers, 214-215
removing, 433-434
replacing, 223-225
table contents, 515
updating in linked objects, 566
Formatting toolbar, 6, 9, 48, 242-244
adding or removing Bold with, 91
alignment buttons in, 67
applying styles with, 490-491
changing indents with, 304
creating paragraph styles with, 491
listing of buttons in, 688-689
selecting fonts with, 231
Forms, 245-252, 596-598
creating, 597-598
creating with Internet Assistant, 671-674
designing, 597
printing only data from, 422
protecting, 246
protecting documents for, 330
saving data only for, 445
Forms of address, 355
Forms dialog box, in Internet Assistant, 672-673
Forms toolbar, 245, 252
displaying, 245
listing of buttons on, 693
Formulas
entering, 173-183
inserting in tables, 511
For...Next logical structure, 615, 616
Four-headed arrow pointer, 18
FoxPro, 253
Fractions
creating, 253
creating with \F in EQ field, 200
replacing automatically with symbols, 86
Fractions with Fraction Character check box, in the Options
dialog box, 86
Frame border, 97
Frame dialog box, 255-256
Frames, 254
aligning, 66
applying borders to, 96-97
and borders, 259
dragging, 259
formatting, 257-259
horizontal position of, 257-258
inserting, 254-255
moving, 255-256

in Page Layout view, 255
removing, 259
setting the size of, 257
sizing, 256-257
vertical position of, 258-259
wrapping text around, 257, 258
Freeform button, on the Drawing toolbar, 155, 691
Full Screen button, 704
in the Print Preview toolbar, 546, 698
Full Screen view, 544
Function keys, 13, 260-262
Functions
allowed in {=} field, 194-195
in WordBasic, 608, 609, 610, 611

G

Gallery Example AutoText entry, 728
General default options, for Word, 263-264
General switches, for fields, 212-215
General tab, in the Properties dialog box, 146
GIF format, 662
Global macros, 622
Global search. *See* Find
Global templates, 522
Glossary feature. *See* AutoText feature
Go To command, 29-30
moving the insertion point with, 374-375
Go to Record button, on the Mail Merge toolbar, 357, 700
Goto logical structure, 613, 614
GOTOBUTTON field, 202
Grammar checking, 41, 265-270
options for, 271-272, 272-273
setting options for, 271
Grammar dialog box, 266
Grammar Options dialog box, 271-273
Grammar rules, setting, 271-272, 272-273
Graph elements
adding, 279
formatting, 279-280
Graphic design, 577-578
Graphic images. *See* Graphics
Graphic import filters, 283
Graphics, 280-283
adding to Web documents, 670
applying borders to, 283
creating with text, 551
cropping, 123, 281-282
displaying in Web pages, 662
editing imported, 283
inserting, 281
inserting with AutoText, 89
inserting into documents, 203
inserting into Word documents, 571
layering, 320-321
positioning, 283

replacing text with, 227-228
rotating, 441
selecting, 281
sizing, 281, 282
Graphics packages, 579
Graphs, 273-280
changing types of, 277-278
creating from tables, 274
creating without tables, 276-277
editing, 274, 276
Greeting cards, 591-593
Gridlines, 284
displaying in tables, 515
in graphs, 279
Group button, in the Drawing toolbar, 156, 692
Gutter text box, 359
Gutters, 56, 579

H

Hand Feeding Pages. *See* Printing
Handles, for sizing frames, 256
Hanging indents, 305. *See also* Indents
Hard disk, space requirements for Word, 678
Hard hyphens, 284-285, 302, 541-542
Hard page breaks, 285, 412
displaying, 414
inserting, 412-413
removing, 412-413
Hard spaces, 285, 541
displaying, 285
Hardware, required for Word for Windows 95, 678
Header and Footer toolbar, 286
listing of buttons on, 699-700
Header source document, creating, 345
Headers, 286
adding page numbers to, 409
at the side of pages, 289-290
creating, 286
creating watermarks as, 290
deleting, 287
editing, 286
formatting page numbers in, 289
horizontally positioning, 288
inserting date or time in, 132
letterheads in, 587
linking, 288
unlinking, 288
vertically positioning, 287-288
Heading levels, 400-401
Heading Numbering dialog box, 406
Heading rows, in tables, 516-517
Heading styles, in outlines, 405
Headings
repeating on each page in tables, 516-517. *See also* Outlines

Headings check box, in the Options dialog box, 85
Help, 291-295
accessing, 19-22
Help button
on the Print Preview toolbar, 546, 699
on the Standard toolbar, 22, 487, 687
Help Index, opening, 291
Help Topics: Microsoft Word dialog box, 291
Help topics, moving among, 20-21
Help Topics window, 20
Help window
keeping on top, 294
showing, 19-20
Help for WordPerfect Users check box, 263, 684
Hidden character style, applying, 296
Hidden paragraph characters, 296-297
Hidden text, 296-297
displaying, 296, 542
printing, 296, 422, 542
Hidden Text check box, 542
Hide Spelling Errors in Current Document
check box, 481
Highlight button, 298
in the Formatting toolbar, 243, 688
Highlight check box, 540
Highlighting, 297-298, 540
HOME, 29, 373
Homonyms, 225-226
Horizontal borders, creating, 85
Horizontal Gridlines button, in the Microsoft
Graph toolbar, 276,
712
Horizontal position, of frames, 257-258
Horizontal ruler, 441
Horizontal Scroll Bar check box, 541
Horizontal scroll bars, 449
Hot zone, 301
Hotspots, 292
.HTM extension, 665
HTML, 659
HTML codes, 299, 659-662
for hypertext links, 661
listing of, 666-668
viewing in Web documents, 669, 671
HTML documents. *See* Web documents
HTML edit toolbar, 663
Hypermedia, 658
Hypertext, 658
Hypertext documents, creating, 299
Hypertext links, HTML codes for, 661
Hypertext Markup Language. *See* HTML
Hyphenation, 299-302
automatic, 300
manual, 300
rules for, 299-300
Hyphenation zone, 301
Hyphens, 581
types of, 302

I

Icons
    displaying embedded/linked objects as, 389
    unassigned, 707
Identifier, in WordBasic, 621
IF field, 203, 251, 351
IF function, allowed in {=} field, 194
If...Then...Else logical structure, 613, 614
IF...THEN...ELSE merge field, 634-635
Imagesetter, 579
Import Chart button, in the Microsoft Graph toolbar, 275, 711
Import Data button, in the Microsoft Graph toolbar, 275, 711
Imported graphics, editing, 283
In-place editing, updating embedded data with, 566
INCLUDEPICTURE field, 203, 571
INCLUDETEXT field, 167, 204, 571
Increase Indent button
    in the Formatting toolbar, 243, 689
    on the Word for Windows 2 toolbar, 695
Indent paragraph format, for temporary margins, 359
Indentations, setting, 53-54
Indented indexes, 308
Indented paragraphs, 68
Indents, 303-305
    changing, 303-304, 443
    setting left, 161
    setting for multiple paragraphs, 442
Index entries
    automatically marking, 307
    marking, 305
Index Entry fields, 305, 308, 310-311
INDEX field, 204, 305, 308-310
Index and Find tabbed sections, 21-22
Index window, 21-22
Indexes, 305-311
    inserting, 307-308
    updating, 308
Infinitives, splitting, 272
INFO field, 204-205
Initials, in the User Info Options box, 538
Inline graphics, in HTML, 662
InputBox function, 617
INS key, 30, 311
    using for Paste, 160
Insert Address button, on the Standard toolbar, 417
Insert AutoText button, 704
Insert Cells button, 705
Insert Chart button, 696, 704
Insert Columns button, 705
Insert Database button, 127, 690
Insert File dialog box, 313
Insert Footnote button, 704

Insert Frame button
    in the Drawing toolbar, 157, 693
    in the Forms toolbar, 245, 252, 693
    on the Word for Windows 2 toolbar, 695
Insert Merge Field button, on the Mail Merge toolbar, 357, 700
Insert Microsoft Excel Worksheet button, on the Standard toolbar, 486, 687
Insert mode, 160, 311
Insert Picture dialog box, 281
Insert Rows button, 705
Insert Sound Object button, 704
Insert Subdocument button, in the Master Document toolbar, 360, 701
Insert Table button
    in the Forms toolbar, 245, 252, 693
    on the Standard toolbar, 486, 508, 687
    on the Word for Windows 2 toolbar, 695
Insert Word Field button, on the Mail Merge toolbar, 357, 700
Insertion point, 6, 10, 315
    moving, 29, 374-375
    moving with the keyboard, 374
Inside Border button, on the Borders toolbar, 689
INT function, allowed in {=} field, 194
Integral sign, creating, 200
Internet Assistant, 315, 658
    creating forms with, 671-674
    creating Web pages with, 662-674
    starting, 663, 664
Interoffice memos, creating, 720-721
Invoice forms, creating, 719
Invoice template, 719
Italic button, 50, 243, 688
Italic character style, 49, 51
Italics character format, 315-316
Items
    in dialog boxes, 618-619
    numbering, 208

JPEG format, 662
Justification. *See* Alignment
Justified paragraphs, 52, 53, 68-69
Justify button, in the Formatting toolbar, 243, 688

Keep Help on Top setting, 294
Kerning, 471, 579
Key combinations, in outlines, 399

Keyboard, 12-13
    assigning macros to, 335
    copying formats with, 121
    moving the insertion point with, 373
    selecting text with, 32, 455, 456
Keyboard options, 317-318
Keyboard shortcuts, 13

L

Label Options dialog box, 628-629
Label Products drop-down list box, 319
Labels, 318-319
    printing, 428
    standard sizes for, 628
Labels tab, in the Envelopes and Labels dialog box, 318
Landscape orientation, 57, 410-411
Landscape printing, 319
Language
    setting in Windows 95, 240. *See also* Foreign Language Support
Language dialog box, opening, 239
Last Modified drop-down list box, 143
Last Record button, on the Mail Merge button, 357, 700
Layering, text and graphics, 320-321
Layout formats, applying to sections, 452-453
Layout view, 42
Layouts, for keyboards, 13
Leading. *See* Spacing
LEFT ARROW, moving the insertion point with, 373
Left Border button, on the Borders toolbar, 689
left indent, setting, 303
Left margins, setting, 359
Left tab alignment, 520
Left-aligned paragraphs, 52, 53, 68
Left-handed mouse, 370
Legal documents, 322, 723
Legal format paragraph numbers, inserting automatically, 87, 195-196
Legal pleadings, creating, 322
Legend button, in the Microsoft Graph toolbar, 276, 712
Letter spacing. *See* Spacing
Letter Wizard, 719-720
Letterheads, 585-588
Letters, templates for, 719-720
Letters & Faxes tab, 186
Ligatures, 581-582
Line breaks, in macros, 610
Line button, on the Drawing toolbar, 155, 691
Line Color button, on the Drawing toolbar, 155, 691
Line Draw, 322
Line numbers, 322-325

Line spacing, 467
    setting, 55, 468. *See also* Spacing
Line Style button
    on the Borders toolbar, 689
    on the Drawing toolbar, 155, 691
Lines
    adding between columns, 111
    counting in documents, 550
    keeping on the same page, 413
    options for spacing, 469
LINK field, 205, 383, 564, 568, 569
Linked data, changing, 567
Linked and inserted documents, 571
Linked objects, 560
    altering in Word, 564-565
    changing settings for, 388-389
    displaying as icons, 389
    editing, 386-387
    inserting, 384
    switching to be embedded, 567-568
    unlinking, 565, 567
    updating, 565-567
    updating formatting in, 566
    in Word documents, 563-570
Linking, 382, 560-562
    data with the Clipboard, 558-559
    existing objects, 559
    footers, 288
    headers, 288
    new objects, 559
    versus embedding, 382-383
Links
    breaking, 389
    locking, 566
    settings for updating, 388-389
    updating, 264, 422, 566
Links command, 567
Links dialog box, 388, 567
List boxes, 15-16, 136
List button, in the Open dialog box, 141
Lists, creating numbered or bulleted, 325-328
Lock Document button, in the Master Document toolbar, 360, 701
Locked links, 566
Locking
    documents, 246, 329-332
    fields, 192
    master documents, 331
    templates, 246
Logic, adding to macro commands, 334
Logical structures, in WordBasic, 609, 612-616
Long form, for citations, 499
Look In Favorites button, 186
Look In list box, 391
Lotus 1-2-3 spreadsheet program, 332

M

Macintosh files, opening, 332
Macro button, on the Macro toolbar, 333, 702
Macro commands, inserting, 606-607
Macro documentation, 617-618
Macro Record toolbar, 333, 336
Macro recorder, 604
Macro Text style, 607, 723
Macro toolbar, 332-334
    editing macros with, 604-606
    listing of buttons on, 702
    testing macros with, 605-606
MACROBUTTON field, 205, 334, 337, 523-524
Macros, 334, 604
    assigning, 335
    assigning to buttons, 336-337
    building blocks of, 608-618
    copying to other templates, 337-338
    creating with WordBasic, 607-618
    debugging, 623-624
    editing, 338-339, 604
    execution priority for, 623
    inserting commands for, 606-607
    mapping the logic of, 608
    mistakes to avoid, 611
    models supplied with Word, 339-340
    moving to other templates, 337-338
    planning, 607-608
    problems with writing, 611
    recording, 334-336
    renaming, 338
    running, 336
    saving with templates, 522
    storing, 622-623
    testing, 605, 623-624
Magnification, changing, 544
Magnifier button, 545, 546, 698
Magnifying glass pointer, 545
Mail as Attachment check box, 264
Mail merge, 340-357, 624-637
    prompt during, 195
    for records with fax numbers, 186-187
Mail Merge button, on the Mail Merge toolbar, 358, 701
Mail Merge Helper button, on the Mail Merge toolbar, 357, 700
Mail Merge Helper dialog box, 342-343, 624
Mail Merge Main Document button, 127, 690
Mail Merge toolbar, 343, 357-358
    listing of buttons on, 700-701
Mail. *See* Electronic mail
Mailed documents, merging revisions to, 439
Mailers. *See* Brochures
Mailing labels
    creating with Mail Merge, 627-629, 630.
      See also Labels
Main Dictionary Only check box, 481
Main document, creating for a merge, 342-343

Manage Fields button, 126, 127, 128, 690
Managing documents. *See* Document management
Manual option button, from the Links dialog box, 566, 567
Manual template, 720
Manual updates, of links, 388
Manuals, creating, 720
Margins, 55, 56, 358-360
    changing, 358-359, 441
    establishing temporary, 359
    settings for, 56-57
Margins tab, of the Page Setup dialog box, 56-57
Mark Index Entry dialog box, 306-307
Mark revisions feature, 646
Master Document toolbar, 360-361
    listing of buttons on, 701
Master Document view, 544
Master Document View button, on the Outline toolbar, 407, 698
Master documents, 361, 647, 648
    creating, 361-362, 647-648
    formatting, 362-363
    locking, 331
    page numbering in, 365
    printing, 363
    reorganizing, 363-364
    and sections, 454
    unlocking, 331
Masthead, 599-600, 601
Match All Word Forms check box, 144
Match Case check box, 144, 223
Math calculations, 365
MathType, 180, 182
MAX function, allowed in {=} field, 194
Maximize button, 6, 17, 366
Maximized window, 5
Maximizing windows, 365-366
Measurement units
    changing default, 103
    selecting, 264
Meetings, creating agendas for, 715, 716
Memo templates, 721
Memo Wizard, 720-721
Memory, minimum required, 5
Menu bar, 6, 7-8
    activating, 71
Menu commands, shortcut keys for, 178, 179
Menus
    activating, 5
    assigning macros to, 335
    customizing in Word for Windows 95, 366-368
    entering fields with, 188-189
Merge fields, 341
    chevrons surrounding, 346, 347
    inserting, 345-348
    selecting from data sources, 357
Merge Revisions button, 438

Merge. *See* Mail merge
Merge Subdocument button, in the Master Document toolbar, 360, 701
Merge to New Document button, on the Mail Merge toolbar, 358, 701
Merge to Printer button, on the Mail Merge toolbar, 358, 701
Merged documents
    distributing with e-mail, 354
    printing, 428
MERGEFIELD fields, 205, 346, 368
MERGEREC field, 205, 351, 368, 635-636
Merges
    executing, 348-349
    problems with, 636-637
MERGESEQ field, 205, 351, 368, 635-636
Microsoft Access, 64
Microsoft Access button, on the Microsoft toolbar, 694
Microsoft Binder. *See* Binder
Microsoft Excel button, on the Microsoft toolbar, 694
Microsoft Exchange, 163, 368
Microsoft FoxPro button, on the Microsoft toolbar, 694
Microsoft Graph, 273
Microsoft Graph toolbar, buttons on, 275-276
Microsoft Mail, routing documents with, 654
Microsoft Mail button, on the Microsoft toolbar, 694
Microsoft Paint, 369
Microsoft PowerPoint button, on the Microsoft toolbar, 694
Microsoft PowerPoint. *See* PowerPoint
Microsoft Project button, on the Microsoft toolbar, 694
Microsoft Project. *See* Project
Microsoft Publisher button, on the Microsoft toolbar, 694
Microsoft Publisher. *See* Publisher
Microsoft Schedule+, 164
Microsoft Schedule+ button, on the Microsoft toolbar, 694
Microsoft toolbar, listing of buttons on, 694
Microsoft Word. *See* Word for Windows 95
MIN function, allowed in {=} field, 194
Minimize button, 6, 18, 369
Minimizing windows, 369
Mirror margins, 56, 359
Misspellings
    fixing marked, 477. *See also* Spell Check
Mistakes, finding and replacing, 225-226
MOD function, allowed in {=} field, 194
Model macros, supplied with Word, 339-340
Monospaced fonts, 49
    measuring the size of, 105
Monthly calendars, creating, 717
Most Recently Used list, of documents, 447

Mouse, 11-12
    cropping graphics with, 281-282
    customizing, 369-371
    moving the insertion point with, 374
    selecting text with, 31, 454-455
    sizing graphics with, 281
    techniques for using, 372-373
Mouse button, designating the primary, 11
Mouse pointer, 6, 371, 372
    shapes for, 12
Move command, for moving windows, 18-19
Move Down button, in the Outline toolbar, 402, 697
Move Up button, in the Outline toolbar, 402, 697
MRK indicator, in the status bar, 114, 646
MsgBox statement, 616
MSSP2_EN.EXC file, 483
Multilevel bullets, appearance of, 327
Multiple Pages button, in the Print Preview toolbar, 546, 698

N

Names, for documents, 37, 446
Navigation keys, changing to WordPerfect, 684
Navigation Keys for WordPerfect Users check box, 263, 684
Negative cropping, 97, 282
Negative indents, 304-305, 375
Negative numbers, formatting, 214-215
Nesting, fields, 190
Networks
    file-locking features, 649
    routing documents on, 644-645
    Word for Windows 95 on, 643-645
New button
    on the Standard toolbar, 24, 377, 485, 686
    in the Word for Windows 2 toolbar, 694
New command, 37
New dialog box, 24
New Window button, 706
Newsletter template, 722
Newsletter Wizard, 721-722
Newsletters, 598-602
Newspaper-style columns, 109
NEXT field, 205, 352, 377, 635
Next Record button, on the Mail Merge toolbar, 357, 700
NEXTIF field, 205, 352, 378, 635
No Border button, on the Borders toolbar, 689
Nominative case, 269
Non-variable text, ensuring the correctness of, 354-356
Nonbreaking hyphens. *See* Hard hyphens
Nonbreaking spaces. *See* Hard spaces
Nonprinting characters, 378-380
    display codes for, 378

displaying, 379, 541-542. *See also*
Characters
Normal saves, 444
Normal style, 231, 380
assigning to text, 434
to assigning text, 434
Normal template, 714, 722-723
prompting about saving changes to, 445
storing macros in, 622-623
Normal view, 42, 43, 237, 543-544
appearance of columns in, 110
switching to, 43
NOT function, allowed in {=} field, 194
Note reference marks, 233, 236
Note separators, types of, 235-236
NOTEREF field, 206, 380
NOTEREF field type, 238
Notes, 381. *See also* Footnotes, Endnotes
Notes pane, 234
Number of Columns text box, 111
Number of Copies text box, 424
Number picture switch (\#), 213-215
Number pictures, elements of, 215
Number text form field, 247
Numbered lists, creating, 326
Numbering, adding automatically, 85
Numbering button, 326
in the Formatting toolbar, 243, 688
on the Word for Windows 2 toolbar, 695
Numbering systems, for captions, 101
Numbers
adding to outlines, 403-404
positioning, 328
removing, 326
rules for entering, 26
setting the appearance of, 328
superscripting text after, 85. *See also* Line
numbers; Page numbers
NUMCHARS field, 381
Numeric formulas, in macros, 612
NUMPAGES field, 381
NUMWORDS field, 381

O

Object Anchors check box, 540
Object Linking and Embedding (OLE). *See* OLE
Objective case, 269
Objects
embedding, 166
embedding in Word documents, 199
linking, 382
linking and embedding existing, 559
linking and embedding new, 559
ODBC (open database connectivity) driver, 354
Odd pages, forcing in sections, 453
Office Binder. *See* Binder
Offset printing, 579

OK command button, 14, 137
OLE, 382-390, 558, 563, 564
OLE(_)LINK bookmark, 569
One Page button
in the Print Preview toolbar, 546, 698
on the Word for Windows 2 toolbar, 696
Online forms, 245, 251, 391
Online help, 391
Open button
on the Standard toolbar, 485, 686
in the Word for Windows 2 toolbar, 694
Open command, 37, 38-39
Open Data Source dialog box, 344
Open dialog box, 140-141
options in, 141-145
Open Subdocuments button, 706
Operators
allowed in {=} field, 194
in the IF field, 351
in macros, 612
Optical center, of a page, 580
Option buttons, 16, 136-137
Optional hyphens, 302
displaying, 284, 541
Options, 394-395
for grammar checking, 271-272, 272-273
setting default, 533
startup, 487-488
OR function, allowed in {=} field, 194
Ordinal numbers, superscripting text after, 395
Ordinals (1st) with Superscript check box, in
the Options dialog
box, 85
Organizer feature, 395-397, 493
Orientation
and page size, 410-411
setting for pages, 57
Orphans, 413-414, 548
Outline branches, 400
deleting, 403
moving, 402
promoting or demoting to other levels,
402-403
selecting, 401-402
Outline format paragraph numbers, inserting
automatically, 87
Outline numbering, changing the style of, 406
Outline Numbers, adding, 403-404
Outline toolbar, 398, 407
listing of buttons on, 399, 696-698
Outline view, 407, 544
moving quickly through large
documents with, 405
switching to, 398
Outlines, 397-406
automatically numbering paragraphs in,
195, 196
creating documents from, 405
creating new, 398-399

printing, 405
Outside Border button, on the Borders toolbar, 689
Overstriking, with \o switch in EQ field, 201
Overtype mode, 30, 311
Overtype Mode check box, 160
OVR indicator, 30, 160, 311

P

Padlock. *See* Master Documents
Page breaks, 412
    controlling in tables, 517
    displaying, 414
PAGE DOWN, moving the insertion point with, 373
PAGE field, 206, 407
    adding to documents, 409
Page layout options, 46
Page Layout view, 544
    appearance of columns in, 110
    endnotes in, 237
    footnotes in, 237
    with frames, 255
    switching to, 43
Page numbers, 408-409
    adding to headers or footers, 409
    formatting in headers and footers, 289
    inserting, 408-409
    restarting, 377
Page Numbers button, on the Header and Footer toolbar, 286, 289, 699
Page Setup button, on the Header and Footer toolbar, 286, 287, 289, 699
Page Setup dialog box, 55
Page size
    and orientation, 410-411
    settings for, 57
Page structure codes, in HTML, 660-661
PAGE UP, moving the insertion point with, 373
PAGEREF field, 206, 412
PAGEREF field code, 124
Pages
    centering, 103
    changing the orientation of, 57
    counting in documents, 550
    first in documents, 229
    formatting, 55-57
    inserting the total number of, 208
    moving to specific, 29-30
    numbering in master documents, 365
    optical center of, 580
    repaginating, 263
    restarting numbering, 377
    returning the number in a document, 381
    selecting for printing, 424
Pagination, 412-414
    automatic, 414

turning off automatic, 412
Paintbrush. *See* Microsoft Paint
Palettes, for entering equations, 175
Panes
    splitting document windows into, 149
    splitting windows into, 545
Paper size, setting, 57
Paper Size drop-down list box, 410
Paper Size option, selecting double-sided printing with, 151
Paper source, 415-416
Paragraph alignment, reverting to the default, 67
Paragraph borders, 96, 97
Paragraph characters, hidden, 296-297
Paragraph dialog box, 52, 67
Paragraph formats, 416
    copying, 121
Paragraph formatting, removing, 434
Paragraph marks
    displaying, 541. *See also* Nonprinting characters
Paragraph Marks check box, 541
Paragraph numbers, inserting automatically, 87
Paragraph spacing, 467, 468, 469
Paragraph styles, 489, 491-492
Paragraph symbol (), 27
Paragraph-based word processor, 682
Paragraphs, 68
    alignment settings for, 52-53
    applying borders to, 96-97
    automatically numbering in an outline, 195, 196
    centered, 68
    changing spacing between, 55
    changing spacing within, 54-55
    counting in documents, 550
    ending, 27
    formatting, 46, 51-55
    indented, 68
    justified, 68
    keeping at the top of page, 413
    keeping together, 413
    left-aligned, 68
    numbering, 325
    right-aligned, 68
    selecting, 31
    setting indentations for, 53-54
Parallel columns. *See* Columns
Password protection, for documents, 445-446
Passwords, 331
    protecting documents with, 71-72
    saving documents with, 329-330
Paste button
    in the Microsoft Graph toolbar, 275, 711
    on the Standard toolbar, 107, 486, 686
    on the Word for Windows 2 toolbar, 695
Paste command, 34
Paste Special dialog box, 107-108, 385

Pasting
annotations into text, 75
with the original format, 107-108
Path, 229
Pattern button, in the Microsoft Graph toolbar, 276, 712
Pattern Matching, 223, 224
Pause, in the Macro Record toolbar, 336
Pen Annotation button, 704
Personal address book, 417
PGDN, 29
PGUP, 29
Pica, 580
PICT files, 417
Picture dialog box, 281
Picture Editor check box, 161
Picture frame, creating, 158
Picture Placeholders check box, 540
Pictures
applying borders to, 97-98
editor for, 161. *See also* Graphics
Pie charts, 418
Pitch, 418
Placeholders, 418, 540
Pleading Wizard, 322, 723
Plotter fonts, 232
Plurals, rules for creating, 80
Pointer tracking speed, adjusting, 370
Pointer trails, showing, 370
Pointing, 11
Points, 49, 97, 580
Points drop-down list box, 231-232
Pop-up menus, displaying, 460
Popular symbols, shortcut keys for, 178, 180
Portrait orientation, 57, 410-411
Position settings, for text, 50-51
Positive form, of adjectives and adverbs, 267
Positive numbers, formatting, 214-215
Possessive case, 269
POSTNET bar code, 170, 196
PostScript, 419
PowerPoint, 419
Preferences, 419-420
Preprinted forms, printing, 422
Preserve Formatting During Updates check box, 191
Press releases, templates for, 723
Preview button, in the Open dialog box, 141
Preview. *See* Print preview
Previous Record button, on the Mail Merge toolbar, 357, 700
Primary sort key, in merges, 353
Print button
in the Print Preview toolbar, 546, 698
on the Standard toolbar, 425, 486, 686
on the Word for Windows 2 toolbar, 696
Print command, 41
Print dialog box, 142, 424-425
PRINT field, 206, 420

Print folder, 41
Print merge. *See* Mail merge
Print order, reversing, 422
Print Preview, 427, 544
working in, 545
Print Preview button, on the Standard toolbar, 486, 686
Print Preview command, 43-44
Print Preview toolbar
buttons on, 545, 546
listing of buttons on, 698-699
Print queue, displaying, 138
Print shop, 580
Print tab, in the Options dialog box, 421
PRINTDATE field, 423
Printed forms, 245, 250-251
Printer cartridges, 103
Printer fonts, 232, 423
Printers
changing settings for, 424
confirming selected, 428
inserting envelopes into, 170
problems with, 425-427
sending instructions to, 206
Printing, 423-429
annotations, 75
documents, 41, 424-425
double-sided, 151-152
drafts, 428
envelopes, 428
field codes, 192
hidden text, 296
labels, 428
merged documents, 428
multiple documents, 428
options, 421-423
outlines, 405
Prior editing locations, returning to, 437
PRIVATE field, 207, 429
PRODUCT function, allowed in {=} field, 194
Professional associations, rules for abbreviating, 356
Professional dictionaries, 483
Professional Fax template, 719
Professional Letter template, 720
Professional Memo template, 721
Professional Press Release template, 723
Professional Report template, 724
Professional Resume template, 725
Program icons, 6
displaying the menus for, 17
Programs, 429-430
Project, 430
Promote button, on the Outline toolbar, 402, 696
Prompt for Document Properties option, 445
Prompt to Save Normal Template option, 445
Pronouns, rules for, 269-270
Proofing, 430
Properties, 430

creating for documents, 147
of documents, 142, 145-148
Properties button, in the Open dialog box, 141
Properties dialog box
inserting data from, 199, 204-205
tabs in, 146-147
Proportional fonts, 49
Protect Document command, 246
Protect Form button, in the Forms toolbar, 245, 246, 252, 693
Protected documents, 71
Protecting, documents, 329-332
Publisher, 430
Purchase Order template, 723-724

Q

QBasic. *See* WordBasic
Quadruple spacing, 55
Queries, 431
Query options, specifying, 352-353
Query Options dialog box, setting options in, 129
Quick keys. *See* Shortcut keys
QuickTips, 291, 431
Quotation marks, 431
replacing, 85
rules for, 463
QUOTE field, 207, 431

R

Radical sign, creating with \R in EQ field, 201
Radio buttons. *See* Option buttons
Ranges of cells, inserting from spreadsheets, 315
Raster images, 283, 578
RD field, 207, 432
Read-only documents, 330, 331, 432
Read-write documents, 331
Readability statistics, 266
Readability Statistics dialog box, 273
Recently Used File List check box, 264
Recompiling, 432
Record button, on the Macro toolbar, 333, 607, 702
Record Next Command button, on the Macro toolbar, 333, 607, 702
Records
creating with additional data fields, 354
displaying, 357
entering new into a database, 126, 127, 128
filtering for databases, 129
skipping while merging, 352, 636
sorting for databases, 129
specifying for merging, 348

Rectangle button, on the Drawing toolbar, 155, 691
Redo actions, 536-537
Redo button, on the Standard toolbar, 486, 687
Redundancy, rules for correcting, 227
REF field, 207, 433
REF field code, 124
References. *See* Cross-references, footnotes, endnotes
Registered symbol, 582
Registration
of document types, 573
online, 679
Registry, 433
Regular hyphens, 302
Regular text form field, 247
Remarks, in macros, 617
Remove Subdocument button, in the Master Document toolbar, 360, 701
Renaming, documents, 434
Renumbering, 434
Reorganizing an outline, 434
Repagination, 434-435
Repeat button, 703
Repeat command, 435
Replace, 219-228
Replace dialog box, 220
Replace Text As You Type check box, 473
Replace Text as You Type option, in AutoCorrect, 82
Replacement typing. *See* INS key
Replacements, undoing, 226-227
Replacing text. *See* Find
Reports, 593
creating, 595-596
designing, 593-594
templates for, 724
Reset Picture Boundary button, 707
Reshape button, in the Drawing toolbar, 156, 692
Resizing, 436
Resolution, 580
Restore button, 18
Restoring, 437
Resume Wizard, 724-725
Resumes, templates for, 725
Return address, setting the style and position of, 170
Return addresses, entering, 168
Return Characters. *See* Nonprinting characters
RETURN key, 26
Reusable entries. *See* AutoText
Reveal Codes screen, in WordPerfect, 682
Reverse Print Order option, 422
Reversing print order. *See* printing
Review AutoFormat Changes dialog box, 84
Review Revisions button, 705
Review Revisions dialog box, 646, 647
Revision marks, 114, 115, 646

adding, 114-115
designating settings for, 116
hiding, 117
merging current, 438-439
Revisions
accepting/rejecting, 116-117
compiling all, 439-440
protecting documents for, 330
reviewing, 116
undoing, 116-117
REVNUM field, 440
RFT-DCA format, 440
Rich Text Format (RTF), 440
RIGHT ARROW, moving the insertion point
with, 373
Right Border button, on the Borders toolbar, 689
Right indent, setting, 303
Right margins, setting, 359
Right tab alignment, 520
Right-aligned paragraphs, 52, 53, 68, 69
Right-clicking, 11, 373
Right-pointing arrows, 541
Rotate Left button, 707
Rotate Right button, in the Drawing toolbar,
156, 692
Rotating, text and graphics, 441
ROUND function, allowed in {=} field, 195
Rounded Rectangle button, 706
Routing, documents, 164-165
Routing Slip button, 703
Routing slips, adding, 645
Rows
adding in tables, 512
selecting in tables, 510
setting options for in tables, 513
RTF format, 440
Ruler, 6, 9, 441-443
adjusting column widths with, 112
changing indents with, 303-304
changing margins with, 359
displaying, 442
hiding, 442
opening dialog boxes with, 443
symbols on, 442
Rules, 580
Run-in indexes, 308

S

Same as Previous button, on the Header and
Footer toolbar, 286,
289, 699
Sans serif fonts, 48, 580
Save As command, 36-37, 38
Save As dialog box, 108-109, 444, 446-447
Save button
on the Standard toolbar, 446-447, 486, 686
on the Word for Windows 2 toolbar, 695

Save command, 37, 38
Save Data Only for Forms option, 445
Save Native Picture Formats Only option, 445
Save options, setting, 444-446
Save Search dialog box, 144
Save as Type drop-down list box, 216
SAVEDATE field, 446
Scalable fonts, 49, 231-232
Scaling graphics. *See* Graphics
Scrap icon, 449
Scraps, 35, 448-449
Screen fonts, 86, 232, 449. *See also* Fonts
Screens, 580
Scroll arrows, 450
Scroll bars, 6, 9-10, 449-450
moving the insertion point with, 374
Scroll boxes, 6, 9, 450
Scrolling, 450
Search options, in the Open dialog box, 143-145
Searches, saving, 144
Secondary files. *See* Data sources
Section breaks
copying, 454
deleting, 453
finding, 454
inserting, 451-452
SECTION field, 208, 451
Section number, inserting, 208
SECTIONPAGES field, 208, 451
Sections, 451-454
applying layout formats to, 452-453
and master documents, 454
Select Case statement, 615
Select Drawing Objects button, in the Drawing
toolbar, 156, 691
Selecting text, 454-457
Selection bar, 31
Send Backward button, 706
Send Behind Text button, in the Drawing
toolbar, 156, 320, 692
Send Mail button, 703
Send to Back button, in the Drawing toolbar,
156, 692
Sentence text box, 266
Sentences
capitalizing the first letter of, 82
selecting, 31
Separator, 235, 236
SEQ field, 208-209, 458, 505, 506
Sequence numbers, in indexes, 310
Serial number, retaining for Word for Windows
95, 679
Serif fonts, 47-48, 580
Server applications, 383, 563
Service bureau, 580-581
SET field, 209, 352, 458
Sets, numbering items of, 208
Setup program, 678-680
Shading

applying, 96
applying in tables, 516
fields, 190
Shading button, on the Borders toolbar, 689
SHIFT, 26
drawing with, 154, 157
SHIFT+CTRL+F6, 149, 549
SHIFT+CTRL+F11, 192
SHIFT+DEL, 459
SHIFT+DOWN ARROW, 456
SHIFT+END, 32, 456
SHIFT+F1, 260, 291, 460
SHIFT+F2, 261
SHIFT+F3, 100, 261, 460
SHIFT+F4, 219, 261
SHIFT+F5, 30, 261, 437
SHIFT+F6, 261
SHIFT+F7, 261, 460, 525
SHIFT+F8, 32, 261
SHIFT+F9, 190, 261
SHIFT+F10, 262, 460
SHIFT+F11, 192, 262
SHIFT+F12, 37, 262, 446
SHIFT+HOME, 456
SHIFT+INS, 459
SHIFT+LEFT ARROW, 455, 456
SHIFT+PAGE DOWN, 456
SHIFT+PAGE UP, 456
SHIFT+RIGHT ARROW, 281, 456
SHIFT+TAB, 304, 509
SHIFT+UP ARROW, 456
Short citations, matching, 499
Shortcut keys, 458-460
assigning, 317
changing indents with, 304
changing for symbols and special
characters, 473-474
entering fields with, 189-190
for Equation Editor, 178-180, 181-182
for selecting menu commands, 459-460
setting alignment with, 67-68
Shortcut menus, 460
in Microsoft Graph, 276
opening, 11
Shortcuts. See Favorites folder
Show First Line Only button, 403, 698
Show Formatting button, on the Outline
toolbar, 698
Show Me button, on the TipWizard toolbar, 703
Show Next button, on the Header and Footer
toolbar, 286, 287, 289
Show options, 539-541
Show Previous button, on the Header and
Footer toolbar, 286, 287,
289, 699
Show Variables button, on the Macro toolbar,
333, 624, 702
Show/Hide button, on the Standard toolbar,
379, 487, 687

Show/Hide Document Text button, on the
Header and Footer toolbar,
286, 289, 700
Shrink to Fit button, in the Print Preview
toolbar, 546, 698
Sidebars, right-alignment in, 69
SIGN function, allowed in {=} field, 195
Single Space button, 705
Single spacing, 469
Size settings, for fonts, 49
Sizing buttons, 6
SKIPIF field, 209, 352, 461, 636
Slots, 174
Small Caps button, 705
Small Caps character format, 461-462
Small Caps character style, 50
Smart Cut and Paste, 31, 462
Smart quotes, 85, 462-463
Smart/curly quotes, 581
Snaking columns. See Columns;
Newspaper-style columns
Snap to Grid button, in the Drawing toolbar,
156, 692
Soft fonts, 232
Soft page breaks, 412, 414
Sort Ascending button, 127, 690
Sort Descending button, 127, 690
Sort keys, 353
Sort Records, selecting, 129
Sorting, 463-466
documents in the Open dialog box, 143
in tables, 516
Sorts, undoing, 465
Sound, adding to Word documents, 466
Sound annotations. See Voice annotations
Sound objects, adding embedded, 466-467
Sounds Like check box, 223
Source applications, 382
Sources, changing for links, 389
SPACEBAR, aligning text with, 28
Spaces
displaying, 541
removing intelligently, 161
Spacing, 54, 467-469
between characters, 470-471
changing between paragraphs, 55
changing within paragraphs, 54-55
settings for, 54-55
Spacing text box, for columns, 111
Special characters, 471-474
automatically inserting, 473
entries for finding, 222
inserting, 472
searching and replacing, 221, 222
Special indents, setting, 303
Specialized characters, rules for, 581
Spelling, 39-40, 474-480
Spelling button
on the Standard toolbar, 475, 486, 686

on the Word for Windows 2 toolbar, 696
Spelling dialog box, checking spelling through, 475-476
Spelling errors, hiding, 481
Spelling options, setting, 480-484
Spelling tab, in the Options dialog box, 480-482
Spike, 484-485
    cutting text to, 33-34
Spin box, 15
Split box, 73
    dragging, 545
Split command, 545
Split Infinitives drop-down list box, 272
Split Subdocument button, in the Master Document toolbar, 360, 701
Split Window button, 706
Spooling, 41
Spreadsheets, 485
    importing documents from, 572
    inserting, 314-315
SQL database queries, inserting into Word documents, 198
Standard styles, 487, 494-495
Standard toolbar, 6, 8-9, 485-487
    creating columns with, 110-111
    listing of buttons on, 686-687
Start button, 10
    on the Macro toolbar, 333, 702
Starting locations, for sections, 453
Startup options, 487-488
Statements, in WordBasic, 608, 609-610
States, two-letter abbreviations for, 171
Statistics tab, in the Properties dialog box, 146
Status bar, 6, 10
Status Bar check box, 541
Step button, on the Macro toolbar, 333, 606, 624, 702
Step Subs button, 333, 606, 624, 702
Stop button
    on the Macro Record toolbar, 336
    on the Macro toolbar, 333, 702
Straight Quotes to 'Smart Quotes' check box, in the Options
dialog
    box, 85
Strikethrough button, 704
Strikethrough character format, 488-489
Strikethrough character style, 50
String expressions, in macros, 612
String variables, in macros, 612
Strings of text, in macros, 610
Style aliases, 494
Style area, 495
    opening, 541
Style button, in the Formatting toolbar, 242, 688
Style families, 494
Style Gallery, 494, 523, 723
Style names, 494

displaying in a style area, 495
    in documents, 495
Style rules, in grammar checking, 272
Style sheets, 489
STYLEREF field, 209, 489
Styles, 489-490
    applying with the Formatting toolbar, 490-491
    applying with the menu, 491
    copying, 397
    copying between documents and templates, 493
    copying from templates, 494
    creating, 491-492
    deleting, 396
    editing, 492
    families of, 494
    for headings in outlines, 405
    for master and subdocuments, 362-363
    in the Normal template, 722-723
    printing, 427
    removing from documents, 493
    renaming, 397, 493
    selecting for Web documents, 665, 668, 669
    standard, 487
    switching, 495-496
Styles check box, in the Options dialog box, 86
Subdocuments, 361, 647
    accessing, 365
    creating, 648
    deleting, 364, 649
    displaying in Master Document view, 648-649
    locking, 331
    merging, 364
    moving in master documents, 363
    naming, 649
    opening, 363
    renaming, 363
    splitting, 364
    unlocking, 331
    working in, 648-649
Subentries, creating for indexes, 306
Subject document property, returning, 496
SUBJECT field, 496
Subroutines, 613
    in macros, 617
Subscript button, 705
Subscript format, 496
    adding and removing with menus, 497
Subscript text, 50
Subscripts, creating with EQ field, 201
SUM formula, in tables, 511
SUM function, allowed in {=} field, 195
Summary information, printing, 422, 426
Summary tab, in the Properties dialog box, 146
Superlative form, of adjectives and adverbs, 267
Superscript button, 705

Superscript format, 496
 adding and removing with menus, 497
Superscript text, 50
Superscripts, creating with EQ field, 201
Switch Between Header and Footer button, on
 the Header and Footer toolbar, 286, 289, 699
Switches, for fields, 212-215
Symbol Characters with Symbols check box, in
 the Options dialog
 box, 86
SYMBOL field, 210, 497
Symbol font, characters in, 472
Symbol fonts, 76
Symbols, 474
 entering in Equation Editor, 175
 inserting, 471-472
Synonyms, selecting, 525
System information, 497

T

TA field, 210, 501
TAB, 27-28
 adding a new last row with, 70, 512
 aligning text with, 28
 changing indents with, 304
 moving in a table with, 509
 moving to slots with, 174
Tab Alignment button, 519
 on the Ruler, 442
Tab alignments, effect of, 520
Tab Characters check box, 541
Tab stops, 27-28
 clearing, 443
 deleting, 519
 for headers and footers, 288
 on the Ruler, 442
Tabbed sections, 17
Table of authorities, 498-502
Table AutoFormat, 514-515, 706
Table columns, 109
Table commands, 502
Table of contents
 adding entries in, 505
 creating, 503-504
Table of figures, creating, 504
Table Gridlines button, 706
Table gridlines. *See* Gridlines
Table Wizard, 508, 725-726
Tables, 507-508
 adding cells to, 512
 aligning entries in, 515
 applying borders to, 98, 99
 converting text to, 509
 converting to text, 510
 as databases, 518
 deleting cells from, 512-513
 displaying gridlines in, 515

 formatting the contents of, 515
 inserting, 508
 inserting formulas in, 511
 merging, 514
 merging cells in, 514
 moving in, 509
 numbering cells in, 516
 page breaks in, 517
 referencing cells in, 517-518
 selecting, 511
 selecting in, 510
 sorting, 464
 sorting in, 516
 splitting, 514
 splitting cells in, 514
Tables of authorities, 79
Tabs, 518-520
 changing the interval for default, 518
 in dialog boxes, 137
 displaying, 541
 setting, 443, 519
 setting for multiple paragraphs, 442
TC field, 210, 505
Technical dictionaries, 483-484
TEMPLATE field, 520
Templates, 24-25, 520-524, 651-652, 714
 altering, 727
 attaching new, 521-522
 conflicting settings in multiple, 522-523
 copying styles from, 494
 creating, 521, 654, 728
 creating documents from, 714-715
 creating for letterheads, 586-588
 in the Equation Editor, 174
 location of, 523
 locking, 246
 for memos, 721
 modifying existing, 652-653
 modifying from documents, 523
 opening, 376
 registering, 573
 saving macros with, 522
 selecting in Equation Editor, 175
 special features for creating, 523-524
 storing macros in, 622-623
Text
 aligning, 28
 assigning bookmarks to, 209
 automatically replacing with
 AutoCorrect entries, 82
 changing the capitalization of, 100
 collapsing, 109
 converting tables to, 510
 converting to a table, 509
 copying, 35, 156
 copying by dragging and dropping,
 32-33, 153

creating graphic images with, 551
cutting to the Clipboard or the Spike, 33-34
deleting, 134-135
deleting all instances of, 228
deleting selected, 33-34
editing with drag and drop, 160
entering, 25-28
entering faster, 87
finding, 219
finding sounds like, 223
inserting, 34-35
inserting from another document, 204
inserting as possible code, 207
kerning, 471
layering, 320-321
moving by dragging and dropping, 32-33, 153
pasting annotations into, 75
position settings for, 50-51
repeating, 435
replacing, 220
replacing with graphics, 227-228
rotating, 441
selecting, 31-32, 454-457
selecting columns of, 113, 457
selecting for printing, 424
shifting on a line, 195
size settings for, 49
subscript, 496-497
superscript, 496-497
unattached in graphs, 279
underlining, 535-536
wrapping around frames, 257, 258
wrapping at the end of windows, 540.
    See also Hidden text
Text boundaries, displaying, 540
Text Boundaries check box, 540
Text Box button
    on the Drawing toolbar, 155, 691
    on the Microsoft Graph toolbar, 276, 712
Text boxes, 14-15, 135-136
Text color, 524
Text fields, 247-248
Text files, 525
Text Form Field button, in the Forms toolbar, 245, 252, 693
Text or Property drop-down list box, 143
Text strings, in macros, 610
Text-based word processor, 682
Thesaurus, 525-527
Thesis template, 726-727
TIFF format image, 167
Time, 130-133
Time button, on the Header and Footer toolbar, 286, 289, 699
TIME field, 211
    in a header or footer, 132
Times, formatting the display of, 213, 214

Tip of the Day, 19
TipWizard, 527-528
TipWizard Active check box, 264
TipWizard Box button, on the TipWizard toolbar, 703
TipWizard button, on the Standard toolbar, 487, 687
TipWizard toolbar, listing of buttons on, 703
Title, in graphs, 279
Title bar, 6, 7
TITLE field, 528
TOA fields, 211, 502, 528
TOC field, 211, 505-506, 528
Toggle case option, 100
Toggle Field Codes, 190
Toggles, 50
Toolbars, 530-532
    assigning macros to, 335
    designing new, 528-530
    displaying, 531
    hiding, 531
    modifying, 528-530
    moving, 532
    selecting buttons on, 531
ToolTips, 534
Top Border button, on the Borders toolbar, 689
Top margins, setting, 359
Topics
    moving back to, 294
    printing, 294
    selecting from the Help index, 293
Trace button, on the Macro toolbar, 333, 606, 624, 702
Trademark symbol, 582
Triple spacing, 55
Triple-clicking, for selecting paragraphs, 31
TRUE function, allowed in {=} field, 195
TrueType fonts, 49, 232
    embedding in saved documents, 445.
    See also Fonts
Type. *See* Document type
Typing Replaces Selection check box, 160

U

Unassigned icons, 707
Unattached text, in graphs, 279
Underline button, 50
    in the Formatting toolbar, 243, 535, 688
Underline character style, 49, 50, 51
Underline style, applying, 535
Underlining, 535-536
    adding and removing, 535
Undo, after replacing, 227
Undo actions, 536-537
Undo button
    on the Microsoft Graph toolbar, 275, 711
    on the Standard toolbar, 486, 536, 687

on the Word for Windows 2 toolbar, 695
Undo command, 35-36, 536, 537
Ungroup button, in the Drawing toolbar, 156, 692
Uniform Resource Locator. *See* URL
Unlinking
    fields, 192-193
    footers, 288
    headers, 288
Unlock Document button, on the Master Document toolbar, 649-650
Unlocking
    fields, 192
    master documents, 331
UP ARROW
    moving the insertion point with, 373
    moving in a table with, 509
Update Automatic Links at Open check box, 264
Update Field, 191
Update Fields button, 127, 690
Updating links. *See* OLE
Uppercase
    allowing accented, 161
    displaying all characters as, 69-70
UPPERCASE check box, 481
URL (Uniform Resource Locator), 661
Use the INS Key for Paste check box, 160
Use Smart Cut and Paste check box, 161
Use Tab and Backspace Keys to Set Left Indent check box, 161
User
    information about, 537-538
    prompting for text entry, 202
User address, inserting, 211
USERADDRESS field, 211, 538
USER.DAT file, 538
USERINITIALS field, 211, 538
USERNAME field, 211, 538

V

Values, comparing two, 203
Variables
    in macros, 612
    in WordBasic, 609
Vector images, 283, 581
Verbs, problem, 526-527
Versions, comparing, 114-117
Vertical alignments, for sections, 453
Vertical Gridlines button, in the Microsoft Graph toolbar, 275, 711
Vertical lines. *See* Borders and shading
Vertical position, of frames, 258-259
Vertical ruler, 441, 541
Vertical Ruler check box, 541
Vertical Scroll Bar check box, 541
Vertical scroll bars, 449

View buttons, 6, 10
View Datasheet button, in the Microsoft Graph toolbar, 275, 711
View Field Codes button, 704
View Merged Data button, on the Mail Merge toolbar, 357, 700
View options, 539-542
View Ruler button, in the Print Preview toolbar, 546, 698
Viewing, documents, 543-547
Views
    changing, 42-44
    switching, 543-544
Voice annotations
    creating, 75-76, 467
    reviewing, 75-76

W

Watermarks, 547-548
    creating as headers or footers, 290
Web documents
    adding graphics to, 670
    converting Word documents into, 664-665
    creating with Internet Assistant, 663-664
    viewing HTML codes in, 669
Weekly Time Sheet template, 727
White text on blue background, 263
Whole words, finding, 221-222
Widows, 413-414, 548
Wild card characters, in spelling, 479-480
Window menu, listing of documents currently open, 25
Window selections, under View options, 541
Windows, 548-549
    arranging, 549, 550
    closing, 19
    maximizing, 17, 366
    minimizing, 17-18, 369
    moving, 18-19
    moving between, 549
    moving to another, 549
    opening multiple, 549
    opening on the same document, 545
    restoring, 18
    sizing, 17-18
    splitting into panes, 545. *See also* Document Windows
Windows Clipboard. *See* Clipboard
Windows OLE. *See* OLE
Windows print spooler, 41
Windows registry. *See* Registry
Windows taskbar, 6, 10
Wizards, 549-550
    creating, 549
    registering, 573
WMF format image, 167

Word application window, 5-10, 17
Word count, 550-551
Word Dialog Editor. *See* Dialog Editor
Word documents
    adding existing as subdocuments, 364
    adding sound to, 466-467
    converting into Web documents, 664-665
    as embedded data, 569
    exporting, 185
    faxing directly, 186
    inserting graphics into, 571
    as linked data, 569
    linked and inserted, 571
    linked into Excel, 562
    opening, 391-392. *See also* Documents
Word fields, 341, 349-350
    field codes inserted for, 350
    inserting, 346-348
    selecting, 357
Word processor
    paragraph-based, 682
    text-based, 682
Word TipWizard. *See* TipWizard
Word Underline button, 704
Word for Windows 2.0 toolbar, 551
    listing of buttons on, 694-696
Word for Windows 95
    comparison with WordPerfect, 682
    creating new folders from, 122
    customizing, 125
    customizing menus in, 366
    ending, 5
    exiting, 185
    hardware required for, 678
    installing, 678-680
    listing of buttons, 686-712
    on networks, 643-645
    printing outside of, 429
    protection features of, 645
    starting, 4-5
    updating, 679-680
WordArt, 551-552, 553
WordArt button, 704
WordArt toolbar, buttons on, 553, 709-710
WordBasic, 552, 604
    creating macros with, 607-618
Wordiness, rules for correcting, 227
WordMail, 552
WordPerfect, 552, 554
    enviroment defaults, changing in Word,
      172
    features conversion list to Word, 682-684
    Help, 296

    help in Word for Windows 95, 684
    skills, translating, 20
    switching to Word from, 682-684
    users, help for, 263
Words
    automatic marking of misspelled, 476
    counting in documents, 550
    deleting, 134
    finding all forms of, 223
    finding whole, 221-222
    matching all forms of in document
      searches, 144
    returning the number in a document, 381
    selecting, 31
    selecting part of, 160
Words with Numbers check box, 481
Words Only underlining, 536
Workgroup, 640
    scenarios for activities, 641-643
Workgroup features, 554
Working folder, 392, 554
Worksheets, 485, 554
Workspace, arranging, 17-19
World Wide Web, 658-659
WP, in the status bar, 684
WPH, in the status bar, 684
WPN, in the status bar, 684
Wrap to Window check box, 540

X axis, labels for, 278, 279
XE fields, 211, 308, 554

Y-axis labels, in graphs, 279

Z

Zoom 100% button, on the Word for Windows
    2 toolbar, 696
Zoom Control button, 704
    on the Print Preview toolbar, 546, 698
    on the Standard toolbar, 487, 687
Zoom Page Width button, on the Word for
    Windows 2 toolbar, 696
Zooming, documents, 544

Revolutionary Information on the Information REVOLUTION

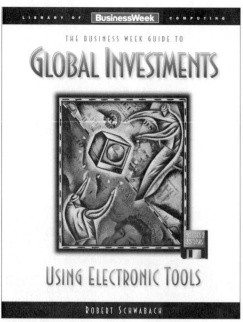

The Business Week Guide to Global Investments Using Electronic Tools
by Robert Schwabach
Includes Three 3.5-Inch Disks
$39.95 U.S.A. ISBN: 0-07-882055-3

Alluring opportunities abound for the global investor. But avoiding investment land mines can be tricky business. The first release in the Business Week Library of Computing lets you master all the winning strategies. Everything is here—from analyzing and selecting the best companies, to tax planning, using investment software tools, and more. Disks include MetaStock, Windows On WallStreet, and Telescan, the leading investment analysis software.

The Business Week Guide to Multimedia Presentations
Create dynamic presentations that inspire.
by Robert Lindstrom
Includes One CD-ROM
$39.95 U.S.A.
ISBN: 0-07-882057-X

The Internet Yellow Pages
Second Edition
by Harley Hahn and Rick Stout
$27.95 U.S.A.
ISBN: 0-07-882098-7

Fundamental Photoshop: A Complete Introduction Second Edition
by Adele Droblas Greenberg and Seth Greenberg
$27.95 U.S.A.
ISBN: 0-07-882093-6

Multimedia: Making It Work, Second Edition
by Tay Vaughan
Includes One CD-ROM
$34.95 U.S.A.
ISBN: 0-07-882035-9

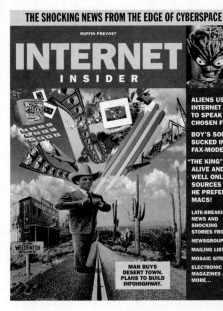

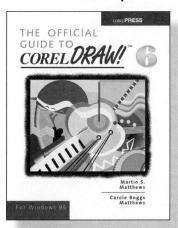

The NEW CLASSICS

ORACLE DBA HANDBOOK

by Kevin Loney

Every DBA can learn to manage a networked Oracle database efficiently and effectively with this comprehensive guide.

Price: $34.95 U.S.A.
Available Now
ISBN: 0-07-881182-1
Pages: 704, paperback

ORACLE: THE COMPLETE REFERENCE,

Third Edition

by George Koch and Kevin Loney

Get true encyclopedic coverage of Oracle with this book. Authoritative and absolutely up-to-the-minute.

Price: $34.95 U.S.A.
Available Now
ISBN: 0-07-882097-9
Pages: 1104, paperback

ORACLE BACKUP AND RECOVERY HANDBOOK

by Rama Velpuri

Keep your database running smoothly and prepare for the possibility of system failure with this comprehensive resource and guide.

Price: $29.95 U.S.A.
Available Now
ISBN: 0-07-882106-1
Pages: 400, paperback

ORACLE POWER OBJECTS HANDBOOK

by Bruce Kolste and David Petersen

This book is the only one available on Oracle's new single/multi-user database product.

Price: $29.95 U.S.A.
Available August, 1995
ISBN: 0-07-882089-8
Pages: 512, paperback

ORACLE® *Oracle Press*™

Driving Your Information Systems for Optimal Performance

The NEW CLASSICS

ORACLE DBA HANDBOOK

by Kevin Loney

Every DBA can learn to manage a networked Oracle database efficiently and effectively with this comprehensive guide.

Price: $34.95 U.S.A.
Available Now
ISBN: 0-07-881182-1
Pages: 704, paperback

TUNING ORACLE

by Michael J. Corey,
Michael Abbey and
Daniel J. Dechichio, Jr.

Learn to customize Oracle for optimal performance and productivity with this focused guide.

Price: $29.95 U.S.A.
Available Now
ISBN: 0-07-881181-3
Pages: 336, paperback

ORACLE WORKGROUP SERVER HANDBOOK

by Thomas B. Cox

Take full advantage of the power and flexibility of the new Oracle Workgroup Server and Oracle7 for Windows with this comprehensive handbook.

Covers Oracle7 for Windows

Price: $27.95 U.S.A.
Available Now
ISBN: 0-07-881186-4
Pages: 320, paperback

ORACLE: A BEGINNER'S GUIDE

by Michael Abbey
and Michael J. Corey

For easy-to-understand, comprehensive information about Oracle RDBMS products, this is the one book every user needs.

Price: $29.95 U.S.A.
Available Now
ISBN: 0-07-882122-3
Pages: 560, paperback

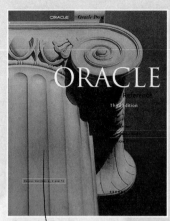

ORACLE: THE COMPLETE REFERENCE

Third Edition

by George Koch
and Kevin Loney

Get true encyclopedic coverage of Oracle with this book. Authoritative and absolutely up-to-the-minute.

Price: $34.95 U.S.A.
Available Now
ISBN: 0-07-882097-9
Pages: 1104, paperback

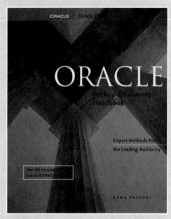

ORACLE BACKUP AND RECOVERY HANDBOOK

by Rama Velpuri

Keep your database running smoothly and prepare for the possibility of system failure with this comprehensive resource and guide.

Price: $29.95 U.S.A.
Available Now
ISBN: 0-07-882106-1
Pages: 400, paperback

ORACLE POWER OBJECTS DEVELOPER'S GUIDE

by Richard Finkelstein,
Kasu Sista, and Rick Greenwald

Integrate the flexibility and power of Oracle Power Objects into your applications development with this results-oriented handbook.

Price: $39.95 U.S.A.
Includes One CD-ROM
Available September, 1995
ISBN: 0-07-882163-0
Pages: 656, paperback

ORACLE POWER OBJECTS HANDBOOK

by Bruce Kolste
and David Petersen

This is the only book available on Oracle's new single/multi-user database product.

Price: $29.95 U.S.A.
Available August, 1995
ISBN: 0-07-882089-8
Pages: 512, paperback

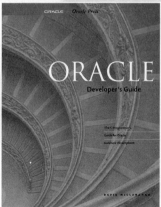

ORACLE DEVELOPER'S GUIDE

by David McClanahan

Learn to develop a database that is fast, powerful, and secure with this comprehensive guide.

Price: $29.95 U.S.A.
Available November, 1995
ISBN: 0-07-882087-1
Pages: 608, paperback

BC640SL

The NEW CLASSICS

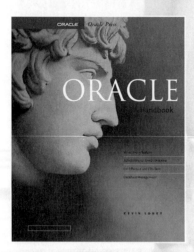

ORACLE DBA HANDBOOK

by Kevin Loney
Every DBA can learn to manage a networked Oracle database efficiently and effectively with this comprehensive guide. Oracle Magazine columnist Kevin Loney covers everything a DBA needs to manage Oracle, from architecture to layout considerations to supporting packages. A command reference and configuration guidelines are included as well as scripts and tips. The **Oracle DBA Handbook** is the ideal support and resource for all new and existing DBAs.

Price: $34.95 U.S.A.
Available Now
ISBN: 0-07-881182-1
Pages: 704, paperback

TUNING ORACLE

by Michael J. Corey, Michael Abbey, and Daniel J. Dechichio, Jr.
Learn to customize Oracle for optimal performance and productivity with this focused guide. Michael Corey, president of the International Oracle Users Group, and Michael Abbey and Daniel Dechichio, recognized Oracle experts, teach strategies and systems to help administrators avoid problems, increase database speed, and ensure overall security. For a powerful and versatile database, **Tuning Oracle** is your ultimate resource for making Oracle reach its full potential.

Price: $29.95 U.S.A.
Available Now
ISBN: 0-07-881181-3
Pages: 336, paperback

ORACLE WORKGROUP SERVER HANDBOOK

by Thomas B. Cox
Take full advantage of the power and flexibility of the new Oracle Workgroup Server with this comprehensive handbook. Thomas Cox helps users master the intricacies of this relational database management system, including creating a database, developing queries, and using SQL as well as explaining and defining declarations, referential integrity, and more. Perfect for both users and administrators, the **Oracle Workgroup Server Handbook** is the one authoriative book.

Price: $34.95 U.S.A.
Available Now
ISBN: 0-07-881186-4
Pages: 320, paperback

ORACLE® *Oracle Press*™

Driving Your Information Systems for Optimal Performance

BC604SL

EXTRATERRESTRIAL CONNECTIONS

THESE DAYS, ANY CONNECTION IS POSSIBLE...
WITH THE INNOVATIVE BOOKS FROM LAN TIMES AND OSBORNE/McGRAW-HILL

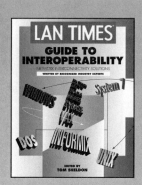

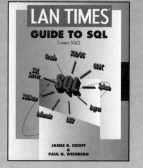

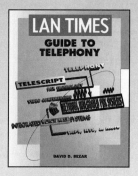

ORDER BOOKS DIRECTLY FROM OSBORNE/McGRAW-HILL

For a complete catalog of Osborne's books, call 510-549-6600 or write to us at 2600 Tenth Street, Berkeley, CA 94710

☎ **Call Toll-Free: 1-800-822-8158**
24 hours a day, 7 days a week in U.S. and Canada

✉ **Mail this order form to:**
McGraw-Hill, Inc.
Customer Service Dept.
P.O. Box 547
Blacklick, OH 43004

📠 **Fax this order form to:**
1-614-759-3644

💻 **EMAIL**
7007.1531@COMPUSERVE.COM
COMPUSERVE GO MH

Ship to:

Name _____

Company _____

Address _____

City / State / Zip _____

Daytime Telephone: _____
(We'll contact you if there's a question about your order.)

ISBN #	BOOK TITLE	Quantity	Price	Total
0-07-88				
0-07-88				
0-07-88				
0-07-88				
0-07-88				
0-07088				
0-07-88				
0-07-88				
0-07-88				
0-07-88				
0-07-88				
0-07-88				
0-07-88				
0-07-88				

Shipping & Handling Charge from Chart Below		
Subtotal		
Please Add Applicable State & Local Sales Tax		
TOTAL		

Shipping & Handling Charges

Order Amount	U.S.	Outside U.S.
Less than $15	$3.50	$5.50
$15.00 - $24.99	$4.00	$6.00
$25.00 - $49.99	$5.00	$7.00
$50.00 - $74.99	$6.00	$8.00
$75.00 - and up	$7.00	$9.00

Occasionally we allow other selected companies to use our mailing list. If you would prefer that we not include you in these extra mailings, please check here: ☐

METHOD OF PAYMENT

☐ Check or money order enclosed (payable to Osborne/McGraw-Hill)

☐ AMERICAN EXPRESS   ☐ DISCOVER   ☐ MasterCard   ☐ VISA

Account No. ☐☐☐☐☐☐☐☐☐☐☐☐☐☐☐

Expiration Date _____

Signature _____

In a hurry? Call 1-800-822-8158 anytime, day or night, or visit your local bookstore.

Thank you for your order   Code BC640SL